Counseling and Psychological Services for College Student-Athletes

Counseling and Psychological Services for College Student-Athletes

Edward F. Etzel

WEST VIRGINIA UNIVERSITY

— Editor —

Fitness Information Technology
A Division of the International Center
for Performance Excellence
262 Coliseum, WVU-PASS, PO Box 6116
Morgantown, WV 26506-6116

Earlier versions of the following chapters appeared in *Counseling College Students: Issues and Interventions* (1996; 2002). Their contents reflect the contributions of the current authors and the following:

   Chapter 1, Christopher Lantz
   Chapter 5, Trent Petrie
   Chapter 13, Dan Gould
   Chapter 15, John Lard and Bart Lerner

Library of Congress Card Catalog Number: 2008937707

ISBN 13: 978-1-885693-91-4

Production Editor: Valerie Gittings
Cover Design: Craig Hines
Typesetter: Craig Hines
Proofreader: Maria denBoer
Indexer: Maria denBoer
Printed by Sheridan Books
Cover Photos © bigstockphoto.com and istockphoto.com

10 9 8 7 6 5 4 3 2 1

Fitness Information Technology
A Division of the International Center for Performance Excellence
West Virginia University
262 Coliseum, WVU-PASS
PO Box 6116
Morgantown, WV 26506-6116
800.477.4348 (toll free)
304.293.6888 (phone)
304.293.6658 (fax)
Email: fitcustomerservice@mail.wvu.edu
Website: www.fitinfotech.com

CONTENTS

FOREWORD

It is a privilege and an honor to be asked to write the foreword to a book of such high quality and caliber. As a psychologist who has worked in a university counseling service for thirty years and who, as a former college athlete, has long advocated for student-athletes and the unique set of struggles they encounter, this is an invitation I accept with humility and much gratitude. In reading *Counseling and Psychological Services for College Student-Athletes* I was immediately impressed by the fact that this is a volume of considerable magnitude and truly a must read for any professional working with college student-athletes. It provides a treasure trove of information, well researched and well written by authors with substantial practical experience in the field. This will no doubt become the go-to reference for anyone working with this population. The editor has pulled together an outstanding team of contributors to make this happen.

While one is left with a myriad of positive impressions from this reading, several observations deserve mentioning. First, although written about student-athletes and for those who serve them, I believe this book has much crossover value for professionals who work with university students in general. This is especially true of counselors and psychotherapists who will find the chapters on counseling women and male college student-athletes, working with the African-descendent college athlete, and working with the GLBTQ athlete especially illuminating. In the end, all students, even if they are not athletes, compete on the playing field of academia, social life, and their emerging careers. Second, this work will be of substantial value and interest to all professionals who interface with student-athletes. The clinician (counselor or psychotherapist) immediately comes to mind, but it will also amply inform trainers, rehabilitation specialists, career and academic advisors, coaches and other athletic administrators, as well as those serving in sports medicine. Finally, as A. P. Ferrante and Edward Etzel underscore in their opening chapter, it strongly advocates for a holistic approach in serving student-athletes, thereby bringing together the combined skills of all professionals to work on behalf of the athlete. As the authors note, the NCAA'S CHAMPS/Life Skills "Challenging Athletes' Minds for Personal Success" is a model that offers much hope. Inviting all support programs into this endeavor and bringing together university personnel to assist student-athletes integrate into campus life and into the educational fabric of the university is one of the book's primary objectives.

The first chapter sets the stage for the wealth of information that follows. While all students face major developmental challenges in their college years, the student-athlete does so on center stage. Not only do student-athletes struggle with the mixed blessings of notoriety, time demands, physical demands and injury, they must also manage academic and social expectations and the temptations of alcohol and drugs. And, all too frequently, the student-athlete does so in isolation with little support to reach out to others for assistance. Certainly this is a population at risk for emotional and personal upheavals.

An overarching emphasis in this book is the centrality of working ethically. Managing sensitively and ethically the challenges of confidentiality, privacy, and third-party inquiries is essential in establishing and maintaining trust with a population that is already aware of being administered, directed, and, in many instances, controlled by those in authority. Closely associated with the focus on ethics is the emphasis placed on being knowledgeable about the struggles of the population we serve. What is it like to be a female or male or African-descendent or GLBTQ student-athlete, or to be learning disabled or injured, or to suffer from disordered eating? The unique issues that these groups bring to helpers are challenging and require multiculturally sensitive professionals who embrace diversity and seek ongoing continuing education. Being personally aware of our biases, misperceptions, and prejudices is a key ingredient to effective intervention. The challenge made by William Parham that we become sensitive to micro aggression, while imperative in our work with African-descendent athletes, can also be broadened as a guiding principle in working with the other student-athlete populations previously identified. Equally important is our awareness of the emotions student-athletes experience in response to the biases and stereotyped reactions expressed toward them by others.

An additional and essential theme discussed is the significant barrier that so many athletes feel with respect to applying for and receiving counseling and psychological services. Hence, the student-athlete is often faced with a "no-win" dilemma: being a person whose very existence as a student-athlete brings with it threats and challenges not likely experienced by his or her non-athlete peers; and, in many instances, being resistant to seek out help. As several of the contributors observe, the "heroic" image and status of the athlete as independent, self-sufficient, and capable of resolving all personal worries and challenges tends to impede the student-athlete from engaging counseling and psychological services. And regretfully, there is often limited support for doing so by coaches, trainers, and fellow athletes. By contrast, being "forced" into counseling services, generally as a part of disciplinary action, does nothing to advance our services as safe and trusted resources. This makes building positive relationships with student-athletes an essential component of their care. Being empathic with student-athletes and recognizing the compromise they feel they are making in seeking help becomes crucially important.

Readers will find the chapters on the specific problems that afflict student-athletes especially useful. Discussions deserving a special thumbs-up include the chapters on depression, learning disabilities, counseling the injured and disabled, and the presentation addressing the damaging influences of alcohol and drugs.

There is obviously much work left to be done and many obstacles and challenges to overcome in the work we do to serve college student-athletes. However, this book leaves me with a sense of optimism and hope. By developing increased sensitivity and awareness and by broadening and deepening the quality of our knowledge and intervention skills and continuing to coordinate our professional efforts, much good can be achieved. I believe this is a central message of this book, and it has been accomplished.

Rolffs Pinkerton, Ph.D., ABPP

Staff Psychologist, Counseling and Psychological Services, Duke University
Associate Clinical Professor of Medical Psychology, Department of Psychiatry and
Behavioral Sciences, Duke University Medical Center

ACKNOWLEDGMENTS

Overseeing an edited book is both a joy and an enormous challenge. The final product is an amazing thing to have in one's hand. Whatever your line of work or interests, I hope that you find this new book a useful resource. May it enable you to better understand and help college student-athletes find their way into adulthood. In retrospect, I believe that the crafting of this book has been a successful adventure. The end product offers you what our many wise contributors have learned, experienced, and continue to do well. I would like to acknowledge and thank the many people who made this venture possible.

First, a very grateful tip of the editorial hat needs to go out to each of the contributing authors who voluntarily devoted their precious time to share their knowledge and expertise writing for you. Please do take a moment to visit their bios. I am sure you will be impressed with who has contributed to this book and the remarkable backgrounds they have brought to this publication!

Certainly, I want to extend my sincere appreciation to everyone at Fitness Information Technology Publishing, Inc. (FIT) for their support and assistance over the course of producing this book. In particular, I want to very sincerely thank the ever gracious and cheerful Val Gittings, FIT's resident editorial expert for her tireless support and guidance. This book is well organized and reads clearly because of her many hours of skillful effort. I also want to extend my sincere appreciation to Dr. Andy Ostrow, FIT's now happily retired director, a dear colleague and friend who supported the concept of this book when I first proposed it.

Finally, I want to extend my gratitude to Dr. Rolffs Pinkerton from Duke University's CAPS for taking time out of his very busy professional life to review this book and author the foreword.

Edward F. Etzel, Ed.D.
Psychologist/Associate Professor
West Virginia University

1

COLLEGE STUDENT-ATHLETES AND COUNSELING SERVICES IN THE NEW MILLENNIUM

A. P. Ferrante
Edward F. Etzel

Few people will argue with the premise that attending college can have a profound effect on one's life. With the possible exception of getting married and having children, few choices have more far-reaching implications than the decision about college. (Astin, 1977, p. 1)

Astin's comments from over 30 years ago still ring true today. College students and most student-athletes of The New Millennium remain young people caught up in a "profound" and emotionally taxing set of life transitions—some of which are predictable and developmental in nature (Medalie, 1981) and some that are not so foreseeable. Student-athletes are a diverse group who must confront the formidable challenges of modern-day life. Like their non-athlete peers, they are trying to find their way in a very rapidly changing, high-tech world that is, in many ways, significantly more complex than the world of their predecessors from the 1980s and 1990s, whom we have previously written about (Howe & Strauss, 2000).

While inhabiting a changed, faster paced world, present-day student-athletes have lifestyles that stand in contrast to the lifestyles of their on-campus non-athlete counterparts. These young women and men must function in the commercialized, very competitive, and controlling milieu of intercollegiate athletics of today. The most recent Knight Commission (2001) report on intercollegiate athletics, "A Call to Action," described some of the undercurrents associated with the professionalization of contemporary intercollegiate athletics and student-athlete participation:

> Under the influence of television and the mass media, the ethos of athletics is now professional. The apex of sporting endeavor is defined by professional sports. This fundamental shift now permeates many campuses. Big-time college basketball and football have a professional look and feel—in their arenas and stadiums, their luxury boxes and financing, their uniforms and coaching staffs, and their marketing and administrative structures. In fact, big-time programs have become minor leagues in their own right, increasingly taken into account as part of the professional athletics system. (Knight Commission, 2001)

Within this complex commercialized system, student-athletes' highly structured lifestyles present a distinctive set of daily personal, academic, and physical demands under a growing degree of university, athletic department, and public scrutiny. Athletes' sometimes complementary roles as both students and performers serve to complicate their experiences (Brent, Erikson-Cornish, Leslie-Toogood, Nadkarni, & Schreier, 2006; Fletcher, Benshoff, & Richburg, 2003; Potuto & O'Hanlon, 2006) and have the potential to both help and hamper their academic success (Long & Caudill, 1991; Briggs, 1996), their overall adjustment to college life, and perhaps most importantly, their personal development (Blann, 1985; Chartrand & Lent, 1987; Henschen & Fry, 1984; Hood, Craig, & Ferguson, 1992; Lewis, 1991; Nelson, 1983; Quarforth, Brewer, Petitpas, Champagne, & Cornelius, 2003). It appears that the consequences of participation in the intercollegiate athletics experience, both positive and negative, can have a considerable impact on many aspects of the general health, mental health, and psychosocial development of student-athletes (Etzel, Watson, Visek, & Maniar, 2006; Harris, 1993).

From a positive perspective, the intercollegiate athletics experience seems to provide a set of opportunities that can be useful to individual growth as a person. Some of the potentially transferable life skills that may be acquired from involvement in the athletics experience include: challenging oneself, setting and following through on goals, testing personal limitations, managing time, dealing with authority figures and others one may not always like, accepting criticism and feedback, handling success and failure, and developing effective coping strategies (Danish, D'Augelli, & Ginsberg, 1983). An assortment of academic, health, and developmental struggles also appears to influence the lives of student-athletes (Donahue, Covassin, Lancer, Dickens, Miller Hash, & Gent, 2004; Selby, Weinstein, & Bird, 1990). However, as Zimbalist (1998) has observed, "it is apparent that there is a fine line between the psychosocial benefits and detriments that are engendered by college sports" (p. 51).

Over the past two decades or so, it appears that helping professionals and researchers have continued to acquire a more clear understanding of the lifestyles and needs of college student-athletes (Andersen, 2002; Brent et al., 2006; Danish, Petitpas, & Hale, 1995; Etzel, Ferrante, & Pinkney, 1991, 1997; Etzel, Pinkney, & Hinkle, 1995; Fields, 1999; Hipple, 1991; Hood, Craig, & Ferguson, 1992; Hosick, 2005; Howard-Hamilton & Watt, 2001; Jordan & Denson, 1990; Kimball, & Freysinger, 2003; Kirk & Kirk, 1993; Lewis, 1991; Murray, 1997; Parham, 1993; Shriberg & Brodzinski, 1984; Shirka, 1997; Stone & Strange, 1989; Swan, 1990). This evolving literature, specialized training programs and opportunities, and increased sensitivity to the plight of student-athletes have combined to better position counselors, psychologists, advisors, athletic trainers, and sports medicine professionals to provide professional support. Awareness of the needs of these young people also seems to have been increased by the introduction of the NCAA's CHAMPS/Life Skills program across the country (Carr & Bauman, 1996; NCAA, 2007a; also see Chapter 4).

On the other hand, some commonly held biases may still hinder efforts to provide support to this population. For example, although student-athletes are often respected as heroes and heroines for their physical skills and accomplishments (Watt & Moore, 2001), they are often typecast as a homogeneous group of "athlete-students," "dumb jocks," and sometimes "thugs" who are spoiled, unmotivated, and/or out of control (Edwards, 1984; Engstrom, Sedlacek, & McEwen, 1995; Remer, Tongate, & Watson, 1978; Zingg, 1982), whose primary motivation for attending college is to "major in eligibility," play their sport, and go pro. Although this may be true for numerous "athlete-students," (e.g., some of those involved in high-profile, so called revenue-generating sports), it does not seem to be a fair assessment of the majority of those who participate in intercollegiate athletics. Sadly, it is apparent that many under-prepared participants in intercollegiate athletes today are "specially" admitted to the university for their athletic prowess alone and therefore have a poor chance, if any, to graduate (Eitzen, 2003; Knight Commission, 2001). Helping professionals need to be prepared to encounter clients who can meet the rigors of academics, athletics, and personal life, as well as those clients who are at great risk to fail.

These stereotypes may stem from the portrayal of student-athletes as "problem children" in the media and the behavior of some in the classroom, on campus, and in the community. One need not search long to find examples of objectionable behavior among student-athletes in the media today. In fact, there are websites that focus on the behavior of athletes (e.g., www.badjocks.com). We have long held the belief that to be effective in working with this group, it is important for helping professionals (e.g., counselors, psychologists), sports medicine staff, academic advisors, and faculty to be sensitive to any biases they may have regarding student-athletes, and as best they can, mindfully "check them" at their office doors. Hopefully, helping professionals and others will then be able to better recognize and respond more effectively to the range of concerns presented by student-athlete clients.

The current authors also remain advocates of a holistic approach to helping college-age people that recognizes the uniqueness of each of our clients. Counseling should emphasize facilitating the adjustment and development of each person within the context of the general collegiate and intercollegiate athletics experience whenever possible. Based upon our professional experiences, as well as interactions with other professionals in the field over time, our view is that this perspective seems to be at variance with that of some athletic department personnel toward student-athletes and their personal counseling issues.

Stressors Student-Athletes Face

The psychological issues of college student-athletes have been overlooked for some time; however, the National Collegiate Athletics Association (NCAA) has of late come to recognize the significance of counseling and mental health issues in the lives of student-athletes (Hosick, 2005). The severity and range of presenting concerns of student-athlete clients are extensive, likely reflecting a mental health crisis that exists on campus today (Benton, Robertson, Tseng, Newton, & Benton, 2003; Brent et al., 2006; Etzel, 2003; Grayson & Meilman, 2006; Hinkle, 1994; Kadison & DiGeronimo, 2004). Recently, Maniar, Carter, and Smith (2003) reported data about student-athlete clients who had recently sought psychological consultation at a large mid-western university. Over a two-year period, student-athletes expressed concerns with significant issues such as: adjustment to college and athletics, alcohol and other substance abuse, anxiety, depression, eating problems and disorders, sexual assault, and coping with sport injury. Other common presenting concerns are relationships with intimates, peers, and coaches; grief and loss; time management; test anxiety; learning disabilities; academic major selection; career searching; competitive pressures; and under-recovery from training (Etzel, 2003).

Academic Demands

Student-athletes must tackle the considerable academic responsibilities that their non-athlete peers must attend to (e.g., attending classes and labs, doing required studying, completing homework and projects, passing exams) around a schedule that is not typical of non-athlete peers. Tiring and time consuming for every student, these day-to-day tasks demand time and energy that student-athletes regularly have very little of vis a vis their athletic commitments and training requirements. These commitments have regrettably become for many (perhaps for a majority these days) a set of year-round "voluntary-mandatory" responsibilities. The good news is that student-athletes in general appear to be successful in the classroom. Unfortunately, those who do thrive there are "virtually invisible" (Burke, 1993). A recent sample survey of 18 NCAA Division I institutions and approximately 900 student-athletes suggested that many were satisfied with the quality of their education and that it had prepared them well for post-graduate life (Potuto & O'Hanlon, 2006). Interestingly, those data also revealed that a large percentage (58%) viewed themselves as athletes first more than students first. Perhaps this revelation should not be startling, given the observation that many tend to "foreclose" on their identities rather early in life, leaning more toward a stronger athletic identity than toward a self-view associated with other endeavors (Murphy, Petitpas, & Brewer, 1996). Thus, this athletic identity becomes the "lens" or context through which they tend to view themselves and their world. For example, when clients are asked who they are, they frequently will begin with some reference to being a swimmer, soccer, football, or baseball player and then perhaps add other information about their background, versus starting off describing themselves as an English or biology major from a particular region or hometown.

Despite the fact that numerous universities and athletics departments continue to provide an expanding range of academic and other support services intended to promote success in the classroom, helping professionals should be prepared to work not only with academically successful and satisfied athlete clients, but also with those who are feeling discouraged, are less prepared, and do not perform well academically (American Institutes for Research, 1988). Many are quite unfocused and are not as motivated to succeed in the classroom as they are motivated to do well in their sport (Simons, Van Rheenen, & Covington, 1999). Many are also less career-mature than their non-athlete peers (Kornspan & Etzel, 2003). Their academic performance may have been impacted by the assumption that they are somehow academically inferior to their non-athlete peers (Howard-Hamilton & Sina, 2001).

After younger, less-prepared student-athletes experience a college workload, they may be compelled to re-evaluate and adjust their academic goals, because the demands of the college classroom typically exceed those of high school. Unfortunately, some further distance themselves from their roles as students (Adler & Adler, 1985) and invest more in athletics. These students, typically freshmen and sophomores, represent the so-called "retention risks." For example, Downey (2005) found that a sample of Division I freshmen student-athletes were considerably less committed to earning their undergraduate degrees than a sample of non-athletes, when surveyed at the middle and end of their first semester. Other research suggests that some specific groups of student-athletes are possible retention risks: basketball and football players, in particular, historically have not been as well prepared as other student peers to function successfully in the classroom (American Institutes for Research, 1988; Pascarella et al., 1995; Purdy, Eitzen, & Hufnagel, 1982; Sedlacek & Adams-Gaston, 1992; Sellers, 1992). Also, it appears that male athletes may not fare as well as females in the classroom (Simons, Rheenen, & Covington, 1999). Some data further suggests that participation in athletics, in particular for males and for those who are involved in basketball and football, can have a detrimental impact on student learning in general and, more specifically, upon mathematics skill development and reading comprehension (Pascarella, Bohr, Nora, & Terenzini, 1995; Pascarella & Terenzini, 2005). Overall, however, it seems risky to generalize about the academic achievement of today's student athletes from different backgrounds and sport groups. Consequently, it may be most useful to closely consider the individual client's academic history, interests, and aspirations to minimize any personal biases the helping professional may own.

Nevertheless, helping professionals may see academically challenged clients at more academically rigorous institutions or where special admissions policies permit entrance to individuals who would not ordinarily be admitted to the university, given their marginal academic credentials. These kinds of student-athletes are often referred for counseling and/or learning disability testing (see Chapter 14), or they present on their own because they are struggling to survive in the classroom. They often report feeling overwhelmed for various reasons, wanting to stay athletically eligible, or trying to keep up with their more academically adept athlete or non-athlete peers. Helping professionals should also be prepared to encounter athletes who are the first in their families to attend college, as well as clients with varying academic and sport-related motives (Gaston-Gayles, 2004). Indeed, many academically distressed clients may lack a sense of purpose or focus, may have been unsure about going on to college after high school, may have found themselves in college simply by default, or may not have even had the opportunity or the desire to attend college if it were not for the fact that they were athletically gifted and consequently had been recruited to attend and play for "the U."

It appears that today's student-athletes, much like other students, may experience even more pressure than in the past to perform well in the classroom so as to meet their institutions' academic standards (Kadison & DiGeronimo, 2004), to prepare as best they can for the competitive world of work (whether they eventually graduate or not), and for some, to possibly go on to attend graduate school. However, additional pressure for student-athletes to do well academically has arisen in recent years with the advent of the NCAA's "Academic Progress Rate" (APR) requirements, ostensibly implemented by NCAA member institutions to enhance the academic achievement of student-athletes and increase their graduation rates (NCAA, 2007b). In view of this, academic progress is closely monitored by athletics compliance officers and is of considerable interest to coaches today, given both their substantive financial incentives for raising graduation rates and the spectrum of penalties for teams that do not fare well academically.

Another area of academic control is linked to the practice of having student-athletes sign a so-called pre-participation document, that "voluntarily" authorizes examination of their academic records (typically protected under the Federal Educational Right to Privacy Act [FERPA], 1974) by athletics staff members (e.g., athletic academic advisors/counselors, rules compliance staff, coaches) who have a need to know (Etzel & Watson, 2007). If the authorization is not freely signed, would-be athletes are not allowed to participate. In light of this practice, which results in the athlete's academic life (and sometimes health history, if part of the agreement) becoming an open book, helping professionals need to be aware that their student-athlete clients may not be immediately trusting and forthcoming, and that they may be quite suspicious of people in authority because it has been those people who have routinely un-empowered them. In fact a so-called "trust gap" often exists between authority figures and student-athletes. For this reason, at the onset of the initial counseling session, helping professionals must make it clear to student-athlete clients that without their expressed permission, the helping professional not only will not, but cannot communicate personal information shared in counseling with athletic department staff members, or for that matter, any others who claim to have a need to know.

As noted above, helping professionals who work with student-athletes need to keep in mind that it is rather common for their course and major selection, class attendance, and studying to be closely overseen and/or controlled by athletics staff (e.g., academic advisors, assistant coaches, and compliance officers). This oversight seems to be particularly common at larger NCAA Division I schools, in the high-profile "revenue" sports, and with freshmen and academically marginal students.

Helping professionals would likely benefit from appreciating how athletics department micromanagement of academics has the potential to diminish the frequency and influence of guidance provided by other university staff (e.g., academic advisors) and faculty. This monitoring is seen by some student-athlete clients as "no big deal" because they have habituated to it; others see it as being intrusive or even confusing, given the mixed messages they sometimes receive from different sources of official and unofficial direction. Indeed, some of our clients have reported that they really do not know who their official faculty advisors are, or (mistakenly) that their advisors are athletics department staff members or coaches. From a developmental perspective, academic micromanaging, while perhaps serving in some ways to foster academic progress, may not be useful to student-athletes in the long run. They may not learn to think, plan, and act independently; deal with uncertainty; take stock of their interests and values; develop a sense of purpose; and assume personal responsibility for their choices and behavior in and out of the classroom. Over the years, we have worked with student-athlete clients who reported having compromised, willingly or unwillingly, their personal academic interests and performance to keep up with athletics—some with the hope of going on to professional sports. Even though the odds of going pro are very poor (i.e., approximately 2%), it is not uncommon to learn that a student-athlete is a "pre-NFL," "pre-NBA," or "pre-MLB" major. Athletes may choose majors that are less challenging to them, because these areas of study are less demanding and allow for more time to be devoted to regular training, travel, and competition (Suggs, 2003). Others report avoiding or having been steered away from other meaningful courses or majors of interest because they directly conflicted with athletics activity or were considered too demanding and consequently a potential threat to remaining eligible.

Recently, Jim Harbaugh (former University of Michigan quarterback, professional football player, and currently head coach for the Stanford University football program) commented: "Michigan is a good school. I got a good education there. But the athletic department has ways to get borderline guys in, and when they are in, they steer them to courses in sports communications" (Oller, 2007). Although in some instances it may be helpful (at least to the athletics program or university) to have "academic friends" of the athletic department, in other instances where there is pressure to excel athletically, some less capable or less academically motivated student-athletes needing to remain eligible may find themselves considering previously unacceptable behaviors as a means of maintaining their active player status (e.g., having others write papers or complete projects for them, or otherwise cheating).

Sadly, too, we have encountered clients who reported that they were misled during the recruiting process about what they could really study while participating in athletics (i.e., they were fed the old "bait and switch"). Indeed, while the frequency of such practices is uncertain, a basketball or football player who studies pre-medicine or engineering and who graduates from such a major appears to be a rather rare bird. Clearly, there are between-school and major differences that exist in the academic offerings and quality of education available to students. It also seems that the extent that academics are emphasized and supported in intercollegiate athletics varies. It has been observed that a gap is growing between the educational missions of colleges and universities and so-called big-time intercollegiate athletics (Bowen & Levin, 2003). One could argue that while appearing pro academics (e.g., APR), intercollegiate athletic programs are perhaps gradually moving away from this position in practice as they acquire more of a stake in student-athletes' academic lifestyles. For example, one author was encouraged by a head coach's apparent interest in screening all incoming freshmen for possible learning disabilities. When the psychologist shared this with another coach on staff, the coach scoffed at the idea, saying that the head coach didn't really care and was just interested in keeping athletes eligible as long as possible by identifying those athletes who might require a greater level of oversight due to the possibility of their being eventually lost to the team.

Unfortunately, academic rules are sometimes bent or adjusted to assist athletes, particularly the talented ones (Lipka, 2006; McGraw &

Reeves, 1997). Failure to thrive in the classroom can have pervasive consequences. For example, academic underachievement or collapse can create personal and interpersonal distress and jeopardize academic and athletic standings, compromising the client's current levels of functioning and psychological well-being. Those who do not survive academically (i.e., do not make adequate "academic progress") may not be able to afford to continue to attend school on their own and/or may lose their annually awarded athletic financial aid (i.e., "scholarships"), if they received such support. This is apparently not an unusual phenomenon (Berg, 1989). Failure to meet minimum academic requirements will likely impact clients' futures. For example, the authors have seen many clients who sought counseling because they were overwhelmed with the demands that life and athletics circumstances placed upon them and the impact on performance in the classroom, putting them at risk for ending their time in school. The opposite situation is also a possible scenario one may confront in consultation. Helping professionals should also be prepared to assist clients who did not graduate in a timely fashion, perhaps gave professional sport a go, and who returned some time later to complete their degrees. Whether they recognize and/or admit it, student-athletes' abilities to meet their academic responsibilities has personal relevance because their lives likely will be affected well beyond the end of their involvement in collegiate athletics; that is to say, their academic ability, lack of it, or failure to apply it will likely shape their occupational prospects, career growth, personal lives, and sense of self.

Physical and Mental Demands

It is safe to say that various life stressors create an atypical collegiate experience for many student-athletes (Etzel, 2003; Ferrante, 1989; Humphrey, Yow, & Bowden, 2000; Kimball & Freysinger, 2003; Shirka, 1997). Both positive and negative stressors seem to make them more vulnerable than many other college students to encounter frequent and higher levels of personal-social and health-related distress than other students (Ferrante, Etzel, & Lantz, 1996). Pinkerton, Hinz, and Barrow's (1987) observations support this view, suggesting that student-athletes form an "at-risk" group who are likely more predisposed than their peers to experiencing psychological distress due, to a large extent, to the unique trials and tribulations of the athletic lifestyle. The impact of stress represents another noteworthy factor that can adversely influence a student-athlete's daily and long-term functioning inside and outside the classroom, which helping professionals should inquire about at intake and monitor over the course of their work with their clients (Wilson & Pritchard, 2005).

Although no person is immune to the effects of stress, freshmen who are adjusting to a new lifestyle and transitioning from high school, family, and friends at home to a more independent university life may be particularly vulnerable to stress (Gruber, 1999; Medalie, 1981; Papanikolaou, Nikolaidais, Parsiaouras, & Alexopoulos, 2003). Transfers from other universities and junior colleges may be at risk, too, given the adjustments they face. Seniors, who are in the process of disengaging from school, sport, and established relationships and heading out to the world of work, graduate school, and new, often-uncertain commitments, also seem to be quite vulnerable and prone to struggle on their way out of the university during a period of "prolonged adolescence" (Eichler, 2006). Lanning (1982) observed that student-athletes who receive athletic scholarships may have additional stresses that at times make it useful for them to seek confidential consultation from helping professionals. This may link to performance expectations associated with receiving athletics-related financial aid and maintaining that award. He maintained that student-athletes could sometimes benefit from direct counseling aimed at self-concept, peer relationships, injury, career choice, study skills, and time management. The authors have also found that some student-athletes seek consultation when they are in jeopardy of losing their scholarships for various reasons.

In a large-scale descriptive study of student-athletes at a medium-size land-grant (NCAA Division I-A) institution, Etzel (1989) investigated the patterns of life stress sources, stress reactions, and perceptions of personal control over life situations of 263 male and female student-athletes. Participants reported that, in comparison to non-athletes, they perceived experiencing significantly greater amounts of overall life stress and cognitive stress symptoms (e.g., anxiety, worry, irritability) and reported possessing a chance-oriented, external locus of control. A 2003 very large-scale survey of nearly 21,000 female and male student-athletes across the three NCAA divisions provided some remarkable insight into aspects of the reported emotional status of the respondents

(NCAA, 2003). When asked how often they had experienced various emotional states during the previous three months, the percentage of those who in combination answered "Some of the time" and "A lot of the time" were as follows: nothing could cheer me up (43%); nervous (85%); restless and fidgety (69%); hopeless (28%); worthless (22%); helpless (29%); and that everything was an effort (23%). Although the sources of these emotional reactions were not specified, the data suggest that these young people were probably struggling with a range of life stress.

Blinde and Greendorfer (1992) (cited in Gill, 1995) have identified four varieties of difficulties associated with "mismatches" that both female and male college athletes often struggle with: (1) role conflict (i.e., meeting student-versus-athlete role expectations); (2) role strain (i.e., distress associated with meeting the expectations of powerful others like parents, coaches, teachers); (3) value alienation (i.e., struggling with one's sport-related and personal values); and (4) exploitation (i.e., predominance of athletic responsibilities that prevent adequate attending to student or personal responsibilities). Alone or in combination, such mismatches and unusual lifestyle demands can drain one's energy and compromise coping skills and abilities. Struggling clients may fail to attend to daily responsibilities and may express discouragement and dissatisfaction, as well as encounter a range of possible health and mental health disorders as noted above (Andersen, 2002; Huebner & Lawson, 1990; Lewis, 1991; Shell & Ferrante, 1996; Stone & Strange, 1989). In view of the range and magnitude of stress sources that these young people may encounter, it is remarkable that so many of them manage to perform successfully, become well-functioning adults, and ultimately graduate.

Counseling sessions and informal interactions with student-athletes as well as senior exit surveys have, over time, revealed that many student-athletes are regularly in a state of mental and physical distress. They report various recurrent health problems and are frequently nursing nagging injuries (Etzel, Watson, Visek, & Maniar, 2006; Humphrey, Yow, & Bowden, 2000; McAllister, Motamedi, Hame, Shapiro, & Dorey, 2001; Selby, Weinstein, & Bird, 1990). Many report having limited energy to devote to their personal and family lives, as well as other areas of interest (hobbies), responsibility (school work), and long-term value (career-planning). Interestingly, a recent, large sample of nearly 700 NCAA Division I and Division II student-athletes revealed that healthy athletes had a more positive view of their physical and mental health status than did same-aged non-athletes (Huffman, Park, Roser-Jones, Senett, Yagnick, & Webner, 2008).

Although these typically healthy, fit young people are quite resilient, it should not be difficult to appreciate how participation in such activities associated with this lifestyle can be experienced as stressful (Kimball & Freysinger, 2003; Pinkerton, Hinz, & Barrow, 1987) and may leave these young people chronically "under-recovered" from all of it (Kellmann, 2002). Under-recovery can be thought of as "the failure to fulfill current [training] recovery demands" that results from "excessively prolonged and/or intense exercise, stressful competition or other [life] stressors" (Kellmann, 2002, p. 3). Under-recovered athletes may present with symptoms of negative affect (e.g., depression, irritability, anxiety), various somatic complaints, and other phenomena such as low energy, sleep problems, poor self-efficacy, a lack of accomplishment, and interpersonal conflict (Kellmann & Kallus, 2001).

Recent literature reflects a greater than ever interest in the mental health of student-athletes (Etzel, Watson, Visek, & Maniar, S. 2006; Hosick, 2005; Maniar, Chamberlain, & Moore, 2005). Tragic cases such as the death of Kyle Ambrogi seem to have heightened awareness to an area of health care that was not emphasized much until the past few years (Drehs, 2007). It has been estimated that approximately 10% of student-athletes experience some sort of mental health concern that necessitates the use of professional assistance (Hinkle, 1994; Broughton & Neyer, 2001). Given an increased awareness of the importance of psychological problems with this population (Maniar et al., 2005), the NCAA has recently published a handbook for dealing with athlete mental health issues (NCAA, 2007c). This document can be useful for athletics staff, helping professionals, and student-athletes themselves.

When conducting an initial interview, helping professionals need to inquire about general health, eating/dietary habits, injury history, alcohol and drug use, and assess for possible under-recovery in addition to standard mental health questions. An effective interview also would involve inquiring about any other symptoms that may be present that may negatively impinge upon the student-athlete's psycho-social functioning or otherwise impede the return to a balanced state. Counselors and psychologists working with student-athletes who routinely administer symptom checklists or athlete-specific screening instruments (Steiner, Pyle, Brassington, Matheson, & King, 2003) may also want to have on hand an instrument to assess training recovery such as REST-Q Sport (Kellmann & Kallus, 2001) or the Brief Assessment of Recovery and Stress (Keeler, Etzel & Blom, under review).

Developmental Tasks

Student-athletes are faced with mastering the so-called "developmental tasks" associated with the college years—tasks that are quite formidable in their own right for all older adolescents and young adults (Astin, 1977; Chickering, 1969; 1981; Chickering, & Reisser, 1993; Erikson, 1968; Farnsworth, 1966; Medalie, 1981; Pascarella & Terenzini, 1991, 2005; Sweet, 1990). Initially, the normally immature late adolescent faces the challenge of becoming competent in a number of areas, while evolving from a position of relative dependence upon parents and other significant influential adults and peers to a position of relative independence. Also, during these four to six years, students are challenged to make major life decisions relating to a sense of purpose (e.g., an academic major; eventually an occupation and career path or transition to graduate school), cultivating lasting and meaningful relationships, and identifying and solidifying personal values regarding love, sexuality, friendship, spirituality, and trust. Learning to recognize, accept, and meet responsibilities, as well as how to set personal limits, and deal effectively and cooperatively with authority figures are other tasks that must be mastered by the young person who is simultaneously engaged in mastering the demands of being a student-athlete.

Clearly, every college student has faced the pressures to overcome academic, personal, and educational challenges and along the way resolve the developmental tasks of young adulthood in her or his own way (McGrath, 2006). However, most non-athletes do not have to do so in addition to training and performing under the stress that the athletics lifestyle imposes, which typically exceeds "normal" college life demands. Today's student-athletes are challenged to somehow keep in relative balance three major areas of responsibility (i.e., personal life, academics, and athletics). Many lack the wherewithal to meet these challenges to self-efficacy and confidence independently (Street, 1999). Still others may at certain times become overwhelmed in one or more of these areas, leading to imbalance that often results in increased levels of psychosocial distress. Helping professionals' jobs involve anticipating, supporting, and responding to the needs of student-athletes, and ideally to prevent or minimize such imbalances through psycho-educational outreach programming and consultation that is aimed at helping them maintain or quickly regain a sense of balance in stressful times.

Some research suggests that involvement in intercollegiate athletics may delay the accomplishment of the normal developmental tasks that college-age people usually work through in a timely fashion (Kornspan & Etzel, 2003), but this may not always be the case (Valentine & Taub, 1999). For example, research from the rather distant past by Blann (1985), Kennedy and Dimick (1987), and Stuart (1985) found that samples of student-athletes were less able to formulate mature educational and career plans than other college students. Sowa and Gressard (1983) reported significant differences between student-athletes and non-athletes on three subscales of the Student Developmental Task Inventory (Winston, Miller, & Prince, 1979) (i.e., educational plans, career plans, and mature relationships with peers). Melendez (2006) observed gender and athletic status differences can have a significant impact on student-athlete adjustment to college. Other research by Brown (1993), Bulling (1992), Smallman and Sowa (1996), and Martens and Cox (2000) provided further evidence for the potentially detrimental influences of sport participation on student-athlete career development.

Most student-athletes appear to find a way to more or less succeed in the classroom, in sport, and in their personal lives. They are a remarkably resilient lot. However, some generally or situationally less resilient student-athletes may be handed a set of daily and long-term responsibilities that they are not able to meet or are sometimes prevented from meeting vis-a-vis their extraordinary lifestyles. For some, awareness of the scope and extent of these responsibilities may become apparent early in their freshman year, when the typically higher levels of sport related training and academic accountability reveal themselves. For others, this reality sets in gradually over time or when some destabilizing life event or series of events occurs.

There are several theories and models of college student development (King, 1994). However one chooses to conceptualize this complex process, it is important to keep in mind that student-athletes' accomplishment of developmental tasks may actually be both helped and hampered in part by participation in collegiate athletics (Valentine & Taub, 1999). More than a few other salient factors may serve to contribute to an atypical or erratic rate of development. As is true for college students in general, athlete clients bring to campus individual attributes, disorders, habits, and an array of experiences that interact with the mix of life's "immediate stressors" that are linked to social life, self-care, change, and the diversities of college life (Grayson, 2006). The time required to condition, train, and practice, to attend film sessions and meetings, to learn sport-specific material, and to travel to and from competitions can have great potential impact on clients' lives and general physical and mental health status. The stress of competition, travel away from school, and the responsibility to perform well can be both exciting and disturbing. The physical effort expended on a daily basis often leaves athletes exhausted and hurting. The constellation of sport-related experiences is usually not the sole cause of their difficulties, deficiencies, and/or special needs, however. Rather, their family backgrounds and life experiences combined with their personalities, intellectual capabilities, psychosocial development, vulnerability to stress, and coping skills prior to matriculation must all be taken into account in the effort to understand and effectively assist athlete clients and the systems in which they function.

Scrutiny

Student-athletes tend to be quite identifiable both on campus and in the community. Indeed, many have described involvement in inter-collegiate athletics as living "in a fishbowl." Many student-athletes (sometimes referred to as the university's most "visible ambassadors") must constantly attend to their public image, which presupposes that their behavior is being regularly scrutinized both on and off the playing field. The DUI or altercation downtown or the leaked positive drug test (i.e., "team rule violations") that would go relatively unnoticed with their non-athlete peers becomes front page news in the case of the athlete. Even fumbles, errors, missed field-goals, dropped passes, and technical fouls are examples of sporting events that can haunt the student-athlete for some time to come. Although such issues are not collectively shared by all student-athletes vis-a-vis the sport in which they participate, it is quite apparent that student-athletes live, study, play, and develop under conditions that frequently make a "normal," rather private college life difficult, if not at times impossible. As such, these difficulties are likely compounded for those who participate in so-called "revenue-producing" sports, and for those involved in highly competitive programs that receive regular national and regional media coverage (e.g., NCAA Division I institutions).

Injury

Another common source of life distress is athletic injury. Data from the NCAA's Injury Surveillance System (ISS) details increases in reported training and competition injury rates (Copeland, 2007). Recent ISS data reveals that athletes are exceptionally vulnerable to injury during their "pre-season" build-up training period and in competitions. Of note to helping professionals is the fact that roughly 25% are considered severe, resulting in at least 10 days out of participation. These serious injuries that have increased in frequency, such as anterior cruciate ligament tears and head trauma, may warrant a referral from sports medicine staff for psychological intervention (e.g., evaluation, counseling, neuropsychological testing).

What has prompted an increased occurrence of injury in current times? Perhaps some causes are the intensity of training, the fact that it often occurs year-round today (which does not allow for adequate recovery), the implementation of sophisticated strength and conditioning methods, and better sport nutrition practices and regular supplement use that have produced stronger and faster athletes that may tend to repeatedly "push the limits." Whatever the causes, it is also known that stressful life events can occasion vulnerabilities that predispose athletes to suffer sport-related injuries (Andersen & Williams, 1988; Etzel, Zizzi, Newcomer-Appeneal, Ferrante, & Perna, 2007; Heil, 1993; Pargman, 2007; Petitpas & Danish, 1995; Rotella & Heyman, 1993; Williams, 2001) and can prolong the complex process of rehabilitation (Podlog & Eklund, 2007). The physical and psychological effects of sport-related injury, or even the specter of injury, can be and often are disruptive and distressful (Etzel & Ferrante, 1993; Etzel et al., 2007; Kleiber & Brock, 1992; Pargman, 2007; Selby, Weinstein, & Bird, 1993). Indeed, rehabilitation, which can involve multiple daily treatment sessions, can become more time consuming than sport participation itself; treatment may discourage and alienate the injured athlete (Ermler & Thomas, 1990).

Given the amount of exposure to training stress and competition, college student-athletes are placed at risk to experience high frequencies of physical impairment—ironically within a system that wants very much to keep them healthy and prevent injury. These young people are quite vulnerable to losses in physical functioning that often not only remove them from athletic activities, but also force them to cope emotionally with those losses—often on their own. Many of these normally active and healthy people are not prepared to deal with injury-linked loss because they have little or no history of such loss in their lives, limited coping skills, or perhaps a lack of social support in these unwelcome situations. Regrettably, some college athletes have been injured quite a bit over time, which may be either useful or not to their rehabilitation. From an oddly beneficial perspective, the client who has been injured, especially in the same or similar way (e.g., a second ACL tear), has a sense of what the path to return to play will be in general (if this is the chosen path), and the coping skills and resources she or he will need to rehabilitate. In contrast, the athlete who has no such history, or a limited one, can be overwhelmed and benefit perhaps even more from professional consultation and different forms of social support (e.g., listening, informational, emotional) (Richman, Hardy, Rosenfeld, & Callanan, 1989).

Psychologists and counselors providing support to college student-athletes should be on the lookout for "sub-clinical" reactions to injury (e.g., apprehension, low level changes in mood, worry, interpersonal problems) (Gardner & Moore, 2006). In cases of more serious injury with greater impairment, a diagnosable disorder (e.g., adjustment disorder, posttraumatic stress disorder; cognitive disorder not otherwise specified) may be observed (Shell & Ferrante, 1996). Helping professionals should inquire about alcohol and other drug use with clients who may be self-medicating in an effort to cope. Clearly, individual differences in response and impact on the rehabilitation process, as well as overall personal functioning (e.g., self-care, mobility, school, relationships), will be seen that are influenced by the severity of the injury (Brewer, 1994; May & Sieb, 1987; Taylor & Taylor, 1997). Although mental health professionals can be very helpful to injured and disabled athletes, their services may unfortunately not be used or they may be sought out only as a resource of "last resort" (Brewer, Van Raalte, & Petitpas, 2007; also see Chapter 15).

Drugs and Alcohol

Like their non-athlete peers, most student-athletes consume alcohol and some other recreational drugs (AOD) (NCAA, 2003; Knight, Wechsler, Meichen, Seibring, Weitzman, & Schuckit, 2002; Wechsler, Davenport, Dowdall, Grossman, & Zanakos, 1997). (See Chapter 16.) In general, alcohol is clearly the drug of choice on campus and its ab/use is linked to numerous behavioral, health, and legal problems (Meilman, Lewis, & Gerstein, 2006). Sometimes students engage in these behaviors to try to cope with their life difficulties, boredom, or stress or for other purposes (e.g., to fit in with peers). Obviously, this strategy can, in fact, both cause and exacerbate problems. Also, as noted earlier, for student-athletes who are required to participate in drug testing (e.g., participants in NCAA associated programs), AOD use may contribute to the denial of problems and reluctance to seek help from service providers. The student-athletes may not trust professionals with personal information about their private habits for fear it may not remain confidential. In still other instances, they may realize that to seek assistance may ultimately result in confronting their need to cease or change the problematic behavior, and they do not want to do so just yet. Obviously, AOD use by student-athletes can make the professional's job of helping to resolve their problems a difficult and frustrating one. Helping professionals should obtain special training in this area in order to become competent to assist athletes with commonly encountered AOD issues (Berg & Reuss, 1998; Miller & Rollnick, 2002).

Ferrante (1989) observed some time ago that mandatory drug testing in intercollegiate athletics provides student-athletes with yet one more stress source (i.e., constant surveillance of private behavior and serious sanctions for positive tests). This requirement possesses the potential to both positively and negatively affect their collegiate experience and beyond. To more fully empower student-athletes, Ferrante proposed that they could benefit from the availability of confidential alcohol and drug education programs, which the NCAA now requires be offered during the academic year, and the incorporation of specific informational or psycho-educational components into existing and future program curricula (e.g., assertiveness training, values clarification, communication skills, self-exploration, and one-on-one counseling). Further, suggesting a preventive approach to these health issues, he advocated for drug testing programs and policies to be supportive and ameliorative rather than punitive in nature. Such alcohol and drug education programs and confidential personal counseling are examples of efforts to assist student-athletes by assessing, identifying, and addressing substance use/abuse as a potential risk to the health (and the future) of these young people, rather than to punish them for their private, albeit possibly illegal and potentially harmful, behavior. Although this notion is especially applicable to interventions with student-athletes who have tested positive for drugs for the first time, individuals who produce repeated positive drug tests, by virtue of their obvious and apparent reliance upon substances in the face of negative consequences, demonstrate a clear need for immediate, more in-depth assistance (e.g., ambulatory detox, intensive out-patient, or even inpatient treatment) that would likely preclude their participation in athletics and possibly finishing the current academic semester. (See Chapter 16.)

Overcoming Obstacles to Accessing Counseling Services

Most colleges and universities today offer a wide range of student services (e.g., counseling, career, disability, health) typically available to all fee-paying students through their respective divisions of student life. These services and their respective staffs offer considerable potential benefit to student-athletes. Although the literature offers rather limited insight into the use of helping services by student-athletes, overall it appears that this group may be rather reluctant to seek help and typically underutilizes such services (Bergandi & Wittig, 1984; Carmen, Zerman, & Blaine 1968; Pierce, 1969; Pinkerton, Hinz, & Barrow, 1987; Reinhold, 1973; Segal, Weiss, & Sokol, 1965; Vaughn & Emener, 1993; Watson, 2005). Unfortunately, several obstacles make it quite difficult or unfeasible for many student-athletes to access or to be inclined to utilize helping services. These include: (1) the student-athlete's visibility on campus; (2) time limitations; (3) myths about the athletics system linked to helping student-athletes; (4) the restricted nature of athletic cultures; (5) personal attributes, behaviors, and expectations of student-athletes; and (6) the potential of loss of status for seeking psychological consultation (Ferrante, Etzel, & Lantz, 1996).

Visibility

Student-athletes appear to be less inclined to visit or schedule an appointment at a counseling center or psychological services agency than non-athletes (Watson, 2005). Many do not want to be seen in the waiting rooms of such an agency or even walking into the office of a (sport) psychologist or counselor conveniently located at athletics facilities for fear of revealing a personal weakness or perceived need for help. (Interestingly, many tend to wear university athletics gear, sometimes with their names on their back, that nonetheless makes them readily identifiable.) Those who do seek assistance sometimes ask to be seen after hours, in private, at alternative settings, or come to services through the "back door." Furthermore, there are real concerns over the possible assumptions that other students, coaches, or teammates might make about the student-athlete should she or he be seen (for example, his or her ability to perform or to handle pressure or to be an effective leader or stable person can come into question) (Linder, Brewer, Van Raalte, & DeLange, 1991). Clearly, seeking professional help and guidance for most students should be and is a largely private act. This may not be so, however, for identifiable student-athletes. In fact, seeking help can quickly become a public act for them—an act that may generate considerable gossip and impinge upon their lives and privacy.

Among many other sticky ethical issues associated with consultation in the intercollegiate athletics environment, helping professionals need to be sensitive to visibility and confidentiality issues (Etzel & Watson, 2007; Watson & Etzel, 2004). They should pay special attention to the potential detrimental implications of both their private and public interactions, even casual ones, with student-athletes. In particular, to be more effective service providers, helpers must be careful when interacting with student-athletes publicly to safeguard the client confidentiality. We recommend simply asking the student-athlete in the initial session if she or he is comfortable and willing to be seen with or informally interacting with the counselor or psychologist at practice, rehabilitation sites, or elsewhere out in public. Our standard practice is to discuss confidentiality and boundaries with our clients in the initial session, and explain that should we inadvertently come into contact outside the counseling room, that we will only engage or otherwise acknowledge them if they initiate such interaction (in an effort to preserve their confidentiality). In addition to this approach being appropriate, it serves to empower the student-athlete and often speeds and enhances rapport and trust. Professionals also must be willing to consider making other accommodations when offering and scheduling formal and informal counseling sessions and where those sessions will be conducted (e.g., at training sites or alternative offices). Clear boundaries must be established in non-traditional consulting situations (Brown & Cogan, 2006).

Time Limitations

In the fairly distant past, a very large sample of student-athletes reported that they invested extensive amounts of time in athletics-related activities (i.e., in excess of 30 hours per week and more), nearly as much as one would performing a full-time job (American Institutes for Research, 1988). Currently, National Collegiate Athletic Association (NCAA) regulations officially limit practice time to no more than 20 hours per week. Yet, despite the fact that there are growing numbers of "compliance" staff, there seem to be exceptions—ways to bend—the rules. Depending on their particular sport and the competitive level of their school's program, student-athletes frequently report investing up to and in excess of 20 hours per week in structured, sport-specific activities (e.g., "voluntary" strength and conditioning workouts, strength and conditioning classes for credit, team meetings, "captain's practices," care of minor physical problems/rehabilitation). Athletes are compelled to engage in training sessions, which for some sports (e.g., swimming) may be held twice a day. So-called "pre-season" workouts and camps are often used to separate the athletic wheat from the chaff, and they may involve all-day activities that start in the early mornings and go into the evenings. Student-athletes can be and often are strongly encouraged to attend other informal sport-related activities as well (e.g., mental preparation for competitions, meetings with coaches, watching game DVD/video, interaction with media, and community service).

Strength and conditioning sessions, practices, rehabilitation, study halls, travel, and competition can drastically limit the amount of free time and energy student-athletes have available for accessing assistance when needed. In fact, some research and data from senior exit surveys over time indicate that many student-athletes in general spend more time, on the average, involved in athletic activities than they devote to preparing for and attending class (American Institutes for Research, 1988). To compound the problem of access, student affairs services and programs are typically offered at times when most classes are in session (mornings and sometimes evenings) and when practices occur (afternoons). For the student-athletes, mornings and early afternoons are characteristically jam-packed with classes that fit into time slots that will not conflict with practices or other athletically related activities. Even an early morning session may be challenging to make because many athletes are engaged in strength and conditioning sessions or sometimes early practices (e.g., in the cases of swimming and diving, rowing). The availability of direct-service contact (i.e., one-on-one counseling) is also usually limited because the majority of service center staff members end their working day at 5:00 p.m. and are no longer on campus except in crisis situations. Although evening consultations and groups may be available to some student-athletes, they are offered at times when many student-athletes are unlikely to be able to benefit from the content (i.e., when they are tired) or when their schedule is still tied into other required activities (e.g., night classes and study hall sessions). It would seem that offering considerably late afternoon and evening consultation hours (post training) would be useful. One may also expect to see athletes on their seemingly limited "off days" when there is no training or when their teams are not traveling to and from competitions.

Even if these accommodations are made, student-athletes may not take advantage of them. Given limited free time to relax and recover, the student-athlete may be much more inclined to take advantage of social and recreational opportunities, perceived as far more attractive than seeking help for academic or personal reasons. Involvement in more pleasurable and necessary recovery activities (e.g. sleeping, watching television, hanging out with friends) may be regarded by the student-athlete as both stress reducing and much more personally appealing.

Institutions often make efforts ostensibly to enhance the leadership abilities of student-athletes by having them involved in activities such as public appearances at university events, various speaking engagements, and other forms of community service. Such activities can be useful, but they are also time consuming and limit the opportunity to engage in useful help-seeking activity. Although public speaking and community service hold potential benefit for some student-athletes, it would seem that the kinds of participatory opportunities that should be offered first would be those that could help the student-athlete develop and maintain personal balance. At the very least, it remains clear that student-athletes who are required to participate in service activities are faced with yet one more demand to be added to an often already overtaxed daily schedule.

Offering alternative opportunities for personal development would perhaps benefit student-athletes more than engaging in aforementioned activities. For example, given the time to participate, student-athletes may benefit from team or community activities such as leadership skills training and peer mentoring and from participation in health-related programs (e.g., healthy eating/sports nutrition, alcohol/drug education, career development). Merely giving them more free time to attend to academics on their own or to simply have additional "down time" to lead some semblance of a normal college life would appear to make sense.

System Myths

Several myths about student-athletes and the athletics system persist, and if believed, would argue against providing helping services to student-athletes much, if at all. For example, if one were to assume that an athletic department's own staff or in-house programming are meeting the needs of their student-athletes, outreach efforts from and referral to student affairs service providers are rather unlikely. This seems to be an assumption held by many personnel inside and outside athletic departments (i.e., faculty, administration, and other students). It has been our experience that many athletics staff do not have much of an idea, if any in some cases, of what support services are actually available for students outside or sometimes even inside a department of intercollegiate athletics. Consequently, they may not know where to send or refer student-athletes even if it would seem useful to do so. Some athletics staff members may consciously avoid referring student-athletes for assistance outside of their "program" even when the referral is indicated and would likely be useful. The "We can take care of this ourselves" approach remains rather common. Referrals may not be made, too, due to a concern that the referral may be perceived by others as an indication of failure or ineptness on the staff's part.

However unfortunate, it appears that many athletics staff, especially those associated with the high-profile sports, like their student-athletes, seem to live in a world divorced from the university; so much so that oftentimes even student affairs administrators and staff may not be particularly aware of what goes on within athletics either (Etzel et al., 2006). In all fairness, it is probably the responsibility of helping professionals to regularly communicate with others to inform them of the range of services available to student-athletes, why and when they might consider referring someone, and how to go about doing so. Despite differences in objectives, perspective, expectations, and philosophies, collaboration with coaches and other departmental potential referral sources is essential to effective and responsible student service provision (Weustenberg, 1999). However, this is often not an easy task.

Unfortunately, a gap seems to exist still today among many athletic department staff, student services providers, and faculty, which may be expanding. Perhaps this is a reflection of the culture of athletics departments becoming more "disengaged' from the rest of the academy (Comeaux, 2007). Nevertheless, from a student affairs and faculty perspective, it would seem useful for those personnel outside of athletics to have an appreciation of student-athlete lifestyles and of some of the basic NCAA rules and regulations that athletes must follow, in order to better understand and support those they encounter from intercollegiate athletics (Fletcher, Benshoff, & Richburg, 2003; Hill, Burch-Ragan, & Yates, 2001; Watt & Moore, 2001). Faculty and student affairs staff who hold critical views of intercollegiate athletics and participants may benefit from outreach efforts from athletics to try to bridge this gap and establish useful connections with athletes, before they need guidance or are in some sort of personal crisis (Brent et al., 2006). Outreach programming intended to bridge such gaps seems to have considerable potential for professional staff working with university counseling and psychological services centers that provide therapy and psycho-social counseling to student-athletes.

Another important yet sometimes overlooked issue involves the identity and qualifications of athletic department staff service providers. In an early attempt to examine the roles, responsibilities, and professional preparation of athletic counselors, Brooks, Etzel, and Ostrow (1987) found that athletic advisors and counselors surveyed at the NCAA Division I level reportedly were predominantly male ex-athletes with master's degrees in education. Their major charge and time commitment were focused on academic advising. In a replication of this study (Etzel, Weaver, & Ostrow, 1995), data revealed that the job responsibilities and the backgrounds of athletic advisors and counselors had not significantly changed over the course of nearly ten years. If these findings are generalizable, then little time, energy, and professional expertise were or are being made available to assist student-athletes "in house" with their personal, social, and developmental concerns. If so, this may be because maintenance of academic eligibility commands a high priority or because internal staff are not generally trained, credentialed, or officially tasked to provide personal counseling services to student-athletes. If true, it may be so because staff who are not counseling or psychology professionals (e.g., coaches, academic advisors, athletic trainers, CHAMPS/ Life Skills coordinators) are informally providing counseling assistance on their own. Feedback from several years of senior exit surveys at a Division I school overseen by one author indicates that student-athletes are inclined to seek support from friends, family, coaches, athletic trainers, and spiritual advisors before they seek the consultation of mental health professionals and sport psychologists.

Over time, it seems that such staffing patterns may be gradually changing as awareness grows regarding the psychosocial needs of athletes and their potential impact on academic and athletic performance. More trained psychologists are being hired by athletic departments to provide assistance to student-athletes in areas such as substance abuse and career and personal counseling (Brent et al., 2006). Over the past few years, the authors have observed increasing numbers of athletic department and university counseling and psychological service centers adding full-time or part-time sport psychologists to their health care teams. This encouraging trend may stem in part from the NCAA's recognition of the psychological needs of student athletes (Hosick, 2005).

Student-athletes are often seen as a pampered group with extraordinary personal privileges that may include special admissions criteria, special academic advising, separate training tables, preferential class scheduling, and free medical care, study centers, and tutoring (Burke, 1993; Engstrom, Sedlacek, & McEwen, 1995; Hipple, 1993; Lanning, 1982). Some time ago, Remer, Tongate, and Watson (1978) observed that student-athletes are more likely a group truly in need of help but often unaware of their needs. This is probably still true today. This finding may hold particular relevance to athletic department staff who may also be unaware of student-athlete personal/psychosocial needs or are more concerned with other pressing problems (e.g., complying with NCAA rules, ticket sales, fund raising, coaching to win) (Heyman, 1993).

Another myth that seems to remain quite alive today is that coaches, athletic department staff members (e.g., academic counselors, athletic trainers), teammates, friends, or family are somehow meeting all of the student-athlete's needs. For example, many coaches seem to wear many hats at different times and are often empowered and quite willing to serve informally as confidante/counselor, psychologist, academic advisor, sports nutritionist, etc. Over time, student-athletes may begin to assume that they need not seek external help and therefore may not know or trust service providers outside the athletic "family." Coaches and athletic department personnel may also openly or indirectly discourage student-athletes from seeking available campus services by implying that the student-athlete's situation may not be understood, cared about, or otherwise handled to their liking by outsiders. Some personnel may be concerned that potentially sensitive information might be communicated to others outside of the team or athletic department "family." The attitude of "We can take care of our own problems" (except perhaps when emergencies arise or individual situations are left exposed) is frequently sensed by outside and sometimes departmental professionals. Therefore, to their detriment, athletic department staff can be very protective and controlling when it comes to their student-athletes and their "turf" (Heyman, 1993). We have seen this to be generally more true for men's than women's sport teams over the years, although this trend may be changing given the increasingly more competitive and commercialized nature of women's sport today. The astute professional should keep in mind that this disinclination to refer a student-athlete to extra-departmental helpers may be an obstacle that is very difficult to overcome; possibly even insurmountable.

Restrictive Environments

Sperber (1990) observed that colleges and universities have created complex, controlling systems that focus their efforts primarily on recruiting, training, and retaining groups of skilled, academically eligible performers, for the purpose of producing highly visible and, hopefully, profitable winning teams. This perception does not seem to have changed much in the increasingly competitive business of intercollegiate athletics today (Duderstadt, 2000; Knight Commission, 2001). Interestingly, it has been further argued that the intercollegiate athletics system has generally served to undermine the quality of undergraduate education in the United States (Sperber, 2000).

Ironically, Walter Byers, past executive director of the NCAA, observed: "Today, professional coaches, professional managers and money-minded presidents have total control [over student-athletes]" (Byers, 1995, p. 398). Accordingly, the intercollegiate athletic system today seems to resemble "total institutions" (Goffman, 1961). Such institutions (e.g., the military, prisons, mental institutions) control all or most aspects of a person's life, in a shared setting, under the close supervision of persons of authority, for the purpose of fulfilling the goals of the institution, leading to changes in the persons involved in the institution (Homer, 1981). Today, coaches often control when the student-athletes on their teams wake, eat, train, attend class, and go to sleep. Those new to working with student-athletes should not be surprised to hear from clients that they are involved in total-institution, athletics-related activities eight or more hours a day—especially "in-season." For example, participants in football often have required strength-and-conditioning training early in the morning, return to watch film in the early afternoon, get taped up, practice, receive treatment post practice, and eat dinner. Some also attend required study halls during the week. Selection of majors, guided by athletic academic advisors and sometimes by coaches, is commonly restricted to those that fit the football training schedule.

Whether it is fact or fiction, many athletic departments function as autonomous entities, curiously separated from the rest of the university. These departments are quite closed to those who are not part of the athletics "family"—except of course, on game days. Thirty years ago, Remer et al. (1978) described collegiate athletics as a self-perpetuating system that is difficult for outsiders to enter. Some maintain that athletic

departments, especially "big-time" departments, are in fact independent on-campus businesses, "auxiliaries" of the university that have very
little, if any, connection to the other functional activities of the school
(Bowan & Levin, 2001; Sperber, 1990, 2000; Zimbalist, 1999).

Student-athletes often report that they feel rather isolated from other
parts of the campus (Lubker, 2006; Potuto & O'Hanlon, 2006). Other
than attending classes with non-athlete peers, they may have limited
contact with the mainstream of campus life. They tend to be discon-
nected from non-athlete peers and generally associate with their athlete
peers from the same "subculture" much more than others on campus or
the community at large (Lanning & Toye, 1993). In fact, they typically
spend a considerable amount of time together, not only in sport-related
activities but also in groups of athletes that live together (e.g., in the
"hockey house"), attend many of the same classes, are clustered into
"jock majors" (Suggs, 2003), and socialize together. Remer et al. (1978)
concluded that even though many student-athletes are supported by
the intercollegiate athletics system, they may not necessarily be helped
by it as much as they could be, except in areas of athletic performance
and academic eligibility that must be maintained if the individual athlete's performance is to be showcased at all.

Interestingly, Bergandi and Wittig (1984) reported that 75% of the
athletic directors they surveyed claimed to have held positive attitudes
about the usefulness of support service programs for their student-
athletes. As a result of growing awareness of the special needs of
student-athletes on the part of the NCAA, many NCAA-affiliated institutions have since adopted models for student-athlete programming
such as CHAMPS/LifeSkills (NCAA, 2007a) on their campuses. (See
Chapter 4.) Nevertheless, it is important to recognize that people and
systems are generally resistant to change; intercollegiate athletics seems
to be no exception. Consequently, helping professionals must appreciate that, if an opportunity arises, the process of implementing a program of support services for student-athletes will likely take a long
time to develop and may likely require persistent effort to maintain
(Ferrante, Etzel, & Pinkney, 1991).

Both the restrictive environments so typical of university athletic departments and their sometimes well-intentioned efforts to microman-
age student-athletes are seen as potentially beneficial and detrimental to

the well-being of these developing young people. At the very least, oversight and control simply do not provide many student-athletes with the opportunities and freedom that non-athlete students have to explore various academic and experiential options and learn to assume personal responsibility through experience. However well meaning, such efforts can shelter student-athletes from the process of learning to make thoughtful, independent choices and from anticipating the logical consequences of their behavior—a shelter that for many may inhibit personal development and the acquisition of a sense of "how the real world works."

Because contemporary student-athletes may function in a total-institution context, helping professionals conducting initial intake interviews with them would do well to inquire about the restricted systems they are involved in (Fletcher, et al., 2003), their unusual lifestyles, daily responsibilities, pressures, and training and recovery requirements to better understand, empathize with, and hopefully provide a more broad-based quality of assistance to these young men and women.

Personal Attributes, Behaviors, and Expectations

Student-athletes themselves can create and cling to barriers to services routinely available to them and used by the general student population. Athletes may ignore seeking help by learning to rely on powerful others (e.g., coaches, friends, family) or by having a developmentally normal yet false sense of self-reliance. As noted above, exit surveys over the years point to a disinclination to seek help from mental health providers and an inclination to reach out to family, friends, teammates, coaches, and spiritual advisors first. Some student-athletes seem to own an unrealistic faith in the ameliorative powers of the athletic lifestyle. That is to say, they believe that as long as they put forth a consistent, high degree of effort and play reasonably well, they will somehow exercise control over their lives and everything else will work out fine.

Many student-athletes, usually males, also cling to and project a "macho" attitude characterized by toughness, apparent insensitivity, invulnerability, and interpersonal distancing. Macho student-athletes may deny problems and be very reluctant to seek help for their personal concerns because they believe that only weak people admit that they could benefit from someone else's help (Linder, Brewer, Van Raalte, &

Delange, 1991; Linder, Pillow, & Reno, 1989; Van Raalte, Brewer, Brewer, & Linder, 1992). If they seek consultation, they often do so as a last resort or when they are compelled to do so. Those who provide assistance to student-athletes (in particular male student-athletes) should expect to encounter these kinds of situations, attitudes, and behaviors. (See Chapter 6.) Such presentations may be seen and understood in part as being related to these college students' developmental striving to become independent. Still others may be reluctant to access professional helping resources because of a perceived mistrust of authority or because they are fearful that their seeking of assistance, if known, could create problematic questions about them if and when they pursue a career as a professional athlete in the future.

As noted above, the sheltering of student-athletes is common. This treatment may stem from differential attention and special care provided by significant others from earlier in life. For example, as children, athletically talented young people may have been cared for by people who have identified with them and directly or indirectly supported the athletic system (e.g., youth coaches, teachers, principals, and parents). Often these adults were reinforced and ego gratified as a function of their affiliation with and support for the talented youngster, as well as by the sense of indebtedness the athlete maintained toward them. One author is aware of a high school football star whose parents openly spoke of his being an A/B student; the young man revealed in counseling, however, that he rarely attended a class for almost the entirety of his junior and senior years (while receiving these grades). Such adult care can foster in student-athletes a dubious sense of personal specialness and power, as well as a dependency upon or a neurotic need to please influential others. Many student-athletes seem to believe that these supportive adults will be able to get them out of trouble, erasing or otherwise softening the consequences of their unacceptable, inappropriate, or even illegal behavior. This adult-fostered, student-athlete point of view often appears to develop by high school and frequently follows the student-athlete to college and beyond. Ultimately, we have seen that the apparent reinforcement of this dysfunctional perspective through life can (and often does) lead to problems in living for the current or former student-athlete. Frequently, it is following such undoing that these individuals seek help for depression, relationship problems, domestic violence, addictions, and various legal problems.

Early in their athletic experience, encouragement or insistence on their spending large amounts of time in sport-related activities may actually discourage children, teens, and eventually college-age athletes from participating in a wider range of life experiences (e.g., socialization outside of sport circles, early work experiences, and exploration of alternative academic paths). In a sense, young student-athletes-to-be may be shaped to acquire an external locus of control that is associated with various life skill deficits, as well as immature and unrealistic values, goals, and expectations. These can be carried with them to the college campus, creating difficulties for them. Young athletes may acquire a strong athletic identity that discourages age-appropriate exploratory behavior (Murphy, Petitpas, & Brewer, 1996; Petitpas, 2002). Some athlete clients come to counseling who reveal a narcissistic sense of "entitlement" (i.e., because I am an athlete, I am special; I have previously received and deserve to receive continued special treatment, and/or need not be held to the same standards of behavior as others on campus or in the community) (Lanning & Toye, 1993).

Misconceptions about Help-seeking and Counseling

Another common barrier to service provision is the stereotypic misperception of counselors and psychologists as "shrinks" who work only with sick, disturbed, or crazy people. For example, one author has had the dubious honor of being tabbed "the head man" for the department of intercollegiate athletics. In fact, a head coach would not even enter the athletic department psychologist's office, insisting (perhaps in jest) that she or he was not crazy. If student-athlete peers, coaches, athletic trainers, or others closely involved with student-athletes hear and hold these mistaken views, the chances of a timely referral or self-referral are quite low. Despite outreach efforts to dispel these misunderstandings and to emphasize the usefulness of counseling, long-standing anti-counseling/psychology stigma are often very difficult if not impossible to change. Perhaps the best way to correct this inclination is to do good work with athlete clients, who then tend to encourage others in need to seek assistance. Clearly, a positive, professional relationship with coaching and athletics staff, particularly sports medicine and athletic training personnel, can prove to be invaluable in generating timely referrals, identifying individuals "at risk," and maintaining continuity of care (Compton & Ferrante, 1991). Further, if allowed, attending regular sports medicine/athletic training, patient staffings, and clinical case consultations, as well as actively seeking opportunities for and inviting collegial participation in collaborative research, are excellent avenues for the enhanced comprehensive care of student-athletes, relationship building among helping professionals, professional development, and making valuable contributions to the professional literature.

Another potential roadblock to helping the student-athlete is the expectation of a "quick fix." This refers to the unrealistic assumption by many referral sources or clients that personal or performance concerns can be resolved in a very brief period of time. Although some personal and developmental difficulties can be overcome somewhat quickly, it seems that oftentimes student-athletes and athletic staff do not appreciate the complexity of certain presenting problems (e.g., eating disorders, mood disorders, identity issues, trauma) or the methodical nature of counseling or psychotherapy. Consequently, they may expect the helping professional to correct the student-athlete's difficulties with a dose of simple advice, which has often already been provided by coaches, family, and peers to no avail.

Brief, problem-focused counseling/psychotherapy appears to be the most common model of service provision on campus today. Pinkerton and Rockwell (1994) reported that university mental health service data indicate that about half of college students seen at counseling services visit for five or fewer sessions. Brief interventions have also been shown to be an effective approach that is consistent with the help-seeking requirements of students (Gallagher, 2004). For the most part, it seems that brief work is preferred by busy student-athletes these days. Brief models of helping students on campus have likely evolved from the significantly increased requests for services in recent times (Benton et al., 2003; Kadison, 2005), coupled with limitations in staff to meet those demands. Those who work with this population should be actively engaged in efforts to educate student-athletes and athletic department referral sources about the nature (e.g., individual and group counseling/psychotherapy, outreach programming, emergency or crisis counseling) and the limitations of the assistance that can be reasonably provided.

Fear of Loss of Status

Some student-athletes may be quite reluctant to seek counseling assistance because they fear that their help-seeking behavior may be seen by significant others (e.g., coaches, teammates, family, intimate partners) in a light that somehow threatens or diminishes their position on their team and in their relationships with these influential others. Indeed, some evidence suggests this concern is legitimate. Van Raalte, Brewer, Brewer, and Linder (1992) examined athletes' perceptions of an athlete who consulted with a sport psychologist, a coach, or a psychotherapist for performance-related issues. They found that other athletes did not derogate peer athletes who consulted with a sport psychologist (i.e., someone who they perceived as having sport-related expertise). The authors observed that athletes who consulted with a sport psychologist on performance enhancement issues apparently were not violating normative behavior. However, athletes who sought the assistance of a psychotherapist (i.e., a professional who is perceived to lack sport expertise) may have been seen as deviating from normative behavior in the eyes of other athlete peers (Linder, Brewer, Van Raalte, & DeLange, 1991; Linder, Pillow, & Reno, 1989; Van Raalte, Brewer, Brewer, & Linder, 1992). Therefore, it may be useful for professionals to market themselves as "sport counselors" or "sport psychologists," provided they are appropriately trained, competent, and are credentialed/licensed to engage in such practice and to legally use these titles.

It has been our experience and the experience of colleagues that some coaches may take a disapproving view of student-athletes who reveal that they are struggling with problems with living and/or that they have sought assistance from counselors or psychologists. Student-athletes may be made to feel ashamed that they somehow cannot deal with life events on their own and that they are weak, dependent people. We see some coaches' attitudes revealed in the language they use to describe these young people. They are sometimes referred to as "head cases," "unmotivated," "coach killers," or "malingerers." In view of the possibility of this bias, it is important for helping professionals to provide outreach education and training to coaches, administrators, athletic trainers, and other sports medicine professionals about the nature, scope, and potential benefits of counseling for student-athletes. Indeed, it appears that many athletic department staff members are not very well informed about what it is like to be a student-athlete today, about mental health issues, and about the usefulness and applicability of counseling support services and other on-campus services. Further, the careful safeguarding of the confidentiality of student-athletes whose coaches are not "user-friendly" is critical to protecting team status and to the positive well-being of clients.

Overall, research and clinical lore indicate that many student-athletes today possess a wide range of psycho-social and health needs that may be supported by involvement in counseling or therapy. Unfortunately, they can be in/directly discouraged from accessing many of the services that colleges and universities provide to meet their varied and changing needs. Certainly, it is to the benefit of the student-athletes and the institutions they so visibly represent to have the willingness to both invest in and more effectively promote the adjustment, personal growth, and individual development of the student-athlete as a whole person. Well-adjusted student-athletes will likely master the developmental tasks of young adulthood, actively pursue a course of study that possesses relevance to their lives, realize a positive and healthy collegiate experience, and hopefully graduate in a timely fashion.

Summary

Student-athletes in the New Millennium continue to represent a distinctive, diverse college population with particular regard to their roles on campus, atypically demanding lifestyles, and varied counseling needs. Certainly, the increased "professionalism" of intercollegiate athletics and the potential for exploitation today (Wertheimer, 2007) serve to complicate their lifestyles and daily experiences during their four to six years on campus. They are a group of students who face unique mounting challenges, problems, and pressures that can both facilitate and impede their success in and outside the classroom and into the future. Many people who are in positions to positively influence student-athlete policies and practices (e.g., university presidents, trustees, university and athletic department administrators, faculty, student affairs professionals, sports medicine practitioners) need to be aware of the various factors that contribute to the frequently imbalanced lifestyles and vulnerabilities of these young people. Based upon what we have learned about student-athletes from our years of work with them, we believe that their unique psychosocial needs and the obstacles they face can both promote and inhibit their development. It is clear that helping professionals are challenged to provide both innovative thinking and timely support that invites the ongoing study of this population and leads to continued constructive action on their behalf.

Given the increasingly commercialized intercollegiate athletics system as it exists, although controversial, it is arguable that student-athletes can be seen, perhaps more than ever, as employees of their institutions; therefore, they should be considered and treated as highly valuable "human assets." As a group, their efforts often generate substantial amounts of publicity and revenue for their schools. In light of what we have learned about student-athletes, and because colleges and universities continue to choose to support and expand the business of intercollegiate athletics to entertain the public and market their institutions, it seems reasonable to expect that these institutions would willingly assume increased responsibility and the financial commitment to provide expanded care and professional services for their student-athletes (much like the services that businesses invest in on behalf of their workers through employee assistance and business coaching services). These services, however, should continue to extend beyond financial aid, coaching, strength and conditioning training, rehabilitation, and academic advising and should take the form of comprehensive professional counseling and (sport) psychological support service programming. Since the 1980s, the current authors have sought to call attention to the plight of student-athletes and to promote holistic counseling and other support service provision to them. Today, we remain hopeful that changes will continue to take place, as evidenced by recent encouragement from the NCAA in the CHAMPS/Life Skills and mental health programming areas (Hosick, 2005; NCAA, 2007a; NCAA, 2007c).

In particular, the NCAA's CHAMPS/Life Skills "Challenging Athletes' Minds for Personal Success" model for student-athlete programming continues to show great promise (see Chapter 4). The stated mission of CHAMPS/LifeSkills is "to maintain intercollegiate athletics as an integral part of the campus educational program and the student-athlete as an integral part of the student body." With this in mind, the CHAMPS/Life Skills Program was created to support the student-athlete development initiatives of NCAA member institutions and to enhance the quality of the student-athlete experience within the context of higher education (NCAA, 2007a).

This program, which is functioning in one form or another on the majority of NCAA-affiliated campuses, is designed to facilitate a high-quality collegiate athletic experience and, more importantly, to promote the holistic development and success of student-athletes. Although the movement to provide life skills is a positive step, such programming should not be seen as a panacea. Ideally, other high-quality services (e.g., personal counseling, psycho-social educational services, career development, sports nutrition consultation, sports medicine services) must be available to assist the student-athlete. We see both group programming and individual direct services as being useful complementary components of a comprehensive student-athlete support program.

Hopefully, institutions will begin to recognize and make the necessary commitments to meet the ongoing needs of this unique group as the "big business" of intercollegiate athletics continues to grow, for better or for worse, at an astonishing rate (Isadore, 2006). We hope that institutions sponsoring intercollegiate athletics recognize the value of meeting the personal developmental needs of their student-athletes and make expanded human services and professional resources available to them. It is important that this be done, because we see the potential for student-athletes (especially those involved in highly competitive programs) to become devalued and exploited by intercollegiate athletic systems—by those very people who are entrusted with the promotion of student-athlete welfare (Sellers, 1993).

Much more seems to be asked of college student-athletes today than most university personnel, alumni, and fans imagine. We encourage university presidents, administrators, athletic department staff, faculty, the NCAA, and commited helping professionals to work together on behalf of student-athletes to identify, develop, and implement innovative programs and support services that will help student-athletes have the best opportunity to grow and succeed as young people in college and later in life. The transition from childhood to adulthood is tough enough—and even tougher today in the New Millennium.

References

Adler, P., & Adler, P. A. (1985). From idealism to pragmatic detachment: The academic performance of college athletes. *Sociology of Education, 58*, 241–250.

American Institutes for Research. (1988). Summary results from the 1987–88 National Study of Intercollegiate Athletics. (Report No.1). Palo Alto, CA: Center for the Study of Athletics.

Andersen, M. B. (2002). Helping college student-athletes in and out of sport. In J. Van Raalte & B. Brewer (Eds.), *Exploring sport and exercise psychology* (2nd ed., pp. 373–393). Washington, DC: American Psychological Association.

Andersen, M. B., & Williams, J. M. (1988). A model of stress and athletic injury: Prediction and prevention. *Journal of Sport and Exercise Psychology, 10*, 294–306.

Astin, A. (1977). *Four critical years.* San Francisco: Jossey-Bass.

Benton, S., Robertson, J., Tseng, W., Newton, F., & Benton, S. (2003). Changes in counseling center client problems across 13 years. *Professional Psychology: Research and Practice, 34*, 66–72.

Berg, I., & Reuss, N. (1998). *Solutions step by step: A substance abuse treatment manual.* New York: W. W. Norton.

Berg, R. (1989). Are college athletes making the grade? *Athletic Business, 13*(10), 30–34.

Bergandi, T., & Wittig, A. (1984). Availability of attitudes toward counseling services for the collegiate athlete. *Journal of College Student Personnel, 25*, 557–558.

Blann, W. (1985). Intercollegiate athletic competition and students' educational and career plans. *Journal of College Student Personnel, 26*, 115–118.

Blinde, E., & Greendorfer, S. (1992). Conflict and the college sport experience of women athletes. *Women in Sport and Physical Activity Journal, 1*, 97–113.

Bowen, W., & Levin, S. (2003). *Reclaiming the game: College sports and educational values.* Princeton, NJ: Princeton University Press.

Brent, M., Erikson-Cornish, J., Leslie-Toogood, A., Nadkarni, L., & Schreier, B. (2006). College student mental health and special populations: Diversity on campus. In S. Benton & S. Benton (Eds.), *College mental health: Effective services and strategies across campus* (pp. 213–224). National Association of Student Personnel Administrators.

Brewer, B. (1993). Self-identity and specific vulnerability to depressed mood. *Journal of Personality, 61*, 343–364.

Brewer, B. (1994). Review and critique of models of psychological adjustment to athletic injury. *Journal of Applied Sport Psychology, 6*, 87–100.

Brewer, B., Van Raalte, J., & Petitpas, A. (2007). Patient-practitioner interactions in sport injury rehabilitation. In D. Pargman (Ed.), *Psychological bases of sport injury* (3rd ed., pp. 80–94). Morgantown, WV: Fitness Information Technology.

Briggs, C. (1996, October). *Differences in degree aspirations and attainment outcomes between football or basketball players and other intercollegiate athletes.* Paper presented at the meeting of the Association for the Study of Higher Education, Memphis, TN.

Brooks, D., Etzel, E., & Ostrow, A. (1987). Job responsibilities and backgrounds of NCAA Division I athletic academic advisors and counselors. *The Sport Psychologist, 1*, 200–207.

Broughton, E., & Neyer, M. (2001). Advising and counseling student-athletes. In M. Howard-Hamilton & S. Watt (Eds.), *Student services for athletes* (pp. 47–55). San Francisco: Jossey-Bass.

Brown, C. (1993). The relationship between role commitment and career developmental tasks among college student-athletes (Doctoral dissertation, University of Missouri). Dissertation Abstracts International, 55, 1429A.

Brown, C. (2006). Injuries: The psychology of recovery and rehab. In S. Murphy (Ed.), *The sport psychology handbook* (pp. 215–236). Champaign, IL: Human Kinetics.

Brown, J., & Cogan, K. (2006). Ethical clinical practice and sport psychology: When two worlds collide. *Ethics and Behavior, 16*(1), 15–23.

Bulling, A. (1992). The relationship of involvement in intercollegiate athletics and other extracurricular activities to personal development (Doctoral dissertation, University of Nebraska). Dissertation Abstracts International, 54, 0101A.

Byers, W. (1995). *Unsportsmanlike conduct: Exploiting college athletes.* Ann Arbor: University of Michigan Press.

Carmen, L., Zerman, J., & Blaine, G. (1968). Use of Harvard psychiatric service by athletes and non-athletes. *Mental Hygiene, 52,* 134–137.

Carr, C., & Bauman, N. (1996). Life skills for collegiate student-athletes. In E. Etzel, A. P. Ferrante, & J. Pinkney (Eds.). *Counseling college student-athletes: Issues and interventions* (pp. 281–307). Morgantown, WV: Fitness InformationTechnology.

Chartrand, J., & Lent, R. (1987). Sports counseling: Enhancing the development of the student-athlete. *Journal of Counseling and Development, 66,* 164–167.

Chickering, A. (1969). *Education and identity.* San Francisco: Jossey-Bass.

Chickering, A. (1981). *The modern American college.* San Francisco: Jossey-Bass.

Chickering, A., & Reisser, L. (1993). *Education and identity.* San Francisco: Jossey-Bass.

Compton, R., & Ferrante, A. P. (1991). The athletic trainer sport psychology connection. In E. Etzel, A. P. Ferrante, & J. Pinkney, J. (Eds.), *Counseling college student-athletes: Issues and interventions* (pp. 221–230). Morgantown, WV: Fitness Information Technology.

Copeland, R. (2007). Athletic trainers' ISS work charts future directions. *NCAA News.* Retrieved June 22, 2007, from http://www.ncaa.org/wps/portal/!ut/p/kcxml/ 04_Sj9SPykssy0xPLMnMz0vM0Y_QjzKLN4g3NPUESUGYHvqRaGLGphhCjg gRX4_83FR9b_0A_YLc0NCIckdFACrZHxQ!/delta/base64xml/L3dJdyEvUUd3Qn dNQSEvNElVRS82XzBfMTVL?New_WCM_Context=/wps/wcm/connect/NCAA/ NCAA+News/NCAA+News+Online/2007/Association-wide/Athletic+trainers%27+ ISS+work+charts+future+directions+-+06-04-07+NCAA+News.

Danish, S., D'Augelli, A., & Ginsberg, M. (1983). Life development intervention: Promotion of mental health through the development of competence. In *Handbook of counseling psychology* (pp. 520–544). New York: Wiley.

Danish, S., Petitpas, A., & Hale, B. (1995). Psychological interventions: A life development model. In S. Murphy (Ed.), *Sport psychology interventions* (pp. 19–38). Champaign, IL: Human Kinetics.

Downey, P. (2005). An exploration of the adjustment to college of freshmen student-athletes and non-athlete students. Retrieved June 28, 2007, from https://etd.wvu. edu/etd/controller.jsp?moduleName=documentdata&jsp_etdId=3960

Drehs, W. (2007) Tragic turn. ESPN.com. Retrieved June 24, 2007, from http:// sports.espn.go.com/espn/eticket/story?page=ambrogi

Duderstadt, J. (2000). *Intercollegiate athletics and the American university. A university president's perspective.* Ann Arbor, MI: University of Michigan Press.

Edwards, H. (1984). The black "dumb jock": An American sport tragedy. *The College Board Review, 131,* 8–13.

Eichler, R. J. (2006). Developmental considerations. In P. Grayson & P. Meilman (Eds.), *College mental health practice.* (pp. 21–41). New York: Routledge.

Eitzen, D. (2003). *Fair and foul: Beyond the myths and paradoxes of sport*. New York: Rowan & Littlefield Publishers, Inc.

Engstrom, C., Sedlacek, W., & McEwen, M. (1995). Faculty attitudes toward male revenue and non-revenue student-athletes. *Journal of College Student Development, 36*, 217–227.

Erikson, E. (1968). *Identity: Youth and crisis*. New York: Norton.

Ermler, K., & Thomas, C. (1990). Interventions for the alienating effect of injury. *Athletic Training, 25*(3), 269–271.

Etzel, E. (1989). *Life stress, locus of control, and competition anxiety patterns of college student-athletes*. Unpublished doctoral dissertation, West Virginia University, Morgantown.

Etzel, E. (2003). *Characteristics of university student-athletes seeking sport psychology/ counseling services*. Paper presented at the American Psychological Association Annual Convention, Toronto, Ontario, Canada.

Etzel, E., & Ferrante, A. (1993). Providing psychological assistance to injured and disabled college student-athletes. In D. Pargmam (Ed.), *Psychological bases of sport injuries* (pp. 265–283). Morgantown, WV: Fitness Information Technology.

Etzel, E., Ferrante, A. P., & Pinkney, J. (Eds.). (1991). Counseling college student-athletes: Issues and interventions. Morgantown, WV: Fitness Information Technology.

Etzel, E., Ferrante, A. P., & Pinkney, J. (Eds.). (1996). Counseling college student-athletes: Issues and interventions (2nd ed.). Morgantown, WV: Fitness Information Technology.

Etzel, E., Pinkney, J., & Hinkle, S. (1995). College student-athletes and needs assessment. In S. Stabb, S. Harris, & J. Talley (Eds.). *Needs assessment for college and university student populations* (pp. 155–172). Springfield, IL: Charles C. Thomas.

Etzel, E., & Watson, J. (2007). Ethical challenges for psychological consultations in intercollegiate athletics. *Journal of Clinical Sport Psychology 1*, 304–317.

Etzel, E., Watson, J. Visek, A., & Maniar, S. (2006). Understanding and promoting college student-athlete health: Essential issues for student affairs professionals. *NASPA Journal, 43*(3). http://publications.naspa.org/cgi/viewcontent.cgi?article=1682&con text=naspajournal

Etzel, E., Weaver, K., & Ostrow, A. (1995, Spring). Job responsibilities and backgrounds of NCAA Division I athletic advisors and counselors: A replication. *Athletic Academic Journal*, 1–10.

Etzel, E., Zizzi, S., Newcomer-Appeneal, R., Ferrante, A., & Perna, F. (2007). Providing psychological assistance to college student-athletes with injuries and disabilities. In D. Pargman (Ed.), *Psychological bases of sport injuries* (pp. 151–169). Morgantown, WV: Fitness Information Technology.

Farnsworth, D. (1966). *Psychiatry, education, and the young adult*. Springfield, IL: Charles C. Thomas.

FERPA general guidance for students (2007). Retrieved April 15, 2008, from http://www.ed.gov/policy/gen/guid/fpco/ferpa/students.html.

Ferrante, A. (1989). Glory or personal growth: The plight of the student-athlete. *ECU Report, 20*, 6.

Ferrante, A., Etzel, E., & Pinkney, J. (1991). A model for accessing student-athletes with student-affairs resources. In E. Etzel, A. Ferrante, & J. Pinkney (Eds.). *Counseling college student-athletes: Issues and interventions* (pp. 19–30). Morgantown, WV: Fitness Information Technology.

Fields, T. (1999). Counseling the student-athlete: History, problems, and possible interventions. In S. Robinson (Ed.), *Gaining the competitive edge: Enriching the collegiate experience of the new student-athlete* (pp. 11–18). Columbia, SC: National Resource Center for the First Year Experience and Students in Transition.

Fletcher, T., Benshoff, J., & Richburg, M. (2003). A systems approach to understanding and counseling college student-athletes. *Journal of College Counseling, 6*(1), 35–45.

Gallagher, R. (2004). *National survey of counseling center directors.* Alexandria, VA: International Association of Counseling Services.

Gardner, F., & Moore, Z. (2006). Future directions. In F. Gardner & Z. Moore, *Clinical sport psychology* (pp. 239–249). Champaign, IL: Human Kinetics.

Gaston-Gayles, J. (2004). Examining the academic and athletic motivation among student-athletes at a Division I university. *Journal of College Student Development, 45,* 75–83.

Gill, D. (1995). Gender issues: A social-educational perspective. In S. Murphy (Ed.), *Sport psychology interventions* (pp. 205–234). Champaign, IL: Human Kinetics.

Goffman E. (1961). *Asylums: Essays on the social situation of mental patients and other inmates.* Harmondsworth: Penguin.

Grayson, P. (2006). Overview. In P. Grayson & P. Meilman (Eds.), *College mental health practice* (pp. 1–20). New York: Routledge.

Gruber, C. (1999). The first-year female student-athlete: Characteristics and interventions. In S. Robinson (Ed.), *Gaining the competitive edge: Enriching the collegiate experiences of the new student-athlete* (pp. 105–115). Columbia, SC: National Resource Center for the First Year Experience & Students in Transition, University of South Carolina.

Harris, M. (1993). Developmental benefits of athletics. In W. Kirk & S. Kirk (Eds.), *Student athletes: Shattering the myths and sharing the realities* (pp. 3–12). Alexandria, VA: American Counseling Association.

Heil, J. (Ed.). (1993). *Psychology of sport injury.* Champaign, IL: Human Kinetics.

Heller, T., Bloom, G., Graham, N., & Salmela, J. (2005). Sources of stress in NCAA Division I women ice hockey players. *Athletic Insight: The On-line Journal of Sport Psychology, 7*(4). Retrieved May 2, 2007, from http://www.athleticinsight.com/Vol7 Iss4/SourcesofStress.htm

Henschen, K., & Fry, D. (1984). An archival study of the relationship of intercollegiate athletic participation and graduation. *Sociology of Sport Journal, 1,* 52–56.

Heubner, L., & Lawson, J. (1990). In D. Creamer & Associates (Eds.), *College student development: Theory and practice for the 1990s* (pp. 127–151). Alexandria, VA: American College Personnel Association.

Heyman, S. (1993). When to refer athletes for counseling or psychotherapy. In J. M. Williams (Ed.), *Applied sport psychology: Personal growth to peak performance* (2nd ed., pp. 299–309). Palo Alto, CA: Mayfield.

Hill, K., Burch-Ragan, K., & Yates, D. (2001). Current and future issues and trends facing student athletes and athletic programs. In M. Howard-Hamilton & S. Watt (Eds.), *Student services for athletes* (pp. 65–80). San Francisco: Jossey-Bass.

Hinkle, J. (1996). Depression, adjustment disorder, generalized anxiety, and substance abuse: An overview for sport professionals working with college student-athletes. In E. Etzel, A. Ferrante, & J. Pinkney (Eds.). *Counseling college student-athletes: Issues and interventions* (2nd ed., pp. 109–136). Morgantown, WV: Fitness Information Technology.

Hipple, J. (1991). Do athletes have special counseling needs? *Texas Personnel and Guidance Association, 19*(2), 57–62.

Homer, J. (1981) Total institutions and the self-mortifying process. *Canadian Journal of Criminology, 23.*

Hood, A., Craig, A., & Ferguson, B. (1992). The impact of athletics, part-time employment, and other activities on academic achievement. *Journal of College Student Development, 33,* 447–453.

Hosick, M. B. (February, 2005). Forum places psychological focus on mental health issues. The NCAA News. Retrieved May 16, 2007, from http://www1.ncaa.org/membership/ed_outreach/health-safety/forummentalhealthpdf.pdf.

Howard-Hamilton, M., & Sina, J. (2001). How college affects student athletes. In M. Howard-Hamilton & S. Watt (Eds.), *Student services for athletes* (pp. 35–46). San Francisco: Jossey-Bass.

Howard-Hamilton, M., & Watt, S. (Eds.). (2001). *Student services for athletes.* San Francisco: Jossey-Bass.

Howe, N., & Strauss, W. (2000). *Millennials rising: The next great generation.* New York: Vintage Books.

Huffman, G., Park, J., Roser-Jones, C., Senett, B., Yagnick, G., & Webner, D. (2008). Normative SF-36 values in competing NCAA intercollegiate athletes differ from values in the general population. *The Journal of Bone and Joint Surgery, 90,* 471–476.

Humphrey, J. H., Yow, D. A., & Bowden, W. W. (2000). *Stress in college athletics: Causes, consequences, coping.* Binghamton, NY: The Haworth Half-Court Press.

Isadore, C. (2006, November 10). College sports' fuzzy math. *CNN Money.* Retrieved May 25, 2008, from http://money.cnn.com/2006/11/10/commentary/sportsbiz/index.htm

Jordan, J., & Denson, E. (1990). Student services for athletes: A model for enhancing the student-athlete experience. *Journal of Counseling and Development, 69,* 95–97.

Kadison, R., & DiGeronimo, T. (2004). *College of the overwhelmed: The campus mental health crisis and what to do about it.* San Francisco: Jossey-Bass.

Keeler, L., Etzel, E., & Blom, L. (2008). *Initial validation of a brief assessment of recovery and stress (BARS).* Manuscript.

Kellmann, M. (2002). Underrecovery and overtraining: Different concepts—similar impact? In M. Kellmann (Ed.), *Enhancing recovery: Preventing underperformance in athletes* (pp. 3–24). Champaign, IL: Human Kinetics.

Kellmann, M., & Kallus, K. (2001). *Recovery-stress questionnaire for athletes*. Champaign, IL: Human Kinetics.

Kennedy, S., & Dimick, K. (1987). Career maturity and professional sports expectations of college football and basketball players. *Journal of College Student Personnel, 28*, 293–297.

Kimball, A., & Freysinger, V. (2003). Leisure, stress, and coping: The sport participation of collegiate student-athletes. *Leisure Sciences, 25*, 115–141.

King. P. (1994) Theories of college student development: Sequences and consequences. *Journal of College Student Development, 35*, 413–422.

Kirk, W., & Kirk, S. (Eds.). (1993). *Student-athletes: Shattering the myths and sharing the realities*. Alexandria, VA: American Counseling Association.

Kleiber, A., & Brock, S. (1992). The effects of career-ending injuries on the subsequent well-being of elite college athletes. *Sociology of Sport Journal, 9*, 70–75.

Knight Commission tells presidents to use their power to reform the "fundamental premises" of college sports. (1991, March). *The Chronicle of Higher Education*, pp. A1, A33.

Knight Commission (2001). *A call to action: Reconnecting college sports and higher education*. Report of the Knight Foundation Commission on Intercollegiate Athletics, June 2001. Retrieved March 14, 2007, from http://www.knightcommission.org/about/a_call_to_action_ten_years_later/

Knight, J., Wechsler, H., Meichen, K., Seibring, M., Weitzman, E., & Schuckit, M. (2002, May). Alcohol abuse and dependence among U.S. college students. *Journal of Studies on Alcohol, 263*–270.

Kornspan, A., & Etzel, E. (2003). What do we know about the career maturity of college student-athletes? A brief review and practical suggestions for career development work with student-athletes. *Academic Athletic Journal, 17*, 15–33.

Lanning, W. (1982). The privileged few: Special counseling needs of athletes. *Journal of Sport Psychology, 4*, 19–23.

Lewis, M. (1991). Athletes in college: Differing roles and conflicting expectations. *College Student Journal, 10*, 195–200.

Linder, D., Brewer, B., Van Raalte, J., & DeLange, N. (1991). A negative halo for athletes who consult sport psychologists: Replication and extension. *Journal of Sport and Exercise Psychology, 13*, 133–148.

Linder, D., Pillow, D., & Reno, R. (1989). Shrinking jocks: Derogation of athletes who consult a sport psychologist. *Journal of Sport and Exercise Psychology, 11*, 270–280.

Lipka, S. (2006). Auburn U. announces new academic-quality policy after inquiry into courses taken by some athletes. Retrieved on May 20, 2007, from http://chronicle.com/daily/2006/08/2006081105n.htm

Long, J., & Caudill, S. (1991). The impact of participation in intercollegiate athletics on income and graduation. *Review of Economics and Statistics, 73*, 525–531.

Lubker, J. (2006). Athlete's feeling of isolation and separateness as determined by campus design: A theoretical perspective. *Athletic Academic Journal, 19*(1), 56–68.

Maniar S. D., Carter, J., & Smith, L. (2003, October). Characteristics of university student-athletes seeking sport psychology services, Part I. In S. D. Maniar (Chair),

Getting creative with university-based sport psychology services: Typical issues in an atypical field. Symposium presented at the 17th annual meeting of the Association for the Advancement of Applied Sport Psychology, Philadelphia, PA.

Maniar, S., Chamberlain, R., & Moore, N. (November, 2005). Suicide risk is real for student-athletes. NCAA News. Retrieved May 26, 2007, from http://www1.ncaa. org/ membership/ed_outreach/health-safety/suicide.pdf.

Martens, M., & Cox, R. (2000). Career development in college varsity athletes. *Journal of College Student Development, 41,* 172–180.

May, J., & Sieb, G. (1987). Athletic injuries: Psychological factors in the onset, sequelae, rehabilitation, and prevention. In J. May & M. Asken (Eds.), *Sport psychology: The psychological health of the athlete* (pp.157–185). Great Neck, NY: PMA Publishing.

McAllister D. R, Motamedi A. R., Hame S. L, Shapiro M. S., & Dorey F. J. (2001). Quality of life assessment in elite collegiate athletes. *American Journal of Sports Medicine, 29,* 806–810

McGraw, M., & Reeves, G. (1997, October 10). Sacrificing academics for victories: Rules bent for talented athletes. *The Kansas City Star,* p. A1.

McGrath, R. (2006). Stress. In P. Grayson & P. Meilman (Eds.), *College mental health practice* (pp. 135–151). New York: Routledge.

Medalie, J. (1981). The college years as a mini life cycle: Developmental task and adaptive options. *Journal of American College Health Association, 30,* 75–79.

Meilman, P., Lewis, D., & Gerstein, L. (2006). Alcohol, drugs and other addictions. In P. Grayson & P. Meilman (Eds.), *College mental health practice* (pp. 195–215). New York: Routledge.

Melendez, M. (2006). The influence of athletic participation on the college adjustment of freshmen and sophomore student athletes. *Journal of College Student Retention: Research, Theory and Practice, 8,* 39–55.

Miller, W., & Rollnick, S. (2002). *Motivational interviewing: Preparing people for change* (2nd ed.). New York: The Guilford Press.

Murphy, G., Petitpas, A., & Brewer, B. (1996). Identity foreclosure, athletic identity, and career maturity in intercollegiate athletes. *The Sport Psychologist, 4,* 261–274.

Murray, M. A. (1997). The counseling needs of college student-athletes. *Dissertation Abstracts International Section A: Humanities and Social Sciences, 58,* 2088.

NCAA. (2003). 2003 NCAA national study on collegiate sports wagering and associated behaviors. Retrieved June 28, 2007, from: http://www.ncaa.org/library/research/ sports_wagering/2003/2003_sports_wagering_study.pdf

NCAA. (2006). NCAA student-athlete race and ethnicity report. Retrieved April 27, 2007, from http://www.ncaa.org/library/research/ethnicity_report/2004-05/2004-05_race_ethnicity_report.pdf

NCAA. (2007a). CHAMPS/LifeSkills program. Retrieved 16 May, 2007, from http:// www.ncaa.org/wps/portal/!ut/p/kcxml/04_Sj9SPykssy0xPLMnMz0vM0Y_QjzKLN 4j3CQXJgFjGpvqRqCKOcAFfj_zcVH1v_QD9gtzQiHJHRUUAc0tpTA!!/delta/bas e64xml/L3dJdyEvUUd3QndNQSEvNElVRS82XzBfTFU!?CONTENT_URL=http ://www1.ncaa.org/eprise/main/membership/ed_outreach/champs-life_skills/program .html

NCAA. (2007b). Academic reform. Retrieved 2 June, 2007, from http://www2.ncaa.
org/portal/academics_and_athletes/education_and_research/academic_reform/index.
html

NCAA. (2007c). Managing student-athletes' mental health issues. Retrieved June 25,
2007, from http://www.ncaa.org/library/sports_sciences/mental_health/2007_man-
aging_mental_health.pdf

Nelson, E. (1983). How the myth of the dumb jock becomes a fact: A developmental
view for counselors. *Counseling and Values, 27*, 176–185.

Oller R. (2007, October 9). Big upset could send Harbaugh to Michigan. *The Columbus Dispatch, Sports Section.*

Papanikolaou, Z., Nikolaidais, D., Patsiaouras, A., & Alexopoulos, P. (2003.) The freshman experience: High stress—low grades. *Athletic Insight: The On-line Journal of Sport
Psychology, 5.*

Pargman, D. (Ed.). (2007). *Psychological bases of sport injury* (3rd ed.). Morgantown,
WV: Fitness Information Technologies.

Parham, W. (1993). The intercollegiate athlete: A 1990s profile. *The Counseling Psychologist, 21*, 411–429.

Pascarella, E., Bohr, L., Nora, A., & Terenzini, P. (1995). Intercollegiate athletic partic-
ipations and freshman-year cognitive outcomes. *Journal of Higher Education, 66*,
369–387.

Pascarella, E., & Terenzini, P. (1991). *How college affects students.* San Francisco: Jossey-
Bass.

Pascarella, E. T., & Terenzini, P. T. (2005). *How college affects students: A third decade of
Research.* San Francisco: Jossey-Bass.

Petitpas, A. (2002). Counseling interventions in applied sport psychology. In J. Van
Raalte & B. Brewer (Eds.) *Exploring sport and exercise psychology* (2nd ed.,
pp. 253–268). Washington, DC: American Psychological Association.

Petitpas, A., Buntrock, C., Van Raalte, J., & Brewer, B. (1995). Counseling athletes: A
new specialty in counselor education. *Counselor Education and Supervision, 34*,
21–219.

Petitpas, A., & Danish, S. (1995). Caring for injured athletes. In S. Murphy (Ed.), *Sport
psychology interventions* (pp. 225–281). Champaign, IL: Human Kinetics.

Pierce, R. (1969). Athletes in psychiatry: How many, how come? *Journal of American
College Health, 12*, 244–249.

Pinkerton, R., Hinz, L., & Barrow, J. (1987). The college student athlete: Psychological
consideration and interventions. *Journal of American College Health, 37*, 218–226.

Pinkerton, R., & Rockwell, W. (1994). Very brief psychological interventions with university students. *Journal of American College Health, 13*, 344–357.

Podlog, L., & Eklund, R. (2007). Psychological considerations of the return to sport following injury. In D. Pargman (Ed.), *Psychological bases of sport injury* (3rd ed.,
pp. 110–130). Morgantown, WV: Fitness Information Technology.

Potuto, J., & O'Hanlon, J. (2006). National study of student athletes regarding their experiences as college students. Retrieved May 15, 2007, from http://www.ncaa.org/
library/research/student-athlete_experiences/2006/2006_s-a_experience.pdf

Purdy, D., Eitzen, D., & Hufnagel, R. (1982). Are athletes also students? *Social Problems, 29*, 439–448.

Quarforth, S., Brewer, B., Petitpas, A., Champagne, D., & Cornelius, A. (2003). College adjustment of football players: Predictors of first semester adjustment to college among NCAA Division III intercollegiate football players. *Academic Journal, 17*, 1–7.

Remer, R., Tongate, F., & Watson, J. (1978). Athletes: Counseling the over-privileged minority. *Personnel and Guidance Journal, 56*, 626–629.

Richman, J., Hardy, C., Rosenfeld, L., & Callanan, R. (1989). Strategies for enhancing social support networks in sport: A brainstorming experience. *Applied Sport Psychology, 1*, 150–159.

Rotella, R., & Heyman, S. (1993). Stress, injury, and the psychological rehabilitation of athletes. In J. Williams (Ed.), *Applied sport psychology: Personal growth to peak performance* (pp. 338–355). Palo Alto, CA: Mayfield.

Sedlacek, W., & Adams-Gaston, J. (1992). Predicting the academic success of student-athletes using SAT and non-cognitive variables. *Journal of Counseling and Development, 70*, 724–727.

Segal, B., Weiss, R., & Sokol, R. (1965). Emotional adjustment, social organization, and psychiatric treatment rates. *American Sociological Review, 30*, 545–556.

Selby, R., Weinstein, H., & Bird, T. (1990). The health of university athletes: Attitudes, behaviors, and stressors. *Journal of American College Health, 39*, 11–18.

Sellers, R. (1992). Racial differences in the predictors for academic achievement of student-athletes in Division I revenue sports. *Sociology of Sport Journal, 9*, 48–59.

Sellers, R. (1993). Black student-athletes: Reaping the benefits or recovering from the exploitation. In D. Brooks & R. Althouse (Eds.), *Racism in college athletics: The African-American athlete's experience* (pp.143–173). Morgantown, WV: Fitness Information Technology.

Shell, D., & Ferrante, A. P. (1996). Recognition of adjustment disorder in college athletes: A case study. *Clinical Journal of Sports Medicine, 6*(1), 60–62.

Shriberg, A., & Brodzinski, F. (Eds.). (1984). *Rethinking services for student-athletes.* San Francisco: Jossey-Bass.

Simons, H., Van Rheenen, D., & Covington, M. (March/April 1999). Academic motivation and the student athlete. *Journal of College Student Development, 40*, 151–162.

Skirka, N. (1997). The relationship of hardiness, sense of coherence, sports participation, and gender to perceived stress and psychological symptoms among college students. *Dissertation Abstracts International Section A: Humanities and Social Sciences, 58*, 0120.

Smallman, E., & Sowa, C. (1996). Career maturity levels of male intercollegiate varsity athletes. *Career Development Quarterly, 44*, 270–277.

Sowa, C., & Gressard, C. (1983). Athletic participation: Its relationship to student development. *Journal of College Personnel, 24*, 236–239.

Sperber, M. (1990). *College sports inc.: The athletic department vs. the university.* New York: Henry Holt.

Sperber, M. (2000). *Beer and circus: How big-time college sports is crippling undergraduate education.* New York: Henry Holt.

Steiner, H., Pyle, R., Brassington, G., Matheson, G., & King, M., (2003). The college health related information survey (H.H.R.I.S.-73): A screen for college student athletes. *Child Psychiatry and Human Development, 34,* 97–109.

Stone, J., & Strange, C. (1989). Quality of student experiences of freshman intercollegiate athletes. *Journal of College Student Development, 30,* 148–154.

Street, J. (2000). Self-efficacy: A tool for providing effective support services for student-athletes. In S. Robinson (Ed.), *Gaining the competitive edge: Enriching the collegiate experiences of the new student-athlete* (pp. 19–30). Columbia, SC: National Resource Center for the First Year Experience & Students in Transition, University of South Carolina.

Stuart, D. L. (1985). Academic preparation and subsequent performance of intercollegiate football players. *Journal of College Student Personnel, 26,* 124–129.

Suggs, W. (2003, January, 17). Jock majors: Many colleges allow football players to take the easy way out. *The Chronicle of Higher Education,* A33–34.

Swan, P. R. (1990). *An analysis of support services for student-athletes attending Division I institutions of higher education.* Ann Arbor, Michigan: University Microfilms International.

Sweet, T. W. (1990). A study of an intensive developmental counseling program with the student-athlete. *College Student Journal, 9,* 212–219.

Taylor, J., & Taylor, S. (1997). Psychological problems in rehabilitation. In J. Taylor & S. Taylor, *Psychological approaches to sports injury rehabilitation.* Gaithersburg, MD: Aspen Publishers.

Valentine, J., & Taub, D. (Fall, 1999). Responding to the developmental needs of student athletes. *Journal of College Counseling, 2,* 164–179.

Van Raalte, J., Brewer, B., Brewer, D., & Linder, D. (1992). NCAA Division II college football players' perceptions of an athlete who consults a sport psychologist. *Journal of Sport and Exercise Psychology, 14,* 273–282.

Vaughn, J., & Emener, W. (1993). Rehabilitation counseling with college athletes: A hypothesis-generating study. *Journal of Rehabilitation Counseling, 23,* 30–35.

Watson, J. C., & Etzel, E. F. (2004). Ethical issues affecting psychologists, counselors and sport psychology consultants' work with collegiate student athletes. *Professional Studies Review, 1*(1), 49–60.

Watson, J. (2005). College student-athletes' attitudes toward help-seeking behavior and expectations of counseling services. *Journal of College Student Development 46*(4), 442–449.

Watt, S., & Moore, J. (2001). Who are student-athletes? In M. Howard-Hamilton & S. Watt (2001). *Student services for athletes* (pp. 7–18). San Francisco: Jossey-Bass.

Wechsler, H., Davenport, A., Dowdall, G., Grossman, S., & Zanakos, S. (1997). Binge drinking, tobacco, and illicit drug use and involvement in college athletics. *Journal of American College Health, 45,* 195–200.

Wertheimer, A. (2007). The exploitation of student-athletes. In W. Morgan (Ed.), *Ethics in sport* (2nd ed., pp. 365–37). Champaign, IL: Human Kinetics.

Williams, J. (2001). Psychology of injury risk and prevention. In R. Singer, H. Hausenblas, & C. Janelle (Eds.), *Handbook of sport psychology research* (2nd ed., pp. 766–786). New York: John Wiley & Sons.

Wilson, G., & Pritchard, M. (2005). Comparing sources of stress in college student athletes and non-athletes. *Athletic Insight.* Retrieved May 10, 2007, from http://www.athleticinsight.com./Vol7Iss1/StressAthletesNonathletes.htm

Winston, R., Miller, T., & Prince, J. (1979). *Student developmental task inventory* (2nd ed.). Athens, GA: Student Development Associates.

Wuestenberg, P. (1999). Essential components for successful collaboration between coaches and athletics academic advisors. In S. Robinson (Ed.), *Gaining the competitive edge: Enriching the collegiate experiences of the new student-athlete* (pp. 31–39). Columbia, SC: National Resource Center for the First Year Experience & Students in Transition, University of South Carolina.

Zimbalist, A. (1998). *Unpaid professionals: Commercialism and conflict in big-time college sports.* Princeton, NJ: Princeton University Press.

Zingg, P. (1982). Advising the student-athlete. *Educational Record, 63,* 16–19.

2

CONSULTATION IN INTERCOLLEGIATE ATHLETICS

Deborah N. Roche
Douglas M. Hankes

Consultation is a comprehensive term used across many professional disciplines. Archer and Cooper (1998) described consultation in a college counseling center setting as any activity provided by a counseling center staff member that involves advice or assistance utilizing psychological principles to a clearly defined client. There are many factors to consider in creating one's own personal model of consultation, especially in the realm of intercollegiate athletics. The purpose of this chapter is to provide the reader with an overview of the issues and skills associated with the provision of psychological consultation to the various customers who are involved in the system of intercollegiate athletics. Armed with this basic understanding of consultation, the reader hopefully will be better prepared to explore and navigate the often complex and sensitive dynamics and challenges of psychological consultation in this unique setting. After reading this chapter, the helping professional will have a better basic understanding of the structure of athletics, what he or she can offer as a consultant, ways to approach the consulting relationship based upon expertise, potential barriers and challenges he or she may confront when consulting, and recommendations for successful consultation in college athletics.

Models

Researchers in the counseling and mental health disciplines have examined how to initiate interventions and consultation with individuals and with larger groups or populations (Caplan & Caplan, 1993; Morrill,

Oetting, & Hurst, 1974). In this literature, several issues repeatedly emerge as important factors to consider when developing the consultation relationship. These include: (1) who is the "target" of the consultation? (2) what is the goal of the consultation? and (3) what skills or methods will the consultant use to reach the target population?

The target of the consultation can range from an individual, a group (primary or associated), or an institution/community. The goal and methods of delivery will vary accordingly (Morrill et al., 1974). Others have suggested that the model may involve: (1) direct services to a specific client (e.g., student-athlete); (2) indirect services to a specific athlete client referred by a consultee; (3) service to specifically assist the consultee; or (4) service to a system (e.g., the athletics department) (Meyers, Parsons, & Martin, 1979). Relatedly, Caplan and Caplan (1993) categorize four types of consultations each targeting a different consultee. These are: (1) client-centered; (2) consultee-centered; (3) program-centered administrative; and (4) consultee-centered administrative case consultations. For example, in a client-centered case consultation, the basic goal of the consultation is to assist the consultee in identifying ways to help the consultee's client (Caplan & Caplan, 1993). In the realm of intercollegiate athletics, this type of consultation could be communicating with a coach on increasing his or her knowledge of the female athlete triad so he or she can refer an athlete with a suspected eating disorder. Here the target of the intervention is the coach.

The target could also be a population such as a group of professionals in an athletics department (e.g., administrators) who interact with athletes in various capacities. In this situation, the target is that group of allied professionals, not the student-athletes with whom they work. In collegiate sport, this could include the training of sports medicine professionals to identify signs and symptoms of depression to facilitate referrals to psychologists working at a counseling service.

It is important not only to consider the target of your consultation, but also to think about the method of delivery of consultation (Caplan & Caplan, 1993). There are numerous ways to provide consultation, including direct service, consultation and training for professionals and paraprofessionals, and using the media (Morrill et al., 1974). Helping professionals must decide which method appears most appropriate in a given situation. This decision may be impacted by training, expertise, circumstances of the consultation, and how people communicate. In the previous example of the coach and an eating-disordered athlete, the most effective service would likely be a direct, face-to-face method. In contrast, it may be initially useful to communicate information via e-mail or at a coaches' meeting to those with whom one is consulting.

The goals and purposes of any intervention are also essential to consider when providing consultation services. Some examples of this are remediation, prevention, development, improving professional functioning, collecting and analyzing data, and much more (Caplan & Caplan, 1993; Morrill et al., 1974; Parsons & Meyers, 1984). The goal of any consultation may vary depending upon which of the four types of consultation is being used. For instance, in the program-centered administration example, the identified problem is a difficulty an individual has that occurs in planning and administration. Here the helping professional's goal is to use her or his knowledge of social systems and program development to assist administrative personnel in executing a viable plan of action (Caplan & Caplan, 1993).

As a consultant to intercollegiate athletics, the helping professional has to develop his or her own approach to this process. The resources outlined in this chapter are seen as a starting point for the readers to build their own models. Some factors to consider in developing and refining such a model over time should include knowledge about the target(s) of consultation (e.g., the athletics system, person seeking consultation), methods to best approach the consultation process with individuals or within the athletic department culture and system, and one's current knowledge and consulting proficiency (Hays & Brown, 2004; Terenzini, 1993 in Hays & Brown).

Structure of Athletic Departments

Whether one is employed by an intercollegiate athletic department, has been approached by such an organization to provide psychological consulting services, or is initiating a relationship with collegiate athletics, a basic understanding of the organization and culture of the department of athletics is invaluable. Most athletic departments are made up of numerous entities including administration, support staff, coaches, athletes, etc. The reporting lines of these entities and the operations will vary from school to school (Andersen & Brewer, 1995).

To be reasonably effective in the initial stages of consultation, a consultant must attempt to ascertain, as much as possible, what these lines are and appreciate some of the nuances of the units and the people who work there. Because some athletics department personnel are often not particularly forthcoming, the consultant may not learn a lot about these things before entering into this professional relationship. However, as the consultant is establishing himself or herself during initial contacts, close observation, asking questions, and gaining an appreciation for the various units' functions will be important. For example, getting a sense of the makeup of the department can help the consultant better identify the individual(s) responsible for decision making, as well as payment for the services the consultant provides if one is a private service provider.

Understanding the basic athletic department structure will often enable the consultant to make appropriate and timely internal and external referrals (e.g., sports medicine). Also, knowing about department components and with whom the consultant will (potentially) interact will likely help the consultant ascertain that he or she is not duplicating efforts. Finally, understanding the organization and culture of the department will help the consultant, in the initial consultation, to feel as confident as possible when embarking on this work.

Administration

The administration of athletic departments is usually made up of several persons. Departments will vary from school to school and by size, budget, and NCAA Division. Athletic directors (AD), associate and assistant ADs, senior women's administrators (SWAs), and in some institutions directors of compliance can all represent upper-level administration. At smaller schools, some administrators will function in more than one of these roles. It has been observed that these administrators are key to the consultant's provision of services to athletes (Andersen, 2002; Ferrante, Etzel, & Pinkney, 1991). They have described how the support of the ADs, especially, can facilitate networking on campus as well as within the department of athletics. According to Ferrante et al. (1991), "The AD is perhaps the most important person behind the success of any efforts to assist student athletes" (p. 21). Given the critical role ADs can play in establishing and supporting the consultation relationship, it is wise to regularly interface with these administrators, if possible, as one develops the role as a consultant. Some in the field have gone so far as to state that the AD is the consultant's ultimate client. Since the AD is the organization's official representative and final authority, all consultant actions should support this person's interpretation of the agency's interests (Portenga & Aoyagi, 2007).

In addition to the assistance that members of the higher administration can provide the consultant, appreciating their roles and the pressures they face may also be beneficial to the consultant's provision of services. For example, athletic departments often operate as an independent entity on campus (Fletcher, Benshoff, & Richburg, 2003; Sperber, 1990). Fletcher et al. (2003) attributed this to the significant external fiscal support that athletic departments receive from corporate sponsors, boosters, media contracts, and other private donors. Further, they stated that "intercollegiate sports are not all the same, and there can be tremendous differences among different sports even at the same institution" (p. 37). An appreciation of these differences is instrumental to successful consulting, as is an awareness of the pressures on upper administrators to solicit funding and manage their staff regarding the allocation of this funding. This information may assist consultants in determining how to establish their rates for compensation if they are private practitioners.

Sperber (1990) and Telander (1996) describe the ways in which the AD is similar to a chief operating officer in business. Operational duties are wide-ranging and include such responsibilities as deciding how many games are to be played in a season across sports, and keeping the athletic program in good financial and NCAA standing. The responsibility for the entire operation ultimately falls on the AD, but there can be many perks as well (Sperber, 1990). Sperber addressed the fact that ADs sometimes have celebrity standing on their campuses and can be viewed as incredibly powerful, in some cases even more so than the university presidents. As a consultant, it is crucial to understand the basic roles of the AD, the perception of the AD's power, and the reality of that power, both within the department and campus-wide.

Making personal contact with such authority figures in the institution is often vital to consulting (Caplan & Caplan, 1993). This can be applied to athletics, where in many cases the AD is the ultimate authority. Furthermore, it is useful for the consultant to become familiar with the norms, values, and beliefs at the institution in which he or she is working, in order to be potentially helpful at many levels (Fletcher et al., 2003). A careful understanding of the institution will help consultants avoid stepping on toes or insulting those with whom they are working. Avoiding the occasional landmines inherent in the departmental structure and politics can foster trust and perceived credibility in the consultants' work.

Coaches

Similar to administrative organizations, coaching staff structures can be complex and vary dramatically from school to school (Fletcher et al., 2003). The NCAA creates limits on the number of coaches for each sport, depending upon the division (NCAA, 2007a). Teams can vary from having as many as 11 full-time coaches in Division I football to having only two full-time coaches in Division I golf (NCAA, 2007a). Although the NCAA allows a certain number of coaches for each team, each university determines for itself how many coaches will actually be assigned. Clearly the resources of these different teams will vary, sometimes substantially even on the same campus.

The need and ability to support consulting services for athletes on teams may vary. For example, a team with a larger budget may be able to support a consultant from its own budget, whereas less financially endowed teams may not. Andersen, Van Raalte, and Brewer (2001) addressed the frequency of universities not setting aside funds for psychology services. Understanding the means available to the department, as well as individual programs, helps the consultant to make decisions about fees prior to engaging in services when setting rates can be more difficult. When payment does not take place, compensation can occasionally take the alternate form in tickets for games and athletic gear. This may raise the issue of barter for professionals. Those navigating such a situation are encouraged to consult the profession's ethical guidelines.

Consultants may also be counselors or psychologists who are generally employed by the university (e.g., counseling service staff) or perhaps in rare instances, actually be members of the athletic department staff. The nature of internal and external consultants is discussed later in this chapter.

Another factor that is important to consider when dealing with coaches is their openness to psychology services. In the authors' experience, coaches' views of psychology services vary. Some are put off or threatened by sport psychology consultants. They may believe that the team belongs to them, and external help is not welcome. On the other hand, the authors have experienced coaches who are exceptionally inviting to consultants and welcome their services. Before one enters the consulting relationship, one must acquire a sense of the coach's perspective on the usefulness of psychology services. This will boost the chances of a successful initial contact and continued relationship with the team and its members.

Sports Medicine Staff and Athletic Trainers

Many athletic departments have a team of physicians, athletic trainers, and other medical-related practitioners (e.g., orthopedists, dentists, physical therapists, and nutritionists) who work with student-athletes (Andersen, 2002). The makeup of a sports medicine staff typically varies from school to school. Many smaller departments unfortunately do not have the luxury of this range of support. Sports medicine colleagues can be a tremendous source of information, assistance, and referrals. They can also thwart a consultant's efforts. To avoid conflicts, it is important that the consultant is familiar with the sports medicine staff's services and basic policies when initiating the consultative relationship.

The relationship between the sports medicine staff and psychology consultant can be complex. The role of each entity of the sports medicine team, designation of authority, supervisory structure, as well as accountability of this group for health care delivery to the student-athletes, can all be quite complicated (Andersen & Brewer, 1995). For example, the team physician at some universities reports to the chief of student health and the athletic director. In the authors' experience, the members of the sports medicine team often have an intimate understanding of the dynamics of an athletic department, as well as a significant understanding of the student-athlete experience. It is important to keep in mind that these professionals may have greater credibility with athletic department administration and staff than do counselors and psychologists. This group also has a powerful voice on important decisions that affect the student-athlete. For example, the sports medicine physician is ultimately responsible for removing a student-athlete from play because of certain medical indicators such as injury, illness, or pregnancy (NCAA, 2007b).

Academic Support Services

Many athletics departments provide a range of academic support services (e.g., advising, tutoring, mentoring) for athletes. This office and the staff are important to understanding the student-athlete experience. Depending upon the reporting lines to and from this office, their roles and interactions with students and others in athletics and on campus will vary. At some universities the physical location of this office is outside of the athletic department on another part of campus (Gabbard & Halischak, 1993). Other schools have their athlete support services housed in athletics but reporting administratively to another unit on campus (e.g., academic advising center, counseling center) (Denson, 2002; Jordan & Denson, 1990).

Academic support services assist athletes with numerous issues. Usually their primary function is to address academic issues including overseeing NCAA academic rules and regulations, academic monitoring, tutorial services, study hall, and career development to name a few (Brougthon & Neyer, 2001; Denson, 2002). This office may also provide informal counseling, academic development workshops, and consultation with coaches, faculty, parents, and recruits on academic matters (Broughton & Neyer, 2001; Jordan & Denson, 1990). Depending upon the size of the institution and amount of support provided by the athletic department and/or university, this office may contain many advisors or a few individuals who are responsible for the coordination of these services for the athletes at an institution. Andersen (2002) captured the significant influence of this office in his encouragement of consultants to develop relationships with this unit's staff members, stating that "forming a liaison with academic athletic counselors is probably one of the smarter moves a university counseling center psychologist (or any other practitioner) could make" (p. 387).

CHAMPS/Life Skills

In addition to the academic development unit, numerous athletics departments also often have a CHAMPS (Challenging Athletes' Minds for

Personal Success)/Life Skills program and CHAMPS/Life Skills coordinator. This person is responsible for coordination of the NCAA CHAMPS/Life Skills program as it has been uniquely implemented on a particular campus. The CHAMPS/Life Skills program began its development in 1991 and was officially launched to the NCAA membership in 1994 when 40 institutions joined and spearheaded this initiative (NCAA, 2007c). According to the NCAA, the mission of this program is to:

> maintain intercollegiate athletics as an integral part of the campus educational program and the student-athlete as an integral part of the student body. . . . CHAMPS/Life Skills Program was created to support the student-athlete development initiatives of NCAA member institutions and to enhance the quality of the student-athlete experience within the context of higher education. (NCAA, 2007d)

There are five "commitment" areas within the CHAMPS/Life Skills model for programming: (1) academic excellence, (2) athletic excellence, (3) personal development, (4) career development, and (5) community service (NCAA, 2007d). Each university develops its own program to address the five commitment areas. CHAMPS/Life Skills programs often provide many opportunities for consultants to assist student-athletes. Consultants may have the opportunity to provide psycho-educational programming on various topics (e.g., stress management, mental health issues, and alcohol and other drug use). Carr and Bauman (2002) reported that some athletes may divulge clinical concerns to CHAMPS/Life Skills coordinators (e.g., eating disorders, depression, relationship problems). Establishing a relationship with the program coordinator of CHAMPS can help the consultant understand the issues at a particular institution as well as facilitate timely referrals to a consultant.

Athletes

Student-athletes are clearly the most important group of people within the athletic department. Without their participation and various needs, the entities described above would have no reason to exist on campus. The NCAA addresses the expectation of the student who participates in NCAA-sponsored sports in the core values section of its mission statement, which describes a commitment to:

> The collegiate model of athletics in which students participate as an avocation, balancing their academic, social and athletics experiences, the highest levels of integrity and sportsmanship, the pursuit of excellence in both academics and athletics. (NCAA, 2007e)

The NCAA views participation in intercollegiate athletics as an important choice and privilege and, in its mission statement, acknowledges the many demands the students have as they balance their academic, social, and athletic responsibilities. The NCAA suggests that student-athletes pursue excellence in every domain in which they participate. Though the values promoted in the NCAA mission statement are exemplary and certainly noble goals for all student-athletes, balancing the various demands can be quite a challenge for them. Student-athlete welfare is an issue many researchers have explored (Broughton & Neyer, 2001; Etzel, Watson, Visek, & Maniar, 2006 ; Hill, Burch-Ragan, & Yates, 2001). The demands placed upon this populace are tremendous, which affects their overall well-being (Broughton & Neyer, 2001; Etzel et al., 2006; Jordan & Denson, 1990). As such, it is essential for consultants to be aware of these often competing demands and stressors on this population if they are to effectively assist this group. In addition, consultants must appreciate the structure that is in place to protect these students. Because of their status and value to the university, and specifically to the athletic department, this group can be at risk for numerous physical and mental health issues (Etzel et al., 2006; Pinkerton, Hinz, & Barrow, 1989).

Organizations introduced to protect and give student-athletes a voice are the Student-Athlete Advisory Councils or Committees (SAAC) or Student-Athlete Advisory Boards (SAAB) (NCAA, 2007f). Each institution determines the basic mission and bylaws for its council. These councils may have different names at different institutions, but the overall purpose remains essentially the same. SAACs typically conduct regular meetings at which student-athletes have an opportunity to discuss their concerns and often have an opportunity to communicate with administration (e.g., ADs, faculty athletics representatives [FARs]). Council members also have the opportunity to vote on relevant NCAA legislation (NCAA, 2007f). Each school sends one representative to the conference SAAC, and then one member of the conference SAAC represents that conference at the national SAAC. The mission of the national SAAC is "to enhance the total student-athlete experience by promoting opportunity, protecting student-athlete welfare and fostering a positive student-athlete image" (NCAA, 2007f). This organization can be a very important one for student-athletes. To get a better appreciation of the needs of the student-athletes, consultants may want to seek permission from athletics administration to attend and present at SAAC/SAAB meetings, as well as network with their leaders and the administrator(s) who oversee this group.

In summary, the structure of an athletic department is typically complex and challenging. No two are organized in exactly the same way. The services provided by consultants from the helping professions of counseling and psychology have considerable benefit to consultees and clients. Basic familiarity with each of these units, with the manner in which they function, and with the people who work within them, is useful to effectively consult within the department of athletics. Below, the potential needs of these entities are discussed, as well as potential areas for entry for the consultant and ways in which the consultant can help.

The Need

Depending on the competencies of the consultant, the needs of consultees, and resources offered by an athletic department, consultants may be afforded the opportunity to offer and provide a variety of services. Assistance may be useful not only to athletes, but also to other personnel within the athletic department. This section will explore potential needs that may exist for each entity and how a consultant might meet them.

It would likely benefit consultants to enlist the assistance of the department of athletics and as many of its members as are willing to participate at the identified institution in an evaluation of its perceived needs (Etzel, Pinkney, & Hinkle, 1995). To create a "needs assessment," consultants could draw upon the numerous issues raised throughout this book, as well as include open-ended inquiries about the participants' needs and ways in which consultants could help. Other potential contributors that could be contacted include retired staff members, graduating athletes, former faculty athletics representatives, and other members of the athletics community who are moving on from the university.

In particular, annual surveys or interviews with graduating (i.e., "exiting") athletes are required by the NCAA. This data may be made available to consultants by the administration. These individuals can provide unique perspectives that could be valuable to consultants and their work.

By engaging in this type of university-specific needs assessment, consultants demonstrate that they are invested in understanding the community and want to assist only where needed. In addition, in the authors' experience, this simple task is an excellent way to meet many parties in the athletic department in a non-threatening way, facilitating entry into the often closed system of athletics.

Administration

There can be a great deal of overlap of perceived issues and needs that each athletic department entity struggles to address. Their particular stake in these issues and the approaches they take or have taken to deal with them may be quite varied. Administration may use assistance from a counseling or psychology consultant for several issues: adjustment to school, mental health problems, drug testing, counseling, sexual health and assault, organizational issues, Life Skills programming, psychoeducational and career counseling, and learning disabilities (Etzel et al., 1995; Etzel et al., 2006, Gabbard & Halischak, 1993; Hill et al., 2001; NCAA, 2007g; Parham, 1993).

Organizational issues linked to assisting student-athletes are also a potential area in which a consultant may be able to intervene with upper level administration (e.g., a systems consultation) (Parham, 1993). At times, administration may be initiating new programs, developing a new organizational structure, or adding new middle- or upper-level employees to the division. When these large-scale projects or new hires occur, organizational issues may arise in which lower-level employees and staff are unhappy with or confused about the new mission and attendant changes. A consultant who is competent in this area can intervene in this case by assisting one or more members of the administration to evaluate plans, implement them smoothly, and evaluate their impact over time.

Sports Medicine Staff and Athletic Trainers

There are two obvious areas in which psychology consultants can provide assistance to the sports medicine staff and athletic training staff
with regard to consultation that addresses student-athlete psychological
issues. First, they can provide training to these staff and their trainees
to help them recognize when student-athletes are struggling with psychological issues and to help them understand how to make appropriate referrals for mental health problems. Andersen (2002) described a
study done by Francis, Andersen, and Maley (2000) in which athletic
trainers and sports physical therapists requested more training in psychology and more psychological services provided within the sport medicine setting. This finding is encouraging. It appears that there is some
desire on the part of members of these disciplines to work collaboratively to address psychological issues as they relate to the medical issues
they address.

The second way consultants can provide assistance to sports medicine
staff and athletic trainers is by working collaboratively with them when
clinical issues of a medical and psychological nature emerge. One example of this is eating disorders. Petrie and Cogan (2002) stress the importance of the mental health provider having relationships across the
sports medicine disciplines, in order to provide comprehensive care to
the student-athlete. Sports medicine staff and athletic training staff can
also work in concert with a psychology consultant when dealing with
issues of injury. According to Tunick, Etzel, Leard, and Lerner (2002),
athletic trainers in particular often notice changes in a student-athlete's
emotional state when coping with injury. Athletic trainers are in an excellent position to monitor these changes and make referrals when necessary. Referrals from athletic trainers to psychological consultants can
be quite useful to the injured athlete. Consultants can assist athletic
trainers and sports medicine staff as part of the injury rehabilitation
process (Taylor & Taylor, 1997).

Substance abuse is another area of concern among athletes (Hill et
al., 2001; NCAA, 2007g; Wechsler et al., 1997). Given the substantial
amount of time that the sports medicine staff and athletic trainers
spend with athletes, they may be privy to issues of substance abuse and
observant of behavioral indicators in an athlete. Being able to consult

with a psychology consultant with competence in such cases can be very helpful to intervening and assisting the athlete.

Finally, head injury is another area in which sport psychology consultants can assist the sports medicine staff and athletic trainers. Neuropsychology assessment can be very valuable to athletes who participate in sports where head injury is common (e.g., football, soccer, wrestling). Consultants possessing training and experience in neurological assessment could offer useful pre/post-season or post-injury evaluation to athletes who have incurred a head injury. Also, consultants with experience in assessment may be able to perform other evaluations such as screening for learning disabilities and additional related issues. The NCAA outlines resources available to athletes who struggle with these challenges (NCAA, 2007h). The growing number of student-athletes who come to campus already diagnosed with clinical issues presents a viable professional opportunity for consultants competent in this area.

Coaches

Just like the other personnel noted above, coaches too have needs that could be met by psychology consultants. Grant and Darley (1993) presented the role of the coach as one that includes educator, lay counselor, and mentor. With the significant amount of time they spend together weekly, the coach provides a consistent adult relationship in the life of the athlete. The psychology consultant can intervene with this group by teaching coaches basic counseling skills and communication skills (Gabbard & Halischak, 1993; Hinkle, 1994). Interested coaches can learn how to communicate more effectively with their athletes; training can also help coaches when talking with their athletes about sensitive issues that may require referral. Coaches engaged in this type of interaction with their student-athletes should also be educated about potential dual relationships (Brewer, 2000).

Recently, coaches have requested support and education about issues that fall outside of their expertise. For example, Klossner (2005) discussed issues that athletes are now facing with greater frequency: hazing, eating disorders, depression, substance abuse, and head injury. In a survey conducted by the NCAA, female athletes' coaches were asked what was helpful when dealing with eating disorders among their student-athletes: 68% reported consultants on campus, 60% said educational materials, and 59% said referral information (Klossner, 2005).

These are all areas in which appropriately trained psychology consultants can assist. Given recent events of student-athlete suicides, also needed are the support and assistance of coaches in identifying signs and symptoms of depression and suicidal ideation (Maniar, Chamberlain, & Moore, 2005). Consultants with training and expertise in clinical issues can certainly assist in this educational effort and treatment of athletes with these types of serious concerns.

Performance enhancement will likely interest many coaches and is an obvious area in which the psychology consultant might intervene on both an individual and a team level. Though there are opportunities within this area, it is very important to bear in mind NCAA regulations that can affect these consultations (Andersen, 2002). Working with the coaching staff and department compliance office, the consultant can ascertain that the services are provided within the limitations of the NCAA rules and regulations. Athletes and coaches who utilize psychological skills training to improve athletic performance may also find this to be a less threatening entrée to address more serious issues at a later date, after trust has been established in the consultant.

Another way a consultant can assist coaches is through a coaches' discussion group (Gabbard & Halischak, 1993). To identify topics for workshops, the needs assessment can be a great resource. The authors have conducted numerous workshops with coaches addressing various issues. Some topics were initiated by the coaches and others were initiated by the consultants as a proactive measure, given incidents on campus or in the media. Topics for workshops included mental health and the college student-athlete, working with the millennial athlete, and developing responsible social networking behaviors among student-athletes (e.g., Facebook and MySpace). Participation in these workshops was open to coaching staff as well as athletic trainers, strength and conditioning coaches, and sports medicine staff. The format was informal, allowing for participation from those in attendance. Lunch was often provided, and the workshop usually ran for 60 to 90 minutes. Research suggests that this type of peer support can be beneficial to coaches (Gabbard & Halischak, 1993). This kind of interaction allows the consultant to meet with the staff informally, outside of a crisis, which may improve relationships and ultimately increase referral sources and opportunities to provide psychological services.

Athletes

Parham (1993) predicted that the face of athletics would change in the near future. Opportunities afforded to college students today, both academically and athletically, have grown considerably. For example, the Atlantic Coast Conference (ACC) now spans from Florida to Massachusetts; it is not the only conference to encompass such a large area. Smaller conferences, like the Colonial Athletic Association spans from Georgia to Massachusetts and most of those programs run on significantly smaller budgets than their ACC counterparts. These changes include more media exposure, additional travel time, and potentially more missed class time by student-athletes than in the past.

In addition to the changes in the athletic structure like conference size, today's student-athletes differ from those of the 1980s and 1990s in other ways. They report more pressure than their predecessors, loss of enthusiasm for their sport, feelings of exhaustion, and overtraining (Etzel et al., 2006). In our work with student-athletes, many frequently report that obtaining an athletic scholarship was their goal, that they have lost passion for participation in their once exciting sport, and that they are now playing only so that their parents will not have to pay for their otherwise expensive education.

Outside of athletics, pressure to succeed can come from parents who have afforded their children many opportunities and raised the bar of expectation, leaving the student-athlete feeling quite overwhelmed (Kadison & DiGeronimo, 2004). Mental health professionals also report an increase in students with diagnosed mental health issues, learning disabilities, and an increase in the use of medication to manage these conditions (Kadison & DiGeronimo, 2004). Student-athletes are not immune to this trend. Some suggest they may be more at-risk than their non-athlete peers (Maniar et al., 2005).

Among other changes over the past 20 years is the explosion of technology. Numerous benefits to student-athletes are a direct result of this boom (e.g., being able to engage in distance learning classes, having access to class notes and other academic materials via the Internet while traveling) (Hill et al., 2001). In the authors' experience, there are also considerable drawbacks to the information superhighway. While student-athletes may be hyper connected via cell phones and the Internet, they may have minimal time to interact face-to-face. Websites created to defame athletes, like badjocks.com, can make student-athletes vulnerable to media scandals from which they were previously more protected. A bad decision one night in a bar can be the next morning's YouTube favorite.

When consulting with this population one must consider the potential impact of any and all of these influences on student-athlete clients. They are remarkably resilient given the stressors they endure but are also quite fragile at times. Many authors encourage those in positions of responsibility on campus to act in ways that protect the welfare of the athlete and facilitate a positive, more well-rounded college experience (Etzel et al., 2006; Hill et al., 2001).

The needs and associated consulting services for athletes can range widely. Other sections of this book elaborate on these specific needs. The ways in which consultants address each of these issues will depend upon the training, expertise, and availability of the consultants; the willingess of referral sources to encourage service use; and the interest, time, and motivation of individual clients to engage in consultation. Clearly, there are many ways that a psychology consultant can enter into a relationship with consultees and clients in intercollegiate athletics. Coaches, athletes, administrators, and sports medicine staff all can benefit from the expertise offered by a psychology consultant. Consultants will also learn much about their lifestyles and needs from these people, knowledge that will make them better consultants. With such understanding, how can the consultant help?

Consulting Agreements

So far, we have discussed the people a consultant may work with, the context of consultation, and certain identified needs. Now we will explore how consultants can proceed with helping various entities. Prior to beginning any consultation, crafting a consulting contract or agreement is an essential task. Sperry (2005) provides useful basic guidance on issues associated with developing agreements with various organizations and agencies. This process may be completed in one step, but more likely it will require negotiation, with several drafts between the consultant and the entity of intervention, which is frequently athletics administration, including the business office (Caplan & Caplan, 1993).

One may establish an open-ended verbal or written agreement allowing the consultant initially to enter the system and evaluate the needs linked to potential avenues for intervention. More specifically, Sperry (2005) recommended that consultants consider the following at the onset of consultations: (1) the context of the request for help; (2) the reason(s) for seeking help at that particular time; (3) the apparent stage of readiness to change of service recipients; (4) the ability of the consultant to deliver competent services that are the focus of the consultation; and (5) whether the consultant can provide those services in an ethical manner. After these have been addressed and an operationalized definition of the problem(s) has been established, a specific contract can be created in a written form. This might include goals for the intervention and types of services, (e.g., individual counseling to student-athletes), duration of services (e.g., during the fall and spring semesters of the academic year), and remuneration (e.g., hourly fee if appropriate for external consultants).

Having such a contract or agreement is in the best interest of both the consultant and the athletic department. A clear and fair agreement will hopefully begin to establish a shared climate of trust relative to the services to be provided. Contacts should be reviewed with some frequency to ensure that all parties are content with services, to ensure that they meet changing client needs, and/or to modify agreements.

With the contract in place, the consultant can begin to provide requested services. Using the needs assessment, the consultant can develop an intervention or set of interventions in response to particular issues or problems. The intervention may include implementation of a method to address the problem, training in the system, and evaluation of the system put in place. For example, if the needs assessment demonstrates a problem with mental health referrals to the counseling center, then the consultant could create a system for referrals, train staff in how to recognize symptoms that require counseling and how to refer someone, and finally an evaluation measure that would assess how successful the training and referral system were.

Depending upon the needs or problems addressed, the interventions the consultant uses will vary. However, regardless of whether the services provided is group training, individual counseling, or individual consulting to athletics staff, the consultant should evaluate the intervention's efficacy. Without follow-up evaluation, the consultant will have no way of knowing what, if any, impact her or his work has had. This protects consultants in that they are able to provide consumers with evidence of change and benefits, by demonstrating that the expected goals indicated in the initial contract were met.

There may be instances after an initial evaluation and agreement when the consultant senses that the problems presented by clients are beyond his or her scope of practice (e.g., neuropsychological testing, substance abuse treatment). If this is the case, it is prudent to refer the athletic department to another practitioner who is better suited to meet the perceived and assessed needs of clients. A consultant may also realize after a while that too much business is on his or her plate and should arrange for additional consulting services.

Consultant Variables

There are some basic factors that impact the type and quality of consultation a practitioner can provide in athletics. In particular, two variables within the consultant include: (1) background training, experience and competence, and (2) location as an internal or external service provider.

Background

As noted by Sperry (2005), before entering into a consulting relationship one must identify the scope of proficient practice. Many authors have discussed the expertise required to serve ethically as a psychology consultant in the field of sport (Andersen, Van Raalte, & Brewer, 2001; Brown & Cogan, 2006; Hays, 2006; Packard, 2007). In the Monitor on Psychology, Division 47 President Elect Christopher Carr describes the two primary training routes for psychologists working with athletes and in sport settings:

> One is to complete graduate work in clinical or counseling psychology with additional training in the issues athletes face, including academic preparation in sport sciences and sport psychology, and the other is to gain graduate degrees in physical education or kinesiology departments. (Packard, 2007, p. 62)

Depending upon their training, the type of consultation helping professionals can competently provide will vary. What is most important is that they are practicing ethically and within their areas of expertise. Hays (2006) described important aspects to consider when evaluating consulting competence: the need for formal academic training in assessment, therapy skills, counseling, and cognitive behavioral approaches, to name a few. She also emphasized the importance of post-degree training in areas relevant to work with a particular client population (e.g., college students, student-athletes) but may not have been in the reader's degree program of study and training.

Informal training is another way to keep current using topical readings, continuing education, personal experiences, collaborative consultations, and creating supervisory relationships with colleagues (Hays, 2006). Brown and Cogan (2006) emphasized that licensed mental health providers should not assume they are somehow competent to work in the milieu of sport psychology: "This is a specialized domain and requires specialized training to become a competent practitioner" (p. 21).

Division 47 of the American Psychological Association has also examined and provided guidance on the range of skills and training necessary to be a proficient provider in sport psychology (Division 47, 2007). Outlined in this abstract are areas of competence, including knowledge of theory and research in the social, historical, and cultural development of sport psychology, training in counseling of athletes, a knowledge of biological bases for sport and exercise physiology, and others. In addition, Division 47 proficiency explores those populations who benefit from this , as well as principal areas of intervention, including psychological skills training, eating disorders and weight management, team building, leadership training, moral development, etc. (Division 47, 2007).

In line with the foregoing, it is also important for consultants to take stock of their current competence to work with the issues presented by today's college students and student-athletes. Persons who participate in athletics have unique developmental needs and engage in lifestyles that are quite different than non-athlete students (see Chapter 1). Just as one needs special knowledge and experience to work with other special populations (e.g., children, older adults, persons from different ethnic backgrounds), consultants should be proficient to work with older adolescents and young adults. Although it may provide some degree of credibility, consultants should not assume that having been student-athletes themselves makes them competent to consult with student-athletes and others within the athletics system. They should seek supplemental training, supervision, and consult with other competent professional peers before and while they work with this group and in this setting. Considering the aforementioned factors will better enable the consultant to provide high quality services and meet the needs of student-athlete clients and others most effectively.

Internal vs. External

Beyond training considerations, another factor that affects consultation is whether one is an "internal" or an "external" consultant (Tobias, 1990). For example, a consultant may be a university counseling center employee and not an employee of the athletic department. In contrast, one may be an outside independent contractor who provides consultation to the athletic department. A few universities have psychologists who are employed solely or in part by athletics departments. Each of these arrangements has pros and cons. Ferrante et al. (2002) described the possibility of athletics being a closed environment. Gaining access and building and maintaining trust can be a challenge from either an internal or external perspective. Sometimes being an outside consultant can be an advantage. One does not necessarily have the pressures of athlete performance issues as the focal point or primary undercurrent of consultation and intervention (Denson, 2002). For example, as a member of the counseling center providing consultation, one could be freer to address other issues, such as transition to college, academics, mental health, etc. (Denson, 2002). Conversely, since athletics can be a closed domain, as an outsider a consultant may not be seen as trustworthy as someone who is internal to the department—a member of the family.

The "Good" Consultant versus the "Bad" Consultant

There are some traits that are agreed upon as integral to successful consultants in the sport psychology field. Hays and Brown (2004) conducted research to investigate what consultant traits are seen as important by executives, athletes, and performers in the arts. They developed a set of common characteristics of "good" consultants that include: (1) having personal performance experience (i.e., competitive performance experience in any domain); (2) being capable of demonstrating empathy for their clients; (3) taking time to understand the client's environment even if the consultant is not personally familiar with it; (4) establishing credibility and competence; (5) working collaboratively with their clients; (6) being able to establish a trusting relationship fairly quickly; and (7) being accessible and available to clients for significant periods of time at different levels of involvement. Other authors have echoed the importance of these traits, emphasizing that a trusting relationship with the student-athlete as well as staff affiliated with student-athletes is crucial to the success of the consultant with clients. The consultant "must be genuinely interested in working with student-athletes, truly aware of the uniqueness of the student-athletes' experience, and willing to learn about applied sport psychology" (Ferrante et al., 1991, p. 22). In contrast to the characteristics of "good" consultants, Hays and Brown (2004) also asked the executives, athletes, and performers what constitutes a poor consultant. Traits associated with indicated poor consultants include: (1) undermining the clients' confidence by not recognizing their strengths; (2) not knowing what is appropriate for the individual in his or her unique setting; (3) not assessing and working toward realistic goals; (4) using inappropriate pacing or mismatching interventions to the client; (5) being unable to provide adequate support and follow through; (6) ignoring unique traits of the individual; (7) creating an atmosphere of overdependence on the consultant; (8) being a "fan" rather than a professional; (9) providing technical feedback on performance elements; (10) practicing outside one's area of competence; and (11) an inability to "practice what you preach" (Hays & Brown, 2004, p. 246).

Although the above does not represent an exhaustive set of traits, it would appear useful to take into consideration both the desirable and undesirable characteristics associated with consultation. Clearly, each consultant brings to the table unique personal strengths as well as shortcomings. To increase the probability of successful consultation, being genuine and honest with oneself as well as clients about what services one can and cannot provide and how to do so is a best practice. Self-assessment based upon feedback from consultees and clients is an excellent way to work toward being more of a "good" consultant in the realm of intercollegiate athletics. One way to do this is to take a personal inventory of one's ever-changing competencies and experiences.

Challenges and Recommendations

There are several challenges to the provision of psychological consultation to clients in intercollegiate athletics today. They include: (1) establishing and maintaining trust; (2) working within the relatively closed system of athletics; (3) dealing with ethical concerns; and (4) working within the scope of NCAA rules (Andersen et al., 2001; Andersen, 2002; Brown & Cogan, 2006; Ferrante et al., 1991; Hayes, 2006; Hays & Brown, 2004; Whelan, Meyers, & Elkins, 2002). In the following section these challenges and barriers will be explored. Suggestions will be provided about how to address these issues if or when they arise in practice.

Accessibility

With any consultation, being available to clients is essential to the success of the work. Earlier we explored the issues surrounding serving as an internal or external consultant to athletics. As an internal consultant one may have more access to clients. Denson (2002) discussed the ways this can be beneficial for the Student Services for Athletes' model. Housed in athletics, the psychologist or counselor is more readily available to student-athletes and perhaps better able to offer services at times that meet the schedules of athletes. As an outside entity, however, the consultant sometimes faces challenges that make it difficult to be accessible to student-athletes because of their demanding schedules. Another issue that may affect a consultant's work is the sometimes unreasonable expectation that one be available for consultation whenever needed.

> The logistics of the timing and location of sport psychology service offer a range of possibilities for when and where sport psychologists will work. Time commitments, however, can be exhausting. For example, a sport psychology delegate with an Olympic team is essentially on call 24 hours a day for the duration of the competition. (Andersen et al., 2002, p. 14)

Although this example involves Olympic athletes' expectations, it is becoming somewhat more common in intercollegiate athletics for the sport psychology consultant to be available 24 hours a day, seven days a week. After-hours phone calls, text messages, and emails are not uncommon. When something happens to athletes after hours (e.g., crises, arrests), it is not unusual for consultants to be contacted at any time to assist athletes, administrators, or staff. It is important that consultants be aware of this potential expectation and work within the parameters established by their consulting contracts. If this expectation goes beyond the contracted time limitations or the consultant's comfort level, then it will be necessary to clarify the limits of accessibility or work out a shared on-call system with another consultant (e.g., counseling service staff).

Trust

Trust is essential to any successful consulting relationship. Gaining the trust of the athletic department, athletes, coaches, and sports medicine staff is a very significant issue. As mentioned, the athletics system can be closed to consultants, and gaining trust can be quite difficult to do (Ferrante et al., 1991). To build and maintain trust, it is essential that the consultant spend regular time with clients in their environment (Andersen et al., 2001; Andersen, 2002). From our personal experience, we note that various factors have an impact on trust in relationships with different entities in athletics: the length of time the consultant has been affiliated with the athletics program, past experiences of staff members with consultants, the consultant's ability to manage confidentiality concerns, perceived success with previous consultations, and lastly, the consultant's training.

In the authors' experience, trust has been established with student-athletes in shorter periods of time than it has with athletics staff. Possibly because they are young, student-athletes are more trusting, but in personal feedback, they report their past experience with other members of the office, word-of-mouth from teammates, and informal contacts as reasons they have developed trust. The chief predictors of success in trust building and maintenance appear to be demonstration of genuine concern, accessibility to clients, and ethical practice.

Ethical Considerations

Probably the most challenging aspect of consultation in intercollegiate athletics is ethical practice. Consultants may encounter numerous ethical issues in their work in intercollegiate athletics. (See this book's chapter on ethics by Watson et al.) Clearly, one cannot anticipate all potential challenges that may arise (Andersen et al., 2001). Discussing these issues at the onset of a consulting relationship creates a starting point for discussion and education with consultees and their clients. This can help create and maintain a high standard of care for clientele.

Confidentiality. One common ethical concern practitioners face is confidentiality (Andersen et al., 2001; Brown & Cogan, 2006; Klossner, 2005; Gabbard & Halischak, 1993; Hays, 2006; Whelan et al., 2002). In general, these authors agree that it is vital to ensure (1) that the participants involved in the consultation are aware of the boundaries of confidentiality, and (2) that those boundaries are maintained (Andersen et al., 2001; Brown & Cogan, 2006; Hays, 2006; Watson & Etzel, 2004; Whelan et al., 2002). This is essential for several reasons, beyond the obvious need of consultants to adhere to their professional ethical codes. Andersen et al. (2001) described athletes' possible perception of psychology consultants, initially, as untrustworthy, because the consultants have a relationship with coaches or other staff members; student-athletes may assume that consultants will therefore share sensitive information about the nature of their interactions. To avoid this, it is critical to make sure that guidelines concerning confidentiality are set early and explained to all parties.

Hays (2006) reported that athletic directors, coaches, and other staff working with athletes may assume that confidential information can and perhaps should be shared among all persons who have a need to know. Although this may be the case in other areas of consultation (e.g., injury status), in which a pre-participation waiver is often signed by athletes, it is important to remind the parties involved in a consultation that there are distinct limits as to what information, if any, one can and cannot share (Etzel & Watson, 2007).

Gabbard and Halischak (1993) emphasized that it is the responsibility of the consultant to educate administrators, coaches, and other division staff about confidentiality limits and why it is integral to a trusting consultant-client relationship. A useful way to prevent misunderstanding about the ethical boundaries is to ensure that there is an informed consent document as part of the consulting agreement wherein all parties, at onset of consultation, are made clearly aware of what the standard of care will be and the limitations of confidentiality (Andersen et al., 2001; Hays, 2006).

Hays (2006) reminded us that in any kind of professional relationship it is important that the client understand the benefits and risks of the service being provided. Consultation in athletics is no different.

From the very beginning with informed consent all the parties (coaches, athletes, administrators) knowing who the client is and what confidentiality means can serve as a foundation to reflect back on when concerned parties feel the need for information on their investments (the athletes) (Andersen et al., 2001).

Electronic communication. Beyond direct face-to-face contact, clients may seek consultation via email or the phone when they are on campus or perhaps traveling (Hays, 2006). This brings up potential problems of security, privacy, confidentiality, and documentation (Etzel, Watson, & Zizzi, 2004). However, working with this generation, not using these technologies can potentially distance or alienate the consultant from clients. Making sure one is aware of these potential ethical risks, addressing them with the client, and acting within the ethical guidelines is the best the consultant can do.

Multiple relationships. Another common ethical issue that arises when providing psychological consultation is the potential for multiple or dual roles (Andersen et al., 2001; Hays, 2006; Whelan et al., 2002). A consultant may be a member of the university community, for example, as a professor or part-time faculty member. This individual may also work with the athletic department as a consultant in addition to his or her other role on campus (Etzel & Watson, 2007). It is common that in this situation the faculty member who also serves as a consultant may have a student-athlete with whom the consultant has worked (or worse, is currently working with) enroll in his or her class (Etzel & Watson, 2007). Managing this type of situation can be complicated. Whelan et al. (2002) remarked:

> For the professional, the difficulty lies in avoiding dual-role relationships; however, no rules exist that clearly delineate all possible dual-role relationships. The professional must operate from general principles, with a view toward clearly defining future dual-role relationships. (p. 518)

Unfortunately, there are times when such situations cannot be avoided. Although it is not ideal, working in all capacities of multiple or dual roles may not necessarily be unethical.

Referrals. Referral is another area in which ethical considerations can arise. Knowing that one is moving beyond his or her scope of practice necessitates considering referral to another competent practitioner. Van Raalte and Andersen (2002) remarked:

> A central issue in deciding whether or not to make a referral is the determination of the limits of one's competence. Competence is not defined by degree titles, departmental affiliates, or even licensure; competence is an issue of knowledge and skills. (pp. 329–330)

Brown and Cogan (2004) described the problem of referral sources expecting that treatment information will be shared with them. Obviously, a release of information is necessary in these situations. As with the other ethical concerns, when consultants are unsure whether they are entering a domain outside of their expertise, the best thing for them to do is to consult with a knowledgeable professional in order to protect themselves and their clients (Andersen et al., 2001; Hays & Brown, 2004).

Who is the client? Another challenge consultants confront in college athletics is determining "who is the client?" Hays (2006) described the complexity of the consultation relationship:

> Who is consenting to the service and who is the service for? . . . Consultation typically involves three layers: the consultant, the consultee or consultee system, and the client or clients affected by the consultee. Although the consultee may be more or less involved, depending in part on the performance domain, service and practitioner, that intermediary is at least implicitly involved. (p. 227)

Here Hays (2006) began to explore the challenge for psychology consultants in facilitating consultation. As noted above, there are many layers in athletic departments. Sometimes it may be important for numerous entities to be involved (e.g., a crisis situation involving athletes, coaches, and sports medicine staff). There may be other, perhaps more common, times when multi-person involvement is not necessary, and the information will need to remain solely between the consultant and the client.

This issue can become complicated when the consultant is an external one and must deal with payment for services (e.g., learning disability testing). In these cases, the athletics department pays for the consultation. As described in the section on confidentiality, the division consultees sometimes believe that this arrangement entitles them to information about treatment. Whelan et al. (2002) addressed this circumstance:

> This is an example in which issues of confidentiality become clouded; even though the professional is under contract by the university, the professional's primary fiduciary responsibility lies with the athlete. (p. 517)

The consultant's primary responsibility is to the athlete as the client, despite the fact that the consultant is being paid by the athletic department for services (Whelan et al., 2002).

Another challenging situation occurs when consultants are approached by athletics staff members regarding athletes they are concerned about because of a possible problem (e.g., an eating disorder, alcohol/drug abuse, depression) and who are not already clients. In such an instance, the consultant is initially providing service to the athletic staff member or the coach. At this point, the athlete is not the client; however, the consultant is now privy to potential issues of danger to self. This can be a rather complicated situation, and how the consultant responds will depend upon many factors. As with any other ethical issue, consultation with another professional is the best way for the consultant to determine how to proceed ethically.

Marketing services. In addition to the different challenges to providing services there are also challenges to the marketing of services, connecting with clients, and developing and nurturing the consultation relationship. For each consultant and athletic department, the marketing strategy will be somewhat different. Whether the consultant is internal or external to the university will change how marketing is done. For example, when working on an external basis, consultants need to establish relationships within the athletics department independently. Consultants who are already involved in the university (e.g., a counseling service staff member) may find it easier to develop relationships and market their services.

In some ways, student-athletes and the athletic department can be viewed as simply one of many campus entities (e.g., resident halls, Greek organizations, international students) deserving of outreach efforts from the counseling center. If the counseling center has a staff member who is expert (and has interest) in working with student-athletes and their unique issues, then it makes a great deal of sense for this consultative relationship to occur. Working on an internal basis, consultants can more easily attend practices, games, meets, and matches and network with other university professionals who can introduce them and help them gain entry to the department.

We have found that one of the simplest and most effective means to facilitate relationships within the athletic department is to invite coaches for informal lunches. Coaches are often the gatekeepers to services that student-athletes utilize as resources. Coaches who have been educated about confidentiality, who acknowledge the importance of confidentiality in counseling relationships, and who are comfortable with a counseling center staff member are more likely to encourage their student-athletes to access the counseling center.

External consultants need to approach the relationship and make initial contacts differently. For example, external consultants can write introductory letters to ADs describing their credentials and the services they can offer. This can be followed up with letters to the directors of each entity within athletics outlining the services the consultants can provide that may be beneficial to their unique needs. The efforts of external consultants to gain entrée are more like salespeople making cold calls. If a consultant has a contact at a university, then that would help him or her get a foot in the door. A disadvantage to being external is that it is more difficult to gain access and to learn about the values of the athletic department, who the players are, and the internal politics of the program; however, this external status can be beneficial too. Consultants who are able to gain entrée and do a needs assessment from an outsider's view can then offer a unique perspective that is highly valued. In addition, consultants will be able to gather data about the different parts of the athletic department and use this opportunity to familiarize themselves with the various players.

Consultants who are thoughtful about the approach they take to consultation and relationships increase their chances of being successful. Being truthful about what they can provide, their expertise, their training, and their experience can only help them build rapport and begin successful consultative experiences.

NCAA Rules and Regulations

The NCAA has numerous rules when it comes to participation in college athletics (NCAA, 2007a). Extensive rules govern all facets of athletics, including recruitment, provision of special privileges to athletes, practice times, and academic standards that are cryptic to the lay person. It is important when working in this domain that the consultant has at least a working knowledge of these rules, in particular those that apply to consulting.

Andersen (2002) described the potential ramifications of violating these rules: "Depending on the NCAA rule infraction, the consequences can range from a warning to the loss of a student's eligibility to the whole team being placed on probation or worse" (p. 385). Such consequences are certainly one motivation for being familiar with these rules; another is that it will allow consultants to recognize where they can provide assistance. Team meetings, individual sessions, and consulting with coaches are all legal in the eyes of the NCAA; however, required team meetings must be counted toward the 20 hours that teams are allotted for their weekly practice (Andersen, 2002). Individual sessions, as long as they are initiated by the athlete and not mandated, would not count toward this 20-hour rule (Andersen, 2002). When in doubt, consultants have a resource they can contact regarding these rules—the university's compliance coordinator (Andersen, 2002), who will be able to answer most questions. Consultants can also consult with the NCAA to make sure interactions are legal (Andersen, 2002).

Summary

Consultation in college athletics can be a complicated yet rewarding set of experiences. This chapter exposes some of the challenges and barriers sport psychology consultants face when engaged in this type of work. This chapter serves only as an introduction. It is the consultants' responsibility to fill in the gaps in their practices and to seek out additional training, supervision, and professional consultation when they are confronted with these complexities, to assure that they are practicing in an effective, ethical manner.

References

Andersen, M. (2002). Helping college student-athletes in and out of sport. In J. L. Van Raalte & B.W. Brewer (Eds.), *Exploring sport and exercise pychology* (2nd ed., pp. 373–393). Washington, DC: American Psychological Association.

Andersen, M., & Brewer, B. (1995). Organizational and psychological consultation in collegiate sports medicine groups. *Journal of American College Health, 44*(2), 63–70.

Andersen, M., Van Raalte, J. L., & Brewer, B. W. (2001). Sport psychology service delivery: Staying ethical while keeping loose. *Professional Psychology: Research and Practice, 32*(1), 12–18.

Archer, J., & Cooper, S. (1998). *Counseling and mental health services on campus.* San Francisco: Jossey-Bass.

Brewer, B.W. (2000). Doing sport psychology in the coaching role. In M. B. Andersen (Ed.), *Doing sport psychology* (pp. 237–247). Champaign, IL: Human Kinetics.

Broughton, E., & Neyer, M. (2001). Advising and counseling student athletes. *New Directions for Student Services, 93*, 47–53.

Brown, J. L., & Cogan, K. (2006). Ethical clinical practice and sport psychology: When two worlds collide. *Ethics and Behavior, 16*(1), 15–23.

Caplan, G., & Caplan, R. (1993). *Mental health consultation and collaboration.* Long Grove, IL: Waveland Press Inc.

Carr, C., & Bauman, N. J. (2002). Life skills for collegiate student-athletes. In E. Etzel, A.P. Ferrante, & J.W. Pinkney (Eds.), *Counseling college student athletes: Issues and interventions* (2nd ed., pp. 281–307). Morgantown, WV: Fitness Information and Technology, Inc.

Denson, E. (2002). An integrative model of academic and personal support services for student athletes. In E. Etzel, A. P. Ferrante, & J. W. Pinkney (Eds.), *Counseling college student athletes: Issues and interventions* (2nd ed., pp. 247–280). Morgantown, WV: Fitness Information and Technology, Inc.

Division 47 of the American Psychological Association. (2007). A Proficiency in Sport Psychology. Retrieved November 13, 2007, from http://www.psyc.unt.edu/ap adiv 47/APA %20Div%2047%20(3)/Proficiency/Proficiency.html.

Etzel, E., Pinkney, J., & Hinkle, S. (1995). College student-athletes and needs assessment. In S. Stabb, S. Harris, & J. Talley (Eds.), *Needs assessment for college and university student populations* (pp. 155–172). Springfield, IL: Charles C. Thomas.

Etzel, E., & Watson, J. (2007) Ethical challenges for psychological consultation in intercollegiate athletics. *Journal of Clinical Sport Psychology, 1*, 228–241.

Etzel, E., Watson, J. C., & Zizzi, S. (2004). A web-based survey of AAASP members' ethical beliefs and behaviors in the new millennium. *Journal of Applied Sport Psychology, 16*, 236–250.

Etzel, E., Watson, J., Visek, A., & Maniar, S. (2006). Understanding and promoting college student-athlete health: Essential issues for student affairs professionals. *NASPA Journal, 43*(3), 518–546.

Ferrante, A. P., Etzel, E., & Lantz, C. (2002). Counseling college student athletes: The problem, the need 1996. In E. Etzel, A. P. Ferrante, & J. W. Pinkney (Eds.), *Counseling college student athletes: Issues and interventions* (2nd ed., pp. 3–26). Morgantown, WV: Fitness Information and Technology, Inc.

Ferrante, A.P., Etzel, E., & Pinkney, J. (1991). A model for accessing student-athletes student-affairs resources. In E. Etzel, A. Ferrante, & J. Pinkney (Eds.), *Counseling college student athletes: Issues and interventions* (pp. 19–30). Morgantown, WV: Fitness and Information Technology, Inc.

Fletcher, T. B., Benshoff, J. M., & Richburg, M. J. (2003). A systems approach to understanding counseling college student athletes. *Journal of College Counseling, 6,* 35–45.

Gabbard, C., & Halischak, K. (1993). Consulting opportunities: Working with student-athletes at a university. *The Counseling Psychologist, 21*(3), 386–398.

Grant, C. H., & Darley, C. F. (1993). Reaffirming the coach-athlete relationship: A response from intercollegiate athletics. *The Counseling Psychologist, 21*(3), 441–444.

Hays, K. (2006). Being fit: The ethics of practice diversification in performance psychology. *Professional Psychology: Research and Practice, 37*(3), 223–232.

Hays, K. F., & Brown, C. H. (2004). *You're on! Consulting for peak performance.* Washington, DC: American Psychological Association.

Hill, K., Burch-Ragan, M., & Yates, D. (2001). Current and future issues and trends facing student athletes and athletic programs. *New Directions for Student Services, 93,* 65–80.

Hinkle, S. (1994). Sport counseling: Helping student-athletes. Eric Digest, Article ED379532. Retrieved November 14, 2007, from http://www.ericdigests. org/1996-1/ sports.htm

Jordan, J., & Denson, E. (1990). Student services for athletes: A model for enhancing the student-athlete experience. *Journal of Counseling and Development, 69,* 95–97.

Kadison, R., & DiGeronimo, T. F. (2004). *College of the overwhelmed: The campus mental health crisis and what to do about it.* San Francisco, CA: Jossey Bass.

Klossner, D. (2005). *Mental health in sport.* Association for the Advancement of Applied Sport Psychology Annual Conference, Miami, FL.

Maniar, S., Chamberlain, R., & Moore, N. (2005, November 7). Suicide risk is real for student-athletes. NCAA News. Retrieved November 13, 2007, from http://www. ncaa.org/wps/ncaa?ContentID=15249

Meyers, J., Parson, D., & Martin, R. (1979). *Mental health consultation in the schools: A comprehensive guide for psychologists, social workers, psychiatrists, counselors, educators and other human services professionals.* San Francisco: Jossey-Bass.

Morrill, W. H., Oetting, E. R., & Hurst, J. C. (1974). Dimensions of counselor functioning. *Personnel Guidance Journal, 52,* 354–359.

National Collegiate Athletics Association. (2007a). Division I Manual. Retrieved November 9, 2007, from http://www.ncaa.org/library/sports_sciences/sports_med_ handbook/2007-08/2007-08_sports_medicine_handbook.pdf

National Collegiate Athletics Association. (2007c). CHAMPS Life Skills History. Retrieved November 9, 2007, from http://www.ncaa.org/wps/ncaa?ContentID=13

National Collegiate Athletics Association. (2007d) CHAMPS Life Skills Program. Retrieved November 9, 2007, from http://www.ncaa.org/wps/ncaa?ContentID=13

National Collegiate Athletics Association. (2007e) NCAA Our Mission. Retrieved November 9, 2007, from http://www2.ncaa.org/portal/about_ncaa/overview/mission.html

National Collegiate Athletics Association. (2007f) NCAA Student Athlete Advisory Committees. Retrieved November 9, 2007, from http://www1.ncaa.org/membership/membership_svcs/saac/index.html

National Collegiate Athletics Association. (2007h) Academic Services and Resources-Disability Information. Retrieved November 9, 2007, from www.ncaa.org/wps/ncaa?ContentID=3439

Packard, E. (2007). Sports authority. *Monitor on Psychology, 38*(32), 62.

Parham, W. (1993). The intercollegiate athlete: A 1990s profile. *The Counseling Psychologist, 21*(3), 411–429.

Parsons, D., & Meyers, J. (1984). *Developing consultation skills.* San Francisco: Jossey-Bass.

Petrie, T., & Cogan, K. (1996). Counseling college women student-athletes. In E. Etzel, A. P. Ferrante, & J. W. Pinkney (Eds.), *Counseling college student athletes: Issues and interventions* (2nd ed., pp. 77–106). Morgantown, WV: Fitness Information and Technology, Inc.

Pinkerton, R., Hinz, L., & Barrow, J. (1987). The college student athlete: Psychological consideration and interventions. *Journal of American College Health, 37*, 218–226.

Portenga, S. T., & Aoyagi, M. W. (2007). Ethical practice for consultants working directly for university athletic departments. Paper presented at the 22nd annual meeting of the Association for Applied Sport Psychology, Louisville, KY.

Sperber, M. (1990). *College Sports Inc.: The athletic department vs the university.* New York: Henry Holt and Company, Inc.

Sperry, L. (2005). Establishing a consulting agreement. In G. P. Koocher, J. C. Norcross, & S. S. Hill (Eds.), *Psychologist's desk reference* (2nd ed., pp. 666–669). New York: Oxford University Press.

Taylor, J., & Taylor, S. (1997). Psychological problems in rehabilitation. In J. Taylor & S. Taylor, *Psychological approaches to sports injury rehabilitation.* Gaithersburg, MD: Aspen Publishers.

Telander, R. (1996). *The hundred yard lie: The corruption of college football and what we can do to stop it.* Urbana and Chicago: University of Illinois Press.

Terenzini, P. (1993). On the nature of institutional research and the knowledge and skills it requires. *Research in Higher Education 34*, 1–10.

Tobias, L. (1990). *Psychological consulting to management.* New York: Bruner Mazel.

Tunick, R., Etzel, E., Leard, J., & Lerner, B. (1996). Counseling injured and disabled student athletes: A guide for understanding and intervention. In E. Etzel, A. P. Ferrante, and J.W. Pinkney (Eds.), *Counseling college student athletes: Issues and interventions* (2nd ed., pp. 157–184). Morgantown, WV: Fitness Information Technology, Inc.

Van Raalte, J. L., & Andersen, M. B. (2002). Referral process in sport psychology. In J. L. Van Raalte & B.W. Brewer (Eds.), *Exploring sport and exercise psychology* (2nd ed., pp. 325–337). Washington, DC: American Psychological Association

Watson, J. C., & Etzel, E. F. (2004). Ethical issues affecting psychologists, counselors and sport psychology consultant's work with collegiate student athletes. *Professional Studies Review, 1*(1), 49–60.

Wechsler, H., Davenport, A. E., Dowdall, G. W., Grossman, S. J., & Zanakos, S. I. (1997). Binge drinking, tobacco, and illicit drug use and involvement in college athletics. *Journal of American College Health, 45*(5), 195–200.

Whelan, J. P., Meyers, A. W., & Elkins, T. D., (2002). Ethics in sport and exercise psychology. In J. L. Van Raalte & B.W. Brewer (Eds.), *Exploring sport and exercise psychology* (2nd ed., pp. 503–523). Washington, DC: American Psychological Association.

3

ETHICS AND COUNSELING PRACTICE WITH COLLEGE STUDENT-ATHLETES

Jack Watson
Edward F. Etzel
Jamie Shapiro

Ethical practice in college counseling, psychotherapy, and consultation is the foundation of principled, high-quality service provision. Because of the numerous and often frequent challenges that helping professionals who work with college student-athlete clients are likely to encounter, it is essential that they be ethically well versed. The central premise of ethical practice is to do no harm to the young people being served. Those helping professionals who work within intercollegiate athletics or who see clients from athletic departments recognize that the setting and culture offer a set of regular, sometimes unique threats to ethical practice connected to various consultative "undercurrents" (Etzel & Watson, 2007). The reader will no doubt come across frequent opportunities to do harm to clients—often in simple, unintentional ways (e.g., breaches of confidentiality, multiple relationships). Helping professionals who provide consultation to student-athletes must be able to recognize these ethically challenging dilemmas as they evolve, and be able to resolve these situations in a responsible and competent manner.

In this chapter, the authors will use the term "helping professional" to describe the variety of practitioners who work with college student-athletes in one or more helping capacities. Examples of these professionals are counselors, psychologists, and sport psychology consultants, as well as sports medicine professionals. Helping professionals may also be supervised graduate students from any of the abovementioned domains engaging in practica and internships. Although people from allied but different professions have their own codes of ethics to know and follow, all of the ethical issues discussed in this chapter are generally applicable to licensed professionals as well as professionals in training. In addition, all of these professions have their own ethics codes (e.g., Association of Applied Sport Psychology, n.d.; American Counseling Association, 2005; APA, 2002). Because two of the authors of this chapter are licensed psychologists, we have chosen to primarily make use of the American Psychological Association (APA) code.

Ethical Challenges and Ethics Codes

On any given day, helping professionals who work with student-athletes can encounter circumstances that test their values-based thinking and behavior in the workplace. Even the most experienced professional's ethical mettle is tested by these often spontaneous, unpredictable, and sometimes complex turns of events. Regrettably, many of the responses to these situations are not at all clear cut or particularly easy to make. Within the mix of collegiate and athletic cultures, some decisions may be obviously right or wrong (e.g., whether or not to engage in an intimate relationship with a client), or may be less obvious (e.g., sharing information with a coach about an athlete referred for sport performance issues). One thing is certain: ethically challenging situations will occur again and again when working with this population.

Clearly, the decisions that helping professionals must make can have a great impact upon the well-being of the clients with whom they are working, as well as on their individual reputations and the collective reputation of their profession. Consequently, it is essential that helping professionals be aware of and knowledgeable about the code(s) of ethics of their profession(s), as well as willing and able to make sometimes multifaceted ethical judgments.

Codes

Ethics codes can be thought of as a set of guidelines or overarching principles that direct the behavior of individuals in line with the fundamental values of an organization or group (Bersoff, 1995). These codes serve as guides to protect the public by helping members resolve the moral problems they face. The current codes of ethics in psychology and applied sport psychology are comprised of an introduction, preamble, general principles, and ethical standards (AASP, n.d.; APA, 2002). The initial "preambles" and general "principles" of codes are "aspirational" in nature, and designed to encourage members to hold themselves to the highest possible level of behavior, useful to ethical decision making (APA, 2002). In contrast, ethical "standards" are designed to more specifically guide member thinking and behavior in an enforceable manner across a wide variety of professional situations.

Confidentiality and Privacy

Confidentiality is an agreed-upon standard of professional behavior that obliges a helping professional not to discuss information about a client with anyone. This practice is regarded as the "cornerstone of trust on which the therapeutic relationship is built" (Glosoff, Herlihy, Herlihy, & Spence, 1997, p. 573; Koocher & Keith-Spiegel, 1998). Although confidentiality is a widespread ethical concept, it may or may not also be consistent with the practice of law in some states and provinces.

Helping professionals on campus need to be able to differentiate between confidentiality and privacy as these pertain to practice. As noted above, it is important to bear in mind that confidentiality is typically an ethical standard: it may or may not be the law in one's own state or province. In contrast to confidentiality, *privacy* is a fundamental legal right in the United States that limits the extent to which client information is available and communicated with others (Fisher, 2003; Koocher & Keith-Spiegel, 1998). Privacy is central to the Health Insurance Portability and Accountability Act of 1996 (HIPAA) discussed below (United States Department of Health & Human Resources, n.d.).

Professionals must be aware of the ethical principles and standards of their profession concerning confidentiality, and they must also understand and follow the laws that pertain to the practice of counseling, psychology, or other allied professions in the state/province in which they practice. Lacking a strong foundation of trust and rapport, any counseling or psychological relationship or set of interventions, no matter how useful or innovative, would likely be short-lived and ineffective. Therefore, confidentiality and privacy are of the utmost importance to building and maintaining trusting relationships in order to be effective as helpers with individual student-athletes and group/team clients.

Release of Confidential and/or Private Information

The Health Insurance Portability and Accountability Act of 1996 (HIPAA) is intended "to assure that individuals' health information is protected while allowing the flow of health information needed to provide and promote high quality health care and to protect the public's health and well being" (United States Department of Health & Human Resources, n.d.). As such, this law protects the transmission of all individually identifiable information related to past, present, or future physical or mental health services, the current provision of mental health services, and the past, present, or future payment for such health services. The HIPAA Privacy Rule permits communication between healthcare providers on existing treatment teams providing collaborative consultations (e.g., from a team physician to department or campus psychologist). Based upon this law, practitioners must make clients aware of their rights under this law and take every effort to protect client information from others who are not intended to see such information.

Third-Party Inquiries

As noted above, the college and athletic environment and cultures today pose several potential ethical challenges to consultation with individual athletes and teams. One such challenge involves determining "Who is the client?" This issue is in reality quite commonly faced in a setting with many so-called "players." For example, an athlete may be referred by one or more members of the athletic department staff, including a coach, athletic trainer, team physician, academic advisor, and/or administrator. Further complicating the matter, the athletic department or team may also be paying the salary or fees for the helping professional.

As a result, some referral sources or other third parties may believe they are entitled to know any and sometimes all information about "their" athlete, especially if it relates to the performance of high-profile or scholarship athletes (Etzel & Watson, 2007). It should not come as a surprise to a helping professional to be asked by a coach in a hallway or on the phone about how Brandon or Brandy is doing. In general, clients provide "informed consent" for their own treatment, with certain exceptions (e.g., threats to self or other; child or elder abuse). Within such legally binding contacts with clients, information about appointments, personal issues, progress, and so on must remain confidential unless a release of information has been provided by the client.

When such arrangements exist with third-party referrals, practitioners should initially clarify their professional roles and responsibilities to each party, as well as the limits to confidentiality before providing any services to the athlete (APA Ethical Principle B and Standards 3.07, 3.11a, 4.02a, 4.02b, 2002). During the initial session with a client, the limits of confidentiality should be reviewed (e.g., self/other harm, self/other abuse), as well as very specifically what, if anything, the athlete would want to be disclosed to an inquiring, identified third party. For example, a client might agree that a third party such as her head coach can be made aware only of attendance at counseling sessions and no more. If clients want information to be shared, it is necessary to have them sign a written release of information to be kept on record along with the informed consent form, which specifies these limits to confidentiality (APA Ethical Standard 3.10, 2002). Even if the athlete signs a more general release of information, helping professionals are encouraged to disclose as little as possible to designated third parties and only what is relevant to the purposes of the release (APA Ethical Standard 4.04a; Moore, 2003). In our experience, it has been constructive to encourage clients to discuss any issues they feel comfortable discussing directly with concerned third parties. This allows them to control the information that they would like to be released.

Athletes may be referred by caring but sometimes intrusive "helicopter" parents (i.e., parents that hover around their children and make decisions for them). Indeed, college is sometimes the first time that parents have had to deal with not being privy to their child's health or academic information, not to mention their status as athletes. This can be quite a surprise and source of consternation to caring but uninformed parents of student-athletes who are over the age of 18 and who are therefore no longer legally "minors." Helping professionals should keep in mind that they may occasionally encounter clients who are below the age of 18. In these rather rare situations, parents and guardians in some states may still have a right to know about the helping professional's work with their son or daughter. As coaches do—but often for different reasons— parents will inquire about how their daughter or son is doing: "Is he or she still coming to see you?" "How can we be helpful?" Helping professionals need to be able to respond in a respectful yet ethical way to an e-mail message or phone call from an athlete's parent or guardian that may jeopardize the confidential relationship with the client. The ethical helping professional needs to be gently assertive to protect the boundaries of client confidentiality, even in the face of sometimes temperamental inquirers. Parents and coaches alike are often supportive of athlete clients, but they are sometimes part of young people's problems.

There are also times when coaches or other third parties recognize that the athlete has improved in performance, affect, or attitude and may inquire about what strategies or techniques the practitioner used to help the athlete. Although such inquiries are most likely well intended, professionals should again protect the confidentiality of the consultation, and instead of possibly offending the coach by stating the rules of confidentiality, simply refer the coach or parent to the athlete. For instance, one might say, "I'm glad you've seen that Joe has improved. Perhaps you could ask him what he learned that may have been helpful to him." This would allow the client to make a decision about what information to discuss (Brown & Cogan, 2006).

NCAA Rules

Another issue that is unique to helping professionals working within or for an athletic department is the reporting of possible National Collegiate Athletic Association (NCAA) rule violations. The 2007–08 NCAA Division I "Manual" is nearly 450 pages long (National Collegiate Athletics Association, 2007a). Although this publication is not a code of ethics per se (ironically, only one page is devoted to principles of ethical conduct), it is a document that can have some occasional influence on the helping professional's work with student-athletes. All athletic department personnel, including psychologists or counselors who may be part of the athletic department staff, must annually sign a statement stating that they will follow NCAA rules and dutifully report any violations to the athletic department compliance office. Ethical dilemmas may emerge from consultations with athletes who divulge information about participating in or observing behaviors that may seem to constitute NCAA violations (e.g., practicing for too many hours).

In general, helping professionals, whether members of the athletic department staff or not, should be aware of NCAA rules. If infractions are identified, they should inform the athlete that these acts are possible NCAA violations, and then work with the athlete to make educated decisions about how to respond, if at all, to the behaviors in question. Helping professionals should initially be direct with athletic department staff regarding the protection of information related to possible NCAA rule violations, citing the guidance of the APA ethics code, other professional codes, and state law. However, as per initial informed consent agreements with clients, helping professionals should treat information as confidential given that the ethics code and the law represent higher standards of practice by which counselors or psychologists must abide (APA Ethical Standards 1.02 and 1.03, 2002; Etzel & Watson, 2007).

Records

Appointment histories and detailed clinical records, as well as miscellaneous notes, must be protected. Although different agencies and professionals use differing formats, useful guidance is provided on this subject by Koocher (2005). This critical information should be stored in a safe and secure place (APA Ethical Standards 4.01, 4.02a, 4.02b, 6.01, 6.02, 2002; Moore, 2003). If these records are electronic, they should be password protected and located on a secure computer server. HIPAA guidelines indicate that hard copy files should also be kept in a locked file and behind a locked door. Although there appear to be different practices associated among agencies and states, records are generally kept on average seven to ten years prior to appropriate disposal.

Competence

Although all helping professionals would like to believe they are quite competent to serve their clients, this may not be the truth. Competence is something that takes considerable time, effort, and work to develop. Further, once achieved, competence is not static. Practitioners must continually strive to update their knowledge and skills. The ethical standard of competence includes: (1) practicing within the boundaries of one's education, training, and supervision; (2) providing services to only those populations with whom one is trained to work; (3) keeping up with new developments in one's field; and (4) knowing when personal problems might interfere with one's work (APA Ethical Standard 2, 2002). Many issues related to competence arise when considering working with an athlete population on campus.

Backgrounds

It is safe to say that helping professionals working in intercollegiate athletics come from varying backgrounds with different types and levels of training. Because of these training differences, defining competence becomes an important ethical matter when working with this population. Whereas the services provided by these professionals may overlap, there are important distinctions related to their training and expertise. Those individuals using the term "psychologist" or "counselor" within the United States must meet the requirements set forth for that title by their state or the federal government. For example, the title "psychologist" is protected in all 50 states and the District of Columbia. In general, "psychologists have a doctoral degree in psychology from an organized, sequential program in a regionally accredited university or professional school" (American Psychological Association, 2003), and such degrees are most commonly in clinical, counseling, child, or industrial/organizational psychology. The combination of these qualifications and having completed a licensing process within their state allows them to practice psychology within the bounds of their competence. Many licensed psychologists are trained in assisting their clients with mental health issues. In light of licensing requirements, some who have earned a terminal degree in applied sport psychology or a related field may not be able to call themselves "sport psychologists" unless they are licensed psychologists. The exception to this practice is if they are employed as a psychologist by a state or federal government organization, such as a university or prison system, where they would be able to call themselves psychologists only within those settings.

Counselors are in many ways similar to psychologists in terms of training and areas of competence. Although the title "counselor" is not protected in all states, it communicates a high level of professional training and competence. Professional counselors often receive master's and/or doctoral level training from programs in counseling or counselor education. These professionals are trained to provide mental health services to individuals of all ages and backgrounds, but often have different competency areas than psychologists. Counselors often focus on the growth and development of individuals by utilizing both prevention and remediation to help them lead productive lives (American Counseling Association, 2007). As with psychologists, counselors can bill third-party agencies and can address issues found within the Diagnostic and Statistical Manual for Mental Disorders, 4th edition (DSM-IV: American Psychiatric Association, 1996).

Credentials

Student-athletes and athletic department staff may not be clear about the credentials and competencies of helping professionals. Those persons who do not possess the appropriate training in psychology and/or counseling should not use professional titles. They should not allow other people to misrepresent them by referring to them by incorrect titles (e.g., team psychiatrist versus psychologist; media guide bios). Further, they should quickly correct people who do misrepresent them.

Although it may be disappointing to some, individuals who were trained in the traditional sport sciences/applied sport psychology/physical education model of sport psychology and not licensed or credentialed should not be involved in the provision of counseling and therapy to student-athletes, unless they are employed by a state university or federal government organization for the purposes of providing such services. In order to practice within the law and scope of the ethical codes of their professions (e.g., Association of Applied Sport Psychology [AASP]), such professionals must only teach educational sport performance enhancement skills to athlete clients who present with performance enhancement issues. Similarly, those individuals with training specifically in psychology and counseling should be very careful when working with sport performance enhancement issues if they do not have an established competency area within sport (i.e., education, training, and supervision). For a more complete review of the differences in training and services provided by the above professions, see Watson and Etzel (2004).

Presenting Concerns

Is one helping professional really competent to do career counseling, brief psychotherapy, crisis intervention, drug and alcohol counseling, trauma therapy, and learning disability testing? Indeed, it can be tempting to try to be all things to all people, and sometimes in a pinch professionals are asked to be so. However, doing so regularly is a risky stretch; in some instances it may be unethical and possibly even illegal.

It is therefore imperative that helping professionals know what issues and problems they are competent to work with.

When in doubt, ethical helping professionals seek supervision from a colleague if there is any question about their competency within a specific area of their work with student-athletes. Ethical professionals must also know what assessment measures and interventions they are trained to use (e.g., a Myers-Briggs Type Indicator, Beck Depression Inventory-2, Beck Anxiety Inventory, and Minnesota Multiphasic Personality Inventory-2) and when to employ or not employ them with clients. When practitioners determine that client needs are outside the boundaries of their professional training and expertise, they should consult with a competent trusted colleague and consider referring the client to another professional who is competent to handle these issues. Having an up-to-date set of consulting and referral resources on hand (e.g., for learning disability testing or a neuropsychological assessment) is a key to providing high-quality service.

Populations

Another aspect of competence relates to being sufficiently trained to work with the population requesting services. Although attending to common features that college student-athletes share is quite important, it is just as significant for helping professionals to be aware of potential visible and invisible differences among and between these young people (Loughran & Etzel, under review). Accordingly, an ethical helping professional should have a good working "understanding of the factors associated with age, gender, gender identity, race, ethnicity, culture, national origin, religion, sexual orientation, disability, language, and socioeconomic status" (APA, 2002, p. 5). If a counselor or psychologist is perhaps not comfortable or knowledgeable in working with a client from a particular background, or if the client is not comfortable working with the professional, then the professional should consult with one or more competent colleagues, discuss these issues with the client, and/or make a referral to another professional.

As described in other chapters in this book, student-athletes are considered by some to be a unique on-campus population. They are also a diverse group of individuals (perhaps the most diverse on campus) and should not be lumped into one category. Therefore, before starting to work with student-athletes, counselors, psychologists, and professionals in the making should acquire some knowledge about and experience with this population through graduate coursework, continuing education, and/or supervised experiences under the guidance of a helping professional who is competent to provide such supervision (Loughran & Etzel, under review). Having been an athlete or sports fan does not make a professional competent to work with athlete clients. If not sufficiently competent to work with the presenting concerns of student-athletes, professionals should refer them to someone with training and competence in the appropriate field (Brown & Cogan, 2006). Since counseling and/or psychology professionals proficient in this area may not be readily available at many colleges, a psychologist or counselor should at least consult (i.e., via e-mail or phone) with a qualified sport psychology professional regarding the athlete's concerns. Such consultations should always be handled in an anonymous and confidential manner.

Continuing Education

As noted above, ethical helping professionals should practice only within the confines of their competence and not outside those limits. Further, competence can change over time, as a result of work experience, inactivity, or personal difficulty. Although a terminal degree may serve as evidence of competence in one's field, the "half-life" of a doctorate in psychology has been estimated to be 10–12 years (Dubin, 1972, as cited in Koocher & Keith-Spiegel, 1998). The ethical professional "makes a life-long commitment to learning and professional growth" (Watson & Etzel, 2004, p. 58). Therefore, it is essential that professionals continue their education and training beyond graduate school to ensure that they keep up with the latest developments in the field and are providing high quality assistance to their student-athlete clients (APA Ethical Standard 2.03, 2002; Watson & Etzel, 2004).

Continued education can be accomplished by attending conferences and lectures, reading, taking additional courses, and regular consultation with colleagues and supervisors. Ethical helping professionals who work with student-athletes would benefit from regular updating on common issues and interventions associated with the lifestyles of student-athletes. Essential topics include the impact of year-round training, injury risk and response, academic demands, learning disabilities, social networking, and the growing incidence of other psychological disorders that college students present with (e.g., alcohol and substance use, depression, suicidality, anxiety disorders, disordered eating and eating disorders, sexual assault and promiscuity) (Kadisson & DiGeronimo, 2005; National Collegiate Athletic Association, 2007b).

A rather recent ethical concern regarding competence comes with an increasingly popular form of higher education—online courses and degrees. These programs have expanded access to certain areas of practice and subject matters, but they bring up potential ethical problems for practitioners. A key concern is for those who choose to complete an entire degree online and wish to practice counseling or (sport) psychology. Training for these professions requires that the student be supervised through an internship. In an on-line distance-learning program, "direct" supervision (i.e., direct observation) can be quite difficult if not impossible at times. Because supervisors are ultimately responsible for supervisees' work (APA Ethical Standard 2.05, 2002), those who supervise students in on-line programs should be sure to engage in as much direct supervision as possible from a distance, such as through video recordings of counseling sessions. Those who obtain degrees on-line from these programs must be very careful that they apply their degree only within the boundaries of their education, training, and supervision.

Self-Care

Counseling and therapy work with college students can be quite demanding in its own right; personal life developments, health problems, addictions, attractions, and other issues can take their toll on the mental and physical health of helping professionals. Other issues (e.g., attraction, aversion, staleness, burnout, work conditions, and relationships with others) can negatively influence the quality of work with clients (Koocher & Keith-Spiegel, 1998; Pope & Tabachnick, 1993). As a result, ethical counselors and psychologists need to be self-aware and monitor how their personal and working lives may be influencing their work. When professionals experience personal problems creating impairment, they should seek out assistance and determine whether they should continue or suspend working with clients (APA Ethical Standard 2.06, 2002). Ethical helping professionals also have an obligation to approach peers who appear to be "impaired" and, if so, may be jeopardizing their own welfare. Many professional organizations (e.g., state counseling and psychological associations) have colleague assistance programs in place to help those in need (Schoener, 2003).

Overidentification

In the stimulating and sometimes seductive world of modern intercollegiate athletics, it is easy to get wrapped up in clients or their teams' performance. Some have a need to be seen with these young people, "hang out" at competitions, insist on being included in media guides, and/or display athlete photos and team memorabilia in their offices. This phenomenon is similar to parents who "live through" their children and overidentify with their accomplishments. Those who succumb to this role risk compromising their objectivity and competence. Helping professionals must monitor the extent to which they overidentify with the teams and athletes with whom they work. Ethical helping professionals maintain appropriate distance from their athletes and resist the temptation to become enmeshed with athletes' teams and perhaps gain special recognition for services.

Multiple Relationships

Multiple relationships exist when a helping professional "is in a professional role with a person and: (1) at the same time is in another role with the person; (2) at the same time is in a relationship with a person closely associated with or related to the person with whom the [helping professional] has a professional relationship; or (3) promises to enter into another relationship in the future with the person or a person closely associated with or related to the person" (American Psychological Association, 2002, p. 1065). The major problems associated with multiple relationships include the ability of a person who is in a position of influence (i.e., consultant or therapist) misusing that influence, either knowingly or unknowingly, resulting in harm to clients. Within the fields of counseling and psychology, multiple relationships generally have the potential to distort the working relationship and the consulting process (Pope & Vasques, 1991). Such relationships are typically frowned upon (Kitchener, 1988). However, exceptions are seen in unusual situations (e.g., emergencies, lack of other resources) and when harm is very unlikely to happen to the client or the professional's work quality and/or objectivity.

Given a generally consistent negative view of multiple relationships, it may not be surprising to find that, when surveyed, professionals from counseling and psychology working within the sport domain reported more often than non-licensed professionals that multiple roles are never appropriate and that they had never taken part in multiple role relationships (Watson, Clement, Harris, Leffingwell, & Hurst, 2006). Moreover, this same sample of mental health professionals with a background in sport and exercise psychology were more likely than non-practitioners to report significantly higher levels of concern for both the practitioners and clients engaging in multiple role relationships (Watson et al., 2006).

Because of the relatively small number of qualified service providers in sport psychology, many tend to be employed by or around universities where they often both teach and consult with student-athletes (Watson & Etzel, 2004). This suggests a greater than normal chance for the development of multiple relationships with student-athletes and perhaps others involved with athletics. For example, it is not uncommon for a consultant to teach a course that has enrolled in it an athlete from a team that the consultant currently works with, has worked with in the past, or may work with in the future. Additionally, psychologists are sometimes approached to provide consultation to coaches and athletic trainers, which can rapidly transform into a request for personal assistance.

When true multiple relationships exist as described by the APA definition above, they often bring with them the potential for uncomfortable and distressful interactions and potentially unconstructive outcomes. Indeed, if both parties are not able to separate the two roles, it is possible for athlete clients to perceive that what happens in one of the relationships may affect the relationship in the other role. For example, a poor grade on an exam could be perceived as the consultant not valuing or supporting the athlete (Watson & Etzel, 2004).

Other possible multiple relationships in university settings that may affect student-athletes extend beyond that of teacher-consultant. Such roles may include that of consultant-coach and teacher-coach. As is the case with the teacher-practitioner multiple role relationship, there are some potential benefits but also many problems that can result from a teacher-coach relationship (Figone, 1994) and the coach-consultant relationship (Buceta, 1993). Examples of such problems and benefits could include a potential loss of trust in both roles due to behavior in one domain, and the ease with which rapport can be developed.

Some recent literature suggests that the onus of responsibility in such multiple role relationships falls upon the helping professional much more so than the student-athlete (Watson et al., 2006; Watson & Etzel, 2004). The major considerations associated with possibly getting involved in or disengaging from such situations need to be the welfare of the client and clarification of the boundaries of the relationship (Watson et al., 2006). As such, suggestions have been made for the two parties to meet early and frequently to discuss potential hazards, the creation of open and honest lines of communication, and limits for public interaction (Watson & Etzel, 2004).

Although the frequency of multiple role relationships in traditional college counseling and psychology work with student-athletes is unclear, such contacts may be more likely to occur in sport and exercise psychology settings (e.g., consultations with student-athletes). The campus and surrounding community environment presents many opportunities to interact with clients in several professional and non-professional capacities. It is a small—sometimes very small—world, after all. However, many interactions with clients, students, or others may not be necessarily unethical and damaging to the client and consultant. In fact, Sonne (2004) pointed out that there is considerable uncertainty and debate related to so-called "non-sexual" multiple relationships (e.g., loaning a client a self-help book, shaking a client's hand on the way in or out of a counseling session, a benign self-disclosure in session, unintentional encounters at games, walking down the street, or in a store or health service) and other harmless communications, contacts, and "boundary crossings."

Marketing

Unfortunately, many barriers to service provision exist within sport and intercollegiate athletics (see Ferrante and Etzel in this book). Marketing is an important aspect of working around or reducing barriers, as well as building and maintaining a professional psychology or counseling practice. Whether one is an employee of the department of intercollegiate athletics, a member of a counseling service staff, or perhaps a private practitioner, information about the specific nature and method of accessing counseling and psychological services available to student-athletes is critical to service access and utilization. Useful guidance on marketing for consultants applicable to work in athletics but beyond the scope of this chapter is offered by Hays and Brown (2004) and Lesyk (1998).

Overall, helping professionals need to present their services and themselves in an accurate, positive light to make potential clients and referral sources aware of their services. The ethical standards of both the APA and AASP suggest that practitioners need to make honest and truthful claims about their training and competence, degrees, credentials, affiliations, fees (if any), and services when marketing their services.

With this in mind, ethical professionals will be specific as to what degrees and titles they hold. For example, printing "Dr. Jack Smith" on a business card is vague and does not tell clients in what degree or field Dr. Smith was trained. However, "Jack Smith, Ph.D., Licensed Psychologist" is a better representation of what Dr. Smith was trained to do. Further, helping professionals need to be responsible for making sure that their advertisements are truthful and should take steps to correct any misunderstandings related to their marketing (e.g., in any printed matter or on-line).

Several opportunities to network and communicate about the nature of their services and themselves to potential clients and referral sources may exist for those who work with student-athletes. Often, pre-season, "pre-participation" team meetings are held at the beginning of the school year for teams during which information is shared about health services, NCAA compliance issues, etc. Coaching staff meetings are sometimes organized by athletic administrators surrounding various topics of concern. Athletic departments and counseling centers typically have web sites on which information about available services can be posted. With the consent of the athletic department compliance office and administration, helping professionals can distribute flyers to student-athletes, coaches, and staff.

In marketing counseling services, it has become rather common practice, regrettably, to use the testimonials of former clients, especially when such clients are high-profile athletes. Testimonials should be used only if offered without prompting by the former client. Such testimonials perhaps add instant credibility to the practitioner's credentials, but it should be noted that, although such testimonials are not inherently unethical, they should be used with great caution. Testimonials should never be solicited by a practitioner. Indeed, it is probably most prudent for professionals to avoid testimonials altogether and let satisfied clients provide them, entirely on their own, to prospective clients.

Unique Service Settings

The unique settings in which helping professionals may be called upon to consult with collegiate athletes and their teams also pose several ethical challenges and concerns (Anderson, Van Raalte, & Brewer, 2001). For example, an athlete might wish to speak to a helping professional during practice, on the sidelines during a competition, or perhaps in the strength and conditioning or athletic training rooms. Engaging "face time" at practices (if welcomed by coaches) and being available in the event of a student-athlete needing some assistance is often encouraged to develop relationships (consultants need to be aware of NCAA rules that may limit such interactions and should seek consultation from athletic department compliance staff). On campus, a helping professional may also run into athletes in the hallways of academic buildings or in the student center or library, where they may or may not want to talk about their concerns.

Consulting in these non-traditional settings presents some out-of-the-ordinary ethical challenges to confidentiality. Friends, faculty, fans, other members of the team, and staff or students may recognize the athlete and consultant or may see the athlete seeking consultation, perhaps may even be close enough to hear what is being discussed. In these instances, ethical professionals should always consider the best interests of the client when determining if the contact should be initiated at all, moved to a more private place, or discontinued. If the need is immediate and brief intervention is warranted, it may be best to continue the conversation in as discreet a manner as possible and possibly schedule a follow-up meeting for a later date. It is also useful to consider that some athletes are more comfortable than others talking to a psychologist or counselor in such settings. In any case, the ethical professional should inquire about an athlete client's wishes to interact or not interact in these situations at the outset of their work together (Watson & Etzel, 2004).

The opportunity to travel with college teams to and from competitions (which does not seem commonplace in collegiate settings but nevertheless occurs) also presents some ethical challenges unique to work with student-athletes (e.g., confidentiality issues and blurring of boundaries and roles) (Anderson et al., 2001; Brown & Cogan, 2006; Moore, 2003). When helping professionals travel with a team, they may consult formally or informally on a bus, while waiting for a plane, during team meals, or in hotels. In these potentially awkward situations, practitioners should consider where they can best serve the athlete, that is, what is in the client's best interest, taking into account who is around and the perceived comfort level of the client. For example, a hotel lobby with many people present might seem like a better option than a hotel room, which presents its own risks. Although conversation in a hotel room is more private, others may perceive it as a potentially sexual rather than a professional encounter (Moore, 2003).

Traveling with a team likely presents the opportunity to build rapport and may help the helping professional learn more about team dynamics and how to better intervene with the team and team members; however, such situations are ethically tricky with much higher potential for ethical challenges to arise than likely would exist during office sessions. If a helping professional does engage in travel, these situations are likely unavoidable; the ethical professional should have a plan for how to handle them should they occur (Brown & Cogan, 2006). For example, a psychologist can discuss the logistics of the transportation and hotel arrangements prior to the trip with the coach(es), and discuss a plan with them (and/or the team) for how the consultation will work while traveling. This way, the coaches and athletes will know what to expect and can address any concerns in advance.

Just as the athletic environment lends itself to nontraditional settings for consultation, it also lends itself to nontraditional lengths of consultations (Etzel & Watson, 2007; Moore, 2003; Watson & Etzel, 2004). Sessions may be formal or informal and may be shorter or longer than the traditional 50-minute session. For example, athletes may want to quickly vent frustration or raise a performance concern on the sidelines, at practice, or when they see the consultant in the hallway. Although such meetings are often unplanned and informal, the ethical professional should keep brief notes of what was discussed, even if only writing a couple of sentences in the client's file (Etzel & Watson, 2007). A consultation could also be quite extensive, depending on the athlete's concern. For example, to prepare for an upcoming game, an athlete might need a consultation that is longer than the traditional 50 minutes. Helping professionals need to be careful about making such arrangements the norm and what that might communicate to clients and about the relationship with clients (e.g., overidentification, attraction).

Although there are a variety of sites in which a helping professional may consult with athletes, practitioners usually have an office located somewhere on campus (e.g., at a counseling center, sometimes in athletics facilities). Given options, what is the optimal place for the office to be located? In fact, it is a challenge to find a location that is both confidential and convenient for athletes. An office in athletic facilities may be more accessible to athletes than in a counseling center since athletes spend so much time there. However, there is a high potential for other athletes and coaches to see the athlete walk in or out of an office in athletics.

Having an office in a university counseling center typically offers more privacy from coaches and other athletic personnel. On the other hand, it is often less convenient for an athlete to access (Watson & Etzel, 2004). In fact, one of the authors finds that he sees more athletes now that his office is in the athletic department than when it was located in the college counseling center. Some athlete clients report feeling uncomfortable in waiting rooms with others who might recognize them. High-profile student-athletes may be particularly reluctant to walk into a counseling center for fear of being seen by others in the campus community and having information that they are receiving counseling somehow "leaked" to others. Regardless, confidentiality is a major concern when it comes to others seeing athletes enter or exit an office, whether it is located in an athletic department or somewhere else on campus. As one of the authors does after a counseling session is over, one can look outside into the hallway before student-athlete clients leave, to make sure that others are not around to see them.

Consultants may also need to be somewhat flexible in terms of the hours they consult with athletes (Watson & Etzel, 2004). Since athletes typically have class during the day and then practice in the afternoon, they may be available only in the evenings to meet with a counselor.

Meeting at a late time can reduce the concern about confidentiality; however, the professional should be cautious since there may not be others around (colleagues, etc.) in case of an emergency (Etzel & Watson, 2007). These types of arrangements also present some risk in terms of the potential for conveying an unintended message (e.g., more romantic or accommodating) to the student-athlete.

Finally, many professionals working in a college setting will likely have to deal with running into clients in the community (Etzel & Watson, 2007). A professional may see a client in the grocery store, mall, coffee shop, restaurant, bar, etc. It can be an uncomfortable situation for both client and professional when each decides whether or not to acknowledge the other. A suggestion would be to wait for the client to acknowledge the helping professional first and to make the contact as brief as possible. As noted earlier, to prevent an uncomfortable and awkward situation, an ethical professional should discuss the possibility of such encounters with clients upfront in their consultations and ask them how they would like to be acknowledged (or not acknowledged) in such situations (Etzel & Watson, 2007).

Working in a college athletic environment also presents the possibility of encountering situations involving alcohol, particularly for young professionals or graduate students working with teams. Professionals may also be invited to functions or coaches' meetings at a restaurant where the staff may be drinking. Although being in such social situations can build rapport, particularly with coaches, a consultant should make smart personal and professional decisions when alcohol is involved. For example, one can be the designated driver so as not to decline an invitation to an event with coaches but still remain professional without the influence of alcohol (Brown & Cogan, 2006).

Tele-Consulting

As a general rule, college students today are very technologically savvy. They have grown up in an era in which information is available to them with just a few key strokes. They are able to listen to music, search the Internet for pertinent information, chat on-line, and IM and text message with friends, often simultaneously. This "digital native" lifestyle has in many cases created the expectation that all information can be found very quickly and easily. Collegiate athletes often travel to compete, and may want or need to have contact with their consultants while traveling. If they have a desire or need to "meet" with their consultants while on the road, there are few options outside of the telephone and Internet.

Although the thought of consulting with a client over the telephone or Internet may not have been considered 15 years ago, recent technology has made these forms of communication more accessible and manageable. In fact, research has shown that 35% of sport psychology practitioners rated the Internet as moderately to very important to their practices, and that non-certified consultants viewed the Internet as more important and reported using it more than those who were certified by AASP (Watson, Lubker, & Zakrajsek, 2006). Furthermore, respondents to this survey also frequently expressed the belief that the use of the Internet for consulting presents many potential ethical challenges.

Given the above information, helping professionals working with this population may be drawn to use the Internet more often in their practices. Such uses of the Internet may include marketing and dissemination of information, supervision, collaboration with colleagues, professional development, research, distance learning, referrals, or even consulting itself (Watson & Etzel, 2000; Watson, Tenenbaum, Lidor, & Alfermann, 2001). However, this technology is not without its problems. Potential problems associated with the Internet in consulting include an inability to identify clients, difficulties establishing a therapeutic relationship, assessing content and affect, the lack of assumed confidentiality with client contact, the potential for miscommunications and misunderstandings, and practicing across state lines when consulting with clients in a different area of the country. Some other possible problems include the quality and quantity of information found on the Internet that clients must sift through, appropriate training of consultants to use the Internet effectively, and the validity of information with regard to assessments (Watson & Etzel, 2000; Watson et al., 2001).

Although the current ethical standards of AASP (n.d.) and APA (2002) do not directly address the use of the telephone and Internet in consulting, many of the standards do appear to apply to such practices. As such, there are several considerations that helping professionals may want to be aware of before engaging in "teleconsulting" with student-athletes. Such considerations might include: (1) making a determination as to whether one is legally allowed to consult with the client based upon geographic location and licensure restrictions; (2) making clients aware that confidentiality cannot be guaranteed in either telephone and e-mail conversations (use of client waiver would help with this); (3) making clients aware of traditional consulting hours and the length of response time; (4) taking reasonable steps to confidentially store client information on a server or hard drive; (5) identifying clients and making sure that they are eligible to consent to such services; (6) maintaining knowledge of events local to the client; (7) taking steps to clarify possible misunderstandings; and (8) dealing only with cases that can realistically be handled appropriately from a distance (e.g., performance anxiety vs. an eating disorder). Finally, helping professionals should be very cautious with the amount of identifiable client information they provide when requesting consultations over the Internet and with specific information and guidance they provide when responding to requests for consultation over the Internet (Behnke, 2007).

Ethical Decision Making

Although a basic understanding of ethics and the ethics code(s) that impact the practice of helping professionals is important, this information alone will not guarantee that good decisions will be made, even by those individuals with considerable experience or who act with the best of intentions. For this reason, it is important that helping professionals also be familiar with ethical decision-making models that may help them make effective decisions to guide their thinking and action in work with student-athletes.

One commonly employed ethical decision making model was developed by Forester-Miller and Davis (1996) for the American Counseling Association. This model outlines a sequential, seven-step approach that can be used to help guide practitioners' thinking in times of uncertainty and perhaps confusion. The first step involves identifying as much information about the problem as possible. The second step encourages the application of the appropriate code of ethics to this information. Third, decision makers are directed to determine the nature and dimensions of the dilemma by reviewing any applicable moral principles, consulting with colleagues, and reviewing relevant literature. The fourth step in this logical process involves brainstorming potential courses of action for dealing with the situation. Fifth, decision makers are encouraged to estimate the potential consequences of all considered options and make a decision about a specific course of action. The sixth step involves evaluating the selected course of action for any potential problems. If the course of action decided upon in the previous step is appropriate, the seventh and final step is to implement this action.

Another commonly used process for making decisions was developed by the Canadian Psychological Association (Hadjistavropoulos & Malloy, 2000). This model is similar to the model developed by the American Counseling Association, but it was developed to work within a hierarchically organized code of ethics using a multidimensional approach within each stage. The first of seven steps involves identifying the issues and potential reactions that are related to the situation. The second and third steps involve the development of alternative ways of dealing with the situation and assessing the short- and long-term risks and benefits of these possible courses of action. Upon review of the potential courses of action, the fourth step involves choosing a course of action, after taking into account the appropriate ethical codes and principles. The fifth step involves implementing the action decided upon and taking responsibility for the outcome of the action. After such action is taken, the sixth step involves evaluating the consequences of the action, and the seventh step involves taking appropriate steps to correct any inappropriate consequences of the action (See case at the end of chapter for an example of a situation where the use of these decision making strategies would be particularly prudent).

Conclusion

Awareness of the nature and regular ethical challenges of working with college student-athletes is essential to responsible, competent service provision to promote the welfare of clients and to do no harm to them. It is critical for helping professionals to understand and consistently apply, as best they can, the values of their professions as incorporated into the ethical codes they agree to follow. In reality, no one is immune from making ethical mistakes. However, with knowledge, experience, and consultation, most ethical challenges, as identified above, can be sensed in advance and avoided.

References

American Counseling Association. (2005). ACA Code of Ethics. Retrieved August 23, 2007, from http://www.counseling.org/Resources/CodeOfEthics/TP/Home/CT2.aspx

American Counseling Association. (2007). An Overview of Counseling. Retrieved July 25, 2007 from http://www.counseling.org/Resources/ConsumersMedia.aspx?AGuid =8fa66290-45d6-4239-97aa-4a30b2f0ec62

American Psychological Association. (2002). Ethical principles of psychologists and code of conduct. *American Psychologist, 57,* 1060–1073.

American Psychological Association. (n.d.). About APA. Retrieved August 2, 2007, from http://www.apa.org/about/

Anderson, M. B., Van Raalte, J. L., & Brewer, B. W. (2001). Sport psychology service delivery: Staying ethical while keeping loose. *Professional Psychology: Research and Practice, 32,* 12–18.

Association for Applied Sport Psychology. (n.d.). Ethical Standards. Retrieved August 2, 2007, from http://aasp.orca-cms.com/about/ethics/code

Behnke, S. (2007). Ethics and the Internet: Requesting clinical consultations over listserves. *Monitor on Psychology, 38*(7), 62–63.

Brown, J., & Cogan, K. (2006). Ethical clinical practice and sport psychology: When two worlds collide. *Ethics and Behavior, 16*(1), 15–24.

Buceta, J. (1993). The sport psychologist/athletic coach dual role: Advantages, difficulties, and ethical considerations. *Journal of Applied Sport Psychology, 5,* 64–77.

Etzel, E. F., & Watson, J. C. (2007). Ethical challenges for psychological consultations in intercollegiate athletics. *Journal of Clinical Sport Psychology, 1,* 304–317.

Figone, A. (1994). Origins of the teacher-coach: Idealism, convenience, and unworkability. *The Physical Educator, 51,* 148–156.

Fisher, C. B. (2003). *Decoding the ethics code: A practical guide for psychologists.* New York: Sage.

Forester-Miller, H., & Davis, T. E. (1996*). A practitioner's guide to ethical decision making.* Alexandria, VA: American Counseling Association.

Glosoff, H. L., Herlihy, S. B., Herlihy, B., & Spence, E. B. (1997). Privileged communication in the psychologist-client relationship. *Professional Psychology: Research and Practice, 28,* 573–581.

Hadjistavropoulos, T., & Malloy, D. C. (2000). Making ethical choices: A comprehensive decision making model for Canadian psychologists. *Canadian Psychology. 41*(2), 104–115.

Hays, K. F., & Brown, C. H. (2004). *You're on! Consulting for peak performance.* Washington, DC: American Psychological Association.

Kitchener, K. S. (1988). Dual role relationships? What makes them so problematic? *Journal of Counseling and Development, 67,* 217–221.

Koocher, G. (2005). Prototype mental health records. In G. Koocher, J. Norcross, & S. Hill III (Eds.). *Psychologist's desk reference* (2nd ed., pp. 649–652). New York: Oxford University Press.

Koocher, G. P., & Keith-Spiegel, P. (1998). *Ethics in psychology: Professional standards and cases* (2nd ed.). New York: Oxford University Press.

Lesyk, J. L. (1998). *Developing sport psychology with your clinical practice: A practical guide for mental health professionals.* San Francisco: Jossey-Bass.

Loughran, M. J., & Etzel, E. (under review). Ethical practice in a diverse world: The challenges of working with differences in the psychological treatment of student-athletes.

Moore, Z. E. (2003). Ethical dilemmas in sport psychology: Discussion and recommendations for practice. *Professional Psychology: Research and Practice, 34*, 601–610.

National Collegiate Athletic Association. (2007a). 2007–08 NCAA Division I Manual. Indianapolis, IN: Author.

National Collegiate Athletics Association. (2007b). *Managing student-athletes' mental health issues.* Indianapolis: Author.

Pope, K., & Tabachnick, B. (1993). Therapists' anger, hate, fear, and sexual feelings: National survey of therapist responses, client characteristics, critical events, formal complaints, and training. *Professional Psychology: Research and Practice, 24(2)*, 142–152.

Pope, K., & Vasques, M. (1991). *Ethics in psychotherapy and consulting: A practical guide for psychologists.* San Francisco: Jossey-Bass.

Schoener, G. R. (2003). Recognizing, assisting, and reporting the impaired psychologist. In G. Koocher, J. Norcross, & S. Hill III (Eds.), *Psychologist's desk reference* (2nd ed., pp. 620–624). New York: Oxford University Press.

Sonne, J. L. (2004). Nonsexual multiple relationships: A practical decision-making model for clinicians. Retrieved August 2, 2007, from http://kspope.com/site/multiple-relationships.php

United States Department of Education. (n.d.). Family Education Rights and Privacy Act (FERPA). Retrieved August 2, 2007 from http://www.ed.gov/policy/gen/guid/fpco/ferpa/index.html

United States Department of Health & Human Resources. (n.d.). Summary of the HIPAA Privacy Rule. Retrieved August 2, 2007 from http://www.hhs.gov/ocr/privacysummary.pdf

Watson, J. C., II (2000, October). The Internet: Ethical implications for the field of sport psychology. A symposium presented at the 2000 Annual Conference of the Association for the Advancement of Applied Sport Psychology, Nashville, TN.

Watson, J. C., Clement, D., Harris, B., Leffingwell, T., & Hurst, J. (2006). Teacher-practitioner multiple role issues in sport psychology. *Ethics and Behavior, 16*, 41–59.

Watson, J. C., & Etzel, E. F. (Fall 2000). Considering ethics: Using the Internet in sport psychology. *AAASP Newsletter, 15*(3), 13–16.

Watson, J. C., & Etzel, E. F. (2004). Ethical issues affecting psychologists, counselors and sport psychology consultants' work with collegiate student athletes. *Professional Studies Review, 1*, 49–60.

Watson, J. C., II, Lubker, J., & Zakrajsek, R. (2006, August). Ethical issues of Internet use in practice of sport psychology. Presented at the 2006 Annual Convention of the American Psychological Association, New Orleans, LA.

Watson, J. C., II, Tenenbaum, G., Lidor, R., & Alfermann, D. (2001). Ethical uses of the Internet in sport psychology: A position stand. *International Journal of Sport Psychology, 32*, 207–222.

Case Study

Now that you have read about ethical issues that may arise while working with teams and athletes, read the following case and identify the ethical concerns:

> Dr. Smith is a professor of clinical psychology in the psychology department at U Tech and a former nationally ranked collegiate wrestler. Dr. Smith has never worked with athletes before for performance enhancement purposes, but has definitely stayed interested in sports since his days as an athlete. One day, he is contacted by his former coach at State U (located in a different state), who wants to know if Dr. Smith could consult with a wrestler at State U. The coach tells Dr. Smith that the athlete has not reached his potential during his first three years. This athlete has returned to school for his senior year with much less body fat and a sculpted physique. Further, this athlete seems to be much more aggressive while on the mat. Although these changes are in the positive direction, the coach is concerned about the methods used to make these changes over a relatively short period of time.
>
> The coach has heard of sport psychology, believes that Dr. Smith could be of some assistance to the athlete, via telephone or e-mail, and hopes that he will be able to help him before the match next week. He is concerned that the athlete has been using performance-enhancing substances and could either hurt himself or test positive for the substances. During the conversation, the coach states that he is not sure if his athlete wants to work with a sport psychologist, but states that he could "certainly make the athlete take part in this endeavor if it will help." The coach also believes that if Dr. Smith is successful with this athlete that he would be able to get him work as a sport psychologist with several other athletic teams at State U.

Ethical Issues

- Competence: Does Dr. Smith have any training in sport psychology? Just because he is a former athlete does not mean he has had training in working with athletes on similar issues. Does he have training in counseling or is he a psychologist? The athlete's body changes may be related to the use of performance-enhancing substances. If Dr. Smith has not had education, training, or supervision in any of these areas, he should refer the athlete to someone with more expertise.

- Who is the client? The coach contacted Dr. Smith but wants him to work with his athlete. Because this is a third-party referral, Dr. Smith must specify the limits to confidentiality at the outset of providing services.

- Consulting from a distance: If Dr. Smith is a licensed professional, his license may not be valid across state lines. Can he work as a psychologist via the Internet or telephone if he is not licensed in the state where the client resides? Is substance (ab)use an issue that should be undertaken from a distance?

- Tele-consulting: Because Dr. Smith will be consulting via telephone or e-mail, he will be unable to observe the client directly and therefore unable to observe nonverbal behavior and affect. Consulting via telephone or e-mail is also not entirely secure; therefore, complete confidentiality cannot be ensured. What steps can Dr. Smith take to ensure that he is actually talking with the person who he is intending to talk with?

- Multiple relationships: The coach is a former coach of Dr. Smith's (and someone whom Smith may consider a "friend" if they keep in touch a lot). This may result in a blurring of boundaries between the two.

- Appropriate information: The coach seems to believe that sport psychology consultations are a quick fix. It would be appropriate to correct this misassumption.

- Coercion: The athlete may not be a voluntary participant. It would be appropriate to discuss the athlete's desires to participate in the sessions. Decisions about whether to continue may need to be made, based upon the athlete's thoughts.

- Title: The coach has made inferences to Dr. Smith being a sport psychologist. Such a title is not appropriate for Dr. Smith to use, given his training and background. Dr. Smith should correct this misuse of title quickly.

4

LIFE SKILLS FOR COLLEGIATE STUDENT-ATHLETES: DEFINING THE NEED AND MODEL PRACTICES

Rebecca Ahlgren-Bedics
Samantha Monda

Managing the multiple demands of being a collegiate student-athlete can be challenging, but the benefits of participating in collegiate sports also can be very valuable to the personal development of student-athletes. During this critical period of development in which young people are transitioning from childhood to adulthood, athletics can serve as an arena where a student-athlete can learn, develop, and grow personally and professionally into a productive citizen. The challenges and relationships that student-athletes encounter through sport help them to learn valuable life skills that can be used outside of and after their athletic experience.

Dr. Myles Brand, president of the National Collegiate Athletic Association (NCAA), asserts that the NCAA is not a sports organization but, rather, a higher education association with an athletic focus. This view supports the NCAA's long-standing position that fostering athletic experiences in environments that develop the entire person, and not just the athlete, results in well-rounded individuals who are equipped with the skills to be successful in both sport and life.

This chapter will begin by providing an overview of contextual factors and student-athlete needs that are unique to participation in collegiate athletics today. This discussion does not provide a comprehensive list of potential issues. Rather, it highlights topics of particular importance to those working with student-athletes on life skills issues. The other chapters in this book provide additional, in-depth discussions of these and other topics related to counseling and working with student-athletes. Next, we will discuss the rationale and strategies for colleges and universities addressing these issues. We will also include a brief history of the NCAA CHAMPS/Life Skills Program and model practices from universities across the county. We will also review results from a recent survey of current NCAA CHAMPS/Life Skills Coordinators. Finally, we will introduce selected topics and life skills issues on the horizon about which colleges and universities should stay vigilant to support and enhance the well-being of collegiate student-athletes.

Student-Athletes' Unique Lifestyles and Needs

Student-athletes have unique psychological, contextual, and behavioral circumstances that need to be taken into account as part of the process of facilitating life skills development. As a result of their additional athletic role, student-athletes can experience a variety of challenges that often differ from challenges faced by college students who are not involved in athletics.

Role Conflict and the Athletic Lifestyle

Student-athletes have the challenging responsibility of living the roles of both student and athlete. As students, individuals must attend classes, meet deadlines, adjust to large amounts of reading, and develop the skills to eventually pursue a career. As athletes, individuals must develop their schedule around multiple practices and competitions, travel, participate in physically grueling training sessions, and cope with increased pressure to perform well in all arenas (Giacobbi, Lynn, & Wetherington, 2004). In order to be successful, student-athletes must meet the demands and expectations of both roles. However, student-athletes typically have limited time and energy to devote to both roles. When these two roles compete for the same resources, some may experience the stresses of role conflict linked to the responsibilities associated with those roles. In order to cope with the conflict, they may focus more on the demands of the athlete role and minimize the student role. The opposite may be true at different times during the academic year, too.

It has been suggested that some student-athletes may initially over-identify with the athlete role by investing more time in sport than in academics (Lally & Kerr, 2005; Miller & Kerr, 2003). If a student-athlete does not reduce the discrepancy between the two roles, it can have a negative effect on his or her well-being (Killeya-Jones, 2005; Settles, Sellers, & Damas, 2002). However, by the junior and senior years in college, many student-athletes will shift or at least begin to shift their attention to the demands of the student role and focus on a career after college (Adler & Adler, 1987; Lally & Kerr, 2005; Miller & Kerr, 2003). Mastering the balance between the two primary responsibilities of school and sport can help student-athletes make the most of their collegiate experience and continue to be a valuable skill for balancing multiple future roles, such as that of parent, employee, friend, and member of the community.

Transitions

The college experience has been likened to a "mini-life cycle" in which students experience many more or less predictable changes, challenges, and events (Medalie, 1981). During their time as intercollegiate athletes, most student-athletes will experience two major transitions (Schlossberg, 1984) that will require them to adjust to changes in their academic, athletic, and personal lives. Although transitioning from high school to college and transitioning out of sport typically occur at opposite ends of the collegiate career, the developmental processes that are necessary to adjust are similar. The transition process in both situations requires a student-athlete to adapt to the demands of new circumstances. Additionally, both situations are prime opportunities for interventions and support from significant others and student development professionals in the student-athlete's life.

Transition into College

Student-athletes enter college during a period of development considered to be emerging adulthood (Arnett, 2000). The college environment serves as living laboratory where individuals aged 18–25, no longer adolescents, but not yet adults, can explore potential life directions. During this phase, emerging adults are learning to achieve independence from their parents, trying on alternative social roles, clarifying their interests and values, and planning their future careers.

During their first year, student-athletes learn to manage the different demands and unfamiliar challenges of their new and diverse roles. As students, they must declare a major, develop and refine study skills, and learn to be responsible for their own learning and behavior. As athletes, they must adapt to a higher level of play, greater time commitments, and increased travel (Ridinger & Pastore, 2000). On a personal level, first-year students must adjust to living with a roommate, making new friends, making their own decisions, and in many cases navigating a new community. These demands may exceed a student-athlete's pre-college expectations, which can lead to a significant amount of stress and a potentially poor adjustment (Prancer, Hunsberger, Pratt, & Alisat, 2000).

Because many of these challenges are being experienced for the first time, first-year students may not know how to deal with them, so they must acquire or experiment with different coping skills, mechanisms, and choices to determine which ones are the most appropriate and adaptive (Giacobbi et al., 2004). Some of the choices may be positive, such as joining campus organizations to meet people, or seeking part-time employment to improve their personal financial situations. However, some choices made by first-year students (not solely student-athletes) may compromise their health and well-being, such as engaging in risk-taking behaviors (e.g., alcohol abuse, disordered eating behaviors, unhealthy sexual practices, gambling), associating with negative-influencing peers, or making poor financial decisions, such as abusing credit cards. It is primarily because of issues such as these that life skills training and programs are necessary and can be quite valuable in assisting with the adjustment process.

Involvement in organized activities, such as collegiate sports, can help facilitate positive adjustment to the college environment. Among students who had a difficult time adjusting to the college environment during their freshman year, some who were involved in organized activities reported lower rates of loneliness and social dissatisfaction (Bohnert, Aikins, & Edidin, 2007). Although being a member of an organized support group on campus, such as an athletic team, may help first-year student-athletes adapt to college life, they can still experience a great amount of life stress. Balancing the increased demands of school, sport, and personal life can be difficult to manage for an emerging adult. For example, a group of first year Division I swimmers reported their greatest sources of stress were training intensity, high performance expectations, interpersonal relationships, being away from home, and academics (Giacobbi et al., 2004). Another account of first-year Division I student-athletes found that balancing school and sport, coping with the athlete "stigma," and experiencing physical exhaustion from sport were significant sources of stress (Ortez, 1997). In addition, higher athletic identity in freshman college student-athletes has been correlated with higher levels of life stress (Quarforth, Brewer, Petitpas, Champagne, & Cornelius, 2003).

Student-athletes' experiences in sport may also impact how well they adjust in other realms of their rapidly changing lives. For example, a recent study of Division III football players found that reported sport satisfaction as well as the quality of roommate relationship significantly predicted positive adjustment to college (Quarforth et al., 2003). Therefore, it is important for life skills programming to address not only the multiple roles of the student-athlete, but also the potentially complex interactions and impacts those roles may have.

Transition Out of Sport

Sport career retirement is another transition that can impact a student-athlete's development. The majority of college student-athletes do not go on to compete at the professional level. Therefore, the end of collegiate eligibility marks the end of most student-athletes' competitive sport careers. Most appear to adjust to this transition out of athletics reasonably well, especially when the transition is planned and anticipated. However, some student-athletes' college careers may end unexpectedly by a career-ending injury, deselection, or in some cases dismissal from the team due to breaking team, university, or NCAA rules. These unexpected terminations can be more difficult to adjust to and can produce short- and long-term distress (Sparkes, 1998; Webb, Nasco, Riley, & Headrick, 1998; Zuk, 2004). For example, Zuk (2004) looked at the retirement experiences of collegiate gymnasts and found that those who retired prematurely from their sport reported experiencing more emotional distress three years after their retirement than gymnasts who did not retire prematurely.

Whether the end of the sport career is planned or not, when student-athletes do not adjust well to the changes in their life, they seem to be at greater risk of experiencing problems such as psychological distress, physical illness, injury, drop out, poor academic performance, or immature career behaviors (Dyson & Renk, 2006; Erpic, Wylleman, & Zupancic, 2003; Grove, Lavallee, & Gordon, 1997; Murphy, Petitpas, & Brewer, 1996). Consequently, it is essential that these young people acquire and develop appropriate coping skills, support networks, and planning strategies to adjust properly to either anticipated or unanticipated transitions (Lally, 2007). Although some believe that gradually reducing the amount of time participating in the sport (e.g., finding and engaging in other meaningful activities) to replace athletics will help ensure a positive transition (Lavallee & Robinson, 2007), the reality is that most collegiate student-athletes will not significantly change their involvement to their sport until the last point is scored. This is important to keep in mind for life skills administrators who are promoting and assisting with proactive planning for life after sport. Exploring and facilitating the development of alternative options to the familiar athletic role are other important ways to helping a student-athlete transition smoothly out of his or her sport career.

Athletic Identity

As student-athletes choose to reprioritize non-athletic interests and social activities in order to dedicate more time to sport, a stronger identification with athletics can develop through athletic participation (Brewer, Van Raalte, & Linder, 1993). College is a period of time where young people can try out different identities and determine how they want to define themselves (Arnett, 2000). It is common for those with athletic talent to define themselves by their athletic accomplishments without exploring other potential identities. Although there is potential for a strong athletic identity to be helpful in developing team cohesion, confidence, and global self-esteem, much of the research suggests that a strong athletic identity can prevent student-athletes from investing in other dimensions of their life (Brewer, Van Raalte, & Linder, 1993; Cornelius, 1995; Kornspan & Etzel, 2003; Lavallee & Robinson, 2007; Marsh, Perry, Horsely, & Roche, 1995). Athletes who over-identify with the athlete role and have perhaps not explored or been discouraged from exploring other roles may be more at risk for transitional difficulties over time.

Career immaturity, in part a consequence of over-identifying with the athlete role, has been thought to occur in individuals who have not explored alternative roles. Empirical support for this concept of identity foreclosure has been mixed. Some research findings suggest that student-athletes may have less career maturity than non-athletes, but other studies have found that this discrepancy may not be as large as originally thought (Brown, Glastetter-Fender, & Shelton, 2000; Ihle Helledy, 2006; Kornspan & Etzel, 2003; Rivas & Quinones, 2003). One study examining the career maturity of college men found that levels of athletic identity and divisional level had no impact on levels of career maturity (Brown & Hartley, 1998). These mixed results warrant closer examination of some of the predictive factors for career maturity. They also support the case for conducting proactive life skills programs addressing athletic identity and life after sport issues.

Relationships, Stereotypes, and Visibility

The emerging adult phase of life is a time for college students to develop friendships, intimate relationships, and social and professional networks (Arnett, 2000). Student-athletes' roles in collegiate athletics can have both positive and negative influences on their development of relationships with others. By their association with the sport, student-athletes have a ready-made social support network of teammates and coaches (Kimball & Freysinger, 2003). Sport participation gives them access to various sources of social support and provides opportunities to develop meaningful relationships outside of their families and high school friends. However, due to the time commitment required by their sport, student-athletes also may have difficulty finding time to develop and nurture relationships with their professors and non-athlete peers (Kimball & Freysinger, 2003).

Stereotypes of student-athletes can sometimes act as a barrier to developing relationships with professors and academic faculty. Some faculty members may perceive all athletes to be "dumb jocks" or members of an "over privileged minority" (Ferrante, Etzel, & Lantz, 1996). They may assume that some student-athletes do not care much about their education and are at the university only to participate in athletics. Research suggests that these stereotypes may keep student-athletes, particularly in Division I and Division II, from approaching faculty for help and may impede them from developing useful mentoring relationships with professors. They also may prevent faculty members from reaching out to establish those relationships (Baucom & Lantz, 2001; Engstrom,

Sedlacek, & McEwen, 1995; Ferrante, Etzel, & Lantz, 1996). These situations can sometimes create a strained relationship between faculty
and the department of athletics as student-athletes often communicate
with one another regarding which professors are "student-athlete
friendly" (e.g., accept travel letters, will work with the student-athletes
to make up missed work due to travel) and which are not. In addition,
if a team has garnered a negative reputation with particular professors
based on the conduct of a few members, that reputation may carry over
to future members of that team, warranted or not. Although there may
be some student-athletes who fit negative stereotypes, most do not;
still, these assumptions may lead to some student-athletes feeling isolated from the academic community. It is in these situations that the
NCAA-required Faculty Athletics Representative (FAR) should have a
great deal of input. It is his or her responsibility to work with both the
faculty and the department of athletics to ensure that both groups are
being regarded with respect for the work they do.

The celebrity status on campus and the media spotlight put on some
student-athletes may serve as another barrier for some to develop meaningful friendships and intimate relationships. Some people may want to
be friends with student-athletes because of their celebrity status and the
perceived social benefits that it may bring, rather than because of their
personalities or common interests. In turn, a student-athlete may have
a difficult time establishing true relationships because he or she may be
unsure of the other person's motives.

The high visibility of collegiate student-athletes on many campuses
makes it even more important that they remain vigilant about those
with whom they associate. Although college is a time to learn from
one's mistakes, the decisions a student-athlete makes are highly visible
to the public. There may be pressure for student-athletes not only to
represent themselves and their teams, but to be the "poster child" for
the entire athletic program and the university. Public and sometimes private behaviors of student-athletes are made open to scrutiny by others.

Engaging with others has become increasingly "tricky business" with
the anonymous and non-exclusive nature of the Internet and social networking sites. What once happened behind closed doors and became
campus gossip or legend can now be well documented and world-wide
on sites such as MySpace.com, Facebook.com, or BadJocks.com. Even

photos or information voluntarily placed on websites created by the student-athlete can become distorted or used for negative purposes, such as heckling by an opposing team. There have also been situations in which individuals have used information from social networking sites to stalk student-athletes in an effort to get close to them. With cameras found on every phone and PDA and in every bar and nightclub, life skills programming needs to address how student-athletes in particular must be attentive to their surroundings and of how their actions may appear on video or the Internet, intentional or not.

Time Demands

The roles of student and athlete may conflict in a student-athlete's life because each one requires a significant amount of time. Per NCAA by-laws, Division I and II student-athletes commit themselves to not more than twenty hours per week of in-season training and competition and eight hours per week of off-season training (Division III does not legis-late such restrictions). There has been criticism by some athletics admin-istrators and student-athletes that the "20-hour rule" is not strictly and consistently enforced and does not take "volandatory" practices into ac-count (i.e., a combination of the terms "voluntary" and "mandatory" that applies to practices that are strongly suggested by a coach, but it not considered as a countable, athletically related activity).

Although NCAA bylaws state the maximum amount of time that Division I and II student-athletes can participate in sport-related activ-ities, this rule does not extend to travel time to and from competitions or to practices. It also does not cover the training and preparation that an athlete chooses to do on his or her own time. Some student-athletes feel that they must train all year in order to stay competitive with peers and opponents, and they are encouraged by their coaches to do so. This cycle of continual training can present a problem for student-athletes because they are constantly juggling a time commitment that can be considered equivalent to that of a part-time job. Although this bylaw is in place to ensure that academics comes before athletics, its enforce-ment (as with all NCAA bylaws) is at the discretion of each institution, making it difficult to be completely certain how much time is truly being spent on athletics. The NCAA has taken measures to educate coaches on the qualifications of this rule, but in some circumstances, student-athletes still devote more than twenty hours per week to their sport (Rays, 2006).

Currently, the training time restrictions do not apply to Division III schools, although studies have shown that Division III student-athletes appear to devote similar but slightly less time to their sport than those participating in Division I or II (NCAA, 2007). In addition to the amount of time required to compete at a higher level of athletics, some student-athletes find that the timing of their practices has an effect on how they can balance their schedules. Because facilities may be used by multiple groups (e.g., campus recreation, physical education classes, several athletics teams), sometimes practices are held at undesirable times, such as late in the evening or early in the morning in order to accommodate the various groups.

Subsequently, some student-athletes are devoting a substantial amount of their time to the development of their athletic careers, requiring reprioritization of time choices related to engagement in other activities. This reprioritization can also affect the choice and type of employment a student-athlete engages in during his or her college years, as well. For example, in order to accommodate a practice-heavy schedule and stay close to the pool during the summer break, a swimmer may decide to teach swim lessons and to lifeguard at the pool instead of pursuing an office job or other type of employment, potentially limiting the work experiences he or she may have prior to deciding on a major or career path.

Long-term Educational Impact

The schedule of a student-athlete often makes it difficult to follow the typical 4–5 year educational timeline to graduation. In order to balance academics and athletics, it is often necessary for student-athletes to schedule courses around their sport responsibilities and seasons. Therefore, during the championship season of their sport (considered "in season"), some student-athletes may not take as many courses or the specific courses necessary, such as lab courses, to graduate within four years. Many student-athletes use a post-eligibility fifth year to participate in internships and practica. Thus, it may take a student-athlete five years or more to complete his or her degree.

In addition to the concern of graduating in a timely fashion, participation in sport may make it difficult to complete the requirements of certain majors (Wolverton, 2007). Student-athletes in majors that require attendance at afternoon lab sessions, internships, or student teaching requirements may experience logistical conflicts with their sport schedules. Therefore, student-athletes must either learn how to manage these logistical problems in order to reach their academic goals. However, it is important to note that the 2006 NCAA Study of College Outcomes and Recent Experiences (SCORE) student-centered graduation rates indicated that student-athletes are graduating, as well as earning graduate degrees, at rates higher than their non-student-athlete cohort.

Physical Demands

In addition to the mental and emotional demands of school and sport, student-athletes must manage the physical demands of participating in athletics. In order to compete, a student-athlete will devote a significant amount of time to training, which includes grueling aerobic, strength training, and skill development workouts. Some coaches require student-athletes to train and practice twice per day, sometimes early in the morning before classes and again after class at the end of the day. Competitive seasons can range from a few months to almost a full academic year, during which student-athletes must maintain or improve their physical condition. During the off-season, student-athletes typically have reduced and self-imposed training schedules, but most continue training to some degree in order to be adequately in shape to compete in the upcoming season. Under certain circumstances, the physical demands of participating in sport can lead to negative consequences such as exhaustion, illness, or injury. Because of a variety of uncontrollable, extraneous life variables, many student-athletes tend to become "overtrained." In general, overtraining can be associated with undesirable health, academic, and performance outcomes (e.g., staleness, slumps, and burnout) that are the *opposite* of what athletes and coaches want.

Injury

Most observers of intercollegiate athletics recognize that the risk of injury is very common in athletics. However, some may not recognize that injuries incurred by collegiate athletes vary in frequency and severity, as well as by sport and time of year. In some sports (e.g., golf, rifle) injury rates are lower, whereas in other, collision sports (e.g., football, soccer, gymnastics) as many as two athletes per game may be reported as injured to a degree that they are missing significant playing or practice time (National Collegiate Athletic Association, 2005b). It is has been reported that almost half of all collegiate football players in the United States lose playing time due to serious injury and that one in ten collegiate female soccer and basketball players will suffer an ACL injury (Brown, 2004). When an athlete is injured, he or she may experience physical as well as psychological distress. Some athletes may require surgery or go through a painful rehabilitation process. Injured student-athletes may experience pain that keeps them from participating in their daily activities and may have to rely on medications to help them function (Granito, 2001). In addition, those with recent sport-related concussions may have cognitive impairments such as delayed memory and lower attention spans (Killam, Cautin, & Santucci, 2005). These factors are important to consider in relation to the student-athlete's academic endeavors.

Body Image

Sport participation can have an impact on the body image of both male and female college student-athletes that can contribute to the development of disordered eating behavior. Females may feel pressure to meet the societal ideal of a small and slender woman when, in reality, female athletes may need to be bigger and have more muscle mass in order to compete in their sport. It can be stressful for some female athletes when others perceive their athletic bodies as masculine or unfeminine (Kimball & Freysinger, 2003).

Some female athletes may be concerned that they must adhere to a certain body type in order to perform best. Those in lean body sports have been thought to be more susceptible to this body image issue, but more recent research does not support this claim (Sanford-Martens, Davidson, Yakushko, Martens, Hinton, & Beck, 2005). Athletes in lean body sports may not be any more susceptible to eating disorders than athletes in non-lean body sports. For male athletes, the desire to appear larger and have more muscle can influence their body image. Males may perceive a larger body to be ideal, increasing their risk of using supplements to achieve their ideal size (Raudenbush & Meyer, 2003).

The perceived pressure to meet certain body ideals for men and women can contribute to disordered eating behaviors and can increase a student-athlete's chances of developing a diagnosed eating disorder. It has been reported that at least one fifth of Division I male and female collegiate athletes have symptoms of an eating disorder (Sanford-Martens et al., 2005). In order to elicit a positive reaction and increase attendance at programming to address these issues, life skills coordinators may want to steer away from titling workshops related to this issue for student-athletes as "Eating Disorder Workshops" and may want to instead promote them as "Eating for Performance" or a similar, positive theme.

Drugs and Alcohol

Because binge drinking remains a primary concern on college campuses, it is necessary to address this topic with student-athletes. Although student-athletes typically lead healthy lifestyles, research suggests that student-athletes drink more per week than non-athletes (Nelson & Wechsler, 2001). This can be problematic for several reasons, such as alcohol's effect on performance, public consequences that can occur if a well-known collegiate student-athlete has a negative situation arise from alcohol or drug use and the potential long-term health consequences of engaging in risk-taking behaviors.

The culture of collegiate sports also has an influence on the drinking behaviors of student-athletes. Athletes tend to drink less during their competitive seasons potentially because of a lack of time and the effect it could have on their athletic performance (Martens, Dams-O'Connor, & Duffy-Paiement, 2006). Because they are often drinking less during the competitive season, student-athletes may feel pressure to "make up for lost time" and increase their alcohol consumption in the off-season. Social norms developed within specific sports teams may also influence student-athletes to increase their alcohol consumption (Martens, Dams-O'Connor, Duffy-Paiement, & Gibson, 2006). These norms are particularly strong for male athletes and can vary by sport. Swimmers and divers have been shown to be particularly at risk for heavy alcohol use and abuse (Martens, Watson, & Beck, 2006). When addressing these issues, whether the topic is alcohol or any other subject, it is important to keep the material relevant to the student-athletes. One way to achieve this is to take team-specific norms into consideration when presenting life skills workshops to individual teams.

With regards to drug use and abuse, student-athletes may encounter both illegal and performance-enhancing drugs during their time on campus. Steroid and performance-enhancing drug use is a visible problem in the collegiate and professional sports world, but studies investigating the concept of social norming show that the majority of student-athletes reject the use of performance-enhancing drugs in intercollegiate athletics and support drug testing (Diacin, Parks, & Allison, 2003). Also, student-athletes are less likely than non-athletes to smoke cigarettes or use marijuana but have a greater risk of chewing tobacco and binge drinking (Wechsler & Davenport, 1997). Since 1997, the NCAA has found that student-athletes' use of recreational drugs such as alcohol, chewing tobacco, marijuana, and hallucinogens has decreased (NCAA, 2001). Although the numbers are promising, it is still crucial that life skills programming contain pointed, specific information regarding the use of both legal and illegal drugs and alcohol on a student-athlete's performance, health, and potential behavioral consequences.

Why Is Life Skills Training the University's Responsibility?

As described in the previous section, student-athletes compete, live, and socialize in unique circumstances. The intent is not to characterize all student-athletes as at-risk, dependent time bombs balancing on the brink of despair, but it is important to note that there are several factors to consider when providing life skills programming and training to collegiate student-athletes. A review of the mission statement of several universities finds phrases such as "development of a productive citizen," "education of the whole person," and "development of the mind and body." University mission statements are intended to be inclusive of all students, including student-athletes. Students participating in intercollegiate athletics should not be considered a "special population" or "protected class." Therefore, it is inclusive in the mission of most universities to provide this kind of "whole person" education to all students, and we advocate doing so, with consideration of the student-athlete's unique context as described to this point.

Like most of their non-student-athlete peers, student-athletes begin college when they are around 18 years old, eagerly awaiting the challenges and experiences that lie before them. While SAT and ACT scores and high school GPAs may help student-athletes get in the door, there are no entry tests for creating and balancing a budget; dealing with authority; balancing work, athletics, and a social life; or adjusting to life as a "small fish in a big pond" after living in the possibly reverse scenario for four years. These challenges are met by learning and enhancing life skills. Providing education and training of these skills, in consort with programming introduced by the residence hall staff and other student support programs, supports the university mission. Although support services on campus exist to assist all students with these skills, they do not necessarily take into consideration the unique context and needs of student-athletes. The importance of partnering with others on campus will be discussed in further detail later in this chapter.

NCAA CHAMPS/Life Skills Program History

In 1991, the Division 1-A Athletic Directors Association and the NCAA Foundation (then the fundraising branch of the NCAA) were conducting separate conversations regarding the psychosocial developmental needs of collegiate student-athletes. Through the use of focus groups, institutional interviews, and surveys, the two groups were independently gaining a perspective of the state of intercollegiate athletics from the student-athlete developmental point of view. A clear need to provide services to student-athletes to better align the department of athletics' mission with the university's mission emerged. In addition, the NCAA and the Division 1-A Athletic Directors Association felt it was important to mitigate the perception that student-athletes, especially Division I-A (now referred to at the Football Bowl Subdivision [FBS]) student-athletes, were being exploited for their athletic achievements. Subsequently, a partnership between the NCAA and the Division 1-A Athletic Directors Association was formed and is still very strong. The CHAMPS (Challenging Athletes' Minds for Personal Success)/Life Skills Program was created to provide student-athletes with much-needed support in five specific commitment areas: (1) academics, (2) athletics, (3) career development, (4) personal development, and (5) service to the community. In 1994, the inaugural orientation class of 46 institutions was conducted. Since then, 40 institutions and conference offices, on average, have joined the program annually. As of this writing, more than 630 NCAA institutions and conference offices participate in the NCAA CHAMPS/Life Skills Program, with new inductees every year.

Membership in the CHAMPS/Life Skills Program is open to active NCAA member institutions and conference offices. Benefits of participation include access to CHAMPS/Life Skills program modules and materials, registration on the listserve composed of Life Skills Coordinators from across the country to share resources and programming ideas, and the opportunity to attend the annual Orientation Conference for new life skills coordinators and the Continuing Education Conference for all CHAMPS/Life Skills coordinators to network and share best practices.

Strategies for Life Skills Programming

Although athletics may have formally begun to incorporate life skills programming through the CHAMPS/Life Skills Program about fifteen years ago, coaches have been working with life skills issues for much longer than that. Anecdotes abound regarding coaches providing "charm and etiquette lessons" for female baseball players in the 1940s All-American Girls Professional Baseball League and of coaches requiring their teams to learn to tie a necktie or work on their public speaking skills before addressing the press (AAGPBLPA, 2005). In fact, intentionally or not, many academic advisors, coaches, and sport psychology consultants incorporate basic life skills training into their work with student-athletes on a daily basis, just by discussing future plans, class attendance, and the importance of maintaining a balance among athletics, academics, and socializing. Additionally, these important others in student-athletes' lives are life skills role models to student-athletes. On an informal basis, student-athletes, consciously or not, learn how to conduct themselves professionally from their interactions with their academic advisors, faculty, coaches, and life skills coordinators.

For a more structured and formalized approach to life skills training, however, recognition must be given to professionals who work in the field of student affairs. Organizations such as the National Association of Student Personnel Administrators (NASPA) and the Association of College Personnel Administrators (ACPA) are at the forefront of trends in college student development, research, and applied strategies. Since before athletics took a formal approach to life skills training, student affairs departments and personnel have been offering support to college students in the areas of financial planning, dealing with conflict, adjustment to college, diversity and inclusion, selecting a major, career planning, personal counseling, relationship building, healthy behaviors, and decision-making skills, among others. Student personnel administrators on campus are experts in their respective fields and are excellent resources for life skills administrators.

However, programs currently offered on campus do not necessarily take the above-mentioned, student-athlete specific factors into account when conducted. This disconnect highlights the need for student affairs and departments of athletics to collaborate in order to provide relevant, expert life skills programming for student-athletes. Combining the content expertise of the student affairs personnel with the student-athlete context-specific knowledge of the athletics administrator can result in dynamic, current, and relevant life skills programming.

For example, if a campus career counseling center conducts excellent resume-writing workshops for all students, yet usually offers them only during normal business hours, concluding before 5:00 p.m., student-athletes would most likely not be able to attend, as they are usually in practice or competition until early evening. A compromise might be for the career counseling center to stay open late or offer those seminars at later times in the evening once or twice per month to accommodate *all* students on campus who may have atypical schedules. In return, the department of athletics can help publicize the service to the student-athletes. In doing so, the center would expand its reach to 250 or so more students (depending on the size of the student-athlete population) and student-athletes and interested others could attend the sessions, as well.

Where to Start?

The NCAA conducts a biennial survey of NCAA CHAMPS/Life Skills coordinators as related to their personal demographics, program description, and requests for resources from the NCAA. The following sections will discuss the fundamental elements of building a life skills program and detail some of the related results from the 2007 survey.

Staffing

If done properly, the responsibility of coordinating a life skills program should be undertaken by a university staff member who is full-time and works either in the department of athletics or in a student affairs unit. Some life skills programs are administered by an intern or graduate assistant, which can become complicated when the individual leaves, as people in these positions regularly do. By designating an individual who is a full-time employee of the university to coordinate life skills programming, the program can benefit from the consistency and credibility that comes with having a point person with some leverage and accountability. It should be noted that the majority of NCAA CHAMPS/ Life Skills coordinators (i.e., 70%) are assigned to life skills as 50% or less of their job description. Although it may be ideal to have someone assigned to life skills programming full-time, as discussed in this chapter, much can be accomplished when those responsible for life skills programming partner with others on campus to create programming.

According to the 2007 NCAA survey, the typical CHAMPS/Life Skills coordinator is a Caucasian female with a master's degree in education who is a former Division I student-athlete. Although this is the profile of the typical CHAMPS/Life Skills coordinator, perhaps more important than the earned degree or the athletic experience is the individual's ability to connect to and form relationships with others on campus who can support the mission of the life skills program.

Needs Assessment

Whether or not an institution has a well-established life skills program (NCAA CHAMPS/Life Skills or otherwise), the first place to start every year is to "take the temperature" of the current student-athlete population by administering a needs assessment (Etzel, Pinkney, & Hinkle, 1995). It is recommended that this needs assessment be completed annually by every student-athlete. For example, it is not useful to suggest that the results of the needs assessment of last year's freshman class can be generalized to this year's freshman class.

With the rapid pace of issues such as changing technology, class requirements for majors, and creation of new and potentially illegal substances to "increase athletic performance," to name a few, it is important to learn what the important issues are for every group of students on a frequent basis. Additionally, as student-athletes mature and move through college, their needs change with them. For instance, it might not be as relevant to discuss weighing the importance of medical benefits in a job offer with first-year students as it is to discuss that topic with juniors and seniors.

The NCAA provides a needs assessment for institutions participating in the CHAMPS/Life Skills Program. However, regardless of access to this inventory, most college counseling centers can assist in providing or developing a similar tool to assess the life skills needs of its student-athletes. The inventory should address perceived needs as well as topic knowledge (e.g., "I would know what to do if I thought my teammate had an eating disorder"). The results can be stratified by team, gender, year in school or whatever variable desired, but results of a needs assessment should only be part of the foundation on which life skills programming is based. From that point, input should be gathered from several sources, including the campus Student-Athlete Advisory Committee/Council (SAAC), campus counseling center, and coaches and other athletics administrators. This will be discussed in greater detail later in this chapter.

Topics and Programming

A simple but important question may be: What constitutes life skills subject matter? Although there may be common needs expressed by the assessment, there is no commonly accepted definition of life skills. The NCAA provides resource materials for topics to cover under the life skills umbrella, but it is by no means an inclusive list and institutions are encouraged to develop their own topics, as well. The development of life skills presentation topics is another good opportunity for partnering with student affairs professionals on campus.

Table 1 contains a list of recommended life skills topics for which the NCAA provides materials to its CHAMPS/Life Skills Program member institutions. Again, it is recommended that each institution tailor its programming to the needs of its student-athlete population, rather than use a blanket approach to providing general seminars and workshops for all student-athletes.

According to the 2007 NCAA survey of CHAMPS/Life Skills coordinators, topical programming constitutes the majority (88%) of life skills activities, and many universities sponsor other activities under the life skills umbrella. The following activities are conducted as part of CHAMPS/Life Skills Programming by at least 50% of the respondents

Table 1. Recommended Topics for NCAA CHAMPS/Life Skills Programs

Commitment to Academic Excellence	Commitment to Athletic Excellence	Commitment to Career Development	Commitment to Personal Development	Commitment to Service
Academic Integrity	Coping with Injury	Agents	Addictive Behaviors	Establishing and Maintaining Campus Partnerships
Applying for Scholarships/ Internships	Disordered Eating	Dressing for Success	Alcohol Use Choices and Consequences	Fundraising
Goal Setting	Exit/Continuing Participation Interviews	Developing Effective Work Relationships	Conflict Management	Peer Mentoring
How to Work with Academic Advisors	Leadership	Interviewing Skills	Dealing with Authority	Reaching Out to the Community
How to Work with Faculty	Nutrition for Performance	Job Search Process	Decision Making	Student-Athlete Advisory Committees
Presentation Skills	Performing Under Pressure	Life After Sport	Depression and Grief	Youth Mentoring
Study Skills	Sportsmanship	Mentors	Diversity and Inclusion	
Time Management	Supplements/ Performance Enhancing Drugs	Networking	Electronic Presence, "Netiquette"	
	Team Building	Résumés and Cover Letters	Establishing Relationships	
		Selecting a Major	Fiscal Responsibility	
			Interpersonal Communications	
			Manners and Etiquette	
			Media Relations	
			Self-Esteem	
			Sexual Responsibility	
			Stress Management	
			Violence Prevention	

to the 2007 survey: (1) academic advising (52%), (2) tutoring (51%), (3) freshman student-athlete orientation (65%), (4) leadership training (53%), and (5) community service opportunities (88%). About one-third of CHAMPS/Life Skills Coordinators report conducting student-athlete mentoring programs and sport psychology/mental skills training programs under the life skills umbrella, as well.

Partnerships

It may seem like an overwhelming task to create and conduct life skills programming for the entire student-athlete population at a university. In reality, it can be, if one tries to do it all on his or her own. With most things in athletics, successful teamwork is a primary contributor to success; conducting a successful life skills program is no different. It is not expected that one person would be able to conduct expert programming on such a wide variety of topics. In fact, the most effective life skills coordinators create partnerships with those who are experts in each field, such as student affairs personnel, to deliver specific programming.

According to the NCAA 2007 survey, more than 95% of CHAMPS/Life Skills coordinators partner with another office on campus to conduct life skills programming. The most frequently named partnerships were between athletics and career services (83%) and campus counseling services (74%). More than 40% partner with the university health service (49%), residence life (46%), campus academic advising offices (43%), and leadership programming (42%). Other valuable partnerships include campus safety, disability services, Greek affairs, international student affairs, multicultural affairs, and the campus women's center. These partnerships are often mutually beneficial as student-athletes learn from the expertise of other professionals on campus and the student affairs offices can reach a potentially new audience with student-athletes.

Another significant reason for partnerships between athletics and other offices on campus is to share financial resources. Unfortunately, most life skills programs do not have an extensive designated budget. In fact, the 2007 NCAA study revealed that 55% of CHAMPS/Life Skills programs do not have *any* designated budget. Of the remaining 45%, 25% have a designated budget of $7,500 or less and 20% of programs have a budget of $7,500 or more to put toward CHAMPS/Life Skills programming. Put another way, this means that of those schools that have a designated budget, an average of $11.50 is budgeted for each student-athlete's annual life skills programming, and this does not include personnel salaries. The hope is that this designated budget is not the only resource that is provided for life skills programming. Rather, this amount of money, however small, in combination with services already provided on campus by student affairs professionals can start to provide a strong foundation for life skills programming.

The lack of designated budget is sometimes the result of directors of athletics expecting the life skills coordinator to partner with colleagues on campus, as previously described, and thus not requiring as much financial support from the department of athletics. More often than not, however, budget designation is a result of prioritization of all areas in the department of athletics, including life skills. Athletics administrators whose institutions do not support a life skills program often will attribute the lack of involvement in the program to a shortage of resources such as personnel, funding, and time. Although having a full-time staff and fully funded program is ideal, there are several ways to support life skills that do not necessarily require adding staff, a large budget, and an extensive time commitment by one or more individuals. Creating and maintaining partnerships within the department of athletics and across campus is a great place to start.

Advisory Team

One of the recommended strategies for enhancing a life skills program, while not draining resources, is to establish a life skills advisory team. The purpose of this team is to assist the coordinator with creating and conducting life skills programming. In order for the team to be useful to the coordinator, it is recommended that the team include representatives from diverse areas of a student-athlete's life. According to the 2007 NCAA survey, at least 50% of CHAMPS/Life Skills coordinators include representatives from the following groups on their advisory teams: athletics administration (90%), student-athletes (63%), campus counseling center (62%), coaches (59%), athletics trainers (56%), and the athletics compliance office (50%). Other groups represented include faculty (46%), student health (38%), residence life (35%), multicultural affairs and nutritionist (23% each), and judicial affairs (19%). Members of the international students' office, sport psychology consultants, and the office of disability services are also represented on some life skills advisory teams.

Each institution should tailor the advisory team's composition to the needs of the student-athletes and the campus culture. A point of emphasis is that it is certainly appropriate to include a student-athlete or two on the advisory team. The student-athletes do not necessarily need to attend every meeting, but it is prudent to request their advice and counsel when planning programs and topics. Student-athletes are, after all, the reason why these programs exist.

The level of involvement of the advisory team members in the institution's life skills program can vary from institution to institution and also among members within each advisory team. Team members can teach a section or lesson as part of a life skills class for first-year students or provide topic suggestions and support for individual workshops and programs. The value of having various campus entities represented on the department of athletics' life skills advisory team is the ability to gain a campus-wide perspective of hot topics and issues. If something is affecting the general student population on campus, it is, by definition, affecting student-athletes. Quite possibly, because of the extensive size and well-established communications network of student affairs staffs on most campuses, campus issues can be identified and addressed by the rest of campus before athletics personnel are even aware that they are issues. Supporting an advisory team for the life skills program that includes student affairs personnel increases the chance that the department of athletics will stay "in the loop" on important campus issues.

For example, if the university information technology services has detected a high frequency of Internet gambling activity on university computers in the library and computer labs, that knowledge may be passed on to student judicial affairs and other campus administration. It may not be shared directly with athletics administrators, though, in spite of the fact that if student-athletes are involved in gambling, it could impact their eligibility. However, if this was presented at a life skills advisory team meeting, it could be addressed and supported by the department of athletics in conjunction with university policy and protocol.

In addition to developing a formal advisory team and working closely with the campus Student Athlete Advisory Council/Committee (SAAC) on life skills programming, it is recommended that those in charge of life skills seek other qualified and interested parties to support their work. As mentioned, there should not be an expectation that the life skills coordinator be the expert and sole provider of all life skills programming. The life skills program should be closely linked with student affairs units on campus as they have common goals, common missions, and of course, common target populations—college students.

The goal of the department of athletics' life skills program should *not* be to create a "separate but equal" program, but rather, to facilitate integration of student-athletes into campus activities and programming. Those who work in residence life, multicultural affairs, the counseling center, health services, disability services, career counseling services, and leadership development programs can be very helpful by collaborating with the department of athletics in the design and implementation of life skills programming. Concurrently, athletics can support educational and life skills programs already in place on campus by promoting them to student-athletes and encouraging their attendance.

"Model" Life Skills Programming

The staff at the NCAA is often asked to describe the "model life skills program." This is a difficult task because each institution is in a different situation in terms of finances, personnel, and—most critically—the needs of its student-athletes. Because each program should be based on the unique needs of its student-athletes, there is no standard or benchmark by which programs can be compared with one another. Even within NCAA divisions, programs with similar resources still conduct their programs differently. Varieties in programming include, but are not limited to: offering life skills classes for university credit, holding mandatory versus voluntary workshops or seminars, hosting guest speakers on a variety of topics, varying degrees of community service projects, scope and breath of inventories such as coach evaluations, exit interviews, academic support programs, and the involvement of the campus SAAC in program planning and execution. Some life skills programs incorporate all of these—others, just a few.

An adage from exercise psychology states that the best exercise for any particular person is any particular exercise that the person will actually do. This concept is analogous to life skills programming. The "best" programming for life skills is the one that meets the unique needs of the student-athletes on each particular campus and that those student-athletes will attend. Life skills professionals can increase their chances of developing and maintaining a successful life skills program that generates excitement among student-athletes, coaches, and athletics administrators by creating and utilizing an advisory team, communicating with SAAC, gaining support of athletics administrators (including coaches), and keeping programming current and relevant to the changing needs of today's collegiate student-athletes. This is a challenging task, indeed, but not impossible considering the important purpose.

Issues on the Horizon

There have been many changes in the world of collegiate athletics since the NCAA CHAMPS/Life Skills Program was implemented. For example, the original life skills financial planning materials did not include information such as factors to consider when choosing a cellular telephone plan or the potential budget drain of daily four-dollar coffees and frequent Internet music downloads. In addition to changes in the financial landscape, current and future administrators of life skills programs need to stay current with issues and with the environment in which student-athletes live. The best resources on the college student experience are, of course, the students themselves. Life skills administrators need to maintain open lines of communication with student-athletes and ensure that they are modifying their programming to meet current needs on an ongoing basis.

Decision-making skills related to alcohol, drugs, and sexual responsibility remain a crucial part of most life skills programming. Life skills administrators should also remain aware of additional issues on the horizon, including (in no particular order): (1) electronic presence, (e.g., MySpace, Facebook, etc.); (2) potential risk-taking behaviors such as hazing, gambling, athletics recruiting; (3) mental health issues; and (4) leadership training. Although this is not an exhaustive list, it covers a wide range of topics and is a good foundation for life skills programming.

Electronic presence refers to online behavior, including use of social networking sites and e-mail and text messaging protocol. Some institutions have banned any use of social networking sites for student-athletes, and some have instituted restrictions on what student-athletes can and cannot post on their personal profile pages. Student-athletes may express that it is their "right" to maintain a profile on these sites. Departments of athletics, however, will often defend their restrictions by emphasizing that it is not a "right" but a "privilege" to participate in intercollegiate athletics; therefore, student-athletes can choose to represent themselves without restriction, but that might mean relinquishing their association with the university's athletic team. These websites are not going away and are increasing in number almost on a daily basis. Athletics administrators at each institution need to focus on how they want to address these sites as well as any repercussions their use may incur.

Although issues surrounding hazing, gambling and athletics recruiting are not necessarily new, their prevalence has been dramatically increased by their amplified visibility on the Internet. What used to happen behind closed doors and was limited to reaction from those on campus or the local community is now available for international review via websites such as badjocks.com and ncaahazing.com (not affiliated with the National Collegiate Athletic Association) among others. Additionally, the increased availability of gambling sites and online recruiting "specialists" who target pre-college students hoping to participate in collegiate athletics have created a variety of ethical, athletic eligibility, and safety concerns for student-athletes and the helping professionals who assist them.

Finally, mental health issues and leadership training are also not new issues to collegiate student-athletes or those in the life skills profession (Hosick, 2005). However, as mentioned previously in this chapter, partnerships between the department of athletics and student affairs units who specialize in these issues (such as counseling and psychological services and service learning or community outreach departments) must continue to be strengthened in order to provide comprehensive service to student-athletes. With budgets and job descriptions stretched to the limit, partnerships are a necessity.

Summary

In one form or another, a core mission of most colleges and universities is to develop young people into competent, engaged citizens. Conducting life skills programming for student-athletes supports that mission and personalizes it that much more to connect with the unique elements of the student-athlete experience and circumstances. As employees of the university, life skills coordinators are educators and in a perfect position to identify and work to address the developmental needs of student-athletes through educational opportunities.

This chapter has described the context in which collegiate student-athletes study, compete, and socialize. Because of their unique circumstances, the need exists for life skills programming that is specific to the student-athlete population. Even among student-athletes, there should not be a "one size fits all" approach to programming. The NCAA provides an instrument to assess the needs of student-athletes from institutions that participate in the CHAMPS/Life Skills Program. It is used to tailor programming to the needs of the student-athletes at each particular institution. Even if institutions do not participate in the NCAA program, in order to conduct relevant, current, and necessary life skills programming, it is recommended that an inventory be employed to assess the psychosocial, developmental needs of the student-athletes on that campus.

A final point of emphasis is that life skills programs should not be conducted completely separate from the rest of the university campus. Rather, they should be coordinated with assistance from content experts on campus and integrate the student-athlete into the university as much as possible. Although there are definitely reasons to modify the content and, at times, the workshop logistics to meet the specific needs of student-athletes, the benefits of establishing partnerships with other campus offices should be emphasized and not overlooked. As always, the well-being of the student-athlete should be paramount when considering the mission and strategy for implementing any life skills program.

References

Adler, P., & Adler, P. A. (1987). Role conflict and identity salience: College athletics and the academic role. *The Social Science Journal, 24*, 443–455.

All-American Girls Professional Baseball League. (2005). *Charm School* [On-line]. Retrieved July 9, 2007, from http://www.aagpbl.org/league/charm.cfm

Arnett, J. J. (2000). Emerging adulthood: A theory of development from the late teens through the twenties. *American Psychologist, 55*, 469–480.

Baucom, C., & Lantz, C. D. (2001). Faculty attitudes toward male Division II student-athletes. *Journal of Sport Behavior, 24*, 265–276.

Bohnert, A. M., Aikins, J. W., & Edidin, J. (2007). The role of organized activities in facilitating social adaptation across the transition to college. *Journal of Adolescent Research, 22,* 189–208.

Brewer, B. W., Van Raalte J. L., & Linder, D. E. (1993). Athletic identity: Hercules' muscles or Achilles' heel? *International Journal of Sport Psychology, 24,* 237–254.

Brown, C., Glastetter-Fender, C., & Shelton, M. (2000). Psychosocial identity and career control in college student-athletes. *Journal of Vocational Behavior, 56,* 53–62.

Brown, C., & Hartley, D. L. (1998). Athletic identity and career maturity of male college student athletes. *International Journal of Sport Psychology, 29,* 17–26.

Cornelius, A. (1995). The relationship between athletic identity, peer and faculty socialization, and college student development. *Journal of College Student Development, 36,* 560–573.

Diacin, M. J., Parks, J. B., & Allison, P. C. (2003). Voices of male athletes on drug use, drug testing, and the existing order in intercollegiate athletics. *Journal of Sport Behavior, 26,* 1–16.

Dyson, R., & Renk, K. (2006). Freshman adaptation to university life: Depressive symptoms, stress, and coping. *Journal of Clinical Psychology, 62,* 1231–1244.

Engstrom, C., Sedlacek, W., & McEwen, M. (1995). Faculty attitudes toward male revenue and non-revenue student-athletes. *Journal of College Student Development, 36,* 217–227.

Erpic, C. S., Wyllemann, P., & Zupancic, M. (2003). The effect of athletic and nonathletic factors on the sports career termination process. *Psychology of Sport & Exercise, 5,* 25–59.

Etzel, E., Pinkney, J., & Hinkle, S. (1995). College student-athletes and needs assessment. In S. Stabb, S. Harris, & J. Talley (Eds.), *Needs assessment for college and university student populations* (pp. 155–172). Springfield, IL: Charles C. Thomas.

Ferrante, A., Etzel, E., & Lantz, C. (1996). Counseling college student-athletes: The problem, the need. In E. Etzel, A. Ferrante & J. Pinkney (Eds.), *Counseling college student-athletes: Issues and interventions* (pp. 3–26). Morgantown, WV: Fitness Information Technology, Inc.

Giacobbi, P. R., Lynn, T. K., & Wetherington, J. M. (2004). Stress and coping during the transition to university for first-year female athletes. *Sport Psychologist, 18,* 1–20.

Granito, V. J. (2001). Athletic injury experience: A qualitative focus group approach. *Journal of Sport Behavior, 24,* 63–82.

Grove, J. R., Lavallee, D., & Gordon, S. (1997). Coping with retirement from sport: The influence of athletic identity. *Journal of Applied Sport Psychology, 9,* 191–203.

Hosick, M. B. (February, 2005). Forum places psychological focus on mental health issues. The NCAA News. Retrieved May 16, 2007, from http://www1.ncaa.org/membership/ed_outreach/health-safety/forummentalhealthpdf.pdf

Ihle Helledy, K. L. (2006). Exploration of the factors related to the career development of collegiate student-athletes. *Dissertation Abstracts International Section A: Humanities and Social Sciences, 67,* 914.

Killam, C., Cautin, R. L., & Santucci, A. C. (2005). Assessing the enduring residual neuropsychological effects of head trauma in college athletes who participate in contact sports. *Archives of Clinical Neuropsychology, 20*, 599–611.

Killeya-Jones, L. A. (2005). Identity structure, role discrepancy, and psychological adjustment in male college student-athletes. *Journal of Sport Behavior, 28*, 167–185.

Kimball, A.C., & Freysinger, V. (2003). Leisure, stress, and coping: The sport participation of collegiate student-athletes. *Leisure Sciences, 25*, 115–141.

Kornspan, A. S., & Etzel, E. F. (2003). What do we know about the career maturity of college student-athletes? A brief review and suggestions for career development work with student-athletes. *Academic Athletic Journal*, 15–33.

Lally, P. (2007). Identity and athletic retirement: A prospective study. *Psychology of Sport and Exercise, 8*, 85–99.

Lally, P., & Kerr, G. A. (2005). The career planning, athletic identity and student role identity of intercollegiate student athletes. *Research Quarterly for Exercise & Sport, 76*, 196–219.

Lavallee, D., & Robinson, H. (2007). In pursuit of an identity: A qualitative exploration of retirement from women's artistic gymnastics. *Psychology of Sport & Exercise, 8*, 119–141.

Marsh, H. W., Perry, C., Horsely, C., & Roche, L. (1995) Multidimensional self-concepts of elite athletes: How do they differ from the general population? *Journal of Sport & Exercise Psychology, 17*, 70–83.

Martens, M. P., Dams-O'Connor, K., & Duffy-Paiement, C. (2006).Comparing off-season with in-season alcohol consumption among intercollegiate athletes. *Journal of Sport &Exercise Psychology, 28*, 502–510.

Martens, M. P., Dams-O'Connor, K., Duffy-Paiement, C., & Gibson, J. T. (2006). Perceived alcohol use among friends and alcohol consumption among college athletes. *Psychology of Addictive Behaviors, 20*, 178–184.

Martens, M. P., Watson, J. C., & Beck, N. C. (2006). Sport-type differences in alcohol use among intercollegiate athletes. *Journal of Applied Sport Psychology, 18*, 136–150.

Medalie, J. (1981). The college years as a mini-life cycle: Developmental tasks and adaptive options. *Journal of the American Health Association, 30*, 75–90.

Miller, P. S., & Kerr, G. A. (2003). The role experimentation of intercollegiate student athletes. *The Sport Psychologist, 17*, 196–219.

Murphy, G. M., Petitpas, A. J., & Brewer, B. W. (1996). Identity foreclosure, athletic identity, and career maturity in intercollegiate athletes. *The Sport Psychologist, 10*, 239–246.

National Collegiate Athletic Association. (June, 2001). *NCAA study of substance use habits of college student-athletes*. Paper presented to the National Collegiate Athletic Association Committee on Competitive Safeguards and Medical Aspects of Sports.

National Collegiate Athletic Association. (2007). *Student-athlete perspectives on their college experience: Preliminary findings from the SCORE and GOALS studies* [Online]. Retrieved November 9, 2007, from http://www2.ncaa.org/portal/media_and_events/events/convention/2007/sessions/score_goals/slides.pdf

National Collegiate Athletic Association. (2007). [Study of NCAA CHAMPS/Life Skills Coordinators]. Unpublished raw data.

Nelson, T. F., & Wechsler, H. (2001). Alcohol and college athletes. *Medicine and Science in Sports and Exercise, 33*, 43–47.

Ortez, J. R. (1997). *Generation impacts of freshman student-athletes on their perceptions of the college experience.* Unpublished doctoral dissertation, University of Washington.

Prancer, S. M., Hunsberger, B., Pratt, M. W., & Alisat, S. (2000). Cognitive complexity of expectations and adjustment to university in the first year. *Journal of Adolescent Research,15*, 38–57.

Quarforth, S. C., Brewer, B. W., Petitpas, A. J., Champagne, D. E., & Cornelius, A. E. (2003). College adjustment of football players: Predictors of first semester adjustment to college among NCAA division III intercollegiate football players. *Academic Athletic Journal, 17*, 1–14.

Raudenbush, B., & Meyer, B. (2003). Muscular dissatisfaction and supplement use among male intercollegiate athletes. *Journal of Sport & Exercise Psychology, 25*, 161–170.

Rays, J. (2006). Time to be candid about the 20-hour rule. *NCAA News, 43*, 4.

Ridinger, L. L., & Pastore, D. L. (2000). International student-athlete adjustment to college: A preliminary analysis. *NACADA Journal, 20*, 33–41.

Rivas Quinones, L. A. (2003). Career maturity, exploration, and identity foreclosure of student-athletes. *Dissertation Abstracts International Section A: Humanities and Social Sciences, 64*, 811.

Sanford-Martens, T., Davidson, M. M., Yakushko, O. F., Martens, M., Hinton, P., & Beck, N. (2005). Clinical and subclinical eating disorders: An examination of collegiate athletes. *Journal of Applied Sport Psychology, 17*, 79–86.

Schlossberg, N. K. (1984). *Counseling adults in transition.* New York: Springer.

Settles, I. H., Sellers, R. M., & Damas, A. J. (2002). One role or two?: The function of psychological separation in role conflict. *Journal of Applied Psychology, 87*, 574–582.

Sparkes, A. C. (1998). Athletic identity: An Achilles' heel to the survival of the self. *Qualitative Health Review, 8*, 644–664.

Webb, W. M., Nasco, S. A., Riley, S., & Headrick, B. (1998). Athletic identity and reactions to retirement from sports. *Journal of Sport Behavior, 21*, 338–363.

Wechsler, H., & Davenport, A. E. (1997). Binge drinking, tobacco, and illicit drug use and involvement in college athletics. A survey of students at 140 American colleges. *Journal of American College Health, 45*, 195.

Wolverton, B. (2007). Athletics participation prevents many players from choosing majors they want. *Chronicles of Higher Education, 53*, A36–A37.

Zuk, J. (2004). The psychological implications of forced retirement of female, collegiate gymnasts. *Dissertation Abstracts International: Section B: The Sciences and Engineering, 64*, 5244.

5

COUNSELING WOMEN COLLEGE
STUDENT-ATHLETES

Karen D. Cogan
Ariane Smith Machín

Psychologists, counselors, and other helping professionals have advocated for identifying college student-athletes as a unique population with distinctive needs and have encouraged specialized training for those who counsel or consult with athletes (Danish, Petitpas, & Hale, 1993; Fletcher et al., 2003; Pinkerton, Hinz, & Barrow, 1989). In recent years, researchers and practitioners have recognized that varied academic, personal, and sport-related experiences exist even for different subgroups of athletes and that there is a need to address diversity within the athlete population itself (Chartrand & Lent, 1987; Parham, 1993; Fletcher et al., 2003; Parham, 1996).

Gender is one area of diversity that has received attention lately, both in sport psychology applications (e.g., Savoy, 1993) and research (Duda, 1991; Krane, Choi, Baird, Aimar, & Kauer, 2004; White, 1993). In addition, psychologists and other counseling professionals have an ethical mandate to be sufficiently trained to competently serve diverse populations, such as women athletes (American Psychological Association [APA], 2002; Fitzgerald & Nutt, 1986).

Before proceeding, it is important to clarify some terminology and address certain limitations that exist within the literature that will affect the presentation of material in this chapter. Concerning terminology, "sex" and "gender" often are used interchangeably, but some subtle differences exist between these two terms. According to Matlin (1993), sex refers to the biologically based aspects of a person. Gender, on the other hand, "refers not only to biological sex but also the psychological, social, and cultural features and characteristics that have become strongly associated with biological categories of male and female" (Gilbert, 1992, p. 385). The term "gender" will be used throughout this chapter.

Given this background, the purposes of this chapter are threefold: (1) to examine how women student-athletes may uniquely experience the sport environment; (2) to consider some of the psychological and developmental issues these athletes may face at the collegiate level; and (3) to provide recommendations for effectively counseling and consulting with collegiate women athletes. For more in-depth information, readers are referred to the reference list and encouraged to seek consultation or supervision from colleagues knowledgeable in the desired area.

In general, research on a variety of gender-related characteristics has highlighted the similarities between men and women, concluding that more similarities than differences exist (Deaux, 1985; Moss, 1974). Even so, situational factors, such as socialization and the adoption of gender roles, create environments that are unique for men and women. It has been noted that women, in general, have qualitatively different life experiences than men do (Hyde, 1992; Parham, 1993). Gill (1986) suggested that women experience the sport environment differently as well. Despite the similarities between men and women, this chapter will focus on college women athletes' unique experiences and highlight how the college and sport environment may be different for them.

Social and Developmental Considerations

Before examining the collegiate female's sport experience, it is helpful to consider factors that may have influenced her development as a woman in the United States. A primary factor, socialization, is defined by Weiss and Glenn (1992) as:

> The process whereby individuals learn the skills, values, norms, and behaviors enabling them to function competently in many different social roles within their group or culture. More specifically . . . socialization occurring through sport refers to attitudes, values, or behaviors that may be acquired as a result of participation. (p. 140)

Over time our society communicates messages through many media (e.g., school, family, television) that shape the gender roles children are expected to adopt. Boys usually are taught to be competitive, aggressive, active, and independent, characteristics that are congruent with the general sport environment. Girls, however, are generally expected to be nurturing, kind, beautiful, cooperative, and even passive. Although females may not view the general sport environment as consistent with their gender identity, certain sports, such as gymnastics and figure skating, may fit this ideal female gender profile better than others (Csizma, Wittig, & Schurr, 1988; Metheny, 1965).

Competitive sport experiences (e.g., intercollegiate athletics) also tend to convey strong messages about masculinity and femininity and have traditionally been viewed as a domain where men are encouraged to pursue a masculine gender role identity (Miller & Levy, 1996; Nixon & Frey, 1996). Males who choose not to participate in sports are often seen as deviant, while female competitive sport participation has largely been viewed as inappropriate (Lantz & Schroeder, 1999). These messages are conveyed beginning in childhood, where the groundwork is laid for future athletes to determine how they will participate in sports. In their model of activity choice, Eccles, Alder, Futterman, Goff, Kaczala, Meece, and Midgley (1983) proposed that gender-role stereotypes, as well as beliefs and behaviors of significant socializers, mediate expectancies and activity choices. The gender-role stereotypes held by significant individuals in children's lives can easily influence their development of self-concept, perceived value of various activities, and performance expectations. Likewise, the beliefs and behaviors of important figures in a child's world can influence the child's self-perception. Research on this model using kindergartners through seventh graders indicates that girls express more negative assessment of their general athletic ability than boys do. These gender differences at such young ages appear to be more a consequence of gender role socialization than of natural attitudinal differences (Eccles & Herold, 1991).

However, in 1972, Title IX legislation was passed prohibiting sex discrimination in educational institutions, including the areas of athletic and recreational programs. Following the passage of Title IX, the U.S. Department of Education issued its regulation for compliance, indicating that all institutions that receive federal funds need to abide by this federal law. Although there was resistance to this law, including private schools that argued they did not receive public funding and therefore did not need to abide by this federal law, the enforcement of these regulations has impacted the number of women and girls participating in sports which has risen at all competition levels (Himmelberg, 1992). Due to this policy shift, a generation of girls has grown up learning competitive team sports early enough to develop the skills required for professional-level games, which is a huge social change (Huffman, Tuggle, & Rosengard, 2004). These girls and young women play sports and, with their families, attend sporting events and watch sports on television. According to the Women's Sport Foundation, women 25 years and younger are three to four times more likely than previous generations to be actively involved or interested in sports (Women's Sport Foundation, 2008). In addition, since the inception of Title IX and movement toward gender equity, female college athletic participation has increased 456% (Women's Sport Foundation, 2007). Thus, although traditional gender role socialization may be present, perhaps there is an on-going positive shift in the attitudes and behaviors within younger males and females regarding sport participation.

Even if attitudes and behaviors within childhood are becoming more flexible, girls approaching adolescence often learn that general achievement and femininity are somehow incompatible and believe they need to make a choice between the two (Hyde, 1992; Gurian, 2002). A girl may find her interests evolving from sport and competition to dating and developing interpersonal relationships. After all, girls are taught to be cooperative and to focus on social relationships. The message appears to be "Be an athlete or develop relationships" rather than "Consider doing both." Such a pervasive and limiting message may discourage some talented young athletes from persisting in sport (Allison, 1991).

College

The traditional college years (ages 18–22) are viewed as a transitional stage between adolescence and adulthood (Grayson, 1989, 2006). Both male and female students are shifting from dependence on family to individuation and independence. Moving into the collegiate environment can be a stressful time as students are experiencing normative developmental tasks such as forming sexual and nonsexual relationships, separating from family and friends, increasing their sense of identity (Eichler, 2006; Lacey, Coker, & Birtchnell, 1986; Smolak & Levine, 1996), and meeting academic demands (Levine, Smolak, Moodey, Shuman, & Hessen, 1994). On top of these normative tasks, other stressors exist, such as establishing friendships, gaining autonomy from family, changing social support networks, and increasing financial responsibility (Stein, Saelens, Counchis, Lewczyk, Swenson, & Wilfey, 2001). Parham (1993) argued that student-athletes face additional challenges that make the resolution of these normal developmental tasks even more difficult, including balancing academic and athletic pursuits, being isolated from mainstream campus activities due to sport activities, managing athletic successes and failures, maintaining physical health for injury prevention and optimal athletic performance, and terminating an athletic career.

Researchers have suggested that, as a result of the pressures of balancing what often appear to be potentially conflicting roles, student-athletes experience more stressors than do their non-athlete counterparts (Parham, 1993; Fletcher et al., 2003). In spite of an apparent need, athletes tend to underutilize the counseling services available to them at university counseling centers (Watson, 2005). Previous research (Hinkle, 1994) has conservatively estimated that 10% to 15% of student-athletes suffer from distress that warrants clinical attention. In light of these claims, student-athletes appear to remain an underrepresented population in counseling service settings on campuses nationwide (Maniar, Curry, & Sommers-Flanagan, 2001). Assumptions related to the underutilization of services suggest that student-athletes are hesitant to seek help because they have skeptical views about counseling and are apprehensive of being stigmatized by coaches, teammates, student peers, and fans (Brewer, Van Raalte, Petitpas, Bachman, & Weinhold, 1998; Linder, Brewer, Van Raalte, & DeLange, 1991; Wrisberg & Martin, 1994). In general women are more likely to seek counseling than men (Pederson & Vogel, 2007). Therefore, it is possible that of the athletes who seek services, more will be women. Counselors, then, must be competent in treating issues specific to women.

Athletes may be under the impression that current helping services offered to student-athletes do not match their specific needs (e.g., counselors may not have an understanding of unique student athlete needs, or the times that services are offered conflict with class and practice schedules). Further, athletic departments often have their own academic advisors or informal counselors who meet some of the personal needs of the student-athletes (e.g., a caring person who will listen and help them find solutions to better cope in a university environment). These advisors may, in turn, serve some of the functions that counselors in a counseling center do. Although most utilization studies have focused on male athletes, Pinkerton et al. (1989) suggested that, with greater equality in women's sports, women are likely to experience the same pressures and have similar needs for assistance in coping with stressors. In addressing gender-specific stressors, Parham (1993) noted that female athletes might be more likely to struggle with issues of eating disorders or weight management, the ramifications of participating in sports that generally operate with smaller budgets such as fewer scholarships and less media exposure, and the general societal biases that exist concerning women's participation in sport.

Role Conflict and Body Image for Women in Sport

Research examining one type of societal bias concerns the construct of role conflict, which refers to the conflict between a woman's femininity (e.g., submissiveness, grace, beauty) and attributes needed to succeed in her sport (e.g., strength, achievement, aggressiveness). Sportswomen in the United States live in two cultures: (1) the sport culture that is inherently masculine and (2) the larger social culture where femininity is celebrated for women (Krane et al., 2004). Although female athletes must meet general sociocultural ideals regarding body size and shape (i.e., westernized society's "thin ideal"), they are also under pressure to compete at optimal levels of performance. For instance, athletes participating in certain sports may experience enhanced performance when they have a more muscular, bulky body type (e.g., rowing, softball, hockey, track and field) whereas athletes in other sports may experience success in performing with a leaner, thinner body type (e.g., diving, gymnastics, figure skating, running). The "ideal" female conforming to cultural standards is that of a woman who is thin (and possibly emaciated) and beautiful. Although the "pale, frail, female" standard for women may have shifted in recent years, it still remains that an "attractive" (i.e., wanted, admired) woman may have muscle tone, but nothing too big or muscular (Thompson & Sherman, 1993). To some female athletes, these conflicting messages may leave them in a state of confusion about their bodies and their feelings toward themselves. For example, in downhill skiing, the emphasis is on speed, and heavier, more muscular skiers go faster. Therefore, coaches will encourage muscle weight gain, which is directly opposite to the pressures women may feel to maintain a thinner frame. An athlete in this case might experience an internal conflict between the goal of increasing mass to please the coach and augment her performance and the desire to maintain a more "feminine" body type outside of the ski venue.

Further, female student-athletes must navigate the typical social pressures associated with college, including forming dating relationships and friendships and engaging in comparisons with others (Smolak & Levine, 1996). Thus, they are likely to make comparisons with peers and think about socially desired body types and standards of attraction when developing potential friendships and intimate partners. Research has suggested that social comparative pressure to be thin fosters body dissatisfaction (Krones, Stice, & Batres, 2005). Out of the sport environment where their bodies are valued, these female athletes may experience heightened awareness, sensitivity, confusion, and dissatisfaction regarding their appearance and body type while interacting with nonathlete peers.

This greater complexity of the awareness and internalization of the thin-ideal and sport-ideal presents unique challenges within this college-age population, and these athletes also may compromise their athletic performance if the sociocultural thin-ideal is pursued. Even if a female athlete has a very solid and stable self-concept, the "sociocultural ideal" versus the "athletic ideal" may begin to take effects in the form of compensatory dieting or restricting behaviors. Thus, the athlete's confusion may take the form of disordered eating behaviors that has the potential to eventually develop into a diagnosable eating disorder.

Sexual Orientation

Another societal issue concerns negative stereotypes held toward female sport participants. Unfortunately, women athletes often are viewed as lacking femininity or questioned about their sexual orientation or both (Krane et al., 2004; Snyder & Spretizer, 1983). In one study, athletes expressed that being feminine conflicted with being athletic. They further conveyed that as athletes, they were marginalized and perceived as different from "normal" women. Yet, they were also proud of their strong, developed bodies and expressed feelings of empowerment that generalized beyond the sport context (Krane et al., 2004). Females who participate in sports such as basketball, softball, and track and field often are stigmatized and viewed as unfeminine (Pederson & Kono, 1990; Snyder & Spreitzer, 1983). Some sports, however, such as gymnastics, tennis, and swimming are considered more socially "acceptable" or "appropriate" for women (Pederson & Kono, 1990; Snyder & Spreitzer, 1983). Women who participate in such gender-appropriate sports are chosen more often as dating partners by men and as best friends by women than are those who participate in less gender-appropriate sports (Kane, 1988). Again, society's biases have added an extra burden for women who participate in certain sports.

Women also have different athletic-related career opportunities than men do. On a positive note, women currently have more opportunities than ever to participate at a collegiate level, although athletic budget disparities still exist (Women's Sport Foundation, 2007). Unfortunately, women still have limited possibilities for professional sport or coaching careers (e.g., Acosta & Carpenter, 1992; Suggs, 2001) and continue to experience this aspect of sport involvement differently than men do. For example, Suggs (2001) reported that only 9% of Division I athletic directors were women. Because women have fewer athletic career opportunities, they place more emphasis on obtaining an education, as a degree will be necessary for their success (Meyer, 1990). Although women may experience a "pro-academic" culture, they may receive little campus-wide support for being student-athletes, certainly less than many males receive for being athletes. Women also may continue to face negative stereotypes from society or the campus community concerning their involvements as female athletes (Griffin, 1992; Krane et al., 2004).

Intervention Strategies

Student-athletes face a range of unique challenges that result in qualitatively different collegiate experiences than those experienced by other students (Ferrante, Etzel, & Lantz, 1996; Etzel, Watson, Visek, & Maniar, 2006). Although student-athletes attract honors and praise for their successes, they also at times experience resentment due to their perceived privileges and special status (Fletcher et al., 2003). In considering the general development of females and the more specific transitions and stressors associated with collegiate sport, we offer the following basic suggestions for counselors who work with female athletes or in female sport environments.

Counselor Attitudes

First and foremost, helping professionals (e.g., counselors, psychologists) who provide counseling and therapy to student-athletes should examine their general attitudes toward college sports and their participants (e.g., viewing athletes as pampered, lacking intellectual potential), as well as their specific feelings toward women's sports and female student-athletes (e.g., the acceptability of women being competitive and physically strong). Engstrom and colleagues (Engstrom & Sedlacek, 1991; Engstrom, Sedlacek, & McEwan, 1995) reported that both faculty and students exhibited prejudicial and stereotypical attitudes toward student-athletes, especially in terms of academic performance. Additionally, some faculty regarded student-athletes' academic abilities as less positive compared to non-athlete students and expressed disapproval and anger in situations in which additional privileges or services are granted to student-athletes (Engstrom et al., 1995). Thus, counselors may want to speak with coaches, former athletes, or current student-athletes to better appreciate the athletic lifestyle today and thus gain an understanding and some empathy for what female student-athletes face during their collegiate experience.

Advocacy

As noted above, female athletes may have to deal with negative societal biases, stereotypes, and possible mistreatment. For example, sexual harassment and abuse of female athletes are issues that have recently received media attention (Heywood, 1999). Thus, counselors might adopt an advocacy role to help educate colleagues, student-athletes, coaches, and the general university community concerning the damage caused by these negatively held beliefs. Helping professionals who believe that female athletes are treated unfairly can serve as advocates by voicing professional concerns and opinions about policies and procedures set by the

organization (NCAA, 2001; Fletcher et al., 2003). Additionally, counselors can appeal to offices of social justice on campus and to athletic
department administration if they become aware that coaches are not
acting in the best interest of athletes. Through consultation and outreach programming to athletic teams, helping professionals can assist
student-athletes in gaining a better understanding of their team culture
and assessing interpersonal and communication skills, as well as fostering leadership behaviors (Fletcher et al., 2003). Such advocacy efforts
and increased dialogue may not result in immediate benefits, but may
be a first step in improving the university community for future student-
athletes.

Outreach and Consultation

Given the pressures associated with maintaining multiple roles (e.g.,
athlete, student, quasi-employee, young person), female athletes may
need additional support or guidance. Because fewer athletes than non-
athletes appear to seek existing services in university counseling centers
(e.g., individual counseling), helping professionals on campus are encouraged to be proactive by offering educational workshops to athletes
and coaches concerning relevant issues, such as time management,
study skills (Gabbard & Halischak, 1993), and men's and women's issues. Counselors and psychologists can support struggling female athletes by making themselves more accessible to athletes, by visiting practices, if invited by coaches, and by being available for consultation at
less traditional times such as in the evening.

In response to the developmental needs of college student-athletes,
the National Collegiate Athletic Association (NCAA, 1998) developed
and implemented the CHAMPS Life Skills Program (Carr & Bauman,
1996). Specifically, the NCAA CHAMPS Life Skills Program provides
student-athletes with a model for optimizing their college experiences,
promoting academic achievement, supporting students' meaningful
contributions to their communities, and facilitating successful transitions from college to professional careers or graduate school (Clarke &
Parette, 2002). This program also provides athletic departments with
resources and guidance to help them assist student-athletes to engage
more fully in the collegiate experience (National Collegiate Athletic
Association, 1998; Robinson, 1998) and can be used to assist women

athletes in particular. Helping professionals are often well suited to consult and conduct outreach programming through CHAMPS Life Skills on a range of topics (e.g., adjustment to school, stress management, healthy eating, time management, un/healthy relationships) that are useful to the student-athletes in general and female student-athletes in particular.

Career Opportunities

Given the limited but somewhat increasing availability of competitive post-collegiate sport opportunities, female athletes may experience psychological distress concerning their retirement from sport (Baillie, 1993; Suggs, 2001). Female athletes may need additional support, understanding, and guidance as they attempt to redefine themselves outside of the sport domain and head into the world of work or graduate school. In a proactive vein, psychologists and counselors might organize and offer workshops or discussion groups to provide student-athletes with the chance to connect with other "retiring" women athletes. Helping professionals also can assist transitioning female athletes with other timely life and post-college career issues they may not have considered until the end of their time on campus (e.g., career counseling). Personal counseling and career counseling may be useful concurrent events that may benefit female student-athletes in transition (Pinkerton, Etzel, Rockwell, Talley, & Moorman, 1990). With these general issues in mind, we move to an examination of other salient topics that counselors may encounter in their work with female student-athletes.

Ethical Issues in Counseling Female Student-Athletes

A male counseling center psychology intern, Daniel, is working with an attractive female volleyball player, Tara. Tara just broke up with her boyfriend and is tearful when recounting the events in the session. She feels there is something wrong with her and that she is unlovable. She asks Daniel for a hug.

As in any area of psychological practice, ethical issues arise in counseling women athletes. Counselors who work with women athletes will want to be aware of these issues and special concerns inherent in the sport environment. The next section will highlight some areas of which counselors should be aware as a means of avoiding ethical conflicts.

Working in Area of Expertise

APA general ethical guidelines charge therapists to work only in their area(s) of expertise. Two of the Division 17 principles (Fitzgerald & Nutt, 1986) state:

> Counselors/therapists should be knowledgeable about women, particularly with regard to biological, psychological, and social issues that have an impact on women in general or on particular groups of women in our society. (p. 181)

In addition, counselors must have the ability to use intervention skills geared toward helping women in general and subgroups of women in particular. To be effective in working with a collegiate female athlete client, helping professionals must also have some knowledge of how college age women's lives in general and sport-related experiences are unique.

Attraction

General attraction (i.e., feelings of friendship, caring) and sexual attraction between counselor and client happens very often within the counseling relationship. General attraction is a natural occurrence and often enhances the therapeutic work. When the attraction becomes sexualized, however, it becomes an important therapeutic issue to be addressed. Of course, sexual activity on the part of counselors and therapists with their female clients is clearly unethical (APA, 2002; Fitzgerald & Nutt, 1986; Heiden, 1993). Unfortunately, a nationwide survey of 900 ethical complaints reported to 32 state counselor licensing boards revealed that the second most frequent ethical violation was engaging in sexual activity with a client (Neukrug, Healy, & Herlihy, 1992). Male, more than female, therapists report previous sexual involvement with clients (Pope, 1988; Pope, Sonne, & Holroyd, 1993) with the majority of male therapist attraction being toward female clients (Rodolfa, Hall, Holmes, Davena, Komatz, Antunez, & Hall, 1994). Such activity is always detrimental to the women (Committee on Women in Psychology, 1989), often leading to impairment in ability to trust, feelings of emptiness and isolation, and increases in suicidal risk (Pope, 1988; Somer & Saadon, 1999).

Petrie and Buntrock (1995) conducted a study regarding counselors' sexual attraction and sexual behavior with the athlete population. Approximately 4% of the male counselors who responded reported that they had at one time become sexually involved with an athlete client. However, female respondents engaged in these unethical behaviors substantially less frequently. Because sexual behavior with clients is so taboo, these reported percentages of sexual attraction and behavior are likely to be underestimates of the actual prevalence of sexual or romantic intimacy between psychologists and college athletes (Holroyd & Bouhoutsos, 1985).

The same ethical guidelines (APA, 2002) that generally apply to mental health professionals need to be exercised by counselors who work with women athletes. Appropriate professional boundaries, without any romantic or sexual involvement, must be established at the beginning of a counseling or consulting relationship and steadfastly followed throughout. To avoid ethical misconduct and malpractice, therapists must be able to identify and cope with the feelings of attraction that arise.

Multiple Roles

Ethical guidelines also address multiple-role issues and discourage inappropriate counselor-client relationships (APA, 2002; Brown & Cogan, 2006). Counselors who work with athletes are in unique positions because they may function in capacities outside of the traditional one-on-one office sessions, such as when visiting rehabilitation rooms, attending practices and competitions, and traveling with teams or individuals. Such involvements offer the opportunity for the counselor and athlete to become more personally acquainted and could be construed as a multiple-role issue. We are not suggesting that counselors avoid such contacts with athletes. However, it is essential for the counselors to be aware of the potential to develop special friendships or become overinvolved with the athlete's life. Boundaries must be professionally maintained, and if boundary issues emerge, appropriate supervision or consultation must be sought.

In the case scenario at the start of this section, there is the potential for the male counselor to cross a boundary by giving a hug. He must be very clear about his role as a counselor and the message a hug sends, especially when this athlete is vulnerable. If there is any type of sexual attraction, a hug can serve to further develop the attraction and could lead to inappropriate behavior. At the same time, the male therapist needs to be sensitive to how much rejection the athlete might feel if he does not give her the hug she asks for, given her current negative feelings about herself. He will need to approach this situation sensitively and openly to make the interaction as therapeutic as possible and seek supervision or consultation as needed. Finally, it is important to keep in mind that both male and female psychologists are vulnerable to the dilemmas surrounding dual relationships and attraction to female athletes.

Confidentiality

Confidentiality is an indispensable component of any trusting therapeutic relationship. Work with female athletes is no exception. But what are the bounds of confidentiality when consulting with female clients and women's athletic teams and who determines what information is released? The coach? Individual athlete? Team? Athletic department? For example, consultants may find themselves providing consulting, psychoeducational, or team-building services to sport teams in which the normal limits of confidentiality are not clear.

There are several types of situations in which confidentiality can be compromised. First, upon initial meetings with teams to "try out" the services of a helping professional, athletes may not have signed consent forms or been briefed on confidentiality guidelines. If issues of a personal nature arise in that session for an athlete, then the entire team is aware and may not be sensitive to the need to keep that information in the room. Women athletes often seem more willing to disclose emotional issues or have a history of concerns such as abuse or eating disorders that could emerge depending on the content of the session. Female athletes may be more likely to bring issues related to sexual abuse, harassment, or unplanned pregnancies to counseling. These issues are particularly sensitive, further increasing the importance of maintaining a confidential environment. Second, if an athlete approaches a consultant about an issue in public others can easily become aware of the concern. Third, in a public setting, a consultant could offhandedly ask an athlete how she is doing, and if she is struggling with a concern, she may unintentionally express emotions about it. These issues have the potential to arise because of the unique setting in which sport psychology services are offered. Thus, it is essential to clearly establish such limits prior to beginning the consulting relationship, even eliciting clients' consent to treatment in writing. In addition, consultants must realize that the nature of their job opens them up to potential compromises in confidentiality. Consultants might also provide impromptu services in more public areas (e.g., lobby of a hotel or living area of a condo where the team is staying) and must be sensitive to the fact that they are not in private, soundproof environments. Athletes may be less forthcoming or more uncomfortable, and a change in venue may be necessary. In addition, athletes may have a tendency not to trust professionals who work outside of the athletic realm (e.g., counseling service staff, private practitioners). Emphasizing confidentiality may allow an athlete to take the risk to trust those outside of athletics.

Men Working with Female Student-Athletes

Fitzgerald and Nutt (1986) recommended that therapists be sensitive to circumstances in which a woman would work best with a female counselor and make referrals as needed. This guideline is applicable in counseling female athletes as well. With some issues, such as sexual abuse or eating disorders, a woman athlete may feel more comfortable working with a female psychologist or counselor. We are not suggesting that males are not capable of working competently with female athletes. In fact, some women athletes may relate better to, or be more comfortable working with, a male helping professional.

In instances in which a male counselor is unsure of the client's level of comfort in the cross-gender pairing, we encourage him to discuss the issue with the athlete. When in doubt . . . ask! Such an approach demonstrates respect for the athlete and allows her to communicate her needs concerning counseling. If a counseling relationship is established, it is important to be sensitive to the unique factors in a woman's athletic experience, some of which are highlighted in this chapter. Male psychologists and counselors should seek supervision or consultation or additional training as needed.

Women Working with Female Student-Athletes

A female counselor may find much in common with collegiate women athletes. In fact, the counselor may feel an affinity for the athletes and desire such contact because of her own interest or involvement in sport.

In addition to potential unethical friendships, same-gender attractions and other counter-transference issues may develop. Here the same cautions are in order as for male professionals. Boundaries must be clear from the beginning; a counselor should never become intimately involved with an athlete. Counselors will want to monitor these inclinations, and if attractions or other issues do arise, supervision should be sought in order to discuss the issue and determine how to intervene to avoid damage to the athlete.

Mental Health Issues Affecting Women Student-Athletes

As with any other female college student, female athletes are not immune to general mental health concerns. With the combined pressures of their sport, school, and personal lives, emotional concerns can emerge and often need to be treated within the context of the sport.

> Anita, a female basketball player, was referred by her coach because her performance had apparently been deteriorating. No one seemed to know what was wrong, as this athlete had previously been a good performer. She told the counselor that she had not been interested in practicing because it had become boring. She did not care about basketball that much anymore, though she used to live her life around it. In general, she had no motivation to do much of anything and her performance had slacked off in other areas, such as school.

This case represents a somewhat typical initial presentation. The concerns are vague, requiring exploration and detailed questions from the counselor to determine what the athlete is facing. The concerns could reflect depression, anxiety, or another concern. In any case, more information must be gathered during intake and over time. The following sections address issues of depression and anxiety in athletes.

Depression

Depression is a common complaint among the general population of women; the lifetime risk for major depression in a community sample ranges from 10% to 25% (American Psychiatric Association, 2000). The DSM IV-TR also reports that depression is twice as common in adolescent and adult females as in adolescent and adult males. One study reported that 21% of female college athletes met the criteria for mild depression, which is consistent with general population prevalence (Carr & Plane, 2005). Another study on collegiate athletes reported that female athletes had 1.32 greater odds of experiencing symptoms of depression than male athletes (Yang, Peek-Asa, Corlette, Cheng, Foster, & Albright, 2007).

There are numerous signs and symptoms of depression that include: (1) low/sad mood; (2) irritability or anger; (3) feelings of worthlessness, (4) appetite changes (more or less); (5) sleep disturbances (more or less); (6) decreased energy level; (7) decreased ability to focus or concentrate; (8) social withdrawal; (9) negative thinking; and (10) suicidal thoughts (American Psychiatric Association, 2000). Depression can have a pervasive, negative impact on overall functioning in general and on academic and athletic performance in particular because many of the symptoms of depression (e.g., poor concentration, decreased motivation, and negativity) clearly lead to performance difficulties (Thompson & Sherman, 2007).

Depression can be caused by a specific event or set of events in an athlete's life (e.g., death of a loved one, breakup of a relationship) or by events related specifically to sport, such as a serious injury. Depression also can be more biological in nature. For example, women often feel depressed due to hormonal imbalances. When depression is at its worst, an athlete may experience suicidal thoughts or even attempt suicide. Because college is a time of transition often accompanied by a host of new stressors, an initial depression can emerge or an existing depression can worsen. In addition, female athletes may feel pressure to achieve a specific physical appearance for their sports and can develop disordered eating patterns or even Female Athlete Triad (i.e., disordered eating, amenorrhea, and osteoporosis). These sorts of eating concerns may be accompanied by depressed mood. In addition, athletes who overtrain without including sufficient recovery into their routine can experience symptoms of depression.

Anxiety

Anxiety is another common presenting concern. In clinical settings it is diagnosed more frequently in women than men (55–60% are female) and has a lifetime prevalence rate of 5% for the general population of men and women (American Psychiatric Association, 2000). In a female athlete sample, Carr and Plane (2005) reported that the prevalence of anxiety was 33%, much higher than for the general population.

As with depression, most people experience some symptoms of anxiety during their lives. For some, anxiety becomes extremely difficult and even debilitating. Symptoms of anxiety include: (1) excessive worry or fears; (2) sleep disturbances; (3) changes in appetite, feeling anything from uneasiness to immobilization, pounding heart; (4) sweating or shaking, (5) impaired concentration; (6) feeling out of control; (7) and fear of dying or going crazy. There are different types of anxiety, including generalized anxiety disorder, panic attacks, obsessive compulsive disorder, and phobias. For specific descriptions of each, the reader is referred to the DSM-IV-TR (American Psychiatric Association, 2000). Often other conditions, such as depression, alcohol/drug abuse, or history of trauma, exist comorbidly with anxiety. Counselors will want to get a thorough history when the presenting concern is anxiety to truly understand what has led to these symptoms.

Anxiety is a central feature of sport participation (Hackfort & Spielberger, 1989). Often anxiety is viewed negatively, but not all anxiety is bad. In fact, with athletes, some anxiety often helps them increase their energy levels to be prepared for a high-level performance. In high risk sports such as gymnastics, anxiety helps athletes stay focused on what to do to adequately execute skills and stay safe. Too much of any good thing, however, can backfire, and when athletes experience too much anxiety, performance can be negatively affected. Most performance-related anxiety is subclinical and can be addressed through performance enhancement interventions (e.g., relaxation training). In some cases, however, anxiety is severe and warrants clinical attention (Brewer & Petrie, 2002). In such a case, a counselor will want to have the appropriate training to treat a clinical level of anxiety or to refer.

Interventions for Depression and Anxiety

Any competent counselor working with female athletes must be well versed in recognizing, assessing, and treating depression and anxiety. Often female athletes present with vague complaints about poor performance or questions about continuing in their sport. Sometimes depression and/or anxiety are behind this complaint, and counselors need to be attuned to the existence of these underlying conditions as they screen during sessions. For instance, in the case scenario, the athlete is rather vague about what is behind the performance decrement and the coach seems baffled as well. In a case such as this, it is helpful to screen for symptoms of depression and/or anxiety. On the surface, the case example above would suggest that some form of depression is possible (e.g., adjustment disorder, dysthymia, or major depression). It would be important to screen for anxiety too, as anxiety and depression often co-exist and some symptoms may be the same (e.g., sleep or appetite problems).

Medication

If depression and/or anxiety are present at a clinical level, medication can be considered, and a referral to a psychiatrist or other medical doctor would be necessary. After medications have been prescribed, the counselor can help monitor the effectiveness of the medication and the athlete's compliance in taking the medication. Of course, the prescribing physician would need to make any changes in dosage or be notified if significant difficulties with side effects persisted. Many of the current antidepressants will reduce both anxiety and depression and are non addictive. However, some psychoactive drugs can have a detrimental impact on athletic performance (Schwenck, 1997).

Cognitive Behavioral Therapies

Cognitive behavioral therapies (CBT) have acquired much empirical support as effective treatments for depression and anxiety (Freeman, 2005) and can be useful to therapy with women student-athletes. For depression, research indicates that Beck's Cognitive Therapy is as effective as medications. Both show a reduction in symptoms of depression (Strunk & DeRubeis, 2001). Cognitive behavioral therapy is the most empirically supported psychological treatment for anxiety disorders as well (Meadows & Butcher, 2005). Treatment using CBT usually focuses on changing physiological, behavioral, and cognitive responses to anxiety.

Crisis Intervention

Depression in particular can become severe and debilitating. If it becomes too severe, an athlete may experience suicidal thoughts or even create a suicidal plan. If the counselor is skilled in crisis intervention, then immediate action and treatment must be taken. If a counselor is uncomfortable working with such severe symptoms, then an immediate referral is in order.

Sexual Abuse or Violating Acts Against Female Athletes

This section addresses issues related to abusive acts female athletes may experience in college. Specifically, the prevalence of, effects of, and interventions for sexual abuse and harassment are examined. Although a thorough examination is not possible within the limits of this chapter, basic information is provided and readers are referred to other resources for further study.

> A new male coach, Andrew, took over coaching a university's women's swim team. He began the year with new ideas and was very energetic and friendly. After the first few months he began to ask three athletes (Megan, Stacie, and Jennifer) to stay late after practice; none of them knew he had made this request of the other two. He began by complimenting their performance and work ethics, asking how they liked his coaching style and what suggestions they might have for his work with the team. In the following weeks he took each one to dinner and was physically affectionate with them (hugging and touching). The athletes felt uncomfortable but did not want to defy the coach and jeopardize their spots on the team. Eventually he began to fondle and kiss the athletes. Megan finally mentioned it to Stacie and Jennifer, who admitted that the coach had done the same thing to them.

Sexual victimization is a common issue in college mental health work (Resnick & Indelicato, 2006). Women college students are at a particularly high risk for being victims of rape, particularly date rape or acquaintance rape. The peak age of victimization for women is 16–19 years, while the second highest age-range for victimization is 20–24 years (Bureau of Justice Statistics, 1995). Twenty years ago researchers estimated that approximately 28% of women experienced an event that met the legal definition of rape (Koss, Gidycz, & Wisneiwski, 1987). More recent statistics suggest that now one in six American women are victims of sexual assault. In addition, since 1993, sexual assault has fallen by over 69% (Rape, Abuse and Incest National Network, 2007). These lower incidence rates appear to be a trend in the right direction, though the data may reflect some women's tendencies not to identify the act as rape. In any case, college women still experience sexual assault and the subsequent emotional effects.

Being an athlete does not make a woman immune to these types of sexual violations. Jackson (1991) surveyed 50 female collegiate athletes and found that 24% had been fondled against their will, 14% were coerced into sex, and 10% were assaulted on dates. However, none actually acknowledged having been raped.

As a specific college population, athletes are often exposed to beliefs and patterns of behavior that create an atmosphere conducive to sexual abuse. This atmosphere can become an integral part of their collegiate experience (Holcomb, Savage, Seehafer, & Waalkes, 2002). There is also increasing evidence suggesting that men and women athletes are a population requiring special attention regarding the issue of sexual abuse (Benson, Charlton, & Goodhart, 1992; O'Sullivan, 1991). For many male athletes in particular, these beliefs and behaviors are reinforced by training in aggression (more so with some sports, such as football or hockey), their high social status on campus, behavior of women fans, alcohol and other drug use, and the peer pressure inherent in most male groups (Parrot et al., 1994). Although the extent to which male athletes endorse these beliefs varies, it has been suggested that male athletes who tend to do so are more likely to consider sexual assault as acceptable behavior (O'Sullivan, 1991; Berkowitz, 1992). In understanding such abuse, it is important to note that these violations can be perpetrated by parents, other relatives, family friends, strangers, coaches, and teammates or other athletes. In addition, perpetrators can be males or females.

In the case scenario, the coach gradually set up an environment in which he had the power to abuse female athletes. The athletes felt uncomfortable with his requests but did not want to refuse them because he was the coach. Only after the abuse had progressed and athletes learned that it was happening to several of them did they feel they could come forward and report it. In a situation such as this case a counselor can assist the athletes in facing the emotional impact of the coach's actions and making decisions about how to address it or report it.

Intervention Strategies

Not every counselor will feel comfortable or be competent in counseling athletes with a history of distant or recent sexual victimization. If an athlete discloses such sensitive information, however, she likely has some degree of trust and developed rapport with the counselor. In such circumstances, it is imperative that the counselor respond very sensitively and openly to the athlete and the information she has shared, because it will likely be a disturbing topic. In fact, the counselor may be the first person with whom the athlete has discussed this very private information. If the counselor felt unprepared to conduct an in-depth exploration of the abuse, a referral to a knowledgeable colleague would be necessary. Still, the athlete would need some immediate support and acknowledgment from the counselor concerning her disclosure. Recognizing this fact, we outline some strategies for discussing abuse with an athlete (adapted in part from Bass & Davis, 1988; Courtois, 1988).

Co-Morbid Conditions Associated with Sexual Abuse

Research has suggested that survivors of sexual abuse are more likely than non-abused female clients to have a history of substance abuse; be re-victimized in adulthood (e.g., battered); attempt suicide; report dissociative experiences; experience sleep disturbances; feel isolated, anxious, and afraid; experience problems controlling anger; have sexual difficulties; and engage in self-destructive behaviors (Briere & Runtz, 1987). Similarly, Courtois (1993) described the after-effects of sexual abuse, such as symptoms of post-traumatic stress, emotional reactions (e.g., anxiety, anger), and disturbances in sexual, interpersonal, and social functioning. These accompanying concerns must be considered as well when a counselor intervenes with an athlete. The next section suggests some basic intervention ideas.

Requests for Help and Appropriate Resources

Counselors should be alert to clues that the athlete has been abused and wants to discuss it. If the topic is ignored, her request for help is as well. Such avoidance may represent a recapitulation of earlier attempts to disclose to other adults. Listening closely to the client's story is an important first step and a means of furthering trust. If the athlete discloses, the counselor should ask questions about the abuse such as: Was there any other perpetrator? Did anything else similar ever happen in her past? How has she coped until now? What supports does she currently have? Who has she communicated with (e.g., family, law enforcement)? Has she visited the student health service or emergency room? The athlete should be supported in seeking appropriate help, such as referral to a skilled therapist, support or therapy groups, or both, and possibly legal assistance.

Issues to Consider in Conducting Counseling

The athlete should be assisted in discussing and validating her emotions, which may be strong. Some women may need time to vent past feelings, whereas others may need to focus on how emotions influence their current reactions to life events. These reactions may persist and possibly interfere with school work and sport performance, which may cause further distress. She may need additional help in therapy or a support group to process her emotional reactions.

Counselors should be very careful about physical contact with survivors of trauma. As past physical contact was violating, any current physical contact may feel like a further violation and lead to flashbacks and lack of trust. For example, placing what seems to be a benign hand on her shoulder may bring back memories of unsafe touch. As a general guideline, counselors should not initiate touch. If the athlete asks for a hug or touch, and the counselor is comfortable with that, then touch can be appropriate but must be on the athlete's terms.

It is important not to blame the survivor. The responsibility should be placed firmly on the abuser. Likewise, therapy should not focus on trying to understand the abuser. It is more useful to explore the survivor's reactions and help her establish coping strategies.

Counselors should examine their own attitudes about sexual abuse. If they do not believe it can happen, they may not be helpful to an athlete discussing her experiences. Counselors should not attempt to minimize the abuse. The survivor has probably done enough of that herself. These experiences have influenced her life, sometimes in critical ways. The abuse is no minor event.

Harassment

All types of abuse and harassment occur in sport as they do in many other institutional contexts such as government, religious organizations, or the workplace. There is a relative lack of studies addressing the experience of sexual harassment in the sport environment. Among the earliest studies of sexual harassment in sport are Lackey's (1990) survey of 264 Nebraska women college and university athletes, and Yorganci's (1993) survey of 149 female athletes in the U.K. Lackey (1990) found that at least 20% of female athletes he surveyed identified harassment as occurring in each of three categories: (1) profanity; (2) intrusive physical contacts (e.g., "slapping on the butt" [p. 23]; and (3) demeaning language (e.g., language that is "embarrassing, derogatory, or containing sexual innuendos that male athletes are superior to females" [p. 23]. He also found that participants accepted much of the harassing behavior as "part of the game" (p. 24), with only 17% acknowledging sexual harassment as a problem. In Yorganci's (1993) study, 54% of the participants had experienced or knew of athletes who had experienced demeaning language, physical contact, verbal intrusion, fondling, or pressure to have sexual intercourse from their male coaches. Of these participants, 43% felt that the behavior was not harassment. Similar findings have been reported by other researchers (Lenskyj, 1992; Kirby & Greaves [cited in Smith, 1996]; Tomlinson & Yorganci, 1997; Volkwein et al., 1997) suggesting that sexually harassing behaviors occur consistently.

The conclusions from these studies suggest that women in sport, like those studied in other contexts, are not only unwilling to take formal action against their harassers (Cairns, 1997; Thomas & Kitzinger, 1997), they are also unwilling to label the behaviors as sexual harassment. In the United States, under Title VII of the Civil Rights Act and Title IX of the Education Amendment Acts of 1972, sexual harassment is illegal sex discrimination. The U.S. federal agency charged with the enforcement of Title VII defines sexual harassment in the context of athletics and fitness as follows:

Sexual harassment consists of unwelcome sexual advances, requests for sexual favors, and other verbal or physical conduct of a sexual nature when:

(a) submission to such conduct or communication is made either explicitly or implicitly a term or condition of an individual's (employment or) status in a course, program, or activity,

(b) submission to or rejection of that conduct by an individual is used as a factor in decisions affecting that individual; or

(c) such sexual conduct has the purposes or effect of unreasonably interfering with an individual's (work) educational or athletic performance, or of creating an intimidating, hostile, or offensive environment for (working) learning or the development of athletic skills.

Overall, the majority of harassment study results highlight the need for transformation within the sport environment, specifically a movement toward empowering women themselves. Female athletes need to be able to resist sexual harassment by not considering it acceptable and actively reporting incidents to prevent future occurrences. By reporting, female athletes can send a message that the behaviors will not be tolerated and can help reduce harassing behaviors in the sport environment for future generations.

Interventions

If an athlete believes she has been sexually harassed within the sport context, she should be encouraged to report the incident immediately to the appropriate office on campus. This office has different titles on different campuses (e.g., Dean of Students or Student Rights and Responsibilities), but counselors who work with athletes need to have this information available or at least know who to ask. The athlete also needs to know that, in the end, it is her decision about whether to make the report. The counselor should discuss confidentiality with the athlete as she will need to know where the information might go if she informs another professional on campus. Whatever she decides, the counselor can play a key role in helping her cope with her emotions and making decisions about how to address the incident.

We recognize that these suggestions on intervening with abuse or harassment cases do not (and cannot within the scope of this chapter) cover every aspect of intervening with athletes who experience these incidences. Counselors who would like additional information are referred to the references provided at the end of this chapter and are encouraged to seek supervision from a knowledgeable colleague.

Pregnancy and Abortion

Risky sexual behavior is a major social concern among young adults and can lead to negative outcomes such as sexually transmitted diseases, pregnancies, and victimization. Female college athletes, who are balancing the demands of sport and academics, are not immune to the potential negative consequences of risky sexual behavior. Further, female athletes also may be more at risk as they are balancing academics with high-level sport participation and, consequently, an athletic scholarship that is likely funding part or all of their college education.

In an effort to understand the connection between athletic participation, sexual behavior, and pregnancy, the Women's Sport Foundation conducted a nation-wide study derived from multiple sources of data, including: (1) the Youth Risk Behavior Survey of the Centers for Disease Control and Prevention and (2) the Family and Adolescent Study, a New York State Research Institute on Addiction study. Specifically, the WSF study concluded that female athletes were less than half as likely to get pregnant as female non-athletes (5% and 11%, respectively), with significantly reduced rates of pregnancy in the subsamples of African-American, Caucasian, and Latina-Hispanic female athletes. In addition, female athletes were more likely to be virgins, have their first intercourse later in adolescence, have sex less often, have fewer sex partners, and were more likely to use contraceptives than female non-athletes. Overall, the results suggested that, for girls, sports may be used as a potential help to reduce risky sexual behavior that often accompanies their particular age group.

As female athletes enter and progress through college, their sexual behavior patterns from adolescence tend to persist. In a recent study, further confirmation of female sport involvement and less risky sexual behavior was verified (Lehman & Koerner, 2004; Sabo et al., 1999). Research suggested that adolescent women's involvement in organized team sports was associated with less sexual risk-taking behavior, more sexual/reproductive health-seeking behavior, and overall sexual/reproductive health.

Although the majority of the literature supports female sport involvement and healthier sexual behaviors in late adolescence and young adulthood (Women's Sport Foundation, 1998), pregnancy within the female student athlete population does occur. It has been suggested that educational institutions, national sport governing bodies, and athletic organizations should adopt policies concerning pregnancy that protect both the health and rights of pregnant female athletes to participate in sport and physical activity (Women's Sport Foundation, 2006). The situation can become more complex if the female athlete is on a scholarship and cannot participate because of her pregnancy, in relation both to her status on the team and to her ability to attend classes and complete necessary schoolwork. Because of challenges with school and sport, the female athlete may decide that abortion may be the best option at this particular point in time.

Interventions

As the female athlete is progressing through her decision-making process while simultaneously trying to balance the demands of her life, it may be imperative that she feel supported and has someone in whom she can confide about her feelings and options. As with any young woman facing an unexpected pregnancy, it is helpful to approach the female athlete in a nonjudgmental fashion and assist her in exploring her options. Also, it is important to recognize that pregnancy will take a physical toll and affect her sport involvement, which may also be her livelihood (through a scholarship). A counselor can advocate for continued financial support that any other athlete who would be out due to physical limitations (e.g., injury) would receive. The counselor can also help her explore her options for the pregnancy: keep the child, choose adoption, or abort. She will need to find the option with which she feels most comfortable, whatever that might be.

Conclusion

This chapter has reviewed female athletes' general development and socialization as well as specific concerns, including ethics, depression, anxiety, sexual abuse, harassment, and pregnancy. The number of female athletes participating in sport at the collegiate level has continued to grow, and counselors are likely to see more of the issues addressed in the chapter in female athletes who seek their services. It behooves the counselor to view women athletes as a unique population and to learn how to sensitively and effectively intervene. Although some information could not be covered in this chapter given space limitations, what has been offered provides the basis for beginning to understand the unique issues women athletes might face. Counselors are encouraged to consult other resources or professionals if more detailed information is desired and to continue their educational training.

References

Acosta, R. V., & Carpenter, L. J. (1992). As the years go by—coaching opportunities in the 1990s. *Journal of Physical Education, Recreation, and Dance, 63,* 36–41.

Allison, M. T. (1991). Role conflict and the female athlete: Preoccupation with little grounding. *Journal of Applied Sport Psychology, 3,* 49–60.

American Psychological Association. (1992). Ethical principles of psychologists and code of conduct. *American Psychologist, 47,* 1597–1611.

American Psychiatric Association. (2000). Diagnostic and statistical manual of mental disorders: IV-TR (4th ed.). Washington, DC: Author.

Baillie, P. H. (1993). Understanding retirement from sport: Therapeutic ideas for helping athletes in transition. *The Counseling Psychologist, 21,* 399–410.

Bass, E., & Davis, L. (1988). *The courage to heal.* New York: Harper & Row.

Benson, D., Charlton, C., & Goodhart, F. (1992). Acquaintance rape on campus: A literature review. *Journal of American College Health, 40,* 157–165.

Berkowitz, A. (1992). College men as perpetrators of acquaintance rape and sexual assault: A review of recent research. *Journal of American College Health, 40,* 175–181.

Brewer, B. W., & Petrie, T. A. (2002). Psychopathology in sport and exercise. In J. L. Van Raalte & B. W. Brewer (Eds.), *Exploring sport and exercise psychology* (pp. 307–324). Washington, DC: American Psychological Association.

Brewer, B. W., Van Raalte, J. L., Petitpas, A. J., & Weinhold, R. A. (1998). Newspaper portrayals of sport psychology in the United States, 1985–1993. *Sport Psychologist, 12,* 89–94.

Briere, J., & Runtz, M. (1987). Post sexual abuse trauma: Data and implications for clinical practice. *Journal of Interpersonal Violence, 2,* 367–379.

Cairns, K. (1997). Femininity and women's silence in response to sexual harassment and coercion. In V. Krauchek & B. Ranson (1999), Women's experiences and perception of sexual harassment in sport. *Canadian Review of Sociology and Anthropology, 36,* 585–600.

Carr, C., & Bauman, N. J. (1996). *Life skills for collegiate student-athletes.* In E. F. Etzel, A. P. Ferrante, & J. W. Pinkney (Eds.), *Counseling college student-athletes: Issues and interventions* (2nd ed., pp. 3–26). Morgantown, WV: Fitness Information Technology.

Carr, K. E., & Plane, M. B. (2005). Division I Female College Athlete Health Studied by DFM Researcher. Retrieved 7/18/2007 from http://www.fammed.wisc.edu/research/news0504c.html

Chartrand, J. M., & Lent, R. W. (1987). Sport counseling: Enhancing the development of the student-athlete. *Journal of Counseling and Development, 66,* 164–166.

Clarke, M., & Parette, P. (2002). Student athletes with learning disabilities: A model for effective supports. *College Student Journal, 36,* 47–62.

Coakley, J. J. (1990). *Sport in society: Issues and controversies* (4th ed.). St. Louis, MO: Times Mirror/Mosby.

Committee on Women in Psychology. (1989). If sex enters into the psychotherapy relationship. *Professional Psychology: Research and Practice, 20,* 112–115.

Courtois, C. A. (1988). *Healing the incest wound: Adult survivors in therapy.* New York: Norton.

Courtois, C. A. (1993). Adult survivors of sexual abuse. *Family Violence and Abusive Relationships, 20,* 433–446.

Csizma, K. A., Wittig, A. F., & Schurr, K. T. (1988). Sport stereotypes and gender. *Journal of Sport Psychology, 10,* 62–74.

Danish, S., Petitpas, A., & Hale, B. (1993). Life development for athletes: Life skills through sports. *The Counseling Psychologist, 21,* 352–387.

Deaux, K. (1985). Sex and gender. *Annual Review of Psychology, 36,* 49–81.

Duda, J. L. (1991). Perspectives on gender roles in physical activity. *Journal of Applied Sport Psychology, 3,* 1–6.

Eccles, J., Adler, T. F., Futterman, R., Goff, S. B., Kaczala, C. M., Meece, J. L., & Midgley, C. (1983). Expectations, values and academic behaviors. In J. T. Spence (Ed.), *Achievement and achievement motivation* (pp. 75–146). San Fransisco: W. H. Freeman.

Eccles, J. S., & Herald, R. D. (1991). Gender differences in sport involvement: Applying the Eccles' expectancy-value model. *Journal of Applied Sport Psychology, 3,* 7–35.

Eichler, R. J. (2006). Developmental considerations. In P. Grayson & P. Meilman (Eds.), *College mental health practice* (pp. 21–41). New York: Routledge.

Engstrom, C. M., & Sedlacek, W. E. (1991). A study of prejudice toward university student-athletes. *Journal of Counseling & Development, 70,* 189–193.

Engstrom, C. M., Sedlacek, W. E., & McEwen, M. K. (1995). Faculty attitudes toward male revenue and nonrevenue student-athletes. *Journal of College Student Development, 36,* 217–227.

Etzel, E., Watson, J. Visek, A., & Maniar, S. (2006). Understanding and promoting college student-athlete health: Essential issues for student affairs professionals. *NASPA Journal, 43*(3), 518–548. Retrieved July 3, 2008, from http://publications.naspa.org/cgi/viewcontent.cgi?article=1682&context=naspajournal

Ferrante, A. P., Etzel, E., & Lantz, C. (1996). Counseling college student-athletes: The problem, the need. In E. F. Etzel, A. P. Ferrante, & J. W. Pinkney (Eds.), *Counseling college student-athletes: Issues and interventions* (2nd ed., pp 3–26). Morgantown, WV: Fitness Information Technology.

Fitzgerald, L. F., & Nutt, R. (1986). The Division 17 principles concerning the counseling/psychotherapy of women: Rationale and implementation. *The Counseling Psychologist, 14,* 180–216.

Fletcher, T., Benshoff, J., & Richburg, M. (2003). A systems approach to understanding and counseling college student-athletes. *Journal of College Counseling, 6,* 35–45.

Freeman, A. (2005). *Encyclopedia of cognitive behavioral therapy.* New York: Springer Science & Business Media, Inc.

Gabbard, C., & Halishchak, K. (1993). Consulting opportunities: Working with student-athletes at a university. *The Counseling Psychologist, 21,* 386–398.

Gilbert, L. A. (1992). Gender and counseling psychology: Current knowledge and directions for research and social action. In S. Brown & R. Lent (Eds.), *Handbook of counseling psychology* (pp. 383–411). New York: J. Wiley.

Gill, D. L. (1986). *Psychological dynamics of sport.* Champaign, IL: Human Kinetics Publishers.

Grayson, P. (2006). Overview. In P. Grayson & P. Meilman (Eds.), *College mental health practice* (pp. 1–20). New York: Routledge.

Grayson, P. A. (1989). The college psychotherapy client: An overview. In P. Grayson & K. Cauley (Eds.), *College psychotherapy* (pp. 8–28). New York: The Guilford Press.

Griffin, P. (1992). Changing the game: Homophobia, sexism, and lesbians in sport. *Quest, 44,* 251–265.

Gurian, M. (2002). *The wonder of girls.* New York: Artia.

Heiden, J. M. (1993). Preview-prevent: A training strategy to prevent counselor-client sexual relationships. *Counselor Education and Supervision, 33,* 53–60.

Heywood, L. (1999). Despite the positive rhetoric about women's sports, female athletes face a culture of sexual harassment. *The Chronicle of Higher Education,* p. B4.

Himmelburg, M. (1992). Sexism still rampant. *Nieman Reports, 46,* 38–41.

Hinkle, J. S. (1994). Integrating sport psychology and sports counseling: Development programming, education, and research. *Journal of Sport Behavior, 17,* 52–59.

Holcomb, D. R., Savage, M. P., Seehafer, R., & Waalkes, D. M. (2002). A mixed-gender date rape prevention intervention targeting freshman college athletes. *College Student Journal, 36,* 165–179.

Holroyd, J., & Bouhoutsos, J. C. (1985). Biased reporting of therapist-patient sexual intimacy. *Professional Psychology: Research and Practice, 16,* 701–709.

Huffman, S., Tuggle, C. A., & Rosengard, D. S. (2004). How campus media cover sports: The gender-equity issue, one generation later. *Mass Communication and Society, 7,* 475–489.

Hyde, J. S. (1992). *Half the human experience: The psychology of women* (2nd ed.). Lexington, MA: D. C. Heath and Company.

Jackson, T. L. (1991). The university athletic department's rape and assault experiences. *Journal of College Student Development, 32,* 77–78.

Kane, M. J. (1988). The female athletic role as a status determinant within the social systems of high school adolescents. *Adolescence, 23,* 253–264.

Koss, M. P., Gidycz, C. A., & Wisneiwski, N. (1987). The scope of rape: Incidence and prevalence of sexual aggression and victimization in a national sample of higher education students. *Journal of Consulting and Clinical Psychology, 55,* 162–170.

Krane, V., Choi, P. Y., & Baird, S. M. (2004). Living the paradox: Female athletes negotiate femininity and muscularity. *Sex Roles, 50,* 315–329.

Krones, P. G., Stice, E., & Batres, C. (2005). In vivo social comparison to a thin-ideal peer promotes body dissatisfaction: A randomized experiment. *International Journal of Eating Disorders, 38,* 134–142.

Lacey, J. H., Coker, S., & Birtchnell, S. A. (1986). Bulimia: Factors associated with its etiology and maintenance. *International Journal of Eating Disorders, 5,* 475–487.

Lackey, D. (1990). Sexual harassment in sports. *Physical Educator, 47,* 22–26.

Lehman, S. J., & Koerner, S. S. (2004). Adolescent women's sport involvement and sexual behavior/health: A process-level investigation. *Journal of Youth and Adolescence, 33,* 443–455.

Lenskyj, H. (1991). Combating homophobia in sport and physical education. *Sociology of Sport Journal, 8,* 61–69.

Lenskyj, H. (1992). Sexual harassment: Female athletes' experiences and coaches' responsibilities. *Sports, 12,* 1–5.

Levine, M. P., Smolak, L., Moodey, A. F., Shuman, M. D., & Hessen, I. D. (1994). Normative development challenges and dieting and eating disturbances in middle school girls. *International Journal of Eating Disorders, 15,* 11–20.

Linder, D. E., Brewer, B. W., Van Raalte, J. L., & DeLange, N. (1991). A negative halo for athletes who consult sport psychologists: Replication and extension. *Journal of Sport & Exercise Psychology, 13,* 133–148.

Maniar, S. D., Curry, L. A., & Sommers-Flanagan, J. (2001). Student athletes' preferences in seeking help when confronted with sport performance problems. *Sport Psychologist, 15,* 205–223.

Matlin, M. W. (1993). *The psychology of women* (2nd ed.). Orlando, FL: Harcourt, Brace and Jovanovich.

Meadows, E. A., & Butcher, J. (2005). Adult-anxiety. In A. Freeman (Ed.), *Encyclopedia of cognitive behavioral therapy* (pp. 33–35). New York: Springer Science & Business Media, Inc.

Metheny, E. (1965). Symbolic forms of movement: The feminine image in sports. In *Connotations of movement in sport and dance* (pp. 43–56). Dubuque, IA: Wm. C. Brown.

Meyer, B. (1990). From idealism to actualization: The academic performance of female collegiate athletes. *Sociology of Sport Journal, 7,* 44–57.

Meyers, A. (1995, Winter). Ethical principles of AAASP. *AAASP Newsletter, 10,* 15–21.

Miller, J., & Levy, G. (1996). Gender role conflict, gender-typed characteristics, self-concepts, and sport socialization in female athletes and nonathletes. *Sex Roles, 35,* 111–122.

Moss, H. A. (1974). Early sex differences and mother infant interactions. In R. Friedman, R. Richard, & R. Vande Wiele (Eds.), *Sex differences in behavior* (pp. 149–163). New York: J. Wiley.

National Collegiate Athletic Association. (1998). Gender equity in intercollegiate athletics. Retrieved March 31, 2008, from http://www.ncaa.org/library/general/gender_equity/gender_equity_manual.pdf

National Collegiate Athletic Association. (2001). *2001–2002 NCAA Division I manual.* Overland Park, KS: Author.

Neukurg, E. S., Healy, M., & Herlihy, B. (1992). Ethical practices of licensed professional counselors: An updated survey of state licensing boards. *Counselor Education and Supervision, 32,* 130–141.

O'Sullivan, C. S. (1991). Acquaintance gang rape on campus: In A. Parrot & L. Bechofer (Eds.), *Acquaintance rape: The hidden crime* (pp. 140–156). New York: Wiley.

Parham, W. D. (1993). The intercollegiate athletes: A 1990s profile. *The Counseling Psychologist, 21,* 411–429.

Parham, W. D. (1996). Diversity within intercollegiate athletics: Current profile and welcomed opportunities. In E. Etzel, A. P. Ferrante, & J. Pinkney (Eds.), *Counseling college student-athletes: Issues and interventions* (2nd ed., pp. 27–53). Morgantown, WV: Fitness Information Technology.

Parrot, A., Cummings, M., Marchall, T. C., & Hofner, J. (1994). A rape awareness and prevention model for men athletes. *Journal of American College Health, 42*, 179–184.

Pederson, D. M., & Kono, D. M. (1990). Perceived effects on femininity of the participation of women in sport. *Perceptual and Motor Skills, 71*, 783–792.

Pederson, E. L. , & Vogel, D. L. (2007). Male gender role conflict and willingness to seek counseling: Testing a mediation model on college-aged men. *Journal of Counseling Psychology, 54*, 373–384.

Petrie, T., & Buntrock, C. (1995). Sexual attraction and the professional of sport psychology. *Journal of Applied Sport Psychology, 7*, 98–107.

Pinkerton, R. S., Etzel, E., Rockwell, W. J., Talley, J., & Moorman, J. C. (1990). Psychotherapy and career counseling: Toward an integration for use with college students. *Journal of American College Health, 39*, 129–136.

Pinkerton, R. S., Hinz, L. D., & Barrow, J. C. (1989). The college student-athlete: Psychological considerations and interventions. *Journal of American College Health, 37*, 218–226.

Pope, K. S. (1988). How clients are harmed by sexual contact with mental health professionals: The syndrome and its prevalence. *Journal of Counseling and Development, 67*, 222–226.

Pope, K. S., Sonne, J. L., & Holroyd, J. (1993). *Sexual feelings in psychotherapy: Explorations for therapists and therapists-in-training.* Washington, DC: American Psychological Association, 304.

Rodolfa, E., Hall, T., Holms, V., Davena, A., Komatz, D., Antunez, M., & Hall, A. (1994). The management of sexual feelings in therapy. *Professional Psychology: Research and Practice, 25*, 168–172.

Sabo, D. F., Miller, K. E., Farrell, M. P., Melnick, M. J., & Barnes, G. M. (1999). High school athletic participation, sexual behavior, and adolescent pregnancy: A regional study. *Journal of Adolescent Health, 25*, 207–216.

Savoy, C. (1993). A yearly mental training program for a college basketball player. *The Sport Psychologist, 7*, 173–190.

Smith, B. (1996). Abuse prevalent in elite sport, survey indicates. In V. Krauchek & B. Ranson (1999). Women's experiences and perception of sexual harassment in sport. *Canadian Review of Sociology and Anthropology, 36*, 585–600.

Smolak, L., & Levine, M. P. (1996). Adolescent transitions and the development of eating problems. In M. P. Mussell, R. B. Binford, & J. A. Fulkerson, Eating disorders: Summary of risk factors, prevention programming, and prevention research. *The Counseling Psychologist, 28*, 764–796.

Snyder, E. E., & Spreitzer, E. (1983). Change and variation in the social acceptance of female participation in sports. *Journal of Sport Behavior, 6*, 3–8.

Somer, E., & Saadon, M. (1999). Therapist-client sex: Clients' retrospective reports. *Professional Psychology: Research and Practice, 30*, 504–509.

Stein, R. I., Saelens, B. E., Lewczyk, C. M., Swenson, A. K., & Wilfey, D. E. (2001). Treatment of eating disorders in women. *The Counseling Psychologist, 29*, 695–732.

Strunk, D. R., & DeRubeis, R. J. (2001). Cognitive therapy of depression: A review of its efficacy. *Journal of Cognitive Psychotherapy: An International Quarterly, 15,* 289–297.

Suggs, W. (2001). Gender in athletic administration. In T. Fletcher, J. Benshoff, & M. Richburg (2003). A systems approach to understanding and counseling student athletes. *Journal of College Counseling, 6,* 35–45.

Thomas, A., & Kitzinger, C. (1997). "It's just something that happens": The invisibility of sexual harassment in the workplace. *Gender, Work, and Organization, 1,* 151–161.

Thompson, R. A., & Sherman, R. T. (1993). *Helping athletes with eating disorders.* Champaign, IL: Human Kinetics.

Thompson, R. A., & Sherman, R. T. (2007). Managing student athletes' mental health issues. National Collegiate Athletic Association online publications. Retrieved 03/31/08 from http://www.ncaa.org/library/sports_sciences/sports_med_handbook/2007-08/ 2007-08_sports_medicine_handbook.pdf

Tomlinson, A., & Yorganci, I. (1997). Male coach/female athlete relations: Gender and power relations in competitive sport. *Journal of Sport and Social Issues, 21,* 134–155.

Volkwein, K., Schnell, F., Sherwood, D., & Livezey, A. (1997). Sexual harassment in sport: Perceptions and experiences of American female student-athletes. *International Review for the Sociology of Sport. 32,* 283–295.

Watson, J. (2005). College student-athletes' attitudes toward help-seeking behavior and expectations of counseling services. *Journal of College Student Development, 46,* 442–449.

Weiss, M. R., & Glenn, S. D. (1992). Psychological development of females' sport participation: An interactional perspective. *Quest, 44,* 138–157.

White, S. A. (1993). The relationship between psychological skills, experience, and practice commitment among collegiate male and female skiers. *The Sport Psychologist, 7,* 49–57.

Women's Sport Foundation Report: Sport and Teen Pregnancy, 1998.

Women's Sport Foundation Report: Equity in Women's Sports—A Health and Fairness Perspective, 2006.

Women's Sport Foundation Report: Women in Intercollegiate Sport, A Longitudinal National Study Thirty-One Year Update: 1977–2008.

Wrisberg, C. A., & Martin, S. B. (1994). *Attitudes of African-American and Caucasian athletes towards sport psychology consultants.* In J. Watson (2005), College student-athletes' attitudes toward help-seeking behavior and expectations of counseling services. *Journal of College Student Development, 46,* 442–449.

Yorganci, I. (1993). Preliminary findings from a survey of gender relationship and sexual harassment in sport. In C. Brackenridge (Ed.), *Body Matters: Leisure Images and Lifestyles* (pp. 197–203). Brighton: Leisure Studies Association.

6

COUNSELING MALE COLLEGE STUDENT-ATHLETES

Mark A. Stevens
Robin Scholefield

This chapter will provide the reader with some general guidelines about counseling male college student-athletes. The salient context of the chapter is the client as a member of two significantly influential and intersecting cultural groups: as a male and as a student-athlete. What is perhaps most significant about these two cultures are their similarities. How we socialize men and how we socialize our high performing athletes bear remarkable resemblances. Male student-athletes come in for therapy for all the same reasons as do non-athlete college students, plus more (Englar-Carlson & Stevens, 2006). Stress, time management, relationship management, performance issues, relationship issues, depression, anxiety, learning disabilities, anger management, sexual responsibility, eating disorders, drug and alcohol use and abuse, retirement, and bereavement are some of the more presenting concerns of male student-athlete clients.

Space considerations will limit the authors' ability to contextualize the student-athlete in terms of his sport, type of university, ethnicity, sexual orientation, and socio-economic status. It should be noted, though, that these contexts are quite important when considering diagnosis and treatment interventions.

The authors will begin with identifying and briefly summarizing some key aspects of the interpersonal and intrapersonal lives of male student-athletes. The next section of the chapter will include a discussion about the intersection of male socialization and being a student-athlete. The authors will then highlight how male student-athletes are commonly referred to counseling, and they will follow that information with some practical suggestions for counseling male student-athletes. Finally, the authors will present two case vignettes of short-term therapy with male student-athletes along with commentary about the cases.

Culture of Male Student-Athletes

We are listing for the reader some key aspects of the interpersonal and intrapersonal lives of male student-athletes. These features are not always apparent to counselors unfamiliar with the circumstances behind the scenes in college sports.

Developmental Acceleration and Arrest

College student-athletes are among the most elite young athletes in the United States (Finch & Gould, 1996). Most of them have dedicated a huge amount of time and effort and made many sacrifices in order to excel in their sport. These sacrifices are social and academic in nature, and include the free time to "just be a kid." It is not uncommon for freshman athletes to arrive on their college campus and say they are tired and/or burnt out and wish they could "just be a normal student." Student-athletes have had to develop toughness and determination sometimes far beyond what is characteristic of their peers. They were generally very successful in high school and/or club sports and they were accustomed to being a leader in their sport at home. Often they were favored by coaches, and sometimes parents, over other children. These child athletes typically received a lot of attention from peers, parents, friends, teachers, and sometimes local media. Occasionally, they obtained extra privileges at school or home, which not surprisingly may have led to a sense of entitlement. On the road to success, parents often paved the way by providing extra support that generally non-athlete students must provide for themselves. Thus, it is understandable how college student-athletes are independent and mature in some ways and, at the same time, dependent and immature in other ways.

While male student-athletes proceed with the normal developmental challenges (e.g., independence, values clarification, relationship choices) all young men face as they become adults, male student-athletes are also required to sustain a very high level of toughness as the stakes get bigger and increasingly more public. This is in contrast to the experience of most young men, who typically slowly decrease their participation in sport and gradually supplant their interests with more intellectual, social, and professional pursuits. Although the student-athletes' ongoing participation in high-level competition tends to affirm their masculinity, it also prolongs their exposure to the idea that some of their more stereotypical masculine traits (e.g., competitiveness, aggressiveness, and emotional restrictiveness) will have a greater impact on their ultimate happiness than is likely the case. Male student-athletes may generalize their use of "win-loss" philosophies into non-competitive and relational aspects of their lives (for instance, how do you win in a close loving relationship? How can I be vulnerable and not be afraid of being seen as weak?). As opposed to women, who must find support for their femininity outside sport, participation in sport for men asserts their masculinity. Status as a student-athlete in college also tends to prolong the belief that it is their physical prowess and/or aesthetic that will bring them the augmentation in esteem that will result in deeper satisfaction in life.

Finances and Security

The lifestyle of a student-athlete has changed dramatically over the past few decades. This often starts with what amounts to fairly high-level financial negotiations around scholarships. These contractual obligations, which were once rather secure guarantees of at least a four-year college education, are now largely annual contracts that can be adjusted among team members or taken away entirely on an annual basis. These contractual commitments with the athletic department include duties to perform and train, as well as to fulfill other team responsibilities. They also include expected standards of behavior and attitude. Non-scholarship athletes have basically all the same responsibilities as scholarship athletes without the benefit of money in order to be members of the varsity team. The public perception of student-athletes as getting a "free ride" is a myth. Most college student-athletes receive no monetary support for their athletic participation. The time demands for student-athletes can be enormous, and the financial pressures often match those demands.

Time Pressures

Student-athlete orientation to time tends to be both present and future. Every day, every minute counts toward the future. Student-athletes and athletic department staff tend to want everything done yesterday. They often live with a sense of urgency. Their over-scheduled lifestyles contribute to this feeling. At the same time, they often harbor strong beliefs that their future goals will do something very important for them, determine something important about them, or solve some problem for them that others just don't understand. Student-athletes pursue their dreams with intense sacrifice and hard work on a daily basis without knowing what the outcome of their efforts will be. The worry and desire to know how their present athletic endeavors will be rewarded in the future (e.g., playing professionally, making business connections, or gaining fame) can create a type of existential stress that they must manage at a relatively young age.

Restrictions and Responsibilities

Student-athletes may be subject to mandatory study hours, daily monitoring of class attendance and grades, and random drug testing by both the educational institution and the NCAA. Healthy or not, athletes are also subject to an annual physical and often ongoing weight requirements. Obviously, they must also make up class work and tests missed because of travel. Additionally, student-athletes are occasionally required to assist with fundraising events and community service activities and often are required to fulfill team recruiting responsibilities.

Academic Pressures

Competition for admission to the major universities that generally have competitive athletic departments has also changed the environment for many student-athletes. The recent adoption of the NCAA's APR rules may create additional academic pressures within teams that historically have poor academic performance. In particular, data suggests that male student-athletes from basketball and football programs have in the past not been as academically prepared as other student-athletes. Grade point averages and SAT scores have risen at most universities faster than NCAA's minimum entrance requirements. Consequently, the gap between the skills of student-athletes and those of the non-athlete students has widened at many colleges. Some data further suggests that participation in athletics, in particular for men and those who are involved in basketball and football, can have a detrimental impact on student learning in general and, more specifically, in mathematics skill and reading comprehension (Pascarella, Bohr, Nora, & Terenzini, 1995; Pascarella & Terenzini, 2005).

Relationship Stress with Teammates

Although this varies from school to school, many athletic departments either mandate that athletes live together or, out of convenience, house them together. Because the schedules of athletes are generally not their own and booked so full, student-athletes often end up taking a lot of the same classes (those offered not during practice time), eating together, studying together, practicing together, traveling together, sleeping together, and socializing together. This can make for instant friends, but not necessarily one big happy family.

Negotiating Multiple Relationships with Authority Figures On and Off Campus

Student-athletes often have many more times the number of on-campus relationships to manage as non-athlete students. They often have coaches, assistant coaches, managers, athletic academic counselors, regular academic counselors associated with their majors, stipend/financial staff, trainers, equipment managers, strength and conditioning coaches, tutors, teammates, team captains, physicians, nutritionists, and occasionally sport consultants. Student-athletes often feel their behavior is monitored on a microscopic level by a variety of campus and family authority figures. Often these authority figures have conflicting views of what is best for the student-athlete. Relationships with these persons of influence, especially head coaches, can be a source of interpersonal distress. An unspoken "trust gap" frequently exists between coaches and student-athletes. Not surprisingly, many male student-athletes have become fairly skilled at managing people in positions of authority, as well as any individuals they perceive as wanting something from them. For example, student-athletes have learned to say what authority figures want to hear by using a friendly countenance while maintaining a comfortable distance.

Adjustment to College-Level Sport

Although all freshmen have to make adjustments upon their arrival, student-athletes have to make even more (Kirk & Kirk, 1996). Except for the select few, most have to adjust to a new status or hierarchy on the team (Finch & Gould, 1996). The experience of team membership as the top player in high school and potentially the coach's favorite is entirely different from being one of many—on average half of whom are better than you are. It is not uncommon for high school All-American starters to arrive on a college campus and be benched their entire freshman year and longer.

Common Personality Characteristics of Male Student-Athletes

When considering the lifestyles of male student-athletes in college, it is not surprising that they possess some common personality traits and coping strategies. Male student-athletes tend to be focused, task-oriented, and self-disciplined and to have a good work ethic. They generally have good time management skills and can concentrate when they need to. They tend to be optimistic and tenacious. They have often persevered through a variety of challenges to have attained their level of success in sport before adulthood. These strengths can be extremely helpful when working with student-athletes.

However, it is in the over-use of some of these coping strategies that athletes often create issues for themselves. Bearing down, working harder, holding on, denying or minimizing distress, and focusing on a solution are not always helpful when working through family illness, relationship problems, anxiety, and depression. Male student-athletes may also be perfectionist and somewhat stoic, restraining their emotions in fear of appearing weak or vulnerable. This is facilitated by their ability to isolate their emotions fairly effectively, particularly during competition.

Negotiating and Understanding Attention from Women

Quite often male student-athletes are not developmentally prepared to negotiate the attention given to them by females. Men's sports tend to carry the greatest status on campus. On many campuses, football is typically the greatest income producer, thus it is afforded the highest rung on the status ladder. Basketball often lines up second. All these vary by school, but the extra status associated with these two sports is in no way coincidental. Although slim, the potential to earn contracts in the millions of dollars creates a semi-god-like aura around these young men. Any connection with them carries with it perceptions of greatness by association. This is particularly evident in male-female relationships with athletes.

The expectation expressed by many male athletes is that this status will bring them the sexual and relationship opportunities they need to feel fulfilled. For the women (often not student-athletes), there is the belief that the successful male athlete will bring them the potential of financial security and status. It is not surprising that male student-athletes report that women approach them all the time in and out of class, but particularly at parties. This is experienced in an even greater way by the higher profile student-athletes, but it is present to a certain extent for male student-athletes in general. This experience is important in that it coincides with the time in which young men are typically learning to navigate romantic relationships. It is hard to imagine how this experience would not skew their perceptions of healthy intimate relationships. The privilege of extra female attention afforded to male student-athletes is tempered by the significant number of male student-athletes who are accused of date and acquaintance rape (Messner & Stevens, 2002).

First-Generation Male College Students

Student-athletes are often one of the largest groups of first-generation college students on a college campus. This has implications for student-athletes on many levels. The how-to-survive-in-college coping skills passed on by parents who attended college themselves are not available to many entering student-athletes (Sellers & Damas, 1996). Additionally, it is not unusual for the first-generation male student-athlete to be the family icon, upon whom rests the future survival of the entire family. These young men are expected not only to be the breadwinner for whatever family they create, but often also to become the primary breadwinner for their family of origin. This puts immediate and substantial pressure on male student-athletes who have been adults for only a very short while. It is almost as though they skip the developmental stage of young adulthood. These male student-athletes will be called sometimes daily by mom or sister or brother (younger and older) or aunt. They might be asked to come home on a moment's notice, or to use part of their stipend (if obtained) to help pay bills. Time is usually of the essence to these young men. They see their family struggling at home and cannot wait to relieve the strain. They may feel that they are family's only hope and that everyone is counting on them. As opposed to second- and third-generation college student-athletes, first-generation student-athletes may receive less support around the day-to-day rigors of academic work and more pressure to fulfill important family roles while fulfilling all their athletic and academic obligations on campus. Understandably, the pressure may become overwhelming. First-generation college students may be more reluctant to voluntarily utilize the services of a university counseling center based on concerns related to confidentiality and cultural norms about disclosing personal information to persons outside of the family.

Transitioning Out of Sport

Student-athletes transition out of sport for a variety of reasons, including injury, retirement, financial distress, academic and career pursuits, and so on. Often, sport has been a major source of identity for male student-athletes. As one student-athlete said in session, "What if there isn't anything else there?" Another major concern with transitioning to non-athlete status is the idea of being "average." Transitioning out of college for male student-athletes often serves as a defining moment in the young man's life (Petitpas, Brewer, & Van Raalte, 1996). Unfortunately, because of time constraints and focus on his sport, it often goes unexamined until he nears graduation. Other circumstances, such as under-recovery, burnout, or injury, often mask the underlying loss that accompanies transitioning out of their sport. Although student-athletes do not typically enter into counseling to discuss transitioning issues, such issues tend to become a salient therapeutic focus without too much prodding.

Ingroup/Outgroup Dynamics:
Racism, Sexism, and Homophobia

Players on teams that are ethnically diverse will often cite how well the team collaborates despite racial differences. Racist banter among teammates is also often considered a friendly sport in the locker room. However, it is not until the counselor starts hearing about the behavior of teammates off the field, in the residential halls and out in the community, that the intrapersonal impact of racist behavior becomes much more visible. When a teammate calls the comments into question, the male student-athlete may be considered "wimpy" and unable to take a joke. The player is expected to "be a man" and take it and then come back with a witty retort. Either no reaction or an over-reaction may have real social consequences for the male athlete on the team. It is important that the counselor have patience with the male student-athlete, and typically an established relationship is necessary to explore issues surrounding race and ethnicity. This may be even more salient if the ethnicities of the counselor and client are different.

Sport evolved as a male-dominated activity. Therefore, it is not surprising that sexism remains prevalent despite Title IX, the relatively recent growth of women's collegiate athletics, and the ascent of women's professional sports.

It is quite difficult for college-age males to negotiate some of the developmental tasks associated with sexual identity. Male college students in general need support and guidance in how to deal with the variety of perceived dangers of coming out to family and friends. For male student-athletes, often depending on the sport, the coming-out process has significantly more dangers and obstacles. Homophobia is pervasive in the world of intercollegiate athletics. Commonly heard from many of college coaches of male sports is the statement, "We are open to the gay and lesbian population. We just don't have any gay or lesbian athletes here." To the contrary, Parham (1996) suggested that both trends and clinical experience point to an increasing GLBTQ population among student-athletes. Although some sports are more GLBTQ friendly, in general, homophobia remains prevalent in male collegiate sport. From a clinical perspective, it is quite difficult to impossible to be a closeted or openly gay or bisexual male student-athlete. The stress and fear associated with coming out can delay the development of more mature intimate relationships, in addition to complicating the relationships male athletes have with their teammates and coaches.

Role of the Family

A major developmental task for college students is separation and individuation. This will get played out differently depending on a variety of factors including: student's role in the family, birth order, marital status of parents, distance from home, and cultural expectations. It is often assumed that male college students' relationships with their parents are more independent than what they actually are. In many cases, college athletes have spent significant periods of time away from their families through travels and sports camp. Frequently, the hidden dynamic is a type of symbiotic relationship that has clear signs of intense independence and dependence. For example the family, in particular the parents, of the student-athlete have usually played and may continue to play a significant role in the athlete's athletic and academic endeavors. It is not unlikely for student-athletes to initially report that their parents are very supportive and caring. This may change as therapy proceeds. They often have a wish for their parents to back off but still find a way to be supportive. It is common to hear male student-athletes say they want to find a way to accomplish their own goals, not the dreams of their parents.

Male student-athletes are often a major source of pride within the family system as their accomplishments are very visible indications of success. Consequently, in addition to all the traditional male role expectations of young men are heaped even more monumental expectations of glory and grandeur. Sometimes, in an effort to help their male children succeed in sport, mothers and fathers end up stepping in and fulfilling duties that most children would eventually have learned to do for themselves. Some male student-athletes arrive on campus having no idea how to make a meal, do laundry, shop for groceries or clothing, negotiate with teachers, etc. These behaviors lie in sharp contrast to the tough, stoic, brave, capable warriors that male student-athletes tend to represent to the rest of the world and themselves.

Physical Size and Strength

As mentioned previously, student-athletes in general have honed their ability to manage their relationships in a manner that prevents them from being overwhelmed by the demands or issues of others. Consequently, they have radar that is sensitive even to nonverbal cues. This includes reactions from others to their physical size and/or perceived degree of fitness. Typically, counselors have gathered various approaches they have found helpful in addressing racial, ethnic, and sociocultural differences between themselves and their clients. These approaches may be useful in addressing noticeable differences between the counselor and the male student-athlete in physicality as well. Used with care, humor may help initiate discussions of differences in this area. However, it is important to determine whether addressing these concerns is for the benefit of the client or the therapist. The underlying message here is that the natural reactions counselors may have about their male student-athlete's physicality can interfere with the therapeutic process by way of non-intentioned objectification of their client.

Male Socialization and Male Student-Athletes

For many boys, sport is an inextricable part of their socialization as boys and eventually as young men (Messner, 1992). After they have become identified as "athletes," their sport and their performance within their sport continue to define and challenge their masculinity at an even higher level. While they proceed with the normal developmental challenges all young men face as they become adults, male student-athletes are required to acquire and sustain a progressively higher level of toughness as the competition gets stiffer and their performance becomes increasingly more public. Participation in college sport affirms masculinity, but it is also potentially threatening, as most are eventually de-selected from participation over time. Male college athletes have to, once again, make the cut and then perform at the college sport level.

It is important for the reader to understand the intersection of male socialization and male athletes. In most cultures, including that of the United States, many of the rules of masculinity are taught to young men and reinforced by their participation in and observation of sports. It is easier to highlight how the rules of masculinity can have an adverse impact on the lives of male student-athletes. However, there is also a shadow side of these rules that can offer the counselor a window into the resiliency and strength of their male student-athletes as clients.

The rules of masculinity (David & Brannon, 1976) (i.e., be strong, "suck it up," give it your all, no pain–no gain, no sissy stuff, don't show weakness, don't cry) are all messages that are often heard on the court and field and internalized. For many boys (and men) being good at sports is a ticket into the "masculinity club," which gives a type of status that helps build a sense of belonging and importance. The rules of masculinity learned from TV, books, computer games, family, and other institutions are often reinforced and deepened through the boys' involvement in sports. Typically, but not always, the sports that involve more contact and aggressiveness (e.g., basketball, baseball, football, hockey, rugby, and soccer) send out louder and harsher messages about the rules of masculinity.

It is also essential for the reader to appreciate the more positive messages that male gender role socialization can offer male student-athletes. These may include the values and subsequent behaviors associated with high levels of commitment and dedication to improvement, loyalty to their teams and teammates, and male-male friendship and support. How to both compete against your teammate (e.g., for a position or playing time) and also to bond at the same time in a supportive and almost brotherly fashion is a lesson that many male student-athletes learn as a consequence of participating in college-level sports. Understanding and being able to communicate both the positive and adverse aspects of gender-role socialization for male college student-athletes is critical to the therapeutic process.

How Do Male Student-Athletes Get Involved in Counseling?

Perhaps the most influential factor in whether male student-athletes are referred for treatment is the relationship that the university counseling center or counselor(s) has with the athletic department. Male student-athletes are referred to counseling through several different channels. It is of paramount importance that the counselors have a strong relationship with the members of various departments within athletics, such as the trainers, student-athlete academic counselors, financial staff, coaches, nutritionists, and administrators.

Men in general have a difficult time asking for help, particularly when they feel it will be a sign of weakness. This process is only magnified by the culture of athletics, which is antithetical to the idea of seeking help from a mental health professional. Mental toughness is assumed, and the idea that a male student-athlete may need some assistance with "emotional problems" is often threatening to both the coach and the male student-athlete. College coaches may fear that counseling will soften up or take away the competitive edge of their male student-athletes if they refer them for counseling. Counselors' openly sharing their philosophy and approach with coaches and student-athletes helps gain their trust.

One area that coaches are pleased to better understand is how counselors handle student-athletes who come in to complain about their coaches. With regards to differences in personality and/or opinion between a student-athlete and a coach, counselors need to reassure coaches that the general approach is to help the student-athletes find a way to: (1) best communicate with the coach and (2) get the most out of what the coach has to offer. This dialogue will often inspire coaches to make referrals even when they suspect their relationship is contributing to the student-athletes' angst.

Other sources of referral within the larger campus are the office of student conduct or judicial affairs, student affairs, and the student health center. Because student-athletes are tracked so closely by the athletic department personnel, it is rare that a student-athlete is referred by faculty. Self-referrals to counseling are quite common at university counseling centers that have an established counselor with a positive reputation among student-athletes. The hesitation about going to see a counselor is usually mitigated by a shared positive experience from a teammate or fellow student-athlete. Self-referrals are generally more common with female student-athletes because of the socialization messages of permission to share about personal matters, such as in going to see a counselor.

Male student-athletes are sometimes referred through the office of student conduct or judicial affairs. Perhaps the most common reasons students are referred through this office are related to anger management issues, which often involve alcohol. Rarer are the referrals for academic integrity violations and allegations of sexual assault.

Sometimes a student-athlete is not officially mandated to treatment. However, there is so much pressure to comply that attendance may be considered "quasi"-voluntary. Many male student-athletes initially have unstated feelings of being mandated for counseling regardless of the circumstances. The respect for authority as well as fear of not accepting the referral gets played out in some predictable patterns. Usually the call to make an appointment is made by a staff or coach. When the student does make the call, it is usually at the last minute, with the student needing an immediate appointment to please a staff person from the athletic department. After the initial appointment, second appointments are typically cancelled or no-showed, even when the students have seemed very interested in counseling.

Over the past couple of decades, the amount of money in collegiate sport has increased tremendously, as has the celebrity status of some athletes. Not surprisingly, the size of the entourage attached to male student-athletes has also grown, as well as the financial, emotional, and social investment of the entourage. For this reason, it is extremely important for the counselor to go over confidentiality again and again and again. State licensing laws supersede NCAA laws, and therapists are not mandated reporters of NCAA rule violations. It is important for counselors to review this with the student-athlete as well. When the male student-athlete arrives on campus, the size of his support group grows significantly to include not only his parents and friends from his home town, but also college trainers, athletic department academic advisors, university academic advisors, faculty, stipend/financial staff, strength and conditioning staff, new coaches and assistant coaches, equipment managers, nutritionists, new physicians and medical specialists, NCAA compliance officers, roommates, boy/girlfriends, and so on. It is recommended that the therapist use specific examples that demonstrate how a member of the male student-athlete's support group might request information about the client and how the counselor will respond.

Counseling Male Student-Athletes

In general, athletes tend to be respectful of persons in authority, namely coaches and parents. The culture tends to be hierarchical and linear in its thinking. Initially, compliance with counseling is often experienced as something that must be done to please others. Male student-athletes have learned verbal and non-verbal behaviors that suggest they are with the "game plan" of counseling without real intent to follow through.

Trust and confidentiality are of utmost importance to student-athletes. It is for this reason that counselors need to be very clear about their boundaries for treatment. Will the counselor(s) see roommates, boyfriends/girlfriends, or teammates of current clients? Deciding on boundaries, sticking to them, and being upfront with the athletes about the policy is essential to building their trust. It is recommended that the therapist use specific examples that demonstrate how requests for information about the client will be kept in confidence.

Whatever the particular clinical orientation of the counselor, it may be helpful for the counselor to point out genuine strengths he or she observes about the client as soon as possible, preferably early on in the first session. While student-athletes are familiar with receiving direct criticism in the athletic arena, they tend to respond quite well to affirmations about their personal lives. After the counseling relationship is better established, athletes can often take more direct feedback about their behaviors. Student-athletes are quite skillful at taking this type of feedback and integrating it into their lives. It is important for counselors to know that male student-athletes have been very successful at taking direct feedback and transforming it into the healthy outlet of acquiring athletic skills.

There are several guiding principles for counseling men that are applicable to counseling male student-athletes. This next section will highlight approaches to counseling men that can be utilized with male student-athletes.

Counseling Men and Counseling Male Student-Athletes

Approaching counseling with a male student-athlete means taking into consideration both his cultural background as a male and his cultural background as a student-athlete. Obviously, other cultural factors such as race, ethnicity, socioeconomic status, family culture, sexual orientation, academic class, and type of sport are also essential factors to consider.

Being in counseling is both a challenge and an opportunity for male college student-athletes. Masculinity is a focal organizing principle for all aspects of a man's life and is an influential contributor to not only why (or why not) a man is in psychotherapy, but also how he "does" psychotherapy and the expectations he has for therapy outcomes (Englar-Carlson, 2006). Masculinity-sensitive counseling interventions and therapeutic style are critical to the engagement and ultimate success of psychotherapy with male clients. The examination of the differential process of therapy and flexibility of interventions for men is essential (Mintz & O'Neil, 1990).

Over the past two decades researchers and practitioners have developed models for counseling men (Brooks & Good 2001; Englar-Carlson & Stevens 2006; Scher, Stevens, Good, & Eichenfield, 1987; Stevens, 2006). These guidelines or "best practices" can be useful to counselors of male student-athletes. The core of these guidelines includes the importance of building a connection and choosing the appropriate intervention strategy.

Building a Connection with Male Clients

Recognize, acknowledge, and affirm gently the difficulty that men have for entering and being in counseling. It is well documented that men initially experience going to therapy as extremely difficult and will avoid going at almost any cost. Seeking psychological help is usually the last resort (Rabinowitz, 2002). Men often believe they are being coerced into therapy (e.g., by a spouse, employer, or the law) and enter the counseling room with a great deal of resentment. Often men experience going to therapy with shame and fear (Levant, 1997; Park, 2006). Asking for help implies weakness and a failure to be self-sufficient. Men do not want to feel dependent on the therapist. Confronting a man's fears of being in therapy too strongly may actually cause the man to flee.

Help the client save "masculine face." It is important for counselors to communicate their genuine respect for the male student-athlete coming into therapy. Reflecting and contextualizing coming to therapy as a brave, courageous, and honorable behavior is congruent with traditional male socialization (Park, 2006). For many male student-athletes, acceptance as a man is needed before progressing with treatment.

Educate the male student-athlete up front about the process of therapy. Check out his assumptions of what will be expected of him as a client. Clarify your role as the therapist. Explain how one practices psychotherapy. Most male student-athletes don't know how the therapy process works and worry that the therapist will be judgmental or will discover their weaknesses (Stevens, 2006). Male clients often have a fear of not being a "good enough" client. Men perceive therapy as a place where they will need to become emotional. Men often do not feel ready or equipped to do what they believe they will be asked to do in a traditional therapy setting. Most men believe they will be expected to be strong, hide their vulnerability, and not cry in therapy. The mystery and fear of what happens in therapy are potentially present for all clients, but they are often more salient issues for male clients. It is important to understand that because of male gender-role socialization, men are often quite uncomfortable with "just being" with a problem. Often male student-athletes expect and hope for immediate results from therapy.

Be patient. It is important for counselors to be patient and understanding of the walls men have erected if they are to be let inside (Rabinowitz, 2006). Men may slam their emotional doors and leave therapy if confrontation is used too early (Rabinowitz, 2006). Male student-athletes often need to start therapy slow and resist sharing intimate personal details and feelings up front. Rituals of initial engagement through more traditional masculine means are often needed.

Use a therapy language and approach that is congruent with your client's gender role identity. Words substituted for psychotherapy, such as consultation, meeting, or discussion, may be more in line and provide a better way to describe how traditional male student-athletes may want to view their involvement in the process (Robertson, 2006). Feeling words and other types of relational language that psychologists are typically trained to use are often resisted by traditionally trained male therapists. It is important for psychologists to recognize the relational style of men in contrast to their conception of how therapy should proceed (Kiselica, 2006). Creating a male-friendly psychotherapeutic process is critical to the success of treatment.

Be genuine and real. Male clients may want to be treated in ways that feel congruent with their masculine socialization. This can be accomplished by listening carefully and projecting warmth without appearing overly sympathetic (Smart, 2006). Male clients often trust and are more engaged in treatment when they experience their psychologists as "real human" beings, and not professionally detached.

Choosing an Intervention Strategy for the Male Student-Athlete

It is critical that counselors have an understanding of the significant impact that male socialization has on the lives of their clients. Furthermore, it is important to realize the uniqueness of each male student-athlete, as the counselor decides on the types of clinical interventions that will best help that particular male client. Traditional men's socialization and gender-role conflict theories suggest that men are more comfortable and trained to have instrumental and problem-solving ways of addressing mental health issues. Therefore, cognitive and behavioral interventions, at least in the beginning of treatment, may offer the best results in terms of engagement and increase the likelihood that the male client will continue in treatment. According to Mahalik (2001), men who experienced less gender-role conflict did not have a preference for either an emotionally based or a cognitively based type of treatment. Men who had higher levels of gender-role conflict did show a preference for more cognitively based treatments. As the therapeutic comfort level is developed, the bridging to more interpersonal and feelings-oriented interventions will most likely be met with less resistance and can offer positive psychotherapeutic experience. Therapy with men is about both doing and being. Too much being will be too frustrating for the male student-athlete, and too much doing will not give him an opportunity to learn about his inner world and trust that examining this part of him will produce positive results (Rabinowitz, 2006).

Case Vignettes

The final part of the chapter will employ case vignettes as a way to illustrate some of the theoretical concepts discussed thus far. These vignettes are composites of male student-athletes that the authors have counseled at different universities over the past two decades. Each case vignette will provide the reader an opportunity to enter into the counseling room and view how the counselor conceptualized, experienced, and clinically intervened with his or her client.

Case of James

James is a 20-year-old African-American sophomore majoring in communications. He is on an athletic scholarship and plays football at an academically competitive and major public Division I university. He is red shirting this year. He moved more than 1,500 miles to come to the university. He was raised by his mother and grandmother in a middle-class neighborhood. He has excelled in sports his entire life. His athletic accomplishments have been noticed since the seventh grade. Academically, he is an average student. He has dreams of becoming a professional football player. Last year, he had a significant amount of playing time, and he was projected to be a starter for the upcoming year. James had a season- and possible career-ending injury his second week of spring training. His coaches have noticed he has been unusually withdrawn from his teammates. There are rumors he has been drinking quite often. James is referred to counseling.

As expected, James was reluctant to come to counseling. After being "nagged" by his assistant coach and head athletic trainer, he made an appointment. Initially the counselor was aware of several important clinical dynamics that needed to be addressed. James was not ready to be in counseling. He had never been in counseling before. Most of his life, he went to a family member (usually his grandmother or a friend's father) to discuss personal issues. James knew how to appear as if he were interested in counseling. Over the years James had become an expert at appeasing adult authority figures. The first task of the counselor was to find an inroad with James in terms of acknowledging the difficulty of coming into counseling and talking with a stranger about very personal issues. The counselor (a male) let James know everything he had heard about the nature of why he was being encouraged to come to counseling. The counselor placed extra emphasis on the confidentiality of the session. While discussing the "gossip mill" nature of athletic teams and departments, the counselor shared with James the details about how he intended to keep confidentiality, even when the counselor would be challenged by the athletic department to share information. The counselor also shared in some detail about the nature of counseling—how counseling might work and the possible benefits and difficulties associated with being in counseling. Male student-athletes, in particular, are appreciative of straight talk about counseling and explanations that "demystify" the process. They are familiar with hearing about game plans and respond to a type of linear explanation of counseling.

In the first session, James did share with the counselor that he was not really interested in counseling and that he did not see how it would benefit him. James was consumed with worries about his season and possible career-ending injury. The counselor asked James what kind of support he was getting. At first, he shrugged it off and said, "Everyone is being cool with me." The counselor noticed a subtle discomfort in James' eyes. Rather than increase the discomfort, the counselor asked James' permission to find out a little more about the nature of the injury. The timing of confrontational interventions is quite critical. The counselor assumed that James was not comfortable enough to share some of the disappointment he may have felt in terms of the type of support he was receiving. The counselor was aware that, in the sports world, "the game must go on." It is quite common for injured athletes to get lots of attention from their coaches and teammates for a short period of time after the injury. When the attention starts to fade, the student-athlete often is left with some resentment.

Gently, the counselor asked about the injury, when and how it happened, staying curious about the details. James was very comfortable talking about the details of his injury. The comfort of the conversation allowed the counselor to find out more about James in terms of his athletic background and history, how he had dealt with other injuries, the pride he had felt as an athlete, and his dreams and hopes for the future. The counselor aligned with James in terms of the hopes he had for returning to football next year and being stronger than before.

The counselor acknowledged the ease and enthusiasm with which James shared his story. It was very clear to the counselor that athletics had been a huge part of James' life and how frightened he was at the prospect of his dreams being broken. The counselor did not address the drinking rumors or James' withdrawal from the team. James was asked if he would like to come back and talk some more. He said yes and an appointment was made for the following week. James did not show.

The counselor was disappointed that James did not show, but was not surprised. A true connection was felt during the first session. Yet a positive first connection does not always mean a return visit. James' ambivalence and unfamiliarity with counseling seemed to have spoken louder than the connection.

This counselor typically waits a few days after the no-show of a student-athlete and then makes a "reach-out" call. James answered his cell phone and apologetically said he had forgotten about the appointment and he was meaning to call, wanting to reschedule. Another appointment was made for the following week, and James came five minutes late for that appointment. After some small talk, which is often a comfortable way to start out the session with a male student-athlete, the counselor asked James if he had any particular reactions to the first session. The counselor also asked if anyone from the athletic department had asked him about the appointment.

The counselor was struggling with how to address both the ambivalence and desire to come to counseling. James had no obligation to come back for another appointment. The counselor decided to ask James what it was like to sit out in the waiting room with other students. James was quite noticeable as a football player, both in terms of his size and his picture having been in the school and local papers on numerous occasions. The counselor said to James that it might feel strange being noticed in the waiting room of the counseling center. The counselor mentioned casually that "most students waiting cannot be recognized like you." James acknowledged that he was used to getting lots of attention wherever he went, but usually the attention was positive. He was wondering what other students were thinking of his going to counseling. This was a gigantic acknowledgment on James' part. The counselor made mention, without too much enthusiasm, how impressed he was with James' willingness to talk about his vulnerability. This led to a conversation about how James is much more comfortable being vulnerable with females than with men. This, in turn, led to a discussion about his relationship with his father. James was ready to share his story, and the counselor was very interested in listening. James talked freely about how he did not really know his father and up until recently had not had much contact with him. He was quite bitter at his father about what he experienced as his father's irresponsible behavior, saying that his father was unable to "get his life together." Generally speaking, male clients have easy access to their feelings and memories and have a willingness to talk about their relationships with their fathers. James was no exception. Having a male counselor may also have been a condition that allowed for the father material to emerge without much resistance. The counselor was appreciative and a little surprised about James' openness in just the second meeting. The counselor also was aware that to be "too loud" in acknowledging James' openness in session could result in pushing him away.

James came to the next session on time. He was in the middle of finals and seemed distracted. The counselor also knew that James was scheduled for major surgery after his finals. James was planning to have his surgery at a local hospital and, when physically ready, he would fly back home for recovery and physical therapy. James did not want to stay at school during the summer.

The session started out slow with some small talk again. The counselor asked him if there was anything in particular he wanted to talk about that day. James was hesitant at first and then disclosed if he was unable to play football again he may not return to school. James had not told anyone about this except his mother. Coaches, trainers, teammates, and friends were all assuming he would go home for the summer, recover, and return to school. James discussed how he felt subtle pressure to return to school; nobody was talking with him about the possibility of the surgery not being successful. Although James enjoyed the optimism from his teammates and coaches, he felt he did not have permission to talk openly about the "what ifs" of the situation. The counselor asked James directly if he would like to feel more freedom to talk about the "what ifs" and what he would like to say to his teammates and coaches. The counselor gave permission for James to speak up about his "secret" feelings and thoughts in session without the expectation that he actually say anything to his coaches and teammates. James agreed and shared quite articulately a variety of plans he had been thinking about in the event his surgery did not work out.

The session was close to the end, and the counselor acknowledged that it might be the last time they would meet. James was quite appreciative of the sessions. He told his counselor he felt a sense of relief to be able to talk about his life without worrying about being evaluated. He acknowledged that he was surprised how open he was considering that he had really not thought counseling was going to be helpful. Although his future remained as uncertain as the day he had come to counseling, James appeared to benefit from being treated as a "real" person and not just a student-athlete.

Commentary on the Case of James

James' case illustrates many of the classic dilemmas and dynamics of working therapeutically with male student-athletes. As is common with men in general, they often do not seek medical or mental health services without encouragement and/or prodding from others. After they have taken the step to seek services, skepticism tends to remain. In this case, patience with the process part of psychotherapy, psychoeducation, and a willingness to have a "real" relationship (as opposed to strictly a therapeutic one), allowed the male student-athlete to feel comfortable enough with the counselor to acknowledge and address both old and new concerns—those regarding his feelings about his dad and those regarding his potentially career-ending injury—relatively quickly, in about three sessions. To a non-athlete counselor, discussion about the details around one's participation in sport may seem relatively trivial. However, for the male student-athlete, this may be one of the most sensitive and intimate disclosures they make in session. A client's dialogue about his participation in sport may touch upon his purpose and meaning in life, his hopes for the future, issues of gender identity, and possibly the biggest part of his identity to date, namely that of a student-athlete.

Athletic culture is antithetical to seeking mental health help; consequently, student-athletes have one of the highest no-show rates of any clinical population. At times, they are simply overwhelmed by the demands of their schedule. It is important for counselors to have a little more flexibility in their interpretations of no-shows. Often, a "reach-out" call without an agenda, but rather just to "check in," is received very favorably by student-athletes. If they are able to perceive that the counselor has no agenda with regard to their sport performance, but rather concern for them as people, they often find it very refreshing and respond favorably by returning to treatment. At other times, they are very good at acting on suggestion and may only return when they get stuck again. This kind of flexibility often leads to sustained long-term treatment in the end.

Another dynamic some counselors might find surprising is how student-athletes, particularly male student-athletes, are generally extremely hesitant to discuss any doubts about their sport participation with their teammates. Although they may have close bonds with their teammates and be able to discuss a host of topics with some, very few athletes are willing to share openly doubts they have about their physical ability (injury-related or not) and the possibility of retirement. It is very important for counselors not to get overly dramatic in their empathic responses to either of these situations. Additionally, it is crucial that, no matter what direction the male student-athlete seems to be leaning, no assumptions are made. It is extremely helpful for the counselor to facilitate opening the dialogue so that the athlete feels as free as possible at that time to discuss any and all possibilities, but to be very careful not to make any conclusions or push for any decisions from the client. Males are often great problem solvers, and athletes are often great at taking action. It is indeed the process part of decision making that is the most difficult for male student-athletes, and counselors may help facilitate the process as long as they remain patient and sensitive to the pushes and pulls of their male student-athlete clients.

Case of Kevin

Kevin is a 20-year-old European-American male in his junior year, majoring in psychology. He is a member of the varsity swimming team at a highly competitive and small, private, Division I university. The university is not known to be academically difficult. He is on a 50 percent athletic scholarship. Kevin comes from an intact family living 200 miles away. His family has a significant history of alcohol abuse. Kevin's coaches feel he has not been swimming to his ability, and he has not lived up to their expectations in terms of his impact on the team. Kevin is thinking about quitting the team and has been referred to counseling.

Kevin had been in counseling once before during high school, briefly, to talk about his reaction to family conflict around his father's drinking. He attended two sessions with the high school counselor, who was a female. Although he reported feeling some relief in talking with someone, he felt the sessions were basically pretty useless. He had the same expectations for this therapy and was only coming in to get the coach off his back and to give himself some more time to decide what to do.

The counselor met him the waiting room and shook his hand after he extended his hand to greet the counselor. Kevin was about 6'4" with broad shoulders and a long muscular physique that was apparent even under loose athletic clothing. For the female counselor unaccustomed to being around athletes, beginning treatment with a male student-athlete who may be physically much larger than she is may be daunting. It is important to consider potential counter-transference reactions before the initial intake. Male student-athletes are, of course, very attuned to their bodies and are as aware of differences in body size as the potentially much smaller female counselor might be. Honest reflection of differences in size or stature, especially when they are significant, may help keep the relationship real for the male student-athlete. In this case, the counselor (a female) was tall and medium/large in stature and accustomed to working with athletes.

Although Kevin did not appear very anxious about coming to therapy, his demeanor was slightly detached and his mood seemed a little hopeless. His personality was typically pleasant and friendly with some cautiousness around his relationships. Kevin reported that he had a few close male friends (one from high school and two he made since attending university) in whom he confided some of what he was feeling. Otherwise, he did not disclose his true feelings and problems to anyone, including his parents. He got along well with his teammates by staying away from interpersonal conflict and maintaining a friendly countenance but an otherwise closed private or inner world.

The first consideration for the counselor was to find a way of connecting with the client that might give him hope. The counselor allowed the client some room for inquiry into the tenure of her work at the university, which seemed of some interest to him. Male student-athletes seem to prefer working with someone with whom they feel they are having a real relationship (i.e., versus strictly a professional one). The counselor quickly moved the discussion, however, to some general chitchat around athletics that let the client experience a little of the counselor's personality and understanding of sport dynamics. The counselor then gently suggested that it must be frustrating to be asked to come in for counseling after having had a less-than-successful experience in the past. This resulted in Kevin further disclosing that he had also attended one family intervention session around his father's drinking, which "did absolutely nothing" to change his father's behavior, except to make his father upset with everyone for a while. The client agreed verbally and non-verbally with the counselor about his frustration. He then quickly regrouped to let the counselor know that he was not assuming it would be the same with her. In keeping with the client's ability to manage yet another relationship in his life, the client was sensitive to appearing uninterested in or disrespectful an authority figure at least in the moment. This allowed him to avoid confrontation in his relationships that he was only too familiar with, which may have resulted in threats from coaches around lack of compliance or in lectures of the "I'm only thinking of your own good" type from parents and/or other athletic department support staff.

The counselor then acknowledged Kevin's courage and open-mindedness in his choice to come in, despite the fact that he felt quite pressured. Male student-athletes often end up in counseling after some pressure from persons in authority. This often makes them feel powerless and resentful, negates the choice involved despite the pressure, and makes coming in for treatment seem like anything but self-care. In addition, student-athletes often feel their schedules are so packed that they have no flexibility in their time for anything outside of athletics and academics. Helping them experience their day-to-day lives more in terms of choices and alternatives also helps them take more responsibility for their emotional lives and personal responsibilities.

Next, the counselor reviewed her orientation to therapy as a sort of team approach, in which the counselor would be walking or playing next to him in a manner that was open and in no way resembling a "guess what the therapist is thinking" type experience. Anything and everything would be appropriate to discuss in the office. However, what *would* be addressed was only what Kevin was ready and willing to discuss. Confidentiality boundaries were reviewed and examples of how that might be challenged were included.

Inquiry as to why he thought his coaches referred him to counseling led to a discussion of his swimming performance. Following his lead to stick to the facts allowed Kevin to present the problem in a more removed manner that felt more like a professional consultation. This gave him the control over the session that he needed in order to feel comfortable talking about himself. The counselor was patient, and Kevin eventually acknowledged that he had been holding on to serious doubts as to whether he would ever be able to improve upon his personal best swimming times (some from his senior year in high school and some achieved as a freshman in college). The counselor asked him how it had been to hold on to this thought for all this time. He said it had been exhausting, "but you just deal." He was letting the counselor know that a momentary acknowledgment around these feelings was acceptable, but that he was not ready to sit with them at this point. This created an opportunity for initial inquiry into his high school experience and how he had coped with adversity and uncertainty in the past, with the goal of illustrating his emotional competency and strength.

During the session, it was revealed that he had a younger sister who was also a swimmer. They were close, and she was emerging as a very strong sprinter. He felt she had more natural talent than he did. Kevin then confided that he was afraid that he might have already reached his peak. This was a huge admission on his part. He knew the counselor had an athletic background, and he asked how she knew when she had reached her peak. Again, he revealed a closely held secret, but the quickness of the follow-up question let the counselor know that he was not ready to delve too deeply into how it felt to hold on to this uncertainty. Some brief psychoeducation around mental versus physical peaks followed, including the idea that mental peaks often closely reflect how an athlete's values and interests naturally change with time. The counselor decided to be patient and pursue a discussion around what peaking physically meant to him at another opportunity. (This would be an important discussion in that it would serve to de-shame the idea that a physical peak for excellence in a particular sport somehow translated into his being a lesser man.) The counselor was a little nervous about Kevin feeling as though she was putting him off by not answering how she knew when she had peaked, but it was not appropriate for the counselor to answer this question about her own experience at that time.

The above discussion also allowed for the client to experience the clinician as both a female and a counselor. Due to the homophobic culture of sport and masculinity, the female counselor may find that a positive transference develops earlier with some male student-athletes than it might otherwise with a male therapist. Additionally, issues with male authority figures that may come into play in male-male matches do not have to be worked through in male-female client-therapist matches. Early positive transference is perhaps more likely in cases in which the male student-athlete is struggling with what he perceives to be things that a woman would understand better. Kevin may have associated sharing his intimate thoughts with a female as more fitting or permissible and less threatening with respect to any internalized homophobic fears. Seeing the therapist as a counselor, Kevin would have experienced the opportunity to attend to his concerns with *his* objectives in mind and not just with a therapist's intent to make him talk about his feelings, which would only contribute to his feeling insecure and incompetent in the counseling setting.

The discussion about his high school experience revealed that earlier in his career he had overcome fears around his performance after a shoulder injury. He reported staying very close to his teammates and coach during his recovery and doing some of his rehab on the pool deck while the rest of the team was in the water. This helped him feel like he

was part of the team despite the fact that he had to refrain from training for more than a month. During his rehabilitation, Kevin was at
home more often due to his inability to practice. It was during this time
that he became more aware of his father's regular drinking and how it
affected the rest of the family. Although he found himself to be more
disappointed in his father than ever before, Kevin coped by spending
more time with his mother and sister. This information opened up an
opportunity for the counselor to give him encouragement for using
some healthy, positive coping strategies in the face of two challenging
situations. In addition, it suggested that he was indeed emotionally
pretty strong in managing two problematic situations at the same time.
The counselor spent some time processing these two points with Kevin,
allowing the experience of his affect in the first session to be one of
pride and competence in his handling of his emotional life.

The first session ended with the counselor asking the client what he
thought about the session and whether he felt it had addressed any of
his concerns. He reflected that it was not at all like his previous counseling experience in that there was more back-and-forth dialogue. Not
surprisingly, Kevin stated that he felt he had the opportunity to address
some of his concerns; however, that was anticipated, as he was perhaps
still trying to "manage" yet another person in authority in his life. He decided to come in for another consultation and made an appointment
for the next week.

A couple of hours before the next session, Kevin left a message to can-
cel the appointment. He had forgotten he would be traveling. A return
call from the counselor resulted in his rescheduling again for the next
week.

Kevin showed up on time for the next session. He no longer extended
his hand for a shake. His body language was suggestive of some apathy.
He seemed less guarded. He apologized for the last-minute cancellation
the prior week. The counselor felt his apology was more a reflection of
his respect for authority than of connection at this point. Fairly quickly
into the beginning of the session, Kevin acknowledged feeling unmotivated to do much of anything that week. He attributed this to his continuing to feel frustrated about whether or not to quit swimming. He
denied feeling sad or depressed. He was frowning and looked pensive.
The counselor normalized his frustration, especially given the fact that

he had already dedicated a decade of his life to the sport. Because of his demeanor, combined with the sleep difficulties and poor appetite he reported, the counselor was considering a diagnosis of a depressive episode. The counselor's experience had led her to observe depression manifesting more as emotional lability in the male student-athlete than a consistent or regular feeling of sadness. Student-athletes believe they can will themselves into almost any frame of mind, thus trying harder to "just snap out of it." A male student-athlete will sometimes exert great effort to change his attitude. This effort results in moments that seem to go really well or in subjective happiness that abruptly changes to irritation or moodiness, especially in men, around seemingly small issues.

Kevin reported feeling pressure from his coaches. He didn't feel like going to class and he avoided socializing with the team over the weekend because he felt guilty about possibly wanting to quit. The counselor acknowledged how much energy it took to maintain his rigorous schedule even when things were going well. It therefore made sense that he should be somewhat low on energy given his uncertainty about what he was doing. Kevin agreed. The counselor stated that although she believed he had a lot of gifts other than swimming (that had yet to be explored), it would only be natural for him to be having a significant reaction to his dilemma given his history as a nationally ranked swimmer. He nodded his head and seemed to relax a little. The client worried about being perceived as a "quitter" by his teammates if he were to decide to stop swimming. The counselor asked what he considered "a quitter" and Kevin answered typically with "someone who quits." The counselor gave some different scenarios to explore this idea further. The main point was to differentiate between (1) individuals who go through life trying a succession of different sports and giving up as soon as they get difficult and (2) a committed athlete who had demonstrated his dedication by participating in a sport for more than 10 years, including some ups and downs.

When an athlete of this caliber decides that he has had enough, it is "retirement." This is an important reframe and opens the dialogue for a frank discussion around retirement. Ending his participation in sport no longer remains a forbidden topic. It is in the process of feeling free to explore all alternatives without shame that student-athletes are able to better understand their participation in sport. It is important for the counselor not to make any assumptions about where the athlete is going from this point. Any indication that the counselor believes the student-athlete is on his way to retirement will immediately close this door and limit a very important discussion to come, namely what it means to him as a person and as a man to be an elite athlete. This was simply a platform from which to have an open and honest conversation about all the possibilities open to Kevin at the time.

The counselor asked Kevin how he felt about what they had talked about so far. He said it made sense. Kevin stated that he agreed with the counselor, but that his friends would still perceive him to be quitting and not very tough if he decided to retire. This was a very honest statement that suggested to the counselor that a connection was in the works. He wasn't just trying to appease the counselor so much anymore.

Kevin was fixated on trying to figure out how to determine whether he should continue to swim or not. The counselor asked him what he liked about competitive swimming. Without hesitation Kevin replied that what he liked most at the moment were his friends on the team. Although he was open with only a few teammates, his relationships with most of his teammates were enjoyable and important to him at university.

Camaraderie is important in the socialization of men and athletes. However, this does not necessarily include the idea of sharing their feelings in relationships. Male student-athletes may fear being rejected or being perceived as weak if they open up emotionally to another teammate. An added dose of homophobia in the culture of athletics heightens any concerns of being seen as too close to another male friend. A few male athletes get around this by maintaining a certain silence about their closest male relationships. Two or three male student-athletes may have a very close bond, but rarely walk or ride to practice together. From all public appearances, they are nothing more than teammates in how they relate on the field or pool deck or court. However, they may quietly spend a significant amount of time together unbeknownst to much of the team.

Kevin further disclosed that he liked belonging to a specific group on campus. As is often the case with male student-athletes, it was clear that sport participation was not the only issue under consideration, but his identity was feeling threatened as well. This is an important issue for student-athletes as they consider retirement, that is, can I continue to identify myself as an athlete if I am no longer participating in the sport?

From there, the counselor took an athletic history in a low-key manner. Family dynamics come up readily when the counselor takes a thorough *athletic* history. This discussion may also be a useful springboard for helping student-athletes discern healthy boundaries in relationships. However, it was important at this point to continue this discussion with the client's agenda in mind. The counselor felt that if she got off track by commenting on family dynamics at this time, the client's concern about how to figure out whether or not to retire would go unaddressed. Failing to respect the client's request for assistance with his concern at this time might create more frustration for the client in the immediate future, and he might become disillusioned about the usefulness of the therapy process as well.

Here and there Kevin would refer back to his concerns about what others would think of him should he decide to quit. He would fidget in his seat and look down at the floor. Free association allowed him to identify that he thought other teammates would think he was "a wimp" or "a girl" or "a bitch" for not finishing out the season or even for retiring before the end of his senior year. He didn't even flinch when reporting this to the counselor. To him, it was just the way it was. The female counselor may hear misogynistic comments from male student-athletes who at times fail to connect that these statements make reference to the female counselor as well. To "take it like a man" may reflect feelings of power that athletes seek in order to gain a sense of confidence in their sporting endeavors. "You're acting like a girl" may be code for a sense of powerlessness that is loath to the male student-athlete because it suggests that they may not be powerful enough gain victory over their opponents. Indeed these comments may be less reflective to the male student-athlete of the powerless status of women in society, but may be important in understanding the male student-athlete client's environment and internalized sense of control and efficacy in the world.

The session ended with Kevin still deep in thought. He stated that the discussion had gotten him thinking and he needed to think some more. He felt he had a little bit of direction at least for the next week or so.

It is not surprising that issues related to purpose and meaning in sport arise "in season." It is during the beginning of the most competitive part of student-athletes' season that the demands and intensity of sport increase, sometimes dramatically. It is at this time that their drive and confidence assist them the most. When these motivators are missing or starting to wane, it is an unfamiliar and scary experience. In addition, the intensity of the season presses student-athletes just enough to put them in crisis as they are striving to manage and hide their uncertainties about their ongoing participation.

The third session began with the counselor asking Kevin what he thought about the last session. Kevin reported that the last session had gotten him thinking a lot about his athletic career and his family. On the one hand, he was starting to realize how much his parents had sacrificed to support him, from all the traveling they had done to watch him compete to the all the money they had spent. On the other hand, he felt that they were perhaps overly concerned with his performance, not at all unlike his present coach. Kevin reported that his father was usually working and/or traveling for his work. His dad was not very communicative, but he went to every one of Kevin's meets. They talked almost exclusively about sports—Kevin's swimming or whatever professional sport was in season. He believed in hard work and getting the job done—whether it was work or sports. Once or twice, Kevin's father had shown up to an evening final intoxicated. His father had called out in the stands inappropriately and Kevin had felt furious and humiliated. Congruent with the dictates of masculinity in society, it seemed easier for Kevin to talk about his anger toward his dad than his disappointment at his dad's not being more emotionally available to him.

Kevin felt he had a slightly closer relationship with his mother, whom he described as more emotional but also more critical. She was very responsible, but critical of his father and of his drinking. It would have been a mistake for this counselor to assume that Kevin's disclosure about his parents was an invitation to further scrutinize his relationships with his parents. Although he had his complaints, he was still very attached to them and had experienced what he believed to be their honest affection and love for him. When the counselor asked him how this new understanding of his parents related to his swimming career, he credited his parents with having taught him self-discipline. He seemed to be setting a limit for the moment. He still looked frustrated and the counselor reflected this observation back to him. He shrugged his shoulders and said, "So what? I just need to figure out what to do."

Counselors must be careful not to immediately interpret emotional restraint as resistance. As mentioned above, male student-athletes have a lot of justification for guarding their emotions closely. As the therapist is able to help them redefine strength in broader terms that include room for acknowledging their emotional lives, male student-athletes may come to believe that there is strength in acknowledging their affect. A little psychoeducation around the usefulness of identifying his emotional needs may feel empowering to the male student-athlete as he sets his problem-solving skills to coping strategies that better fit those needs. This is especially true if the counselor has helped point out even small examples of how emotionally competent the male student-athlete already is. The counselor may be instrumental at this point in treatment by encouraging the male student-athlete to come up with strategies that help him become someone responsible for his emotional life rather than a victim of it, which would otherwise make him feel out of control. In essence, this technique formulates a new template for "controlling my feelings" that the male student-athlete may find more in line with his identity as a strong, conscientious man who can withstand pressure and absorb pain.

The counselor asked Kevin if he had thought about talking to his parents about his feelings. Kevin shook his head and stated that he thought his parents would be disappointed in him if he retired before the end of his senior year. He mentioned that his dad was very quiet and worked to hold back his irritation after Kevin's swims that did not go so well. The counselor asked what that was like for Kevin, and he replied, "I'm used to it." Although Kevin was able to maintain himself effectively on his own, he was struggling with why he was not able to control his feelings and with what to do about them. He eventually lamented that he wished he was able to talk to his dad about his dilemma because his dad understood his sport really well, but he was sure that his dad would just tell him to tough it out until he graduated. Kevin clearly experienced this as a loss. Kevin's worries about his teammates viewing him as unmanly if he were to retire were particularly troubling to him. The counselor believed that Kevin longed to have his father affirm his masculinity whatever his decision about his swimming career.

The counselor felt that what Kevin was unable to get clarity about, let alone express, was that his parents were so focused on teaching him what he *should* do that he wasn't sure his continued participation in sport was what he *wanted* to do. This confusion was clouding his ability to understand what he wanted to do and affecting his performance.

Over the next couple of sessions, the counselor gradually encouraged Kevin to take stock of his feelings at least briefly, but more regularly to help sort out what he might want to do about this season. He was able to identify that he really loved the activity around his sport, the physicality, the jocularity during practice, and the camaraderie. Kevin decided that he wanted to finish this season and would worry about next year after the NCAA championships. The counselor discussed the difference between a child athletic career and an adult athletic career, plateaus, and so on. This helped Kevin find some peace with respect to his performances of late, while allowing him to discern how his competitive swimming related to his values and identities as a man and as an athlete. At this point in treatment, Kevin really began to relax with the counselor and his sense of humor emerged. He once again made some inquiries about the counselor. The counselor answered some questions, and she interpreted this inquiry as an attempt to connect more deeply with the counselor.

Kevin's preoccupation about whether he had reached his peak had led to tremendous pre-event performance anxiety, which the counselor helped him address with some relaxation exercises and mental imagery strategies. In addition, he was encouraged to try to be a little more open with his two closest friends on the team (who did not swim his events) since he didn't feel he could go to his father at that time. Treatment ended just before division championships when both his athletic and academic schedules were becoming all consuming. He and the counselor agreed he would call during the summer if he was still struggling and/or wanted to pursue some of his thoughts further. He thanked the counselor and again offered her his hand.

Commentary on the Case of Kevin

This case illustrates an integrative and flexible approach by the counselor. Attention to relationship building, psychoeducational interventions, and process comments seemed to be quite effective. Kevin presented with frustration and feelings of confusion and burn-out about his swimming career. The counselor helped Kevin discover that his feelings and perceptions about his current situation had roots in his relationship with his father, his perceptions of masculinity, and his fear of disappointing others. Kevin's case also illustrates some critical dynamics for work by a female counselor and a male client. The awareness that the physical size and strength of the male client may have an impact on the counselor is essential to recognize, even if it never is acknowledged in session. It was clear from the interactions that this particular female counselor had a strong sports history and displayed a level of comfort with her client. Male and female counselors who are not accustomed to being around male athletes are encouraged to notice their personal reactions to the size and strength of their clients and the potential impact that has on their clinical work.

The counselor discussed the importance of the male student-athlete having a sense of the "real relationship" between the counselor and client. This seems particularly important with male student-athletes. There seems to be a no-nonsense type of attitude in sports, and counselors who use too much of a "therapy language" and attention to emotions may turn off their clients who are male student-athletes. The "realness" of the relationship that is felt by the client often translates into increased trust and acceptance, cornerstones of effective intervention. Often counselors are trained to worry about boundary crossings and giving clients the wrong message about the client-counselor relationship. In this case, the counselor was sophisticated enough to know how to walk a rather fine line with Kevin, allowing him to sense the counselor as a person, without compromising the professional nature of the relationship. The counselor, by her actions, was skillful in reducing conceptions that Kevin experienced in therapy as a child and brought to his current work.

The counselor's disclosure of how she approaches doing therapy appeared to be quite beneficial in increasing trust and confidence in the process. Male clients often seem to worry about losing a sense of control in the therapy process. Kevin appeared uncertain as to what would be expected of him in therapy. Knowing that student-athletes are familiar with taking direction and having situations explained, the counselor reduced Kevin's worries and increased his confidence that he would be able to benefit from counseling, by "breaking down" the process of therapy. The counselor showed much patience in providing Kevin a place to struggle with a major life decision about whether or not to continue with his college swimming career. The counselor allowed Kevin to examine and voice the variety of internal and external pushes and pulls he was experiencing around this major decision. She respected Kevin's intense focus on making a decision and did not rush him. As well, the counselor did not take the "bait" that student-athletes often put to counselors, in terms of giving advice. The counselor's knowledge of the culture of male college sports was useful in terms of her ability to understand the context and not personalize the sexist language her male client used when describing what his teammates would say about him if he were to leave the team.

The case also illustrates the roles that various males play in the development and affirmation of a young man's masculinity through sports. This was particularly clear as Kevin described his relationship with his father and potentially his coach. The counselor was skillful in helping Kevin keep the options open about his decision and helped him reframe the usage of the word "quit" to the concept of retirement. Very often, elite male athletes are socialized to excel through the fear of disappointing others, and their internalized voice is often extremely critical. The counselor in Kevin's case was able to bring a nice balance of not pressuring Kevin to stray too far from his cultural roots, while at the same time offering realistic relief valves for him to consider.

Conclusion

This chapter has reviewed many of the unique issues of college male student-athletes. The intersection of gender-role socialization with the culture of male college sports has been a central conceptualizing principle of this chapter. Counseling male college student-athletes can evoke some unique reactions on the part of the counselor. Self-awareness, knowledge of the culture of college sports, and knowledge of the culture of men are essential components of working effectively with male student-athletes. In the near future the authors anticipate a significant increase in the acceptance and usage of counseling services by athletic departments and their student-athletes.

References

Brooks, G. R., & Good, G. (Eds.). (2001). *The new handbook of psychotherapy and counseling with men.* San Francisco: Jossey-Bass.

David, D. S., & Brannon, R. (1976). *The forty-nine percent majority: The male sex role.* Reading, MA: Addison-Wesley.

Englar-Carlson, M. (2006). Masculine norms and the therapy process. In M. Englar-Carlson & M. A. Stevens (Eds.), *In the therapy room with men: A casebook of psychotherapeutic process and change* (pp. 13–47). Washington, DC: American Psychological Association.

Englar-Carlson, M., & Stevens, M. A. (Eds.). (2006). *In the therapy room with men: A casebook of psychotherapeutic process and change with male clients.* Washington, DC: American Psychological Association.

Finch, L. M., & Gould, D. (1996). Understanding and intervening with the student-athlete-to-be. In E. F. Etzel, A. P. Ferrante, & J. W. Pinkney (Eds.), *Counseling college student-athletes: Issues and interventions* (2nd ed., pp. 223–245). Morgantown, WV: Fitness Information Technology, Inc.

Hinkle, J. S. (1996). Depression, adjustment disorder, generalized anxiety, and substance abuse: An overview for sports professionals working with college student-athletes. In E. F. Etzel, A. P. Ferrante, & J. W. Pinkney (Eds.), *Counseling college student-athletes: Issues and interventions* (2nd ed., pp. 109–136). Morgantown, WV: Fitness Information Technology, Inc.

Kirk, Q., & Kirk, S. (Eds.). (1993). *Student-athletes: Shattering the myths & sharing the realities.* Alexandria, VA: ACA Press.

Kiselica, M. S. (2006). Helping a boy become a parent: Male-sensitive psychotherapy with a teenage father. In M. Englar-Carlson & M. A. Stevens (Eds.), *In the therapy room with men: A casebook of psychotherapeutic process and change* (pp. 225–240). Washington, DC: American Psychological Association.

Levant, R. F. (1997). *Men and emotions: A psychoeducational approach.* New York: Newbridge.

Mahalik, J. R. (2001). Cognitive therapy for men. In G. R. Brooks & G. E. Good (Eds.), *The new handbook of psychotherapy and counseling with men: A comprehensive guide to settings, problems, and treatment approaches* (Vol. 2. pp. 544–564). San Francisco: Jossey-Bass.

Mahalik, J. R., Good, G. E., & Englar-Carlson, M. (2003). Masculinity scripts, presenting concerns, and help seeking: Implications for practice and training. *Professional Psychology, 34,* 123–131.

Messner, M. A. (1992). *Power at Play: Sports and the problem of masculinity.* Boston: Beacon.

Messner, M. A., & Stevens, M. A. (2002). Scoring without consent: Confronting male athletes' violence against women. In M. Gatz, M. Messner, & S. Ball-Rokeach (Eds.), *Paradoxes of youth and sport* (pp. 225–240). Albany: State University of New York Press.

Mintz, L., & O'Neil, J. (1990). Gender roles, sex, and the process of psychotherapy: Many questions and few answers. *Journal of Counseling and Development, 68,* 381–387.

Nelson, E. (1993). How the myth of the dumb jock becomes a fact: A developmental view for counselors. *Counseling & Values, 27,* 176–185.

Parham, W. D. (1996). Diversity within intercollegiate athletics: Current profile and welcomed opportunities. In E. F. Etzel, A. P. Ferrante, & J. W. Pinkney (Eds.), *Counseling college student-athletes: Issues and interventions* (2nd ed., pp. 27–53). Morgantown, WV: Fitness Information Technology, Inc.

Park, S. (2006). Facing fear without losing face: Working with Asian American men. In M. Englar-Carlson & M. A. Stevens (Eds.), *In the therapy room with men: A casebook of psychotherapeutic process and change* (pp. 151–174). Washington, DC: American Psychological Association.

Petitpas, A. J., Brewer, B. W., & Van Raalte, J. L. (1996). Transitions of the student-athlete: Theoretical, empirical, and practical perspectives. In E. F. Etzel, A. P. Ferrante, & J. W. Pinkney (Eds.), *Counseling college student-athletes: Issues and interventions* (2nd ed., pp. 137–156). Morgantown, WV: Fitness Information Technology, Inc.

Rabinowitz, F. E., & Cochran, S. V. (2002). *Deepening psychotherapy with men.* Washington, DC: American Psychological Association.

Rabonowitz, F. E. (2006). Thawing the iceman: Coping with grief and loss. In M. Englar-Carlson & M. A. Stevens (Eds.), *In the therapy room with men: A casebook of psychotherapeutic process and change* (pp. 109–128). Washington, DC: American Psychological Association.

Robertson, J. M. (2206). Finding Joshua's soul: Working with religious men. In M. Englar-Carlson & M. A. Stevens (Eds.), *In the therapy room with men: A casebook of psychotherapeutic process and change* (pp. 129–150). Washington, DC: American Psychological Association.

Scher, M., Stevens, M., Good, G. E., & Eichenfield, G. A. (Eds). (1987). *Handbook of counseling and psychotherapy with men.* Thousand Oaks, CA: Sage.

Sellers, R. M., & Damas, A. (1996). The African-American student-athlete experience. In E. F. Etzel, A. P. Ferrante, & J. W. Pinkney (Eds.), *Counseling college student-athletes: Issues and interventions* (2nd ed., pp. 55–76). Morgantown, WV: Fitness Information Technology, Inc.

Smart, R. (2006). A man with a "woman's problem": Male gender and eating disorders. In M. Englar-Carlson & M. A. Stevens (Eds.). (2006). *In the therapy room with men: A casebook of psychotherapeutic process and change* (pp. 319–338). Washington, DC: American Psychological Association.

Stevens, M. A. (2006) *Engaging men in psychotherapy.* Symposium presentation at the American Psychological Association 114th Annual Convention.

Vodde, R. J., & Randall, E. J. (1994). Treatment considerations for men who keep score in the game of life. *Clinical Social Work Journal, 22,* 385–396.

7

AFRICAN-DESCENDENT COLLEGIATE ATHLETES: AN INVITATION TO *RESPOND* TO THEIR VISIBILITY

William D. Parham

Organizing Assumptions and Premises

Several observations guided the organization of the following thoughts and observations regarding today's African-descendent collegiate student-athletes. The implications of these reflections for coaches, athletic training staff, sports medicine physicians, counselors, psychologists, and other service providers working with college athletes of African descent will be shared, along with some suggestions relative to research, practice, and advocacy on behalf of these young people.

The first premise that helps frame an understanding of African-descendent athletes invites consideration of the belief that context is everything. Simply stated, people do not function in a vacuum. It is not possible to arrive at a realistic understanding of a young person seeking consultation without some discussion of the environment(s) within which he or she functions. Understanding the needs of an athlete of African descent/other interaction requires examination of at least three factors: (1) what each individual brings "to the table" (e.g., personality, past and current "baggage," life experiences, self-perceptions, perceptions of personal versus environmental control); (2) an identification of the environmental forces that are influencing the individual; and (3) the hoped-for outcomes of the respective parties. For every action there is a reaction and a resolution of challenges, and concerns that spring forth from person-to-person interactions require both to be addressed.

In essence, a presentation and discussion about counseling collegiate student-athletes of African descent is incomplete without a parallel consideration of the profile of persons (e.g., coach, physicians, psychologists, athletic administrator) and systems (e.g., athletics, media, entertainment, etc.) with whom and with which the athlete is in a relationship. The athlete of African descent and others (e.g., coaches, administrators, team members, family) bring a wide range of defining influences to each interaction. The respective intrapersonal complexity that represents each party, coupled with environmental contexts (e.g., social, athletics, entertainment) within which these transactions take place, influences both the subsequent interaction and the outcome that results from the collective engagement of these entities. In situational interactions involving groups such as teams or families, the intrapersonal complexity becomes exponentially more fascinating. Thus, the interactive complexity of numerous contextual variables at any given point in time makes this premise an important one to consider up front.

The second premise that guides the organization of the following narrative is that race and ethnicity as separate indices do little to inform us about either the African descent athletes or the persons(s) with whom the athlete is interacting. Athletes of African descent are not a homogenous group: there is considerable variability relative to areas such as family heritage, cultural orientation, regional residence, social economic status, and faith-based affiliations. A recent poll published by the Pew Research Center (2007), in association with national Public Radio (NPR), suggested that about one-third of African descendents across ages (i.e., 18–29; 30–49; over 65) support a belief that it is no longer accurate or appropriate to view persons of African descent as a single race.

Likewise, helping professionals and others with whom athletes of African descent interact also are not a homogenous group, in that they represent variations at least on the same aforementioned dimensions. So, the question, "How does a person work with an athlete of African descent?" should be reframed to ask, "How do I interact/intervene with an athlete of African descent at this particular time presenting this particular set of concerns and challenges?" The interplay between athletes of African descent and the persons with whom they interact, in relation to their respective levels of knowledge and their understanding and acceptance of self and of the other, represents an important index for measuring effectiveness of the interaction.

A third premise that guides the forthcoming discussion underscores the importance of conceptualizing African-descended athletes using paradigms that reflect our cultural and ethnic (ethno-centric) world views. Ethno-centric formulations, by and large, provide an alternative lens through which to view athletes of African descent and a portal into a more accurate and qualitatively enhanced understanding of their concerns. For example, traditional African communities thrived and sustained themselves in keeping with laws and expressions of nature that spoke to resilience, strength, and empowerment of self through community connection and alignment with the Creator. Conceptualizing the experiences of athletes of African descent using beliefs and values that are more in alignment with their ancestral and cultural belief and value systems presents an opportunity for the emergence of a richer understanding of their current and likely future struggles as well as their truer essence and spirit. Though valuable, Euro-centric formulations, rooted in race- and gender-based oppressive ideologies but nonetheless alleged by many to be universal, are often fraught with erroneous beliefs and therefore limitations that may cloud the lens through which African-descendent collegiate student-athlete client concerns are perceived. Thus, the question reasserted herein is the degree to which Euro-centric formulations constitute the yardstick by which all human behaviors, feelings, and thoughts are measured.

In view of the above, a statistical profile of African-descendent college student-athletes relative to: (1) their representation in National Collegiate Athletic Association (NCAA) Division I, II, or III; (2) their participation in revenue- vs. non-revenue-producing sports; and (3) their distribution across class level and academic standing and graduation rates will not be discussed here. Further, their racial identity development (Kontos & Breland-Noble, 2002), career aspirations (Brown, 1993), family of origin issues, and profiles of educational attainment, health status, geographical distribution and other "traditional" indices also will not be elaborated on here. Similarly, distribution profiles relative to job classifications, administrative rankings, and years in the coaching industry across ethnicity, race, and other parameters of multiculturalism of coaches, administrators, support personnel, and others will not be discussed here. Readers interested in this potentially useful information are referred to any one of several other sources in the literature (Abney, 1999; Adler & Adler, 1991; Brown, Jackson, Brown, Sellers, Keiper, & Manuel, 2003; Coakley, 2001; Cogan & Petrie, 1996; Corbett & Johnson, 2000; Eisen & Wiggins, 1994; Gaston-Gayles, 2004; Gaston, 2004; Hawkins, 1995; Lapchick & Matthews, 2000; National

Collegiate Athletic Association Publications, 1999, 2005, 2007; Pope, 2000; Sails, 1998; Sellers & Damas, 1996; Shropshire, 1996).

Alternatively, readers of this chapter are invited to consider the ways in which *they respond* to African-descendent athletes with whom they interact as advisors, counselors, psychologists, sport medicine professionals, and perhaps as teachers, mentors, and supervisors. In other words, the onus of responsibility is on those persons responding to student-athletes of African descent, for whatever reason and irrespective of the role or capacity within which the interaction takes place. Student-athlete clients of African descent are not exempt from considering implementation of the forthcoming recommendations. Removing student-athletes of African descent from a targeted spotlight, however, allows for the illumination of opportunities for helping professionals to better consider their positions as persons whose influence on African-descendent student-athletes is clear. With the foregoing as prelude, the challenges experienced by African-descendent collegiate student-athletes juxtaposed to challenges experienced by their Anglo or other counterparts will be briefly discussed. Responses to these often dissimilar experiences by helping professionals and others will also be highlighted. Finally, suggestions for developing improved and hopefully more productive student-athlete/helping professional consultations also will be offered.

Selected Challenges and More Challenges

The challenges inherent in the lives of collegiate athletes have been amply documented (Brooks & Althouse, 2000; Chartrand & Lent, 1987; Etzel, Ferrante, & Pinkney, 1996; Pinkerton, Hinz, & Barrow, 1989; Parham, 1993; Parham, 1996). In brief, profiles of collegiate athletes have been viewed within at least two contexts. First, college student-athletes have been examined by comparing them across various dimensions with their non-athlete peers. From this perspective, there appears to be agreement that non-athletes and athletes usually find ways to: (1) manage separation from home and community while becoming integrated into a new academic and social community; (2) learn to appreciate the evolution of their personal identities; (3) respond to the demands of a challenging school curriculum; (4) prepare for and attend to career aspirations; (5) secure and develop social relationships; (6) identify and address ongoing health care needs; and (7) reconcile spiritual and religious affiliation challenges.

In addition to these across-the-board college student challenges, collegiate student-athletes are also confronted with having to negotiate additional hurdles. Irrespective of factors such as race, ethnicity, gender, sexual orientation, or physical disability, they are faced with balancing academic pursuits, athletic participation, and social development. These challenges take on special significance during their competitive season(s) when the bulk of their waking hours are spent in activities related largely to attending class, managing a full course load, doing homework, logging study hall hours, utilizing tutoring services, accessing computer labs, going to practice, participating in pre- and post-practice activities such as watching game film, getting taped, rehabilitating sore muscles, implementing and managing nutritional regimens and recommendations, and allowing sufficient time for sleep and recovery in order to engage in the exact same balancing act the next day. Often, this sun-up-to-sun-down cycle precludes optimal participation in other areas such as academics and the development of social and friend relationships outside of those established with teammates or other student-athletes within the community.

Managing athletic competitive pressures represents a second set of unique challenges for student-athletes across the board versus their non-athlete peer experience. These competitive pressures on the field of play can be defined as both within-group and intrapersonal. The within-group pressures are manifest in the way student-athletes pursue their personal development and positioning for playing time relative to that of their teammates. Desires to earn a starting spot versus "riding the bench" and the perceived or real short- and long-term implications of these roles are realities that trigger within-group competitive pressures.

Intrapersonal pressures may come in the form of battling "Am I good enough?" demons. These pressures are manifest in the desires to feel and to be seen by others as competent, confident, and as a strong link in the chain of the athletic team on which the athlete wishes to participate. Discovering and learning to value unique talents and harnessing inner confidence, motivation, and the will to persist through external and self-imposed roadblocks define this intrapersonal journey. Struggles with other academic and social pursuits can exacerbate sensitivities in this area.

College student-athletes across the board face the unique prospect of injury on a daily basis (Brewer, 2007; Brewer, Andersen, & Van Raalte,

2002; Parham, 2004). Advances in technology relative to athletic equipment, the fine tuning of knowledge about strength and conditioning, and increased clarity regarding the role nutrition and recovery play in the physical health of the collegiate student-athlete are applied preemptively to circumvent injury. Trend analyses of injury to college student-athletes indicate changes over the last several years in minor and more severe injuries (NCAA, 2007), thus lending credence to the importance of the aforementioned advances. Inevitably, though, injury is experienced by numerous athletes. Learning to navigate the physical as well as emotional and psychological journey that characterizes the response to and recovery from injury can be quite challenging. Injuries are never predicted, always come at a "bad" time, and usually require time away from the sport; depending on the degree of injury, the rehabilitation can feel arduous. Ample research and writing about the injury experience exist (Brewer, 2007; Brewer, Andersen, & Van Raalte, 2002; Parham, 2004), and there appears to be agreement that managing the injury experience includes three foci: (1) knowledge of the degree of physiological compromise; (2) information regarding the anticipated time of healing; and (3) accessing emotional and psychological coping resources. The simultaneous navigation of other challenges, such as academic, social, and familial, adds to the angst college student-athletes experience relative to injury.

An Onerous System

Student-athletes of African descent struggle with a set of challenges that often go beyond the experiences of both their Anglo student-athlete peers and their non-athlete student peers. Whether covert or overt, racism represents the most significant challenge facing today's athletes of African descent. Irrespective of sport, division, or student demographic profile of the institution they attend, overt daily "micro aggressions" are common. Examples of micro-aggressions within athletic communities include beliefs and actions of coaches and sports writers that suggest that African-descendent athletes possess the tools (e.g., quickness, agility, speed) but not the intellect for athletic success (Coakley, 2001; Eisen & Wiggins, 1994; Entine, 2000; Hawkins, 1995; Majors, 1998; Sailes, 1998; Shropshire, 1996). These young people also encounter hostile acts of racial aggression within athletic, academic, and larger social communities that expose past and current racism and discrimination in ways their Anglo peers do not or choose to not comprehend.

In his book, *Days of Grace: A Memoir* (1993), Arthur Ashe identified race as a burden that was not only difficult to manage but felt larger than managing the stigma and related challenges associated with HIV/AIDS. Edwards (2000) spoke to race as a salient 21st century issue within athletics. Sue, Capodilupo, Torino, Bucerri, Holder, Nadal, and Esquilin (2007) and Solorzano, Ceja, and Tara (2007) invited us to consider that "micro-aggressions are brief and commonplace daily verbal, behavioral, or environmental indignities, whether intentional or unintentional, that communicate hostile, derogatory or negative racial slights and insults toward people of color" (p. 273). Further, regardless of the form in which they are expressed (e.g. micro-assaults, micro-insults, micro-invalidations), the effect of micro-aggressions are cumulative and adversely impact the experiences of the targets—athletes of African descent.

The "dumb jock" stereotype, though targeting athletes in general, has added valence when applied to athletes of African descent. These kinds of attitudes are fueled by pre-college academic preparation determined by traditional academic indices (e.g., high school grades, ACT/SAT scores) and college academic performance, including graduation rates, compared to their Anglo student-athlete peers. Micro-aggressions in the larger society include portrayals of nooses and swastikas and other hate-based actions, pejorative classifications (e.g., "those people"), and jokes rooted in stereotypes and group characterizations, a la Don Imus's negative portrayal of the Rutgers University women's basketball team (CBS News, 2007). Collectively, these race-based transgressions add substantively to the environmental realities of collegiate athletes of African descent and experiences, in ways not always understood or appreciated fully by non-targeted groups.

The myriad influences of the campus racial climate on the experiences of college students of African descent have been examined. Several scholars (Guinier, Fine, & Balin, 1997; Hurtado, Milem, Clayton-Petersen, & Allen, 1999) have pointed out that a positive and affirming racial collegiate environment usually includes: (1) a mission statement that illuminates the institution's support of multiculturalism; (2) the presence in critical numbers of African-descended students, faculty, and administrators; (3) active recruitment and retention programs that lead to graduation; and (4) reflections in the curriculum of past and current experiences of persons of color. The absence of these environmental signposts sets the stage for a negative racial climate and resultant experiences by students of color.

Why should the foregoing be important to readers and their work with student-athletes? Current manifestations of racism, discrimination, and intolerance in collegiate athletics represent vestiges of socially sanctioned, race-based practices that framed the collegiate landscape as recently as forty years ago. As is true today, collegiate America was a microcosm of the bigotry and racial injustice perpetrated in society at large. Student-athlete clients of African descent bring these experiences to their work with helping professionals, who must be sensitive to their existence and the impact they have on their clients.

In Times Past

During times past, African-descended athletes, especially those attending predominately Anglo institutions, experienced considerable isolation and loneliness, lower quality living arrangements, few if any social and cultural outlets, and less overall support for academic and personal success in comparison to their Anglo peers. These experiences were exacerbated in academic institutions in the South (Ashe, 1993; Spivey & Jones, 1975; Wiggins, 1991; Wolters, 1975), where conditions were more disparate. Related, it was commonplace for southern institutions to decline participation in games against northern colleges that dressed African-descended players. As a result, African-descended collegiate student-athletes were often asked to sit out games so that their team would be able to compete (Ashe, 1993; Paul, McGhee, & Fant, 1984; Wiggins, 1991). In response to the oppressive and hate-filled environment of college athletics in America, organizations were formed to develop legitimacy for African-descended student-athletes, beginning with the Colored Intercollegiate Athletic Association (CIAA) in 1912.

The prevalence and tolerance for racism and discrimination in society, so not surprisingly in collegiate and professional communities as well, loomed large. From the latter quarter of 19th century until 1965, the "Jim Crow" era contaminated the American landscape: local and state laws, mostly in the southern states, mandated that persons of African descent to be treated "separate but equal." Effectively, these laws required that public places such as schools, transportation venues, and dining establishments include spaces for Anglos that were different than for African-descendents. The accommodations for persons of African descent were generally substandard and usually very inferior to Anglo accommodations. It wasn't until 1954 that the Supreme Court of the United States declared segregation unconstitutional (*Brown vs. Board of Education*), essentially overturning an earlier U. S. Supreme Court ruling (*Plessy vs. Ferguson*, in 1896) that allowed segregation based on race. Jim Crow laws represented society's permission slips to segregate along racial lines, deny economic and other opportunities, support private and public acts of violence, and suppress voting rights for those of African descent. Even with the passage of the 1954 *Brown vs. Board of Education* decision, segregation continued in many southern states. Further, persons of African descent migrating to the North, believing that Jim Crow laws were not as tough to manage there, found bigotry and racial segregation very much present in the fabric of American culture. This discovery was not totally surprising or unpredicted, given the limits of the 1954 *Brown vs. Board of Education* decision that declared racial segregation illegal but provided few, if any, remedies for its continued expression.

The Civil Rights Movement represented a desire to abolish racial discrimination and segregation and level the playing field. The pervasiveness of the "Jim Crow" era environment juxtaposed to the Civil Rights Movement influenced the psyche and behavior of all American citizens. There were strong and passionate supporters of segregation and equally if not stronger and more passionate and determined supporters to abolish the racial divide. Put simply, it was not possible to live during the Civil Rights era and not be affected in many ways by the social disarray and turmoil. Responses by persons of African descent to racial atrocities perpetrated against them are well documented, and the post-situation impact of such hate-based expressions merits ongoing investigation.

In the New Millennium

Collectively, these by-gone eras invite us to consider again today that generations of those associated with intercollegiate athletics have been indoctrinated with beliefs regarding the alleged inferiority of persons of African descent. Attitudes and behaviors that have been patterned and reinforced in our athletic, educational, political, judicial, economic, and other life systems are difficult to break down. Though the fallacy of views supporting cultural and racial inferiority is apparent, aggressive and systematic promotion of such erroneous assumptions frequently results in their believability. Assumptions about genetic inferiority and cultural deprivation and deficiency were marketed so well by those in power that some persons of African descent began to believe these mistruths and thus participated in their own subjugation.

One challenge facing athletes and the service providers with whom they interact, across dimensions of culture, race, and ethnicity, is the realization that *everyone* is a product of environments that have both overtly and covertly devalued persons of African descent. It is not possible to have experienced the denigration of African-descended persons—or American society's collusion with the spread of this social cancer—and emerge unaffected.

Arguably, not much has changed relative to society's expression of racism and discrimination. Numerous hate crimes in recent years have served as chilling reminders of the malicious profile of some American communities. The lack of local, regional, and national response to acts of racism, sexism, anti-Semitism, and homophobia is as chilling as the acts themselves. Although many citizens have called for justice, far too many people have said and done nothing.

Relatedly, in a recent social and demographic trend report released by the Pew Research Center (2007), several findings suggest that African-descendent–Anglo race relations have not really changed much over time. The report suggested a declining sense of optimism among African-descendent communities regarding the society's embrace of fairness and of a level playing field. In this survey, conducted in conjunction with National Public Radio (NPR), just one in five persons of African descent reported that life is better for them now than five years ago (Pew Research Center, 2007). This report also indicated that 44% of African descendents feel that life will get better in the future, but this finding is down from 56% reported in a 1986 survey. Anti-black discrimination is still prevalent, according to African-descendent respondents. The report indicates that 68% of the African-descendent respondents report racial discrimination experiences in at least two of the following categories: buying a house, renting an apartment, applying for a job, applying for college, and shopping or dining out. In contrast, Anglo respondents believed there is a decrease in anti-black discrimination. Persons of African descent said that they have decreased confidence in the fairness of the criminal justice system.

Steele and Aronson (1995) and Steele (1999) reintroduced the notion of "stereotype threat" (introduced by Irwin Katz, 1964), defined as a belief that one's behavior will confirm already held stereotypes of the group with which one identifies and that the fear of this occurring may contribute to impaired performance. Their early studies targeted the academic performance of students of African descent; subsequent work targeted the physiological responses of students of African descent to academic work. All studies, however, confirmed the presence of the stereotype threat and, more importantly, shed light on the emotional power associated with a person's awareness of and perceived affiliation with stereotypes and prejudice. Stereotype threat speaks to the presence of internalized oppression within students of African descent, the full expression of which lays dormant. To what degree does stereotype threat apply to athletic performance? How does stereotype threat impact athletes of African descent relative to their training regimen or in anticipation of their need to "perform" for their coaches, athletic department administrators, sport medicine physicians, sport psychologists, or other allied service providers when called in for a consultation? How might coaches, athletic department administrators, and allied service providers use the stereotype threat phenomenon as a template for understanding their responses to athletes of African descent?

Professionals who interact with student-athletes might consider asking: " To what degree have I been influenced by the social, political, and other system forces that have been antagonistic to persons of African descent?" "As a person unavoidably influenced by racial stereotypes about persons of African descent, am I able to see that they are survivors of systems of oppression?" Finally, "As a person unavoidably influenced by racial stereotypes about persons of African descent, can I shift my thinking from believing deficient- and deprivation-based hypotheses to embracing more positive views?"

The point made here is that the wider and pronounced systemic support of racism has influenced athletes of African descent who have been targets of such hate. It has also influenced those who have been exposed to and have supported racist practices. In other words, America's support of institutional racism has influenced everyone who has encountered it.

Additional Systems of Influence

Student-athletes, student-athletes of African descent, and other "players" in their system (e.g., coaches, administrators, helping providers) all function within and are inescapably influenced by the sports industry, the collegiate sports industry, and mass media. Sport as an organized entity looms large in America and also touches the lives of young and old across the globe. It is promoted as the one activity that bridges cultural divides and provides a respite (albeit brief) from life's chaos and disarray. The International Olympic Committee (IOC), the General Association of International Sports Federations (AGFIS), and the Maccabi World Union (MWU), the organization for Jewish sport associations, are arguably the best examples of sport's universal appeal. In addition to the above umbrella organizations, many countries, poor and rich, find some solace and take pride in their nation's accomplishments as they vie for international sport titles.

Domestically and globally, the marketing of sports as entertainment is a billion-dollar industry. Sport is a product that sells promises of a good time, social connections, and changed lives. Countries, provinces, states, and local communities actively promote sports through construction of arenas and training facilities, sponsorships, ticket sales, advertisements, athlete product endorsements, and licensing merchandise that includes sport memorabilia, sporting goods, books, and video games.

Within collegiate America, sports promotion is also large scale. Many conferences, including the Atlantic Coast Conference (ACC), Big East, Sun Belt, and Conference USA, invest handsomely for advertising media (radio, Internet, television, cable, etc.) to increase audience exposure to their "product" in order to increase revenue for their athletic departments. Typically, advertising dollars are disproportionately invested in football and basketball programs, as they represent the revenue producing sports for most collegiate institutions (Shropshire, 1996).

It is interesting to note that broadcast television ratings for the Big Four networks (ABC, CBS, Fox, and NBC) have witnessed a decade-long decline (Longman, 2004). Reasons cited for this downturn are many and include a racial factor. Increased ethnic diversity among athletes is essentially forcing predominately Anglo and wealthy audiences to pay their money to see non-Anglo (persons of African descent) players. This observation is key, as history reminds us that similar racial phenomena occurred in the mid-1960s: within professional basketball at the time of the NBA/ABA merger; within the collegiate system, illuminated best during the 1965–1966 NCAA season in the championship game that showcased Texas Western versus powerhouse University of Kentucky; and then again in the 1980s. Race, pure and simple, contributes importantly to sport/spectator-fan participation in basketball and likely in other sports. In 1981, 16 of the 23 NBA teams were losing money and were facing tremendous financial challenges, including threats of sale and liquidation procedures (Conrad, 2004). Marketing Larry Bird as "the great white hope" (along with the creating salary cap agreements and revenue sharing programs), professional basketball began to rebound. As fate would have it, race played a key role in the jettison of professional basketball out of its financial struggles. The Anglo-black marketing strategy of using Larry Bird (Anglo) vs. Ervin "Magic" Johnson" (person of African descent) added to the rise in the fan base of professional basketball. (The rivalry between the Celtics vs. Lakers, two storied franchises, was a secondary benefit.) Then came Michael "Air" Jordan, another person of African descent. His exploits on the court were legendary, and fans paid handsomely to witness them.

Race, Class, Media, and the American System of Intercollegiate Athletics

Why is the foregoing important to helping professionals who work with student-athletes of African descent? The study of race involves understanding the biological connections that define human characteristics and traits. Physical characteristics and traits such as skin color and anatomical structures have taken on symbolic meanings that have been transmitted across generations and promoted and believed as truth. Race has been used as a Rubik's cube whose manipulation into patterns that fit hierarchical ordering based on race and class is supported by mechanisms, such as the media and social-economic systems, that have been designed to promulgate such beliefs. Race and class in America and globally have been tied to systems of privilege and elitism. This "haves-and-have-nots" social structure has impacted both the targets of these orchestrated abuses (e.g., persons of African descent) as well as the perpetrators. No group is immune from the pervasiveness of these carefully crafted systems of control.

Mass media adds an important influence to the mix. In *The Black Image in the White Mind* (2000) Entman and Rojecki addressed the portrayals in the media of persons of African descent, and they shared several observations: First, Anglo-Americans learn about persons of African descent largely through media portrayals and less through personal relationships. News regarding persons of African descent tends to focus on themes of crime and poverty, which may bias the views that helping professionals and others form about African descent athletes. Though subtle, themes projecting differences, conflict, and a racial hierarchy that assumes Anglo-America is in a top position also are commonplace. (Readers interested in more detailed analyses of portrayals of persons of African descent in the media are directed to Bogle, 1989; Boyd, 1996; Entman & Constance, 2000; Gray, 1989; and Greenberg & Brand, 2002.)

Thus, African-descendent student athletes, knowingly or unknowingly, contend with the following on a daily basis: (1) a social-political system that contains vestiges of discrimination and injustice based on hierarchical beliefs about race and class; (2) a sports industry defined increasingly as big business entertainment venues, designed to foster the belief that life through direct or vicarious participation in sports is or can be better (i.e., a belief largely inconsistent with life in America for the vast majority of persons of African descent); and (3) a mass media mega-system that sells images, products, and promises by persuading members of the public to embrace a false reality while second-guessing their beliefs about "truth." Each system expresses itself in self-sustaining ways. Their respective and collective expressions influence the ways in which persons respond to the admixture of environmental "reality" and fabrication. (Extended presentations of the inextricable connection between sports and the media, politics, families, education, and the economy can be reviewed in several sources including Coakley, 2001; Coltrane, 2000; Koppett, 1994; Maguire, 1999; Rowe, 1999; Whannel, 2000.)

A Shift in Thinking about Persons of African Descent

Imagine, for a moment, replacing socially created interpretations of race with concepts that are more in keeping with illuminating persons of African descent and other cultural groups (Salaam, n.d.; Abdi, 2006;

Azibo, 2003; Asante, 1998). Specifically, consider a mindset rooted in concepts and principles that emanate from an ethno-centric versus Euro-centric perspective. Beliefs about the universe, mind-body relationships, spirituality, time, and individuality emerged from the African ancestral cradle. These led to larger beliefs about the interconnectedness of all things living and their aspiration to be one with nature. Euro-centric formulations, in contrast, valued separateness, hierarchical ordering of separate phenomena (usually on a continuum anchored with inferior to superior), and control of nature versus harmonious co-existence with "her."

Traditional Euro-centric thinking promoted mind-body dualism, assigning primacy to rational thought. In ancestral Africa, though, mind-body distinctions were less absolute; the focus was on the interrelatedness of the mind, body, and other life forms. "Existence" consisted of both visible (i.e., people, animals, nature) and invisible (i.e., spirit, soul, energy) dimensions. Euro-centric beliefs, on the other hand, devalued that which was vague, intangible, and unseen.

Time, from a Euro-centric perspective, has been viewed metrically and valued as a commodity to be invested wisely. African traditions, on the other hand, have embraced the fluidity of past, present, and future dimensions and recognized that they were connected seamlessly. Finally, survival for traditional Africa was often dependent on the work of the collective. In contrast, Euro-centric thought promoted individualism, survival of the fittest, and pyramid-type thinking. Further, Euro-centric beliefs included the concept of *tabula rasa*, thus one's birth-to-death journey was a quest to add unceasingly to the "blank slate" that needed to be filled. Ancestral African beliefs, in contrast, embodied the idea of existing, innate talents whose discoveries and expressions were triggered by life's challenges.

This compare-and-contrast snapshot of selected variables reasserts scholars' conclusions that persons of African descent never have been inferior. Rather, they have been "inferiorized" by others. Because coaches, administrators, and service providers have been exposed to social-political marketing campaigns that have devalued persons of African descent, they bear some responsibility to examine their own vulnerability to such fallacies.

Coming Full Circle

Race- and class-based formulations of human behavior have adversely impacted generations of players, coaches, administrators, sport medicine physicians, psychologists, and other allied service providers. Given this reality, Anglo service providers will need to confront several questions regarding their culpability in maintaining race- and class-consciousness: Is it possible for anyone to escape the influences of a race-and class-conscious society? If yes, then how? If no, then what, if any, responsibility do participants bear in recalibrating their responses? Should the service providers, the athletes of African descent, or both be challenged to question the one-size-fits-all models of professional practice? Who should stand and confront the presence or absence of policies and procedures that support fair and equitable treatment of athletes of African descent relative to issues of class and race? Who bears the responsibility for understanding the "inheritability factor" of past thinking and practices relative to race and class?

Non-Anglo service providers will need to confront a slightly different set of questions: "Given that society continues to advocate race- and class-consciousness, and that I function in sport and mass media environments that are framed by the same parameters, how do I identify the ways in which my interactions with both Anglos and non-Anglos have been influenced?" "Are there alternative ways of responding to these two groups that avoid collusion with society's tolerance for race-class distinctions and thus foster enriched communication and understanding?"

Student-athletes

Student-athletes of African descent also are invited to seek resolution with the following question: "Given that society continues to advocate race- and class-consciousness, and that I function in sport and mass media environments that are framed by the same parameters, how do I come to terms with my status as an ongoing target of social discomfort?" Equally important questions to address include: "Am I even aware of the cultural and social factors that influence the perceptions I have and the decisions I make relative to school, athletics, and social engagements?" "If aware of these influences, then in what ways do I knowingly or unknowingly collude with the very systems that shape how I think, feel, and behave?"

Counseling Student-Athletes of African Descent: Some Best Practices

In addition to asking self-reflective questions, coaches, administrators, sport medicine and mental health professionals, and other allied service providers may want to take inventory of their awareness, knowledge, and skills relative to their interactions with student-athletes of African descent. Given their findings, they can establish concrete and behavioral plans to address the discrepancies in these areas. For example, their inventory may pose questions about their ability to listen appropriately to concerns expressed by athletes of African descent. Relatedly, their inventory may seek to identify cultural filters that frame the questions student-athletes of African descent ask. They might then ask themselves to what degree they are able to use such filters as aids in understanding what is being communicated.

Those who may be in a counseling position can challenge themselves to better understand the families, communities of origin, and academic environmental realities that influence African-descendent student-athletes in ways that may not affect their Anglo peers. It also seems useful for these groups to understand that environmental realities may impact student-athletes of African descent in ways they may not even recognize. Participation in continuing education courses and seminars that address challenges faced by African-descendent student-athletes is recommended as a way for professionals to become and remain educated.

All of the aforementioned groups are invited to promote within their colleges and universities an examination of institutional polices and practices that violate fairness and inclusiveness. They can advocate for the hiring and retention of African-descendent professionals (e.g., coaches, administrators, faculty, staff, etc.), for the safeguarding of an inclusive work environment, and for compensation systems that are based on performance and not on race, ethnicity, or other dimensions of multiculturalism.

Student-athletes of African descent also bear some responsibility in their relationships with others; counselors might encourage them to ask themselves the same self-assessment questions recommended above for coaches, administrators, and service professionals. Counselors might suggest that, in addition to taking courses based on their majors, these student-athletes may want to take advantage of life skill courses and seminars that address real-world realities of sport and coaching as professions that operate as businesses that are judged in large part on the products (e.g., titles, championships, increased alumni dollars, etc.) they produce.

Finally, counselors can encourage student-athletes of African descent to think "big picture" and to seek at every stage of their academic and athletic careers an understanding of the roles and responsibilities of the professionals with whom they interact, which will position them to feel increased confidence in the instruction they receive and about the academic and athletic direction in which they want to head.

Summary

The author decided to forego a presentation of African-descendent student-athletes using traditional approaches that include generating profiles, drawing inferences, and suggesting ways to better understand *them*. Traditional presentations lead often to prescriptive beliefs and practices, perpetuation of stereotypes, definitions of *differences* as non-affirming and negative, and recycled observations. The invitation, herein, was sent as an encouragement to coaches, administrators, sport medicine physicians, sport psychologists, and allied service providers to examine their *responses* to athletes of African descent with whom they interact.

The discussion was predicated on several assumptions. First, race and class are institutionalized experiences from which no one is immune and about which everyone has developed assumptions, beliefs, and biases. Second, it would have been impossible for the current generation of student-athletes and the persons who provide support services to them not to have inherited attitudes about race and class from preceding generations. Third, beliefs about race and class are learned, not innate; thus they can be unlearned and reformatted. Relatedly, current expressions of race-hate and hierarchical class status are *influenced* by like expressions of past generations but are not connected *causally* to those past expressions. Fourth, beliefs about race and class are expressed consciously and unconsciously. Fifth, whether expressed as heinous acts or as acts of unconscious micro-aggression, race-hate and beliefs about hierarchical class status adversely impact the mental, psychological, and spiritual health of both the targets and the perpetrators of such acts. The targets and the perpetrators also have the opportunity to acknowledge their culpability in colluding with hate-fueled legacies and to re-calibrate current responses to be more aligned with beliefs about inclu-siveness and fair play.

Intercollegiate athletics represents an arena wherein student-athletes of African descent, coaches, administrators, and allied service providers respond to the enactment of life's challenges, following rules that were designed to create an imbalance on the playing field. The promotion of the status quo relative to beliefs about race and class is as evident in the play of all of the game's participants as is the success of many who are combating the influences of socially created fallacies. As long as the final whistle relative to hierarchical beliefs about race and class has not blown signaling that the game is over, time remains for all parties to modify those beliefs and to refocus their respective game plans in hopes of achieving a win-win situation for all involved.

References

Abdi, A. A. (2006). Eurocentric discourses and African philosophies and epistemologies of education: Counter-hegemonic analyses and responses. *International Education, 36*(1), 15–31.

Abney, R. (1999). African-American women in sport. *Journal of Physical Education, Recreation and Dance, 70*(4), 35–38.

Adler, P. A., & Adler, P. (1991). *Backboards and blackboards: College athletes and role en-gulfment.* New York: Columbia University Press.

Asante, M. K. (1998). *The Afro-centric idea.* Philadelphia, PA: Temple University Press.

Ashe, A. (1988, 1993). *A hard road to glory.* (Vols. 1–3). New York: Amistad.

Ashe, A. (1996). *Days of grace: A memoir.* New York: Ballantine Books.

Azibo, D. A. (2003). *African-centered psychology: Culture focusing for multicultural com-petence.* Durham, NC: Carolina Academic Press.

Banet-Weiser, S. (1999). Hoop dreams: Professional basketball and the politics of race and gender. *Journal of Sport & Social Issues, 23*(4), 403–420.

Bogle, D. (1989). *Blacks in American film and television: An encyclopedia.* New York: Simon & Schuster.

Boyd, H. (1996). African-American images on television and film. *Crisis, 103(2),* 2–25.

Brewer, B. W. (2007). Psychology of sport injury rehabilitation. In G. Tenenbaum (Ed.) *Handbook of sport psychology* (3rd ed., pp. 404–424). Hoboken, NJ: John Wiley & Sons.

Brewer, B. W., Andersen, M. B., & Van Raalte, J. L. (2002). Psychological aspects of sport injury rehabilitation: Toward a biopsychosocial approach. In D. L. Mostofsky & L. D. Zaichkowsky (Eds.), *Medical and psychological aspects of sport and exercise* (pp. 41–45). Morgantown, WV: Fitness Information Technology, Inc.

Brooks, D., & Althouse, R. (2000). African-American head coaches and administrators: Progress but . . . ? In D. Brooks & R. C. Althouse (Eds.), *Racism in college athletics: The African-American athlete's experience* (pp. 85–118). Morgantown, WV: Fitness Information Technology, Inc.

Brooks, D. D., & Althouse, R. C. (Eds.). (2000). *Racism in college athletics: The African-American athlete's experience* (2nd ed.). Morgantown, WV: Fitness Information Technology, Inc.

Brown, C. (1993). The relationship between role commitment and career development tasks among college student-athletes (Doctoral dissertation, University of Missouri, 1993). *Dissertation Abstracts International, 55*, 1429A.

Brown, T. N., Jackson, J., Brown, K. T., Sellers, R. M., Keiper, S., & Manuel, L. (2003). There's no race on the playing field. *Journal of Sport and Social Issues, 27*(2), 162–183.

CBS News. (2007, April 12). CBS fires Don Imus over racial slur. Retrieved August 25, 2007, from http://www.cbsnews.com/stories/2007/04/12/national/main2675273_page2.shtml

Chartrand, J., & Lent, R. (1987). Sports counseling: Enhancing the development of the student-athlete. *Journal of Counseling and Development, 66*, 164–167.

Chomsky, N. (2001). *9–11*. New York: Seven Stories Press.

Coakley, J. (2001). *Sport in society: Issues and controversies* (7th ed.). New York: McGraw Hill.

Cogan, K. D., & Petrie, T. A. (1996). Diversity in sport. In J. L. Van Raalte & B. W. Brewer (Eds.), *Exploring sport and exercising psychology* (pp. 355–373). Washington, DC: American Psychological Association.

Coltrane, S. (2000). The perpetuation of subtle prejudice: Race and gender imagery in 1990s television advertising. *Sex Roles: A Journal of Research, 10*, 41–44.

Conrad, M. (2004). Blue-collar law and basketball. In S. Rosner & K. L. Shropshire (Eds.), *The business of sports* (p. 204). Sudbury, MA: Jones & Bartlett Publishers.

Corbett, D., & Johnson, W. (2000). The African-American female in collegiate sport: Sexism and racism. In D. Brooks & R. C. Althouse (Eds.), *Racism in college athletics: The African-American athlete's experience* (pp. 199–226). Morgantown, WV: Fitness Information Technology, Inc.

Daniels, D. (2000). Gazing at the new black woman athlete. *Color Lines, 3*(1) 25–26.

Danish, S. (1985). Psychological aspects in the care and treatment of athletic injuries. In P. E. Vinger & E. F. Hoerner (Eds.), *Sports injuries: The unthwarted epidemic* (pp. 345–353). Boston: Wright.

Dick, R. W. (2004). *National collegiate athletic association injury surveillance system*. Indianapolis, IN: NCAA Publications. (Available: http://www1.ncaa.org/membership/ed _outreach/health-safety/iss/index.html)

Duda, J. L., & Allison, M. T. (1990). Cross-cultural analysis in exercise and sport psychology: A void in the field. *Journal of Sport and Exercise Psychology, 12*, 114–131.

Edwards, H. (2000). Crisis of Black athletes at the millennium on the eve of the 21st century. *Society, 37*(3), 9–13.

Edwards, H. (2000). The decline of the black athlete. *Color Lines, 3*(1), 24–29.

Eisen, G., & Wiggins, D. K. (Eds.). (1994). *Ethnicity and sport in North American history and culture.* Westport, CT: Greenwood Press.

Ellison, R. (1947, 1980). *The invisible man.* New York: Random House.

Entine, J. (2000). *Taboo: Why Black athletes dominate sports and why we are afraid to talk about it.* New York.: Public Affairs.

Entman, R. M., & Rojecki, A. (2000). *The black image in the white mind.* Chicago: University of Chicago Press.

Entman, R., & Constance, L. (2000). Light makes right: Skin color and racial hierarchy in television advertising. In R. Andersen & L. Strate (Eds.), *Critical studies in media commercialism* (pp. 214–224). New York: Oxford University Press.

Franklin, A. J. (2004). *From brotherhood to manhood: How Black men rescue their relationships and dreams from the invisibility syndrome.* Thousand Oaks, CA: Wiley.

Gaston, J. L. (2004). Advising African-American student athletes. In L. A. Flowers (Ed.), *Diversity issues in American colleges and universities: Case studies for higher education and student affairs professionals* (pp. 59–60). Springfield, IL: Charles C. Thomas.

Gaston-Gayles, J. L. (2004). Examining academic and athlete motivation among student athletes at a Division I university. *Journal of College Student Development, 45,* 75–83.

Greenberg, B. S., & Brand, J. E. (2002). Minorities and the mass media: Television into the 21st century. In J. Bryant & D. Zillman (Eds.), *Media effects: Advances in theory and research* (pp. 333–352). Hillsdale, NJ: Erlbaum.

Guiner, L., Fine, M., & Balin, J. (1997). *Becoming gentlemen: Women, law school and institutional change.* New York: Beacon Press.

Hawkins, B. (1995). The Black student athlete: The colonized Black body. *Journal of African-American Studies, 1*(3), 23–35.

Harrison, C. K. (1998). Themes that thread through society: Racism and athletic manifestation in the African-American community. *Race, Ethnicity and Education, 1*(1), 63–74.

Harrison, K. (2000). Black athletes at the millennium. *Society, 37*(3), 35–39.

Heil, J. (1993). *Psychology of sport injury.* Champaign, IL: Human Kinetics.

Hurtado, S., Milem, J., Clayton-Petersen, A., & Allen, W. (1999). Enhancing diverse learning environments: Improving the climate for racial/ethnic diversity in higher education. ASHE-ERIC Higher Education Report, Vol. 26, No. 8, Washington, DC, The George Washington University School of Education and Human Development.

King, M. L. K., Jr. (1967). Beyond Vietnam: Address to the clergy and laymen concerned about Vietnam, Riverside Church. In C. Clayborne & K. Shepard (Eds.), *A call to conscience: The landmark speeches of Dr. Martin Luther King, Jr.* (pp. 133–164). New York: Warner Books.

Koppett, L. (1994). *Sports illusion, sports reality: A reporter's view of sports, journalism and society.* Urbana: University of Illinois Press.

Kontos, A. P., & Breland-Noble, A. M. (2002). Racial/ethnic diversity in applied sport psychology: A multicultural introduction to working with athletes of color. *The Sport Psychologist, 16,* 296–315.

Lawrence, S. M. (2005). African American athletes' experiences of race in sports. *International Review for the Sociology of Sport, 40*(1), 99–110.

Lapchick, R. (1984). *Broken promises: Racism in American sports.* New York: St. Martens/Marek.

Lapchick, R. (1995). Front court (Preface). In V. Fudzie & A. Hayes (Eds.), *The sport of learning: A comprehensive survival guide for African-American student-athletes* (pp. 5–7). North Hollywood, CA: Doubleday.

Lapchick, R., & Matthews, K. (2000). *Racial and gender report card for 1998.* Boston: Center for the Study of Sport and Society Northeastern University.

Maguire, J. (1999). *Global sport: Identities, societies, civilizations.* Cambridge, England: Polity Press.

Majors, R. (1998). Cool pose: Black masculinity and sports. In G. Sailes (Ed.), *African-Americans in sport: Contemporary themes* (pp. 15–22). New Brunswick, NJ: Transaction.

Martens, M. P., Mobley, M., & Zizzi, S. J. (2000). Multicultural training in applied sport psychology. *The Sport Psychologist, 14,* 81–97.

NCAA. (2007). National and Sport Group Three-Year Academic Progress Report Differences. Indianapolis, IN.: NCAA Publications.

NCAA. (1999–2000; 2005–2006) NCAA Student Athlete Race and Ethnicity Report. Indianapolis, IN: NCAA Publications.

NCAA. NCAA Research Report 99-04: Academic Characteristics by Ethnic Group in Division I Recruits in the 1997 and 1998 NCAA Initial Eligibility Clearinghouse. Indianapolis, IN: NCAA Publications.

NCAA. 2005–06 Ethnicity and Gender Demographics of NCAA Member Institutions Athletic Personnel. Indianapolis, IN.: NCAA Publications.

NCAA. NCAA Special Issue. *Journal of Athletic Training, 42*(2), April/June 2007.

Parham, W. D. (1996). Diversity within intercollegiate athletics: Current profile and welcomed opportunities. In E. F. Etzel, A. P. Ferrante, & J. W. Pinkney (Eds.), *Counseling college student athletes: Issues and interventions* (pp. 27–54). Morgantown, WV: Fitness Information Technology, Inc.

Parham, W. D. (2003). Sport psychology and injured athletes. In J. C. DeLee, D. Drez, & M. D. Miller (Eds.), *Orthopedic sports medicine: Principles and practices* (2nd ed., Vol. 1, pp. 493–504). Philadelphia: Saunders.

Paul, J., McGhee, R. V., & Fant, H. (1984). The arrival and ascendance of Black athletes in the Southeastern Conference, 1966–1980. *Phylon, 45,* 284–287.

Pew Research Center. (2007). Blacks see growing values gap between poor and middle class: Optimism about Black progress declines. *Pew Research Center: A Social & Demographic Trends Report, Survey conducted in association with National Public Radio.* November 13: Washington, DC.

Pinkerton, R., Hinz, L., & Barrow, J. (1989). The college student-athlete: Psychological considerations and interventions. *Journal of American College Health, 37,* 218–226.

Pope, R. L. (2000). Relationship between psychosocial development and racial identity of black college students. *Journal of College Student Development, 41,* 301–312.

Rowe, D. (1999). *Sports, culture and the media: The unholy trinity.* Philadelphia: Open University Press.

Sailes, G. (Ed.). (1998). *African- Americans in sport.* New Brunswick, NJ: Transaction.

Salaam, K. (n.d.). *The importance of an African-centered education.* Retrieved August 25, 2008, from http://www.nathanielturner.com/africancenterededucation.htm

Sellers, R. M. (1992). Racial differences in the predictors of academic achievement of Division I student-athletes. *Sociology of Sport Journal, 9,* 48–59.

Sellers, R. M., & Damas, A., (1996). The African-American student-athlete experience. In E. F. Etzel, A. P. Ferrante, & J. W. Pinkney (Eds.), *Counseling college student athletes: Issues and interventions* (2nd ed., pp. 55–76). Morgantown, WV: Fitness Information Technology, Inc.

Shropshire, K. (1996). *In Black and white: Race and sports in America.* New York: New York University Press.

Sinnett, C. (1998). *Forbidden fairways: African-Americans and the game of golf.* Chelsea, MI: Sleeping Bear Press.

Solorzano, D., Ceja, M., & Yosso, Tara (2000). Critical race theory, racial microaggressions and campus racial climate: The experiences of African-American college students. *The Journal of Negro Education, 69*(1), 60–73.

Spivey, D., & Jones, T. (1975). Intercollegiate athletic servitude: A case study of the Black Illinois student-athletes 1931–1967. *Social Science Quarterly, 55,* 939–947.

Steele, C. M. (1999, August). Thin ice: Stereotype threat and Black college students. *The Atlantic Monthly, 284*(2), 44–47, 50–54.

Steele, C. M., & Aronson, J. (1995) Stereotype threat and the intellectual test performance of African-Americans. *Journal of Personality and Social Psychology, 69*(5), 797–811.

Sue, D.W., Capodilupo, C. M., Torino, G. C., Bucceri, J. M., Holder, A. M. B., Nadal, K. L., & Esquilin, M. (2007). Racial microaggressions in everyday life: Implications for clinical practice. *American Psychologist, 62*(4), 271–286.

Thomas, R. (2002). They cleared the lanes: The NBA's black pioneers. Lincoln: University of Nebraska Press.

Whannel, G. (2000). Sports and the media. In J. Coakley & E. Dunning (Eds.), *Handbook of sport studies* (pp. 291–309). London: Sage.

Wiggins, D. (2000). Critical events affecting racism in athletics. In D. Brooks & R. C. Althouse (Eds.), *Racism in college athletics: The African-American athlete's experience* (pp. 15–36). Morgantown, WV: Fitness Information Technology, Inc.

Wolters, R. (1975). *The new Negro on campus: Black college rebellions of the 1920s.* Princeton: Princeton University Press.

Yopyk, D. J. A., & Prentice, D. A. (2005). Am I an athlete or a student? Identity salience and stereotype threat in student athletes. *Basic and Applied Social Psychology, 27*(4), 329–336.

8

COUNSELING THE GLBTQ STUDENT-ATHLETE: ISSUES AND INTERVENTION STRATEGIES

Mary Jo Loughran

- In February, 2007, an undisclosed settlement was reached in the law-suit brought by athlete Jennifer Harris against Penn State University Women's Basketball Coach Rene Portland. The lawsuit had alleged that Harris was dismissed from the team because of Portland's perception that Harris was a lesbian. Portland resigned her position in March, 2007.

- In 2007, former Orlando Magic and Utah Jazz center John Amaechi disclosed his homosexuality in his book *Man in the Middle*. In a subsequent radio interview, retired Miami Heat star Tim Hardaway responded to an inquiry about how he would react to having a gay teammate: "I hate gay people."

- During July of 2006, 11,500 athletes from all over the world competed in 28 sports in the "Gay Games" in Chicago.

- When Michael Muska, a gay man, was hired in 1998 as director of athletics at Oberlin College in Ohio, anti-gay activist Reverend Fred Phelps threatened to demonstrate on the campus at the beginning of the school year.

Attitudes toward gay, lesbian, bisexual, transgendered, and questioning (GLBTQ) individuals have improved drastically in recent years in most elements of society. Recent opinion surveys indicate that the majority of Americans believe that sexual relationships between consenting same-sex partners should be legal. Additionally, most Americans favor workplace protections based upon sexual orientation, and they further believe that gay and lesbian persons should not be banned from any profession (Gallup, 2007).

Despite these gains, collegiate athletics remains a world in which negative attitudes and accompanying discriminatory behavior toward sexual minorities enjoy widespread approval (Wolf-Wendel, Toma, & Morphew, 2001). In contrast, the GLBTQ culture is one in which divergence from the norms of dominant culture is encouraged and celebrated. The result is that the GLBTQ student-athlete must straddle two cultures with sharply contrasting values and norms. Consequently, counseling GLBTQ collegiate athletes requires a specialized set of sensibilities and skills to assist them in navigating between these two salient, but perhaps contentious aspects of their identity. This chapter will outline the challenges facing GLBTQ collegiate athletes and will suggest intervention strategies appropriate for working with this population.

Defining the Population

As is the case with the U.S. population in general, it is nearly impossible to accurately estimate the percentage of collegiate athletes who are GLBTQ. This is true for a variety of reasons, including difficulties with definitions associated with sexual orientation, inadequate or biased sampling techniques, and the tendency of persons not to accurately report sexual behavior (People Like Us, 2003).

Defining sexual orientation is a complex process. What components should be considered in the definition? Should the definition be confined strictly to sexual behavior? Or should sexual attraction and emotional attraction also be considered? Should sexual fantasy be included in the definition? What about the individual's self-identification? Is sexual orientation best classified as a categorical event (i.e., homosexual, bisexual, and heterosexual) or should it be considered along a continuum? Estimates of GLBTQ prevalence will vary, depending upon how sexual orientation is defined.

Several studies illustrate this construct. Using a dimensional scale originally developed by Alfred Kinsey and his associates in the mid-20th century (Kinsey, Pomeroy, & Martin, 1948; Kinsey, Pomeroy, & Martin, 1953), Gangestad, Bailey, and Martin (2000) found in their large-scale sample of Australian twins that 3.6% of men and 1% of women reported being either primarily or exclusively homosexual. Similarly, Lippa (2000) asked a large sample of college students to classify their sexual orientation. His results indicated that of the men, 95% reported being heterosexual, 3% reported being bisexual, and 2% reported having a homosexual orientation. In the same sample, 97% of women reported being heterosexual, 2% reported being bisexual, and 1% reported being lesbians. However, when sexual attraction was considered in addition to self-report, the percentage of respondents who reported any same-sex attraction rose to 19% for men and 24% for women.

Given this context, the best estimates of the prevalence of a gay, lesbian, or bisexual orientation seems to fall between 4% and 17% (Gonsiorek, Sell, & Weinrich, 1995).

The Athletic Culture

Obtaining accurate data regarding the prevalence of GLBTQ individuals in collegiate athletics is further hampered by the widespread homophobia and negative attitudes toward homosexuality permeating that environment (Wolf-Wendel et al., 2001). Athletic departments are generally perceived to be more conservative than other departments on the college campus, espousing values of conformity over individual expression, and aggression over sensitivity. The result is an environment in which sometimes even slight variation from the norm is frowned upon at best and openly condemned at worst. Anecdotal evidence suggests that most GLBTQ athletes do not feel safe enough to disclose their identities to their coaches or teammates or to administrators (Jacobson, 2002).

The pervasiveness of homophobia in the athletic culture has been well documented (Kettman, 1998; Jacobson, 2002; Baird, 2002). One example of homophobic behavior includes the use of slurs such as "sissy" and "faggot" by coaches directed toward players to motivate or to chastise inadequate play (Anderson, 2005). Another example is the practice of "negative recruiting," in which a coach intimates that the other teams attempting to recruit a promising high school athlete are populated by lesbian coaches, lesbian players, or both (Sandoval, 2003). A third example of insidious homophobia in sports occurs in many high schools and colleges across the country in which veteran members of an athletic team initiate the freshman players with "tea-bagging," referring to a ritual in which a male player is held down by his teammates while an upperclassman rubs his testicles in the victim's face and mouth (Simonovich, 2002).

Underlying the concept of homophobia are sexism and misogyny, both historical mainstays in the athletic culture. Anderson (2005) argued that homosexuality threatens the dominant patriarchy and that in order to be characterized as sufficiently masculine, males must eschew all things associated with femininity. Boys learn early in life that displaying interests, behaviors, or emotions deemed to be feminine will result in being labeled "girly," "sissy," or subsequently, "gay." Success in sporting endeavors for both male and female athletes is typically the result of being stronger, faster, tougher, and more dominant than their opponents, all qualities that are traditionally masculine. As a result, the prevailing attitudes of those belonging to the athletic culture tend to support the notion that the masculine is the ideal. Anderson (2005) called this idealization of masculinity "hegemonic," which is based upon the notion that the dominant culture legitimizes its position by obtaining the support of those below it. In other words, even those individuals who do not conform to the stereotypes of the athlete as macho participate in the glorification of masculinity and the oppression of femininity.

The pressure for male athletes to conform to traditional masculinity is overt and strong. For female athletes, the picture is a bit more complicated. By their very participation in sports, female athletes defy the feminine stereotype. The traditional feminine gender role requires women to be soft, nurturing, and noncompetitive, all antithetical to the demands of collegiate athletics. Despite the fact that the number of women participating in intercollegiate athletics has skyrocketed from 32,000 in 1982 to more than 150,000 in 2002 (Bray, 2003), many women athletes continue to experience conflict regarding gender role expectations. Researchers studying gender roles in female athletes have consistently found that these women tend to view themselves as more masculine than their non-athlete counterparts (Miller & Levy, 1996). For many women, this is actually a positive experience. Young and Bursik (2000) found in a sample of women athletes that a masculine self-concept was positively related to higher levels of self-esteem and identity achievement. Krane, Choi, Baird, Aimar, and Kauer (2004) concluded from a series of focus group interviews with female athletes that women who participated in collegiate sports experienced both feelings of empowerment and feelings of marginalization due to their differences from non-athlete women.

Although men in athletic environments tend to be uniformly negative in their attitudes toward GLBTQ individuals, women tend to have more complex responses. Wolf-Wendel, Toma, and Morphew (2001) interviewed student-athletes, coaches, and athletic administrators at several NCAA Division I universities. Their findings revealed that, in contrast to men, women tended to have a higher level of tolerance toward GLBTQ persons. At the same time, however, women in athletic environments went to greater lengths to distance themselves from the perception that they may have a lesbian orientation. Baird (2002) posited that the pervasiveness of the perception that all female athletes are suspect in their sexual orientation is another vestige of sexism, designed to deter women from participating in sports and therefore preserving a greater share of the available resources for the male athletes.

In summary, the athletic culture is one that can be characterized by emphasis on the traditionally male values of strength, dominance, and conformity. Tolerance of behaviors or identities that vary from the prescribed majority is limited. This appears to be the case across the board, but more overtly so for men than for women.

GLBTQ Culture

In recent times it seems difficult to pick up a newspaper or to turn on a television set without coming across some item related to sexual orientation. Movies and television shows regularly include gay or lesbian characters or storylines. Legalized relationships between same-gender partners, whether they are called marriages or civil unions, are becoming more common in the United States. GLBTQ persons are serving in Congress and in many other elected offices across the nation. A majority of Fortune 500 companies offer health care and other benefits to the same-sex domestic partners of their employees (Human Rights Campaign, 2006). The increased visibility of sexual minority persons no doubt has contributed to the changing attitudes in this country toward

GLBTQ persons. In addition, members of the GLBTQ community are changing their attitudes toward themselves to reflect a greater sense of pride and empowerment.

The increased visibility of the GLBTQ community is evident on college campuses as well. Many public and even some religiously affiliated universities have policies prohibiting harassment and discrimination based upon sexual orientation (Getz & Kirkley, 2006). Campus organizations for GLBTQ students and their straight allies are commonplace. On many campuses, academic courses are offered that include GLBTQ content.

Gender roles also influence perceptions of GLBTQ students on campus. The stereotypes associated with the gender roles of GLBTQ persons characterize men as being overly feminine and women as overly masculine. As is often the case with stereotypes, this is an oversimplification. Lippa (2000) conducted a series of studies in which he compared gender roles in gay men and lesbians with heterosexual men and women. His results suggested that gay men and lesbians tended to report vocational and hobby interests that diverged from the gender norms (i.e., gay men displayed greater interest in traditionally feminine hobbies and vocations, while lesbians exhibited greater interest in traditionally masculine hobbies and vocations). Interestingly, self-reports of masculinity and femininity were less predictive of a gay or lesbian orientation, and objective measures of gender role adherence were weaker still. These results suggest that there is more within-group than between-group variability in sexual orientation when it comes to gender role adherence. In other words, a person's sexual orientation does not necessarily dictate his or her behavior in the masculinity/femininity spectrum. In fact, rather than pressuring individuals to conform to the socially prescribed gender norms, the GLBTQ culture is one in which all forms of gender expression are accepted and perhaps even celebrated.

Several models of identity development have been proposed regarding the process by which individuals consolidate their sexual orientation (Cass, 1979; Troiden, 1993). These models have much in common with existing models of racial and ethnic identity development, in that they begin with an individual's growing awareness of being different from members of dominant culture, progress through stages or phases of exploration, lead to the affiliation and identification with the non-dominant culture group, and culminate in a synthesis with the rest of the individual's identity.

"Coming out," the process of becoming aware of a same-gender orientation and sharing it with others, is a central theme in many sexual identity development models. In fact, in some models group affiliation is linked to positive adjustment. Fassinger and Miller (1996), however, cautioned against the use of sexual orientation disclosure as an indicator of psychological health, particularly in light of the potential influence of pressure from external sources, such as race, religion, and geographic location.

The degree to which people are open with others about their GLBTQ orientation has been examined for its relationship to various aspects of psychological adjustment. Griffith and Hebl (2002) demonstrated a link between the degree of "outness" in the workplace with increased job satisfaction and decreased job anxiety. In this study, GLBTQ workers expressed greater willingness to disclose their sexual orientation in the workplace when they perceived supportive attitudes by their coworkers and supervisors. Further, participants in this study were more likely to disclose their sexual orientation in the workplace when they considered their sexual orientation to be a central aspect of their identities.

In addition to the finding that disclosure of sexual orientation contributes to an improved psychological adjustment, there is evidence to suggest that the decision to withhold this information may have deleterious effects on GLBTQ individuals. In a longitudinal study of HIV-negative gay men, Cole et al. (1996) documented increased health risks, including cancer and infectious diseases, in men who kept their identity a secret. Thus, the stress associated with leading a "double life," such as changing the pronouns when referring to a partner or bringing a member of the opposite gender to formal functions to avoid suspicion, may result in severe negative psychological *and even* physical consequences.

The evidence presented above suggests that openness about sexual orientation is linked to positive adjustment and that secrecy regarding GLBTQ identity is linked to negative outcomes. It seems reasonable to conclude that as a non-dominant culture the GLBTQ community is likely to endorse the value of living as openly as possible.

In summary, the GLBTQ subculture has distinctive values that distinguish it from the dominant culture. Nonconformity is an overriding value in the GLBTQ community. Individual expression is preferred over conformity to predefined expectations. Another one of the values esteemed by the GLBTQ culture seems to be a greater freedom of expression regarding gender roles. Additionally, living as openly as possible in terms of disclosure of sexual orientation to others is clearly an optimal situation in this community.

The GLBTQ Athlete as a Bi-Cultural Individual

The experience of the GLBTQ athlete can be characterized as a "clash of cultures." A comparison of the culture of athletics with the GLBTQ culture illuminates considerable differences in norms and values. The GLBTQ student-athlete often faces a difficult task in the attempt to reconcile these potentially competing aspects of identity in an unsupportive environment.

For example, difference between the two cultural norms regarding adherence to gender roles may result in an internal conflict for the gay male athlete. Away from the locker room and playing field, he may feel comfortable expressing more stereotypically feminine emotions and interests. However, the same individual may find himself monitoring (and perhaps censoring) his emotional expressiveness and activities when in the company of his teammates.

Another example of a potential conflict between cultural norms may occur for the lesbian athlete. The value that the GLBTQ community places on disclosure and openness may compel her to come out to her parents, her professors, and her classmates. However, the cultural homophobia in the athletic department may make her think twice about disclosing her lesbian identity to her coaches or teammates.

Interestingly, an additional potential conflict that the GLBTQ athlete may experience is the prejudice that at times faces all members of the athletic community. Engstrom and Sedlacek (1991) documented the negative attitudes that members of the campus community exhibit toward student-athletes. Students in this study were surveyed regarding their perceptions of student-athletes. Their results indicated that some students were suspicious of good grades obtained by student-athletes. Student-athletes also were viewed negatively because of the perception by non-athletes that disproportionate resources were being channeled to the athletes, particularly in the area of academic support services.

Counseling Issues for GLBTQ Student-Athletes

Given the numerous and unique sources of conflict faced by GLBTQ individuals, it is not surprising that research studies have demonstrated that they seek psychological services at rates higher than their heterosexual counterparts (Liddle, 1997; Jones & Gabriel, 1999). Specific reasons for the higher usage of mental health services include the need to combat the stressful effects of societal oppression, diminished social support, and stress related to the coming-out process. There is no evidence to suggest, however, that GLBTQ persons experience lower levels of psychological adjustment attributable solely to sexual orientation status.

It is known that student-athletes seek psychological services at lower rates than their non-athlete counterparts on college campuses (Watson, 2006). Little if any research has been conducted to determine either the relative need for or the utilization of psychological services for the GLBTQ student-athlete in comparison to heterosexual student-athletes and to the larger campus population. It is decidedly possible that either GLBTQ student-athletes do not seek psychological care at the same rate as non-athletes or, in the event that psychological services are sought, they may not disclose their sexual orientation to the care provider. In either case, it would seem essential that the psychological consulting room be made a safe space for the GLBTQ student-athlete. The sport psychologist must take the responsibility for becoming familiar with the GLBTQ culture and the challenges facing its members who are also student-athletes. This expertise is not enough, however. It is also crucial to examine and perhaps modify one's own attitudes and values related to sexual orientation. Sexual orientation is an issue that evokes deep-seated emotional responses, sometimes rooted in religious beliefs or cultural norms. It may be tempting to conclude that the solution to this dilemma is simply to refer these clients to another provider, but there are reasons why this approach may be ill-advised. Primarily, the client may not readily disclose a GLBTQ identity. As we have discovered, disclosure requires trust and may not occur at the outset of the treatment relationship, but may come well after a therapeutic bond has been established. Referral at this point may put the client at undue risk of abandonment.

Also, one must take into consideration the Ethical Principles of the American Psychological Association (APA, 2002). Principle A (beneficence and nonmaleficence) of the Ethical Code begins with the statement, "Psychologists strive to benefit those with whom they work and take care to do no harm." Further, Principle B (fidelity and responsibility) states, "Psychologists establish relationships of trust with those with whom they work." Finally, Principle E (respect for people's rights and dignity) includes the statement, "Psychologists are aware of and respect cultural, individual and role differences, including those based on age, gender, gender identity, race, ethnicity, culture, national origin, religion, sexual orientation, disability, language, and socioeconomic status and consider these factors when working with members of such groups." APA has further clarified the explicit responsibilities of psychologists working with GLBTQ individuals in a therapeutic setting. Specifically, the organization has adopted a policy statement that mandates that the psychologists "take the lead in removing the stigma of mental illness that has long been associated with homosexuality" (APA, 1997).

Resources are available to assist psychologists in gaining the required knowledge and comfort level to work effectively with the GLBTQ student-athlete. Education and advocacy are provided by the APA's Lesbian, Gay, & Bisexual Concern's Office (APA, 2007). In addition, psychologists can remediate any knowledge deficits in this area through continuing education, consultation, and peer supervision.

GLBTQ-Specific Counseling Issues

There is considerable overlap in the issues that confront gay men, lesbians, bisexual individuals, transgendered individuals, and questioning individuals. Each segment of this population also presents with specific concerns that warrant separate discussions.

"G" (Gay)

Like their straight male counterparts, gay men are subject to the same societal messages regarding the narrowly acceptable range of appropriate gender role expressions for men. More specifically, the vast majority of males are acculturated to value success, power, and competition and to limit emotional expressiveness. In addition, however, gay men may experience the added stress of living life outside the bounds of societal acceptance, particularly in regard to prescribed gender roles. For example, men commonly limit their public expression of affection for one another to a handshake or perhaps a pat on the back. Gay men who may be more effusive in expressing affection for one another learn to inhibit their public displays of affection for their male friends and partners to comply with the heterosexual norm. The enthusiastic hugs, high fives, and chest-bumping that are the norm between male teammates on the athletic field may create tremendous tension for the gay male athlete who may be accustomed to censoring affectionate behavior for fear of drawing unwanted attention to himself. Or, if he does hug a teammate, he runs the risk of being accused of "coming on to" or making an unwanted sexual advance.

The gay athlete faces another difficult dilemma in the locker room, a place that is notorious for male bonding. Often this happens as a result of teammates sharing with one another stories of sexual escapades. The gay athlete's options include sharing accurate details about his relationships with men, fabricating stories in an attempt to fit in, or remaining silent. In any of these scenarios he risks alienation or condemnation from his teammates and in the latter two he also risks diminished self-regard.

Counseling the gay collegiate athlete will likely involve assisting him in negotiating situations such as those described above. In doing so, the counselor may find it useful to borrow and adapt from the multicultural counseling literature. For instance, individuals from non-dominant cultures often must engage in "code-switching" as an adaptive strategy for moving between the worlds in which they travel. The term is borrowed from linguistics and refers to the process of seamlessly switching from one language to another. The figure-ground construct of Gestalt psychology is a useful metaphor for the process of code-switching. Figure refers to the part of the picture that is in focus, while ground remains in the picture, although as background. The counselor might help the gay athlete code-switch by putting his "athlete persona" into figure and rendering his "gay persona" into ground while in the pool, the gym, or the locker room and then switching to bring his sexual orientation back into sharper focus when in a more gay-supportive environment.

Internalized homophobia may serve as one obstacle that can hinder the gay athlete's ability to remain centered and grounded in environments in which he feels outnumbered, discriminated against, or invisible. The effective counselor will facilitate the gay athlete's exploration of his feelings about his sexual orientation. In doing so, the counselor's genuine affirmation of the client's gay identity may provide a powerful antidote to the negative messages the athlete may have internalized about himself.

Gay-affirmative counseling also involves assisting the gay athlete to build a strong social and emotional support system by exploring with the client who among his community of family, friends, coaches, teammates, and classmates is supportive and affirming of his sexual orientation. If needed, the counselor can assist the client in identifying ways of expanding the size and scope of his support system. Possible strategies may be to encourage the athlete to come out to those already in his support network or to help him with efforts to widen his social circle to include new friends who are gay-supportive. The counselor must be particularly cautious in encouraging the athlete to come out. Although it is appropriate to gently challenge the client's hesitation and fear around disclosing his sexual orientation, it also is imperative to keep the decision making about coming out firmly in the client's hands.

"L" (Lesbian)

Many of the issues covered in the discussion regarding counseling interventions for gay male athletes are applicable to working with lesbian athletes as well. These topics include addressing internalized homophobia, working to increase a client's social and emotional support system, and cognizance of both the costs and the benefits of coming out. The lesbian athlete also faces a unique concern, however. Specifically, she is, in essence, the victim of dual oppression, first as a woman in a male-dominated sphere and second as a member of a sexual minority group.

The homophobia in men's sport is pervasive and absolute, but in women's athletics the negativity toward lesbianism is slightly more complex. Women athletes seem to be more tolerant of diversity in sexual orientation than their male counterparts, mirroring the greater tolerance toward GLBTQ persons among women in general as compared to men. By the same token, because of the misperception by some that all women athletes are lesbians, homophobia in women's athletics often takes the form of the female athlete's feeling the pressure to overemphasize the appearance of heterosexuality.

Another issue that may become fodder for counseling is the occasional romantic relationship that develops between teammates. Relationships of this nature may develop as a result of the enormous amount of time that teams spend together, coupled with the highly charged emotional bonds that occur between members of a team. Romantic relationships between team members, if discovered, most likely will create significant consternation in the team culture, sometimes resulting in negative reactions from the coaching staff as well as the other members of the team. The counseling role in this instance might be to assist the lesbian athlete in managing the resulting stress. Dissolution of the relationship between team members often complicates matters even further. Here, the counselor's assistance may be required in preserving the necessary relationship between teammates while supporting the athlete's taking the necessary steps to dissolve the romantic aspects of the relationship.

"B" (Bisexual)

By its very definition, bisexuality defies the dualistic notion in our society that all individuals must fit neatly into either a heterosexual or a homosexual category. An individual who identifies as bisexual acknowledges an attraction to both men and women. As with sexual orientation in general, it is important to remember that a bisexual identity is not defined strictly by sexual behavior. In other words, a person who identifies as bisexual may engage in relationships with only men, only women, or men and women both. Likewise, contrary to stereotypes, monogamy is not incompatible with a bisexual identity.

Bisexual individuals are subject to stereotyping and discrimination by both the heterosexual and homosexual communities. The bisexual person may be subject to the same homophobic attitudes and discrimination by non-GLBTQ persons as those directed at their gay and lesbian peers. As an added bias, bisexuality is stereotypically associated with promiscuity and indiscriminant polygamous sexual behavior. In addition, the gay and lesbian community has historically been less than welcoming of bisexual individuals, perceiving them more as indecisive and less as a distinct sexual orientation.

From this dual bias, bisexual athletes faces challenges related to finding affirmation and community perhaps to an even greater extent than their gay and lesbian peers. The temptation to keep one's identity concealed may be stronger, particularly if the athlete is not engaged in a same-gender relationship. Counseling the bisexual collegiate athlete requires providing affirmation for a sexual orientation that is commonly misunderstood by many in both the straight and gay communities. This affirmation might take the form of correcting any wrongly held assumptions or internalized prejudice that the athlete may have toward a bisexual orientation.

Relationship issues may also be a concern of counseling for a bisexual client. Disclosure of a bisexual identity to a dating partner may lead to feelings of insecurity and mistrust. In this situation, the counselor's role would be to assist the client in understanding the distinction between attraction and behavior and in communicating with the dating partner that bisexuality does not preclude monogamy.

"T" (Transgender)

Gender identity is an entirely separate concept from sexual orientation: sexual orientation refers to the aspect of one's identity that pertains to sexual, emotional, and affectional attraction toward *others*; gender identity refers to the individual's *own* conceptualization of being male or female. Gender identity most often coincides with an individual's anatomical sex; however, that is not always the case. Transgenderism occurs when the individual's experience of one's own gender is at variance with his or her biological categorization of sex. Although transgenderism continues to be listed as a mental disorder in the DSM-IV-TR, there is growing debate about whether this is accurate (Lev, 2005). Transgender advocates argue that variations in gender identity are a naturally occurring phenomenon and that labeling transgendered individuals as mentally ill serves as a means of preserving the societal dualistic norms of prescribed gender behavior.

With respect to athletics, the issue of transgendered persons in competition raises the question of unfair physical advantage, particularly for male-to-female individuals. Teetzel (2006) argued that these advantages should not be a determining factor in consideration of an athlete's eligibility to participate and that any advantage of this nature would pale in comparison to the unfair advantages derived from steroid abuse or doping.

Counseling the transgendered student-athlete will depend upon where the individual is in the process of recognizing and embracing his or her emerging gender identity. For the client who is just beginning the exploration of gender identity, counseling most likely will involve consideration of the client's wishes and available alternatives regarding gender identity expression. Hormone treatment and surgical reassignment are options that would allow the individual to transition toward a gender identity more consistent with his or her internal experience. However, as gender is becoming recognized as a dimensional rather than a categorical variable, many transgendered individuals are choosing to forgo medical or surgical interventions. Likewise, these treatments may interfere with an athlete's ability to compete due to side effects and required healing time.

The counselor will undoubtedly need to assist the transgendered client in managing disclosure of his or her gender identity to coaches, teammates, family, and classmates. Unfortunately, concomitant with disclosure comes assisting the client in coping with prejudice, stereotypes, and discrimination that exceed even those faced by the gay, lesbian, and bisexual community. Thus, the building of social support and identity affirmation are essential ingredients to the counseling process.

One caveat: counseling a transgendered individual through the decision-making process involved in transitioning through gender reassignment is an area requiring significant specialized knowledge and skill that may very well fall beyond the scope of many psychologists. Frequently, the best course of action in these cases is to make a sensitive referral to an expert in this field.

"Q" (Questioning)

For many, consolidation of a non-normative sexual orientation or gender identity is a linear process, beginning with a presumption of male or female heterosexuality and journeying to another destination along the continuum, whether it is homosexuality, bisexuality, transgenderism, etc. For some, however, the journey is nonlinear and may not even have an ultimate resting point. Still others refuse any label, considering this to be too limiting or constraining. For those individuals, the catch-all descriptor of "questioning," or in some circles, "queer," has been co-opted to refer to any person occupying the space outside of the dominant, heteronormative culture.

The practitioner who provides counseling to a questioning student-athlete is challenged to resist the urge to encourage, either subtly or overtly, the societal pressure from every direction to conform to pre-existing identity categories. Rather, the counselor's task should be to provide a safe, affirming space free from judgment and peer pressure for the client to explore these fundamental identity issues.

Summary

This chapter has explored the issues pertinent to counseling the GLBTQ collegiate athlete. In essence, the psychologist providing counseling to a GLBTQ student-athlete must possess multicultural competence to understand the pluralistic and perhaps conflicting cultural contexts of the individual's affiliation with both the athletic environment and the GLBTQ community. This includes possessing a fundamental understanding of the norms of both cultures, as well as an appreciation of the unique challenges faced by their members. Finally, an exploration of one's own attitudes about sexual orientation and gender identity as well as the resolution of any internalized prejudice are essential components of the process of developing expertise and effectiveness in working with GLBTQ student-athletes.

References

American Psychological Association. (1997). Appropriate therapeutic responses to sexual orientation. Retrieved March 17, 2007, from http://www.apa.org/pi/lgbc/policy/appropriate.html

American Psychological Association. (2002). Ethical principles of psychologists and code of conduct. Retrieved March 17, 2007, from http://www.apa.org/ethics/code2002.pdf

American Psychological Association. (2007). APA Lesbian, Gay, and Bisexual Concerns Office. Retrieved March 17, 2007, from http?//ww.apa.org/pi/lgbc/office/homepage. html

Anderson, E. (2005). *In the game: Gay athletes and the cult of masculinity.* Albany: State University of New York Press.

Baird, J. A. (2002). Playing it straight: An analysis of current legal protections to combat homophobia and sexual orientation discrimination in intercollegiate athletics. *Berkeley Women's Law Journal*, 31–67.

Bray, C. (2003). *1982–2002 NCAA Sponsorship and Participation Report 65*. Retrieved March 8, 2007, from http://ncaa.org/library/research/participationrates/1982–2002/participation.pdf

Cass, V. C. (1979). Homosexual identity formation: A theoretical model. *Journal of Homosexuality, 4*(3), 219–235.

Cole, S. W., Kemeny, M. E., Taylor, S. E., & Visscher, B. R. (1996). Elevated physical health risk among gay men who conceal their homosexual identity. *Health Psychology, 15*, 243–251.

Engstrom, C. M., & Sedlacek, W. E. (1991). A study of prejudice toward university student-athletes. *Journal of Counseling & Development, 70*, 189–193.

Fassinger, R. E., & Miller, B. A. (1996). Validation of an inclusive model of homosexual identity formation on a sample of gay men. *Journal of Homosexuality, 32*(2), 53–78.

Gallup Poll. (2007). Gallup's Pulse of Democracy: Constitutional Amendment Defining Marriage as Only Between a Man and a Woman. Conducted May 8–11, 2006. Retrieved March 5, 2007 from http://www.galluppoll.com/content/?ci=1651&pg=1

Gangestad, S. W., Bailey, J. M., & Martin, N. G. (2000). Taxometric analyses of sexual orientation and gender identity. *Journal of Personality and Social Psychology, 78*(6), 1109–1121.

Gonsiorek, J. C., Sell, R. L., & Weinrich, J. D. (1995). Definition and measurement of sexual orientation. *Suicide and Life-Threatening Behavior, 25*, 40–51.

Griffith, K. H., & Hebl, M. R. (2002). The disclosure dilemma for gay men and lesbians: "Coming out" at work. *Journal of Applied Psychology, 87*(6), 1191–1199.

Jacobson, J. (2002). The loneliest athletes. *Chronicle of Higher Education, 49*, pA33, 2p, 4c.

Jones, M. A., & Gabriel, M. A. (1999). Utilization of psychotherapy by gay men, lesbians, and bisexuals: Findings from a nationwide survey. *American Journal of Orthopsychiatry, 69*(2), 209–219.

Kettmann, S. (1998). Out of bounds. *The New Republic, 219*(20), 17–18.

Kinsey, A. C., Pomeroy, W. B., & Martin, C. E. (1948). *Sexual behavior in the human male*. Philadelphia: W. B. Saunders.

Kinsey, A. C., Pomeroy, W. B., & Martin, C. E. (1953). *Sexual behavior in the human female*. Philadelphia: W. B. Saunders.

Krane, V., Choi, P. Y. L., Baird, S. M., Aimar, C. M., & Kauer, K. J. (2004). Living the paradox: Female athletes negotiate femininity and muscularity. *Sex Roles, 50*(5/6), 315–328.

Lev, A. I. (2005). Disordering gender identity: Gender identity disorder in the DSM-IV-TR. *Journal of Psychology & Human Sexuality, 17*(3/4), 35–69.

Liddle, B. J. (1997). Gay and lesbian clients' selection of therapists and utilization of therapy. *Psychotherapy, 34*(1), 11–18.

Lippa, R. A. (2000). Gender-related traits in gay men, lesbian women, and heterosexual men and women: The virtual identity of homosexual-heterosexual diagnosticity and gender diagnosticity. *Journal of Personality, 68*(5), 899–926.

Miller, J. L., & Levy, G. D. (1996). Gender role conflict, gender-typed characteristics, self-concepts, and sport socialization in female athletes and non-athletes. *Sex Roles, 35*(1/2), 111–122.

People Like Us. (2003). What percentage of the population is gay? Retrieved March 6, 2007, from http://www.plu.sg/main/facts_05.html

Sandoval, G. (2003, January 24). Going behind the back: College recruiters raise issue of sexual orientation. *The Washington Post*, p. D1.

Simonovich, M. (2002, October 30). Football camp hazing incidents not uncommon. *The Pittsburgh Post-Gazette*, p. B1.

Teetzel, S. (2006). On transgendered athletes, fairness, and doping: An international challenge. *Society & Sport, 9*(2), 227–251.

Troiden, R. R. (1993). The formation of homosexual identities. In L. D. Garnets & D. C. Kimmel (Eds.), *Psychological perspectives on lesbian and gay male experiences.* New York: Columbia University Press.

Watson, J. C. (2006). Student-athletes and counseling: Factors influencing the decision to seek counseling services. *College Student Journal, 40(1)*, 35–42.

Wolf-Wendel, L. E., Toma, J. D., & Morphew, C. C. (2001). How much difference is too much difference? Perceptions of gay men and lesbians in intercollegiate athletics. *Journal of College Student Development, 42*(5), 465–479.

Young, J., & Bursik, K. (2000). Identity development and life plan maturity: A comparison of women athletes and nonathletes. *Sex Roles, 43*(3/4), 241–254.

9

THE COLLEGE STUDENT-ATHLETE EXPERIENCE AND ACADEMICS

James W. Pinkney
Carmen Tebbe

The academic performance and progress of student-athletes today are constantly changing and regularly scrutinized. In fact, recent academic scandals in major university athletic departments have led to more oversight and concern regarding the academic integrity of academic support services and academic progress of student-athletes (Academic Cheating Scandal at Florida State University, 2007; Thamel, 2007). Critics have assumed for some time that many of these young people are merely "dumb jocks," having few academic goals and attending college only to play sports (i.e., majoring in NFL, NBA, MLB)(Lanning, 1982). Regrettably, a number of student-athletes appear to fit this stereotype. However, it is safe to say that most student-athletes truly do want to succeed in the classroom and do so, with some general academic performance indicators (e.g., graduation rates) exceeding those of non-athletes (NCAA, 2008a).

In order to better understand the formidable academic challenges that student-athletes face today, it is essential to understand the general context of their experiences. Like non-athletes, student-athletes must succeed in the classroom. However, unlike their peers, student-athletes are charged with doing so while simultaneously engaging in what amounts to at least a half-time (i.e., 20-hour-per-week) job—training, preparation, and competition in high-level sport. It appears that the norm today for student-athletes is that choices of majors and courses, class attendance, study behavior, and academic advancement are micromanaged. Information about academic matters that is typically private under the Federal Educational Right to Privacy Act (FERPA general guidance for students, 1974) is often freely accessed and shared by athletics personnel, the right to use often provided by pre-participation waivers that student-athletes sign (voluntarily) at the onset of each academic year. In addition to the foregoing factors associated with student-athlete lifestyles and the intercollegiate athletics system, the academic challenges numerous student-athletes face become more complex because many are not well-prepared in comparison to their non-athlete classmates (American Institutes for Research, 1988). Unfortunately, it is likely that many of these young people would not have attended college if they had not been athletically gifted (Etzel & Watson, 2007).

It remains unclear whether or not involvement in the increasingly demanding experiences associated with participation in intercollegiate athletics is beneficial or detrimental to the academic success of student-athletes (Comeaux, 2007). The "educative value" of participation in intercollegiate sports (e.g., promoting character, developing of a sound work ethic) has been repeatedly questioned (Flowers, 2007). Some have argued that the intercollegiate athletic system that has evolved over time makes balancing the athlete and student roles very difficult, tipping the balance more toward athletic responsibilities and less toward academics (Jayakumar & Comeaux, 2006, in Comeaux, 2007). This chapter will provide a general discussion of the college student-athlete academic experience, as well as provide several practical ideas to enhance student-athlete academic success.

The National Collegiate Athletic Association (NCAA) continues to increase off-the-field, academic expectations for collegiate student-athletes. The NCAA's (2007) most recent statement on "academic reform" establishes yearly percentage targets for individual student's progress toward college degree. The focal point of NCAA's academic reform movement for athletic teams and programs is the Academic Progress Rate (APR) (NCAA, 2008b). This is far more directive than merely requiring a minimum grade point average (GPA) for athletic participation. The percentage target means that taking courses toward completion of a major limits the student-athlete's (or the coach's) earlier strategy of selecting courses for easy grades to keep the necessary GPA level for sport participation.

These practices continue the trend toward higher academic expectations, a potentially more career-relevant college experience, and penalizing athletic teams that have graduation rates below 50% that the Knight Commission (2001) proposed. In addition to improved graduation rates, the Commission also suggested that athletic scholarships should be tied to specific athletes until the athlete or the athlete's entering class graduated. This second suggestion implies that, once offered to a specific student-athlete, a scholarship is not portable but committed until graduation. Both of the aforementioned reports evidence a call to support and cultivate the life skills of collegiate student-athletes (NCAA, 1995).

Although the academic expectations of student-athletes are growing, the expectations of their academic preparedness upon admission may not be. For example, in 2003, the NCAA changed initial eligibility criteria for college admission. The requirement regarding the necessary college preparatory courses increased to 16, and will be increased to 18 in 2008. A "sliding scale" was also implemented that allowed lower college entrance exam scores (i.e., SAT, ACT) if a person's high school percentile rank was high enough (Gurney & Weber, 2007). Thus, student-athletes can perform poorly on standardized tests, yet still gain entrance to the university based on their much better high school grades and vice versa.

Although the intent behind these reforms has ostensibly been to improve the chances of student-athletes receiving a solid education, there has been controversy regarding other possible motives for such changes (e.g., the public image of athletics) and how these reforms will be achieved. For example, some suspect that more student-athletes may be diagnosed with learning disabilities to bypass the increased core curriculum requirement. It is also possible that some high schools may have lowered or will lower the academic standards for high school athletes in order to ensure that student-athletes have higher GPAs, thereby diminishing the impact their performance on standardized tests may have on their gaining admission to a university.

Regardless of the factors that lead to student-athletes' admission to the university, once they step on campus, these young people must meet academic standards that are typically greater and often much greater than in high school. These standards are also frequently beyond the requirements of students who are not involved in athletics (e.g., meeting NCAA eligibility requirements). Athletic departments are now faced with the challenge of assisting under-prepared or over-occupied student-athletes to succeed in the classroom, or at least maintain eligibility, while at the same time requiring them to engage in an exhausting lifestyle that frequently involves year-round training and competition.

Clearly, like their non-athlete peers, scores of student-athletes do well academically. As noted above, their graduation rates are in general about the same as or better than non-athletes (2007 NCAA Report on the Federal Graduation-Rates, 2007). However, numerous other participants in intercollegiate athletics struggle mightily with the demands that academics places upon them. Ducey (2006) reviewed learning difficulties and created a taxonomy of what causes such problems. Three of those causes seem especially relevant for student-athletes: (1) study skills, (2) specific prior knowledge, and 3) intrinsic motivation. All three may be affected by the student-athlete's unique situation.

All students, athletes and non-athletes, vary in their academic preparedness for college. Individual differences, learning styles, high school experiences, and other factors all contribute to a student's readiness for college. Unfortunately, the status of being a high school student-athlete may at times lead to grade inflation in an attempt to maintain eligibility for athletic participation. Although grade inflation is difficult to prove, it is a safe assumption that it does occur at times. At the time, it may seem like a short-term solution, but it does indeed have long-term consequences, including the potential for students not to fully develop the meta-cognitive skills necessary to monitor their comprehension. When students achieve grades that they have truly earned, they likely discover the connection between the use of essential study strategies and quality academic performance. However, if students receive grades that they did not earn through much personal effort and the application of necessary study strategies, they will not likely learn this connection (Tebbe, 2007). Thus, high school grade inflation may contribute to student-athletes entering college without mastery of the necessary study strategies to succeed at a higher level. For example, many students do not appear to have a highly developed ability to determine how prepared they are for an exam (Peverly, Brobst, Graham, & Shaw, 2003).

This may be even worse for college student-athletes whose high school experiences did not adequately teach them the meta-cognitive strategies necessary to do so (Tebbe, 2007).

In terms of specific prior knowledge, recent anecdotal data of college student-athletes included reports of not being challenged in high school (Tebbe, 2007). Perhaps high school teachers assumed that because they were athletes, they would not and should not be able to "cut it" as a student; or, perhaps high school teachers believed they were benefiting student-athletes by assisting them in maintaining eligibility and believed grade inflation was acceptable and in the students' best interest.

The type and amount of motivation to attend college and actively engage in the rigors of one's studies would seem to vary from person to person and may be affected by many other factors (e.g., health status, life stress, time of year). Some recent evidence exists that suggests that a large amount of student-athletes value their college education and are highly motivated to be successful in the academic realm (Potuto & O'Hanon, 2006). Helping professionals who work with student-athletes who have learning difficulties should explore clients' academic motivations and their motivational orientation (i.e., intrinsic, extrinsic).

A Student Success Course to Help College Student-Athletes Achieve Academic Success

One possible intervention to assist college student-athletes in achieving academic success is through offering a student success course designed to address the needs of college student-athletes and their experience. Research on one such course offered at the University of North Texas found that student-athletes who were admitted into the university under special conditions, and thus deemed as "at-risk" based on their previous academic performance, earned GPAs during their first and second semesters of college comparable to those of their non-mandated student-athlete cohorts, after they passed a student success course (Tebbe & Petrie, 2006). The course curriculum emphasized the mastery of self-regulatory skills (e.g., goal-setting, motivation, time management) and learning strategies (e.g., note-taking, test-taking, information processing) that have been found to be essential for college success (Kriner & Shriberg, 1992; Petrie & Helmcamp, 1998). Both male and female student-athletes demonstrated improvements in anxiety management, concentration/focusing of attention, information processing, time management, and test-taking strategies (Tebbe & Petrie, 2006).

In a replication and extension of Tebbe and Petrie's (2006) research, Tebbe's study (2007) compared four groups of students in terms of their GPAs over their first two years of college and reported use of study strategies across their first semester of college. The groups included student-athletes and non-athletes who were accepted under individual review status and mandated to take a student success course based on their previous academic performance and student-athletes and non-athletes who did not enter the university under these conditions. Tebbe found that student-athletes who entered the university "at-risk" had lower GPAs compared to student-athletes and non-athletes who were not considered "at-risk," as well as non-athletes who were also considered "at-risk;" however, these differences were not significant. Although student-athletes who took the student success course initially reported less use of study strategies compared to both non-athlete groups, they also demonstrated improvements in most areas across the semester. Specifically, the student-athletes who took the student success course reported significant improvements over the course of the semester in their ability to manage anxiety, direct concentration/attention, identify important information on which they needed additional study time, develop and use study aids, and effective use of self-monitoring and self-testing strategies. Although student-athletes earn similar grades in high school, it appears that some of them, in particular "at risk" persons, may not possess the necessary cognitive strategies to succeed at the rigorous academic challenges of colleges, which supports previous research (Sedlacek & Adams-Gaston, 1992; Sellers, 1992).

Pintrich and De Groot (1990) proposed that students who had more intrinsic motivation to learn the material, beyond just wanting to earn a good grade, were more cognitively engaged in the process. Based on their findings, it seems plausible that if student-athletes believe they are less capable of succeeding in the classroom, they may be less likely to engage in the learning activities required to be successful. Thus, their lack of using essential study strategies may be related to their not believing that they can, as much as to not knowing how (Tebbe, 2007).

Furthermore, it is difficult to discern if such student-athlete beliefs are based on their own limited academic self-efficacy, or if they are perhaps also a product of society believing they cannot succeed off the field. This is related to the common misperception that student-athletes do not care about their academic performance. As noted above, some student-athletes may not care about their academic performance. However, many desire to do well in school, but do not possess the skills to do so. A student success course, such as the course identified above, might be a useful intervention to help these academically under-prepared students learn the self-regulatory and cognitive strategies necessary to succeed at the college level. In addition, it may be an opportunity to assess the student-athlete's level of academic self-efficacy.

Study Strategies for Academic Success

Student-athletes are well aware of the importance of practice for improving and winning on the field or court. Practice also promotes improving and winning in the classroom as a critical component of many career options and eligibility for participation in collegiate athletics. Thus, any intervention or study strategy that is presented to student-athletes must include an emphasis on the importance of practice that leads to a greater chance of success.

Time Management for Studying

Time management is perhaps the most important key to success for student-athletes. A helping professional's didactic presentation of basic concepts about managing study time such as Lakein's (1989) organizing, listing of tasks, prioritizing, and time analysis is unlikely to benefit most student-athletes' academic performance. A brief appraisal of the typical student-athlete's collegiate experience suggests the problems with using a didactic approach.

First, student-athletes are very busy people who truly do not have a lot of free time. For things that are important to them, they manage time just fine. Activities related to their sport participation get managed very well, while activities that are not related to sports or fun get indifferent management. Studying can easily wind up in last place if a busy schedule puts athletic responsibilities first, fun second, and any number of things in front of studying.

Second, given little free time, it is unrealistic to expect student-athletes to study instead of engaging in options that are much more attractive and appealing to them. They are often social magnets because of their high visibility on campus; other students seek them out for many reasons. Saying "no" to friends and acquaintances is next to impossible when studying is not the first choice anyway. After all, time for personal relationships is limited by sport-related commitments just as sport involvement restricts the time available for studying. Obviously, these priorities are not conducive to academic success; however, they are a reality.

Third, playing time and winning are usually the coin of the realm at the collegiate level of competition. Time management for studying may be viewed by the student-athlete as a matter of merely maintaining eligibility to compete in his or her sport. The excellence the student-athlete pursues in athletics does not automatically transfer to the classroom—the minimum time and effort needed to stay eligible may be the student-athlete's target for studying.

Finally, student-athletes at the collegiate level have been coached for years with specific instructions, diagrams, walk-throughs, and hands-on practice. They are not usually accustomed to a verbal instruction approach that does not include physical demonstration of what is expected. The helping professional working with student-athletes' academic performance will not likely see a great deal of change in student-athletes' academic behaviors with traditional approaches to studying and time management.

This does not mean that student-athletes will not or somehow cannot improve their studying effectiveness, test-taking skills, and consequently grades. However, it does suggest that some basic "rules of the game" need to be learned and conscientiously attended to as student-athletes work to strengthen their academic performance. The following rules are critical to being effective in helping student-athletes' classroom achievement.

1. Be very specific about how to use study techniques.
2. Do not expect student-athletes to spend more time studying.
3. Clearly state the advantages of these suggested techniques.
4. Translate these techniques into athletics-related analogies.
5. Promote efficiency of effort as more important than the amount of time spent studying.

When "coaching" student-athletes in using time-efficient test-taking behavior and study techniques, these rules should be kept in mind and made part of the helping professional's "coaching" for more efficient (not longer) studying.

Concise and informative resources about managing time for studying that include the following: Weigand (1974) presented studying by subjects such as science, math, and English. Lengefeld's (1986) brief book about study techniques has excellent tips on studying and has been a helpful, quick review. More comprehensive resources are the master student book by Ellis (1985) and Haynes' (2002) book on personal time management.

The following techniques for efficient studying are typically presented as an hour-long program. Throughout the program the concept of efficiency of effort is brought up. Effective examples from the student-athletes' own experiences are used to reinforce this concept. For example, questions such as the following might be used: Is reading a page three times because you are tired efficient? How well will a person do on a biology test if she or he studies German to get ready for that biology test? Will running backward improve your free throw shooting? What do your coaches have you do in practice, read textbooks or do competition type things?

Differential Study Techniques

Numerous student-athletes seem to have only one way to study: they put their material on a desk or table, sit down, and proceed to study as long as they can stand it or until a friend, cell phone, iPod, computer, or television offers a better option. No, student-athletes do not feel efficient or particularly effective about this kind of studying, but that is how studying has always been done by a majority. Besides, everyone else studies the same way; it is just that some students can do it longer or better than other students. Yes, student-athletes know the frustration and discouragement of being bored silly while studying, but no one has offered them a better way to go about it.

This part of the program is based on the reasonable assumption that what you study should, to a large extent, determine how you study. Good grades are like winning: more likely to happen if you adjust your game plan (studying) to what the competition will let you do best. There are different ways to study, and efficiency of effort suggests some study techniques are better for some courses and have some advantages for the student-athlete. These are strange ideas for most student-athletes. Why do student-athletes get right answers to questions about a multiplication table when they have not studied it for years? In part because of how the table was learned in the first place.

Flash Cards

Everyone remembers the challenge of the teacher holding up "retro" flash cards and the fun of being right. Flash cards as a study approach have some unique advantages for busy student-athletes. The cards can be used anywhere and, given even a few minutes, let the student-athlete immediately study. Flash cards also give the student-athlete a form of studying that takes place in brief periods that are normally wasted or ignored.

The use of flash cards means that the student-athlete does not have to commit blocks of evening time to a course being studied with cards. As the flash cards are made, the student-athlete becomes more involved with the material. Best of all, flash cards automatically streamline preparation for tests. As cards are learned, and that learning is reinforced by successful recall, they are pulled from the deck being studied. This means test preparation time becomes more efficient, because the time is being used exactly where it is needed, on the material that has not yet been learned. (Personal experience with flash cards provides a helpful anecdote. One of the authors used them while studying Chinese in 1981. Not only did the cards result in high test scores, but much of the studying was done during prime-time television commercials.)

Flash cards have been used successfully by students in foreign languages, anatomy, art history, biology, and other courses in which terminology and definitions are important. Cards are not particularly useful for problem courses, philosophy, or courses in which the application of principles is important. Flash cards are easy for student-athletes to relate to because of the importance given to repetitions, or "reps," in their practice for sports.

It is important that student-athletes understand that flash cards are not the solution for every course. A good tip for the helping professional is to have the student-athlete ask the instructor about his or her feelings toward a flash card approach to studying for the course. This forewarns the student-athlete if there is a potential problem. It also opens up the possibility of the instructor directly coaching the student-athlete on how best to study for the course. Student-athletes are very practiced in relating to coaches, and they expect coaching in performance situations, which is what a classroom test certainly is.

Continuity Tracking

For this approach, the student-athlete is asked to consider committing just a small amount of time to a course, say twenty minutes a day. The important point is that he or she commits that time every single day. Most student-athletes are amazed to learn that in the average semester twenty minutes a day adds up to over thirty hours a semester. This is considerably more time than might otherwise be committed to reading for a single course.

If twenty minutes a day seems unreasonable, the same idea can apply to a number of pages per day. The student-athlete can read the syllabus for a course, add up the number of pages that will be covered, and divide that number by how many days remain until the final exam. The result is how many pages a day will keep the student-athlete on track to get it all done. The number of pages needed per day will be ten or fewer for undergraduate courses (except for some English courses or courses with unusual expectations). Anyone can handle five or six pages a day without disrupting his or her life.

Student-athletes have reported that continuity tracking seems to work best when the twenty minutes or six pages can be associated with some everyday event. Just before or after lunch, before going anywhere in the evening, before practice, and before going to bed have been times that have been used successfully. The important issue is that continuity tracking occurs every day to gain the advantages of this approach to studying, and there are several advantages.

The short time frame of continuity tracking means that the studying always occurs with good concentration. Twenty minutes of almost anything can be focused on without stress or boredom. The fatigue and loss of attention associated with cramming or marathon studying are avoided. The daily exposure to the material jogs the memory and slows down forgetting. The student-athlete keeps up with where the instructor assumes he or she is in reading the text. This means the instructor can be approached as an asset rather than as a threat who will ask if the current material has been read. Again, large blocks of evening time are not used, so the penalty of missing out on friends and fun is avoided. Personal experience by one of the authors with continuity tracking for a course in information science illustrates these advantages. At no time during the semester did the textbook leave his office except when he took it to class. There was no time to study or cram for any of the three tests or the final. No social events, athletic games, exercise, or television programs were missed because of the course. But the textbook was always open and on his desk. Over the course of a day, pages would be read or reviewed: the end result was an "A" for the course. Continuity tracking is ideal for courses in which a known amount of reading factual information is going to be learned.

Recorded Studying

Some student-athletes are far more comfortable and effective with information presented in a form that allows them to listen rather than read. For whatever reason, some student-athletes dislike reading, hate to take notes, and avoid learning much from higher education's traditional style of read and remember. Student-athletes can be asked if they like to listen to music, enjoy chatting with friends, do not mind lectures but get bored reading, or enjoy having coaches tell them how to do something better. A counselor or psychologist can acknowledge a student-athlete's preference for audio-based learning and suggest a more compatible way to study with less reliance on visual methods.

For student-athletes who have an audio preference, recorded (i.e., "taped") studying may be a far more efficient way to study. Recorded studying has the student-athlete replace traditional note taking with a recorder. The student-athlete records materials such as brief summaries, definitions of concepts, and other information worth remembering. This audio record of notes is then available for review at a later time. The night before a test, the student-athlete's own voice reminding him or her of what was important may be the most potent recall stimulus for efficient learning.

Recorded studying can be particularly efficient for courses that use essay tests. The note-taking process of vocally recording what is important actually requires that student-athletes do exactly what they will have to do for the test in their own words: convince the instructor that he or she understands the content and has covered the reading. The helping professional can point out that this is a form of direct practice just like in the student-athlete's sport. The student-athlete is telling himself or herself how to remember things that are important. All student-athletes recognize the importance of practicing and its direct relationship to getting better and winning. They may not like it, but they realize that without practice they won't play. And many student-athletes have already proved that if you do not "practice" for courses, you may not play because of poor grades.

Sunshine Studying

Do student-athletes practice at midnight? Are games scheduled for 7:00 a.m.? Of course not. That would be inconvenient for coaches and spectators as well as disruptive for student-athletes. Practice is scheduled for afternoons or early evening for very practical reasons. The student-athletes have finished classes and can concentrate on what they are doing. Games are played on weekends or in the evening because that is when fans can attend. Sunshine studying, or the art of timely convenience, takes advantage of the fact that there is little going on early in the day.

Any studying that gets done before 5:00 p.m. is efficient in a unique way: it will not cost the student-athlete fun. Better yet, the number of distracting options open to the student-athlete is far smaller than during the evening hours when most students assume they should study. It is also the time when the student-athlete is fresh, before being physically tired by long hours of practice. Friends and acquaintances are busy with their own schedules during the day and are unlikely to be readily available, as they will be in the evening.

Although student-athletes may not think of themselves as early birds, neither are they true night owls. It is simply that in the evening diversions and fun activities do not require the same concentration that studying does. This creates the illusion of being more alert at night. It is certainly worth a try to see if sunshine studying might actually be more efficient for some courses. The counselor or tutor should point out that this is particularly the case for problem-oriented courses such as math and science.

A good reason for this is that very little assistance is available in a residence hall or at the study table at 11:00 p.m. If the student-athlete gets stuck on a problem at that hour, study time will be wasted since there is no one to resolve the problem in a way that promotes understanding the material. The best time to study for a problem-solving course is when the instructor has office hours or a graduate assistant/tutor is known to be available.

Sunshine studying lets the student-athlete do problems when a resource can be quickly accessed to figure out a troublesome issue. Student-athletes need to know that it is not really studying to work on a problem for two hours, not solve it, and quit in frustration. It is efficient studying to use resource people in a timely fashion during the day when they are available to help the student-athlete understand the material and concepts. A suggested resource for problem courses is Weigand's (1974) chapters on how to study math and science.

Reading Instructors

Student-athletes read all the time, but not necessarily books. They read "keys," behavior, situations, and other student-athletes' intentions. "He takes a deep breath before throwing a fast ball," "She always claps her hands before spiking down the line," and "He looks at every receiver except his primary one" are examples of the kind of reading that student-athletes do and for which they receive rewards. In athletic competition there is a dramatic advantage in correctly guessing what your opponent is going to do. It makes sense to student-athletes that correct guessing is also an advantage in the classroom where test performance will determine the grade.

Reading a particular instructor is a learnable skill and the clues and cues that an instructor gives can be helpful. It is a universal student maxim that what goes on the blackboard is important and needs to be in one's notes. There are other cues that the helping professional can have the student-athlete begin to look for in lectures by an instructor. The idea of reading the instructor also reinforces and accents the importance of going to class and attending regularly.

Student-athletes are encouraged to use their knack for reading opponents to read the instructor in the classroom. In fact, it should be easier than reading opponents because the instructor is not trying to hide his or her intentions. Instructors want their students to understand what is important, and they give several signals that certain material should be remembered. Student-athletes are well trained to capitalize on this if their athletic reading skills can be reframed for the classroom.

Repeating something verbatim is not an indication of the instructor's senility. It gives the students time to write it down. Most instructors know that the surest way to capture student attention is to move closer to the students—physical proximity draws student attention like a magnet. Raising the voice or slowing the cadence are both ways of making information stand out. Writing on the blackboard is still the most tried and true way of alerting students to the importance of information. Student-athletes need to know, though, that blackboard information is usually a shorthand symbol of the original information and some explanation is needed. Otherwise, by test time the actual comments in the notes may be cryptic to the point of worthlessness.

Student-athletes, like anyone else, will do better when they have actively tried to figure out what is important to the instructor. Everyone does well on a test when she or he knows what will be asked. A good example is what happens when students face their first driver's license examination—the sixteen-year-olds frantically ask the seventeen-year-olds to make their preparation goof proof because the license is so important to them.

Writing Papers

A ten-page, double-spaced term paper is defined by most student-athletes as a monolithic endeavor that requires large blocks of time to complete. But we could also define such a paper as a beginning (introduction), a middle (the researched findings of the student-athlete), and an end (the summary and conclusions). Even more simply, a ten-page, double-spaced paper could also be defined as roughly three paragraphs per page for a total of about thirty paragraphs.

Most student-athletes will agree that writing a paragraph is not a big deal or a major task, nor does it take a large block of time. In fact, given a topic many student-athletes could generate a paragraph in minutes. Once the paper-writing task has been defined as a discrete, known number of paragraphs, the focus of writing a paper becomes task redefinition. A paper is a number of brief writing tasks called paragraphs that each consist of a few sentences.

All of those paragraphs do not have to be written in a single sitting or weekend. In fact, if the paragraphs were spread out over a period of time, then the student-athlete's life would not be disrupted and a "lost weekend" of nothing but writing a paper (and no fun) would not be required. In fact, the helping professional can offer the student-athlete a simple "tool kit" for managing the paragraph production process.

The "tool kit" consists of a five-by-eight-inch index card for each paragraph needed (about three paragraphs per page). This simple kit defines each paragraph as a separate task or step that can be accomplished as a single unit by itself. There is no need (and little or no gain) to do a bunch of paragraphs at any one point in time. Actually, paragraphs done as a separate task are likely to be of better written quality than if several were done at a single sitting.

This approach also means the student-athlete is not trying to simultaneously organize his or her writing into a complete paper. Rather, organizing the material becomes a separate, discrete task of its own. The student-athlete can concentrate on the writing task with less interference. The paragraphs are on separate index cards, and when the student-athlete has enough paragraphs on cards he or she can began exploring how to organize the paper. The paragraph cards can be easily shuffled and different sequences of paragraphs can be considered by the student-athlete and/or the helping professional. The flexibility to experiment with minimum effort (merely rearranging the cards) means several potential arrangements can be considered. Time is not wasted at the typewriter or computer, and input from others can be sought.

Only after the student-athlete has found an arrangement he or she likes is there any need for typing the actual paper. Prior to that, the student-athlete can do proofing and rewriting directly on the cards. The final step is not writing a complete paper in one massive effort, but typing up a finished product that has the advantages of being done over time, without wasting a weekend, in a way that allows each paragraph to be proofread, and without the anxiety of last minute stress or the awareness that a mediocre product is being submitted to the instructor for a grade.

Many of our student-athletes are excellent students and time managers, but for their sports rather than for classroom studying. A time management and study skills program needs to focus on helping them translate their athletic skills and attitudes into efficient studying. Given the student-athlete's time-compressed life style, asking for more study time is typically unproductive; the time is not there without sacrificing more important or more pleasant alternatives.

Mastery Learning

Benjamin Bloom's (1968, 1976) original description of "mastery learning" proposed the consistent use of "formative testing," in which an assessment is made of the student's readiness to be given an evaluative test by an instructor for a grade on required material. Basically, the student has a chance to see if more preparation (and where) is needed before performing for a grade. For student-athletes, this can be presented as a form of practice that allows them to focus their studying where needed for a maximum grade on the instructor's test. So-called "formative" study techniques follow for different types of tests.

Multiple Choice Exams

Multiple choice items require the student-athlete to select a correct answer from four or five similar options. There is a four-step process for maximizing results from studying for a multiple choice test. First, preparation is critical. Exposure to the test material must occur. The critical issue is how to preserve what is learned in the most productive way. A "formative" practice test would do this efficiently and simply. In this case, the student-athlete merely writes down a question from each page studied that he or she thinks might turn up on the instructor's test. As the material is covered over time rather than being "crammed" at the last minute, the questions provide a record of what the student-athlete felt was important.

This record then becomes the second step in studying for a multiple choice test: this "practice" test can be taken the day or night before the instructor's test. It provides an estimate not only of how well the preparation has been done, but where additional work may be needed. Fortunately, the student-athlete included a page number for each question. This allows her or him to either remember the answer to each question or to know where to look it up if it is not recalled. This kind of practice test streamlines the final preparation for the instructor's test that will be graded. It also leads to the third part of studying for a multiple choice test: prediction.

Test-wise students realize that instructors have their own ideas of what is important in the material the students are covering. In fact, predicting an instructor's test questions is part of building the practice test. An active part of successful test preparation then is trying to predict what will be on the "real" test. Making prediction part of studying and lectures also supports better attention and better concentration while studying or taking lecture notes in class. This also helps the student-athlete be ready for the final part of studying for multiple choice tests: pinpointing.

The student-athlete is then encouraged to take his or her practice test, notes, handouts, and textbook to the instructor's in-class test. Immediately after, he or she can go through these materials and put asterisks wherever an instructor's test item is found. There are two primary reasons for pinpointing items immediately after a multiple choice test. First, it provides a guide for selecting future questions for future practice tests. Second, at the end of the semester or quarter it provides a streamlined review process in preparing for the final exam. Students who used this process report that it allowed them to take two final exams on the same day and do well at both!

Essay Exams

The essay test presents the student-athlete with some different and perhaps more difficult challenges: in your own words, prove that you are familiar with the covered material, understand it, and can apply the material correctly when questioned about it. The essay-testing charge is for students to answer the above challenges by creating a written statement in their own words. The grade for an item is improved by having a grammatically correct statement (with accurate spelling) that is responsive to the instructor's question, is well organized, and shows a sufficient grasp of the material being covered by the test.

Pauk and Owens (2004) noted that there are over thirty "key" words in essay questions. Each of these key words suggests how the instructor is envisioning the written statement or answer to his or her question. For example, the key word "list" should immediately cue the student-athlete to first put down numbers so their recall answer matches the instructor's ideal format for the response. The key term "compare and contrast" indicates that similarities should be put into the answer first, and then the differences. In any case, a minimum of two sentences expected.

How is the student-athlete best equipped to deal with essay items? Pinkney (1996) advocated an approach to preparing for essay tests that used a tape (now digital) recorder for taking notes versus the traditional paper-and-pencil notes typically made by students as they read material for an essay test. Although recorded notes were suggested for students who were inclined to learn best by audio delivery, it seems this style of note making also has an appealing aspect for the student-athlete. Essentially, it gives the student-athlete a chance to practice in a different way for the essay test task—in your own words meet the challenges of the essay item format. The student-athlete reads the material, stopping after important information and recording a summary of it. Again, a page number is included as part of the recorded note ("Page 140, the causes of the American Revolution are . . ."). The student-athlete could easily include motivational and coaching comments as part of the recorded notes. For example, "This will be on the test, so reread the night before and think about how the American and French revolutions differed."

The practice aspect of recorded studying might be enhanced by encouraging student-athletes to use key terms as part of their note making. "List the causes . . ., define the . . ., compare and contrast . . ." could easily be incorporated into the recording process and encourage the student-athlete to imagine how the information would be presented for key terms the instructor uses. It might also strengthen the practice nature of recorded notes to clearly explain what an essay item is asking of the student-athlete and what the challenges are for making a good, responsive answer.

Problem-solving Exams

Courses involving abstract problems such as chemistry or calculus place special demands on the student-athlete. Study skills for abstract problem solving may be absent or rusty from disuse if a pattern of avoidance of such courses has occurred. Sometimes, part of the reluctance to taking this kind of course may be disinterest in such topics, a negative history of unproductive studying, and/or a sense that such material is too complicated for the student-athlete to master. Some student-athletes appear to avoid majors (e.g., in the sciences) that can be time consuming and interfere with their athletic commitments.

A related issue is the nature of the teaching approach to abstract problem solving. In class, the student-athlete may have a sense of understanding as the instructor solves problems on the blackboard. Later, trying to do homework problems, the solution may not come even as large blocks of time are invested. The lack of rewards in the form of solutions by successful problem solving may be frustrating and discouraging to the point of the student-athlete dropping the course or perhaps switching majors.

Intrinsic motivation for the student-athlete often revolves around playing time and being eligible for athletic participation. Practice, weight training, game days that last all day or weekend, and other aspects of being a collegiate student-athlete restrict the time available for the rest of a busy college lifestyle. Learning abstract material may appear to take more time and effort than the student-athlete is willing to commit. Studying to do well on abstract problem tests requires some adjustments for the student-athlete.

There is one, and only one, way to ensure that the instructor's test on abstract problems will be taken successfully—success at doing the homework problems. It is not enough to put in two or three hours studying for math or chemistry. It is not sufficient to sit in class and marvel at how the blackboard solution of the instructor makes sense. The only way to be well prepared is to be able to do the homework problems, which are practice for the test problems. For that to happen, the student-athlete needs to adjust to the process of solving abstract problems and to understand and practice that process of solution.

Kozoil's (1989) discussion of the "cognitive Doppler" applies directly to practicing for abstract problem tests. His cognitive Doppler is analogous to the familiar Doppler effect of an approaching train: the closer it gets the louder it gets until it passes. Then it sounds quieter and quieter until it fades away. He observed that abstract problem solving creates the same effect. In the classroom, the instructor's blackboard solution makes sense because the instructor verbally explains the abstract reasoning behind the solution. Unfortunately for most students, the only things included in their notes when they turn to the assigned homework are the concrete solutions from the blackboard. The abstract reasoning that explained how the solution works was verbal, and it quickly faded as time passed.

No matter how long a time is spent in an attempt to do homework problems, the studying or practicing for the instructor's test is usually not productive if solutions do not result from the student-athlete's time and effort. A real problem for doing abstract problem homework is timing. Student-athletes and students in general often assume the best time to do homework for abstract courses is in the evening or on a weekend when a large block of time can be directed to the task. Unfortunately, this usually means no knowledgeable source of help or coaching is available. Because the instructor's verbal explanation of the solution process is often gone, frustration and disinterest can quickly set in. What was understood in the classroom becomes undoable in the evening, as the cognitive Doppler has done its "fade" in the time since class. There are two strategies for studying abstract problem solving material and doing better on the instructor's tests: (1) timing and (2) note taking.

Abstract homework can be done most productively during instructors' office hours when they are available for questions. Being able to quickly clarify the needed solution steps with the instructor as soon as help is needed is efficient and allows the solution process to solve the homework problems. If the student-athlete's other commitments prevent this, the alternative is to identify when and where qualified tutors are available. Many hard science and math departments sponsor labs specific to their abstract material and staff them with graduate students or upper classmen whose purpose is to assist in reconstructing the solution process. The issue is twofold in successful studying for abstract material: (1) do homework as soon as possible after class and (2) do it when an instructor, tutor, or coach is available to help with understanding the reasoning process needed to solve the homework problems.

The note-taking process for most students, including student-athletes, is fairly predictable. Given some indication that information is important, it goes in the student's notes. In an abstract problem course this usually means what is on the blackboard, on an overhead, on a PowerPoint slide, or anything that can quickly be copied by the student. This note-taking strategy works in many lectures but has a critical flaw for an abstract problem solving lecture: the concrete solution from the blackboard is saved but all of the supporting abstract reasoning and explanation is lost. The instructor's verbal discussion of the solution process is left to the cognitive Doppler and quickly begins fading as the student's day moves on. By the time the student-athlete is ready to do homework problems, he or she is left with solutions that are no longer understood.

A more productive note-taking approach focuses on the instructor's verbal explanation of how and why the solution is derived. A graphic way to encourage this change in focus is to divide the note paper in two by drawing a vertical line down the middle. One side is used for the explanation and the other side for the actual solution on the blackboard. If getting both the solution and the explanation is too much for the student-athlete, he or she would more profitably take notes on the verbal explanation as it is given by the instructor. After all, the student-athlete can get the blackboard solution from another student's notes after class.

Studying techniques that allow practicing for tests certainly have an intuitive appeal for student-athletes in the sense that it imitates their behavior in athletic training and performance. Just as student-athletes seem to enjoy obvious improvement from physical repetition and mental rehearsal as forms of practice, the idea that studying can be practice for classroom tests needs to be explored and processed. In and of itself, the gain obtained from using such study techniques will probably be satisfying to the student-athlete.

Tips for Writing a Paper

Student-athletes also appear to be well aware of the concept of breaking down athletic tasks into smaller elements and improving by taking manageable steps before mastering the larger, more complex task. This process can be used to suggest a productive approach to the complex academic task of writing a paper. The process avoids the last minute, all-at-one-time approach often used by college students, which has several disadvantages for the student-athlete. Those disadvantages include needing a large block of time (like a weekend), writing under considerable time pressure, and little or no chance for proofreading and re-writing before turning the paper in for the instructor's evaluation and grading.

The student-athlete who needs to write a paper for a course may need to redefine the task to make it more manageable so as to hopefully improve the quality of the end result. For example, if a ten-page paper is assigned, it may be more productive and helpful to look at the smaller elements involved in this assignment. An average page of double-spaced typing has three paragraphs of about 250 words. The ten-page paper is actually about thirty paragraphs. A paragraph is far more manageable than an entire ten-page paper, and a process for producing individual paragraphs over time is more effective. The ten-page paper becomes four smaller steps: (1) writing paragraphs; (2) finding a cohesive, focused order for the paragraphs; (3) presenting a conclusion based on the content of the paper; and (4) proofreading for typos, misspellings, and grammar.

A deck of 30 blank index cards (5 x 8 inches is a good size) also helps to redefine the writing task. What is needed is not a ten-page paper, but a single paragraph on each card. One could also write one paragraph on a single page of a computer document. An advantage to this approach is that it also lets the student-athlete have a sense of how much has been done and how many paragraphs are still needed. A reasonable goal can be set, say two paragraphs a day, and the ten-page paper has become a series of short, focused writing assignments over time in small steps. As the student-athlete approaches having thirty paragraphs, he or she can begin to start the next phase of putting the paragraphs into order. The second advantage of using index cards becomes apparent to the student-athlete at this point: the cards can be shuffled and rearranged again and again with minimal effort.

The ordering of the paragraphs is a matter of judgment concerning what makes sense. It may be helpful to remind the student-athlete that a beginning, middle, and end are a logical way to look at a paper. The beginning is often a stated position with a summary of relevant facts and literature. The middle may deal with discussion and some conjecture about those facts or literature, and the end reaches some conclusion or finding. A number of arrangements of the paragraphs can be efficiently and quickly considered merely by shuffling the index cards.

At this point, the only additional writing needed is to present the conclusion as a final paragraph. This can be a summary of the preceding paragraphs or an independent opinion about how to interpret the content of the paper. Likely the conclusion or the purpose of the final paragraph has been determined by the actual assignment of the paper in the instructor's syllabus. The student-athlete can also directly ask the instructor about how the paper should end.

If a reasonable time table was established for generating the paragraphs, there should be ample time to take a break before proofing the paper. It is important for the student-athlete to realize that a paper is a scholarly production and needs to be presented as a finished piece of writing. A goal to plan for is to have a period where the paper can be ignored for a few days and reviewed and proofed with a fresh view and a thorough search for mistakes. Many instructors interpret casual mistakes as signs of indifference or writing just to meet the deadline. Neatness and mistake-free writing speak to planning, effort, and concern for producing a paper that meets the intent of the instructor's assignment.

Summary

In support of student-athletes' success in the classroom, this chapter offers discussion of the academic environment for today's student-athletes. In addition, various study techniques were presented that allow and encourage student-athletes to study and to practice for their academic tests and writing papers.

In their exceptionally busy, time-stressed lives, student-athletes need practical study skills that are effective and efficient. Structuring study techniques to practice for different kinds of tests supports the ability to attain grades that maintain eligibility while progressing toward timely graduation. A student success course structured to teach these study strategies, within the context of the unique challenges of student-athletes today, may be an ideal intervention for university athletic departments to adopt to address the ever-increasing challenges of helping athletes truly capitalize on their roles as students.

References

Academic cheating scandal detailed at Florida State. Retrieved October 30, 2007, from http://www.usatoday.com/printedition/sports/20070928/cnotes28.art.htm.

American Insititutes for Research. (1988). Summary results from the 1987–88 national study of intercollegiate athletics (Report No. 1). Palo Alto, CA: Center for the Study of Athletics.

Bloom, B. S. (1968). Mastery learning. *Evaluation Comment, 1*(2).

Bloom, B. S. (1976). *Human characteristics and school learning.* New York: McGraw-Hill.

Comeaux, E. (2007). The student(less) athlete: Identifying the unidentified student. *Journal for the Study of Sports and Athletes in Education, 1*(1), 37–44.

Ducey, C. P. (2006). Academic difficulties. In P. Grayson & P. Meilman (Eds.), *College mental health practices* (pp. 173–193). New York: Routledge.

Ellis, D. B. (1985). *Becoming a master student.* Rapid City, SD: College Survival.

Etzel, E., & Watson, J. (2007). Ethical challenges for psychological consultations in intercollegiate athletics. *Journal of Clinical Sport Psychology, 1,* 304–317.

FERPA general guidance for students. (2007). Retrieved August 6, 2007, from http://www.ed.gov/policy/gen/guid/fpco/ferpa/students.html

Flowers, R. D. (2007). "Win one for the Gipper": Organizational foundations of inter-collegiate athletics. *Journal for the Study of Sports and Athletes in Education, 1*(2), 121–140.

Gurney, G., & Weber, J. (2007). Rethinking the NCAA's academic reform. *College and University Journal, 83*(2), 47–52.

Haynes, M. E. (2002). *Personal time management.* Los Altos, CA: Crisp Publication.

Jayakumar, U., & Comeaux, E. (2006). The mis-education of student-athletes: A case study of an athletic organization. Presented at the annual meeting of the American Educational Research Association, San Francisco.

Knight Commission on Intercollegiate Athletics. (2001). A call to action: Reconnecting college sports and higher education. Retrieved January 15, 2008, from www.Knight-Commission.org

Kozoil, M. E. (1989). The cognitive Doppler. *Journal of Educational Development, 13*, 14–16.

Kriner, L. S., & Shriberg, A. (1992). Counseling center interventions with low achievers. *NASPA Journal, 30*, 39–42.

Lakein, A. (1974). *How to get control of your life and your time.* New York: Signet.

Lanning, W. (1982). The privileged few: Special counseling needs of athletes. *Journal of Sport Psychology, 4*, 19–23.

Lengefeld, U. *The fifty-minute study skills program: How to become a master student.* Menlo Park, CA: Crisp Publications.

National Collegiate Athletic Association. (1995). *The name of the game is LIFE . . .* Overland Park, KS: NCAA Foundation.

National Collegiate Athletic Association. (2007). NCAA backgrounder on academic reform. Retrieved December 14, 2007, from http://www.ncaa.org/wps/portal/!ut/p/kc xml/04_Sj9SPykssy0xPLMnMz0vM0Y_QjzKLN4j3NQDJgFiGph76kRCGN0zM2 BQihFDliC7gEwYX8fXIz03V99YP0C_IDQ0NjSh3BACJjGvD/delta/base64xml/L 3dJdyEvUUd3QndNQSEvNElVRS82XzBfTFU!?CONTENT_URL=http://www2. ncaa.org/portal/academics_and_athletes/education_and_research/academic_reform/ backgrounder_academic_reform.html

National Collegiate Athletic Association. (2008a). Division I graduation success rate; Division II graduation success rate. Retrieved January 22, 2008, from http://www2. ncaa.org/portal/academics_and_athletes/education_and_research/academic_reform/ gsr/index.html

National Collegiate Athletic Association. (2008b). Academic reform. Retrieved January 22, 2008, from http://www2.ncaa.org/portal/academics_and_athletes/education_and _research/academic_reform/index.html

NCAA Report on the Federal Graduation-Rates Data. (2007). Retrieved May 5, 2008, from http://www.ncaa.org/grad_rates

Pauk, W., & Owens, J. (2004). *How to study in college.* Boston: Houghton Mifflin.

Peverly, S. T., Brobst, K. E., Graham, M., & Shaw, R. (2003). College adults are not good at self-regulation: A study on the relationship of self-regulation, note-taking, and test-taking. *Journal of Educational Psychology, 95*, 335–346.

Petrie, T. A., & Helmcamp, A. (1998). Evaluation of an academic study skills course. *Journal of College Student Development, 39*, 112–116.

Pinkney, J. W. (1996). Coaching student-athletes toward academic success. In E. F. Etzel, A. P. Ferrante, & J. W. Pinkney (Eds.) Counseling college student-athletes: Issues and interventions (pp. 309–331). Morgantown, WV: Fitness Information Technology.

Pintrich, P. R. & De Groot, E. V. (1990). Motivational and self-regulated learning components of classroom academic performance. *Journal of Educational Psychology, 82*, 33–40.

Potuto, J., & O'Hanlon, J. (2006). National study of student athletes regarding their experiences as college students. University of Nebraska—Lincoln.

Sedlacek, W. E., & Adams-Gaston, J. (1992). Predicting the academic success of student-athletes using SAT and noncognitive variables. *Journal of Counseling & Development, 70*, 724–727.

Sellers, R. (1992). Racial differences in the predictors for academic achievement of student-athletes in Division I revenue-producing sports. *Sociology of Sport Journal, 9*, 48–59.

Tebbe, C. M. (2007). *The effectiveness of a learning strategies course of college student-athletes' and non-athletes' academic performance, and retention after the first two years of college.* Unpublished doctoral dissertation, University of North Texas, Denton.

Tebbe, C. M. & Petrie, T. A. (2005). The effectiveness of a learning strategies course on college student-athletes' adjustment, learning strategies, and academic performance. *Academic Athletic Journal, 19*, 1–20.

Thamel, P. (2006, July 14). Top grades and no class time for Auburn players, *New York Times*, p. 1A.

Weigand, G. (1974). *How to succeed in high school.* Woodbury, NY: Barron's Educational Series.

10

TRANSITIONS OF THE STUDENT-ATHLETE: THEORETICAL, EMPIRICAL, AND PRACTICAL PERSPECTIVES

Albert J. Petitpas
Britton W. Brewer
Judy L. Van Raalte

As young people make the transition from high school to college, they are faced with a number of developmental challenges. Establishing an identity, developing new relationships, separating from their families of origin, and balancing academic and social priorities are just four of the challenges confronting college students of traditional age (Kadison & DiGeronimo, 2004). Coping with these challenges can be a daunting task for anyone. Unfortunately, college student-athletes face not only these challenges, but also the physical, social, psychological, and time demands inherent in being an intercollegiate athlete (Watt & Moore, 2001). In addition, when most graduating students are preparing to enter into their professional careers through employment or specialized graduate study, most student-athletes also have to cope with the end of their formal sport careers. Ironically, although it appears that college student-athletes must adjust to a number of significant transitions, these transitions have received little attention in the literature.

In this chapter, we describe some of the major transitions faced by intercollegiate athletes and examine these transitions from both theoretical and empirical perspectives. Suggestions are presented for designing interventions, and existing programs for student-athletes in transition are described.

Transitions of the College Student-Athlete

"A transition can be said to occur if an event or non-event results in a change in assumptions about oneself and the world and thus requires a corresponding change in one's behavior and relationships" (Schlossberg, 1981, p. 5). This definition is particularly useful in examining the transitions of student-athletes because it includes the importance of cognitive appraisal and "nonevents." The way in which individuals interpret or appraise a transition may affect their emotional and other responses to the situation. For example, a first-year student who views not making a team as a challenge will likely have a different emotional reaction than one who views the situation as a catastrophe. Likewise, a student-athlete who aspires to a leadership position may be honored and excited to be team captain, a reaction different from that of an athlete overburdened with other tasks and responsibilities. Nonevents happen when individuals anticipate changes that do not occur. Athletes are susceptible to transitional events, such as the athletic team selection process, injury, and retirement, but also must cope with such nonevents as not making the starting team or failing to get more playing time because the coach has decided to go with other players (Danish, Petitpas, & Hale, 1993).

High School to College

Adjusting to college after high school is the first transition faced by college students. Incoming students must grapple with establishing new relationships, adapting to more rigorous academic requirements, and managing their new freedom (Medalie, 1981). Student-athletes have the additional task of adapting to demanding sport participation at the intercollegiate level. Student-athletes who have good-quality roommate relationships and are satisfied with their sport involvement tend to adjust better during their first semester of college (Quarforth, Brewer, Petitpas, Champagne, & Cornelius, 2003).

Perhaps the most challenging change for college student-athletes is the player to nonplayer transition (Lubker & Etzel, 2007; Pearson & Petitpas, 1990). This transition occurs when individuals are "deselected" from the team, incur a career-ending injury, complete their eligibility, or choose to retire from sport participation (Alfermann & Stambulova, 2007). The deselection process is a harsh reality of the sport system.

Each sport season, thousands of highly skilled former high school "superstars" are not selected to teams. Some lack the physical skills necessary to compete at a particular college or university. Others may be "cut" because they do not match the coach's expectations. Still others may lose their team spot to a promising new recruit. Ogilvie and Howe (1982) described this process as "survival of the fittest," and it is clearly a reality in high-level college sport.

Injury

Another reality of life in college sport is injury (NCAA, 2007a). Despite marked improvement in equipment and training methods, the incidence of sport injury has remained high (Lanese, Strauss, Leizman, & Rotondi, 1990), with slightly more than half of all student-athletes reporting an injury during their college careers (Etzel, Zizzi, Newcomer-Appeneal, Ferrante, & Perna, 2007). Many athletes have had their sport careers ended by a serious injury, and many more have had to make adjustments to being out of their sport for weeks, months, or even years due to injury (Rotella, 1984).

Even if student-athletes are successful in making the team and avoiding injury, they cannot escape the end of their collegiate sport career. Whether they are fifth-year seniors or play as graduate students, all intercollegiate student-athletes are limited to four years of eligibility. With less than 2–3% of college student-athletes going on to professional careers (NCAA, 2007b; Ogilvie & Howe, 1986), the end of eligibility marks the termination of the organized sport careers for the vast majority of student-athletes.

Academic Ineligibility

A smaller number of student-athletes forfeit portions of their eligibility by failing to meet NCAA Clearinghouse or institutional academic entrance standards, by failing to attain NCAA or institutional academic progress standards, or by transferring to another college or university. Others may choose to stop playing voluntarily because of family issues, player-coach difficulties, reduced interest in sport, or a desire to spend more time with friends, on academic pursuits, or on outside interests.

Although student-athletes face several transitions in addition to those already faced by the typical college student, this area has received relatively little attention in the literature. A growing number of authors have focused on retirement from professional or elite amateur sport (e.g., Lally, 2007; Lavalle & Wylleman, 2000; Lubker & Etzel, 2007; Stambulova, Stephan, & Jäphag, 2007; Stephan, Torregrosa, & Sanchez, 2007) and have offered several models of sport transition, but few have focused on the college student-athlete. Before we review the empirical literature and offer programming suggestions for student-athletes in transition, it may be helpful to examine several of the theoretical frameworks that have been proposed, namely stage and developmental models.

Theoretical Perspectives

Stage Models

Over the last three decades, the sport psychology literature has seen an increase in interest in transitions in sport (Alfermann & Stambulova, 2007; Gardner & Moore, 2006). Most of the early writings (e.g., Lerch, 1982; McPherson, 1980; Rosenberg, 1982) attempted to adapt theoretical models from social gerontology and thanatology to sport retirement. For example, social and psychological changes involved in retirement from sport were depicted by Lerch (1982) and Rosenberg (1982) as "social death," a form of social withdrawal and rejection from an individual's primary affiliation group. The parallels between the social death of the retiring athlete and the terminally ill patient led several writers to speculate that injured or retiring athletes would go through stages similar to those experienced by a dying person. Various adaptations of Kubler-Ross's (1969) stage model of grief and loss can be found in the sport psychology literature. These adaptations suggest that transitional athletes pass through stages of adjustment that may include shock, denial, anger, bargaining, depression, and acceptance (e.g., Astle, 1986; Lynch, 1988; Ogilvie, 1987; Rotella & Heyman, 1986). Although there is some anecdotal evidence in support of a stage model explanation of athletic transition (Gordon, Milios, & Grove, 1991; Ogilvie, 1987), this theory has not stood up well to empirical scrutiny (Baillie, 1992; Kleiber & Brock, 1992). It has been criticized as oversimplifying a complex process and therefore offering little predictive value (Brewer, 1994; Crook & Robertson, 1991; Swain, 1991; Taylor & Ogilvie, 1994).

Stage models of sport transition assume that every person who experiences a major sport transition would go through the same set of stages of adjustment. Clearly, this assumption is ripe for criticism because it fails to take into account individual, environmental, and social differences (Crook & Robertson, 1991; Danish et al., 1993; Pearson & Petitpas, 1990; Taylor & Ogilvie, 1994). Nonetheless, knowledge of stage models of sport transition can help practitioners understand the general range of reactions that may occur during the disengagement process and assist them in managing situations in which specific patterns of behavior are emerging.

Developmental Models

So-called "developmental models" strive to examine transitions from a variety of domains, taking into account the diversity of individual and environmental factors present. Two models, namely the adaptation to transitions model (Schlossberg, 1981) and the "life development interventions" model (LDI) (Danish, Petitpas, & Hale, 1993), appear to have particular relevance to understanding transitional college student-athletes.

Schlossberg's model was developed to provide a framework for understanding adult life transitions and has been applied to sport transitions by several researchers (Crook & Robertson, 1991; Gorbett, 1984; Pearson & Petitpas, 1990; Swain, 1991). According to Schlossberg (1981), adaptation to transition is a factor of individuals' appraisals of the transition, their personal characteristics, and their life situations. Most transitions can be understood by examining a common set of variables (Gardner & Moore, 2006). Did the transition occur when it was expected to occur ("on-time," e.g., retirement after four years of eligibility) or was it unexpected ("off-time," e.g., getting "cut" from the team as a sophomore)? Did the transition come on gradually or suddenly? Was the duration of the transition permanent, temporary, or uncertain? How much stress was experienced? What role change (gain or loss) occurred? What positive or negative emotions were experienced? Each of these factors provides insight into the nature of a transition. However, coping with the transition is contingent on several additional individual and environmental factors that helping professionals need to take into consideration.

Individual characteristics include age, sex, life stage, health, race/ethnicity, socioeconomic status, value orientation, psychosexual competence, sex role identification, and prior experience with similar transitions. Environmental factors include the interpersonal support system, institutional supports, and the pre- and post-transitional physical settings. These individual and environmental characteristics can have either a facilitating or debilitating affect on the transition (Schlossberg, 1984).

Although Schlossberg's model is seen as multidimensional, several other factors that may affect the transition process of student-athletes have been suggested. These factors include: (a) status loss (Gorbett, 1984); (b) strength and exclusivity of the athletic identity, (c) confidence, (d) locus of control, (e) anticipatory socialization, and (f) coaches (Crook & Robertson, 1991); (g) entitlement (Pearson & Petitpas, 1990;) (h) education, (i) skills, (j) interests, and (k) unanticipated support (Swain, 1991). Extrapolating from Schlossberg's model, Pearson and Petitpas (1990) predicted that the transition process would be most difficult for student-athletes who:

a. have most strongly and exclusively based their identity on athletic performance;
b. have the greatest gap between level of aspiration and level of ability;
c. have had the least prior experience with the same or similar transitions;
d. are limited in their general ability to adapt to change because of emotional and/or behavioral deficits;
e. are limited in their ability to form and maintain supportive relationships; and
f. must deal with the transition in a context (social and/or physical) lacking material and emotional resources that could be helpful (p. 9).

Thus, Schlossberg's (1981) model provides an excellent framework to understand transitional experiences of college student-athletes. It clearly addresses several of the shortcomings of the stage models presented earlier, has been supported empirically (Swain, 1991), and has inspired the sport-specific athletic career termination model (Taylor & Ogilvie, 1994, 2001) and the athletic career transition model (Stambulova, 1997, 2003), both of which focus on personal and situational factors that contribute to the ways in which athletes cope with transition.

The LDI model (Danish et al., 2002, 2003) has much in common with Schlossberg's model. Transitions are viewed as multidimensional events with many biopsychosocial components. Transitions, or "critical life events," are not discrete but are processes that commence when individuals begin to anticipate them and continue through their occurrence until the post-transition aftermath has been determined. Similar to Schlossberg's model, transitions have their own characteristics (e.g., timing, duration, contextual purity) and individuals' reactions to transitions are often a factor of their individual and support resources, their level of preparation for the event (preoccurrence priming), and their past experience dealing with similar events. Although the overlap with Schlossberg's model is obvious, the LDI perspective is particularly helpful because it clearly links transitional theory to an intervention framework. Before elaborating on this framework, we examine empirical studies of college student-athletes' transitions.

Empirical Perspectives

Although thousands of student-athletes make transitions as a function of their sport involvement each year, there have been relatively few systematic investigations on the transitions of college student-athletes. As indicated in a recent review of the literature (Alfermann & Stambulova, 2007), researchers have focused primarily on one type of transition in particular—retirement from sport involvement—at other levels of competition (e.g., elite amateur, junior, masters, professional). The studies that have examined college student-athlete transitions have also focused primarily on adjustment to leaving intercollegiate sport. In this section, we review the empirical literature on student-athlete adjustment to transitions by examining the quality of adjustment to these transitions, exploring factors that affect the quality of adjustment, summarizing the results of intervention studies, and addressing considerations for future research in this area.

Quality of Adjustment

The available research data suggest that, in general, college student-athletes adjust quite well to termination of involvement in intercollegiate sport (Baillie, 1992; Greendorfer & Blinde, 1985; Perna, Ahlgren, & Zaichkowsky, 1999; Snyder & Baber, 1979). Two studies (Blinde &

Stratta, 1992; Hallinan & Snyder, 1987) found evidence of some grief-like reactions in athletes who had been cut from their athletic teams or whose sport programs had been eliminated. But these investigations assessed adjustment a relatively short time after forced disengagement from intercollegiate sport had occurred.

When adjustment has been measured after more time has elapsed since collegiate sport career termination, a different picture has emerged. In the largest empirical study of sport transitions to date, involving 1,124 former NCAA Division I student-athletes, Greendorfer and Blinde (1985) found that "the majority of athletes did not experience feelings of loss or disruption upon leaving sport" (p. 107). Similarly, findings from an investigation of 233 male former intercollegiate student-athletes and a randomly selected sample of 190 nonathlete peers revealed that the former student-athletes demonstrated levels of adjustment comparable to or better than their student-nonathlete counterparts.

Moderators of Adjustment

Although student-athletes tend to cope well with disengagement from college sport, it is clear that this transition can be traumatic for some individuals (Blinde & Stratta, 1992; Hallinan & Snyder, 1987). Even former student-athletes who later demonstrate positive adjustment may experience difficulty in the process of terminating their involvement in intercollegiate sport (Baillie, 1992). With these facts in mind, researchers have attempted to identify factors associated with adjustment to leaving college sport.

One factor that may influence the quality of student-athlete adjustment to sport career termination is the context in which termination occurs. As noted by Blinde and Stratta (1992) and Hallinan and Snyder (1987), aversive reactions to disengagement from college sport may be particularly pronounced when such disengagement is involuntary and unanticipated. Baillie (1992) found that when retirement from collegiate athletics was due to injury or team politics, emotional adjustment was hampered. In a similar vein, Kleiber, Greendorfer, Blinde, and Samdahl (1987) found that having one's college sport career ended prematurely by injury was associated with poor adjustment. Kleiber and Brock (1992) reanalyzed the data of Kleiber et al. (1987), finding that sustaining a career-ending injury affected adjustment negatively only for those student-athletes who were highly invested in playing professional sport.

Webb, Nasco, Riley, and Headrick (1998) reported that student-athletes whose termination of sport involvement was prompted by injury experienced retirement difficulty.

Consistent with the findings of Kleiber and Brock (1992), another factor thought to be associated with adjustment to the transition out of college sport is athletic identity, which is the degree to which an individual identifies with or invests in the athlete role as a source of self-worth (Baillie & Danish, 1992; Blinde & Greendorfer, 1985; Brewer, Van Raalte, & Linder, 1993; Pearson & Petitpas, 1990). In support of this hypothesis, Hinitz (1988) found that former intercollegiate gymnasts who identified strongly with the role of "gymnast" and considered involvement in gymnastics a primary source of self-definition experienced difficulty in adjusting to sport retirement. Ingebritsen (1997) and Webb et al. (1998) reported similar findings for student-athletes in other sports.

The extensive investigation of former University of Southern California football players by Baillie (1992) identified a number of other potential moderators of adjustment to college sport career termination. Mental preparation and planning for retirement were positively related to both emotional and functional adjustment. Factors negatively associated with emotional adjustment included the amount of "unfinished business" in sport, the length of time needed to find a new focus outside of college football, the belief that sport provided pleasure unrivalled in the years since athletic retirement, the length of time after sport career termination spent entertaining thoughts about making a "comeback," and the frequency of thoughts about college football involvement. Perna et al. (1999) essentially replicated Baillie's results for retirement planning, finding that former student-athletes with a career plan reported greater life satisfaction than those without a career plan. The findings of Baillie (1992) and Perna et al. (1999) suggest that career maturity may be an important contributor to the adjustment of student-athletes to sport career termination (see Kornspan & Etzel, 2003 for a review).

Issues for Future Research

There is a clear need not only for more research but also for research of better quality on transitions of college student-athletes. Whenever possible, control groups of students not participating in college athletics should be incorporated into study designs. Control groups allow for comparison against a relevant standard of adjustment (Curtis & Ennis, 1988; Snyder & Baber, 1979). Longitudinal studies with multiple assessments of adjustment (including preretirement) are essential, as they enable researchers to examine temporal aspects of adjustment to sport career termination. Both standardized and sport-specific measures of adjustment (Baillie, 1992) should be used in empirical investigations. Such an approach permits comparison with normative populations of interest, while recognizing the unique characteristics of the sport transition process. In addition to questionnaire assessments of adjustment, objective indices reflecting overt behavioral outcomes (e.g., income, educational attainment) should also be taken to supplement the current focus on the inner experience of sport career transitions. Finally, from a topical standpoint, more qualitative and quantitative research is needed on transitions other than sport career termination, such as the transition from high school to college (Giacobbi et al., 2004; Parker, 1994).

Interventions to Facilitate Adjustment

As the process by which student-athletes adjust to transition has become better understood, interventions to facilitate positive adjustment have been developed and, in several cases, evaluated empirically. In one study, female college students who had concluded their involvement in intercollegiate sport and were experiencing difficulties in adjustment reported being highly satisfied with their participation in a group counseling intervention called Retired Athletes in Transition (Constantine, 1995). Selden (1998) and Stankovich (1998) presented evidence that student-athletes who participated in career development interventions designed to prepare them for intercollegiate sport career termination experienced an increase in career maturity. Both interventions focused on identity exploration, career planning, and goal setting. In a related study, Shiina, Brewer, Petitpas, and Cornelius (2004) found that student-athletes who completed a workshop designed to identify skills gained through sport participation that have value in other domains and augmented with a self-report transferable skills inventory experienced greater increases in career self-efficacy than those who viewed a sports nutrition video or completed a transferable skills workshop that was not augmented with a self-report inventory. Other interventions that have been advocated to facilitate student-athlete adjustment to transitions but are currently without empirical support include family involvement, life skills programs, and mentoring/networking (Levy, Gordon, Wilson, & Barrett, 2005).

Summary

Empirical research has indicated that, for the most part, college student-athletes cope well with sport career termination. It may be that "the transition out of intercollegiate sport seems to go hand-in-hand with the transition from college to work careers, new friendships, marriage, parenthood, and other roles normally associated with adulthood" (Coakley, 1983, p. 4). Some student-athletes do experience difficulty adjusting, however, and several moderators of adjustment have been identified. Additional research is needed to enhance understanding of college student-athletes' transitional processes particularly with respect to transitions other than that out of sport involvement and to further examine the utility of the Schlossberg (1981) and LDI (Danish et al., 1993) models for college student-athletes.

Assisting Student-Athletes in Transition

A large number of academic athletic counseling departments have developed specific programs to assist student-athletes in managing transitions. For example, the National Association of Academic Advisors for Athletics (N4A) (2007) identified the Academic Success Skills Workshop at Elon University, Enhancing the Student Experience at Gonzaga University, HEADS UP at California State University, Long Beach, and Coping with College at Pennsylvania State University as "Model Practices." The goal of this section is to outline a framework for planning athletic transition programs and to provide a description of one that strives to prepare student-athletes for their transition out of college.

An Intervention Framework

Although the overall goal of the Life Development Intervention (LDI) perspective is to enhance personal competence through the acquisition of life skills, it is particularly helpful in designing programs because it links the timing of the transitional experience to an appropriate intervention (Danish et al., 1992, 1993). Interventions that take place before a transition are considered *enhancement* strategies. Those that take place during a transition are *supportive*, and those that take place after a transitional event are considered *counseling* strategies.

Because the LDI perspective is based on developmental-educational theory, the primary intervention is enhancement. *Enhancement* prepares student-athletes to cope with future events by assisting them in anticipating normative and paranormative transitions, by helping them identify transferable skills, by showing them how transferable skills can be used in non-sport domains, and by teaching them a variety of coping or life skills.

Supportive interventions are those that take place during a transition. The goal of support is to buffer the impact of any stressful aspects of a transition and to assist in mobilizing the transitional student-athlete's coping resources. For example, the Peer Counseling Program at the University of Connecticut offers a support group for athletes who are coping with injury (Roberts-Wilbur, Swenson, & Dargan, 1994). Injured athletes have opportunities to meet in small groups that are facilitated by professional counselors who understand the unique needs and experiences of student-athletes. These support groups provide informational support, encouragement, challenge, and the emotional support sometimes required to keep student-athletes focused on their schoolwork, their responsibilities, and their injury rehabilitation process.

Counseling interventions take place after a transitional event and are directed at assisting those student-athletes who may be having difficulty coping with or managing the aftermath of a transition. Often the intervention is geared toward assisting student-athletes in dealing with issues such as withdrawal, substance abuse, or acting-out behaviors, which are frequently the student-athletes' attempts at self-cure or methods for avoiding their own feelings. Athletic department or support service personnel should identify specialists within the college/university or local community who can serve as referral targets for individuals who are having difficulty coping with a transition. Ideally these referral targets are well versed in the problem area (e.g., eating disorders) and espouse an educational rather than a remedial orientation. The goal is to assist individuals in developing resources to better cope with transitions.

Time Line	Type of Intervention
Enhancement Pre-Transition	1. Educate about future transitions 2. Identify transferable skills 3. Teach how transferable skills work in new domains and in coping with transitions 4. Teach new life skills
Support During Transition	1. Develop support network 2. Mobilize student-athlete coping resources 3. Buffer impact of any stress related to transition
Counseling Post-Transition	1. Develop referral network 2. Identify or develop coping resources to manage transition aftermath

Figure 1. Conceptual Model for Planning Transitions

As shown in Figure 1, intervention programs for transitional college student-athletes should be multidimensional and include enhancement, support, and counseling components. The following section contains a more detailed description of an enhancement program that strives to prepare student-athletes for their transition out of college.

CHAMPS/Life Skills

The CHAMPS/Life Skills Program (NCAA, 2007c) was created in 1991 by the NCAA Foundation to support the personal, career, and educational development of student-athletes at member institutions. Using primarily enhancement strategies per the Life Development Intervention model, each participating college or university is provided with educational materials and resources to support student-athlete development in five areas: academics, athletics, personal development, career planning, and community service.

Although the CHAMPS/Life Skills Program provides separate resources for the five development areas identified above, there is considerable overlap among the areas. For example, career planning requires self-assessment that is also critical for personal development. Community service can expose student-athletes to a wide range of career possibilities, but also plays an important role in their personal self-discovery.

The CHAMPS/Life Skills Program is structured according to a framework for developmental programming (Petitpas & Champagne, 1988) that is rooted in the work of noted developmental theorists including Perry (cognitive), Erikson (personal), and Super (career). The framework is based on the belief that many student-athletes enter college with a somewhat narrow and rigid worldview. As such, the goal is to facilitate individuals' personal and career development through a process of exploratory behavior and skill development that begins in the first year at college and continues through graduation.

Most traditional-age students enter college with a stereotypic view that professors have all the answers and their views should not be questioned (Wright, 1992). This dualistic or black-and-white thinking can be strongly reinforced in first-year student-athletes who learn that independent thinking or action is not often accepted by a sport system that expects unquestioned obedience to coaches' directives (Howard-Hamilton, & Watt, 2001). Therefore, the CHAMPS/Life Skills Program is designed to meet the needs of first-year students by providing student-athletes with courses, orientation programs, and workshops in which they can engage in an exploration of their values, needs, interests, and skills through interactions with individuals who come from different cultures, lifestyles, and worldviews. This type of learning experience is most effective when it is open to all students and structured in a manner that encourages self-disclosure and feedback. In this type of forum student-athletes can feel safe enough to begin questioning the absoluteness of authority and become more comfortable with multiplistic viewpoints.

Second-year students often continue the exploration of personal values, needs, interests, and skills, which allows them to develop the self-knowledge necessary to find and/or commit to a major course of study that is appropriate for their future objectives. CHAMPS/Life Skills programming often includes weekly support groups, study halls, and workshops offered by the academic athletic support staff. The support provided by the staff in one-on-one meetings is also an important component of the CHAMPS/Life Skills Program. These various venues provide a forum where student-athletes can discover that they have meaningful alternatives from which to choose. These learning opportunities can also help student-athletes identify and use the skills that they have developed though sport in other aspects of their lives. Goal setting, planning, leadership, and teamwork are just four of the transferable skills that can help student-athletes gain confidence and increase their career self-efficacy (Shiina, Brewer, Petitpas, & Cornelius, 2003). In addition, this continued exploratory behavior can prompt more relativistic thinking as student-athletes begin to explore the advantages and disadvantages of majors that may relate to their evolving career aspirations. Student-athletes who fail to engage in adequate exploratory behavior run the risk of being forced to choose a major in order to comply with NCAA academic progress mandates before they have enough self-knowledge to make an informed decision.

Third-year student-athletes may benefit from connecting with campus support services that supplement the self- and career-exploration strategies provided in the CHAMPS/Life Skills resources. An important goal of the third year at college is to explore the world of work in order to identify possible career options that would be most consistent with the student-athlete's personal values, needs, interests, and skills. Although the time demands associated with intercollegiate athletes, particularly at the Division I level, may interfere with internships and part-time job opportunities, student-athletes should be provided with resources to gather career information from people in the workplace. Shared experience programs in which alumni, coaches, and former athletes come to campus to share their transition-to-work experiences are one example of this type of resource.

In the final year of college, the focus is often on preparing for a transition from college to the workplace. The focus of support services shifts from personal and career exploration to preparing for the termination of one's college career and to making initial career commitments. CHAMPS/Life Skills professionals often meet these needs by working with student-athletes to prepare résumés and cover letters, develop and practice job-interviewing skills, and engage in job-hunting strategies. It can also be helpful to provide opportunities for graduating student-athletes to talk about college experiences and develop support systems for their eventual disengagement from sport.

The CHAMPS/Life Skills Program provides a wealth of resources to help student-athletes develop the skills necessary to manage transitions that they might face during and after their college careers. With staff creating and delivering the programming and offering the necessary support, CHAMPS/Life Skills provides a comprehensive enhancement program for individual student-athletes. To more fully meet the developmental needs of student-athletes, however, colleges should also offer counseling programs for those student-athletes who are struggling to cope with the stress associated with a range of transitions, including career-ending injury, death of loved ones, or other significant events.

Summary

Although we have used Schlossberg's (1981) term "adaptation to transition" throughout this chapter, we strongly support Hopson's (1981) argument that this term can be misleading. Adaptation implies that a crisis has been faced and the individual has returned to a state of homeostasis. Hopson (1981) contends that *responses to transitions* can range "from those which are completely non-adaptive by any definition, to those that imply somehow having survived and gotten through it, to the most effective response by which the mover has actually gained something as a result of the experience" (p. 37). The goal of any intervention program for college student-athletes in transition should be to enhance their ability not only to cope with transitions, but also to grow through the experience (Danish et al., 1993). The purpose of this chapter was to provide the reader with a framework for understanding these transitions and planning interventions that may enhance student-athletes' possibilities to enjoy continued growth through future transitions.

References

Alfermann, D., & Stambulova, N. (2007). Career transitions and career termination. In G. Tenenbaum & R. C. Eklund (Eds.), *Handbook of sport psychology* (3rd ed., pp. 712–733). New York: Wiley.

Astle, S. J. (1986). The experience of loss in athletics. *Journal of Sports Medicine and Physical Fitness, 26,* 279–284.

Baillie, P. H. F. (1992). *Career transition in elite and professional athletes: A study of individuals in their preparation for and adjustment to retirement from competitive sports.* Unpublished doctoral dissertation, Virginia Commonwealth University, Richmond.

Baillie, P. H. F., & Danish, S. J. (1992). Understanding the career transition of athletes. *The Sport Psychologist, 6,* 77–98.

Blinde, E. M., & Greendorfer, S. L. (1985). A reconceptualization of leaving the role of competitive athlete. *International Review for the Sociology of Sport, 20,* 87–93.

Blinde, E. M., & Stratta, T. M. (1992). The "sport career death" of college athletes: Involuntary and unanticipated sport exits. *Journal of Sport Behavior, 15,* 3–20.

Brewer, B. W. (1994). Review and critique of models of psychological adjustment to athletic injury. *Journal of Applied Sport Psychology, 6*, 87–100.

Brewer, B. W., Van Raalte, J. L., & Linder, D. E. (1993). Athletic identity: Hercules' muscles or Achilles heel? *International Journal of Sport Psychology, 24*, 237–254.

Carnegie Council. (1995). *Great transitions: Preparing adolescents for a new century.* New York: Carnegie Corporation.

Catalano, R., Berglund, L., Ryan, J., Lonczak, H., & Hawkins, D. (2002), *Positive youth development in the United States: Research findings on evaluations of positive youth development programs.* Retrieved February 2, 2002, from http://aspe.os.dhhs.gov/hsp/PositiveYouthDev99/index.html

Coakley, J. J. (1983). Leaving competitive sport: Retirement or rebirth? *Quest, 35*, 1–11.

Constantine, M. G. (1995). Retired female athletes in transition: A group counseling intervention. *Journal of College Student Development, 36*, 604–605.

Crook, J. M., & Robertson, S. E. (1991). Transitions out of elite sport. *International Journal of Sport Psychology, 22*, 115–127.

Curtis, J., & Ennis, R. (1988). Negative consequences of leaving competitive sport? Comparative findings for former elite-level hockey players. *Sociology of Sport Journal, 5*, 87–106.

Danish, S. D., Petitpas, A. J., & Hale, B. D. (1992). A developmental-educational intervention model of sport psychology. *The Sport Psychologist, 6*, 403–415.

Danish, S. D., Petitpas, A. J., & Hale, B. D. (1993). Life development intervention for athletes: Life skills through sports. *The Counseling Psychologist, 21*, 352–385.

Etzel, E. F., Zizzi, S., Newcomer-Appeneal, R., Ferrante, A., & Perna, F. (2007). Providing psychological assistance to college student-athletes with injuries and disabilities. In D. Pargman (Ed.), *Psychological bases of sport injuries* (3rd ed., pp. 151–169). Morgantown, WV: Fitness Information Technology.

Gardner, F., & Moore, Z. (2006). *Clinical sport psychology.* Champaign, IL: Human Kinetics.

Giacobbi, P. R., Jr., Lynn, T. K., Wetherington, J. M., Jenkins, J., Bodendorf, M., & Langley, B. (2004). Stress and coping during the transition to university for first-year female athletes. *The Sport Psychologist, 18*, 1–20.

Gorbett, F. J. (1984). Psycho-social adjustment of athletes to retirement. In L. Bunker, R. J. Rotella, & A. S. Reilly (Eds.), *Sport psychology: Psychological considerations in maximizing sport performance* (pp. 288–294). Ithaca, NY: Mouvement.

Gordon, S., Milios, D., & Grove, J. R. (1991). Psychological aspects of the recovery process from sport injury: The perspective of sport physiotherapists. *Australian Journal of Science and Medicine in Sport, 23*, 53–60.

Greendorfer, S. L., & Blinde, E. M. (1985). "Retirement" from intercollegiate sport: Theoretical and empirical considerations. *Sociology of Sport Journal, 2*, 101–110.

Haerle, R. (1975). Career patterns and career contingencies of professional baseball players: An occupational analysis. In D. W. Ball & J. W. Loy (Eds.), *Sport and social order* (pp. 461–519). Reading, MA: Addison-Wesley.

Hallinan, C. J., & Snyder, E. E. (1987). Forced disengagement and the collegiate athlete. *Arena Review, 11*(2), 28–34.

Hinitz, D. R. (1988). *Role theory and the retirement of collegiate gymnasts.* Unpublished doctoral dissertation, University of Nevada, Reno.

Hopson, B. (1981). Response to the papers by Schlossberg, Brammer and Abrego. *The Counseling Psychologist, 9,* 36–39.

Howard-Hamilton, M., & Watt, S. (2001). Student services for athletes. *New Directions for Student Services, 93,* 35–45.

Ingebritsen, D. A. (1997). A qualitative study of the transition process of intercollegiate athletes out of sport. *Dissertation Abstracts International Section A: Humanities and Social Sciences, 57*(7-A), 2938.

Kadison, R., & DiGeronimo, T. (2004). *College of the overwhelmed: The campus mental health crisis and what to do about it.* San Francisco: Jossey-Bass.

Kleiber, D. A., & Brock, S. C. (1992). The effect of career-ending injuries on the subsequent well-being of elite college athletes. *Sociology of Sport Journal, 9,* 70–75.

Kleiber, D., Greendorfer, S., Blinde, E., & Samdahl, D. (1987). Quality of exit from university sports and subsequent life satisfaction. *Sociology of Sport Journal, 4,* 28–36.

Kornspan, A., & Etzel, E. (2003). What do we know about the career maturity of college student-athletes? A brief review and practical suggestions for career development work with student-athletes. *Academic Athletic Journal, 17,* 15–33.

Kubler-Ross, E. (1969). *On death and dying.* New York: Macmillan.

Lally, P. (2007). Identity and athletic retirement: A prospective study. *Psychology of Sport and Exercise, 8,* 85–99.

Lanese, R., Strauss, R., Leizman, D., & Rotondi, A. (1990). Injury and disability in matched men's and women's intercollegiate sports. *American Journal of Public Health, 80,* 1459–1462.

Lavallee, D., & Wylleman, P. (2000). *Career transitions in sport: International perspectives.* Morgantown, WV: FIT.

Lerch, S. H. (1982). Athletic retirement as social death: An overview. In N. Theberge & P. Donnelly (Eds.), *Sport and the sociological imagination* (pp. 259–272). Fort Worth, TX: Texas Christian University Press.

Levy, M. A., Gordon, L., Wilson, R., & Barrett, C. (2005). Career transitions. In J. Taylor & G. S. Wilson (Eds.), *Applying sport psychology: Four perspectives* (pp. 249–266). Champaign, IL: Human Kinetics.

Lubker, J., & Etzel, E. (2007, October). *College adjustment experiences of first-year students: Disengaged athletes, non-athletes, and current varsity athletes.* Paper presented at the annual meeting of the Association for the Advancement of Applied Sport Psychology, Louisville, KY.

Lynch, G. P. (1988). Athletic injuries and the practicing sport psychologist: Practical guidelines for assisting athletes. *The Sport Psychologist, 2,* 161–167.

McPherson, B. P. (1980). Retirement from professional sport: The process and problems of occupational and psychological adjustment. *Sociological Symposium, 30,* 126–143.

Medalie, J. (1981). The college years as a mini-life cycle: Developmental tasks and adaptive options. *The Journal of the American College Health Association, 30,* 75–79.

National Association of Academic Advisors for Athletics. (2007). *Model Practices/Inter-*

ventions Information. Retrieved May 3, 2007, from http://www1.ncaa.org/
member ship/membership_svcs/academic_support/programs/population/index.html

National Collegiate Athletic Association. (2007a). *NCAA Injury Surveillance System.* Retrieved September 28, 2007, from http://www1.ncaa.org/membership/ed_outreach/
health-safety/iss/Report_SelectionByYear

National Collegiate Athletic Association. (2007b). *A career in professional athletics: A
guide for making the transition.* Retrieved September 28, 2007, from http://www.ncaa.
org/library/general/career_in_pro_athletics/2004-05/2004-05_career_pro_athletics.pdf

National Collegiate Athletic Association. (2007c). *Welcome to the NCAA CHAMPS/Life
Skills Program.* Retrieved September 28, 2007, from http://www1.ncaa.org/eprise/
main/membership/ed_outreach/champs-life_skills/index.html

Ogilvie, B. C. (1987). Counseling for sports career termination. In J. R. May &
M. J. Asken (Eds.), *Sport psychology: The psychological health of the athlete* (pp. 213–230).
New York: PMA Publishing.

Ogilvie, B. C., & Howe, M. (1982). Career crisis in sports. In T. Orlick, J. T. Parting-
ton, & J. H. Salmela (Eds.), *Proceedings of the Fifth World Congress of Sport Psychology*
(pp. 176–183). Ottawa, Canada: Coaching Association of Canada.

Ogilvie, B. C., & Howe, M. (1986). The trauma of termination from athletics. In
J. M. Williams (Ed.), *Applied sport psychology: Personal growth to peak experience*
(pp. 365–382). Palo Alto, CA: Mayfield.

Parker, K. B. (1994). "Has-beens" and "wanna-bes": Transition experiences of former
major college football players. *The Sport Psychologist, 8,* 287–304.

Pearson, R. E., & Petitpas, A. J. (1990). Transitions of athletes: Developmental and preventive perspectives. *Journal of Counseling and Development, 69,* 7–10.

Perna, F. M., Ahlgren, R. A., & Zaichkowsky, L. D. (1999). The influence of career
planning, race, and athletic injury on life satisfaction among recently retired collegiate
male athletes. *The Sport Psychologist, 13,* 144–156.

Petitpas, A., & Champagne, D. (1988). Developmental programming for intercollegiate
athletes. *Journal of College Student Development, 29,* 454–460.

Quarforth, S., Brewer, B. W., Petitpas, A. J., Champagne, D., & Cornelius, A. E. (2003).
College adjustment of football players: Predictors of first semester adjustment to col-
lege among NCAA Division III intercollegiate football players. *Academic Athletic
Journal, 17,* 1–14.

Roberts-Wilbur, J., Swenson, D., & Dargan, P. (1994, June). *A group approach to counseling injured athletes.* Workshop presented at the 11th Annual Conference on Counseling Athletes, Springfield, MA.

Rosenberg, E. (1982). Athletic retirement as social death: Concepts and perspectives. In
N. Theberge & P. Donnelly (Eds.), *Sport and the sociological imagination* (pp. 245–258).
Fort Worth, TX: Texas Christian University Press.

Rotella, R. J. (1984). Psychological care of the injured athlete. In L. Bunker, R. J. Rotella, & A. S. Reilly (Eds.), *Sport psychology: Psychological considerations in maximizing
sport performance* (pp. 273–288). Ithaca, NY: Mouvement Publishers.

Rotella, R. J., & Heyman, S. R. (1986). Stress, injury, and the psychological rehabilitation of athletes. In J. M. Williams (Ed.), *Applied sport psychology: Personal growth to peak performance* (pp. 343–364). Palo Alto, CA: Mayfield.

Schlossberg, N. K. (1981). A model for analyzing human adaptation to transition. *The Counseling Psychologist, 9,* 2–18.

Schlossberg, N. K. (1984). *Counseling adults in transition.* New York: Springer.

Selden, F. A. (1998). Career transition groups for college students. *Dissertation Abstracts International Section A: Humanities and Social Sciences, 58*(8A), 3025.

Shiina, S., Brewer, B. W., Petitpas, A. J., & Cornelius, A. E. (2003). Effects of transferable skills workshops on the career self-efficacy of college student-athletes. *Academic Athletic Journal, 17,* 54–64.

Snyder, E. E., & Baber, L. L. (1979). A profile of former collegiate athletes and nonathletes: Leisure activities, attitudes toward work, and aspects of satisfaction with life. *Journal of Sport Behavior, 2,* 211–219.

Stambulova, N. (1997). Sociological sports career transitions. In J. Bangsbo, B. Saltin, H. Bonde, Y. Hellsten, B. Ibsen, & M. Kjaer et al. (Eds.), *Proceedings of the 2nd Annual Congress of the European College of Sport Science* (Vol. I, pp. 88–89). Copenhagen, Denmark: University of Copenhagen.

Stambulova, N. (2003). Symptoms of a crisis-transition. In N. Hassmen (Ed.), *SIPF yearbook, 2003* (pp. 97–109). Örebro, Sweden: Örebro University Press.

Stambulova, N., Stephan, Y., & Jäphag, U. (2007). Athletic retirement: A cross-national comparison of elite French and Swedish athletes. *Psychology of Sport and Exercise, 8,* 101–118.

Stankovich, C. E. (1998). The effectiveness of a career development intervention program designed to assist student-athletes through the sport retirement transition. *Dissertation Abstracts International Section A: Humanities and Social Sciences, 59*(5A), 1475.

Stephan, Y., Torregrosa, M., & Sanchez, X. (2007). The body matters: Psychophysical impact of retiring from elite sport. *Psychology of Sport and Exercise, 8,* 73-83.

Swain, D. A. (1991). Withdrawal from sport and Schlossberg's model of transitions. *Sociology of Sport Journal, 8,* 152-160.

Taylor, J., & Ogilvie, B. C. (1994). A conceptual model of adaptation to retirement among athletes. *Journal of Applied Sport Psychology, 6,* 1–20.

Taylor, J., & Ogilvie, B. C. (2001). Career termination among athletes. In R. N. Singer, H. A. Hausenblas, & C. M. Janelle (Eds.), *Handbook of sport psychology* (2nd ed., pp. 672–691). New York: Wiley.

Watt, S., & Moore, J. (2001). Who are student-athletes? In M. Howard-Hamilton & S. Watt (Eds.), *Student services for athletes: New directions for student services* (pp. 7–18). San Francisco: Jossey-Bass.

Webb, W. M., Nasco, S. A., Riley, S., & Headrick, B. (1998). Athletic identity and reactions to retirement from sports. *Journal of Sport Behavior, 21,* 338–361.

Werthner, P., & Orlick, T. (1986). Retirement experiences of successful Olympic athletes. *International Journal of Sport Psychology, 17,* 337–363.

Wright, S. (1992). Promoting intellectual development during freshman year. *Journal of the Freshman Year Experience, 4,* 23–29.

11

DISORDERED EATING IN COLLEGE STUDENT-ATHLETES

Jennifer E. Carter

Allison sat in the training room, her knee throbbing with pain. She was still wearing her sweaty team uniform, having abruptly left the soccer game midway through the second half. As the team doctor examined her knee carefully, Allison tried to regain her composure, but her breathing was still choppy following the harrowing incident on the field from which she had been carted away a few minutes ago. The score had been tied when she received a crisp pass from a midfielder. Driving toward the goal, she had pivoted to avoid a defender and had felt a strange popping sensation in her right knee. Allison had never sustained a serious injury before, but she knew that something was definitely wrong at that moment. When the physician told Allison that he strongly suspected a torn ACL, Allison felt devastated. She had worked so hard in the pre-season to lose those extra five pounds, and now she would likely be out for six months. Allison panicked and told herself that there was no way this injury would make her fat.

Four months later, Allison again sat in the training room for her physical therapy appointment. She felt very proud of her eating habits the past few months. Although her surgeon only recently had cleared her to tackle more intense exercise, she had managed to lose twenty pounds from her small frame. At first she had eliminated dessert from her diet in an effort to avoid weight gain with her limited physical activity. Then Allison decided to cut out fats since she had heard that athletes should eat a low-fat diet. Gradually eliminating parts of her diet helped her to feel calmer and more in control in spite of the pain and uncertainty of rehabbing her knee. Currently she allowed herself to eat lettuce, cottage cheese, carrots, apples, and turkey; she considered other foods to be unhealthy. Allison was puzzled that the plethora of positive comments about her weight loss had ended, replaced by others' looks of concerns. She found herself feeling moody and had stopped hanging out with her team- mates since all they wanted to do was to eat out at restaurants. For some reason Allison wasn't sleeping very well, and she had started drinking several cups of coffee a day, to keep up her energy. Allison was glad that she had skipped her period the past two months, and that she continued to maintain her 4.0 GPA. She smiled, pleased that she was demonstrating such keen self-discipline. Allison was heading into anorexia nervosa

Unfortunately, stories like Allison's are increasingly common in univer- sity athletic departments. The culture of sport presents particular risk factors as well as protective factors regarding nutritional health. Allison's story highlights a unique risk factor in athletics for the development of disordered eating: injury. Although injury played a role in Allison's par- ticular situation, for some student-athletes, sport has nothing to do with the development of disordered eating. Mental health professionals working with college student-athletes need to be knowledgeable about disordered eating, because such professionals will undoubtedly face this issue. The term *disordered eating*, used throughout this chapter, encom- passes clinical eating disorders, subclinical eating problems (eating dis- order symptoms that do not fit into diagnostic categories), and body image problems.

As defined by the *Diagnostic and Statistical Manual of Mental Disor- ders, Fourth Edition* (DSM-IV; American Psychiatric Association, 1994), clinical eating disorders refer to three diagnoses: (1) anorexia nervosa (AN), (2) bulimia nervosa (BN), and (3) eating disorder not otherwise specified (EDNOS). Although a complete review of the diagnostic cri- teria for each eating disorder is beyond the scope of this chapter, brief summaries follow. Anorexia nervosa (AN) involves a significant weight loss (leaving the individual at roughly a body mass index [BMI] of 17.5

or below), a strong drive for thinness, body image distortion, and loss of menses in women. Bulimia nervosa (BN) involves episodes of binge-eating followed by purging (self-induced vomiting, use of laxatives, over-exercise, etc.) and negative body image. EDNOS is the largest diagnostic category. It consists of a wide range of AN and BN eating/body image problems, including forms of purging without binge eating, or binge eating with no purging behaviors (Wonderlich, Joiner, Keel, Williamson, & Crosby, 2007). It is also feasible to include body dysmorphic disorder and the proposed diagnosis of muscle dysmorphia (Pope, Phillips, & Olivardia, 2000) in the group of disordered eating diagnoses.

This chapter will explore the following five topics related to disordered eating in college student-athletes: (1) prevalence, (2) risk factors, (3) development of an athletic department disordered eating policy, (4) unique aspects of sport on nutritional health, and (5) treatment issues.

Prevalence

Several studies, mostly on female athletes, have found that prevalence rates for college athletes are less than 3% for clinical eating disorders and 15–30% for disordered eating (Beals & Manore, 2002; Carter & Rudd, 2005; Johnson, Powers, & Dick, 1999). There are particular difficulties in measuring the prevalence rates of disordered eating in student-athletes. One issue is that researchers often use different definitions and measures, leading to varied results. For example, researchers would likely find discrepant prevalence rates when using the Questionnaire for Eating Disorder Diagnoses (Mintz, O'Halloran, Mulholland, & Schneider, 1997) instead of the Eating Attitudes Test (Garner, 1982). Studies conducted with a large sample representing a variety of sports are rare, and studies focusing on high-risk sports only may overestimate prevalence rates (Beals, 2004). Although few athlete studies have had large enough samples to compare prevalence rates among various ethnic groups, prevalence studies completed with non-athlete populations indicate that black women are less likely to suffer from eating disorders than are white women (Striegel-Moore & Bulik, 2007). Additionally, athletes may be reluctant to report eating disorder symptoms on questionnaires, leading to an underestimation of prevalence rates (Brownell & Rodin, 1992; Carter & Rudd, 2005).

Do athletes experience more disordered eating than non-athletes? Research exploring this question has produced equivocal results. Some studies have found alarmingly high numbers of disordered eating in female athletes (i.e., 8% of athletes with bulimia nervosa and 8.2% with "anorexia athletica") (Sundgot-Bergen, 1993), and others have found comparable rates in athlete and non-athlete samples (Reinking & Alexander, 2005; Sanford-Martens, Davidson, Yakusho, Martens, Hinton, & Beck, 2005). Some researchers have found similar rates for clinical eating disorders between athletes and non-athletes, but higher rates of subclinical problems in athletes (Petrie, Reel, & Carter, 2005; Sherman & Thompson, 2001). Athletes with subclinical disordered eating may not suffer from severe clinical syndromes, but their eating symptoms can impair their athletic performance and overall health (Beals, 2000). One study found that athletes with subclinical problems were quite similar to those with clinical eating disorders in terms of experiencing weight pressures, sociocultural internalization, and negative mood, indicating that prevention and treatment efforts are just as important for subclinical problems as for clinical syndromes (Petrie et al., in press).

It appears that the type of sport influences prevalence rates, with elite athletes from "lean" sports being more at risk for eating disorders than non-athletes (Smolak, Murnen, & Ruble, 2000; Thompson & Sherman, 1999). Lean sports have been defined as those sports emphasizing thinness for performance reasons (e.g., running, rowing) and/or aesthetic reasons (e.g., gymnastics, diving, and synchronized swimming). One NCAA study found that two sports in particular, gymnastics and wrestling, were associated with increased disordered eating risk compared to other sports (Engel et al., 2003). Two meta-analyses found that high-school and recreational athletes may experience more positive body image (Hausenblas & Downs, 2001) and fewer eating disorders (Smolak et al., 2000) than non-athletes, suggesting that there are also protective factors to sport participation.

There is some evidence that college students are presenting to university counseling centers with more severe psychopathology in recent years (Benton, Robertson, Tseng, Newton, & Benton, 2003; Kadison, & DiGeronimo, 2004). College student-athletes are not immune to mental disorders. It seems that today more student-athletes arrive at college with pre-existing eating disorders as well as experience more severe disorders during their tenure at the university.

Risk Factors

Athletics present certain risk factors in the development of disordered eating. There is a pervasive belief that athletes in each sport must possess a particular type of body to perform successfully. Fairburn, Cooper, and Sharfran (2003) pointed out that interpersonal environments (such as athletics) that magnify weight and appearance pressures tend to represent significant risk factors for disordered eating. For most women's sports, a highly desired body type is one that is quite lean. For most men's sports, the ideal is a very muscular body. However, this emphasis on one ideal ignores evidence that bodies of all types have been successful in sport. One might look at the variety of body types among major league baseball pitchers as an example. Even a particular body composition is not the gold standard for athletic performance. One college swim coach measured body fat percentages for swimmers over a period of twenty years, and found that body fat percentages of national champion swimmers varied from 12% to 30% (Steen, 2004)—quite a broad range.

Additional risk factors in athletics include personality traits that overlap between high-achieving athletes and individuals with disordered eating, such as perfectionism, over-compliance, excessive discipline, and high tolerance for pain (Hausenblas & Carron, 1999). There are likely different risk factors for male athletes than there are for female athletes (Petrie et al., 2007). Wearing revealing athletic uniforms can be a risk factor. Additionally, athletes are more at risk to use performance-enhancing substances such as steroids and supplements (Pope, Phillips, & Olivardia, 2000).

Protective Factors

Although disordered eating risk factors abound in athletics, sport participation also represents a wonderful opportunity to improve body image and nutritional health. Numerous studies have shown the benefits of exercise for (1) reducing depression and (2) coping effectively with negative emotions (Stathopoulou, Powers, Berry, Smits, & Otto, 2006), two effects of exercise that can increase resilience and protect individuals from developing eating disorders. Athletic participation has been shown to increase self-esteem (Spence, McGannon, & Poon, 2005). Achievement in sport actually provides an avenue to improve body image for some individuals. Female athletes who are large and muscular often struggle with negative body image when comparing themselves to underweight models in the media, yet their size and muscularity can help them perform well in sport. One journalist (Granderson, 2007) wrote about this phenomenon specifically in basketball: "A life handcuffed by low self-esteem because she's taller than everyone else in class. A life so desperate to be liked that she'd rather be promiscuous than continue being alone. . . . Basketball gives larger women a place to belong and often starts the healing process from years of psychological abuse" (p. 2). Finally, athletes often seek out nutritional information so that they can effectively fuel their bodies for performance. Athletes may have access to more nutritional resources (e.g., sport dietitians, athletic trainers, and team physicians) than non-athletes do.

Athletic Department Eating Disorder Policy

With the multitude of mental health issues facing college student-athletes, how can athletic departments adequately attend to the prevention of disordered eating? How do athletic organizations manage athletes with severe disordered eating who refuse to get treatment? And, how can large athletic departments facilitate communication among the multiple units involved in helping athletes with disordered eating? One potential answer to these questions is a sound disordered eating policy for the athletic department.

A policy that was developed and revised at The Ohio State University is available at http://hec.osu.edu/sportsnut/policy. Key aspects of an eating disorder policy include sections on prevention/education, identification of disordered eating, intervention approaches, setting weight/body composition goals, treatment issues including noncompliance, and return-to-play issues.

Prevention

Thompson and Sherman (1993) outlined several guidelines for preventing eating disorders in athletes. They recommended that athletic department staff emphasize health and performance over weight, avoiding comments about weight and appearance. One coach they interviewed supported this recommendation in her assertion, "I don't care how much an athlete weighs if she's strong enough and fit enough to do what I want her to do" (Thompson & Sherman, 1993, p. 158). The authors also encouraged athletic organizations to eliminate group weigh-ins, treat each athlete individually, and carefully monitor any attempts by athletes to modify their weight.

Coaches can have a large impact on preventing eating disorders when they send clear messages about healthy body image and behaviors. Psychologists can encourage coaches to emphasize function instead of form regarding athletes' bodies. For example, if an athlete complains that her thighs are too big, coaches can tell her, "Your strong legs allow you to stay balanced and solid on defense." If an athlete complains that his chest is not big enough, coaches might say, "You demonstrate a lot of speed and flexibility in your position." Mental health professionals should encourage coaches to emphasize the athlete rather than the athlete's body (providing feedback such as "You need to work harder"; "I love the way you encourage your teammates"). Coaches should be clear about the acceptability of weight-management strategies ("It is not healthy to fast. Fasting will lead to binge-eating, and both behaviors will harm your performance and health"). The NCAA Coaches Handbook, *Managing the Female Athlete Triad* (Thompson & Sherman, 2005) provides helpful guidance for coaches.

Ideally, athletic departments will offer education and prevention programs to their student-athletes. It is important that such programs avoid glamorizing disordered eating so that there are no iatrogenic effects (Levine & Smolak, 2005). According to Stice et al. (2000), reducing the internalization of the thin ideal in women has led to decreased disordered eating, and educational programs enhancing media literacy by challenging the thin or muscular ideals have shown promise (Levine & Smolak, 2005). Nutritional misinformation and myths are abundant in athletics; therefore effective prevention involves sound nutritional education from sport dietitians (Beals, 2004). Disordered eating can arise not only from misguided demands that student-athletes somehow modify their weight, but also from a lack of guidance as to how they are supposed to go about losing or gaining weight.

Setting Weight/Body Composition Goals

Because the sport culture often emphasizes winning at all costs and views weight/body composition modifications as essential for winning, athletes and coaches frequently set unrealistic weight and body composition goals without proper guidance. "Unfortunately, some have adopted the philosophy that if small weight losses improve performance a little, major weight losses should be even better" (Wilmore, 1992, p. 323). Disordered eating policies might include prohibitions against coaches arbitrarily setting such goals for their athletes, particularly group goals for individuals with varying needs and risk factors. It is not uncommon for coaches to have their own body image and nutrition struggles, and it is rare for coaches to have sound nutritional, medical, and psychological training. Therefore, it is wise to put the goal-setting responsibilities in the hands of those who are well-trained to assess suitable goals and assist student-athletes in reaching these goals healthfully. Manore and Thompson (2000) mentioned the following factors to consider in defining an ideal body weight or composition: one that is individualized, is relatively easily maintained, allows adequate nutrition, is associated with optimal health, and allows optimal performance.

Identification

Policies often include DSM-IV criteria for eating disorders as well as common signs of disordered eating in athletes. Barriers to identifying eating problems include coaches feeling overwhelmed by the complicated factors involved in disordered eating and perhaps feeling partly to blame for eating problems, teammates not knowing how to help, parents lacking information on what their student-athletes need for healthy nutrition and body image, and administrators fearing legal issues and negative publicity (Ryan, 1992). Secondary prevention involves group screening for disordered eating, which can be another method for identifying troubled student-athletes. At The Ohio State University, medical staff members have administered the Questionnaire for Eating Disorder Diagnoses (Q-EDD; Mintz et al., 1997) to the entire student-athlete population, requesting highly symptomatic student-athletes to meet with the psychologist for an assessment. Such a screening necessitates the staff resources and administrative buy-in to be successful (see Carter & Rudd, 2005).

Approaching a Student-Athlete

Teammates, family, and coaches are often bewildered about how to help a student-athlete suffering from disordered eating. Thompson and Sherman (2005) recommended that the eating disorder be treated as an "injury" that requires evaluation and treatment before continuing on with sport participation. The first step frequently includes some type of gentle discussion, in which caring significant others privately approach the identified individual (Thompson & Sherman, 2005). It is helpful to include specific guidelines for such a discussion in a policy, outlining suggested language. "I feel concerned that you skip team meals and often appear tired. I want you to meet with the (psychologist, dietitian, and/or physician) to assess what is going on. I will check back with you in one week to see if you have made the appointment(s)." It is important that the intervening individuals be prepared for possible reactions of denial or even hostility. It is also helpful for supportive individuals to meet together before the discussion, in order to ensure that everyone is on the same page.

For example, the author participated in an intervention with a student-athlete who had lost a significant amount of weight, in which there was misinformation about her engaging in self-induced vomiting. The student-athlete was so upset about being falsely accused of this purging behavior that it took months to build rapport and trust with her in treatment. Often a student-athlete will ask, point blank, "Do you believe me?" or "Do you believe what they are saying about me?" It seems useful to respond to such questions with statements such as, "At this point I may not know the specifics of your behavior, but I am concerned enough about your weight loss (or other disordered eating indicator) to insist that you get an assessment with medical professionals."

Treatment Team

Compared to university counseling centers in which mental health professionals appear to communicate rarely with others about their clients, athletic departments represent a system in which strong communication is essential for treatment and viability of mental health positions. Meetings involving the student-athlete and treatment team, consisting of the psychologist or counselor, dietitian, physician, and athletic trainer, are essential for treatment. Mental health professionals obviously need to follow rules regarding confidentiality and HIPPA, although sometimes with mandated referrals it is necessary to make communication with the treatment team a condition for continued athletic participation. If student-athletes are non-compliant, the treatment team might involve an athletic department administrator in the meetings and/or require a treatment contract.

Contracts and Return to Play

Because of the protective factors presented by sports, continued athletic participation can often be a healing aspect for student-athletes attempting to recover from disordered eating. Preventing student-athletes from playing sports that they love is a difficult task that is not taken lightly. However, there is a point at which continued participation is not medically sound, and team physicians are responsible for determining safety regarding participation. Many psychologists have found it important to be very specific in the contract about expectations and guidelines for return to play.

A sample contract:

> The following are requirements that must be met in order for _____ to have medical clearance to participate in _____ .
>
> - Weigh-ins done by medical team (not coaches) as needed.
> - Meeting with the psychologist _____ times a month.
> - Meeting with the dietitian _____ times a month.
> - A good-faith effort to engage in these meetings and complete counseling assignments.
> - Meeting with the team physician _____ times a month. Labs/other testing as recommended by the team physician.
> - Maintenance of at least _____ lbs. (or % body fat) for participation (including training, practice, and events).
> - Quarterly meetings with the management team.

Unique Aspects of Sport Related to Nutritional Health

Body Image

Student-athletes face competing body image demands from the popular culture and specific sport environment. For female student-athletes, the media emphasizes a very thin build whereas athletics tends to reward a muscular build. This mixed-message dilemma can be seen in some female athletes fearing that weight training will make them too bulky. Male student-athletes experience unique body image pressures, in which many men wish to gain muscularity (Pope et al., 2000) although some men focus on leanness. Whereas women often experience a "drive for thinness" (Garner, Olmsted, & Polivy, 1983), men are more likely to experience a "drive for muscularity" (McCreary & Sasse, 2000), putting them at risk for excessive exercise, steroid and supplement use, and body dissatisfaction.

Complicating Sport Factors

It appears that athletes may use the compensatory behavior of over-exercise as a purging method more frequently than non-athletes. It is difficult to define excessive exercise in a population that views twice-a-day practices or three-hour workouts as the norm, but exercising in addition to normally scheduled practices is one indication of over-exercise. For example, a lacrosse player may exercise for two hours at the student recreation center in the morning, and then attend her two-hour team practice in the afternoon. Not surprisingly, her teammates and coaches might reward such "dedication" and "hard work" without realizing that the additional exercise could be a disordered eating symptom (Petrie & Sherman, 2000).

It is also difficult to define "binge-eating" in an athletic population with such high caloric needs. The DSM-IV defines binge-eating as consuming a significantly larger amount of food than most people would consume in one sitting, combined with a sense of lack of control. Some male athletes need over 4,000 calories a day to maintain their weight, and the large volumes of food needed to reach this calorie total may be difficult to distinguish from a binge. Athletes are competitive people, and they occasionally demonstrate their competitive drive in risky ways, such as binge drinking or binge eating contests. One could argue that

college in general is a time of binges for students and student-athletes—
binge-drinking, binge-eating, binge-studying, etc.

Team = Family

Treatment for eating disorders often involves family intervention. In
fact, the treatment for AN with the best empirical support is a family
treatment (Wilson, Grilo, & Vitousek, 2007). In a college athletic department, the student-athlete's "family" is often her or his team. Effective recovery for a student-athlete typically includes consultation and
education with coaches and teammates, who may be instrumental in
identifying disordered eating and in supporting treatment. It may be
helpful for the student-athlete to communicate her or his needs to particular teammates, with or without the presence of the mental health
professional (as long as the student-athlete grants permission for the
mental health professional to be present). Therapists can assist student-
athletes in identifying positive, supportive teammates whom the student-
athlete can approach to discuss the disordered eating. Depending on informed consent and the relationship between the student-athlete and
coach, it may also be helpful to have the coach attend treatment team
meetings.

It is important not to underestimate the influence of coaches on
student-athletes' lives. Coaches who understand and support treatment
can be a huge motivator for their athletes' recovery. It is very useful to
educate coaches and athletes about the critical voice present with eating
disorders (Claude-Pierre, 1997; Schaefer & Rutledge, 2003). Many
times coaches are trying to help when they tell their athletes they look
better after losing or gaining weight, yet the negative voice can turn any
compliment into a criticism (i.e., an athlete hears her coach say, "You
look good," and might hear instead, "You look fat"). Helping professionals should encourage coaches to focus on performance and internal personality characteristics (work ethic, sense of humor, etc.) instead
of focusing on athletes' appearance.

Insider Culture

Athletics is an insider culture, in which coaches and athletes may not
trust the assistance provided by "outsiders." In the absence of full-time
mental health staff in the athletic department, it is important that administrators, medical staff, and coaches form relationships with univer-

sity and community units. Liaisons with university counseling centers, campus organizations, and community eating disorder treatment centers are essential. Such outside professionals need to understand the athletic culture, including the need for communication and the instant gratification mentality. If athletic personnel do not know whether or not the student-athletes show up for their appointments, or if they have to wait too long for services, they will likely not follow-through with services. At The Ohio State University there is a campus organization called the Body Image & Health Task Force. This group is composed of faculty and staff from the wellness center, community eating disorder center, university counseling center, recreational sports, athletic department, and various academic units. The student-athlete advisory group may also be involved. Although the athletic department is typically insular, athletics and student-athletes can benefit greatly by collaborating with other campus units for planning prevention programs and coordinating treatment.

Treatment

Assessment. Athletic department mental health professionals often field consultations and referrals about worrisome behaviors observed in student-athletes. Physicians, athletic trainers, coaches, teammates, and academic counselors all refer disordered eating student-athletes for assessment and treatment. When the student-athlete arrives, it is important that the mental health professional do a thorough and accurate assessment. Particularly with a suspicion of AN, it may be easy to collude with the student-athlete that she is just fine, especially when it is common to see athletic performance improve in the initial stages of the disorder. To discourage such collusion, a helpful tool is the structured clinical interview The Eating Disorder Examination (EDE; Fairburn & Wilson, 1993), which contains a thorough set of questions that can help professionals arrive at the appropriate diagnosis more easily.

The EDE requires a height and weight measurement, which may be uncomfortable for mental health professionals to obtain. Medical staff or strength coaches normally weigh student-athletes periodically, but mental health professionals may also do the weighing during assessment and treatment. Before weighing, an introduction is helpful: "As part of the assessment, I need to weigh you and measure your height. We tend to use blind weights, meaning that I will ask you to step onto the scale backwards. We do this because we find that the eating disorder part of you might obsess about the number on the scale. Is it okay with you if I take a blind weight right now?" Obtaining a body mass index measure assists with determining the appropriate level of treatment but it should be used with caution in an athletic population. With student-athletes, it is also useful to assess body composition since their increased muscularity makes the body mass index a less meaningful measure. It is unlikely that a muscular student-athlete actively participating in her sport will have a body mass index below 17.5, though she may meet the remaining AN criteria. If intensive outpatient treatment is warranted, typically student-athletes will have to modify their academic or athletic schedule in order to have enough time to complete the treatment. It is more common for student-athletes to engage in weekly outpatient therapy and nutritional counseling, with frequent medical evaluations.

Effective treatments. There is very little evidence for effective treatments for AN, though the Maudsley approach with adolescents does look promising (Wilson et al., 2007). For BN, cognitive-behavioral therapy is an empirically validated treatment, with interpersonal therapy also showing some promise for reducing bulimic symptoms (Mitchell, Agras, & Wonderlich, 2007). Fairburn et al. (2003) proposed a "transdiagnostic" model, examining overlapping maintenance factors in disordered eating to address the spectrum of eating-related problems, including the more commonly diagnosed Eating Disorder NOS. These four maintaining processes are: (1) clinical perfectionism, (2) core low self-esteem, (3) mood intolerance, and (4) interpersonal difficulties (Fairburn et al., 2003). Two of these maintenance factors are quite relevant to treatment with student-athletes: perfectionism and mood intolerance.

It is a challenge to reduce athletes' sense of perfectionism, as they believe that expanding their self-evaluation beyond their achievements or becoming more encouraging in their self-talk may diminish their athletic and academic success. To challenge the effectiveness of the perfectionism for athletes struggling with disordered eating, cognitive restructuring and interpersonal therapy can be helpful. An interpersonal approach might involve examining where the critical perfectionism originated in the family, comparing the past versus current usefulness of perfectionism, and practicing new ways of relating to oneself and others.

Regarding mood intolerance, student-athletes often learn how to cope with success and failure gracefully through the ups and downs of athletic competition. However, athletes with perfectionism and disordered eating often feel absolutely crushed following an athletic defeat. It can be difficult to motivate individuals with AN in treatment, and one early shared goal between the therapist and athlete might be learning how to bounce back from failure more quickly as a means of improving athletic performance. Resistant athletes may buy into this treatment focus more easily because of the intense emotional pain they feel when falling short of their goals.

Education about dieting. In a culture obsessed with dieting, it may be difficult to believe accurate statistics about the efficacy of dieting. However, it is important to educate student-athletes about the facts concerning dieting. There is accumulating evidence that 95% of dieters regain the weight they lost within two years, often ending at higher weights than where they started (Gaesser, 2002). When timely, it may be useful to share findings from Keys' (1950) study of human starvation, in which severe restriction of calories in a group of men led to increased binge-eating, depression, food preoccupation, and social withdrawal.

Pharmacotherapy. Antidepressants such as selective serotonin reuptake inhibitors (SSRIs) have been used at higher doses to treat BN. SSRIs help reduce bulimic and comorbid symptoms, but individuals taking the medications rarely achieve complete abstinence from their disordered eating behaviors (Mitchell et al., 2007). Recently, atypical antipsychotics have been used with some success in treating AN. Kaye et al. (2003) found that abnormally high serotonin levels may be associated with the anxious and obsessional thinking characterizing AN. Severe restriction of nutritional intake can suppress serotonin activity, thereby lowering the anxiety and obsessive thoughts. When individuals with AN begin to re-feed, their anxiety skyrockets. Atypical antipsychotics can assist with keeping anxiety and obsessive thoughts at manageable levels during the re-feeding process.

Counseling Case Study

When Allison met with her athletic trainer, he noticed that she had lost a significant amount of weight. He was also puzzled that her torn ACL was not healing well despite Allison's hard work at rehabilitation. After consulting with the department's sport psychologist about the best way to approach Allison, the athletic trainer told Allison his concerns about her weight loss and slow healing during a rehabilitation session. The trainer asked Allison to schedule appointments with the psychologist and dietitian within a week. At the end of the week, the trainer inquired about the appointments and Allison sheepishly replied that she had not scheduled them. The trainer told Allison that she would not be able to attend practice until she had scheduled the appointments, and he had Allison call both professionals from the athletic training room.

At her first counseling appointment with the psychologist, Allison initially insisted that she was "fine." She felt excited, believing that when she returned to soccer, she would "bend it like Beckham" because of her weight loss. Allison agreed to sign a release of information so that the psychologist could communicate with the treatment team. On the Eating Disorders Examination interview, Allison did admit to cutting back severely on the portion size and variety of her food selections. She also reported that she thought about food over 50% of the day, had difficulty sleeping, wanted a flat stomach, felt more irritable, and had not been menstruating regularly. Her body mass index was 17.9 (height 5'3" and weight 101 lbs.). The psychologist informed Allison that she met criteria for Eating Disorder NOS and recommended further counseling. Allison had difficulty identifying treatment goals, but she wanted to feel less irritable and would do whatever it took to be cleared to participate in her sport.

The psychologist was not surprised when Allison failed to show up for her second counseling session, given her reluctance, with both the psychologist and dietitian, to disclose any problems she was experiencing. The psychologist consulted with the athletic trainer and both decided to join the dietitian and team physician for a treatment team meeting with Allison. At the meeting the health professionals outlined a contract for Allison, who appeared withdrawn and angry, believing that she was being forced into treatment without needing it. She did promise to attend her meetings so that she could continue practicing with the team.

Over the next six months, the psychologist worked on slowly building rapport with Allison. The young student-athlete completed several assignments from Cash's (1997) *Body Image Workbook* and Schaefer and Rutledge's (2003) *Life without Ed*, which facilitated her admitting the negative thoughts and feelings she had about herself. The psychologist and Allison worked on challenging her dysfunctional thinking patterns and improving her communication in relationships. Allison gradually disclosed that she felt pressured by her father's constant nagging for her to perform better in school and soccer. She eventually wrote her father a letter expressing her feelings and a desire to have a better relationship with him. Her father responded surprisingly well, and her parents met with a therapist themselves in order to learn how to be more supportive.

Meanwhile, Allison worked on small goals with the dietitian, adding recovery snacks after practice or training room visits, and gradually adding feared foods into her diet. The treatment team permitted Allison to continue training for her sport because of medical clearance and her compliance with the contract. Her weight was slow to change, but after two months she began making gains. It often felt like one step forward, one step backward, but by the end of six months Allison had gained seven pounds. Her mood was much brighter after her ACL healed and she returned to full participation. Allison continued her recovery over the summer and was able to contribute to her team the next season by scoring eight goals.

Summary

It is important for mental health professionals who work in intercollegiate athletics to be well versed in the identification, prevention, assessment, and treatment of disordered eating in athletes. Related to the particular risk factors and protective factors inherent in sports, athletes appear to have similar rates of disordered eating as do non-athletes. Eating Disorder NOS and subclinical problems are more common than either AN or BN.

Athletic organizations can benefit from implementing a disordered eating policy, outlining identification, treatment, and return-to-play issues. Effectively addressing disordered eating among athletes includes an appreciation of the unique aspects of the sports culture, including demands for leanness and muscularity, excesses in training that mask eating problems, and the importance of educating teammates and coaches. Although it is unrealistic to expect a quick resolution of every conflict in student-athletes' lives, it is often quite encouraging and rewarding to assist in their recovery from disordered eating.

Note: The author is grateful to Roberta Sherman and Laura Hill for their careful review of this chapter.

References

American Psychiatric Association. (1994). *Diagnostic and statistical manual for mental disorder* (4th ed.). Washington, DC: Author.

Beals, K. A. (2000). Subclinical eating disorders in female athletes. *The Journal of Physical Education, Recreation, and Dance, 71*, 23–31.

Beals, K. A. (2004). *Disordered eating among athletes.* Champaign, IL: Human Kinetics.

Beals, K. A., & Manore, M. M. (2002). Disorders of the female athlete triad among collegiate student-athletes. *International Journal of Sport Nutrition and Exercise Metabolism, 12*, 281–293.

Benton, S. A., Robertson, J. M., Tseng, W. C., Newton, F. B., & Benton, S. L. (2003). Changes in counseling center client problems across 13 years. *Professional Psychology: Research and Practice, 34*, 66–72.

Brownell, K. D., & Rodin, J. (1992). Prevalence of eating disorders in athletes. In K. Brownell, J. Rudin, & J. Wilmore (Eds.), *Eating, body weight, and performance in athletes* (pp. 128–145). Philadelphia: Lea & Febiger.

Carter, J. E., & Rudd, N. A. (2005). Disordered eating assessment in college student-athletes. *Women in Sport & Physical Activity Journal, 14*, 62–71.

Cash, T. F. (1997). *The body image workbook: An 8-step program for learning to like your looks.* Oakland, CA: New Harbinger.

Claude-Pierre, P. (1997). *The secret language of eating disorders.* New York: Random House.

Engel, S. G., Johnson, C., Powers, P. S., Crosby, R. D., Wonderlich, S. A., Wittrock, D. A., & Mitchell, J. E. (2003). Predictors of disordered eating in a sample of elite Division I college athletes. *Eating Behaviors, 4*, 333–343.

Fairburn, C. G., Cooper, Z., & Shafran, R. (2003). Cognitive behaviour therapy for eating disorders: A "transdiagnostic" theory and treatment. *Behaviour Research and Therapy, 41*, 509–528.

Fairburn, C. G., & Wilson, G. T. (1993). *Binge eating: Nature, assessment, and treatment.* New York: The Guilford Press.

Gaesser, G. A. (2002). *Big fat lies: The truth about your weight and your health.* Carlsbad, CA: Gurze.

Garner, D. M., Olmstead, M. P., Bohr, Y., & Garfinkle, P. E. (1982). The Eating Attitudes Test: An index of symptoms of Anorexia Nervosa. *Psychological Medicine, 9*, 273–279.

Granderson, L. Z. (2007). Big girls need love too. Retrieved April 15, 2007, from http://www.sports.espn.com

Hausenblas, H., & Carron, A. (1999). Eating disorder indices and athletes: An integration. *Journal of Sport and Exercise Psychology, 21*, 230–258.

Hausenblas, H., & Downs, D. (2001). Comparison of body image between athletes and nonathletes: A meta-analytic review. *Journal of Applied Sport Psychology, 13*(3), 323–339.

Johnson, C., Powers, P. S., & Dick, R. (1999). Athletes and eating disorders: The National Collegiate Athletic Association study. *International Journal of Eating Disorders, 26*, 179–188.

Kadison, R., & DiGeronimo, T. (2004). *College of the overwhelmed: The campus mental health crisis and what to do about it.* San Francisco: Jossey-Bass.

Kaye, W. H., Barbarich, N. C., Putnam, K., Gendall, K. A., Fernstrom, J., Fernstrom, M., McConaha, C. W., & Kishore, A. (2003). Anxiolytic effects of acute tryptophan depletion in Anorexia Nervosa. *International Journal of Eating Disorders, 33*, 257–267.

Keys, A. (1950). *The biology of human starvation.* Minneapolis: University of Minnesota Press.

Levine, M. P., & Smolak, L. (2005). *The prevention of eating problems and eating disorders: Theory, research and practice.* Mahwah, NJ: Lawrence Erlbaum.

Manore, M., & Thompson, J. (2000). *Sport nutrition for health and performance.* Champaign, IL: Human Kinetics.

McCreary, D. R., & Sasse, D. K. (2000). An exploration of the drive for muscularity in adolescent boys and girls. *Journal of American College Health, 48*, 297–304.

Mintz, L. B., O'Halloran, M. S., Mulholland, A. M., & Schneider, P. A. (1997). Questionnaire for Eating Disorder Diagnoses: Reliability and validity of operationalizing DSM-IV criteria into a self-report format. *Journal of Counseling Psychology, 44*, 63–79.

Mitchell, J. E., Agras, S., & Wonderlich, S. (2007). Treatment of bulimia nervosa: Where are we and where are we going? *International Journal of Eating Disorders, 40*, 95–101.

Petrie, T., Greenleaf, C., Reel, J., & Carter, J. E. (2007). Psychosocial correlates of disordered eating among male collegiate athletes. *Journal of Clinical Sport Psychology, 1*, 340–357.

Petrie, T., Greenleaf, C., Reel, J., & Carter, J. E. (in press). An examination of psychosocial correlates of disordered eating among female collegiate athletes. *Research Quarterly.*

Petrie, T., Reel, J., & Carter, J. E. (2005, October). *Disordered eating in college student-athletes: A multi-sport, multi-site study.* Symposium conducted at the annual meeting of the Association for the Advancement of Applied Sport Psychology, Vancouver, BC.

Petrie, T., & Sherman, R. (1999). Recognizing and assisting athletes with eating disorders. In R. Ray & D. Wiese-Bjornstal (Eds.), *Counseling in sports medicine.* Champaign, IL: Human Kinetics.

Petrie, T. A., & Sherman, R. (2000). Counseling athletes with eating disorders. In M. A. Andersen (Ed.), *Doing sport psychology.* Champaign, IL: Human Kinetics.

Pope, H. G., Phillips, K. A., & Olivardia, R. (2000). *The Adonis complex: The secret crisis of male body obsession.* New York: The Free Press.

Reinking, M. F., & Alexander, L. E. (2005). Prevalence of disordered-eating behaviors in undergraduate female collegiate athletes and nonathletes. *Journal of Athletic Training, 40*(1), 47–51.

Ryan, R. (1992). Management of eating problems in athletic settings. In K. Brownell, J. Rudin, & J. Wilmore (Eds.), *Eating, body weight, and performance in athletes.* Philadelphia: Lea & Febiger.

Sanford-Martens, T., Davidson, M., Yakushko, O., Martens, M., Hinton, P., & Beck, N. (2005). Clinical and subclinical eating disorders: An examination of female athletes. *Journal of Applied Sport Psychology, 17*(1), 79–86.

Schaefer, J., & Rutledge, T. (2003). *Life without Ed: How one woman declared independence from her eating disorder and how you can too.* New York: Mc-Graw Hill.

Sheehy, J., & Commerford, M. (2006). Eating disorders. In P. Grayson & P. Meilman (Eds.), *College mental health practice* (pp. 261–280). New York: Rutledge.

Sherman, R. T., & Thompson, R. A. (2001). Athletes and disordered eating: Four major issues for the professional psychologist. *Professional Psychology: Research and Practice, 32*(1), 27–33.

Sherman, R. T., & Thompson, R. A. (200X). Managing the female athlete triad. *NCAA Coaches Handbook,* www.ncaa.org

Smolak, L., Murnen, S. K., & Ruble, A. E. (2000). Female athletes and eating problems: A meta-analysis. *International Journal of Eating Disorders, 27,* 371–380.

Spence, J. C., McGannon, K. R., & Poon, P. (2005). The effect of exercise on global self-esteem. *Journal of Sport & Exercise Psychology, 27*(3), 311–334.

Stathopoulou, G., Powers, M. B., Berry, A., Smits, J. A., & Otto, M. W. (2006). Exercise interventions for mental health: A quantitative and qualitative review. *Clinical Psychology: Science and Practice, 13*(2), 179–193.

Steen, J. (2004). Personal communication.

Stice, E., Mazotti, L., Weibel, D., & Agras, W. S. (2000). Dissonance prevention program decrease thin-ideal internalization, body dissatisfaction, negative affect, and bulimic symptoms: A preliminary experiment. *International Journal of Eating Disorders, 27,* 206–217.

Striegel-Moore, R. H., & Bulik, C. M. (2007). Risk factors for eating disorders. *American Psychologist, 62*(3), 181–198.

Sundgot-Bergen, J. (1993). Prevalence of eating disorders in elite female athletes. *International Journal of Sport Nutrition, 3,* 29–40.

Thompson, R., & Sherman, R. (1993). *Helping athletes with eating disorders.* Champaign, IL: Human Kinetics.

Thompson, R. A., & Sherman, R. T. (1999). Athletes, athletic performance, and eating disorders: Healthier alternatives. *Journal of Social Issues, 55,* 317–337.

Thompson, R. A., & Sherman, R. T. (2005). NCAA coaches handbook: Managing the female athlete triad. Indianapolis, IN: The National Collegiate Athletic Association, www1.ncaa.org/membership/ed_outreach/health-safety/sports_med_education/triad/Handbook.pdf

Wilmore, J. (1992). Body weight standards and athletic performance. In K. Brownell, J. Rudin, & J. Wilmore (Eds.), *Eating, body weight, and performance in athletes.* Philadelphia: Lea & Febiger.

Wilson, G. T., Grilo, C. M., & Vitousek, K. M. (2007). Psychological treatment of eating disorders. *American Psychologist, 62(3),* 199–216.

Wonderlich, S. A., Joiner, T. E., Keel, P. K., Williamson, D. A., & Crosby, R. D. (2007). Eating disorder diagnoses: Empirical approaches to classification. *American Psychologist, 62(3),* 167–180.

12

CLINICAL DEPRESSION AND COLLEGE STUDENT-ATHLETES

Sam Maniar
John Sommers-Flanagan

Kyle Ambrogi couldn't get comfortable. He sat. He stood. He lay down. He grabbed a pillow and squeezed it as tightly as he could. Nothing settled his screaming nerves. Staring into Brad Martinez's eyes, bouncing off the walls of his friend's apartment that day this past August, Ambrogi couldn't explain the dark, numb feeling that was rotting his core. He couldn't organize his thoughts. He couldn't complete a sentence.

"You know, man," he'd begin, "I . . . just . . . feel . . . like . . ."

And then he'd stop. Each second brought more frustration, more pain. He began pulling chunks of hair out of his head, picking at tiny blemishes on his face. His body started to shake. His eyes began to tear up.

"Kyle, what's wrong? What is it? Talk to me," Martinez said. "You can tell me anything."

He could, just not today. Not this.

So Martinez pulled out a piece of paper and a pen. "Here, write it down," he said. Ambrogi grabbed the pen and scribbled down his emotions. He wrote two sentences.

I feel confused and upset. I can't do anything right.

Then he spoke.

"There's something," he told Martinez. "Something really bad. Last night, I stood on the South Street Bridge for an hour and a half . . . wondering if I should jump."

Martinez thought back to a month earlier, when Ambrogi asked

Martinez if he'd be upset if he jumped off a high-rise. "Of course I would," Martinez had said that day. "I'd be friggin' pissed."

Maybe it wasn't such a shock. Maybe the signs were there, but still . . . Kyle? Ambrogi was acting so strangely, pacing back and forth, squeezing his head in his hands, unable to sit still, that Martinez feared Ambrogi might hurt himself. Here. Now.

"I'm stupid," Ambrogi said to Martinez. "I can't do anything right. I'm a terrible friend. I don't even know why you guys are friends with me."

Martinez couldn't comprehend any of it. Kyle Ambrogi was Mr. All-American, the high school football star from nearby St. Joe's Prep with the GQ-cover-boy looks, the artfully chiseled frame and the outgoing, ice-breaking personality. He was a running back on the Penn football team, a senior finance major with a 3.5 GPA in the prestigious Wharton business school, and, perhaps most impressive, the kid everyone else turned to for advice when feeling down. (Drehs, 2006a)

Unfortunately, stories like Kyle Ambrogi's are becoming more common in the world of college sports. We are becoming more aware that athletes, even those who are highly successful, are not immune to depression. Moreover, athletes and student-athletes may not exhibit some of the "telltale signs" of depression that non-athletes might. For these reasons, depression is a key area to address in the care of student-athletes.

Clinical depression is a multifaceted bio-psycho-social-spiritual condition primarily characterized by the core symptom of sadness and/or irritability. At any given time, approximately 6–13% of college students suffer from a depressive condition, depending upon school setting, race, gender, income, and other factors; white students are more likely to be diagnosed with depression than black students; and women reportedly suffer from depression at approximately twice the rate of men (Jonas, Brody, Roper, & Narrow, 2003; Riolo, Nguyen, Greden, & King, 2005; Williams, Gonzalez, Neighbors, Nesse, Abelson, Sweetman, & Jackson, 2007).

Many individuals with depressive diagnoses think about, attempt, or commit suicide (Sommers-Flanagan & Sommers-Flanagan, 2003). For example, in a recent large-scale survey of students at Emory University, over 28% of students with significant depressive symptoms reported having suicidal thoughts within a four-week period (Garlow, Purselle, & Heninger, 2007). Additionally, although males are only half as likely to be diagnosed with a depressive disorder as females, they are about four times more likely to commit suicide (Sommers-Flanagan & Sommers-Flanagan, 2003). As noted by many authors, the monitoring and treatment of depression among college students, including college athletes, is essential (Etzel, Watson, Visek, & Maniar, 2006; Maniar, Chamberlain, & Moore, 2005; Sommers-Flanagan & Sommers-Flanagan, 1995, 2007). Moreover, depression and suicide among student-athletes has received increased attention from the NCAA (Hosick, 2005; NCAA, 2007) and media (e.g., Howard-Cooper, 2006a, 2006b; Drehs, 2006a, 2006b).

For several reasons, including stigmatization, the majority of college students with mental health problems apparently do not seek professional help, even though most depressive symptoms can be improved with treatment (Eisenberg, Golberstein, & Gollust, 2007). This is also true for college athletes, who often have a particular resistance to appearing weak or revealing a need for professional assistance or who may be discouraged from seeking help by the values and practices of the athletic culture (Etzel et al., 2006; Maniar, Curry, Sommers-Flanagan, & Walsh, 2001). The purpose of this chapter is to provide information about clinical depression, its manifestation among athletes, and depression screening, assessment, intervention, and referral guidelines for professionals who work with college athletes.

The Faces of Clinical Depression

Athletes are identified as having "clinical depression" if they qualify for a depressive psychiatric disorder as defined by the fourth edition of the Diagnostic and Statistical Manual of Mental Disorders (*DSM*; American Psychiatric Association, 2000). There are three primary forms of clinical depression in the *DSM*, including: (1) major depression, (2) dysthymic disorder, and (3) adjustment disorder with depressed mood. Additionally, some college athletes with depressive symptoms may be suffering from some form of bipolar disorder.

Major Depressive Disorder (Unipolar Depression)

To obtain a diagnosis of major depression, an athlete must be experiencing the core depressive symptom of sadness or low mood, in combination with at least four of nine additional symptoms (see Table 1). Major depression is further defined as the presence of this sometimes shifting cluster of symptoms for at least two weeks or longer. Athletes may suffer from mild, moderate, or severe forms of major depression. For example, athletes with a mild form of major depression typically report experiencing depressive symptoms of sadness, lack of interest or pleasure in usually enjoyable activities (anhedodia), insomnia or hypersomnia, difficulty concentrating, and decreased energy or motivation on most days over a two-week period. In contrast, athletes suffering from severe major depression might have substantial weight loss or gain, pervasive feelings of worthlessness or guilt, and suicidal thoughts—in addition to the more common symptoms listed below.

Table 1. Major Depression Symptoms
• Feelings of sadness or low mood for most of the day and nearly every day [this symptom is required for someone to be diagnosed with major depressive disorder and, for children/adolescents, the mood may be described as irritable instead of sad]
• Lack of or loss of interest or pleasure in activities that were once enjoyable [hanging out with friends, sport participation, school, sex]
• Hopelessness or significant negative thoughts about the future
• Decreased energy, fatigue, and/or feeling "slowed down"
• Significantly diminished or increased appetite or significant weight loss or weight gain
• Difficulty concentrating, indecisiveness, or memory problems
• Frequent feelings of worthlessness, low self-esteem, hopelessness, helplessness, or inappropriate guilt
• Insomnia or hypersomnia
• Agitation (motor restlessness) or psychomotor retardation (motor slowness)
• Recurrent thoughts of death or thoughts about suicide

Dysthymic Disorder

Dysthymic disorder is a chronic and mild form of clinical depression. Individuals with dysthymic disorder are sometimes seen as having a depressive personality. In other words, their depressive symptoms are chronic but less severe than those of major depressive disorder. To obtain a dysthymic disorder diagnosis, an athlete must experience a sad or depressed mood for most of the day, for more days than not, for at least two years. In adolescents, depressed moods may be characterized by irritability instead of sadness, and the duration must be at least one year. For both adults and adolescents, the core symptom of sadness or irritability must be accompanied by at least two of six additional depressive symptoms (i.e., poor appetite or overeating, insomnia or hypersomnia, low energy or fatigue, low self-esteem, poor concentration or difficulty making decisions, and feelings of hopelessness).

Although dysthymic symptoms are sometimes not disabling (i.e., the student-athlete often remains capable of engaging in his or her daily routine in a mostly productive manner), the individual's overall functioning is adversely affected in assorted ways. Additionally, it is possible for athletes who have been suffering from dysthymic disorder to experience a worsening of depressive symptoms that may also qualify them for a major depression diagnosis. When this pattern occurs, it is typically referred to as "double depression" (i.e., major depressive symptoms superimposed on dysthymic symptoms) (Keller et al., 1995).

Adjustment Disorder with Depressed Mood

An adjustment disorder is an abnormal and excessive reaction to a life stressor, such as starting school, getting divorced, or the death of a loved one, or when the symptoms appear to be excessive relative to the amount of stress present (APA, 2000). For athletes, an injury, a failure, or retirement from athletic participation may trigger depressive symptoms, and in such cases, the athlete might qualify for the diagnosis of adjustment disorder with depressed mood. Unlike major depression and dysthymic disorder, adjustment disorder with depressed mood does not include specific depressive symptom criteria beyond a sad, depressed, or irritable mood.

Bipolar Disorders

The *DSM* includes three forms of bipolar disorder that lie upon a continuum of severity. These three diagnoses, beginning with the most severe, include bipolar I, bipolar II, and cyclothymia, and each afflicts approximately 1% of the population (Lewinsohn, Klein, & Seeley, 1995). Historically, bipolar I has also been referred to as "manic depressive disorder."

Bipolar conditions typically involve "mood swings" ranging from major depressive symptoms to extreme euphoria (also termed "mania"), with intermittent periods of normal mood. Usually mood changes are gradual, but these changes may be rapid (i.e., rapid cycling). To be diagnosed with bipolar I, symptoms of major depression must be present for at least two weeks and a manic episode of at least four days. Manic symptoms associated with bipolar disorder are in Table 2.

Table 2. Manic Symptoms
• Inflated self-esteem or grandiose beliefs in one's worth or ability
• Decreased need for sleep (e.g., feels rested after only three hours of sleep)
• More talkative than usual or pressure to keep talking
• Psychomotor agitation (observable by others, not merely subjective feelings of restlessness or being slowed down)
• Flight of ideas or subjective experience that thoughts are racing
• Distractibility (i.e., attention too easily drawn to unimportant or irrelevant external stimuli)
• Increase in goal-directed activity (either socially, at work or school, or sexually) or psychomotor agitation
• Excessive involvement in pleasurable activities that have a high potential for painful consequences (e.g., engaging in unrestrained buying sprees, sexual indiscretions, or foolish business investments)

Other Depressive Disorders

Athletes may also experience depressive symptoms linked to or associated with other problems. In particular, the *DSM* includes two relevant diagnoses: (1) mood disorder due to a general medical condition, and (2) substance-induced mood disorder. The diagnosis of mood disorder due to a general medical condition is used when the symptoms are the direct result of the physiological mechanisms of an illness. For example, individuals with multiple sclerosis may be prone to depression because the disease directly impacts various parts of the brain (Morrison, 1995). Conversely, an individual who became depressed as a result of being diagnosed with an illness or because of the stress of living with an illness would not meet criteria for mood disorder due to a general medical condition. Likewise, substance-induced mood disorder is used when symptoms are a direct result of substance use, such as manic symptoms from cocaine or amphetamine abuse or depressive symptoms associated with withdrawal from a substance.

Depression among College Student-Athletes

Relatively little research has been conducted on the incidence of depression among student-athletes, but a potential increase in student-athlete suicides and suicidality has prompted athletic departments and university administrators to pay considerably more attention to depression among student-athletes (Etzel et al., 2006; Maniar et al., 2005; NCAA, 2006). Although the data are somewhat inconsistent, research suggests that student-athletes experience depressive symptoms and disorders at similar or higher rates than non-athlete students (Maniar & Carter, 2003; Storch et al., 2005). Moreover, as with non-athletes, research indicates that student-athletes under-utilize mental health services (Bergandi & Wittig, 1984; Eisenberg et al., 2007; Pinkerton, Hinz, & Barrow, 1989).

Depression is a critical issue to address among student-athletes and athlete clients, because it can impact athletic performance as well as academic performance, injury healing, and overall personal well-being. However, mental health issues such as depression among athletes and clinical depression in particular have rather unique and somewhat confusing histories. Over the years, there have been conflicting perspectives and evidence regarding the incidence of depression among athletes and student-athletes. On one hand, research indicates that participation in athletics may decrease the likelihood of depression. For example, numerous studies have shown the salutary effects of exercise on depression (for review, see Tkachuk & Martin, 1999). Originally, Franz and Hamilton (1905) conducted the first known empirical study of the effects of exercise on depression, concluding that exercise "retarded" depression—and their findings have stood the test of time. Additionally, research has suggested that athletes may have greater strength of personality than non-athletes and it seems intuitive that individuals with severe psychopathology might be "weeded out" by the time they reach high levels of sport participation. For example, Morgan (1985) stated, "success in sport is inversely correlated with psychopathology" (p. 71). Consequently, it might be assumed that, because of their high levels of exercise, strength of personality, and athletic success, college student-athletes are at less risk for depression than non-athletes.

On the other hand, more recent research indicates that student-athletes are equally (or more) at risk for depression as non-athlete peers. Storch, Storch, Killiany, and Roberti (2005) found that female college athletes, male college athletes, female college students, and male college students suffered from similar rates of clinical depression. Moreover, Maniar and Carter (2003) reported that college student-athletes presenting for counseling services were diagnosed with major depressive disorder equally as often as non-athlete college students presenting for counseling services. It has also been suggested that because of the increased demands student-athletes face (e.g., time, sport training and competition, school, etc.), they may be *more* at risk for depression than non-athletes.

Overall, as observed by Storch and colleagues, it is important to "underscore the need for early detection and intervention" of mental health issues among athletes (Storch et al., 2005, p. 94). The incidence of depression among student-athletes, combined with student-athletes' traditional tendency to under-utilize mental health services, makes them an at-risk population (Bergandi & Wittig, 1984; Pinkerton et al., 1989).

Unique Causes and Symptoms of Depression among Athletes

Modern formulations of clinical depression include biological, psychological, social/cultural, and spiritual components (Corveleyn, Luyten, Blatt, & Lens-Gielis, 2005). From the biological perspective, depression is hypothesized as being caused by various neurotransmitter deficiencies (e.g., serotonin), genetic abnormalities, hormonal imbalances, general inflammation, and other physiological phenomena. From the psychological perspective, cognitive factors, including persistent negative thoughts about oneself, the world, and the future are seen as a primary cause of depression. Similarly, social isolation, destructive relationship patterns, unemployment and poverty, and an absence of purpose or meaning in life are viewed as social, cultural, and spiritual contributors to depressive conditions. Overall, it is clear that clinical depression is initiated and maintained by a wide range of contributing factors. Additionally, the particular depressive symptoms displayed by individuals are typically related to specific cultural and situational factors. Unique factors that contribute to depression and unique symptom patterns among college athletes are summarized below.

Athletic Culture

Although glorified by some, student-athletes' lives have been described as overprotected (Lanning, 1982), socially depleted and isolated (Golden, 1984), and rigidly structured (Hinkle, 1996). Moreover, some student-athletes may internalize negative evaluations or identities of society (Balague, 1999; Engstrom & Sedlacek, 1991), and others may not have adequate academic preparation to succeed in college (AIR, 1988). Furthermore, many athletes experience stress related to the demands of juggling multiple responsibilities and balancing realistic life expectations with idealistic goals (Smallman, Sowa, & Young, 1991). Finally, although the athletic culture is highly supportive of excellence in performance, it is typically much less supportive when athletes suffer from emotional problems. Former Pittsburgh Steeler quarterback Terry Bradshaw described the athletic culture's response to clinical depression: "We're supposed to be big, tough guys. 'You have depression? Shoot, that's not depression. That's weakness.' That's how the thinking goes" (Wertheim, 2003, p. 76). Overall, in some ways, athletic culture exacerbates depressive problems among athletes.

Injury

Athletic injuries may contribute to depressive symptoms in several ways. An injury may be perceived as a threat to one's athletic identity (Brewer, 1994; Brewer, Van Raalte, & Linder, 1991, 1993; Kolt, 2004; Petitipas & Danish, 1995), and if the threat is not addressed, it may lead to depression. It has been estimated that between 5% and 24% of injured athletes experience clinically significant distress (Brewer & Petrie, 2002), and the most at-risk period may be in the first month following an injury (Newcomer, Perna, Maniar, Roh, & Stilger, 1999). Athletes who have the hardest time coping with an injury usually exclusively identify with their athletic identity. This is referred to as a foreclosed identity (Miller, 2003).

Additionally, some injury conditions in and of themselves seem to contribute to depression. For example, in a recent study, college athletes with mild traumatic brain injury (i.e., concussion) exhibited a significant increase in depression, confusion, and mood disturbances (Mainwaring et al., 2004). These results suggest that when athletes experience a blow to the head during competition or training, it may initiate some depressive symptoms.

Retirement

Similar to injury, athletic retirement can threaten an athlete's identity and therefore contribute to depressive symptoms (Baillie & Danish, 1992; Grove, Lavallee, Gordon, & Harvey, 1998; Lavallee & Andersen, 2000). Many athletes report disappointment and confusion about what they will do with their lives at the end of their athletic career (Brewer, 1993). Interestingly, the opposite may also be the case. Upon graduation, student-athletes may suffer from lower rates of depression than their non-athlete peers because exercise continues while competitive pressures cease. For example, Wyshak (2001) found that, in the years after college, female college athletic activity was negatively correlated with self-reported physician-diagnosed depression. Thus, when intercollegiate competition ends, athletes may feel stress relief. Additional research indicates that athletes' perception of control regarding retirement may impact their adjustment to life after sport (McPherson, 1980).

Performance-Related Stress and Coping

Athletes report both anecdotally and through research about their stresses related to elite performance expectations (Birky, 2007; Maniar & Carter, 2003). This performance-related stress is a well-known contributor to alcohol, drug abuse, eating disorders, and other destructive behavior patterns (Miller et al., 2002). Put simply, when athletes are placed in the spotlight and faced with high performance expectations, it is not unusual for them to begin using destructive coping strategies (e.g., excessive alcohol consumption). Chronic use of destructive coping strategies may, in turn, increase depressive symptoms.

Athlete-Specific Depressive Symptoms

Because of the fight-through-pain and never-show-weakness culture of athletics, some athletes may not be comfortable talking openly about their depressive symptoms (Wertheim, 2003). Further, for similar reasons, athletes may not even be aware of their depressive symptoms until the symptoms become quite severe. Underrecovery from training and other associated life stress may also be reported by athletes who seek consultation (Kellman, 2002). Consequently, it is crucial for coaches and professionals who work with athletes to be aware of some of the less obvious signs of depression among athletes. These signs may include but are not limited to: missed rehab appointments, vague or specific physical complaints, reduced quickness or psychomotor speed, lack of responsiveness to training and performance opportunities, withdrawal from social interactions with other athletes, increased alcohol or drug use, and repeated expression of dissatisfaction or unhappiness with performance or physical attributes/condition. Obviously, in many cases, symptoms from the preceding list are not indicative of clinical depression, but awareness of these potential signs of depression is important.

Assessment

Any assessment for psychological disorders should only be done by a licensed mental health professional (e.g., psychologist, psychiatrist, licensed social worker, licensed professional counselor, licensed marriage and family therapist, etc.). Many mental health professionals are able to make an accurate diagnosis of depressive disorder via an interview or symptom checklist from the *DSM*. However, some clinicians prefer to supplement interviews with assessment measures. Assessment measures have been applauded in assessing mental disorder because they can be more objective than clinician observations, and clients may feel more open to answer honestly because they may not have to directly face the therapist's feedback (Grayson & Cooper, 2006).

Many assessment measures for depression are self-report (i.e., the client fills out a symptom checklist based on their own recollection of their symptoms), while others are structured-interview templates (with scoring) for the clinician to follow. Examples of widely used self-report depression instruments are the Beck Depression Inventory-II (BDI-II; Beck, Steer, & Brown, 1996) and the Center for Epidemiological Studies Depression (CES-D) Scale (Radloff, 1977). The Hamilton Depression Rating Scale (Hamilton, 1960) is a commonly used structured interview assessment. It should be noted that a thorough assessment of depression should also include asking questions about suicidality (NCAA, 2006).

Treatment Options

As a condition with biological, psychological, social/cultural, and spiritual dimensions, it should come as no surprise that there are a number of viable treatment options available to athletes suffering from depression. Below, we discuss both evidence-based treatments and adjunctive treatments—recognizing that for some individual athletes, adjunctive treatments may constitute a perfectly adequate intervention and, in some cases, evidence-based treatments may be completely ineffective.

Evidence-Based Treatments

In 1993, the Division 12 Task Force of the American Psychological Association (APA) published a list of "empirically validated" psychotherapeutic treatments (Chambless & Hollon, 1993). This publication was, in part, an effort to establish psychotherapy treatments as equivalent or superior to existing medical treatments. In particular, because medical treatments (e.g., antidepressant medications) were evaluated by the Food and Drug Administration (FDA) based on randomized clinical trials (RCTs), psychologists sought to use similar standards for evaluating their clinical techniques.

Perhaps not surprisingly, after APA Division 12 published its initial list of "empirically validated" treatments, great controversy followed—primarily because, using medical RCT standards, many common psychotherapy approaches did not qualify as empirically validated (Silverman, 1996). Consequently, at a later date, empirically validated treatments were relabeled as "empirically supported" and the original list was expanded. Additionally, other professional organizations began using different criteria to define empirically supported treatments (Chambless, 2002). Recently, the APA has moved toward a less divisive label of evidence-based practice and acknowledged that it may not be the specific technique or treatment that produces positive change, but instead positive change may be produced by a variety of variables—including "the treatment method, the individual psychologist, the treatment relationship, and the patient" (APA, 2006, p. 275).

In addition to this explanation about the evolution of evidence-based treatments in psychology, the authors also feel compelled to note that the medically oriented RCT model used to provide evidence or support for specific treatment models has been strongly criticized. For the purposes of this chapter, the most important criticism is that RCTs are almost always conducted exclusively on patients who are suffering from a single psychiatric condition (e.g., major depressive disorder). This means that in contrast to real-world college athletes who are often suffering from multiple symptoms and multiple psychiatric conditions in addition to depression (e.g., anxiety disorders, attention-deficit disorder, alcohol abuse, eating disorders, etc.), RCTs are conducted on individuals suffering only from clinical depression. As an example, research indicates that athletes' symptoms of depression may be compounded by pain from injuries (Schwenk, Gorenflo, Dopp, & Hipple, 2007).

What this means is that the following evidence-based treatments may, in reality, be limited in their use with athletes who are experiencing many symptoms in addition to their depressive symptoms. Additionally, although RCTs typically include 20 sessions of uninterrupted treatment (Grayson & Cooper, 2006), as many readers know, student-athletes are usually seen for fewer sessions and in chunks between competition seasons and school vacations (Maniar & Carter, 2003). Accordingly, after listing and briefly describing standard, evidence-based treatments, the authors list and describe a wide range of adjunctive treatments that may be just as appropriate for athletes as evidence-based treatments.

Biomedical Treatments

Biomedical treatments seek to address underlying physical, biological, or genetic conditions that may be causing or contributing to clinical depression. These treatments include antidepressant medications, herbal remedies, light therapy, massage, and physical exercise. The only biomedical treatments for depression that have significant research support are antidepressant medications and electroconvulsive therapy (UK

ECT Review Group, 2003). For the purposes of this chapter, we focus only on antidepressant medication treatment and some selected adjunctive biologically based treatments.

Antidepressant medications. Antidepressant medications are one of the most common treatments for depression within the United States. Given this status, it is no surprise to find there are many proponents and detractors of antidepressant medications. Antidepressant proponents often claim that antidepressant medications are effective in alleviating depression at a 70–80% rate. In contrast, antidepressant detractors suggest that antidepressants are no more effective than a smack to the head with a baseball bat (Breggin & Cohen, 1999). More moderate estimates indicate that antidepressant medications are probably somewhat but not completely effective for about 50–60% of patients with clinical depression (Sommers-Flanagan & Sommers-Flanagan, 2007). In general, the following are five reasonable guidelines for helping professionals to keep in mind relative to psychotropic medication when working with student-athletes who are struggling with depression:

1. Medications are generally recommended for more severe cases of depression.
2. Medications should be used as an *adjunct* to counseling, because medications will not help depressed athletes make choices and changes in their lives to alleviate depression in the future.
3. Medications should be taken and/or stopped only under the direct care of a physician.
4. When the depression appears complex, team physicians should consult with psychiatrists.
5. In all cases, athletes taking antidepressant medications should be monitored closely for agitation, suicidality, and violent thoughts.

In October, 2004, the FDA voted unanimously to begin requiring "black box" warnings on all selective serotonin reuptake inhibitors (SSRI) antidepressant medications. These labels warned that SSRI antidepressants can sometimes increase suicidality in patients 18 and younger. More recently, the FDA extended the warning label to include young adults, ages 19–24 (Friedman & Leon, 2007). Although this decision is not without controversy, it speaks to the fact that SSRI antidepressants—and perhaps all antidepressants—are not a simple quick biological fix for persons suffering from depression. Instead, antidepressant medications may produce uncomfortable side effects and adverse medical reactions; consequently, antidepressant medications should not be used as a sole depression intervention.

A wide variety of antidepressants are prescribed for clinical depression. These medications are generally of four types: selective serotonin reuptake inhibitors (SSRIs), serotonin and norepinephrine reuptake inhibitors (SNRIs), tricyclic antidepressants (TCAs), and monoamine oxidase inhibitors (MAOIs).

Today, SSRIs and SNRIs are the first choice of treatment due to limited side effects and their impact on specific neurotransmitters. Although some improvement in mood may occur immediately upon administration of these medications, in most cases it takes three to four weeks of medication to obtain the full therapeutic effect (NIMH, 2002). It should be noted, though, that with the exception of fluoxetine (Prozac), recent research on adolescents indicates that the risk of suicide may outweigh the potential benefits derived from SSRIs (Whittington et al., 2004).

Herbal remedies. It is relatively easy to find a plethora of herbal remedies for depression at the local health food store or online. Because the chemical action is similar to pharmaceutical products, recently some professionals have begun referring to herbal remedies as herbaceuticals (Ingersoll, 2005). However, some of these products have absolutely no research support for their efficacy. Others have limited support that sometimes makes them worth trying as an adjunctive treatment for depression (Ingersoll, 2005). For example, both St. John's wort and omega-3 fatty acids appear to have some promise in the treatment of depression (Severus, 2006; Simopoulos, 2007). Nevertheless, as with pharmaceutical interventions, herbal supplements should be used with caution and preferably under the supervision of a licensed professional.

Light therapy. Research indicates that light therapy may provide some anti-depressant effects, especially when administered in the morning (Kripke, 1998). Although originally thought to be helpful only in cases of seasonal affective disorder (SAD), recent research indicates light therapy may reduce depressive symptoms in chronically depressed individuals (Terman & Terman, 2005). Additionally, light therapy may have advantages over medication treatment, in that light therapy produces an antidepressant effect more quickly and generally has fewer problematic side effects. Typically, light therapy involves direct exposure to intense artificial illumination delivered through devices marketed and sold as "light boxes."

Massage therapy. There is some evidence that massage therapy may be effective in treating a number of other mental health problems, including clinical depression (for review, see Field, 1998). The exact mechanism underlying massage therapy as a treatment for depression is unknown. However, as an adjunctive treatment for athletes with depression, massage therapy, as long as it is administered by a licensed professional, is a relatively low-risk alternative. Many athletics departments have licensed massage therapists on staff or as referral resources.

Physical exercise. Although physical exercise is a viable treatment for depression in non-athletes, there is no evidence that additional physical exercise is a useful treatment alternative for athletes. However, for athletes who have discontinued their usual exercise regime, re-initiation of the exercise program or the development of an alternative exercise regime may be helpful.

Psycho-Social-Spiritual Treatments

Psycho-social-spiritual treatments seek to address depression through interventions designed to address the client's thinking patterns, social relationships, and spiritual practices. Within this domain, there are three evidence-based or empirically supported therapies. These include cognitive therapy, behavior therapy, and interpersonal psychotherapy.

Cognitive, behavioral, and interpersonal therapies. Cognitive and behavioral therapies focus on helping athletes modify their dysfunctional thoughts, beliefs, and/or behaviors (for review, see Beck, Rush, Shaw, & Emery, 1987). These therapy approaches are generally directive and educational. They are also demanding—in that, to be successful, athletes need to work hard at becoming aware of their self-destructive thinking and behavior patterns. Many professional therapists, as well as graduate students, have substantial training in providing cognitive and behavioral therapy.

In contrast, although it is also an empirically supported treatment, interpersonal psychotherapy (for review, see Teyber, 2005) is a less well-known therapy approach. Consequently, it is more difficult to find professionals who offer interpersonal therapy—although it will be more available in urban areas and through medical school or clinical psychology training programs. Interpersonal therapy involves examining the role of relationships that may cause and/or intensify depression.

Generally, cognitive, behavioral, and interpersonal therapies should be the first choice for treating depression among college-student athletes. Given the success rate of counseling and the potential side effects of medication, we typically recommend counseling as the treatment of choice for mild to moderate depression. For severe depression, a combination of counseling and medication may be the best choice of treatment (TADS, 2004).

Other Therapies

There are many other approaches to counseling and psychotherapy that may be especially beneficial for student-athletes. For example, athletes may gravitate toward solution-focused therapy (for review, see Friedman & Fanger, 1991) because it espouses a very positive philosophy and focuses on what is working, rather than on what is wrong or negative. This perspective is somewhat consistent with the athletic culture.

In addition, as some athletes begin to question whether college athletics or professional sports are a viable option for them, other therapy approaches may be more appropriate. For example, therapies that focus on finding meaning or purpose in life, in mindful acceptance of life as it is, and on connecting with one's culture and faith can be very helpful. These therapies include existential therapy, acceptance and commitment therapy, and multicultural therapy (Sommers-Flanagan & Sommers-Flanagan, 2004).

Bibliotherapy

Bibliotherapy is a fancy name for the use of self-help books for addressing personal problems. Interestingly, there is limited empirical evidence attesting to the efficacy of self-help bibliotherapy for some specific problems, such as anxiety and phobias. Rather than meeting with a "professional," some athletes may prefer an approach that involves working through their depressive symptoms more independently. Examples of bibliotherapy for depression include Burns (1999) and Greenberger and Padesky (1995).

Suggestions for Working with College Student-Athletes Clients with Depression

Athletes with depression and other mental health problems present a particular challenge to coaches, trainers, and athletic programs. Nevertheless, it is a challenge well worth meeting. The following recommendations are offered in an effort to help athletic programs and personnel to develop a system that is sensitive and responsive to athletes with clinical depression.

Develop Procedures and Systems that Encourage Genuine Self-Disclosure

As a matter of course, athletic programs should develop procedures and systems that encourage athlete self-disclosure—even when such disclosure includes depressive content that might traditionally be viewed as signs of weakness. These procedures could include regular times when specific personnel check-in with students on how they are doing off the field, posters that articulate the importance of self-disclosure as a sign of strength, and small-group open forums in which athletes get an opportunity to articulate their concerns as well as positive experiences to administrators and/or mental health professionals. Overall, it is crucial for athletic programs to help fight the stigma that prevents athletes from talking about and seeking help for their depressive symptoms.

Identify Referral Sources in Advance

It is impossible to know, in advance, when a student athlete will need mental health services. Consequently, as advocated by the NCAA (2006, 2007), athletic programs should proactively identify referral sources for athletes with depression. Referral sources may include but are not limited to: (1) athletic department academic support services; (2) athletic department sports medicine or counseling services; (3) university health and counseling services; (4) counseling or medical services offered through university graduate programs or medical schools; and (5) local community resources.

It is often very difficult to get athletes to follow through on contacting referral sources. To address this issue, it is wise for athletic program staff to establish positive working relationships in advance with a member of the university counseling center and/or medical personnel. Ideally, these professionals or professionals-in-training will have previous experience working directly with athletes. This is important, because athletes often view their problems as unique and may devalue assistance from individuals without competitive athletic experience.

Screen and Monitor for Depressive Symptoms

Screening and monitoring for depressive symptoms is not necessarily the responsibility of athletic program personnel. Any screening should be conducted by licensed mental health professionals affiliated with the athletics department. As suggested by the NCAA Depression Guidelines (2006), one potential time to screen athletes for depression is during pre-participation exams using self-report instruments, such as the CES-D Scale (Radloff, 1977) or the BDI-II (Beck et al., 1996). Nonetheless, because athletic personnel may have more contact with athletes than anyone else, it is desirable for all athletic personnel to have a general awareness of the signs and symptoms of depression. One way to accomplish this is to review the symptoms of major depression in Table 1. However, there are also warning signs of depression that do not constitute diagnostic symptoms, but that may signal depression. These include but are not limited to: (1) social withdrawal; (2) recurrent headaches or other body aches and pains; (3) missing classes, practices, or rehabilitation appointments; (4) increased irritability; and (5) increased negativity (e.g., complaints, criticisms, etc.).

Screen and Monitor for Suicide Warning Signs

Although suicide is a rare event, it is very important for athletic personnel to be apprised of two of the most pernicious of all suicide myths. That is: (1) suicidal people do not usually talk about suicide in advance (in fact, they usually do, and this is an important warning sign); and (2) one should never ask about suicide because it might plant the idea of suicide into a depressed person's mind (in fact, asking about suicide is the right thing to do).

It is imperative for athletic personnel to be educated about potential suicide risk factors and warning signs. A suicide risk factor and warning signs checklist is presented in Table 3. When athletic personnel are concerned about moderate to severe depression with or without suicidality, a timely referral to a licensed mental health professional is imperative.

Table 3. Suicide Risk Factor and Warning Signs Checklist
____ 1. Previous suicide attempt
____ 2. Excessive or abusive alcohol/drug use
____ 3. Psychiatric diagnosis of depression is suspected
____ 4. Social isolation (e.g., few friends, too much time alone)
____ 5. Physical injury or significant health problem
____ 6. Recent and significant personal loss (of ability, objects, or persons)
____ 7. Sexual identity issues
____ 8. Past or recent physical or sexual abuse victim
____ 9. Significant anxiety, insomnia, or disinterest in usually pleasurable activities
____ 10. Statements about hopelessness, helplessness, or excessive guilt are present
____ 11. Suicidal talk or thoughts
____ 12. Suicide plan
____ 13. Poor self-control or impulsive behavior
____ 14. Giving away of valuable possessions
____ 15. Recently discharged from a psychiatric facility after apparent improvement
____ 16. Recently prescribed an SSRI and reports agitation and/or violent thoughts

Discussion of Case

The case of Kyle Ambrogi illustrates how excellent athletes, students, and individuals are not spared symptoms of clinical depression and associated suicidal thoughts and impulses. With individuals like Kyle Ambrogi, the emergence of depressive symptoms can seem unbelievable or impossible; it can even seem impossible to the athlete himself (or herself), which usually only leads to deepening shame and dysphoria.

Kyle Ambrogi is also an example of how important it is to educate athletes, coaches, and support personnel about clinical depression. Without education and without encouragement for open communication about internal feelings, thoughts, and impulses, athletes may choose to stay quiet and suffer when they might, instead, seek appropriate informal and professional assistance. They may also not even understand that they are experiencing clinical depression, and they may not know about the many methods for addressing their feelings of alienation and misery. The case of Kyle Ambrogi captures the necessity of educating all athletic personnel, including athletes, about clinical depression and potentially helpful interventions.

Conclusion

Organizations like the National Collegiate Athletics Association (NCAA) have of late recognized the significance of mental health issues in the lives of student-athletes (Hosick, 2005). The severity and range of presenting concerns of student-athlete clients are deep and extensive, likely reflecting a mental health crisis that exists on campus today (Benton, Robertson, Tseng, Newton, & Benton, 2003; Brent et al., 2006; Etzel, 2003; Hinkle, 1994; Kadison & DiGeronimo, 2004). One common presenting mental health concern of student-athletes is depression.

Clinical depression has many faces and is a potentially lethal condition that affects college students in general and athletes in particular. Although it is a great challenge for athletic programs and personnel to remain vigilant for depressive signs and symptoms in their athletes and to treat them with sensitivity and emotional support, it is crucial for helping professionals to work together to meet this important challenge today and in the years to come. This chapter advocates for the development of athletic programs and personnel who are informed about clinical depression and who can address this difficult issue as it affects a growing number of collegiate athletes.

References

American Institutes for Research. (1998). *Summary results from the 1987–1988 national study of intercollegiate athletics* (Report No. 1). Palo Alto, CA: Center for the Study of Athletics.

American Psychiatric Association. (2000). *Diagnostic and statistical manual of mental disorders* (4th ed., text rev.). Washington, DC: Author.

American Psychological Association Presidential Task Force on Evidence-Based Practice. (2006). Evidence-based practice in psychology. *American Psychologist, 61,* 271–285.

Baillie, P. H. F., & Danish, S. J. (1992). Understanding the career transitions of athletes. *The Sport Psychologist, 6,* 77–98.

Balague, G. (1999). Understanding identity, value, and meaning when working with elite athletes. *The Sport Psychologist, 13*, 89–98.

Beck, A. T., Rush, A. J., Shaw, B. F., & Emery, G. (1987). *Cognitive therapy of depression* (rev. ed.). New York: Guilford.

Beck, A. T., Steer, R. A., & Brown, G. K. (1996). *Manual for the Beck Depression Inventory II*. San Antonio, TX: The Psychological Corporation.

Bergandi, T., & Wittig, A. (1984). Availability of and attitudes toward counseling services for the collegiate athlete. *Journal of College Student Personnel, 25*, 557–558.

Breggin, P., & Cohen, D. (1999). *Your drug may be your problem: How and why to stop taking psychiatric medications*. New York: Da Capo Press.

Brewer, B. W. (1994). Review and critique of models of psychological adjustment to athletic injury. *Journal of Applied Sport Psychology, 6*, 87–100.

Brewer, B. W., & Petrie, T. A. (2002). Psychopathology in sport and exercise. In J. L. Van Raalte & B. W. Brewer (Eds.), *Exploring sport and exercise psychology* (2nd ed., pp. 307–324). Washington, DC: American Psychological Association.

Brewer, B. W., Van Raalte, J. L., & Linder, D. E. (1991). Role of the sport psychologist in treating injured athletes: A survey of sports medicine providers. *Journal of Applied Sport Psychology, 3*, 183–190.

Brewer, B. W., Van Raalte, J. L., & Linder, D. E. (1993). Athletic identity: Hercules' muscles or Achilles' heel. *International Journal of Sport Psychology, 24*, 237–254.

Burns, D. D. (1999). *Feeling good: The new mood therapy* (rev. ed.). New York: Avon.

Chambless, D. L. (2002). Identification of empirically supported counseling psychology interventions: Commentary. *Counseling Psychologist, 30*, 302–308.

Chambless, D. L., & Hollon, S. D. (1998). Defining empirically supported therapies. *Journal of Consulting & Clinical Psychology, 66*, 7–18.

Corveleyn, J., Luyten, P., Blatt, S. J., & Lens-Gielis, H. (2005). *Theory and treatment of depression: Towards a dynamic interactionism model*. New York: Lawrence Erlbaum.

Drehs, W. (2006a). Tragic turn. *ESPN.com*. Retrieved August 9, 2007, from http://sports.espn.go.com/espn/eticket/story?page=ambrogi

Drehs, W. (2006b). An inexplicable loss. *ESPN.com*. Retrieved August 9, 2007, from http://sports.espn.go.com/espn/eticket/story?page=ambrogi&num=2

Eisenberg, D., Golberstein, E., & Gollust, S. E. (2007). Help-seeking and access to mental health care in a university student population. *Medical Care, 45*, 594–601.

Elkin, I., Shea, M., Watkins, J., Imber, S., Sotsky, S. M., Collins, J. F., & et al. (1989). National Institute of Mental Health Treatment of Depression Collaborative Research Program: General effectiveness of treatments. *Archives of General Psychiatry, 46*, 971–982.

Engstrom, C. M., & Sedlacek, W. E. (1991). A study of prejudice toward university student-athletes. *Journal of Counseling and Development, 70*, 189–193.

Etzel, E. F., Watson, J. C., Visek, A. J., & Maniar, S. D. (2006). Understanding and promoting college student-athlete health: Essential issues for student affairs professionals. *National Association of Student Personnel Administrators Journal, 43*, 518–546.

Field, T. M. (1998). Massage therapy effects. *American Psychologist, 53*, 1270–1281.

Franz, S. I., & Hamilton, G. V. (1905). The effects of exercise upon the retardation in conditions of depression. *American Journal of Insanity, 62*, 239–256.

Friedman, R. A., & Leon, A. C. (2007). Expanding the black box—Depression, antidepressants, and the risk of suicide. *New England Journal of Medicine, 356*, 2343–2346.

Friedman, S., & Fanger, M. T. (1991). *Expanding therapeutic possibilities: Getting results in brief psychotherapy*. Lexington, MA: Lexington.

Garlow, S. J., Purselle, D. C., & Heninger, M. (2007). Cocaine and alcohol use preceding suicide in African American and white adolescents. *Journal of Psychiatric Research, 41*, 53–536.

Golden, D. (1984). Supervising college athletics: The role of the chief student services officer. *New Directions for Student Services, 28*, 59–70.

Grayson, P. A., & Cooper, S. (2006). Depression and anxiety. In P. A. Grayson & P. W. Meilman (Eds.), *College mental health practice* (pp. 113–134). New York: Routledge.

Greenberger, D., & Padesky, C. A. (1995). *Mind over mood: Change how you feel by changing the way you think*. New York: Guilford.

Grove, J. R., Lavallee, D., Gordon, S., & Harvey, J. H. (1998). Account-making: A model for understanding and resolving distressful reactions to retirement from sport. *The Sport Psychologist, 12*, 52–67.

Hamilton, M. (1960). A rating scale for depression. *Journal of Neurology, Neurosurgery & Psychiatry, 23*, 56–62.

Hinkle, J. S. (1996). Depression, adjustment disorder, generalized anxiety, and substance abuse: An overview for sport professionals working with college student-athletes. In E. F. Etzel, A. P. Ferrante, & J. W. Pinkney (Eds.), *Counseling college student-athletes: Issues and interventions* (2nd ed., pp. 109–136). Morgantown, WV: Fitness Information Technology.

Hosick, M. B. (2005, February 25). Forum places psychological focus on mental health issues. *The NCAA News*. Retrieved August 9, 2007, from http://www1.ncaa.org/membership/ed_outreach/health-safety/forummentalhealthpdf.pdf

Howard-Cooper, S. (2006a, October 8). Pushed to the limit. *The Sacramento Bee*, pp. A1, A12–A13.

Howard-Cooper, S. (2006b, October 9). Pushed to the limit. *The Sacramento Bee*, pp. A1, A14–A15.

Ingersoll, R. E. (2005). Herbaceuticals: An overview for counselors. *Journal of Counseling and Development, 83*, 434–443.

Jonas, B .S., Brody, D., Roper, M., & Narrow, W. E. (2003). Prevalence of mood disorders in a national sample of young American adults. *Social Psychiatry and Psychiatric Epidemiology, 38*, 618–624.

Kaplan, H. I., & Sadock, B. J. (1990). *Pocket handbook of clinical psychiatry*. Baltimore, MD: Williams & Wilkins.

Keller, M. B., Klein, D. N., Hirschfeld, R. M. A., Kocsis, J. H., & et al. (1995). Results of the *DSM-IV* mood disorders field trial. *American Journal of Psychiatry, 152*, 843–849.

Kellmann, M. (2002). *Enhancing recovery: Preventing underperformance in athletes*. Champaign, IL: Human Kinetics.

Kolt, G. (2004). Injury from sport, exercise, and physical activity. In G. S. Kolt & M. B. Andersen (Eds.), *Psychology in the physical and manual therapies* (pp. 247–267). Edinburgh, UK: Churchill Livingstone.

Kripke, D. F. (1998). Light treatment for nonseasonal depression: Speed, efficacy, and combined treatment. *Journal of Affective Disorders, 49,* 109–117.

Lanning, W. (1982). The privileged few: Special counseling needs of athletes. *Journal of Sport Psychology, 4,* 19–23.

Lavallee, D., & Andersen, M. B. (2000). Leaving sport: Easing career transitions. In M. B. Andersen (Ed.), *Doing sport psychology* (pp. 249–260). Champaign, IL: Human Kinetics.

Lewinsohn, P. M., Klein, D. N., & Seeley, J. R. (1995). Bipolar disorders in a community sample of older adolescents: Prevalence, phenomenology, comorbidity, and course. *Journal of the American Academy of Child and Adolescent Psychiatry, 34,* 454–463.

Logan, A. C. (2004). Omega-3 fatty acids and major depression: A primer for the mental health professional. *Lipids and Health Diseases, 3,* 25.

Maniar, S. D., & Carter, J. (2003, October). Characteristics of university student-athletes seeking sport psychology services: Part I. In S. D. Maniar (Chair), *Getting creative with university-based sport psychology services: Typical issues in an atypical field.* Symposium presented at the 17th annual meeting of the Association for the Advancement of Applied Sport Psychology, Philadelphia, PA.

Maniar, S. D., Chamberlain, R., & Moore, N. (2005, November 7). Suicide risk is real for student-athletes. *NCAA News, 42*(23), 4, 20.

Maniar, S. D., Curry, L. A., Sommers-Flanagan, J., & Walsh, J. A. (2001). Student-athlete preferences in seeking help when confronted with sport performance problems. *The Sport Psychologist, 15,* 205–223.

McPherson, B. P. (1980). Retirement from professional sport: The process and problems of occupational and psychological adjustment. *Sociological Symposium, 30,* 126–143.

Miller, P. S. (2003). The role experimentation of intercollegiate student athletes. *The Sport Psychologist, 17,* 196–219.

Morgan, W. P. (1985). Selected psychological factors limiting performance: A mental health model. In D. J. Clark & H. M. Eckert (Eds.), *Limits of human performance* (pp. 70–80). Champaign, IL: Human Kinetics.

Morrison, J. (1995). *DSM-IV made easy: The clinician's guide to diagnosis.* New York: Guilford.

Moyer, C. A., Rounds, J., & Hannum, J. W. (2004). A meta-analysis of massage therapy research. *Psychological Bulletin, 130,* 3–18.

National Collegiate Athletic Association. (2006). Guideline 2o: Depression: Interventions for collegiate athletics. In *2006–07 NCAA Sports Medicine Handbook,* 64–68. Indianapolis: Author.

National Collegiate Athletic Association. (2007). *Managing student-athletes' mental health issues.* Retrieved July 25, 2007, from http://www.ncaa.org/library/sports_sciences/mental_health/2007_managing_mental_health.pdf

National Institute of Mental Health. (2002). *Depression* (NIH Publication No 02-3561). Bethesda (MD): National Institute of Mental Health, National Institutes of Health, U.S. Department of Health and Human Services.

Newcomer, R., Perna, F., Maniar, S., Roh, J., & Stilger, V. (1999, September). Depressive symptomotology distinguishing injured from non-injured athletes. In F. Perna (Chair), *Pre-injury screening and post-injury assessment: Interactions between sport psychologists and the sports medicine team.* Symposium conducted at the 13th annual meeting of the Association for the Advancement of Applied Sport Psychology, Banff, Alberta, Canada.

Petitipas, A., & Danish, S. J. (1995). Caring for injured athletes. In S. M. Murphy (Ed.), *Sport psychology interventions* (pp. 255–281). Champaign, IL: Human Kinetics.

Pinkerton, R. S., Hinz, L. D., & Barrow, J. C. (1989). The college student-athlete: Psychological considerations and interventions. *Journal of American College Health, 37,* 218–226.

Riolo, S. A., Nguyen, T. A., Greden, J. F., & King, C. A. (2005). Prevalence of depression by race/ethnicity: Findings from the National Health and Nutrition Examination Survey III. *American Journal of Public Health, 95,* 998–1000.

Radloff, L. S. (1977). The CES-D Scale: A self-report depression scale for research in the general population. *Applied Psychological Measurement, 1,* 385–401.

Schwenk, T., Gorenflo, D., Dopp, R., & Hipple, E. (2007). Depression and pain in retired professional football players. *Medicine & Science in Sports & Exercise, 39,* 599–605.

Severus, W. E. (2006). Effects of omega-3 polyunsaturated fatty acids on depression. In B. Maisch & R. Oelze (Eds.), *Cardiovascular benefits of omega-3 polyunstaurated fatty acids* (pp. 129–138). Amsterdam, Netherlands: IOS.

Shea, M., Elkin, I., Imber, S., Sotsky, S. M., Watkins, J. T., Collins, J. F., & et al. (1992). Course of depressive symptoms over follow-up. *Archives of General Psychiatry, 49,* 782–787.

Silverman, W. H. (1996). Cookbooks, manuals, and paint-by numbers: Psychotherapy in the 90s. *Psychotherapy, 33,* 207–215.

Simopoulos, A. P. (2007). Omega-3 fatty acids and athletics. *Current Sports Medicine Reports, 6,* 230–236.

Smallman, E., Sowa, C. J., & Young, B. D. (1991). Ethnic and gender differences in student athletes' responses to stressful life events. *Journal of College Student Development, 32,* 230–235.

Sommers-Flanagan, J., & Sommers-Flanagan, R. (1995). Intake interviewing with suicidal patients: A systematic approach. *Professional Psychology: Research and Practice, 30,* 1–7.

Sommers-Flanagan, J., & Sommers-Flanagan, R. (2003). *Clinical interviewing* (3rd ed.). New York: Wiley.

Sommers-Flanagan, J., & Sommers-Flanagan, R. (2007). *Tough kids, cool counseling: User-friendly approaches to working with challenging youth* (2nd ed.). Washington, DC: American Counseling Association.

Storch, E. A., Storch, J. B., Killainy, E. M., & Roberti, J. W. (2005). Self-reported psychopathology in athletes: A comparison of intercollegiate student-athletes and non-athletes. *Journal of Sport Behavior, 28*, 86–97.

Terman, M., & Terman J. S. (2005). Light therapy for seasonal and nonseasonal depression: Efficacy, protocol, safety, and side effects. *CNS Spectrums 10*, 647–663.

Teyber, E. (2005). *Interpersonal process in therapy: An integrative model* (5th ed.). Pacific Grove, CA: Brooks/Cole.

Tkachuk, G. A., & Martin, G. L. (1999). Exercise therapy for patients with psychiatric disorders: Research and clinical implications. *Professional Psychology: Research and Practice, 30*, 275–282.

Treatment for Adolescents with Depression Study Team. (2004). Fluoxetine, cognitive-behavioral therapy, and their combination for adolescents with depression: Treatment for Adolescents with Depression Study (TADS) randomized controlled trial. *Journal of the American Medical Association, 292*, 807–820.

United Kingdom Electroconvulsive Therapy Research Group. (2003). Efficacy and safety of electroconvulsive therapy in depressive disorders: A systematic review and meta-analysis. *Lancet, 361*, 799–808.

Wertheim, L. J. (2003, September 8). Prisoners of depression. *Sports Illustrated*, 71–79.

Whittington, C. J., Kendall, T., Fonagy, P., Cottrell, D., Cotgrove, A., & Boddington, E. (2004). Selective serotonin reuptake inhibitors in childhood depression: Systematic review of published versus unpublished data. *Lancet, 363*, 1341–1345.

Williams, D. R., Gonzalez, H. M., Neighbors, H. Nesse, R., Abelson, J. M., Sweetman, J., & Jackson, J. S. (2007). Prevalence and distribution of major depressive disorder in African Americans, Caribbean blacks, and non-Hispanic whites: Results from the National Survey of American Life. *Archives of General Psychiatry, 64*, 305–315.

Wyshak, G. (2001). Women's college physical activity and self-reports of physician-diagnosed depression and of current symptoms of psychiatric distress. *Journal of Women's Health & Gender-Based Medicine, 10*, 363–370.

13

UNDERSTANDING AND ASSISTING THE STUDENT-ATHLETE-TO-BE AND THE NEW STUDENT-ATHLETE

Laura M. Finch

When young people are admitted to and possibly accept an athletics-related scholarship from their university of choice, both parties enter into a "covenantal" relationship (Hirsch, 2001). The late adolescent student-athletes commit to putting in the substantial time and effort required to be, hopefully, both successful students *and* athletes. Likewise, universities commit to providing adequate resources (e.g., coursework, faculty, laboratories, coaches, related support personnel) to help these young people achieve their academic *and* athletic goals. In most cases, barring significant injury or academic difficulty and depending on the sport/coach, the student-athletes participate in athletics in some capacity for and graduate in approximately four to five years.

However, in too many cases, an increasing number of student-athletes are attending institutions at which there is not an ideal match for this covenantal relationship to be fulfilled (Hirsch, 2001). For example, the incoming student-athletes' preferred or optimal major is sometimes not offered; adequate academic, disability, or other support services are not provided (or taken advantage of); and/or training and travel schedules are excessive. In these cases, it is difficult for some new student-athletes to hold up to their end of the covenantal relationship. Academic support, counseling, psychology, and other helping professionals must be creative in finding ways to add more tools to the student-athletes' coping toolbox to help them manage both their student-athlete and personal roles. Psychological consultation in the forms of counseling, therapy, and sport psychology services is one means that can help student-athletes successfully make the most of this covenantal relationship and their time on campus.

Such consultation can be a helpful service or set of services because adjustment to college and athletics is an exceptionally challenging experience, when added to the academic rigors of school. In particular, the sport experiences of student-athletes (e.g., training, travel, competition, and academic and personal oversight) present not only opportunities but also unique challenges to their psychological development. The helping professional who works with student-athletes at this point in their development should not overlook the potential impact of these experiences. The importance of athletics today is illustrated by the fact that "student-athlete" is the only hyphenated role identity within the academic setting (Goldberg & Chandler, 1995). It is curious that our society does not refer to student-musicians, student-actors, or student-scientists, regardless of the time involvement required for each of these other student endeavors. It is the word at the end of the hyphen, "athletes," that places student-athletes in a high-profile and often stressful situation.

The lure of athletics has skyrocketed at all levels of competition, as sport continues to occupy a front-row seat in many parts of U.S. society. The topic of sport and athletics often has its own section in the newspaper, its own time slot on the local television news, and a multitude of cable stations devoted to its coverage. Numerous Internet websites are also devoted to these activities.

Currently, various counseling and psychology professionals provide services to governing bodies in a variety of Pan American and Olympic sports and in professional sports. Likewise, such helping professionals associated with intercollegiate athletic programs are employed at colleges and universities across North America, ranging from smaller NAIA and NCAA Division-III institutions to the largest NCAA Division-I schools (and athletic programs) such as Duke, Ohio State, Oklahoma, Pennsylvania State, Tennessee, and West Virginia. The availability of these allied services for student-athletes has grown tremendously since the 1980s and 1990s and can be quite useful to new collegiate athletes if they choose to access them.

Help Seeking

Myths about seeking help and using psychology services (e.g., only the crazy or weak-willed tap them) may discourage or prohibit some young student-athletes from seeking assistance, but some sport psychology research suggests that factors such as gender, experience/age, sport type, and athletic status may influence who is more likely to seek out help (e.g., Linder, Brewer, Van Raalte, & DeLange, 1991; Martin, 2005; Martin, Akers, Jackson, Wrisberg, Nelson, Leslie, & Larson, 2001; Watson, 2005). More specifically, certain individual variables/characteristics may influence the decisions of some young people toward or away from seeking consultation. For example, women are thought to be more receptive to seeking out counseling related services than men (Jordan & Quinn, 1997). Women have also been found to have higher expectancies of personal commitment to the sport psychology consulting process than men (Martin et al., 2001). Conversely, male athletes were more likely to stigmatize sport psychology services than female athletes (Martin, 2005). Specifically, men in contact sports such as football and wrestling revealed the greatest stigma toward sport psychology services (versus men in non-contact sports). Thus, when working with new student-athletes, it is important to remember some males may be a bit more of a "slow sell" than females when it comes to seeking counseling or psychological services.

Despite sport psychology's potential to assist young people, Martin (2005) found age differences in relation to seeking out sport psychology services that may generalize to seeking other forms of psychological consultation. Specifically, high school athletes were more likely to have a negative attitude or stigma toward seeking sport psychology services than were college athletes. This research on the stigmas is particularly salient for university support service professionals working with college student-athletes-to-be. At a time when they may well benefit from such help as they transition from high school to college, younger university student-athletes may be fighting unfounded misconceptions about the benefits of seeking help. High school athletes are generally less likely to be exposed to counseling or psychological services than are college athletes, so this reluctance is not surprising. Yet, this reluctance can be overcome with the proper education and encouragement (this will be discussed later in the chapter).

Another type of stigma has been found, based on the type of helping profession from whom the student-athlete was seeking advice. Maniar, Curry, Sommers-Flanagan, and Walsh (2001) found that student-athletes preferred getting sport psychology advice from their coaches, rather than from a sport-titled professional (e.g., sport psychologist, performance enhancement specialist). In addition, student-athletes favored receiving sport psychology assistance from sport-titled professionals *over* counselors and clinicians.

Attitudes toward help-seeking behavior also appear to differ between some student-athletes and non-athletes (Watson, 2005). Specifically, Watson found college student-athletes less likely to have positive expectations about seeking counseling or help-related services than their non-athlete peers. This research suggests it is important to educate coaches about the use of sport psychology services as well as other helping services. It is also important to consider how to best use these resources because student-athletes are likely to be more comfortable seeking advice from their coaches than from people outside their immediate athletic family, such as a clinician.

At times, it seems like an uphill battle for helping professionals, particularly those new to the field or rather unfamiliar with the unique needs and lifestyles of student-athletes. Some new student-athletes may feel uncomfortable seeking help outside of the athletic department from service providers who may not understand special concerns, needs, and pressures faced by student-athletes (Greenspan & Andersen, 1995). Yet, the specialized help a student-athlete might need (for example, to deal with an entire disorder) might be housed outside the athletic department.

Although research suggests some prospective college student-athletes possess a variety of stigmas about sport psychology, these stigmas can be overcome by being armed with knowledge about the student-athletes, sport, and sport psychology. Lewin (1936) summarized this idea in a model that has become a hallmark in social psychology as well as sport psychology. Lewin suggested that behavior (B) is a function (f) of the person (P) and their environment or [B = f(P × E)]. So, to effectively intervene with prospective college student-athletes we must understand student-athletes as people as well as understand their environment (both past and present). The unique environment of competitive athletics, and its place in U.S. culture, places distinctive demands on the college student-athlete.

Schlossberg's transition theory (1981, 1995) is also helpful in understanding how student-athletes manage the shift from high school to college athletics. Schlossberg described transition as any event or non-event that results in changed relationships, routines, assumptions, and roles. Student-athletes experience *anticipated* transitions, such as joining their new teammates on campus, or *unanticipated* transitions, such as injuries or unexpected coaching changes. Schlossberg's model describes three major sets of factors that influence adaptation to transition: (1) the characteristics of the particular transition (such as being anticipated or unanticipated); (2) the characteristics of the pre- and post-transition environments (this could include catalysts, timing, concurrent stress, etc.); and (3) the characteristics of the individual experiencing the transition (e.g., role change, previous experience with similar transitions, assessment of the transition, etc.). The interactions among these three sets of factors produce either a successful adaptation or a failure to adapt. Using concepts related to the athletes and their sports environment, a discussion of various topics related to the transition between high school and college athletics follows.

The Person and the Environment: Understanding the College Student-Athlete-to-Be

At their basic psychological core, both college student-athletes and non-athletes have faced many of the same developmental tasks as they matured from childhood, through adolescence, and into adulthood (Goldberg & Chandler, 1995). Both groups manage the typical teenage struggles of cliques and friendships, the need to balance school work with extracurricular activities, and relationships with their parents and other authority figures. Tracey and Corlett (1995) examined the transition experience of first-year university track and field student-athletes using qualitative research methodologies. They found challenges associated with this transition to include: (1) feeling overwhelmed by new responsibilities, (2) loneliness, and (3) the need to balance freedom and responsibility. This list sounds familiar to entering college students who are not participating in athletics!

Participation in Sport

The sports world in the United States is analogous to a pyramid with a broad base and small, but high, apex. At the base of this pyramid are millions of youth sport participants who will not continue their participation in sport past this youth sport level. It is estimated that over 50 million children participate in competitive sport in the United States, with the majority being younger than 12 years (National Council of Youth Sports, 2000). Historical trends show that the majority of these children (upwards of 85%) discontinue their involvement in sport by the time they are 18 (Petlichkoff, 1992). Thus, as the pyramid narrows toward the apex, fewer young athletes are participating. Consequently, the levels of commitment and competition get more intense.

Additional research suggests less than one-half of 1% of all high school athletes continue their participation at an elite level of athletic competition (Cumming, 2002; Hamstra, Cherubini, & Swanik, 2002). Consequently, the college student-athlete-to-be has successfully navigated through this competitive system to reach near the top of the athletic pyramid. Because of this progression we can safely assume the average entering college student-athlete has experienced a great deal of athletic success by trying out for and making high-caliber teams throughout his or her career. Moreover, collegiate athletes are in all likelihood the more successful participants from their high school programs. For these reasons, "being an athlete" and "being a successful athlete" form an important part of the prospective student-athlete's personal identity.

Sense of Self

Given the apparent importance athletics and athletic accomplishments play in the self-view of prospective student-athletes, most will likely enter college with expectations and dreams of attaining athletic success, as well as hopes linked to the rewards that accompany these achievements. In most cases, however, the prospective student-athlete will probably not have experienced major personal athletic failures during the high school years, such as not starting.

It is also likely the prospective student-athlete has earned valued status from his or her athletic involvements. That is, a benefit of high school athletic participation and especially success is the positive peer and other recognition it brings to the adolescent. As long ago as the 1960s, for instance, Coleman (1974) found that athletic participation was viewed as an important criterion for "leading crowd" status in the schools. In fact, the importance of the athletic status system was such that when forced into a choice, adolescents reported they would rather be successful athletes than scholars in the high school years. More recent studies replicated Coleman's original findings (Duda, 1981; Feltz, 1978; Roberts, 1982), suggesting that this same state of affairs may still hold true.

For some young athletes, athletic status can unfortunately bring about an exaggerated sense of entitlement—a sense of deserving special treatment based on being an athlete (Lanning & Toye, 1993). This sense of entitlement is usually acquired through years of attention provided by a variety of sources including parents, coaches, media, and fans. Such entitlement is often manifested in the athlete's belief that she or he somehow deserves special treatment academically, socially, legally, and/or athletically. When this sense of privilege is excessive, it can be quite dysfunctional (Lanning & Toye, 1993). Unfortunately, some helping services designed to assist student-athletes in their quest for success inadvertently contribute to their sense of entitlement (e.g., financial aid for athletics, advanced preferential registration for classes, class schedules that maximize practice time that can isolate student-athletes from the rest of the student body, tutoring, and sometimes extravagant pre-game meals, among others).

On some university campuses, these benefits (or perceptions of benefits being offered) can create discord between faculty, student affairs personnel, other students, and members of the athletic department staff and athletes. These benefits can further enhance a sense of entitlement in athletes, and/or they can perpetuate negative stereotypes of athletes as recipients of special privileges associated with their athletic status. In either case, being an athlete, particularly in a high-profile NCAA Division I athletic program, carries with it a unique set of identity issues (e.g., "athlete as hero" vs. "athlete as dunce") (Watt & Moore, 2001). In summary, prospective and new collegiate student-athletes are typically adolescents who have experienced substantial athletic success. These individuals are survivors of a system who often have strong athletic identities. Although they may have been challenged in other areas of their personal or academic lives, it is unlikely such individuals faced a great deal of athletic adversity in high school. Therefore, these athletes may not be well prepared for some of the developmental and identity challenges they may encounter for the first time upon starting their collegiate athletic careers.

Developmental Obstacles for the Student-Athlete-to-Be and Freshman Student-Athlete

Prospective student-athletes often face various common lifestyle challenges that can become a developmental crisis. These challenges are similar to the tasks faced by non-student-athletes (e.g., becoming independent, establishing a sense of purpose, clarifying values, dealing with uncertainty, creating new relationships)(see Ferrante and Etzel, Chapter 1) but can be experienced quite differently, serving as potential obstacles to individual development. Athletics-related developmental obstacles make the struggle to resolve the "normal" developmental tasks of becoming a mature young adult even more challenging (Parham, 1993). Examples of these athletics-related developmental obstacles include readjusting athletic expectations, time management concerns, living adjustments, and coping with mistakes and adversity. Each of these obstacles will be discussed in this section.

Adjusting Athletic Expectations

Because high school athletes who enter college have experienced considerable athletic success, they may have unrealistic collegiate athletic and perhaps academic expectations if they did not put forth much effort in this arena. Prior to entering the university they may dream of becoming the stars of their teams as they were in high school, earning a starting position, winning the big game, and/or achieving All-Conference or All-America honors. Seldom do they think about the fact that over 90–95% of those athletes they successfully defeated or beat out to make the team in high school are not competing in college (NCAA, 2007a; Taylor, Ogilvie, & Lavallee, 2006). Many also erroneously assume that the academic load in college is not much different than in high school and subsequently struggle in the classroom.

Similarly, incoming student-athletes typically do not consider that they will be competing for starting positions against other very highly trained athletes with up to four more years of collegiate experience, nor do they consider that their practices and games will be much more intense, demanding, and exhausting than they have ever experienced. They may get frustrated as they try to adapt very quickly to the higher caliber of play that typifies college athletic programs. The typical incoming freshman athlete will likely need to adjust from being the star of his or her high school team to being a sub or scout team player in college, or to being asked to red shirt for a year and to delay competing—but not tough training.

Moreover, their previous role as "big fish, little pond" is frequently reversed as their status drops. Incoming student-athletes may be forced to come to terms with "identity foreclosure" as they adjust to a new, typically more demanding collegiate athletic role out of the high school limelight (Danish, Petitpas, & Hale, 1993). In other words, they may choose or be forced to commit themselves more or exclusively to the role of student-athlete (sometimes athlete-student) without exploring other roles or options. Other new, often unwanted roles present themselves, such as a non-traveling team member, a red shirt, a scout team player, or (in the case of very few) an active team member, or perhaps a new position that the person did not at all anticipate playing in college.

Other new student-athletes end their "careers" soon after matriculation because these adjustments are too much for them to bear. Some of these young people become casualties of the system, leave the university, and return home early in the academic year. Some "hang in" and attempt to adjust to a different lifestyle, sense of self, and social connectivity outside of sport. A few seek psychological consultation or are referred for such support, to help make sense of these radical personal and social changes. Unfortunately cut loose by the athletic "family," they often struggle to find their way, experiencing discouragement, resentment, and considerable unhappiness. In contrast, some find this novel transition quite liberating, investing their considerable energy and talents in other meaningful endeavors.

Successful adaptation through this transitional period is usually facilitated by social support provided by friends, family, and others. These social support systems may not be directly available to assist the student-athlete as they adjust to the college experience and their various new roles. They may live far from their homes, and even if they still live nearby, there are still limitations on precious time to visit given their busy schedules. Alternatively, those social support sources may be available directly or electronically, but they may not quite appreciate how their child is adjusting or why or to what degree their own athletic hero or heroine is having difficulty dealing with the collegiate experience. Although it is common for new freshmen to burn up lots of telephone minutes, many new students are reluctant to reveal their problems, attempting instead to solve them alone in a developmentally normal, independent way. This seems to be behavior particularly characteristic of late adolescent males. Like the student-athlete, many if not most have never experienced such transitions or if they have, they were distant experiences that occurred in a somewhat different context.

Time Management Concerns

Like all other entering college students, student-athletes must learn to manage time efficiently. For many, it will be the first time in their lives they are "really" on their own and have to deal with making the majority of their own decisions. Although students look forward to being independent, they naturally often make many mistakes because of their lack of life experience and limited self-management skills. This may be especially difficult for the young student-athlete who must deal with normal time management concerns associated with academic, athletic, and social involvements in an environment in which two to four hours a day are devoted to sport training. Time management is perhaps the most important survival skill for college students. For student-athletes, time management is critical given their additional athletic responsibilities linked to daily training, team travel, injury rehabilitation, and game preparation.

Academic time-management adjustments to the collegiate schedule are required. In high school, the student-athlete's academic involvement typically runs from approximately 7:30 a.m. to 2:30 p.m. or so, when practice begins. Many collegiate athletes are involved in a mix of academic and athletic activities from 6:00 a.m. to 9:00 p.m. during the week. Although they appear to have more freedom, time management difficulties associated with balancing academics, athletics, and their personal and social lives are common. These time management concerns are reflected in research by Miller and Kerr (2003). Specifically, college student-athlete newcomers discussed difficulty in striking a balance in the time needed between their academic and athletic demands. After athletes had spent more time on campus (i.e., reached their junior and senior years), they generally demonstrated a greater mastery of available time, sometimes as a result of poor academic performances during their early time on campus.

Living Adjustment Concerns

Like all students, new student-athletes must adjust to a novel living environment. They may have a roommate for the first time and may initially experience varying degrees of homesickness. They will also be attempting to meet and make new friends away from the familiar, comfortable confines of home. Many of these distressing experiences may be foreign to the student-athlete who as the high school athletic star was perceived by herself or himself and others as a pillar of strength and center of attention. As noted above, psychology professionals suggest that successful mastery of separation-individuation issues is a critical developmental task for this period (Holmbeck & Wandrei, 1993). That is, student-athletes must successfully adjust to living more independently than they were accustomed to during high school. Research by Miller and Kerr (2003) suggests that the first year on campus is often viewed as (i.e., expected to be) a time of independence, social freedom, and exploration.

Coping with Mistakes and Adversity

Even the most well-adjusted and gifted entering student-athletes will probably find the first few months of college athletics a difficult period of adjustment. They are practicing and competing against a much higher caliber of player. They must learn new, more complicated skills, encounter typically more demanding training, and adjust to new coaches and teammates. In all likelihood this process will be a struggle. This does not mean the entering student-athlete is doomed to failure. Rather, most will successfully adjust to the new demands placed upon them; some will not. Like the majority of maturing young adults, they will be able to adapt to the developmental challenges they must face over time.

Unfortunately, some athletes, especially those who judge their ability and self-worth only on winning and losing (i.e., own an ego orientation), may have greater difficulty coping with the experience of making mistakes and day-to-day adversity (e.g., Duda & Hall, 2001; Roberts, Treasure, & Conroy, 2007). For those who have such difficulty, their confidence will be likely challenged and may decline. Perhaps their anxiety will increase as well. Some research suggests that athletes higher in trait anxiety are more likely to engage in maladaptive coping strategies (Finch, 1993) and be concerned with contest outcome (Hall & Kerr, 1997) than be focused on the process of performing. A common result of such a negative spiral is a decline in athletic and/or academic performance.

In summary, as part of the normal transition from high school to college, the student-athlete will face any number of developmental challenges. These may range from general concerns focusing on time management and living arrangements to sport-specific concerns related to unrealistic expectations and the inability to cope with short-term mistakes and frustration. The student-athlete-to-be must be prepared to cope productively with and use these potential crises as opportunities for growth and development. Toward this end, helping professionals in high schools and universities can play a central role in assisting these young men and women make the transition.

Counseling Strategies for Use with the Student-Athlete-to-Be and Freshman Student Athletes

The transition from high school to college stimulates many new feelings in students. Although most appear to be looking forward to the new challenges college brings, some grieve for who and what were left behind or have been lost (Chickering & Schlossberg, 2002). Family was close by, and high school academic challenges had usually been figured out long before graduation. The students' social roles and places on their athletic teams were typically well defined. Yet, once they arrive on their university campus and begin their first collegiate season, it is time to start figuring it out many of these things all over again.

Although it is highly desirable to prepare the college student-athlete-to-be psychologically for the transition from high school to college, this is unfortunately seldom done. If assistance with this psychological transition is attempted, it usually happens during the student-athlete's first semester on campus (or later) through programs such as the NCAA's Challenging Athletes Minds for Personal Success (CHAMPS) Lifeskills program or perhaps by students seeking out support from others—

family, peers, spiritual persons, or helping professionals on campus. A more productive approach involves preparing these student-athletes for the transition to college during their junior and senior years of high school. This can be accomplished in several ways.

First, high school counseling personnel can offer special transition programs for those athletes who wish to participate in collegiate athletics (e.g., Bailey, 1993; O'Bryant, 1993; Danish, Owens, Green, & Brunelle, 1997; Taylor, Ogilvie, & Lavallee, 2006). Second, coaches, alumni, and athletic personnel can provide advice to these athletes about the typical issues associated with the transition from high school to college athletics. Knowing what to expect when they arrive on a college campus is a key way for student-athletes to reduce stress through preparation and enhanced confidence. Third, helping professionals should consider involving parents in these transition sessions. Including parents will highlight the importance of normal transition struggles and educate a critical support source that will remain involved with the student-athlete throughout the collegiate experience. These interventions presume these individuals understand the obstacles prospective student-athletes may encounter, have a willingness to involve themselves in primary-oriented interventions, and will have and take the time to do so appropriately.

Regardless of the approaches taken to facilitate the transition from high school to collegiate athletics, several other topics are essential to discuss with the prospective college student-athlete. A practical approach is to classify these topics according to the needs of the prospective college student-athlete into various areas (Broughton & Naylor, 2001), many of which are discussed in other chapters of this book. These areas to be discussed here include: (1) perspective training; (2) independence training; (3) time management; (4) goal setting; (5) mistake and loss coping skills/strategies; and (5) stress management skills. The first three areas are often generally thought of as so-called "life skills" or developmental skills, whereas the latter three are generally thought of as psychological skills.

Perspective Training

Perspective training can best be viewed as the philosophical system of values that guides the thoughts and practices of the student-athlete-to-be or new student-athlete, both on and off the field. An important attribute for motivation and success, perspective training is imperative for the success of the prospective college student-athlete. Much as a philosophy of coaching determines every action of a coach (Martens, 2004), so too does the collegiate athlete's perspective on what it means to be a student and an athlete.

From an intervention standpoint, three issues are important to address in helping the college student-athlete-to-be and freshman athlete to develop a healthy and productive athletic perspective. They are: (1) an understanding of the role of academics and athletics; (2) realistic expectations of professional sport opportunities; and (3) the development of a positive mental attitude and outlook.

The Role of Academics and Athletics

In previous decades, college athletics has been the focus of increased criticism regarding the sacrifice of academic standards for athletic success (e.g., Purdy, Eitzen, & Hufnagel, 1982; Sack & Staurowsky, 1998; Sperber, 2002; Sperber, 1990; Thelin, 1996; Zimbalist, 1999). Frequent reports have appeared in the popular press regarding student-athletes who have dubious academic majors, universities with dismal graduation rates for student-athletes, and even reports of functionally illiterate student-athletes who graduated from well-respected institutions of higher education. Fortunately, recent NCAA legislation has helped to curb these egregious academic shortcomings (NCAA, 2007b). For example, student-athletes are now required to complete a certain percentage of credits hours toward their major before entering each academic year and are limited in the number of credits they can pass in summer school.

Although most of the media's attention is focused on these academic abuses at the collegiate level, they are not necessarily confined to that level. In some cases, athletically gifted high school athletes receive academic favors and preferential treatment because of their athletic prowess. If this occurs, the students quickly learn that athletics are a more important priority than academics. They may also come to understand that as long as they are successful athletically, coaches and administrators will somehow ensure they will be taken care of academically, even if this means possibly circumventing the rules. For example, a young student-athlete may become academically ineligible shortly before an important game, but the suspension may be postponed until after the game is played. This is often viewed as justifiable because in the end the student has been penalized for failure to adhere to academic standards. Yet by postponing the suspension, the student-athlete learns to assume that academics are less important than athletic contests and that powerful others will go out of their way to support this mode of thinking. Consequently, the cycle of deteriorating academic standards for the student-athlete continues. In both the short and long run, this type of behavior on the part of faculty and administrators is a clear disservice to the student-athlete.

To prevent such abuses, coaches, teachers, administrators, and helping professionals need to convey clearly to student-athletes that academics are key to their future success. Extracurricular activities such as sports should be viewed as a privilege based on academic success, not a substitute for academics. This privilege will not be available to student-athletes who fail to consistently meet acceptable academic standards. In fact, the NCAA's recent Academic Progress Rate (APR) reforms have significant impacts on teams who fail to meet academic standards, with reductions in scholarships and squad size for teams whose members academically underperform (NCAA 2007b).

Developing an appropriate academic perspective involves more than penalizing the student-athlete for inappropriate behavior. It is imperative that coaches, administrators, family, and influential others take a keen interest in their athletes' academic progress as well. Along with parents, they can have a major impact on the academic value system of high school student-athletes. In addition, helping professionals can help to identify student-athletes who are at risk academically and initiate appropriate intervention programs. Students who have typically struggled in the classroom, have been diagnosed with a learning disability, or whose SAT or ACT scores show great discrepancy (e.g., high verbal, low quantitative) should be identified early on and referred for professional consultation.

Realistic Expectations of Professional Sport Opportunities

One reason many high school student-athletes, in particular those who participate in football, basketball, and baseball, sometimes do not stress academics is their erroneous assumption they will somehow go on to star at the college level and then make a successful transition to professional sports. For example, surveys have suggested that upwards of 66%

of African-American athletes and 39% of white athletes playing college football or basketball expected to play professionally (Kennedy & Dimick, 1987). Unfortunately, for the majority of athletes this dream will not become a reality. Data compiled by Coakley (2004) suggests the odds of making it from the college level to the National Football League are 1:68, and from college to the NBA are 1:74. For women, the odds are even longer, with the odds at 1:208 from college to playing in the WNBA. Moreover, because the average pro career ranges from three to four years, betting on a career in professional sports is a poor career strategy. Thus, both male and female athletes face exceedingly few professional sport opportunities after their collegiate eligibility is completed.

Athletes who over-identify with their athletic role may have difficulty being interested in and understanding what other career options are available to them, or making alternative career plans outside of sports. Murphy, Petitpas, and Brewer (1996) examined the relationship between identity foreclosure, athletic identity, and career maturity in intercollegiate athletes. They found identity foreclosure, athletic identity, and career maturity were inversely related. That is, athletes who were more committed to their athletic role without engaging in exploratory behavior about career options or viewed career planning as a threat to their athletic identity had lower career maturity scores. (See Kornspan and Etzel, 2003, for a review of the topic of career maturity in collegiate athletes.)

In order for aspiring college student-athletes to develop a realistic perspective regarding their athletic participation, advisors, counselors, and coaches should have accurate statistical information available to present to the student-athletes. Similarly, programs should be designed and/or other opportunities developed (i.e., DVDs, streaming video, panel discussion, alumni speakers) in which former athletes whose collegiate and/or professional athletic dreams were not met discuss the need to develop a strong academic and alternate career training base. It would also be useful if successful professional athlete role models emphasized the need for student-athletes to complete their education, even if they do pursue a career in professional sports. The benefits of a college degree are numerous and useful for a variety of activities, from negotiating a contract and a lease to understanding world culture when competing abroad.

Finally, it is important to recognize that this view of reality review does not have to be a sudden ending to what has been a long-term athletic dream. Rather, advisors, counselors, and coaches should explain the need to plan for options in case a professional career does not materialize (and in case professional league draft eligibility rules change, which often negates immediate entry into the pros). Outstanding high school athletes who have solid grades will have many more scholarship offers and university choices available to them than athletes of equal athletic caliber who do not excel academically. Moreover, when this type of information is presented as a group program to all student-athletes in a category (e.g., the junior class), the appearance that someone thinks a particular student-athlete will never achieve a scholarship, professional contract, or tryout may be lessened.

Positive Mental Attitude

One of the most difficult perspective elements to instill in the prospective student-athlete is a positive mental attitude. Sport psychology consultants have long emphasized the need for athletes to use positive affirmations and self-talk such as "I'm strong," "I've practiced hard," or "Stay calm" (Abrams & Hale, 2005; Orlick, 2008; Porter, 2003). However, having a positive mental attitude means much more than espousing a series of memorized positive statements. As Orlick (2008) suggested, it involves knowing oneself, being able to realistically appraise one's strengths and limitations, and realistically believing in one's ability. This is clearly an area in which the helping professional can be of assistance.

Vealey (2005) proposed a helpful model, referred to as "P^3 Thinking," which can help athletes develop the positive mental attitude and mental toughness to be successful and develop appropriate perspective. Essentially a way to help performers think better, it focuses on three important P-words: purposeful, productive, and possibility. *Purposeful* thinking requires athletes to be intentional and deliberate in how they process their thoughts about their performance. *Productive* thinking involves thoughts that are proactive, rational, and facilitative. Lastly, *possibility* thinking involves thinking outside the proverbial box and being innovative. P³ Thinking can assist athletes with developing more control over their thoughts and emotions, which consequently leads to better performances.

The athlete can also develop emotional control by learning how to deal with those situations that arise in athletics (and life) that may be perceived as unfair. Situations such as bad calls from officials, unpopular coaching decisions, and injuries that sideline athletes before big games happen in sport on a regular basis. Over the course of an athlete's career, however, these negative events typically balance out with lucky breaks, favorable calls, and positive coaching decisions. When bad luck and inappropriate calls and decisions occur, athletes must learn to maintain their emotional control and sustain motivation. This is especially difficult to accomplish when athletes are in performance slumps or when their teams are struggling. Many athletes lose control and give up in these situations. Hence, it is important that coaches and counselors discuss the role of luck in sport and the fact that athletes will sometimes face difficult and seemingly unfair situations.

To help the athlete keep a cool head in these situations, psychological skills like relaxation and positive coping thoughts can be used. Additionally, athletes must remind themselves of the need to sustain motivation in these situations. Finally, coaches and helping professionals must continually remind developing athletes of the need to maintain a realistic perspective, including purposeful, productive, and possibility thinking, when they face adversity and setbacks during competitions and practices.

Fostering Independence

When athletes are encouraged to develop a healthy sense of perspective, a sense of autonomy and independence should follow as they are able to practice stronger emotional control. Yet, too often coaches simply pay lip service to the development of independence in their athletes. When changes in the high school athletic system over the last several decades are scrutinized, it is apparent that athletes have been allowed to make fewer and fewer decisions on their own. Gone are the days when a quarterback called his own plays, a gymnast developed her own routine, or a wrestler competed without his coach's continually yelling instructions from the side of the mat. Due in part to increased pressures to win, today's coaches make most of the decisions for the athlete, and hence, the athlete receives little independence training.

If sport (at any level) is to achieve its educational goals, the role of independence training needs to be discussed with coaches. Coaches must provide situations that allow athletes opportunities to make some of their own decisions, whether it is allowing them to call some of their own plays, to have input into game or practice plans, and/or to make team rules. In fact, research suggests athletes who are afforded the opportunity to make these contributions to the team's development are more intrinsically motivated (Amorose & Horn, 2000). Equally important, coaches must assist athletes in this process by providing feedback about the appropriateness of their choices and ways to handle setbacks. Although this is potentially a less efficient process for the coach, it is a proven way to enhance the potential for independent growth in the athlete.

Finally, independence training should not be confined to the playing field or pool deck. Because of their influential status with their athletes, coaches can be invaluable in helping them develop independent behavior off the field. This can be accomplished by purposefully discussing the need to transfer the discipline gained in athletic training rehabilitation to the academic arena, or the need to transfer the discipline needed to execute effectively a complex offensive system to rebuffing peer pressure to experiment with drugs or dangerous supplements or training methods. In essence, independence training is not "caught" by participating in athletics, it is "taught" by knowledgeable, caring coaches and helping professionals who systematically and continually emphasize it.

Time Management Skills

As noted above, time management is a key skill for the college student-athlete to develop. Few high school athletes, however, are given any training in time management. In fact, their athletic practices and contests are typically controlled and scheduled by their coaches (another reason that independence training is necessary). Such control is coupled with parents organizing the student-athletes' lives at home and with tightly scheduled classes—it is no wonder that collegiate first year student-athletes may experience time management problems when left on their own.

Involvement in athletics does not necessarily have to consume too much of the student-athlete's time (Bailey, 1993). It is a challenge, however, for the student-athlete to manage his or her schedule in an efficient manner. High school and university counselors and CHAMPS Life Skills coordinators can provide an important service to these prospective collegiate athletes by providing special sessions on time management and its importance to success in college. Speakers, date books/planners, and courses/orientations about time management are vital to helping student-athletes learn to navigate the complex schedule that is collegiate athletics. The challenge for student-athletes, like their peers on campus who are not competing, is to learn to use their time efficiently and prioritize their obligations effectively for success in both their academic and athletic domains. In fact, research by Tracey and Corlett (1995) suggests that among the primary strategies student-athletes use to maintain perspective are time management and organizational skills.

The three previous strategies (perspective taking, independence training, and time management) are broader approaches that are more universal in nature. The next three approaches (goal setting, mistake and loss coping skills, and stress management techniques) are more discrete in nature and are easy skills to teach to student-athletes. But like any physical skill, both sets of skills must be practiced to be mastered!

Goal-Setting Skills

Goal setting is an extremely valuable skill for any potential college student to learn. It is especially valuable for the student-athlete. Unfortunately, systematic goal-setting procedures are seldom formally taught to prospective collegiate student-athletes. Instead, it is assumed these athletes will somehow automatically develop goal-setting proficiency as a byproduct of participating in high school athletics. Most collegiate athletes do learn something about goal setting as a consequence of meeting long-term general objectives like making the high school varsity team, setting records, winning championships, or going on to play college sports. They often fail, however, to learn simple, systematic goal setting principles that will assist them in their efforts to achieve these long-term objectives.

We are all too familiar with coaches who conduct goal-setting meetings with their team members at the beginning of the season, but then fail to systematically follow-up and evaluate these goals as the season progresses. Unfortunately, goal setting becomes ineffective if done in such a "shotgun" approach. In fact, research on the goal-setting practices used by athletes and coaches supports the premise that many of them do not use goal setting effectively and need additional education to do so (e.g., Burton, Weinberg, Yukelson, & Weigand, 1998; Weinberg, Butt, Knight, & Perritt, 2001).

The use of goal setting in sport parallels effective goal-setting procedures used in other life situations such as academics and business (Burton & Naylor, 2002; Gould, 2006; Locke & Latham, 1990). Numerous guidelines have been offered for effective goal setting (e.g., Gould, 2006; Harwood, 2005; Vealey, 2005; Weinberg, Harmison, Rosenkranz, & Hookom, 2005). For example, sport psychology professionals recommend that athletes set goals in measurable and behavioral terms. Athletes' goals should be difficult but realistic (i.e., challenging), as well as both short- and long-range in nature. Goals should be written out and target dates for attaining goals should be identified. Lastly, specific goal achievement strategies should be identified, and goal support and evaluation need to be provided.

The problem with goal setting does not come from the lack of appropriate goal-setting information available to the developing athlete. In fact, an abundance of information is available throughout the sport psychology literature (see the previous references for examples). Instead, the most difficult aspect of implementing goal setting with prospective collegiate student-athletes is getting them to systematically set and regularly evaluate their goals. Too often at the start of the season goal setting is discussed, and a number of goals are set. After the first few weeks of practice, however, there is little purposeful follow-up and goal evaluation. Coaches often get bogged down in teaching plays, developing fitness, or preparing for opponents (that is, the techniques and tactics of preparation, rather than the psychological side of preparation). Consequently, the goal-setting progression stops, and the student-athlete becomes frustrated or loses interest and stops the goal-setting process.

Because of this, sport psychologists have found it more effective to first expose athletes to goal-setting information while they are in high school or early in their collegiate career, then to set a small number of specific goals with the athlete, monitor those goals over time, and provide evaluative feedback. After athletes learn how to set and achieve a few goals effectively, additional goals can be set (including goals in multiple areas such as skill acquisition and development, fitness, rehabilitation, academics, etc.). In essence, one must teach student-athletes how to set and accomplish a smaller number of goals before implementing goal setting on a widespread basis.

An especially difficult problem encountered when goal setting with athletes is their strong tendency to focus exclusive attention on outcome goals (e.g., winning a game, beating an opponent) rather than performance or technique goals (e.g., personal improvement). Yet mounting evidence suggests focusing sole attention on outcome goals can lead to performance drawbacks (Burton, 1989; Duda & Hall, 2001; Roberts et al., 2007). Specifically, athletes have only partial control over their event outcome, and outcome goals are less flexible than performance goals. Moreover, athletes' focus on contest outcome is often related to increased anxiety (Hall & Kerr, 1997).

Lastly, when a total counseling perspective is considered, there is great potential for teaching the life skill of goal setting through sport. Unfortunately, after athletes learn certain psychological skills through sport such as goal setting, some never learn to transfer these skills to other areas of their lives (Hinkle, 1993). After student-athletes experience the benefits of goal setting in the sport domain, advisors, teachers, coaches, and other helping professionals should work with them to transfer these skills to other situations, such as academic course work, time management, and personal-social development.

Mistake and Loss Coping Skills/Strategies

Even the most skilled athletes will not be able to avoid making mistakes and experiencing losses. As previously mentioned, most entering first-year student-athletes will have experienced considerable athletic success in high school. What they may not be prepared for, however, is the potential adversity they will face when making the transition from high school to collegiate athletics. For some athletes, mistakes and losses can occur on a much more frequent basis in college than they did in high school. These athletes will likely benefit from helping professionals' support and psychological skills to help them cope and learn from these experiences.

Much has been written in the youth sports literature about the importance of providing positive experiences for the young athlete as well as a developmental perspective in sport psychology (e.g., Gould, 1993;

Martens, 2004; Smith, Smoll, & Curtis, 1979; Smoll & Smith, 1996; Weiss, 2004). In fact, seminal research by Smith and his associates (1979) has shown that a positive approach to coaching, which emphasizes the frequent and liberal use of rewarding and encouraging statements, is strongly associated with the young athlete's psychological development. Yet this does not mean that losing and making mistakes are not important learning tools for the developing athlete. High school athletes need to be taught how to cope successfully with defeat, mistakes, and adversity.

An excellent way to teach appropriate coping responses to prospective collegiate athletes is to discuss the meaning of success and failure with them. Success must not be seen solely as winning or losing but as the achievement of personal performance goals (Martens, 2004; Orlick, 2008, Roberts et al., 2007). Similarly, instead of viewing mistakes or losses as terrible, the coach or counselor can help the young athlete view mistakes and losses more productively—as the building blocks of success. Undoubtedly, younger and less experienced athletes will be frustrated after a loss or mistake, and this must be acknowledged. However, to grow and mature, young athletes must learn to analyze why the mistake or loss occurred, learn from it, and move on to the next task. As Halden-Brown (2003) so aptly described it, the best performers focus on *managing* their mistakes rather than never making mistakes. It is irrational to dwell on and catastrophize our errors! But when they happen, as they will, it is also an appropriate time to use the P³ Thinking discussed previously (Vealey, 2005).

The author's experience as an applied sport psychology consultant has shown her that the most productive means of teaching this coping orientation to young and transitioning athletes is by having coaches discuss it with them at the start of each season and reinforce it continually. As the season progresses, coaches should repeatedly remind their athletes about the importance of keeping mistakes and losses in perspective and reward them for using these techniques in frustrating situations. In essence, this involves adopting a task orientation (Roberts et al., 2007). Coaches should stop practices when players become frustrated and react poorly to mistakes, explain the coping orientation again, and encourage their athletes to use it. In addition, athletes who repeatedly become frustrated and have difficulty shutting off negative thoughts following mistakes should be taught thought-stopping skills and realistic positive replacement affirmations.

Finally, referral to a helping professional is another useful option. Helping professionals must be aware of student-athletes' varying coping responses in order to be of assistance. Erroneous conclusions can be made if helping professionals assume student-athletes respond to and cope with both academic and athletic stress in the same manner. Specifically, at-risk student-athletes (e.g., academic or emotional risks) must be identified so their coping resources can be enhanced (Broughton & Neyer, 2001; Parham, 1993). Only through consistent, repeated, and systematic efforts will developing athletes learn a productive coping orientation to help them manage mistakes and losses.

Stress Management Training

An additional psychological skill for the prospective college student-athlete to master is stress management. Fortunately, much has been written about stress and using stress management training in sports, and several classic profiles of the young athlete who is at risk relative to excessive levels of stress are available (e.g., Gould, 1993; Scanlan, 1986). For example, Scanlan (1986) has shown that the at-risk young athlete who is most susceptible to heightened stress is high trait anxious (i.e., has a personality that predisposes him or her to view competition as threatening), has low self-esteem, has low personal and team performance expectancies, experiences less fun and satisfaction, and worries about failure and adult evaluation. These young athletes experience excessive stress in environments as characterized by uncertainty about expectations of others, their ability to perform, and social evaluation. These high-stress environments are also characterized by the importance placed on competitive contest outcomes.

Fortunately, sport psychology professionals have identified specific stress management techniques to use with these at-risk athletes as well as convenient methods of conveying the stress management procedures (e.g., Gould, 1993; Gould & Udry, 1994; Martens, 2004; Orlick, 1993, Orlick, 2008; Vealey, 2005; Williams & Harris, 2006; Wilson, Taylor, Gundersen, & Brahm, 2005). *Cognitive* stress management techniques include monitoring and controlling negative thoughts, focus/attention control, and increasing rational thinking. In comparison, *somatic* stress management techniques include progressive muscular relaxation, deep-breathing techniques, and biofeedback. Advisors, coaches, and helping professionals must work to identify prospective student-athletes who are susceptible to heightened stress and encourage them to seek counseling or sport psychology consultation to acquire and apply stress management techniques such as these.

Summary

This chapter has highlighted the need to provide counseling and applied sport psychology services to prospective college students and new college student-athletes. When prospective student-athletes learn and receive primary prevention services such as perspective training, independence training, time management, goal setting, mistake and loss coping skills/strategies, and stress management skills, they will likely be better prepared to handle the life challenges that characterize the transition from high school to college and intercollegiate athletics. Consequently, normal developmental "stretches" such as readjusting athletic expectations, handling hectic schedules in an independent fashion, living on one's own, and coping with mistakes and adversity will become sources of growth and development—rather than distress—for the college athlete. Moreover, when serious problems do arise, the prospective student-athlete will be better prepared to handle them or seek appropriate professional assistance from helping professionals on campus (e.g., counseling services). Ideally, intervention services for these issues should begin long before the young person arrives on campus.

Regardless of when in the transition process counseling and/or sport psychology services for student-athletes are initiated, the individual needs of each athlete must remain paramount. Although the above-mentioned suggestions can be applied in most settings with most athletes, it is imperative that professionals involved in helping relationships with student-athletes remember the uniqueness of each individual student-athlete and her or his situation. Helping professionals must be knowledgeable of and sensitive to the influential role athletic participation has and will continue to play in the psychological development of these young people.

References

Abrams, M., & Hale, B. (2005). Anger: How to moderate hot buttons. In S. Murphy (Ed.), *The sport psychology handbook* (pp. 93–112). Champaign, IL: Human Kinetics.

Amorose, A. J., & Horn, T. S. (2000). Intrinsic motivation: Relationships with collegiate athletes' gender, scholarship status, and perceptions of their coaches' behavior. *The Sport Psychologist, 22*, 63–84.

Bailey, S. J. (1993). Issues in counseling athletes at the high school level. In W. D. Kirk & S. V. Kirk (Eds.), *Student athletes: Shattering the myths and sharing the realities* (pp. 25–34). Alexandria, VA: American Counseling Association.

Broughton, E., & Neyer, M. (2001). Advising and counseling student athletes. *New Directions for Student Services, 93*, 47–53.

Burton, D. (1989). Winning isn't everything: Examining the impact of performance goals on collegiate swimmers' cognitions and performance. *The Sport Psychologist, 3*, 105–132.

Burton, D., & Naylor, S. (2002). The Jekyll/Hyde nature of goals: Revisiting and updating goal-setting in sport. In T. S. Horn (Ed.), *Advances in sport psychology* (2nd ed., pp. 459–499). Champaign, IL: Human Kinetics.

Burton, D., Weinberg, R., Yukelson, D., & Weigand, D. (1998). The goal effectiveness paradox in sport: Examining the goal practices of collegiate athletes. *The Sport Psychologist, 12*, 404–418.

Cumming, S., & Ewing, M. (2003). Parental involvement in youth sports: The good, the bad and the ugly. Retrieved July 1, 2003, from http://ed-web3.educ.msu.edu/ysi/Spotlight2002/parental_involvement_in_youth_sp.htm.

Chickering, A. W., & Schlossberg, N. K. (2002). *Getting the most out of college.* Upper Saddle River, NJ: Prentice Hall.

Coakley, J. J. (2004). *Sports in society: Issues and controversies* (8th ed.). Boston: McGraw Hill.

Coleman, J. S. (1974). *Youth: Transition to adulthood.* Chicago: University of Chicago Press.

Danish, S. J., Owens, S. S., Green, S. L., & Brunelle, J. P. (1997). Building bridges for disengagement: The transition process for individuals and teams. *Journal of Applied Sport Psychology, 9*, 154–167.

Danish, S. J. Petitpas, A. J., & Hale, B. D. (1993). Life development intervention for athletes. *The Counseling Psychologist, 21*, 352–385.

Duda, J. L. (1981). *A cross-cultural analysis of achievement motivation in sport and the classroom.* Unpublished doctoral dissertation, University of Illinois, Urbana.

Duda, J. L., & Hall, H. (2001). Achievement goal theory in sport: Recent extensions and future directions. In R. N. Singer, H. A. Hausenblas, & C. M. Janelle (Eds.), *Handbook of sport psychology* (2nd ed., pp. 414–443). New York: John Wiley & Sons.

Feltz, D. (1978). Athletics in the status system of female adolescents. *Review of Sport and Leisure, 3*, 98–108.

Finch, L. M. (1993). *The relationships among coping strategies, trait anxiety, and perform-*

ance in collegiate softball players. Unpublished doctoral dissertation, University of North Carolina at Greensboro.

Goldberg, A. D., & Chandler, T. (1995). Sports counseling: Enhancing the development of the high school student-athlete. *Journal of Counseling and Development, 74*, 39–44.

Gould, D. (2006). Goal setting for peak performance. In J. M. Williams (Ed.), *Applied sport psychology: Personal growth to peak performance* (5th ed., pp. 240–259). Boston: McGraw-Hill.

Gould, D. (1993). Intensive sport participation and the prepubescent athlete: Competitive stress and burnout. In B. R. Cahill & A. J. Pearl (Eds.), *Intensive participation in children's sports* (pp. 19–38). Champaign, IL: Human Kinetics.

Gould, D., & Udry, E. (1994). Psychological skills for enhancing performance: Arousal regulation strategies. *Medicine and Science in Exercise and Sport, 26*, 478–485.

Greenspan, M., & Andersen, M. B. (1995). Providing psychological services to student athletes: A developmental psychology model. In S. M. Murphy (Ed.), *Sport psychology interventions* (pp. 177–191). Champaign, IL: Human Kinetics.

Halden-Brown, S. (2003). *Mistakes worth making: How to turn sports errors into athletic excellence*. Champaign, IL: Human Kinetics.

Hall, H. K., & Kerr, A. W. (1997). Motivational antecedents of precompetitive anxiety in youth sport. *The Sport Psychologist, 11*, 24–42.

Hamstra, K., Cherubini, J., & Swanik, B. (2002). Athletic injury and parental pressure in youth sports. *Athletic Therapy Today, 7*, 36–41.

Harwood, C. (2005). Goals: More than just the score. In. S. Murphy (Ed.), *The sport psychology handbook* (pp. 19–36). Champaign, IL: Human Kinetics.

Hinkle, S. J. (1993). Problem solving and decision making. In W. D. Kirk & S. V. Kirk (Eds.), *Student athletes: Shattering the myths and sharing the realities* (pp. 1–80). Alexandria, VA: American Counseling Association.

Hirsch, G. (2001). *Helping college students succeed*. Philadelphia: Taylor & Francis.

Holmbeck, G. N., & Wandrei, M. L. (1993). Individual and relational predictors of adjustment in first-year college students. *Journal of Counseling Psychology, 40*, 73–78.

Jordan, K. B., & Quinn, W. H. (1997). Male and female client perception of session two outcome of the problem—and solution-focused approaches. *Family Therapy, 24*, 25–37.

Kennedy, S. R., & Dimick, K. M. (1987). Career maturity and professional sports expectations of college football and basketball players. *Journal of College Student Personnel, 28*, 293–297.

Kornspan, A., & Etzel, E. (2003). What do we know about the career maturity of college student-athletes? A brief review and practical suggestions for career development work with student-athletes. *Academic Athletic Journal, 17*, 15–33.

Lanning W., & Toye, P. (1993). Counseling athletes in higher education. In W. D. Kirk & S. V. Kirk (Eds.), *Student athletes: Shattering the myths and sharing the realities* (pp. 61–70). Alexandria, VA: American Counseling Association.

Lewin, K. (1936). *Principles of topological psychology*. New York: McGraw-Hill.

Linder, D. E., Brewer, B. W., Van Raalte, J. L., & DeLange, N. (1991). A negative halo for athletes who consult sport psychologists: Replication and extension. *Journal of Sport and Exercise Psychology, 13*, 133–148.

Locke E. A., & Latham, G. P. (1990). *A theory of goal setting and task performance.* Englewood Cliffs, NJ: Prentice-Hall.

Maniar, S. D., Curry, L. A., Sommers-Flanagan, J., & Walsh, J. A. (2001). Student-athlete preferences in seeking help when confronted with sport performance problems. *The Sport Psychologist, 15*, 205–223.

Martens, R. (2004). *Successful coaching* (3rd ed.). Champaign, IL: Human Kinetics.

Martin, S. B. (2005). High school and college athletes' attitudes toward sport psychology consulting. *Journal of Applied Sport Psychology, 17*, 127–139.

Martin, S. B., Akers, A., Jackson, A. W., Wrisberg, C. A., Nelson, L., Leslie, P. J., & Larson, L. (2001). Male and female athletes' and nonathletes' expectations about sport psychology consulting. *Journal of Applied Sport Psychology, 13*, 18–39.

Miller, P. S., & Kerr, G. A. (2003). The role experimentation of intercollegiate student athletes. *The Sport Psychologist, 17*, 196–219.

Murphy, G. M., Petitpas, A. J., & Brewer, B. W. (1996). Identity foreclosure, athletic identity, and career maturity in intercollegiate athletes. *The Sport Psychologist, 10*, 239–246.

Murphy, S., & Ferrante, A. P. (1989). Provision of sport psychology services to the U.S. Team at the 1988 Summer Olympic Games. *The Sport Psychologist, 3*, 374–385.

National Collegiate Athletic Association. (2007a, February 16). *Estimated probability of competing in athletics beyond the high school interscholastic level.* Indianapolis: Author. Retrieved June 15, 2007 from: http://www.ncaa.org/research/prob_of_competing/probability_of_competing2.html

National Collegiate Athletic Association. (2007b). Academic reform. Retrieved on June, 2, 2007, from http://www.ncaa. org/research/prob_of_competing/probability_of_competing2.html

National Council of Youth Sports. (2000). Retrieved March 1, 2007, from http://www.ncys.org/

O'Bryant, B. J. (1993). School counseling and the student athlete. In W. D. Kirk & S. V. Kirk (Eds.), *Student athletes: Shattering the myths and sharing the realities* (pp. 13–24). Alexandria, VA: American Counseling Association.

Orlick, T. (2008). *In pursuit of excellence* (4th ed.). Champaign, IL: Human Kinetics.

Orlick, T. (1993). *Free to feel great: Teaching children to excel at living.* Carp, Ontario: Creative Bound.

Parham, W. D. (1993). The intercollegiate athlete: A 1990s profile. *The Counseling Psychologist, 21*, 411–429.

Petlichkoff, L. M. (1992). Youth sport participation and withdrawal: Is it simply a matter of fun? *Pediatric Exercise Science, 4*, 105–110.

Porter, K. (2003). *The mental athlete.* Champaign, IL: Human Kinetics.

Purdy, D., Eitzen, D., & Hufnagel, R. (1982). Are athletes also students? The educational attainment of college athletes. *Social Problems, 29*, 439–447.

Roberts, G. C. (1982). Achievement motivation in sport. In R. Terjung (Ed.), *Exercise and Sport Science Reviews* (Vol. 10, pp. 236–269). Philadelphia: Franklin Institute Press.

Roberts, G. C., Treasure, D. C., & Conroy, D. E. (2007). Understanding the dynamics of motivation in sport and physical activity: An achievement goal interpretation. In G. Tenenbaum & R. C. Eklund (Eds.), *Handbook of sport psychology* (3rd ed., pp. 3–30). New York: John Wiley & Sons.

Sack, A. L., & Staurowsky, E. J. (1998). *College athletes for hire: The evolution and legacy of the NCAA's amateur myth.* Westport, CN: Praeger.

Scanlan, T. K. (1986). Competitive stress in children. In M. R. Weiss & D. Gould (Eds.), *Sport for children and youth* (pp. 113– 118). Champaign, IL: Human Kinetics.

Schlossberg, N. K. (1981). A model for analyzing human adaptation. *The Counseling Psychologist. 9*, 2–18.

Schlossberg, N. K., Waters, E. B., & Goodman, J. (1995). *Counseling adults in transition* (2nd ed.). New York: Springer.

Smith, R. E., Smoll, F. L., & Curtis, B. (1979). Coaching effectiveness training: A cognitive-behavioral approach to enhancing relationship skills in youth sport coaches. *Journal of Sport Psychology, 1*, 59–75.

Smoll, R. E., & Smith, F. L. (1996). *Children and youth in sport: A biopsychosocial perspective.* Madison, WI: Brown & Benchmark.

Sperber, M. (2000). *Beer and circus: How big-time college sports is crippling undergraduate education.* New York: Henry Holt

Sperber, M. (1990). *College sports inc.: The athletic department vs. the university.* New York: Henry Holt.

Taylor, J., Ogilvie, B., & Lavallee, D. (2006). Career transitions among athletes: Is there life after sports? In J. M. Williams (Ed.) *Applied sport psychology: Personal growth to peak performance* (5th ed., pp. 595–615). Boston: McGraw-Hill.

Thelin, J. R. (1996). *Games colleges play: Scandals and reform in intercollegiate athletics.* Baltimore: Johns Hopkins University Press.

Tracey, J., & Corlett, J. (1995). The transition experience of first-year university track and field student athletes. *Journal of the Freshman Year Experience, 7*, 81–102.

Vealey, R. S. (2005). *Coaching for the inner edge.* Morgantown, WV: Fitness Information Technology.

Watson, J. (2005). College student-athletes' attitudes towards help-seeking behavior and expectations of counseling services. *Journal of College Student Development, 46*, 442–449.

Watt, S. K., & Moore, J. L., III. (2001). Who are student athletes? *New Directions for Student Services, 93*, 7–18.

Weinberg, R., Butt, J., Knight, B., & Perritt, N. (2001). Collegiate coaches' perceptions of their goal-setting practices: A qualitative investigation. *Journal of Applied Sport Psychology, 13*, 374–398.

Weinberg, R. S., Harmison, R. J., Rosenkranz, R., & Hookom, S. (2005). Goal setting.

In J. Taylor & G. Wilson (Eds.), *Applying sport psychology: Four perspectives* (pp. 101–116). Champaign, IL: Human Kinetics.

Weiss, M. R. (Ed.). (2004). *Developmental sport and exercise psychology: A lifespan perspective*. Morgantown, WV: Fitness Information Technology.

Williams, J. M., & Harris, D. V. (2006). Relaxation and energizing techniques for regulation of arousal. In J. M. Williams (Ed.) *Applied sport psychology: Personal growth to peak performance* (5th ed., pp. 285–305). Boston: McGraw-Hill.

Wilson, G., Taylor, J., Gundersen, F., & Brahm, T. (2005). Intensity. In J. Taylor & G. Wilson (Eds.), *Applying sport psychology: Four perspectives* (pp. 33–49). Champaign, IL: Human Kinetics.

Zimbalist, A. S. (1999). *Unpaid professionals: Commercialism and conflict in big-time college sports*. Princeton, NJ: Princeton University Press.

14

COLLEGE STUDENT-ATHLETES WITH LEARNING DISABILITIES

Lisa C. Hamilton

Joe, a 19-year-old red-shirt sophomore defensive back, was referred by his football position coach to visit the counseling center psychologist who worked closely with intercollegiate athletics. A heads-up call from his coach indicated that Joe was a "great kid" who was a "bit scatterbrained at times" and that he had had a "rotten fall semester." The coach and Joe's academic mentor were requiring him to meet with the psychologist to see if he had some sort of learning disability. The young man showed up 20 minutes late for his appointment. He was not particularly forthcoming about his academic struggles and seemed somewhat embarrassed to be meeting with the psychologist. A screening interview pointed to the possibility of a reading disorder and possible ADHD.

Many college student-athletes who struggle with learning problems seek consultation, which complicates further their already exceptionally busy lives. The numerous demands of sport, academics, social interactions, and other life commitments are difficult for any student to juggle. Nonathlete students with learning problems often compensate by putting extra time into their academic work. This is frequently not a viable option for the athlete with significant, chronic learning challenges. Stigma and misunderstandings about learning problems may delay reaching out for potentially useful services. Jay (1990) completed a phenomenological study of four National Collegiate Athletic Association Division I elite male athletes with learning disabilities. In that small sample, each student was undiagnosed before entering college, all made efforts to keep their learning problems a secret, and each had failed to seek the accommodations to which they were entitled. Her small sample reflects the struggles of many student-athletes with learning disorders whom we may meet in any university setting.

The purpose of this chapter is to offer the helping professional working with student-athletes a primer in learning disorders and attention deficit/hyperactivity disorders (ADHD). More specifically, this chapter is intended to (a) help the reader recognize the signs that might suggest a student-athlete is facing these difficulties; (b) help counselors and psychologists to be useful resources to the student-athlete through the steps of assessment, identification, accommodation, and treatment; and (c) assist student-athlete clients as they move toward their goals of success in school, sport, and life.

How Many Student-athletes May Have Disabling Learning Problems?

Prevalence estimates regarding learning disabilities and ADHD among college students vary. The number of identified and accommodated learning disabled students reported by institutions of higher education has varied from .5 % to 10% depending on the demographics of the institutions (Vogel, 1998). General population estimates also vary from 2% to 10% depending on methodology (DSM-IV-TR, 2000, p. 49). These estimates unfortunately do not include the many undiagnosed or unidentified students on college campuses or the number of student-athletes who struggle with these conditions. Similarly, prevalence estimates for ADHD vary with suggestions of 8% or higher incidence in college-age adult populations (Turnock, Rosen, & Karninski, 1998). One study that looked at college student self-reports of ADHD symptoms found between 7% and 8% of students endorsed a significant number of symptoms (Weyandt, Linterman, & Rice, 1995). Certainly, multiple factors are contributing to a steady increase in the number of students with learning problems who are enrolling in post-secondary institutions (Vogel, Leonard, Scales, Hayeslip, Hermansen, & Donnells,

1998; Sitlington 2003). Better evaluation and identification will eventually lead to better prevalence data. However, the population of college students with disabling learning problems is a significant one by any estimate. Many of the students who make up this population are likely student-athletes. Unfortunately, the struggles of these students may or may not be well received by some faculty members and others on campus (Beilke & Yssel, 1999). Vogel, Leyser, Wyland, and Brulle (1999) surveyed faculty about their attitudes and willingness to make accommodations for students with learning disabilities. They found that although for the majority attitudes were positive, there was also significant variability in attitude. They suggested that providing information and training for faculty on special education law, learning differences, teaching strategies, and available support services, among other topics, can help improve their attitudes and increase their willingness to provide accommodations.

What Are Learning Disorders?

There are varying definitions of learning disorders and learning disabilities. There are definitions that guide law and education, as well as definitions that guide diagnosis and treatment. The following definition was outlined in the Individuals with Disabilities Education Act (IDEA) (PL101-476). Although IDEA itself does not apply to college students, and the definition may be imperfect, the author believes this definition is a useful beginning place.

> Specific learning disability means a disorder in one or more of the basic psychological processes involved in understanding or in using language, spoken or written, which may manifest itself in an imperfect ability to listen, think, speak, read, write, spell or to do mathematical calculations. The term includes such conditions as perceptual handicaps, brain injury, minimal brain dysfunction, dyslexia and developmental aphasia. The term does not include children who have learning problems which are primarily the result of visual, hearing, or motor handicaps, of mental retardation, of emotional disturbance, or of environmental, cultural, or economic disadvantage. (34 CFR, Sec. 300.7 (c) (10) (i).

The National Joint Committee on Learning Disabilities (NJCLD) also has developed a definition that is very useful, particularly when we are working with adult learners, including college student-athletes. The NJCLD definition can be found in Table 14.1.

Table 14.1. The NJCLD Definition (NJCLD, 1998)

Learning disabilities is a general term that refers to a heterogeneous group of disorders manifested by significant difficulties in the acquisition and use of listening, speaking, reading, writing, reasoning, or mathematical skills.

These disorders are intrinsic to the individual, presumed to be due to central nervous system dysfunction, and may occur across the life span. Problems in self-regulatory behaviors, social perception, and social interaction may exist with learning disabilities but do not, by themselves, constitute a learning disability.

Although learning disabilities may occur concomitantly with other disabilities (e.g., sensory impairment, mental retardation, serious emotional disturbance), or with extrinsic influences (such as cultural differences, insufficient or inappropriate instruction), they are not the result of those conditions or influences (NJCLD, 1990).

The Five Constructs

1. Learning disabilities are heterogeneous, both within and across individuals. Intra-individual differences involve varied profiles of learning strength and need and/or shifts across the life span within individuals. Inter-individual differences involve different manifestations of learning disabilities for different individuals.

2. Learning disabilities result in significant difficulties in the acquisition and use of listening, speaking, reading, writing, reasoning, and/or mathematical skills. Such difficulties are evident when an individual's appropriate levels of effort do not result in reasonable progress given the opportunity for effective educational instruction and with the recognition that all individuals learn at a different pace and with differing effort. Significant difficulty cannot be determined solely by a quantitative test score.

3. Learning disabilities are intrinsic to the individual. They are presumed to be related to differences in central nervous system development. They do not disappear over time, but may range in expression and severity at different life stages.

4. Learning disabilities may occur concomitantly with other disabilities that do not, by themselves, constitute a learning disability. For example, difficulty with self-regulatory behaviors, social perception, and so-

Table 14.1. (cont.)

cial interactions may occur for many reasons. Some social interaction problems result from learning disabilities; others do not. Individuals with other disabilities, such as sensory impairments, attention deficit hyperactivity disorders, mental retardation, and serious emotional disturbance, may also have learning disabilities, but such conditions do not cause or constitute learning disabilities.

5. Learning disabilities are not caused by extrinsic influences. Inconsistent or insufficient instruction or a lack of instructional experience cause learning difficulties, but not learning disabilities. However, individuals who have had inconsistent or insufficient instruction may also have learning disabilities. The challenge is to document that inadequate or insufficient instruction is not the primary cause of a learning disability. Individuals from all cultural and linguistic backgrounds may also have learning disabilities; therefore, assessments must be designed acknowledging this diversity in culture and language, and examiners who test children from each background must be sensitive to such factors and use practices that are individualized and appropriate for each child. (III 258a–258b)

One of the essential features of most definitions of learning disorders is that they are presumed to be neurological in nature. Generally, diagnosis requires that there are deficits in functioning in some area that would not be predicted by students' (a) measured intelligence; (b) level of educational development; and/or (c) their age. Those deficits should not be better explained by a medical condition, vision or hearing problem, lack of opportunity, or poor education. When the aforementioned conditions co-exist, the learning problems must exceed the expected impact of the problems for a diagnosis of learning disorder to be made (DSM-IV-TR, 2000).

"Basic" reading, writing, and arithmetic skills, the foundations for much of our learning, require remarkable coordination of the systems of perception, memory, recognition, association, analysis, response preparation, inhibition of incorrect output, and production of a correct response. For young adults without learning disorders these multiple tasks are all coordinated in a smooth, seamless, rapid, and automatic process. A "glitch" or failure in any part of this amazing system can result in a

---

Table 14.2. A Personal Exercise

Stop for a moment and think about the reading you are doing right now. It is really a very complicated task to read. As your eyes track along the lines of text, your perceptual functions must all work properly to quickly convey an accurate representation of the symbols on the page to your brain. Then you must briefly hold each unit in working memory while you rapidly retrieve information from long-term memory to provide the sounds and meanings associated with letters and words at a basic level. Now you must draw more information from prior learning and experience to process the new information at a higher level and to derive meaning from it. If you were asked to read this passage aloud there would be the further steps to relay the information to the centers of your brain responsible for speech and motor functions.

---

learning disorder. When we consider how truly miraculous it is that any of us can read, write, and make numerical computations, it should not be surprising that numerous students today have learning disorders.

Terminology

Several learning disorders exist and the faces of these disorders often overlap. Clearly, the language surrounding learning disorders can be somewhat complicated and confusing. The most common terms for learning disorders include reading disorder, mathematics disorder, disorder of written language, and learning disorder NOS (DSM-IV-TR, 2000, pp. 49–56). A brief introduction to each of these conditions follows.

Reading Disorder (Dyslexia)

Reading disorders are perhaps the most familiar learning disorders. They are more likely to be diagnosed in childhood than the others—though certainly not always. A reading disorder in young adulthood may include:

- difficulties in reading fluidly and fluently
- problems in sounding out or decoding unfamiliar words
- difficulty with reading comprehension
- running out of time on tests and reading assignments
- reluctance to read out loud in class activities or presentations

- avoidance of reading assignments
- poor vocabulary development
- problems with over-application of phonological rules (think of "cough," "bough," and "though")
- problems with visually decoding letters, words, and other symbols.

How do these problems link to the academic challenges of college? The student-athlete with a reading disorder may have great difficulty with learning from textbook assignments. Completing true/false and multiple choice exams, for which fast, accurate reading is necessary to discriminate between choices and complete the test on time, may be very trying. "Scantron" or "NCS" answer sheets provide countless opportunities for unintended mistakes in tracking the proper row and column. Additionally, the switching between the answer sheet and test questions can lead to errors. Quickly and accurately reading materials presented on PowerPoint slides or a chalkboard may be problematic as well. Some students with reading disorders may reverse letters, see letters in the wrong sequence, or have problems with left-right orientations or directions. Others may decode accurately, although slowly and painstakingly. A student may not have all of these reading difficulties. However, it is important to remember that by the time we are working with young adults in college, they have doubtless invented many compensatory strategies to work around their reading disorders, and the last remaining sign may be the lack of fluency and fluidity as they labor to complete their reading tasks.

Mathematics Disorder (Dyscalculia)

Although a reading disorder will impact a student in all areas of functioning, a student-athlete with a mathematics disorder has additional problem areas. In a true mathematics disorder the student's "internal calculator" and his or her ability to think quantitatively and to understand numerical values is typically quite dysfunctional. Some of the following challenges are common:

- difficulties with basic "math facts" such as multiplication tables
- numbers and amounts seeming to have little meaning
- math avoidance and/or math phobia
- improbable, incorrect answers to math problems seem to go unrecognized

- problems with sequencing and using formulas or equations
- counting on fingers
- using paper and pencil for even simple calculations
- difficulty making change or balancing a checkbook
- poor time awareness
- problems in learning grammar in adult foreign language courses

These difficulties may impact the student-athlete both in the classroom and outside the classroom in various aspects of daily living or in the athletics realm (e.g., learning plays). Often a student-athlete may have chosen a major for which there are essential math and science course requirements. Although they may be successful in many other courses, their mathematics difficulties present a significant roadblock to completing the selected major. Another often observed occurrence is the student with a mathematics disorder who struggles greatly with passing foreign language course requirements for the major. It appears that for some individuals sequencing problems and difficulty learning to associate symbols with meaning impact both math skills and foreign language acquisition.

Disorder of Written Language (Dysgraphia)

In this disorder the dysfunction is primarily evident in "output" systems. It often appears to be a problem of disconnect or mis-communication between the student's oral language skills and knowledge and their writing skills, which are often required to demonstrate what they think, know, and have learned.

One of the first cues to a disorder of written language may be poor graphomotor skills resulting in very poor or illegible handwriting, or handwriting that appears immature for the student's age. Some of the other common difficulties may include:

- difficulty organizing writing assignments and outlines
- very poor spelling
- poor punctuation and written grammar
- sequencing problems (timelines, storylines, schedules)

Student-athletes with a disorder of written language may truly dread writing assignments and struggle mightily in many, if not most, courses. They might spell in idiosyncratic ways and may spell words in ways that are incorrect, but phonetically "correct," for example, using "wich" for both "witch" and "which." Often, instructors notice a gap between what the young person is able to express orally, in class or office hours, and what he or she is able to produce in papers or essay exams. Student-athletes may limit or restrict their writing to try to use spelling and grammar of which they are the most confident; they cannot fully express themselves because they avoid words and structures of which they are unsure. They also may produce written work much more slowly than their peers. Because of their fear of writing assignments, student-athletes with a disorder of written language may also procrastinate on large writing assignments, term papers, and similar projects, further compounding their academic difficulties. Helping professionals may see these clients when they are faced with deadlines for these responsibilities.

Learning Disorder Not Otherwise Specified (LD NOS)

Many student-athletes' learning problems do not fit neatly into one of the above categories. They may have problems with phonological awareness, or with phonemic and/or graphemic perception that impact reading, math, and written language. They may have a "slow processing speed" or a slow "cognitive tempo" that affects their work across the board but particularly under time constraints (e.g., time-limited exams). There may be problems in short- or long-term memory systems that will impact most, if not all, learning efforts.

The diagnostic category of "LD NOS" allows the assessing clinician to provide a diagnosis when there are problems in all three areas (i.e., reading, math, and written language). Together, these challenges can significantly interfere with academic achievement. It is important for the helping professional to look at the specific individual strengths and problem areas for all students with learning problems, and this is particularly true for the LD NOS student-athlete.

Attention Deficit Hyperactivity Disorder (ADHD)

The student-athlete with ADHD shares many of the challenges of the LD athletes with some challenges unique to the experience of ADHD. Many students (estimates of exactly how many vary) have both an LD and ADHD. Common themes include academic difficulties; decisions and issues regarding use and management of medications; struggles to balance athletics, academics, and social interests; feeling misunderstood; believing life is "unfair," and feeling "not normal" or different from peers (Palmer, 2002). Importantly, student-athletes with ADHD may find their sport provides a source of positive self-esteem that may balance the negative self-perceptions commonly associated with ADHD.

What Is ADHD?

Many people have difficulties with maintaining attention at times and managing their impulses. And many disorders affect attention and concentration. Depression, anxiety, other mood disorders, emotional or physical traumas, some medications, and some substances can cause problems with attention and behavior. However, problems with attention, impulse control, and hyperactivity that are long term, are more severe than "average," aren't better explained by another disorder, and that began in childhood are often diagnosed as ADHD (DSM-IV-TR, 2000, pp. 85–93).

Student-athletes with ADHD are often seen as "problem children." Unfortunately, those who are untreated typically have difficulties in a number of areas, including attention and concentration, impulse control problems, hyperactivity, executive functioning problems, and interpersonal difficulties. (See Table 14.3 for examples of these symptoms.)

It is important to keep in mind that no one person will have all of these problems. The cluster of difficulties an individual struggles with will determine the subtype of ADHD he or she is diagnosed with. The reader should be aware of the fact that there are several subtypes of ADHD.

Attention Deficit/Hyperactivity Disorder, Combined Type

These individuals display problems in attention as well as hyperactive *and/or* impulsive behaviors. This appears to be the most frequent type of ADHD. Anecdotally, it may be over represented in the student-athlete population. This may be the case because (a) these individuals are often steered toward athletics early in life in efforts to "use up the restless energy"; and (b) they may achieve more self-esteem and may experience more reward in athletics, in contrast to the classroom setting, where their problems are less well tolerated by others.

Table14.3. Common Problems and Signs of ADHD

Attention and Concentration

- Difficulty maintaining focus in class or training, although they may have times of "hyper-focus"
- Forgetfulness
- Difficulty sustaining mental effort, giving up on tasks easily
- Lack of concentration even in leisure activities
- Problems "filtering out" sounds, sights, and movements
- Mood difficulties
- Irritability or boredom
- Low tolerance for frustration
- Difficulty managing stress

Impulse Control Problems

- Problems in acting before thinking about the possible consequences
- Difficulty waiting for directions to be completed
- Recklessness

Hyperactivity

- Feeling restless
- Having difficulty remaining seated during long classes
- Frequent unnecessary movement

Other "Executive Functioning" Difficulties

- Disorganization
- Planning problems
- Difficulty with time awareness, deadlines, time frames
- Problems switching between tasks
- Problems with multi-step tasks

Interpersonal problems

- Difficulty "reading" others
- May be blunt, tactless, intruding
- Problems in personal, school, work, and team relationships

(DSM-IV-TR, 2000, pp. 85–93.)

Attention Deficit/Hyperactivity Disorder, Predominantly Inattentive Type

Inattentive student-athlete types usually have a number of the symptoms of being distracted, daydreaming, and having concentration problems without quite as many of the hyperactive or impulsive behaviors. These individuals may be more likely to go undiagnosed for some time because they do not have as many behavioral problems that draw attention to them. They may appear to others as "spacey" or disorganized and forgetful. Helping professionals specializing in learning disabilities often see an overlap of this type with disorders of written language.

Attention Deficit/Hyperactivity Disorder, Predominantly Hyperactive-Impulsive Type

Student athletes with this diagnosis will still have some symptoms of inattention and concentration. However, they will likely present with more symptoms of hyperactive behaviors and difficulties controlling their impulses and "thinking first." Psychologists in our university counseling center assessment program have tended to see this subtype less frequently than the others.

Identification and Assessment of Learning Problems

Concerned counselors, faculty, academic support staff, and coaches are sometimes the first people to realize that there might be a learning disability and/or ADHD compounding the difficulties of a student-athlete. The helping professional's genuine concern and a few questions, along with some encouragement, may help the student-athlete take steps to begin the process toward a more formal, extensive assessment. The description of problem areas for each common type of disorder described earlier in this chapter may guide the reader's observations and the discussion with the athlete.

Some of the following questions may be useful to the helping professional when helping students determine whether a referral for a formal assessment is appropriate. Remember, it is not the counselor's role to complete the assessment or make a diagnosis, only to help the students observe the indicators that there may be a problem that warrants further investigation. Open-ended questions regarding their academic performance, basic skills, and academic history are a good way to start. Table 14.4 offers some specific questions that may be helpful.

Table 14.4. Possible Screening Questions
The helping professional evaluating a student-athlete suspected of having learning problems might ask specific questions, such as: • What concerns do you have about your academic performance? • Were you ever tested for learning problems as a child? • Were you enrolled in any special courses? • Did you or do you receive tutoring? • What are your best and worst subjects? • How many courses have you failed or struggled in? • How much do you like reading? • How do you think your reading speed compares to that of others? • How comfortable do you feel reading out loud in front of others? • How much do you understand of what you read? • How much difficulty do you have remembering what you just read? • How much trouble might you have locating the main idea and the supporting details? • How easy or difficult is it for you to do basic math "in your head"? • How well do you add, subtract, multiply, divide? • How difficult is it for you to balance your checkbook or make change? • How easy or difficult is it for you to sequence multi-step math tasks? • How difficult are upper level math courses for you? • How are foreign language courses for you? • How good are you at spelling, grammar, and punctuation? • How easy or hard is it for you to make an outline and organize a paper? • How much do you fear or dread writing assignments? • How is the quality of your handwriting? • How good do you think your memory is? • How well do you think you perform on tests? • How is your ability to pay attention? • How often do you feel restless in a long class? • How easy or difficult is it for you to settle down to study for a period of time? • How good is your "sense of time"? • What is your experience of any difficulties with hyperactivity?

Indications of problems in more than one or two of the areas noted in Table 14. 4, accompanied by reported significant problems in life and/or academics, may well warrant a referral for a psycho-educational evaluation. It is also frequently useful for the helping professional to offer specific observations and concerns in such a discussion (e.g., I have noticed since we have started our session that you have been fidgety, seem to have had difficulty paying attention during our conversation, etc.).

Some student-athletes may already know or at least sense that they have a learning disability or ADHD. They may have been receiving academic support prior to beginning their college career. In making the transition to college, these "identified" persons may still need significant assistance from a skilled helper. Often, they begin college with hopes that they won't need special services any longer and do not disclose their histories until there are problems or until someone asks. As student-athletes with learning problems make the transition from secondary school to college, there are a number of shifts to navigate, as different laws, policies, and practices apply at the collegiate level. In elementary and high school, the student's accommodations were provided as an entitlement because of the right of every student to receive a free and appropriate public education. At the postsecondary level, the emphasis shifts to providing equal access to educational opportunities. The requirements for assessment and diagnosis change for an adult level, and the students' level of responsibility for seeking, obtaining, and implementing their services increases dramatically (Sitlington, 2003).

Evaluation

A high-quality, formal evaluation serves multiple purposes. First, it helps the student-athlete understand (a) his or her individual strengths and weaknesses; (b) the nature of the problems at hand; and (c) his or her best ways to learn. Second, the evaluation serves the important function of informing the university disability services staff and university instructors how best to help the student achieve academic success with appropriate accommodations. A growing number of campus counseling centers or clinics run by counseling psychology, school psychology, or clinical psychology programs offer assessment services. Often, there are also private external practitioners in the community who offer such services.

A university's Office of Disability Services will likely have clear guidelines for what constitutes a complete evaluation for either LD or ADHD and what will meet their requirements for documentation of the disability. It is important for helping professionals to check these guidelines for their specific universities. Common requirements are that the testing be completed using measures that are normed on adult populations and that the testing was completed within the recent past. For a learning disorder, the assessment must include measures of basic abilities or aptitudes (IQ), achievement (i.e., in all three domains; reading, writing, and mathematics), and information processing (such as processing speed, visual-motor integration, and auditory processes). The assessment battery for ADHD may vary. It may include some of the above measures with an emphasis on information processing and memory systems; some assessment of the symptoms of inattention, hyperactivity, and impulsiveness; perhaps a measure of sustained attention on a task; and tests of "executive functions" such as planning, organizing, concept formation, mental shifting, and mental control. Quick "screening measures" alone are not sufficient for the evaluation. In all cases the assessment must demonstrate what the significant functional impairments resulting from the disorder are, and a definite diagnosis must be provided. "Significant" means that the difficulties place the person's measured performance below that of his or her age mates or another appropriate norm group. The "functional impairments" part of the requirement means that the problems must be causing difficulty in the classroom and everyday life, not just in the assessment room. For ADHD some evidence (often parent and/or teacher reports) of the occurrence of the symptoms during childhood is also required. The Office of Disability Services may also have a list of local or university affiliated providers who are qualified to complete the assessment.

The Accommodation Process

After the assessment has been completed by a qualified professional, the diagnosis has been formally made, and sufficient appropriate evidence is available that there are significant functional impairments, the student-athlete is eligible for academic accommodations under the Americans with Disabilities Act of 1990. The ADA is United States Public Law 101-336, 104 Stat. 327 (July 26, 1990). It provides for equal access to services for persons with disabilities. For helping professionals, that means reasonable and appropriate accommodations must be made to give the student-athlete with a learning disability equal access to educational materials, classroom activities, and learning opportunities.

The student-athletes typically must meet with the disability services staff to identify appropriate individual accommodations that will address their specific functional limitations. Possible accommodations may include suggestions for scheduling classes, materials provided in accessible formats or access to technology that can make the material accessible, priority pre-registration, in-class adjustments such as priority seating or extra time on tests, and substitution of equivalent courses. It is the student-athletes' responsibility to subsequently make appointments with each of their faculty members to discuss which accommodations will need to be implemented in each class and how the arrangements will be made. The student-athletes must still meet the same requirements for their course of study as any other student.

Programming Considerations

Frequently, universities have in place the various resources required to serve students with learning disabilities and ADHD. However, coordination between the various offices with an emphasis on making the services accessible to the disabled student-athlete may be necessary. Identifying persons to serve as liaisons between departments of intercollegiate athletics, counseling and assessment services, disability services, learning centers, and academic advising offices may increase communication between departments and ease the navigation of these resources for the student. These liaisons could also be responsible for reviewing the current state of policies and resources available on campus and evaluating programmatic issues that need to be addressed.

Clark (2002) reviewed the particular challenges of the student-athlete with learning disabilities and proposed a comprehensive model to improve advising and service delivery to meet the complex needs of this population. His program includes recommendations for providing the following components: (a) academic support and transitions; (b) personal and social support; (c) collaboration; and (d) leadership, scholarship, and self-advocacy. His program proposal includes a wide array of suggestions under each domain to increase the probability of meeting the educational and personal needs of the student-athlete with learning problems. This model may serve as a template for post-secondary programs, to develop or improve services for student-athletes with learning problems, as it offers many practical suggestions for policies, programs and supports.

Tutoring and Academic Support

Tutoring services are an excellent adjunct for the student-athlete with an LD or ADHD. The tutor trained to work with LD-diagnosed student-athletes can collaborate with the student to individualize mastery of content and improve study skills. Together, they can play to the athlete's strengths in learning and address problems areas. Hock (1998) looked specifically at the benefits of a tutoring program that included constructing learning strategies and writing strategies for "under-prepared" college athletes including athletes with LD. In his study the students who received the tutoring program performed as well as their "academically prepared" peers in their English 101 courses. Training for the tutors in learning differences, how to establish a tutoring relationship, awareness of possible problem areas, and tutor-tutee matching on shared interests is essential to the success of tutoring programs for students with learning difficulties (Vogel, Fresko, & Wertheim, 2007). Learning centers, study skills support, and other academic supports may all serve to improve academic performance for student-athletes with LD or ADHD.

Treatment Considerations

Education

Educating the student-athlete as well as faculty and staff about disability issues is an important step in achieving success. Outreach and education to de-stigmatize learning problems can help students seek the services they are entitled to. Understanding the nature of their problems in a new way, and particularly understanding their strengths, can give students new confidence and bring fresh motivation to academic endeavors. Educating all involved of the students' legal rights is important to reduce resistance to the accommodation process.

Counseling

Counseling services may be recommended for the student-athlete as well, for many reasons. Years of thinking about oneself in a negative manner can take considerable time to change; counseling can help. Adjusting to the diagnosis and examining beliefs the students hold about their abilities and their disability may be important. Secondary anxiety and phobias around certain subject areas or test situations may have developed over the years and these anxieties respond well to therapy. Various behaviors, such as procrastination or avoidance, can be addressed in counseling also. Finally, some students may have co-morbid mood disorders or other problems that can be addressed with the help of a counselor.

Medication

For any student with attention problems, referral to a physician for medication is an important consideration. The campus student health service, team physicians, or university counseling center staff may all be able to provide names of referrals for a medication evaluation. Students often experience immediate and noticeable improvement in their ability to attend in class, to study, and stay on task with reading and writing assignments when prescribed an appropriate medication. Stimulant medications such as Ritalin, Adderall, Concerta, and Focalin, as well as some classes of antidepressants such as Wellbutrin, have been found to be helpful for many people with ADHD. Strattera is an example of a newer non-stimulant medication the student's physician may consider. Finding the right medication and the right balance for a given individual may take some trial-and-error learning and may require patience on the part of the student-athlete and the treating physician.

The student-athlete who consults with a physician and is considering stimulant medication for ADHD should definitely discuss this issue with the sports medicine staff. Policies vary from institution to institution regarding medication issues for athletes, and certainly, the assessment and documentation to show that the medication is medically necessary or medically recommended should be in place before medication therapy begins. The NCAA does grant medical exceptions for the use of stimulant medications but requires that the medical record and documentation be provided as well as evidence of on-going appropriate medical care (Koloskie, 2008; NCAA, 2007).

A Note Regarding Head Trauma and Athletes with Learning Disorders

Although every effort should be made to prevent the occurrence of concussion or traumatic brain injury for all student-athletes and to provide prompt medical attention if such injuries occur, the student-athlete with pre-existing LD may be more at risk of suffering increased neuropsychological impairments post-concussion. Collins et al. (1999) in a study of 393 athletes from four major football programs found that student-athletes with both an LD and a history of multiple concussions performed significantly more poorly on neuropsychological measures than students with only LD or only multiple concussions. Their study suggested a "detrimentally synergistic" effect of concussions for the LD athlete. Care should be taken to attend to any head injury in a serious manner for these and all student-athletes. Helping professionals should routinely inquire about any history of head trauma as part of a comprehensive intake interview.

The Case of Joe

After his first visit to the counseling center, Joe, the defensive back, was scheduled for a comprehensive evaluation. His test results demonstrated that although he was very intelligent and had particular strengths in his visual-spatial processing and non-verbal reasoning, he did have a reading disorder, with specific difficulties in phonemic awareness, as well as ADHD Inattentive Type. The counseling center psychologist helped with a referral to a psychiatrist, who prescribed an appropriate medication for him. The Office of Disability Services met with Joe and reviewed his test results. Working together, they agreed that a number of accommodations would be useful, including being seated in the front of the class, extra time on tests and reading assignments, note-taking assistance, and some on-campus tutoring through the learning center. His disability counselor assisted Joe in preparing to discuss his accommodations with faculty members and learning to be an advocate for himself without feeling embarrassed. Joe also began some bi-weekly counseling sessions and worked on changing his way of thinking about himself from "dumb, disorganized kid" to "intelligent young man with a reading disorder and ADHD." His counselor also helped Joe with identifying strategies he thought he would like to try, such as using a planner and a schedule to keep track of assignments and activities, and planning ways to use his study time better and to take frequent breaks. His spring final grades were a definite improvement. Over the summer he read some books about succeeding in college with ADHD, and he repeated one class while his tutor helped him with study and reading strategies. In the fall semester Joe's grades improved greatly, demonstrating much more what he could really do. He was well on his way to a more satisfying and successful college experience.

Summary

Today, more than in past years, helping professionals, academic support personnel, faculty, coaches, and others who work with student-athletes need to be very attentive to the academic needs of college student-athletes. Helping professionals must be aware of the most useful approaches for effectively identifying the growing number of student-athletes with suspected and diagnosed learning disabilities in a timely fashion. Those persons should also be well aware of the referral resources both on and off campus that can help those who are diagnosed to receive support services under ADA. These common challenges to learning have a pervasive impact on the general well-being, psychological well-being, and educational attainment of student-athletes in the new millennium.

References

Barkley, R. A. (1998). *Attention deficit hyperactivity disorder: A handbook for diagnosis and treatment* (2nd ed.). New York: Guilford Press.

Beilke, J., & Yssel, N. (1999). The chilly climate for students with disabilities in higher education. *College Student Journal, 33*, 364–371.

Bender, W. M. (Ed.). (1993). *Learning disabilities: Best practices for professionals*. Boston: Andover Medical Publishers.

Clark, M. (2002). Student-athletes with learning disabilities: A model for effective supports. *College Student Journal, 36*, 47–61.

Collins, M. W., Grindel, S. H., Lovell, M. R., Dede, D. E., Moser, D. J., Phalin, B. R., et al. (1999). Relationship between concussion and neuropsychological performance in college football players. *The Journal of the American Medical Association, 282*(10), 964.

Diagnostic and Statistical Manual of Mental Disorders (4th ed., text revision). (2000). Arlington, VA: American Psychiatric Association.

Henderson, C. (1992). *College freshmen with disabilities: A statistical profile.* Washington, DC: Heath Resource Center of the American Council on Education.

Hock, M. F. (1998). The effectiveness of an instructional tutoring model and tutor training on the academic performance of under-prepared college student-athletes (Doctoral dissertation, University of Kansas, 1998). *Dissertation Abstracts International,* 59, 09A, p. 3335.

Individuals with Disabilities Education Act of 1990 (IDEA), Pub. L. No. 101-476, § 602a, 20 U.S.C., 1401.

Jay, C. K. (1999). The college experience of the elite male college athlete with learning disabilities (Doctoral dissertation, University of Texas at Austin, 1999). *Dissertation Abstracts International, 60, 09A,* p. 3235.

Koloski, J. (2008). *NCAA banned drugs and medical exceptions policy.* Retrieved May 23, 2008, from http://www.ncaa.org/wps/ncaa?ContentID=1458

Lyon, G. R. (Ed.). (1994). *Frames of reference for the assessment of learning disabilities.* Baltimore: Paul H. Brooks Publishing Co.

National Collegiate Athletic Association. (2007). *2007–2008 Drug Testing Exceptions Procedures.* Retrieved May 15, 2008, from http://www.ncaa.org/wps/ncaa?ContentID=481

National Institute of Mental Health. (2006). *Attention Deficit Hyperactivity Disorder.* Retrieved May 15, 2007, from http://www.nimh.nih.gov/publicat/adhd.cfm

National Joint Committee on Learning Disabilities. (1998). Operationalizing the NJCLD definition of learning disabilities for ongoing assessment in schools. *Asha, 40* (Suppl. 18).

Palmer, C. G. (2002). College student-athletes' experience of living with attention deficit hyperactivity disorder: A phenomenological analysis (Doctoral dissertation, University of Montana, 2002). *Dissertation Abstracts International, 63,* 07A , p. 2468.

Sitlington, P. L. (2003). Postsecondary education: The other transition. *Exceptionality, 11*(2), 103–113.

Turnock, P., Rosen, L. A., & Karninski, P. L. (1998). Differences in academic coping strategies of college students who self-report high and low symptoms of attention deficit hyperactivity disorder. *Journal of College Student Development, 39*(5), 484–493.

Vogel, G., Fresko, B., & Wertheim, C. (2007). Peer tutoring for college students with learning disabilities: Perceptions of tutors and tutees. *Journal of Learning Disabilities, 40*(6), *485–493.*

Vogel, S. A. (1998). *How many adults really have learning disabilities?* Retrieved May 15, 2007, from http://www.ldonline.org/article/6014

Vogel, S. A., Leonard, F., Scales, W., Hayslip, P., Hermansen, J., & Dennells, L. (1998). The national learning disabilities postsecondary data bank: An overview. *Journal of Learning Disabilities, 31*(3), 234–247.

Vogel, S., Leyser, Y., Wyland, S., & Brulle, A. (1999). Students with learning disabilities in higher education: Faculty attitude and practices. *Learning Disabilities Research & Practice, 14*(3), 173–186.

Weyandt, L. L., Linterman I., & Rice, J. A. (1995). Reported prevalence of attentional difficulties in a general sample of college students. *Journal of Psychopathology and Behavioral Assessment, 17*(3), 293–304.

Further Resources

There are many resources, organizations, and sources of information for the student-athlete dealing with the additional challenges of a learning disability or ADHD. The following is a very brief list of some of the author's favorites.

Books

Some of the author's clients have enjoyed the following books and found them helpful:

Cole, D., and Mooney, J. (2000). *Learning outside the lines: Two Ivy League students with learning disabilities and ADHD give you the tools for academic success and educational revolution.* New York: Simon & Schuster.

Dolber, R. (1996). *College and career success for students with learning disabilities.* Lincolnwood, IL: VGM Career Horizons.

Hallowell, E. M., and Ratey, J. J. (2005). *Delivered from distraction: Getting the most out of life with attention deficit disorder.* New York: Ballantine Books.

Nadeau, K. G. (2006). *Survival guide for college students with ADHD or LD* (2nd ed.) Washington, DC: Magination Press.

Also highly recommended for university and college personnel is the following:

Quinn, P. O., Ratey, N. A., & Maitland, T. L. (2000). *Coaching college students with AD/HD: Issues and answers.* Silver Spring, MD: Advantage Books.

On-line Resources

The National Center for Learning Disabilities (www.ld.org) has an excellent website devoted to education, research, and advocacy with a mission of promoting success for people of all ages with learning disabilities.

The National Institute of Mental Health has an excellent publication on ADHD that can be found at http://www.nimh.nih.gov/health/publications/adhd/complete-publication.shtml. The article covers many topics including signs and symptoms, diagnosis, and treatments.

The ADD WareHouse is a collection of reviewed resources and can be found on-line at http://addwarehouse.com/shopsite_sc/store/html/index.html

Another goldmine of information is LDOnline found at www.ld online.org. Although the title includes only LD, the website has excellent material for ADHD students as well.

Organizations

The Learning Disabilities Association of America (www.ldanatl.org) provides many sources of support and resources, including a bookstore, videos, and many local/state chapters.

The Attention Deficit Disorder Association (ADDA, www.add.org) similarly has a multitude of resources and support services for the student with AD/HD.

15

COUNSELING INJURED AND DISABLED STUDENT-ATHLETES: A GUIDE FOR UNDERSTANDING AND INTERVENTION

Roy Tunick
Damien Clement
Edward F. Etzel

Thousands of college student-athletes are injured during practice and competition each year. Over time, the incidence of athletic injuries and related disabilities experienced by college student-athletes has been increasing. The National Collegiate Athletic Association (NCAA) confirmed this trend by reporting an average increase in the number of injuries sustained in both game and practice situations of the major revenue-producing collegiate sports (e.g., football, men's basketball, and women's basketball) from the 2003–2004 season to the 2004–2005 season (National Collegiate Athletic Association, 2006). This increase, however, has occurred despite the improvement in the quality of athletic equipment, facilities, and physical strength and conditioning methods and practices.

The aforementioned data stands in contrast to the widespread perception that athletes in general, and injured athletes in particular, are somehow "super healthy" and that injury, especially its psychological aspects, should perhaps not be a major concern of student-athletes or professionals who work with injured persons (May & Sieb, 1987). Various authors in sports medicine, counseling, and sport psychology maintain that this assumption is far from the truth (Anderson, White, & McKay, 2004; Ermler & Thomas, 1990; Etzel, Zizzi, Newcomer-Appeneal, Ferrante, & Perna, 2007; McDonald & Hardy, 1990; Meyers,

Peyton, & Jensen, 2004; Leddy, Lambert, & Ogles, 1994; Samples, 1987). Brewer, Linder, and Phelps (1995) observed that some athletes do in fact struggle psychologically as a result of athletic injury.

Mental health conditions (e.g., depression) can predispose athletes to incur injury (NCAA, 2007). Short- or long-term loss of functioning associated with an injury can have a considerable, often unrecognized, impact on student-athletes whose "livelihood," well-being, and futures depend largely upon their physical health and skills. For those who work with student-athletes (e.g., counselors, athletic trainers, and coaches), knowledge about the psychological aspects of injury and its far-reaching effects is something of great value and utility.

Today, several hundred thousand young people participate in intercollegiate athletics at universities, colleges, junior colleges, and community colleges. Among the roughly 1000 universities that belong to the NCAA alone, about 380,000 young people participate in intercollegiate athletics (National Collegiate Athletic Association, 2006). This figure translates to approximately 400 student-athletes per campus. If roughly 50% of these student-athletes are injured at some time during their time on campus, those who provide care in sports medicine and counseling services to student-athletes face the considerable challenge of attending to the psychological needs of hundreds of people with an injury or disability.

Injured student-athletes have many unmet needs as they embark upon the often uncertain road to recovery. Traditionally, athletic trainers and physicians focus on providing the necessary medical assistance needed to ensure that these athletes return to the field of play as soon as possible. Unfortunately, the psychological needs of these injured athletes are typically left unattended. Gotsch (2003) observed that attending to the psychological needs of injured student-athletes can not only assist them during the course of their rehabilitation but can also make the process meaningful, as well as decreasing overall time spent in rehabilitation.

Although some informal supportive counseling is provided by some sports medicine staff members, few are well trained to provide psychological "first aid" to injured student-athletes. Furthermore, the absence of a professional psychologist, counselor, or psychiatrist on the sports medicine staff leaves the athletic trainer as the first line of defense, for not only the physical aspects but also the psychological consequences of injury (Gotsch, 2003). Without psychological rehabilitation, many student-athletes may be unprepared to return to training and competition, feel afraid about doing so, remain vulnerable to reinjury, and demonstrate puzzling performance decrements (Etzel & Ferrante, 1993; Heil, 1993; Rotella & Heyman, 1986). Nevertheless, there are many ways that these professionals can help injured student-athletes psychologically cope with and adjust to their losses subsequent to injury and during the rehabilitation process.

The two central purposes of this chapter are: (1) to re-examine and review definitions and theoretical notions regarding the nature and consequences of injury/disability, examining psychosocial and somatopsychological aspects of injury and disability, and (2) to share and discuss various intervention strategies for helping those who work with injured and disabled college student-athletes. Hopefully, by addressing this frequently neglected topic and giving examples of such interactions, the subsequent information will assist those who work with injured student-athletes to better help them cope with their conditions.

Injury and Disability

Before proceeding much further, it seems fitting to attempt to define two key terms: (1) injury and (2) disability. Although no generally agreed-upon definitions seem to exist for both terms, a useful one is the definition of a "reportable injury" used by the NCAA's "Injury Surveillance System." An injury is considered to be a loss of physical functioning that: (1) "occurred as a result of participation in an organized intercollegiate practice or game," (2) "required medical attention by a team athletic trainer or physician," and (3) "resulted in restriction of the student-athlete's participation for one or more days beyond the day of the injury" (National Collegiate Athletic Association, 2006). As used in this chapter, injury implies that the affected person will probably return to athletic participation. Common examples of injuries viewed in this way are non-surgical sprains or strains, overuse injuries (e.g., torn rotator cuff), and mild traumatic brain injury (i.e., mild concussion).

A central term used in conjunction with injury in the literature is "disability." Here, disability will generally refer to a medically defined state or condition that imposes longer term or permanent limitations or handicaps upon an individual's independent functioning. Disability then is seen as a consequence of a student-athlete's incurring a serious injury. Moreover, disability implies that the injured individual is unable to or limited in the ability to perform various expected roles and tasks (Whitten, 1975). Injury to a paired organ (e.g., eye or kidney) and an anterior cruciate reconstruction are examples of a disabling athletic condition.

Somatopsychology and Related Psychosocial Factors

Injury and disability may not only disturb student-athletes' daily patterns of functioning, but they can also have significant psychosocial impact on those who are struggling to adjust to their changed physical condition, which is typically unexpected and unwanted. Wright (1983) referred to "variations in physique that affect the psychological situation of a person by influencing the effectiveness of this body as a tool for actions or by serving as a stimulus to himself or others" as "somatopsychological" (p. 1). Somatopsychology is a generally accepted theory that presumes somatic disturbances have an effect on one's psychological functioning. Garner (1977) identified several somatopsychic concepts relevant to injured or disabled persons. A few are presented below.

Injury Onset

Life stress research lends some support to the association between significant life stressors and onset and adjustment to injury (Bramwell, Holmes, Masuda, & Wagner, 1975; Cryan & Alles, 1983; Dunn, Smith, & Smoll, 2001; Kerr & Minden, 1988; Petrie, 1992; Williams & Andersen, 1998). Smith, Small, and Ptacek (1990) found a significant relationship between life stress and injury but only in athletes low in coping skills and social support. Therefore, athletes low in coping skills and social support have limited psychological resources available to utilize in coping with a significant life stressor (e.g., injury). Other research has not consistently supported the life stress/injury relationship with collegiate athletes (Laws-Gallen, 2001; Petrie, 1993).

Bergandi's (1985) and Williams' (2001) reviews of the literature on psychological variables relating to the risk and incidence of athletic injury support the fact that the causes of athletic injury are complex. Bergandi determined that many individual variables such as size, strength, level of conditioning, and personality characteristics, combined with the demands of a particular sport, influence the incidence of injury.

Injury Response

An individual's total personality prior to the development of the disturbed structural and physiological functioning can significantly affect the response to injury. All life experiences may be important factors influencing how one adapts and copes with the changes in physical functioning. Some of these factors may include one's developmental history, family, cultural and social experiences, motivation, level of aspiration, tolerance for stress and frustration, and self-concept. Each person will interpret the changed physical condition based on individual personality.

As an aside, the investigation of personality variables as predictors of injury has been a popular avenue of research (Anderson & Williams, 1993; Galambos, Terry, Moyle, Locke, & Lane, 2005). Overall, the research in this area does not point to any highly reliable personality predictors of injury (Rotella & Heyman, 1993; Williams & Andersen, 1998). Pargman (1993) concluded that the association of personality characteristics and injury are nebulous and far from conclusive. He indicated that "this literature, although thought-provoking, has not generated conclusions that coaches, athletes, and trainers may find useful" (p. 8). Some investigators (Ford, Eklund, & Gordon, 2000; Granito, 2001; Junge, 2000; Maddison & Prapavessis, 2005) have observed a relationship between injury and certain psychological factors (e.g., life stress, soft-mindedness, dependency, anxiety, self-concept, introversion, and risk-seeking). Although Hanson, McCulloch, and Tonymon (1992), in a well-conceived study, found support for life stress as an antecedent to injury, they found no personality variables significantly related to injury occurrence. Other researchers (Kerr & Minden, 1998; Abadie, 1976; Brown, 1971; Gover & Koppenhaver, 1965) similarly have found no significant connection between athletic injury and personality. However, some of this research suggests a causal relationship between injury and personality characteristics associated with injury or accident proneness, instead of assuming a somatopsychological relationship (i.e., the effects of bodily function or malfunction on psychological functioning; Wright, 1983). Grove and Cresswell (2007) provided some support for the usefulness of rehabilitating client personality information relative to observed links between hardiness, perfectionism, neuroticism, optimism, and explanatory style with perceptions of stress, injury appraisal, and coping with injury.

Parham (1993) suggested that an athlete's reaction to injury is often quite complex and should be studied on a continuum from mild to very serious. He further advocated that knowledge of how athletes coped with a prior injury or other unexpected life challenges may be an indication of how they will cope with their newly acquired conditions. A student-athlete's previous level of psychological functioning will likely affect his or her unique reaction to a disabling condition (Albinson & Petrie, 2003; Parham, 1993; Samples, 1987; Smith, Smoll, & Ptacek, 1990). The preinjury mental health condition of a person is often referred to as the "premorbid" personality.

The personal meaning of the disturbance caused by injury can have far-reaching implications for injury rehabilitation. One's so-called "cognitive appraisal" of the injury or disabling condition has an impact on affective response and subsequent coping behaviors during the process of healing (Henschen & Shelley, 2007). In general, the greater the severity of the physiological damage and loss of functioning, the greater the somatopsychic influences. Furthermore, it is known that we all value certain parts of our bodies more than others. Therefore, a broken thumb on a quarterback's throwing hand may have some special symbolic significance that may lead to disability disproportionate to the functional loss. It is important to realize that an individual's experience of physical loss can surpass the objective impact on an individual and can produce a different set of damages and often influence self-concept. Furthermore, the same medically defined condition can produce a separate set of psychological problems for different owners (i.e., the impact may be quite different for those who play different sports or positions). Sensitivity to the different response patterns of each student-athlete to injury is an important concept to keep in mind. Helping professionals who work with injured and disabled athletes should inquire in a timely manner about the meaning and implications of changes in physical functioning, social status, sense of self, etc.

Mental Disorders and Psychosocial Factors

The existence of a mental disorder (e.g., anxiety, depression, substance abuse) may predispose athletes to injury (National Collegiate Athletics Association, 2007). Garner (1977) pointed out that anxiety typically accompanies any injury or illness in which physical integrity and self are threatened. Blackwell and McCullagh's (1990) research with injured football players revealed that the injured athletes reported more life stress and anxiety and lower coping resources, as compared to non-injured athletes. Therefore, uncertainties about the nature, consequences, and duration of the impairment are thought to contribute to this anxiety and seemingly have the potential to exhaust the psychological resources of the sufferer.

In addition to the impact of anxiety provoking somatic difficulties on psychological functioning, injured or disabled student-athletes may also have to face an abundance of psychosocial factors in the process of dealing with their injuries/disabilities. Many student-athletes are limited in their ability to continue to participate in their usual routine of attending classes, training and competing with their team, caring for their day-to-day personal responsibilities, and carrying on with their everyday personal lives. However, the impact of injury and disability goes beyond the aforementioned physical restrictions. Other aspects of student-athletes' lives such as academics, social relations, and family relations are also affected, yet these other areas are generally not attended to by those primarily concerned about the student-athlete's physical condition.

Social Impact of Injury on the Student-athlete

In concert with the emotional sequelae experienced by the disabled or injured student-athlete, loss of functioning can have a profound social impact on the person's ability to cope with the condition. As mentioned earlier, Hardy and Crace (1993) and Hardy, Crace, and Burke (1999) asserted that social support (e.g., listening and emotional support, reality confirmation, personal assistance) provided by caring, and sometimes not-so-caring, people may have considerable ramifications for coping and healing. The student-athlete may experience a loss of social status, value strain or loss, isolation, and altered or strained interpersonal relations. Therefore, coping with an injury may result in one of the toughest interpersonal struggles an athlete in her or his late teens or early twenties may have had to confront (Silva & Hardy, 1991).

Social Status

After they have been injured, student-athletes tend to see their social status change. They often sense that they are not a part of the same world they once belonged to. Because these injured student-athletes no longer appear to serve as contributing members of the team, they may not be viewed as they were before their injuries. Removed from the day-to-day activities of the team, the injured athletes often no longer receive the same type and amount of attention from coaches and teammates, or they may be ignored altogether. The "on-the-shelf" or "down" athlete is no longer functionally a part of the team and sometimes of its social activities, unless uncommon efforts are made to keep the individual engaged and involved in team activities. This transition is often rapid and potentially demoralizing.

Injured student-athletes also stand to lose their special status among the student body and the public. Out of the limelight, they have no personal athletic exploits to discuss, no need to respond to admiring interrogatives, and no opportunity to share other customary interpersonal interactions. The injured student-athlete's relative importance to fans and the media may quickly fade as the focus of attention shifts to the new faces and numbers of replacement players. Mental health and sports medicine professionals need to be vigilant about the social transition that affects the injured or disabled student-athlete and should carefully inquire about such transitions in light of the athlete's phenomenological situation during treatment and rehabilitation (Etzel & Ferrante, 1993).

Isolation and Withdrawal

Injured student-athletes may not only be faced with perceived loss of personal value and status, but they also may be subjected to considerable social isolation associated with their new, unwanted physical status. They may struggle with mobility limitations (e.g., inability to drive or negotiate stairs) that contribute to such distancing. Isolation can be exacerbated by teammates' and coaches' avoidance of contact with the injured person. Hence athletes may feel as if they are "quarantined" from their team. The injured athlete may be viewed as somewhat of a threat to other athletes and coaches, in that the injury confronts them with their own vulnerability or uncomfortable memories of past losses. Furthermore, it may also create a situation in which the student-athlete feels "invisible," unable to make sense of the apparent rejection by those who previously valued him or her, and is consequently less likely to maintain contact (Ermler & Thomas, 1990).

An injury can drastically change the usual interaction patterns with others, because the student-athlete cannot train or compete and may not be allowed to travel with the team. Borrowing from epidemiological definitions, the aforementioned isolation can be considered contact isolation (i.e., others may avoid the injured person from a sense of felt awkwardness). Furthermore, coaches or teammates may feel uncomfortable in the presence of the athlete or may not know how to interact with the injured person. This avoidance is often a function of "out of sight, out of mind." Because the injured student-athletes are no longer a part of the team's routine activities, they are not thought about much, if at all. Therefore, others intentionally or unintentionally avoid injured student-athletes, often making them feel discounted, emotionally hurt, and alienated.

The abovementioned examples of isolation should be a concern for all those who had been in usual contact with the athlete prior to the injury. Isolation can be considered to be more externally imposed, whereas withdrawal can be considered to be a more serious internally imposed state, which could result in the athlete's retreat from other support systems and objective reality. Possible examples of withdrawal include, but are not limited to, not attending classes, not attending or complying with rehabilitation protocols (Brewer, 1998; Fisher, 1990; Fisher, Domm, & Wuest, 1988), failure to attend usual daily social occurrences such as dining, restricting oneself to an apartment/dorm room, and avoiding interaction with others. Although isolation is often a difficult state for the injured student-athlete to overcome, there are opportunities for the athlete to have access to, or initiate other mechanisms of, social support (e.g., visit training, travel to competitions). However, withdrawal is seen as more serious and needs immediate intervention. It is therefore important for those working with injured student-athletes to be aware of isolating conditions and withdrawal tendencies. Athletic trainers and trusted peers seem to be in a useful position to monitor these inclinations.

Research has shown that support provided by others is helpful in coping with life stress, mental and physical illness, and other stressors (Bone & Fry, 2006; Bone 2006; Hardy et al., 1993; Manuel 2002; Udry 2002). These authors also found that social support facilitates the recovery process in people in general and in injured athletes as well. Magyar and Duda (2000), Petersen (1997), and Rotella and Heyman

(1993) strongly advocated the need for social support as a critical element of the treatment and rehabilitation of the injured athlete.

Academic and Developmental Concerns

Injury may not only affect the individual's physical, emotional, and social functioning, but it can also have a substantial impact on the student's academic status and development. The injured student-athlete may have to confront new or ignored academic problems and changing priorities. Previously caring and accommodating instructors may now appear to be disinterested, aloof, demanding, or unsympathetic to the young person's condition. At one time, instructors may have afforded the student-athlete additional time to complete required tasks or administered examinations at different times due to unique training or travel demands, but now the instructor may not understand the need for such accommodations. Familiar training, conditioning, and studying routines are usually replaced with different schedule demands of physical rehabilitation, doctor visits, and personal care. These and other changes in routine may create additional problems such as fatigue, lack of motivation, and concentration difficulties, resulting in academic performance challenges.

Disabled student-athletes, particularly those who must cope with a lasting, serious impairment, may be forced to face developmental concerns never before considered or to face such concerns earlier than planned. Confusion about one's self, personal values, life goals, relationships with others, and dealing with ambiguity may emerge. Suddenly, life appears "telescoped," decision making appears more crucial, and academic and career choices more difficult as new concern about other areas of life beyond sport becomes much more important. If physical prowess and athletics have been emphasized over intellectual pursuits, injury/disability will probably have profound implications (Scott & Weinberg, 2001).

Furthermore, those who have "foreclosed" on their identities (Chartrand & Lent, 1987) by having counted on becoming professional athletes can find the loss of functioning potentially devastating. Career and academic goals based on physical assets now must be drastically altered by those whose academic major was "pre-NBA/NFL/MLB." This transition can be a complicated challenge for athlete-students who may be quite career immature (Kornspan & Etzel, 2003). The problem of "Who am I now that I cannot play?" often has more impact on this type of student-athlete than on one who valued and developed both physical and intellectual assets in a more pragmatic, balanced way. Therefore, it is important for those who work with student-athletes to actively encourage them to be realistic in setting long-term goals, to avoid the discouragement of not having their dreams come true.

Phases of Adjustment: A Possible Sequence of Emotional Responses

Emotional reactions to injury and disability are commonly described in terms of "stages" or "phases" of adjustment or in terms of theories of mourning or grieving as it relates to loss. Engel (1961), Kerr (1961), Kubler-Ross (1969), Schlossberg (1981), Schneider (1984), Shontz (1965), and Tunick and Tunick (1982) have characterized common psychological reactions that a disability or loss of functioning can impose on an individual's adjustment to loss. Smart (2001) has criticized the term "adjustment" and instead proposes the term "response" to describe the process the individual experiences. She further suggests that the term "response" is more encompassing, suggesting a process whereas "adjustment" implies just a psychological focus.

More specifically, it is proposed by some that only two stages of adjustment exist (McDonald & Hardy, 1990; Shontz, 1975). Others have proposed a four-phase model of injury response (Petitpas & Danish, 1995; Rose & Jeune, 1993). The process of reacting to loss is perhaps more commonly divided into five phases: (1) shock, (2) realization, (3) mourning, (4) acknowledgment, and (5) coping/reformulation (Kerr, 1961; Tunick et al., 1982). Each phase is associated with certain emotional and behavioral responses that change as an individual progresses through it. It is important to keep in mind that each person reacts to a new condition in a unique manner. Therefore, reactions may vary, resulting in some phases and behaviors not appearing at all, appearing in combination with others, or being repeated or recycled. Nevertheless, Athelstan (1981) and Ford and Gordon (1998) cautioned helpers to be sensitive to these phases and their associated behaviors so that they can be alert to the potential impact a person's psychological responses can have on his or her progress and rehabilitation.

In contrast, Brewer (1994) challenged the notion of stages of adjustment to sport injury. He noted that there is little empirical support for the claims of the various models to identify discrete emotional reactions to athletic injury by means of a stage model. Even though research has not adequately addressed the psychological reactions of injury via a stage model, Livneh and Antonak (1997) attempted to address this oversight by suggesting a three-cluster approach that involves eight phases: (1) early reactions of shock, anxiety, and denial; (2) intermediate reactions of depression, internalized anger, and externalized hostility; and (3) later reactions of acknowledgment and adjustment.

Clearly, there is a lack of consensus among researchers and theoreticians concerning the nature of the adjustment process (i.e., stages a person with an injury or disability experiences) and the empirical validation of the stage model (Brewer, 1994; Parker, Schaller, & Hansmann, 2003; Peititpas, 2002). Perhaps this reflects the reality that people respond in their own way over time. Despite this lack of accord, it is generally agreed that the disability or injury has an effect on the individual's psychological resources and the ability to cope. Hobfoll (1989) concluded that psychological stress results when either there is a loss or a threat of a loss of resources or when coping strategies provide no net resource gain. It is difficult to argue with the premise that response to disability/injury is a function of an individual's perception that includes prior coping experiences. Athletes attempt to organize their view of life on a personal basis.

Injury presents the athlete with a tough opponent—the change and/or loss of physical and psychological resources. Stage models are often inaccurately viewed as having a common sequence of discrete, stepwise emotional reactions that are predictable, having finite cognitive, behavioral, and emotional responses to a given injury or condition. It probably is inaccurate to view them in this manner.

We suggest to the reader that stage models be used as a general guideline to understand an individual's idiographic response to injury and as a basic guide for intervention. A strict adherence to a stage vision of response really can discount a client's unique experience and possibly impose conditions and expectations on recovery efforts that may not exist (Warchal & Metzger, 2005). Injured people will respond in their own ways with features associated with such stage models at certain times during recovery. They may also re-experience these things depending on the progress they make in rehabilitation, support available to them, and other biopsychosocial challenges in life they may encounter over time. Helping professionals need to monitor progressions and regressions of their individual clients/patients over time to do effective work.

The stages and experiences we believe that many injured and disabled clients will often encounter are as follows.

Shock

The shock phase is usually observed soon after an injury. Most often, shock occurs during the first few hours or days after the onset of an injury or disabling condition. The injured individual often experiences muted reactions to the condition, reacting minimally with little apparent understanding that something is physically wrong. The recently injured person may appear to be confused, dazed, numb, and/or stunned (Gunther, 1971). Further, the athlete may deny the condition or be so unaware of it that there is no noticeably demonstrated anxiety. In this state, individuals are still viewing themselves as before the injury, rejecting all incongruence between body and function. The sudden onset, unexpectedness, and seriousness of the athletic injury may intensify the shock reaction.

During this phase, injured student-athletes may reject the assistance of a concerned counselor, athletic trainer, or physician because they view such help as unnecessary. If the defense of denial is being used by the injured person, as it frequently is, helpers should be prepared to feel quite frustrated. Indeed, as Nideffer (1983) told us, it is very hard to develop a working relationship with a person who is avoidant or even laughs at you. Livneh (1991) suggested that individuals react this way in an attempt to direct their psychological resources inward as an effort to salvage the self from a sense of disintegration. Therefore, in such situations, the sport counselor/psychologist may do well to offer little more than friendly support and the willingness to be helpful when needed. Unfortunately, counseling interventions during this phase may have little observable impact on the student-athlete who is now a patient. The helper should be primarily concerned with establishing rapport with the injured person to build a foundation for possible future interventions.

Indeed, this was the response of a student-athlete who had just incurred her second anterior cruciate ligament tear within a few weeks. She voiced little concern and her affect was "flat" as she sat and watched practice. Although her athletic trainer had encouraged her to speak with the school's sport psychologist, she said there was really no need to. Sensing the athlete's perspective, the sport psychologist was content to spend a little time talking, without discussing the injury or the athlete's feelings. He occasionally ran into the player in the training room and at practice for very brief periods of time over the next two weeks. Nearly three weeks later, the injured athlete called for an appointment to meet concerning her situation.

Although this may be a common reaction pattern, it is possible that a needy student-athlete may be quite receptive to assistance during this phase and, consequently, there will be a relative absence of the intense emotionality that is usually confronted in latter phases. It has been our experience that female athletes respond this way more frequently than males. Yet again, it is important to remember that each injured person's response will be unique and that readiness to seek support will vary from person to person.

Realization

In the realization phase, the injured person begins to realize that something is probably wrong. The student-athlete is often confronted with physical limitations and in rare cases mortality—something college-age people typically are not prepared for or accustomed to facing. This realization is usually accompanied by anxiety and in some cases even panic, anger, and depression. It is important to appreciate that in the person's mind, and very often in reality, the injury may create a seemingly insurmountable barrier to leading a "normal life," as the individual begins to recognize that independent functioning and athletic participation are compromised.

The needy student-athlete progressing through this phase may express anger toward others for his or her inability to be cured quickly. At times, the injured person may make statements such as "When I'm well . . ." and "When I get finished with my treatment . . . I am going to . . ." Implicit in these messages is a sense of striving toward goals that were embraced prior to the acquired condition, goals that presuppose a normally functioning body. The astute clinician should be sensitive to the possibility of this anger turning inward, resulting in the person's experiencing a variety of depressive symptoms. For example, an irritated football player who had incurred a career-ending knee injury spoke of petitioning the NCAA for an impossible fifth year of athletic eligibility with his counselor.

During this phase, the injured or disabled student-athlete also may be quite fearful. Helpers need to acknowledge and accept such fear and demonstrate that they will be there for the person when times are tough. Well-intended, but by and large not useful, statements from "well-wishers" such as, "Don't worry, things are bound to get better soon" should be avoided. Instead, it will be more useful to recognize the seriousness of the problem and the injured person's intense reaction to the condition with empathic statements such as, "I realize that this is a scary time for you because you don't know what to expect, but I will help you work with difficulties as they come up. . . . I cannot promise you a miracle, but I can promise you help when you want it." Helpers should be accepting of the student-athlete and attempt to normalize the person's experience when it is appropriate.

Depression and Anger

The depression and anger phase is often characterized by intense distress, reactive depression, and internalized anger (Kerr, 1961; Livneh, 1991; Tracey, 2003). Overwhelmed, the injured/disabled individual may feel hopeless and helpless. The finality of what has been lost has fully entered the person's consciousness. The student-athlete, especially the seriously injured or disabled person, is often convinced that all has been lost and that there is no possibility to achieve life-long ambitions (e.g., participating in a sport engaged in for some time; playing professional sports). The implications of the injury or disability have spread or "metastasized" to several life functions and aspirations. Depression and suicidal ideation and talk are common, and they must be inquired about and attended to by qualified clinicians. Those who are not trained to deal with these reactions should quickly refer the athlete to professionals who are.

Post injury, the disabled athlete's ability to tap available sources of support to cope often waivers or dissipates. As noted above, the student-athlete may avoid contact with others normally associated with, may become uncommunicative, and may even resist treatment as the physical and psychological battle against the condition appears to be a losing one, or even to have been lost. It is important that the astute helper emphasize client personal resources and strengths in an effort to empower the athlete as a personal agent of change in the adjustment to loss and altered status.

During this phase, athletic staff, peers, and others should avoid being critical. Statements such as, "Stop feeling sorry for yourself" or "Tough it out," sometimes said by others, are counter-productive. Statements like these tend to make the individual more introspective and demonstrate to the injured person that indeed others do not understand the situation. Instead, those trying to assist the distressed person need to listen carefully and reflectively, ask open-ended questions, provide consistent support, empathy, and encouragement, and disseminate small doses of accurate information, if known. The purposes of such efforts are to provide emotional and informational social support to the client and to gradually change the "figure-ground relationship" between what can no longer be done and what the person is still capable of at that point in time. Professionals are encouraged to "think small" and to attempt simple interventions, first based on reasonable assumptions (Friedman & Fanger, 1991).

Acknowledgment

In the acknowledgment phase, the injured student-athlete begins to come to grips with the loss of functioning by gradually appreciating the nature of the loss and its associated limitations and implications. These limitations may include the physical, personal, social, familial, vocational, and economic ramifications of the injury (Gunther, 1971). Depression and anxiety may continue to be experienced. The depressed person, particularly someone who has incurred a severe injury and/or endured prolonged hospitalization, may still experience loss of control, choices, independence, and perceived changes in or loss of identity (Greif & Matarazzo, 1982).

It is often mistakenly assumed that depression during the phase of acknowledgment is a necessary prerequisite for adjustment. That is, if depression does not occur the person will never adequately or completely adjust to the condition. Although depression during the acknowledgment phase often occurs, it is not necessarily experienced by everyone, nor is it a prerequisite for adjustment. In some cases, the athlete may experience a sense of relief from the rigors of participation, as the condition presents a time out or, if the injury/disability is career-ending, provides a graceful exit from sport.

Another common feature of this phase is an over-reliance on others for help accomplishing tasks the athletes can likely perform themselves. Here too, the counselor/sport psychologist must listen carefully to the athlete, encourage activities that will likely be self-reinforcing, help identify and call attention to personal resources and progress, as well as allow for the exploration of as many choices as possible (Greif & Matarazzo, 1982). Encouraging the injured student-athlete to assume reasonable personal responsibility and giving the individual the opportunity to do so are important strategies in this phase of recovery. Furthermore, increasing the student-athlete's social contact (i.e., the frequency and variety of visitations from others) may be helpful in working through this stage. This stage reflects the initiation of a restored equilibrium and is characterized by a balance of the individual's internal and external energy investment (Livneh, 1991).

Coping and Reformulation

The coping and reformulation phase normally occurs after some degree of resolution of the injury/disability has occurred. Schneider (1984) stated that this resolution often liberates energy that was once tied to the past. Now the energy is available to broaden personal awareness in ways perhaps never before entertained (e.g., new personal, academic, or occupational interests and options). For example, an athlete may consider quitting participating in sport or change academic majors because more time is available for school than when participating in athletics. Having learned to cope with any residual limitations that may remain, student-athletes reassert themselves emotionally. Having worked through the loss, the person is ready to get on with life. Cognitive reconciliation, with the effects of the injury and its implications for the future, has begun to be assimilated, and the individual has reached the final phase of the coping process (Livneh, 1991).

In this phase, the injury or disability remains mostly in "ground" (i.e., in the background of awareness) as the injured person does not continually attend to the limitations (if any) imposed by the condition. However, at times, the injury/disability may reemerge into "figure" (i.e., becomes the focus of awareness). This regression may be prompted, for example, when the student-athlete sees someone injured in person or on television, encounters a similarly injured person in the training room, or is personally somehow re-injured. When this happens, the student-athlete must face the loss and any related limitations once again. Consequently, the student-athlete may re-experience emotional distress upon being reminded of the past loss and associated experiences.

Reluctance to train or compete, which may involve considerable anxiety even to a phobic degree, and anticipated performance decrements on the part of those who continue to train and perform are sometimes observed. Realistic fears about re-injury typically underlie such responses and may be difficult to overcome. Although they seem irrational to coaches and athletic trainers when the athlete has been cleared to return to training, such fears are very real for the student-athlete and should not be discounted by others. Regardless of the irrationality of the fears, helpers must work to appreciate what the student-athlete is experiencing and work with that person to help overcome the problem. Hopefully, at this stage, the person will utilize experience and personal resources to make the duration of these responses brief. If not, return to play is a dysphoric path.

It is important for the counselor/sport psychologist to help student-athletes normalize these anxieties and regressions so that they can be seen as what they are. That is, anxieties and regressions are to be expected and do not reflect poorly on the person's ability to cope, character, or self-worth. It is also critical for the counselor to avoid using language like, "You need to accept your disability." Thorenson and Kerr (1978) cautioned us to discontinue using terms like "acceptance" when working with persons who are disabled, because the communication has intrinsically derogating aspects. Heil (1993) further recommended that professionals help athletes deal with any fears, appreciate their adaptive value, teach them about the relationship between arousal and fear, emphasize progress that has been made, provide reassurance about the useful nature of any pain experienced, help them recognize safe limits of performance, and consider the use of mental training interventions (e.g., imagery, p.173).

Given the opportunity, counselors/sport psychologists can help educate coaches, teammates, and athletic trainers about the language to use around injured student-athletes. Statements commonly voiced by coaches and teammates like, "Tough it out," or "Suck it up," as well as questions about the person's "giving 100%" are clearly not useful. Rotella and Heyman (1993) pointed out that sport leaders, coaches in particular, need to know that it is essential to make injured athletes feel cared for and important, not as if they are worth less than they were when they were fully functioning. During this critical period, such influential people can foster or destroy trust and confidence by their treatment of the injured. Sport leaders must never ignore or discourage injured or disabled student-athletes.

Intervention—Application of the Transtheoretical Model to Counseling Injured and Disabled Athletes

Much of the chapter, thus far, has focused on the emotional and social impact of injury/disability. However, relatively little emphasis has been placed on the impending rehabilitation regimen into which these student-athletes are usually ushered after the treatment phase of injury process has been completed. Ideally, sport medicine professionals expect that injured/disabled student-athletes will be "ready" for this phase of the recovery process. Although this is true in most situations, depending on the severity of the injury and the time of the season in which the injury/disability was sustained, athletes enter this phase of recovery in varying degrees of readiness to initiate their rehabilitation programs.

Clement and Ostrow (2005) postulated that this varying degree of readiness could possibly be determined via the use of the transtheoretical model (TTM) initially developed by Prochaska and DiClemente (1983). Furthermore, given its previous reported use in investigating how individuals adapt to new behaviors such as exercise (Herrick, Stone, & Mettler, 1997; Marcus, Banspach, Leefebvre, et al., 1992; Prochaska, Velicer, Rossi, et al., 1994) the TTM seems to be quite applicable to rehabilitation since injured/disabled athletes must adapt to and engage in new behaviors (i.e., attending their rehabilitation programs instead of previously normal activities). Wong (1998) stated that athletes "who are about to commence rehabilitation most often experience a change in their pre-injury daily routine" (p. 45).

Prochaska and DiClemente (1983) defined processes of change as the techniques and strategies employed by individuals as they move through the aforementioned stages. These processes can be categorized as either experiential or behavioral. Experiential processes primarily focus on the individual's awareness and the feelings experienced while embarking on the behavior change. Behavioral processes, on the other hand, refer to the overt activities that an individual will engage in during the course of behavior modification.

Self-efficacy is another construct that is linked to the TTM. Self-efficacy refers to the confidence people have in their ability to perform or engage in a behavior (Bandura, 1977). It is assumed that for people to engage in change (e.g., making lifestyle adaptation in response to a career-ending injury) they must believe they are capable of doing so. Helping professionals should encourage discussion about client assumptions and beliefs regarding change, as that may lead to useful or effective choices (Fisher, 1999). Self-efficacy can be fostered by engaging the client in the discovery of a range of possible change solutions, as well as recognition of past and recent successes (Gorski, 2007).

A third "common sense" approach associated with the TTM is "decisional balance," derived from the decision making model of Janis and Mann (1977). Decisional balance is a logical process in which clients examine the pros and cons of behavioral options associated with choices they may need to make before embarking on a new behavior (e.g., counseling) or path (e.g., alternative academic major selection).

Udry, Shelbourne, and Gray (2003) investigated the application of the TTM within the rehabilitation context. In their study prior to anterior cruciate ligament (ACL) surgery, patients were assessed using the TTM. Athletes who were considered ready for their impending surgery reported high levels of self-efficacy, more pros than cons with regards to their surgery, and the use of more behavioral rather than experiential processes linked to change. Thus, it appears that assessment of an athlete's stage of change status could be generally useful to the rehabilitation process, in particular with injuries requiring a longer period of rehabilitation.

Practical Uses of the Transtheoretical Model with Injured and Disabled Athletes

Prior to beginning their rehabilitation programs, injured athletes could be assessed via the different aspects of the TTM (stages of change, processes of change, self-efficacy and decision balance; Clement & Ostrow,

2005). Sports medicine staff such as athletic trainers could be trained to administer these instruments. However, the scoring and interpretation should be done by another appropriately trained professional.

The literature suggests that injured individuals can benefit from the introduction and application of various cognitive strategies to facilitate advancement in their readiness to commence their rehabilitation program (Marcus & Forsyth, 2003). This seems particularly useful when an athlete appears to be in an early stage of change, reports using more experiential versus behavioral processes of change, produces low self-efficacy ratings, and perceives more cons than pros regarding impending rehabilitation. Some of the strategies that can be utilized by sports medicine staff to help such an individual include educating the athlete about the rehabilitation process, helping the individual grasp the benefits of consistently and efficiently participating in rehabilitation, and informing the individual of the inherent risks of not participating in rehabilitation (Clement & Ostrow, 2005). These strategies may have to be delivered more than once over multiple sessions before the injured athlete can utilize the information. Sports medicine professionals need to be mindful that change and movement within the stages of change take time and that many possible progressions and regressions can occur. Marcus and Forsyth (2003) suggested that injured individuals can also benefit from the introduction and application of behavioral strategies prior to commencing their rehabilitation programs. These strategies are more applicable to individuals who have been deemed advanced in the stages of change, i.e., report using more behavioral versus experiential processes of change, have high self-efficacy ratings, and perceive more pros than cons with respect to their impending rehabilitation. Some strategies that can be utilized by athletic trainers and others to help such an individual include: (1) encouraging the athlete to implement a system of goal setting within the rehabilitation program; (2) encouraging athletes to self-monitor rehabilitation progress; and (3) fostering connections among athletes with similar injuries at different stages of their rehabilitation so they can continue to be a source of support for one another (Clement & Ostrow, 2005).

Implications for Helpers

Clearly, injury and disability can have numerous, sometimes profound effects on a student-athlete's psychosocial and academic functioning and future. Injured student-athletes, like other people who experience changes in physical functioning, have many well-wishers during the early phases of their condition. However, as the injury and the recovery period continue, fewer and fewer people make such valuable contact. This often results in a pronounced feeling of isolation and resentment by the student-athlete. Recommendations for those professionals who provide consultation to injured student-athletes, including sports medicine staff, coaches, sport counselors, and psychologists are provided below.

Sports Medicine Staff

Sports medicine professionals (e.g., team physicians, athletic trainers, student athletic trainers) are in a unique position because they interact with student-athletes regularly and some almost exclusively in the early phases of injury. In particular, athletic trainers are the "front line" of helpers and perhaps the people that athletes trust the most on staff. From the start, all members of the sports medicine staff need to provide realistic, concrete information to the injured person regarding the severity of injury, potential and assumed limitations of the injury, the likelihood of a full recovery, and a time line, as well as information on treatment plans. Sports medicine staff must be aware that these issues may need to be addressed repeatedly, because of the disabled athlete's frequent inability to appreciate the implications of the injury at various stages of adjustment and varying stages of change in condition. These professionals not only must be competent medically but, just as importantly, they must also possess excellent interpersonal skills.

Furthermore, sports medicine staff should avoid or disown two common misconceptions: (1) student-athletes are somehow well equipped to cope with their newly acquired condition, and (2) they are somehow more likely than nonathletes to recover fully from a serious injury because of their exceptional premorbid physical condition. The second misconception, in particular, can potentially encourage mistreatment of the athlete, in that one could easily miss or dismiss unusual cognitive, behavioral, and emotional changes in the athlete associated with the adjustment process as being "just not like that person." The injured student-athlete's need for psychological assistance must not be overlooked.

Another recommendation for sports medicine professionals is that, whenever possible, treatment be provided within an athlete's customary environment. When the condition allows for this to be done, the injured person has the opportunity to continue to interact with peers in a familiar setting, thus reducing the sense of isolation from others. Striegel, Hedgpeth, and Sowa (1996) and Weiss and Troxel (1986) suggested the concept of peer modeling to help combat this sense of isolation. Peer modeling involves pairing an injured athlete with another athlete who has successfully recovered from a similar injury. It is believed that through the sharing of the general rehabilitation experience, as well as rehabilitation successes and setbacks, the injured athlete may obtain some realism about the situation. Ermler and Thomas (1990) also recommended providing variability and choices of treatments whenever possible, which can foster a sense of athlete involvement in the healing process and thereby possibly reduce the sense of isolation. In addition, they suggested that athletic trainers avoid treating injured athletes in separate areas; when it is appropriate, continue to conduct strength training for uninjured body parts; and utilize alternative training equipment in order to enhance the athlete's involvement. Setting specific, realistic, short-term rehabilitation goals is also seen as helpful, because they can increase the injured athlete's sense of personal investment and potential satisfaction with the process of recovery (DePalma & DePalma, 1989; Evans & Hardy, 2002).

Athletic trainers almost certainly have more opportunities to interact with injured student-athletes than do any other sports medicine professionals. These high-frequency interactions sometimes allow student athletic trainers to gain additional insight into the athletes' struggles as well as increased awareness about injured student-athletes' psychological make-up (Moulton et al., 1997). As a result, they can use this time not only to treat the student-athlete physically but also to be alert to changes in the student-athlete's psychological status. Athletic trainers, as previously mentioned, serve as the "first line of defense in the identification of psychological conditions" (Ray & Wiese-Bjornstal, 1999, p. 9), thus placing them in the ideal situation of being able to make timely referrals to on-campus mental health professionals or external consultants to promote athletes' psychological well-being.

As we have suggested earlier, sports medicine staff should be very careful when communicating with injured student-athletes. Communication needs to take place in a way that ensures that the injured student-athlete is as receptive as possible and accurately understands the information being delivered by the sport medicine professional. Kahanov and Fairchild (1994) reported significant discrepancies in what athletes understood about their injuries as told to them by their athletic trainers. In those cases, athletic trainers perceived athletes to have understood the information much more accurately than the student-athletes actually did.

Athletic trainers also should avoid communicating negative, judgmental attitudes regarding athletes' conditions or efforts or perhaps discouragement with their behavior or progress, by avoiding statements that convey disability, disappointment, or inferiority. For example, phrases such as, "Move your bad knee," "Lift your broken hand," or "Push off with your good foot," may serve to communicate an unhelpful message to the athlete regarding his or her condition. Alternatively, specific language such as, "Move your left knee," does not convey a judgment about the athlete's condition. Another, more nonverbal, approach involves the athletic trainer placing a hand on the athlete's body part and asking the person to move that particular part of the body during an exercise.

As noted above, athletic trainers can also assist the injured person by providing concrete information concerning the prescription of treatment, realistic rate of recovery, changes in range of motion, and any somatosensory experiences that may occur during treatment. This information should be provided in a manner that is easily understood by the injured athlete, with limited use of athletic training/medical jargon. This can help reduce the anxiety the injured student-athlete experiences. Sports medicine staff should also be realistic in communicating about what to expect from a forthcoming treatment intervention. They should avoid phrases such as, "This shouldn't hurt much," when pressure and some pain are the usual reaction and expected response.

Sports medicine professionals should be reasonably adept at identifying clients who would likely benefit from psychological consultation and at making referrals to mental health professionals. Although some are inclined, comfortable, and skilled at this process, it appears many are not, or they are reluctant to do so. Useful guidance on how to make such referrals is readily available (see Andersen & Tod, 2006). Sports medicine staff who may need assistance may wish to consult with referral personnel on- and off-campus about ways to effectively do so.

Coaches

As teachers, parental figures, and sometimes disciplinarians, coaches have many direct and indirect influences on the injured/disabled student-athlete. When a student-athlete is hurt, the coach is in a position to facilitate or hinder the adjustment process of the athlete to the impairment. Understandably, the coach must be concerned about and responsible for more than one athlete. However, injured student-athletes need to know from coaches that they are still part of the team or "family" even though injury has changed their ability to function as before. The coach needs to act as an advocate for the athlete and demonstrate that the coaching staff is concerned about the student as a person and not just as a performer.

Many simple actions on the part of the coach can go a long way toward communicating concern and serve as a helpful source of social support. Merely going onto the field or court with athletic trainers when a person is injured is an important initial gesture that many coaches unfortunately eschew. Other ways in which to assist student-athletes in their adjustment process are for coaches to involve them as resources for other athletes and to have them attend practices and competitions on the bench or sidelines with their teammates. Coaches can also use injured athletes' presence at practices and competitions as a means of obtaining valuable feedback about sessions and strategies being used (Pargman, 2007). The coach should also encourage the athlete to continue physical rehabilitation activities, emphasizing that the most important function an injured athlete serves is to "commit to an effective rehabilitation program, thus facilitating a timely return to the team" (Hardy, Burke, & Crace, 1999, p. 190). Coach encouragement for the use of counseling and sport psychology services can also be supportive of the athlete in the short and long run.

Avoiding injured athletes appears to be rather common but is certainly not useful practice. The longer the coach and/or the sport staff keep away from or neglect the injured athlete, the greater the likelihood the athlete will feel devalued and isolated. Athlete clients who have experienced this distancing also report feeling confused, angry, and discounted by coaches they previously trusted. At the very least, a busy head coach should instruct his assistant coaches, graduate assistants, and non-injured team members to make periodic contact with the student-athlete in order to assess his or her progress and express the staff's interest. For the most part, the coach or an assistant coach usually has some time and the means with which to make at least brief periodic contact with injured student-athletes to update their physical and emotional status. Just spending a few minutes with them and asking how they are progressing can go a long way.

The Sport Counselor/Psychologist

A sport counselor/psychologist can be a helpful person to call upon to assist the student-athlete either after an injury, in particular a serious one, or during rehabilitation (e.g., when emotional disturbance is observed or when the student-athlete does not seem to respond well to treatment), or when return-to-play issues exist. Although sports medicine professionals are typically interested in the assistance that sport counselors/psychologists can provide, the mental health professionals are often persons of last resort. However, as noted earlier, the sport counselor/psychologist should ideally be involved with the injured student-athlete as early as possible in the injury and recovery process. This allows the professional to be in a position of support and guidance for the injured student-athlete throughout the rehabilitation process.

Sport counselors/psychologists need to be aware that they may have limited time in which to impact the injured student-athlete due to the athlete's reluctance to make or show up for an appointment as a result of initial denial, doubt, anxiety, shame, or coach/peer rejection of psychological interventions and other barriers to assisting student-athletes (see Chapter 1). Regardless of the time available to meet with an injured student-athlete, we believe that it is critical to create a therapeutic environment that establishes trust, begins to rapidly advance the student-athlete's well-being, helps the individual to recognize the potential to change, and encourages positive outcomes. Moreover, it is important for helpers to avoid having preconceived notions about what student-athletes may be thinking, feeling, or may need and thereby imposing "therapeutic agendas" on them. Sport counselors/psychologists need to meet athletes where they are at.

The sport counselor/psychologist should resist the temptation to try to rescue, cure, or "solve everything." Instead, we encourage care-givers to make a "paradigm shift," that is, one that focuses on solutions and possibilities, current coping resources, and personal assets rather than on problems or "what's wrong" (Friedman & Fanger, 1991). From this "possibility" perspective, professionals work to engage the student-athlete in the process of adapting to "normal" reactions to loss of functioning and life change. Professionals utilizing this approach are active, flexible, and practical. Further, they work to initiate and maintain small changes with the help of any available sources of social support (e.g., athletic trainers, family members, teammates, and partners) to foster client hope.

When timely, the sport counselor/psychologist needs to encourage student-athletes to express themselves both affectively and cognitively concerning their rehabilitation. The meaning and implications that loss may have for them should be explored. The injured person may need to consider aspects of life outside of athletics including school, relationships, and avocational interests that can have an impact on the adjustment process.

Although previous decision making may have been avoided or ignored, the injured student-athlete's life has been abruptly disturbed. The individual may now be in the position of having to confront many life decisions at, it may seem to the athlete, an accelerated pace. The sport counselor/psychologist is well suited to assist the injured athlete in reframing the crisis of loss as an opportunity for challenge and growth. By helping the disabled individual cope and readjust, the sport psychologist can help move the disability from "figure" to "ground," thus allowing the injured athlete to view what is happening in a more realistic, healthy light.

Berg and Miller (1992) also emphasized a solution-focused approach to counseling and suggest five basic, but useful, techniques that are geared toward helping the individual identify coping resources, establish possible solutions, and construct or reframe future directions. These paths of inquiry are also part of "motivational interviewing" (Gorski, 2007; Miller & Rollnick, 2002). They suggest that counselors/psychologists assist the injured athlete by using the following techniques. Highlight pre-session change by asking questions that attempt to have the individual acknowledge his or her coping and psychological resources (e.g., a question such as, "Tell me what positive changes you have noticed since you have requested an appointment").

This may facilitate an athlete's self-exploration. The counselor is also urged to look for exceptions in an attempt to identify the athlete's psychological/coping resources (e.g., a question like, "Tell me about those times when things are going well for you"). This encourages the athlete to reframe the current situation and place the injury into "ground" and coping resources in "figure."

The use of the "miracle question" is advocated to try to establish direction and generate hope (e.g., a question like, "Imagine that a miracle would happen. Your problems are gone. What would life be like for you?"). This technique strives to have the injured athlete identify current and future goals and values. The use of scaling questions is also advocated to assist the injured athlete in perceiving the situation in a more objective manner (e.g., a question like, "On a scale from 1 to 10, how are you managing since your injury?"). The last technique is referred to as the "coping question" (e.g., "How have you been able to cope with your condition?"). This type of question suggests that the athlete explore and identify coping or adaptive mechanisms while deemphasizing succumbing behaviors.

From time to time, resistant or uncooperative athletes who do not want to become involved in physical treatment or counseling may be referred to the sport counselor/psychologist. Unfortunately, these people are often dismissed as unmotivated and untreatable, thus absolving others of responsibility in their treatment. The resistant person's problem often lies within the framework of interpersonal and environmental influences. Some of these determinants may involve conflicting pressures from coaches, peers, athletic trainers, physicians, and parents. Other factors may consist of obstacles such as time requirements for physical rehabilitation and a demanding course of study. Cognitive limitations can contribute to resistance brought about by stress, affecting the student-athlete's ability to concentrate, comprehend, or execute appropriate expected behaviors, resulting in actions and moods that appear to be uncooperative, resistant, or based in precontemplation/shock. Then too, the student-athlete may be resistant because he or she does not understand the purpose and meaningfulness of recommended treatments and, therefore, does not become involved in or complete them. This may be more of an obstacle in problem-oriented treatment as opposed to a solution-oriented approach.

In order to work effectively with an injured person, various strategies need to be employed. First, a positive relationship between the student-athlete and the sport psychologist must be developed, providing the student-athlete with realistic support, encouragement, and reinforcement. Second, it is important that the student-athlete understand the rationale for suggested treatment approaches. Such information needs to be dispensed in small bits and reviewed often. Third, the student-athlete should have clear guidelines as to what must be done, what can realistically be expected from treatment, and what is expected of him or her. Fourth, a well-organized daily, weekly, and monthly schedule needs to be developed so that the student-athlete can have a reasonable routine to follow and look forward to, thus providing environmental structure and security for the athlete. Lastly, the sport psychologist needs to help appropriately normalize the athlete's emotional responses to the condition, communicating to the athlete that what he or she is experiencing is consistent with what others have also weathered. The clinically trained sport counselor/psychologist can serve as an especially useful resource for everyone concerned.

An involved helping professional could help model this process and promote the importance of contact by coaches after injury and during recovery. Indeed, spending some time regularly to visit the athletic training room or to chat with injured athletes on the sideline can be an influential, supportive endeavor. Contact with teammates and other athletes not only helps the injured person but can also assist others confront their own vulnerability.

Summary

In this chapter, the authors have attempted to address the common psychosocial consequences related to the acquisition of and response to an injury and/or disabling condition and provided suggestions about how to provide consultation to student-athlete clients who have been injured within the milieu of intercollegiate athletics. Research about the stages of adjustment to injury has painted an inconsistent picture of reaction patterns. However we believe that, in response, a solution-based approach to counseling and the TTM, a well-researched and highly utilized model can be incorporated into the rehabilitation process to increase sports medicine professionals' understanding of the obstacles to behavior change and may help them in assisting athletes to recover holistically. Sports medicine professionals, coaches, and mental health professionals who work with collegiate athletes also need to be mindful that injured or disabled persons reflect varying degrees of readiness and eventual compliance with their rehabilitation programs. More practitioner-driven research using both quantitative and qualitative designs may provide the field with some interesting questions and additional research directions in working with and understanding the injured or disabled athlete.

Some fundamental factors regarding this chapter need to be highlighted. Clearly, without psychological rehabilitation, many student-athletes may be unprepared to return to training and competition, feel afraid about doing so, remain vulnerable to re-injury, and demonstrate puzzling performance decrements (Etzel et al., 2007; Heil, 1993; Rotella & Heyman, 1993). An injured athlete's total premorbid personality prior to injury affects the response to that condition. Moreover, all life experiences may be important factors that influence how one is affected by injury. The personal meaning of the disturbance can have far-reaching implications for injury rehabilitation and should be explored. In general, the greater the severity of the physiological damage and loss of functioning, the greater the somatopsychic influences. It is important to realize that an individual's experience of physical loss can surpass the objective impact on an individual and can produce a different set of damages and often influence self-concept. Additionally, the same medically defined condition can produce a separate set of psychological problems for different student-athletes. Sensitivity to the different response patterns of each student-athlete to injury is an important concept to keep in mind.

Typically, anxiety accompanies any injury or illness in which physical integrity is threatened (Garner, 1977). It is important to keep in mind that each person reacts to a new condition in a unique manner. Therefore, reactions may vary, resulting in some phases and behaviors not appearing at all, appearing in combination with others, or being repeated or recycled.

It is important for helpers to avoid having preconceived notions about what student-athletes may be thinking, may be feeling, or may need and thereby imposing "therapeutic agendas" on them. Helpers need to work with athletes where the athletes are and not where helpers may want them to be.

Sport counselors/psychologists should resist the temptation to try to rescue, cure, or "solve everything." They also need to be aware that they may have limited time in which to have an impact on the injured athlete. Finally, we encourage counselors/psychologists, when working with injured student-athletes, to focus on solutions and possibilities, current coping resources, and personal assets, rather than solely concentrating on what is wrong.

References

Abadie, D. A. (1976). *Comparison of the personalities of non-injured and injured athletes in intercollegiate competition.* Dissertation Abstracts, *15(2)*, 82.

Albinson, C. B., & Petrie, T. A. (2003). Cognitive appraisals, stress, and coping: Pre-injury and postinjury factors influencing psychological adjustment to sport injury. *Journal of Sport Rehabilitation, 12*, 306–322.

Andersen, M., & Tod, D. (2006). When to refer athletes for counseling and psychotherapy. In J. Williams (Ed.), *Applied sport psychology: Person growth to peak performance* (pp. 483–504). Champaign, IL: Human Kinetics.

Andersen, M. B., & Williams, J. M. (1988). A model of stress and athletic injury: Prediction and prevention. *Journal of Sport and Exercise Psychology, 10*, 294–306.

Anderson, A. G., White, A., & McKay, J. (2004). Athletes' emotional responses to sport injury. In D. Lavallee & M. Jones (Eds.), *Coping and emotion in sport* (pp. 211–224). Hauppauge, NY: Nova Science Publishers.

Athelstan, G. T. (1981). Psychosocial adjustment to chronic disease and disability. In W. C. Stover & M. R. Clower (Eds.), *Handbook of severe disability* (pp. 13–18). Washington, DC: U.S. Government Printing Office.

Bandura, A. (1977). Self efficacy: Towards a unifying theory of behavior change. *Psychology Reviews, 84*, 191–215.

Berg, I. K., & Miller, S. D. (1992). *Working with the problem drinker: A solution-focused approach.* New York: W. W. Norton.

Bergandi, T. A. (1985). Psychological variables relating to the incidence of athletic injury. *International Journal of Sport Psychology, 16*(2), 141–149.

Blackwell, B., & McCullagh, P. (1990). The relationship of athletic training to life stress, competitive anxiety, and coping resources. *Athletic Training, 25*, 23–27.

Bone, J. B. (2006). The influence of injured athletes' perceptions of social support from ATCs on their beliefs about rehabilitation. *Journal of Sport Rehabilitation, 15*, 156–167.

Bone, J. B., & Fry, M. (2006). The influence of injured athletes' perception of social support from athletic trainers on their beliefs about rehabilitation. *Journal of Sport Rehabilitation, 15*, 156–169.

Bramwell, S., Holmes, T., Masuda, M., & Wagner, N. (1975). Psychosocial factors in athletic injuries: Development and application of the social and athletic readjustment scale (SAARS). *Journal of Human Stress, 1*, 6–20.

Brewer, B. (1994). Review and critique of models of psychological adjustment models to athletic injury. *Journal of Applied Sport Psychology, 6*, 87–100.

Brewer, B., Linder, B., & Phelps, C. (1995). Situational correlates of emotional adjustment to athletic injury. *Clinical Journal of Sport Medicine, 5*, 241–245.

Chartrand, J., & Lent, R. (1987). Sports counseling: Enhancing the development of the student-athlete. *Journal of Counseling & Development, 66*, 167.

Clement, D., & Ostrow, A. (2005). *Psychological readiness: Is this assessment valuable to athletic trainers in understanding athletes' adherence and compliance?* Unpublished master's thesis. West Virginia University.

Cryan, P. O., & Alles, E. F. (1983). The relationship between stress and football injuries. *Journal of Sports Medicine and Physical Fitness, 23*, 52–58.

DePalma, M. T., & DePalma, B. (1989). The use of instruction and the behavioral approach to facilitate injury rehabilitation. *Athletic Training, 24*, 217–219.

Dunn, E. C., Smith, R, E., & Smoll, F. L. (2001). Do sport-specific stressors predict athletic injury? *Journal of Science and Medicine in Sport, 4*, 283–291.

Engel, G. (1961). Is grief a disease?: A challenge for medical research. *Psychosomatic Medicine, 23*, 18–27.

Ermler, K. L., & Thomas, C. E. (1990). Intervention for the alienating effects of injury. *Athletic Training, 25*(3), 269–271.

Etzel, E., Zizzi, S., Newcomer-Appeneal, R., Ferrante, A. P., & Perna, F. (2007). Providing psychological assistance to injured and disabled college student-athletes. In D. Pargman (Ed.), *Psychological bases of sport injuries* (3rd ed., pp. 151–169). Morgantown, WV: Fitness Information Technology.

Evans, L., & Hardy, L. (2002). Injury rehabilitation: A goal-setting intervention study. *Research Quarterly for Exercise and Sport, 73*, 310–319.

Fisher, A. C. (1990). Counseling for improved rehabilitation adherence. In R. Ray & D. Wiese-Bjornstal (Eds.), *Counseling in sports medicine* (pp. 275–292). Champaign, IL: Human Kinetics.

Fisher, A. C. (1990). Adherence to sports injury rehabilitation programs. *Sports Medicine, 9*, 151–158.

Fisher, A. C., Domm, M. A., & Wuest, D. A. (1988). Adherence to sports injury rehabilitation programs. *The Physician and Sportsmedicine, 16*, 47–52.

Ford, I. W., Eklund, R. C., & Gordon, S. (2000). An examination of psychosocial variables moderating the relationship between life stress and injury time-loss among athletes of a high standard. *Journal of Sports Sciences, 18*, 301–312.

Ford, I. W., & Gordon, S. (1998). Perspectives of sport trainers and athletic therapists on the psychological content of their practice and training. *Journal of Sport Rehabilitation, 7*, 79–94.

Friedman, S., & Fanger, M. (1991). *Expanding therapeutic possibilities: Getting results in brief psychotherapy*. New York: Lexington Books/Macmillan.

Galambos, S. A., Terry, P. C., Moyle, G. M., Locke, S. A., & Lane, A. M. (2005). Psychological predictors of injury among elite athletes. *British Journal of Sports Medicine, 39*, 351–354.

Garner, H. H. (1977). Somatopsychic concepts. In R. P. Marinelli & A. E. Dell Orto (Eds.), *The psychological and social impact of physical disability* (pp. 2–16). New York: Springer.

Gorski, T. (June, 2007). Motivational interviewing. West Virginia University Addiction Training Institute. Morgantown, WV.

Gotsch, K. (2003). *Attitudes of certified athletic trainers concerning formal sport psychology education*. Unpublished master's thesis. Ball State University.

Gover, J. W., & Koppenhaver, R. (1965). Attempts to predict athletic injuries. *Medical Times, 93*(4), 421–422.

Granito, J. V. (2001). Athletic injury experience: A qualitative focus group approach. *Journal of Sport Behavior, 24*, 63–83.

Greif, E., & Matarazzo, R. G. (1982). *Behavioral approaches to rehabilitation*. New York: Springer.

Grove, J. R., & Cresswell, S. L. (2007). Personality correlates of appraisal, stress, and coping during injury rehabilitation. In D. Pargman (Ed.), *Psychological bases of sport injuries* (3rd ed., pp. 53–77). Morgantown, WV: Fitness Information Technology.

Gunther, M. (1971). Psychiatric consultation in a rehabilitation hospital: A regression hypothesis. *Comprehensive Psychiatry, 12*(6), 572–585.

Hanson, S., McCullough, P., & Tonyman, P. (1992). The relationship of personality characteristics, life stress, and coping resources to athletic injury. *Journal of Sport and Exercise Psychology, 14*, 262–272.

Hardy, C., & Crace, R. (1993). The dimensions of social support when dealing with sport injuries. In D. Pargman (Ed.), *Psychological bases of sport injuries* (pp. 121–148). Morgantown, WV: Fitness Information Technology.

Hardy, C. J., Crace, R. K., & Burke, K. L. (1999). Social support and injury: A framework for social support-based interventions with injured athletes. In D. Pargman (Ed.), *Psychological bases of sport injuries* (2nd ed., pp. 175–198). Morgantown, WV: Fitness Information Technology.

Heil, J. (1993). *Psychology of sport injury*. Champaign, IL: Human Kinetics.

Henschen, K. P., & Shelley, G. A. (2007). Counseling athletes with permanent disabilities. In D. Pargman (Ed.), *Psychological bases of sport injury* (3rd ed., pp. 183–192). Morgantown, WV: Fitness Information Technology.

Herrick, A., Stone, W., & Mettler, M. (1997). Stages of change, decisional balance, and self efficacy across four health behaviors in a worksite environment. *American Journal of Health Promotion, 12*, 49–56.

Hobfoll, S. (1989). Conservation of resources: A new attempt at conceptualizing stress. *American Psychologist, 44*, 513–524.

Janis, J., & Mann, L. (1977). *Decision making: A psychological analysis of conflict, choice and commitment*. New York: Free Press.

Junge, A. (2000). The influence of psychological factors on sports injuries. Review of the literature. *The American Journal of Sports Medicine, 28*, S10–15.

Kahanov, L., & Fairchild, P. C. (1994). Discrepancies in perceptions held by injured athletes and athletic trainers during the initial injury evaluation. *Journal of Athletic Training, 29,* 70–75.

Kelley, M. (1990). Psychological risk factors and sports injuries. *The Journal of Sports Medicine and Physical Fitness, 30,* 202–221.

Kerr, G., & Minden, H. (1988). Psychological factors related to the occurrence of athletic injuries. *Journal of Sport and Exercise Psychology, 10,* 167–173.

Kerr, N. (1961). Understanding the process of adjustment to disability. *Journal of Rehabilitation, 27*(6), 16–18.

Kornspan, A., & Etzel, E. (2003). What do we know about the career maturity of college student-athletes? A brief review and practical suggestions for career development work with student-athletes. *Academic Athletic Journal, 17,* 15–33.

Kubler-Ross, E. (1969). *On death and dying.* New York: Macmillan.

Laws-Gallien, D. Y. (2001). *The relationship of life stress, social support systems, and coping behaviors associated with athletic injury and performance in women's intercollegiate softball teams.* Unpublished dissertation, University of Houston.

Leddy, M. H., Lambert, M., & Ogles, B. M. (1994). Psychological consequences of athletic injury among high-level competitors. *Research Quarterly for Exercise and Sport, 65,* 347–354.

Livneh, H. (1991). A unified approach to existing models of adaptation to disability: A model of adaptation. In R. Marinelli & A. Dell Orto (Eds.), *The psychological and social impact of physical disability* (3rd ed., pp. 111–138). New York: Springer.

Livneh, H., & Antonak, R, (1997). *Psychosocial adaptation to chronic illness and disability.* Austin, TX: PRO-ED.

Maddison, R., & Prapavessis, H. (2005). A psychological approach to the prediction and prevention of athletic injury. *Journal of Sport and Exercise Psychology, 27,* 289–311.

Magyar, T., & Duda, J. L. (2000). Confidence restoration following athletic injury. *Sport Psychologist, 14,* 372–390.

Manuel, J. C. (2002). Coping with sports injuries: An examination of the adolescent athlete. *The Journal of Adolescent Health, 31,* 391–393.

Marcus, B., Banspach, S., Leefebvre, R., Rossi, J. S., Carleton, R. A., & Abrams, D. B. (1992). Using the stages of change model to increase the adoption of physical activity among community participants. *American Journal of Health Promotion, 6,* 424–429.

Marcus, B., & Forsyth, A. (2003). *Motivating people to be physically active.* Champaign, IL: Human Kinetics.

May, J. R., & Sieb, G. E. (1987). Athletic injuries: Psychosocial factors in the onset, sequelae, rehabilitation, and prevention. In J. R. May & M. J. Asken (Eds.), *Sport psychology: The psychological health of the athlete* (pp. 157–185). New York: PMA.

McDonald, S., & Hardy, C. (1990). Affective response patterns of the injured athlete: An exploratory analysis. *The Sport Psychologist, 4,* 261–274.

Meyers, C. A., Peyton, D. D., & Jensen, B. J. (2004). Treatment acceptability in NCAA Division I football athletes: Rehabilitation intervention strategies. *Journal of Sport Behavior, 2,* 165–169.

Miller, W. R., & Rollnick, S. (2002). *Motivational interviewing* (2nd ed.). New York: Guilford Press.

Moulton, M. A., Molstad, S., & Turner, A. (1997). The role of athletic trainers in counseling collegiate athletes. *Journal of Athletic Training, 32*, 148–150.

National Collegiate Athletic Association. (2006). *NCAA Injury Surveillance System* (ISS). Retrieved June 26, 2006, from www.ncaa.org

National Collegiate Athletic Association. (2007). Managing student-athletes' mental health issues. Retrieved June 25, 2007, from http://www.ncaa.org/library/sports_sci ences/mental_health/2007_managing_mental_health.pdf

Nideffer, R. (1983). The injured athlete: Psychological factors in treatment. *Orthopedic Clinics of North America, 14*(2), 373–385.

Pargman, D. (1993). Social support and injury: A framework for social support-based interventions with injured athletes. In D. Pargman (Ed.), *Psychological bases of sport injury* (pp. 5–14). Morgantown, WV: Fitness Information Technology.

Pargman, D. (2007). Introduction. In D. Pargman (Ed.), *Psychological bases of sport injury* (3rd ed., pp. xvii–xxvii). Morgantown, WV: Fitness Information Technology.

Parham, W. (1993, August/September). More than physical. *Réhabilitation Management, 13*, 53–54.

Petersen, K. (1997). *Role of social support in coping with athletic injury rehabilitation: A longitudinal investigation.* Presented at the Association for the Advancement of Applied Sport Psychology, San Diego, CA.

Petitpas, A. (2002). Counseling interventions in applied sport psychology. In J. Van Raalte & B. W. Brewer (Eds.), *Exploring sport and exercise psychology* (2nd ed. pp. 253–268). Washington, DC: American Psychological Association.

Petitpas, A., & Danish, S. J. (1995). Caring for injured athletes. In S. M. Murphy (Ed.), *Sport psychology interventions* (pp. 255–281). Champaign, IL: Human Kinetics.

Petrie, T. A. (1992). Psychological antecedents of athletic injury: The effects of life stress and social support on female collegiate gymnasts. *Behavioral Medicine, 18*, 127–138.

Petrie, T. A. (1993). The moderating effects of social support and playing status on the life stress injury relationship. *Journal of Applied Sport Psychology, 5*, 1–16.

Prochaska, J., & DiClemente, C. (1983). Stages and processes of self-change in smoking: Toward an integrative model of change. *Journal of Consulting and Clinical Psychology, 51*, 390–395.

Prochaska, J., Velicer, W., Rossi, J., Goldstein, M. G., Rakowski, W., Reddy, C. A., Rosenblum, D., & Rossi, S. R.(1994). Stages of change and decisional balance for twelve health behaviors. *Health Psychologist, 13*, 161–190.

Ray, R., & Wiese-Bjornstal, D. (1999). *Counseling in sports medicine.* Champaign, IL: Human Kinetics.

Rose, J., & Jeune, R. (1993). Psychosocial processes associated with athletic injuries. *The Sport Psychologist, 7*, 309–328.

Rotella, R., & Heyman, S. (1986). Stress, injury and the psychological rehabilitation of athletes. In J. M. Williams (Ed.), *Applied sport psychology: Personal growth to peak performance* (pp. 343–362). Palo Alto, CA: Mayfield.

Samples, P. (1987). Mind over muscle: Returning the injured athlete to play. *The Physician and Sportsmedicine, 15*, 172–180.

Schlossberg, N. K. (1981). A model for analyzing human adaptation to transition. *Counseling Psychologist, 9*, 2–18.

Schneider, J. (1984). *Stress, loss, and grief.* Baltimore: University Park Press.

Scott, S. L., & Weinberg, R. S. (2001). Relationships among athletic identity, coping skills, social support, and the psychological impact of injury in recreational participants. *Journal of Applied Sport Psychology, 13,* 40–59.

Shontz, F. C. (1965). Reaction to crisis. *Volta Review, 67,* 364–370.

Shontz, F. C. (1975). *The psychological aspects of physical illness and disability.* New York: Macmillan.

Silva, J., & Hardy, C. (1991). The sport psychologist: Psychological aspects of injury in sport. In F. Meuller & A. Ryan (Eds.), *The sport medicine team and athletic injury prevention* (pp. 114–132). Philadelphia: F. A. Davis.

Smart, J. (2001). *Disability, society, and the individual.* Gaithersburg, MD: Aspen Publishers.

Smith, R., Small, F., & Ptacek, J. (1990). Conjunctive moderator variables in vulnerability and resiliency: Life stress, social support, and coping skills, and adolescent sport injuries. *Journal of Personality and Social Psychology, 58,* 360–370.

Striegel, D. A., Hedgpeth, E. G., & Sowa, C. J. (1996). Differential psychological treatment of injured athletes based on length of rehabilitation. *Journal of Sport Rehabilitation, 5,* 330–335.

Thorenson, R. W., & Kerr, B. A. (1978). The stigmatizing aspects of severe disability: Strategies for change. *Journal of Applied Rehabilitation Counseling, 9*(2), 21–26.

Tracey, J. (2003). The emotional response to the injury and rehabilitation process. *Journal of Applied Sport Psychology, 15,* 279–293.

Tunick, R. H., & Tunick, R. (1982). Content narratives for "the disability experience" for the Institute of Information Studies adapted to multimedia computer programs for the Control Data Corp.

Udry, E. (2002). Staying connected: Optimizing social support for injured athletes. *Athletic Therapy Today, 7,* 42–43.

Udry, E., Shelbourne, K., & Gray, T. (2003). Psychological readiness for anterior cruciate ligament surgery: Describing and comparing the adolescent and adult experiences. *Journal of Athletic Training, 38,* 167–171.

Warchal, J., & Metzger, G. (2005). What counselors need to know about physical disabilities: Lessons learned. In G. R. Walz & R. K. Yep (Eds.), *VISTAS Compelling Perspectives on Counseling.* Alexandria, VA: American Counseling Association.

Weiss, M., & Troxel, R. (1986). Psychology of the injured athlete. *Journal of Athletic Training, 2,* 104–109, 154.

Whitten, E. B. (Ed.). (1975). *Pathology, impairment, functional limitation and disability: Implications for practice, research program and policy development and service delivery.* Washington, DC: National Rehabilitation Association.

Williams, J. M. (2001). Psychology of injury risk and prevention. In R. Singer, R. Hausenblaus, & H. C. Janelle (Eds.), *Handbook of sport psychology* (2nd ed., pp. 766–786). New York: John Wiley & Sons.

Williams, J. M., & Andersen, M. B. (1998). Psychosocial antecedents of sport injury. Review and critique of the stress and injury model. *Journal of Applied Sport Psychology, 10,* 5–25.

Wong, I. E. (1998). *Injury rehabilitation behavior: An investigation of stages and processes of change in the athlete-therapist relationship.* Unpublished master's thesis, University of Oregon.

Wright, B. (1983). *Physical disability: A psychological approach* (2nd ed.). New York: Harper & Row.

Yatabe, K., Fujiya, H., Kato, H., Seki, H., Kohno, T., Kumazawa, Y., & Aoki, H. (2005). Personality and emotional responses to sports injury in U-14 soccer players who participated in the JFA elite-program. *Japanese Journal of Clinical Sports Medicine, 13,* 246–256.

Case Study

Ben was a 19-year-old sophomore and an elite wrestler at ABU. During the fall build-up part of the team's season, he was working out with a training partner in the wrestling room in the late afternoon. Near the end of the practice session, his training partner took him down to the mat and accidentally fell hard on Ben's right leg. Ben winced in pain and had a tough time standing up. A senior athletic training student quickly came over to investigate what had happened to Ben. After a minute or so, Ben was assisted to the training room near the wrestling room. After Ben was examined by the head athletic trainer, it was determined that he had incurred a significant high ankle sprain. Ben was still feeling considerable discomfort and seemed angry about the news.

First Session

Athlete: At practice yesterday I twisted my ankle, and I am not feeling really good about it, and worst of all, I don't know what is going to happen for the rest of the season.

Athletic Trainer (ATC): Sounds like you are pretty upset, Ben. What seems to be the most troubling part of this whole thing?

Athlete: Well, the fact that I was doing so well in practice, and I had a shot at really contributing to the team. Now this happened, and it hurts a lot.

ATC: So you really had a lot of high expectations, and you're in major pain.

Athlete: Yeah, this was going to be the season that I was going to do well, and I'm hurting. Honestly, I'm kind of angry and unhappy about the whole deal.

ATC: How long do you think your rehab is going to take?

Athlete: Well, I'm not real sure, but I had a friend who had a similar injury and his rehab took about two months to heal. Man, I don't have two months! If I miss practice for two months, everyone is going to be so much more advanced than I am. I'll have some major catching up to do.

ATC: So it's not that you are worried as much about doing the rehab itself, but you maybe are more worried about the length of time it's going to take for you to get back to the mat?

Athlete: Probably, it is going to take too long for me to get back, and I don't know if I can stay out that long because I really need to practice. I'm mixed up about the whole thing, to be honest with you.

ATC: Together, we can take care of the physical rehab stuff here, and that's really important, but some of your other concerns may be worked on best with our university's sport psychologist.

Athlete: There is nothing wrong with my mind.

ATC: We know that there is nothing wrong with your mind. Maybe now is not the best to talk about this. Just something to think about.

Athlete: If coach finds out I'm going to see a sport psychologist, he might think something is wrong with me and might put me further down the team. Wrestling's for real tough guys, you know.

ATC: So even though you said you're mixed up, kind of angry, and unhappy, it's an option you don't want to consider right now.

Athlete: Well, I hate to admit it, but yes. Maybe you can tell me how a sport psychologist could help me. Maybe I might think about it.

ATC: Okay, I would be happy to give you information about that, and we can explore that tomorrow when you come back to treatment.

It is obvious that the athlete is concerned about his physical condition, his ability to compete this year, and the perceptions of his coach. At this time these previous factors are preventing the athlete from looking at the entire situation objectively, resulting in his denying that he needs any assistance with his emotional response or physical condition.

Second Session (next day)

ATC: Ben, good to see you! How are you doing since we met yesterday?

Athlete: My ankle is still killing me! I hope whatever you are going to do today can really help me with this pain.

ATC: On a scale from 1–10 with 10 being you can't tolerate the pain and 1 being minor discomfort, how is your pain?

Athlete: 8–9. So, what are we going to do today?

ATC: Standard treatment for your injury until the swelling goes down a bit, and then we will progress into rehab. Any other concerns before we start?

Athlete: Well, I have been thinking about how this leg thing is going to mess up my season. I was supposed to go see my coach this morning, but I told him my ankle was hurting too much and I couldn't make it. I don't really want to see coach. I also really don't want to see my teammates. It's kind of upsetting—embarrassing.

ATC: Seems like you're feeling a lot of stuff. What's up with not wanting to be around others?

Athlete: I mean, we used to hang out with each other all of the time, but I really can't even move around with them, so they go do their thing. They all went out last night and I had to stay home and eat and study a little by myself. It sucks.

ATC: Some things have really changed. I don't want to put words in your mouth, but it sounds like you are feeling a little down.

Athlete: Let's just say I am not feeling normal. Like, what is there to feel normal about?

ATC: Remember yesterday I tossed out the idea about possibly talking to someone about this situation and your feelings?

Athlete: Like I said yesterday, I'm not sure if I want to do that. When I think of going to see a psychologist, I think of people who are not right mentally, weak, you know—crazy or something.

ATC: In a way you are worried that something is wrong with you, about how others might think about you—maybe what meeting with a psychologist would be like?

Athlete: Yeah, I'm worried about what someone like that would do and say, what my teammates would say if they find out, what coach would do, and how that might impact my status on the team when I get back. My stock has already dropped big time.

ATC: So right now you are in pain, not feeling great, and kind of isolated. Well, today we are going to continue with your treatment for your ankle. But first, I want you to know that we care about how you are doing emotionally too. Many injured athletes (no names mentioned) have found that meeting with our sport psychologist has been a relief for them. I sense you're uncertain about talking to this person, but I don't want to push you into that. Please think a bit overnight about that option, though, as a part of your rehab. Sometimes it's very useful to meet just once with him. Keep in mind that seeing him is truly confidential. Your coaches, teammates, and others will not know you have met unless you want to tell them.

Athlete: Well . . . I can talk to you, I can tell you anything, but a psychologist? I don't know him. Does he really want to help me? I don't think I can really tell a stranger how I feel. I can tell you how I am feeling, but I really don't know him so it will be kind of hard to do that. It's not a wrestler, guy thing to do. You know?

ATC: Kind of sounds uncertain and uncomfortable for you to think about talking to a stranger, even if he is a trusted department professional?

Athlete: Yeah, it would be a real stretch talking to someone I don't know about how I feel.

ATC: That's a normal thing to think. Given the time we have today, let's move on with treatment. Please do keep giving me feedback about the physical parts of rehab, and if you wish, what's going on with your other personal feelings.

There appears to be some change occurring since the athlete reports a change in emotional and social status. Within the TTM, the athlete is verbalizing that his life is changing and appears more receptive to having some outside help and, hence, a movement toward the contemplation stage. The athletic trainer is careful to maintain communication and not label the athlete's emotional state as being depressed and/or anxious. The athletic trainer also is operating within his area of expertise, being supportive and acting as a source of information. Because athletic trainers have such frequent interactions, they are in an ideal position to be supportive and observant of the athlete's overall functioning.

Third Session (after one week)

ATC: How are you doing today, Ben?

Athlete: (Silence)

ATC: I noticed that you have not shown up for your last few treatments. What's been going on?

Athlete: I don't know. I can't deal with it anymore. It's too much. My ankle is really hurting. I am missing my sport. I still can't really hang out with my teammates anymore. Things I use to do I am not really doing anymore, and worst of all I don't think my ankle is getting any better.

ATC: So you are not seeing any improvements on your own yet?

Athlete: No, I kinda think I am feeling worse.

ATC: In what ways?

Athlete: I don't want to go to class, don't want to talk to anyone, sometimes I don't feel like eating anything. All I can do and think about is the fact that I am hurt, and I am not able to practice, and I am not going to be able to compete.

ATC: You're feeling really down.

Athlete: Down is an understatement.

ATC: So what do you do when you feel that way?

Athlete: I sleep a lot, and I try to come to treatment. As you know, sometimes I do and sometimes I don't.

ATC: We need to make sure you come to treatment every day. Please give me a call if you are having trouble getting here.

Athlete: This is not working. I have not seen any improvement in a week. Why should I keep coming if I am not seeing any progress?

ATC: It sounds like you have been thinking about this a lot.

Athlete: Yeah, that's all I have been thinking about. I can't think about anything else. That's what I came here to do, be a wrestler, and if I can't be a wrestler then what good am I?

ATC: So now your school work is suffering, friendships are suffering, and you are feeling isolated?

Athlete: Everything has been thrown off.

ATC: What do you think we can do about that together?

Athlete: You tell me what I should be doing. You are the expert.

ATC: While it's up to you, I mentioned the possibility of talking to somebody who works with us in athletics who can help you deal with these issues.

Athlete: You mean the sport psychologist. You think talking to him can really help?

ATC: I honestly think it world be worth meeting with him—even one time.

Athlete: I really don't know, but I really don't think things are going to get any better, and maybe if you think it is going to work, I will give it a shot.

ATC: I can give you Dr. Smith's contact information, or maybe I can have him stop by briefly to visit us when you are getting treatment.

Athlete: I want you to be here.

ATC: Okay!

The athlete appears to be exhibiting early symptoms associated with a mood disorder. He is reporting and has exhibited a lack of treatment compliance, poor class attendance, sleep disturbance, social withdrawal, and an overall worsening of symptoms. The athlete acknowledges life is not what it used to be and he is clearly in the contemplation stage. Athletic trainers need to be vigilant about athletes' adherence to physical treatment and any change in academic, social, and emotional functioning.

Fourth Session (one week later)

ATC: How have you been?

Athlete: Same as yesterday. I don't think anything has changed since we talked.

ATC: Okay, today we are going to go through treatment, and toward the end of treatment I've asked Dr. Smith to come visit. And I will be here too, if that is okay with you?

Athlete: I don't know if it is going to work, but if you think it will help me, I will do it.

The athlete acknowledges a need for help and is more receptive to meeting informally with the sport psychologist with the athletic trainer present. This suggests a movement from the contemplation to the preparation stage.

Fifth Session (informal meeting with sport psychologist)

SPC: Hi, Ben. I am Dr. Smith. Your ATC asked me to visit with you today. How are you doing?

Athlete: I have been better. I hurt my ankle a couple of weeks ago, and it hurts a lot, and things are just not feeling normal. Things I used to do I don't want to do. I can't hang out with my friends, I am missing practice really badly, and I don't want to go to class.

SPC: So a lot of things have happened since you have hurt your ankle, and I appreciate your giving me a history of your situation.

Athlete: Too many.

SPC: Kind of feel isolated a little bit?

Athlete: I don't even know if I am going to be here anymore.

SPC: So you are kind of worried about your status on the team?

Athlete: I mean, I am not wrestling, so what's my purpose?

SPC: Sounds like you are feeling down?

Athlete: Yeah, down, depressed whatever you want to call it, just not feeling normal.

SPC: That's pretty common to feel depressed and frustrated when obstacles have been placed in front of you. You know, you had nice plans for yourself, and now things are altered and you need to readjust to what has happened to you.

Athlete: I need to do something, because I can't stay like this.

SPC: So it sounds like you don't know what to expect, but you are willing to do something about how you are feeling

Athlete: Hold on, hold on. Am I going to be lying down on a couch, and are you going to analyze me?

SPC: No, we got rid of the couch a long time ago (in a laughing manner).

Athlete: Well, I have to go to practice, I have treatment, and I have class, and I don't know when I can see you again.

SPC: Tell me what times work for you?

Athlete: Um, I don't know. Well, the time that I come to treatment would work.

SPC: Before or after that?

Athlete: Well, I have to get a ride to treatment, and after treatment I have to get a ride home because I can't really walk. I can't drive, and before treatment will not work since I usually get here just on time. I don't know. It looks a little bit tight. Maybe sometime next week I can skip a class or something.

SPC: I'd rather you not skip a class. Let's see what we can work out. Let's try to figure out a time right now.

Athlete: How about I give you a call when I can get a ride sometime. Right now I can't see how this can fit into my schedule.

SPC: So when can I expect your call?

Athlete: Some time in the next day or two.

SPC: Today is Wednesday, so by Friday I should expect your call?

Athlete: Yes.

SPC: Good enough, then I look forward to hearing from you.

The athlete is really aware that he needs to do something but is fearful because it is something he has never done before. The sport psychologist is mindful that the athlete is reluctant to participate in starting a therapeutic relationship. The athlete, although he had previously been in the preparation stage, may have relapsed or regressed to the precontemplation/contemplation stage.

Session with Sport Psychologist and Athlete

SPC: Good to see you Ben. I am glad you gave me a call.

Athlete: Yeah, I think I need to do something about my injury.

SPC: Please tell me about your injury and how you have been coping.

Athlete: I have not been feeling well enough to do anything. I have not been eating. I don't want to see my teammates. I don't want to see coach. I think I saw him last week for the first time in a long time. I have been avoiding him, been avoiding practice, and not going to class. I don't even want to talk to my parents and my family.

SPC: So a lot of things have not been going well for you, then?

Athlete: Nothing has been going well for me.

SPC: Kind of all as a result of the injury?

Athlete: Everything is as a result of the injury.

SPC: So things seem to be piling up?

Athlete: Yes, I don't even want to go to class, if I make it to one of my classes a week that's good. I don't have the drive to do anything.

SPC: So I will assume that your performance in classes isn't doing too well either.

Athlete: I don't know. I have not been there. Kind of hard to focus on something else when I have all of this going on.

SPC: So it sounds like a lot of things have been going though your mind, your athletic career?

Athlete: That's the only thing I think about.

SPC: When I first met you, you told me you felt isolated.

Athlete: Not a lot has changed. I am feeling worse now. I don't even want to come out of my room, don't feel like doing anything at all. I am not really into this talking thing, but it's been two weeks now, and things are not getting any better.

SPC: Tell me a little bit about some of the things you think about.

Athlete: I think about if I will ever get back to the form I once had. I worked out really hard this summer and I came into camp in great shape.

SPC: Had a lot of high expectations?

Athlete: From coach and myself, family, friends, and now this came and happened, and I don't know if I can get back to that level. I have never been hurt like this before. This is all new to me.

SPC: So a lot of doubts have crept in there, doubting yourself in a number of areas?

Athlete: Yes, everything is bad right now.

SPC: Let's kind of take a look at the opposite of that. Yes, you told me that a lot of things are not going good for you. I want to see if we can identify things that are still going well for you.

Athlete: I can't think of anything.

SPC: Can't think of anything? Just kind of feel stuck, huh?

Athlete: No practice, my foot hurts. Can you think of something that is going good for me?

SPC: I need to hear that from you first. Think about right now. It's all kind of concentrating on a great disappointment. Well, let's take a look at another view of the situation.

Athlete: Another view of the situation? Well, the athletic trainer has been good to me.

SPC: So, basically you have been making some progress with your treatment?

Athlete: It is feeling a little bit better. It is not hurting as much as it used to, but it should be a lot better by now.

SPC: I guess what you are saying is that you want it to heal faster?

Athlete: If I could come to treatment and my foot could get better every day, maybe I could get back a little bit quicker. It is feeling better, but too slowly. Definitely not as quickly as I would want it.

SPC: Some of the dangers of getting you back too quickly would be what?

Athlete: I guess I would hurt my ankle again, and I don't want that. I really can't think of anything else.

SPC: So when you get into your moods when you are feeling down or depressed, tell me some of the things you think about.

Athlete: Why me? Why did this happen to me when it did? And I guess I still think I could have done something to prevent it, and I guess what I could be doing to get better faster.

SPC: So you are kind of angry at yourself a bit?

Athlete: Yeah, I should not have let this happen. I have been wrestling for a long time, and I have not gotten hurt like this. I am sure I could have done something to prevent this.

SPC: Looking back on it you kind of blame yourself in a way?

Athlete: Yes, I should have known better.

The athlete is being much more open to the difficulties he is confronted with. The athlete may be at an increased risk for self-harming behaviors, including suicidal ideations and academic sabotage. The sport psychologist needs to be mindful of these and take appropriate action. The sport psychologist also facilitates the athlete's acknowledgment that progress in one part of his life is being made. The athlete realizes that change needs to be made in his life and that maintaining the status quo has not been successful. This can be considered to be between contemplation and preparation.

Follow-up Session with Sport Psychologist

SPC: How have you been doing since we last met?

Athlete: I guess I have been thinking about some of the things we talked about the last time, and I was thinking that it was maybe not my fault I got hurt. Realistically, I don't think I had control over where I was going to put my foot. I am beginning to think that maybe it was not my fault that I got hurt.

SPC: And when you think that way, does it take away some of that down feeling from you?

Athlete: Yes, yes. I mean, I really don't think I could have done anything, and if I could not have done anything, I don't see why I should be feeling bad about it. I have been feeling a little bit better just using that thought process.

SPC: And your sleeping?

Athlete: The sleeping is still bad. I don't sleep as much, and I have been eating a little bit better, and I hung out with my roommates yesterday for the first time in a long time. I didn't just go to my room and lie down in my bed.

SPC: So you are reconnecting with them, but you are still not sleeping well?

Athlete: Yes, I am trying to. It is still not easy, but I need to try and do something.

SPC: So you are beginning to realize that accidents can happen, and the improvement in your ankle has you feeling better?

Athlete: Definitely, those are the things I have to draw on to feel better.

SPC: That's good, kind of taking a little bit more control of your situation.

Athlete: I am trying to do something to get myself out of this funk.

SPC: You told me that you have increased your contacts with your teammates and roommates. Hopefully sometime soon you are going to talk to your coach.

Athlete: That's going to be the big one, if I can talk to coach and maybe start back going to practice.

SPC: And what is your athletic trainer saying?

Athlete: He says I am making good progress. I don't think I am moving as fast as I should, and if I keep up this, maybe within the next couple of weeks I can stop using my crutches.

SPC: Maybe start being weight bearing again?

Athlete: It is looking kind of good, but two weeks is a long time.

SPC: How long has it been?

Athlete: It's been about three and half weeks.

SPC: So it's only about two weeks more and you are kind of getting close to the end then?

Athlete: Yes, I have never looked at it like that before.

SPC: So what would you like to work on in the next couple of weeks?

Athlete: I know I am feeling better, but I know I can feel a little bit better. I want to concentrate on the things I have control over because these past three weeks I have been bumming out myself over the things I have not had control over, and in talking to you I realized this. I know that I need to do my exercises at home, ice my ankle, and come to treatment in both the morning and afternoon and talk to coach to find out my status on the team.

SPC: Sounds like you have been putting into use some of the things we talked about?

Athlete: Yes, it helps, and since I am feeling better, I am more likely to think in this way than I would have before.

The athlete is clearly in the action stage in most of the matters that are of concern to him, except he has been reluctant to meet with his coach. In that aspect, he is really in contemplation. There may be behaviors that are in different stages even though these behaviors are associated with the overall problem. Subsequent sessions with the athlete addressed his concerns about meeting with the coach and returning to the mat. Some additional issues surfaced involving the athlete's family and loss of a family member. The above case study and abbreviated transcripts can hopefully serve as a guide for athletic trainers and sport psychologists using a cooperative approach in treating injured or disabled athletes. The abbreviated transcripts also highlighted the use of the transtheoretical model as well as a solution-focused approach to treatment.

16

ALCOHOL AND DRUG USE AMONG COLLEGE ATHLETES

Matthew P. Martens
Jason R. Kilmer
Niels C. Beck

Problems associated with alcohol and other illicit drug (AOD) use affect a considerable portion of the population (e.g., Grant et al., 2004a), and college athletes are not immune from these difficulties. For some substances, such as alcohol, college athletes may in fact be more at risk than other students for experiencing problems related to its use, while athletes may be less likely than other students to use certain illicit drugs (e.g., marijuana and cocaine). For other substances, such as steroids and other performance enhancing drugs, there are clear, sport-related factors that may contribute to their use among college athletes. A host of research studies have supported the efficacy of certain types of prevention programs in reducing AOD use among college students in general (see Larimer & Cronce, 2002; Larimer, Kilmer, & Lee, 2005), but a number of unique challenges exist in attempting to implement such programs among college athletes.

The purpose of this chapter is therefore threefold. First, we review the literature on AOD use among college athletes, focusing on prevalence rates and reasons for use. Second, we discuss strategies for preventing problems associated with AOD use among athletes, including ways that interventions may be best targeted for college athletes. Third, we discuss some of the challenges associated with implementing AOD prevention programs within athletic departments, and provide suggestions for overcoming such issues.

Prevalence Rates of AOD Use

Alcohol

There are a number of large-scale, national studies that have addressed the prevalence rates of alcohol use among intercollegiate athletes in the United States. Some of these studies (NCAA, 2006) sampled only athletes, but other studies (Leichliter, Meilman, Presley, & Cashin, 1998; Nelson & Wechsler, 2001; Wechsler, Davenport, Dowdall, Grossman, & Zanakos, 1997) included both athletes and nonathletes. These latter studies involved large samples of both athletes (N = 2,088–8,749) and nonathletes (N = 10,605–51,483), and provide the best data on prevalence rate differences between these groups.

Results from these studies indicate that the percentage of college students reporting any alcohol use at all in the past year is similar between athletes and nonathletes—approximately 80%. Among those using alcohol, though, quantity and frequency of heavy use are higher in athletes than nonathletes. For example, Leichliter et al. (1998) found that college athletes averaged significantly more drinks per week than nonathletes (7.57 vs. 4.12), with differences relatively consistent for men (9.85 vs. 6.37) and women (4.59 vs. 2.79). Research has also shown that a greater percentage of college athletes than nonathletes reported engaging in a "heavy episodic" drinking episode (typically defined as at least four or five drinks in one sitting) in the preceding two weeks, and that athletes were more likely to have engaged in frequent heavy episodic drinking (typically defined as at least three heavy episodes) in the same time frame (Leichliter et al., 1998; Nelson & Wechsler, 2001; Wechsler et al., 1997). Approximately 53%–57% of athletes reported heavy episodic drinking and 27%–28% frequent heavy episodic drinking, compared to 38%–43% and 16%–21% of nonathletes, respectively. Athlete-nonathlete differences were again consistent for both men and women. Finally, research has shown that athletes were more likely than nonathletes to experience a host of negative consequences as a result of using alcohol (Leichliter et al., 1998; Nelson & Wechsler, 2001). These data clearly suggest that intercollegiate athletes represent an "at-risk" population for heavy alcohol use and resulting negative consequences.

Recreational Drugs

In contrast to findings regarding alcohol use, research on recreational drug use (i.e., illicit drugs not taken to directly improve one's performance) indicates that college athletes are either as likely as or less likely than nonathletes to use such substances. In the only large-scale study comparing college athletes to nonathletes, Wechsler et al. (1997) found that fewer male athletes than nonathletes reported marijuana use in the preceding 30 days (12% vs. 16%), although prevalence rates for female athletes were similar to nonathletes (10% vs. 11%). Similarly, a study by the NCAA (2006) on almost 20,000 college athletes found that in the past year 20.3% had used marijuana, 2.4% psychedelics/hallucinogens, and 2.1% cocaine or crack cocaine, rates that are lower than prevalence rates from a national study of college students conducted around the same time (Johnston, O'Mally, Bachman, & Schulenberg, 2006). Taking into account limitations associated with making comparisons across different samples, the research in general seems to indicate that illicit drug use among college athletes is most likely lower than that of the general college student population.

Performance-Enhancing Drugs

Research seems to indicate that the overall percentage of college athletes who use performance-enhancing drugs is relatively small, although prevalence rates may be higher than in the general college student population. The NCAA (2006) reported that only 1.2%, 1.2%, and 1.0% of Division I, II, and III athletes, respectively, used steroids in the past 12 months, but those percentages were higher than those reported in a national sample of 19–22 year olds (approximately 0.5%; Johnston et al., 2006). The NCAA data also suggest sport-type and gender differences in steroid use, with the highest prevalence rates among athletes participating in water polo (10.5%), women's ice hockey (2.4%), baseball (2.3%), and football (2.3%). On average, men's sports had higher prevalence rates than women's sports. One-year prevalence rates for amphetamine and ephedrine use among college athletes from the NCAA (2006) data were 4.1% and 2.5%, respectively, and this rate of amphetamine use is less than that reported in a national sample of college students (6.7%; Johnston et al., 2006). Research on performance enhancing drugs outside of steroids is more difficult to quantify, as many of theses substances (including amphetamines) can also be used for recreational purposes, while national data on prevalence rates of some substances (e.g., illicit painkiller use, nutritional supplements) is lacking.

Reasons for AOD Use

A number of theoretical explanations exist for AOD use among college athletes, especially in terms of why this group may be more at risk than other college students for heavy use of certain substances (especially alcohol). Unfortunately, empirical research on many of these explanations is relatively scarce, and most of the existing research examines only alcohol use. Below we discuss several potential explanations for the aforementioned patterns of AOD use among college athletes, including excessive stress, various sport-related "cultural" factors, certain personality characteristics (especially impulsivity), and performance considerations.

Excessive Stress

One of the most well-known theories of substance abuse involves the tension reduction hypothesis, which posits that individuals use alcohol and other drugs to cope with negative affect (Khantzian, 1985). A number of theorists (e.g., Damm & Murray, 1996; Tricker, Cook, & McGuire, 1989) have speculated that college athletes experience more stress, pressure, and subsequent anxiety than the typical nonathlete, so they may be more likely to engage in AOD use to cope with such stressors. Research, though, has not provided strong support for this premise. For example, several studies have found low endorsement rates among college athletes for coping-related drinking motives (Bower & Martin, 1999; Evans, Weinberg, & Jackson, 1992; Green, Uryasz, Petr, & Bray, 2001). Further, one study found that sport-specific coping motives were not associated with alcohol consumption after controlling for the effects of other relevant variables (Martens, Watson, Royland, & Beck, 2005). Another study found no college athlete-nonathlete differences on a measure of "drinking to relax" (Wilson, Pritchard, & Schaffer, 2004). Although many of these studies suffer from measurement and other methodological limitations (e.g., samples for a single institution), research to date has not supported the premise that heightened stress and anxiety is a major cause of heavy AOD use among college athletes.

Sport-Specific Cultural and Environmental Factors

There are a number of factors unique to the sporting environment itself outside of excessive stress or pressure, which we define as cultural or environmental in nature, that could also be associated with heavy AOD use among college athletes. One factor involves the social status of college athletes, in that college athletes may be afforded more extensive social opportunities than the typical nonathlete (Harvey, 1999; Tricker et al., 1989). A second factor involves the internal social environment of athletic teams. Some researchers have speculated that college athletes are susceptible to a "work hard, play hard" mentality (Leichliter et al., 1998), and research has documented that perceptions of drinking among peers is positively associated with personal alcohol use (e.g., Borsari & Carey, 2003). Therefore, perhaps the perception that heavy drinking is "normal" among college athletes contributes to excessive alcohol use in this group. A third factor involves the seasonal rhythm of a college athlete's year. College athletes may, for a variety of reasons (e.g., team rules, concerns about performance), consciously limit their AOD use during their competitive seasons, but may then compensate for this restrictive behavior by drinking more heavily in the off-season. Although most college athletes train throughout the year, we suspect that factors such as less formal supervision from the coaching staff and the lack of formal competitions are associated with greater substance use during this time period.

Research on these sport-specific cultural and environmental factors has been relatively sparse and generally only focused on alcohol use, although a handful of studies do provide some support for the contentions discussed above. One study (Wilson et al., 2004) found that college athletes were more likely than nonathletes to report endorsing social reasons for drinking, which could be a function of more social opportunities than the typical college student. Similarly, a recent study found that intercollegiate athletes were more likely to participate in drinking games than nonathletes, which is generally a highly social activity (Grossbard, Geisner, Neighbors, Kilmer, & Larimer, 2007). Martens, Dams-O'Connor, Duffy-Paiement, and Gibson (2006) found that perceived drinking among friends who were either athletes or nonathletes predicted one's own use of alcohol among female college athletes, but among male college athletes one's own use of alcohol was predicted only by perceived drinking among friends who were also athletes. Interpreted in the context of social norms theory (Perkins, 2002), these findings suggest that part of the explanation for heavy alcohol use among college athletes may involve an effort to meet the perceived expectations of their athletic peers. One study supported the existence of a team-specific drinking motives construct, although scores on the measure assessing this construct were not associated with alcohol use after controlling for the effects of other drinking motives (Martens et al., 2005). Finally, several studies have found that college athletes consumed more alcohol outside of their competitive seasons than when in-season (e.g., Bower & Martin, 1999; Thombs, 2000). This research includes a recent longitudinal study that found that the average number of drinks per week approximately doubled from in- to off-season (Martens, Dams-O'Connor, & Duffy-Paiement, 2006), suggesting that college athletes may be particularly at risk for heavy drinking outside of their competitive seasons. Taken together, this research indicates that a number of broad cultural and environmental factors associated with athletics may be potential explanations for heavy alcohol use among college athletes. It is unknown, however, if similar factors are associated with use of other substances among this group.

Personality Characteristics

Research has consistently shown that the personality construct of impulsivity is positively associated with heavy AOD use and risk for a substance use disorder (e.g., Butler & Montgomery, 2004; Casillas & Clark, 2002; Fischer, Anderson, & Smith, 2004; Sher, Walitzer, Wood, & Brent, 1991). A handful of research studies have also examined "impulsive" behaviors among college athletes, and found that athletes engaged in more risky or sensation-seeking behaviors than nonathletes (Nattiv & Puffer, 1991; Nattiv, Puffer, & Green, 1997). Other studies have found that athletes scored higher than nonathletes on measures of sensation seeking (Gundersheim, 1987; Schroth, 1995). Sensation seeking is often conceptualized as an important component of impulsivity (e.g., Whiteside & Lynam, 2001), so it is possible that the elevated use of some substances by college athletes is associated with higher levels of the impulsivity personality factor within this group.

Performance Considerations

A final explanation for substance use among college athletes is relatively simple and primarily associated with performance-enhancing substances: the desire to improve one's athletic performance or recover from injury. Results from the NCAA (2006) indicated that the primary reason the majority (51.0%) of those athletes who used steroids in the past year chose to do so was for performance-enhancing purposes, although a relatively high percentage also did so to improve appearance (15.9%) or recover from injury (15.8%). Smaller studies have also found that athletes reported that performance or other pressures from their coaches was also a factor in the decision to use steroids (Diacin, Parks, & Allison, 2003; Tricker & Connolly, 1997). Similarly, college athletes may overuse or abuse painkillers in an effort to live up to an expectation that one must continue to compete in one's sport despite being injured (Tricker, 2000). For example, a survey of collegiate athletes found that only 6% reported that they stopped training when they were injured and 29% did not change their training regimen at all (Selby, Weinstein, & Bird, 1990). Such pressures, attitudes, and behaviors related to one's ability to perform as an athlete may impact a college athlete's decision to engage in certain types of drug use and abuse.

Preventing AOD Abuse in College Athletes

Considering the prevalence of alcohol and other drug use among college students, and with the documented consequences associated with this use, prevention and intervention efforts play an important role on the college campus. Although there are unique factors to consider with student-athletes, they nevertheless are college students with many of the same challenges other students face. Consequently, an examination of "what works" in responding to college student substance use in general is indicated. Additionally, only a handful of studies have addressed prevention efforts specifically among college athletes. We therefore first review the literature on preventing AOD abuse among college students in general, and follow that with a discussion of research specific to college athletes.

Prevention Strategies among College Students in General

The most well-studied AOD prevention efforts among college students have occurred in the area of alcohol use. In 2002, the National Institute on Alcohol Abuse and Alcoholism (NIAAA) commissioned a group of scientists to review the literature on college student drinking prevention efforts and intervention strategies to determine what had demonstrated effectiveness in reducing alcohol use and/or related consequences. The researchers utilized a "3-in-1 Framework" that suggested that any strategic plan for prevention needed to consider the various targets of any prevention message, policy, or intervention strategy. These included efforts targeting "at-risk" drinkers, the student body as a whole, and both the college itself and the surrounding community.

Following the literature review, the report then conceptualized the effectiveness of potential strategies along four tiers. Tier I strategies had evidence of effectiveness among college students; Tier II strategies had evidence of effectiveness in the general adult population that could be applied to college environments; Tier III strategies had evidence of logical and theoretical promise but required more comprehensive evaluation; and Tier IV strategies had evidence of ineffectiveness (NIAAA, 2002). Within Tier I, several components were identified across the effective strategies. The components included cognitive behavioral skills training, norms clarification, motivation enhancement approaches, and challenging alcohol expectancies.

Cognitive behavioral skills training. Cognitive-behavioral skills training involves teaching students specific strategies that are utilized for making changes in behaviors associated with drinking or with possible reasons for drinking. These often include a specific emphasis on the strategies students could utilize if they decided to abstain or, if they were to make the choice to drink, to drink in a less dangerous, less risky, more moderate way. Examples of these skills include blood alcohol level discrimination (i.e., training in recognizing the effects associated with various blood alcohol levels), strategies for drinking in moderation (e.g., drink pacing; avoiding drinking games or other high-consumption alcohol settings), and strategies for avoiding alcohol use (e.g., drink refusal strategies) (Dimeff, Baer, Kivlahan, & Marlatt, 1999; Larimer & Cronce, 2002). Cognitive behavioral skills training can also include general life skills that could be used if a person were to decide to make a change in alcohol consumption, such as relaxation or stress management skills, assertiveness skills, and general lifestyle balance skills.

Norms clarification. Some recent research (e.g., Borsari & Carey, 2003; Perkins, 2002) has consistently demonstrated that college students often overestimate the prevalence of drinking by their peers, and that the degree of overestimation is associated with one's own use of alcohol. Recently, randomized controlled trials have shown that social norms interventions designed to correct this perceived norm were effective at reducing high-risk drinking (DeJong et al., 2006; Neighbors, Larimer, & Lewis, 2004). These interventions typically involve providing students with accurate information regarding the drinking behaviors of their fellow students, through means such as posters on campus, newspaper advertisements, email messages, and other media that deliver the messages to the intended target group. Theoretically, students then reduce their own drinking by conforming to the actual drinking norm, which is lower than their initial, incorrect perceived drinking norm (Perkins, 2002).

Motivational enhancement strategies. Motivational enhancement strategies are those that attempt to elicit personally relevant reasons for changing one's behavior, particularly if a person is ambivalent about change. Perhaps the most well-known motivational enhancement strategy is Motivational Interviewing (MI) (Miller & Rollnick, 2002). MI is a non-judgmental, non-confrontational approach that attempts to meet individuals where they may be in terms of their readiness to change a behavior, and seeks to explore and resolve ambivalence about change. One of the basic principles of MI is to develop discrepancies between how a person sees himself or herself and what might actually be occurring for the individual, or between a person's values and goals for the future in comparison to the status quo. Through a conversation with a provider, by considering information about alcohol's effects as it relates to the person, or by actually receiving personalized feedback about one's use, it is often the case that a "hook" will emerge that highlights what the individual stands to gain by changing his or her behavior. Other factors often included in MI-based interventions include reviewing self-reported consequences from alcohol use, exploring issues such as the personal financial costs of alcohol use and the number of calories consumed from alcohol, and documenting the typical degree of intoxication. Meta-analyses have documented the overall effectiveness of MI-based interventions in preventing substance abuse (e.g., Burke, Arkowitz, & Menchola, 2003; Miller, Andrews, Wilbourne, & Bennett, 1998), including a number of studies with the college student population (e.g., Borsari & Carey, 2000; Larimer et al., 2001; Marlatt et al., 1998).

Challenging alcohol expectancies. A fourth strategy involves attempting to alter students' expectancies about the effects of alcohol. College students often assume that consuming alcohol will have a number of beneficial social effects, such as making it easier to talk to others and having a better time at a social gathering. Research studies have shown, however, that participants who expect alcohol but receive a placebo nevertheless demonstrate the social effects commonly attributed to drinking, and studies evaluating challenging alcohol expectancies as an intervention strategy among college students have demonstrated significant reductions in alcohol use (Darkes & Goldman, 1993, 1998).

Multi-component programs. Although these four strategies are all in some way associated with effective alcohol prevention interventions among college students, the NIAAA report highlighted three specific individual strategies or combinations of strategies that have clear demonstrated effectiveness in college students. These include: (1) combining cognitive-behavioral skills training with norms clarification and motivational enhancement interventions, (2) offering brief motivational enhancement interventions, and (3) stand-alone challenging alcohol expectancies interventions (NIAAA, 2002). Below we briefly discuss two specific programs that have been evaluated in the context of college student alcohol prevention and incorporate the NIAAA recommendations.

The Alcohol Skills Training Program (ASTP) is an example of an intervention that combines the elements of cognitive-behavioral skills training, norms clarification, and motivational enhancement. Developed, implemented, and evaluated at the University of Washington by G. Alan Marlatt and colleagues, participants in the ASTP experienced significant reductions in drinking rates and associated problems (Baer, et al., 1992; Kivlahan, Marlatt, Fromme, Coppel, & Williams, 1990). A second program, the Brief Alcohol Screening and Intervention for College Students (BASICS), was also developed by Marlatt's group (Dimeff et al., 1999). BASICS is designed to increase students' motivation to change their drinking habits by providing personalized feedback on topics such as their current drinking quantity and frequency, how their drinking compares to that of other students, and consequences experienced as a result of drinking. A BASICS intervention also includes modules on cognitive-behavioral skills training and expectancy challenges. A number of studies have shown that BASICS interventions are effective at reducing alcohol-related problems and drinking rates among college students (e.g., Borsari & Carey, 2000; Larimer et al., 2001; Marlatt et al., 1998).

Prevention strategies for other substances. For drugs other than alcohol, there are not clear "gold standards" that seem to work in reducing use and related consequences for college students (Larimer et al., 2005). In part, this could be because alcohol, as the most widely used substance by college students, has been the primary target of prevention efforts and studies. Much as NIAAA introduced the idea of Tier II strategies (i.e., strategies with demonstrated effectiveness in the general adult population that could be applied with college students), it is possible to examine the literature assessing the impact of interventions for drugs other than alcohol to consider what theoretically could be extended to a college setting. Larimer et al. (2005) noted that treatment approaches using MI and other cognitive behavioral therapy approaches have been successful in reducing use, consequences, or both use and consequences for a range of substances (e.g., Marijuana Treatment Project Research Group, 2004; Stephens, Roffman, & Curtin, 2000). Future studies will need to develop, implement, and evaluate prevention efforts and interventions targeting drugs other than alcohol in the college or university setting.

Prevention Strategies among College Athletes

Research seems to indicate that many, if not most, college athletes receive some type of AOD prevention efforts (for a review see Martens, Dams-O'Connor, & Kilmer, 2007). For example, Martin (1998) found that as many as 85% of NCAA Division I female athletes participated

in some type of alcohol prevention programming. Much of this programming is typically educational and informational in nature, yet the
efficacy of such approaches has not been well established despite being
widely used. Trenhaile, Choi, Proctor, and Work (1998) noted in their
review of the literature that providing information about the harmful
effects of steroids to athletes in a high school setting actually increased
the students' interest in trying these substances. They also noted that
subsequent research exploring the impact of more balanced information (i.e., information on the harmful effects along with what could be
perceived as potential benefits) also failed to impact students' attitudes.
These findings are consistent with data from college students that suggest that education-only programs are generally ineffective at reducing
substance use (Larimer & Cronce, 2002; Larimer et al., 2005). Finally,
many of the typical programs adopted by athletic departments across the
country (e.g., the NCAA CHAMPS/Lifeskills program) are often highly
educationally based and have not been evaluated in controlled trials.

Descriptions of a number of AOD prevention programs specifically
for college athletes that go beyond educational information-only have
been published in the literature. Meilman and Fleming (1990) described a prevention program that provides information about the consequences of performance enhancement drug use, information about
the impact of alcohol and drug use on athletic performance, a presentation made by a former athlete now in recovery, a discussion of warning signs of problematic use, and strategies for approaching a teammate
if one is concerned about is or her use. Similarly, Baum (1998) described
an outpatient consultation-liaison model in which the presence of a psychiatrist in a sports-medicine clinic in addition to consultation with staff
would help to identify high-risk athletes in need of intervention for a
range of issues (including substance abuse and steroid use) and would
assist in follow-up following referral. Finally, Curry and Maniar (2004)
described an academic course entitled "Principles of Optimal Performance" that targets a range of performance and health behaviors. Alcohol use is addressed in a program component covering sports nutrition,
hydration, supplements, and eating disorders. In all three instances,
however, no outcome data on program effectiveness were provided.

There have, however, been a handful of studies that present outcome
data from AOD prevention programs with college athletes, with mixed

results. One study indicated that an information and skills training program was not effective at reducing substance use (Marcello, Danish, & Stolberg, 1989), while another study using a broad social norms reeducation campaign also found no effect in reducing alcohol use (Thombs & Hamilton, 2002). Both of these studies, though, had a number of limitations in their design and administration that suggested that more thorough evaluations of prevention efforts were still warranted. Perna and colleagues (2003) developed a general cognitive behavioral stress management program and evaluated its impact on 34 varsity and junior varsity rowers. They found that participants in the program reduced their alcohol use, although not significantly more than those in the control condition.

More recently, Perkins and Craig (2006) developed a social norms campaign to target alcohol use by student-athletes at an NCAA Division III institution. The program used a variety of intervention formats, including newspapers, posters, emails, screen savers, a multimedia program, peer health educators, and a CD with schedules, highlights, and other information, to promote information about actual athlete-specific alcohol norms. The authors reported significant decreases in athletes' alcohol use after program exposure among a range of outcome variables, including drinking twice per week or more often, exceeding a peak BAC of .08%, consuming ten or more drinks at parties or bars, and experiencing frequent negative consequences of alcohol use. Further, they reported that intervention impact was greater among student-athletes with the highest level of program exposure. Although there were several limitations to this study (e.g., the athletes were from a single Division III school, there was no randomized matched control group, and only cross-sectional rather than individual longitudinal analyses were conducted), the results are nonetheless promising for this AOD prevention strategy among college athletes.

Modifying existing programs for college athletes. Given the effectiveness of brief interventions like BASICS and skills-training programs like the ASTP among college students in general, it is likely that these approaches would also be effective among college athletes. It is possible, though, that modifying these programs and making them more specific to the college athlete population would enhance their efficacy among this group. For example, in a BASICS-style intervention that uses personalized drinking feedback, providing feedback on both sport-specific negative consequences (e.g., performing poorly because of alcohol use; missing a practice because of a hangover) and consequences applicable to all students (e.g., getting into trouble with campus authorities, performing poorly academically) might be more effective than providing feedback that does not include the sport-specific consequences. Similarly, research has shown that the more proximal the reference group (e.g., close friends versus students in general), the stronger the relationship between perceived normative behavior and one's own behavior (Borsari & Carey, 2003). Therefore, interventions that provide drinking norms that are specific to intercollegiate athletes (e.g., Perkins & Craig, 2006) may be more effective than interventions that use norms for college students in general. Finally, reviewing the potential consequences of alcohol use on one's athletic performance, including off-season training (e.g., decreased oxygen consumption, decreased psychomotor coordination, increased injury risk, see the American College of Sports Medicine, 1982; Gutgesell & Canterbury, 1999; O'Brien & Lyons, 2000), could be especially effective with the college athlete population.

AOD Use and Other Mental Health Problems

It is important to note that individuals experiencing problems with alcohol and other drugs often experience co-morbid psychological problems (e.g., Dansky, Brewerton, & Kilpatrick, 2000; Grant et al., 2004b, 2004c). National studies of the adult population in the United States have shown that those with substance abuse disorders are more likely to experience personality, anxiety, and mood disorders (Grant et al., 2004b, 2004c), and a host of studies have shown that substance abuse problems (especially heavy drinking) and eating disorders or eating disorder symptoms often co-occur (Danskey et al., 2000; Ross & Ivis, 1999). Counselors working with athletes who have presented for a range of mental health issues may find that substance use is a clinically significant factor relevant to the presenting problem, which highlights the need for assessment of these behaviors. For example, a number of studies have shown that female athletes, especially those in sports in which aesthetics are critical or being thin has a distinct competitive advantage, are more at risk than other athletes and nonathlete college students for engaging in disordered eating behaviors (Hausenblaus & Carron, 1999; Smolak, Murnen, & Rubble, 2000). Considering the aforementioned co-occurrence of such behaviors with heavy alcohol use, clinicians working with athletes experiencing these and other types of mental health issues should also routinely screen for heavy AOD use.

Implementing AOD Prevention Programs in the Context of an Athletic Department

Because of the unique nature of collegiate athletic departments, there are a number of logistical and environmental challenges associated with implementing a substance abuse program in such a setting. Below we review some of these challenges, but also provide strategies and recommendations for those interested in developing and implementing AOD prevention programs in an athletic department setting.

Challenges Associated with Implementing AOD Programs

The implementation of alcohol and drug abuse treatment and prevention programming for college athletes has received relatively little attention in the professional and scientific literature. Only a handful of AOD prevention programs have been subject to empirical evaluation (e.g., Marcello et al., 1989; Perkins & Craig, 2006; Thombs & Hamilton, 2000), and considerable limitations exist to these studies (e.g., small sample sizes, lack of randomized control groups). Although we have previously reviewed and discussed a variety of programs that have established track records of effectiveness or show considerable promise among the general college student population, it remains unclear how many, if any, of these programs are being used in the context of college athletic departments. Further, it is likely that the extent to which any alcohol and drug use treatment and prevention services are available to college athletes varies widely from institution to institution.

There are a number of reasons for this state of affairs. The fact that athletic programs have not widely and uniformly adopted empirically supported treatment and prevention strategies should come as no surprise to those who are familiar with the literature on the adoption of evidence-based treatments in more formal health care settings. This literature indicates that even in the most research-oriented and scholarly institutional contexts, state of the art therapeutic procedures are not always incorporated into day-to-day treatment service delivery programs (Chambless et al., 1998).

Additionally, implementing substance abuse treatment and prevention programming within college athletic departments needs to take into account the unique nature of these organizations, as well as their relationships with the rest of the university community. For example, many athletic programs tend to function more or less as independent entities, with organizational and funding features that separate them from university academic leadership, except at the highest level (Andersen & Brewer, 1996; Sperber, 1990; Zimbalist, 1999). At many universities athletic departments contain their own academic and health service providers, and there is an implicit understanding that college athletes will get virtually all of their needs taken care of within the athletic department. Such climates may foster some degree of resistance for any types of services provided by "outsiders," especially in such a sensitive area as AOD issues. We suspect that many, if not most, athletic departments do not have personnel trained specifically in preventing AOD abuse. Additionally, given the importance of and penalties associated with NCAA and/or university drug tests, it is possible that many prevention efforts among college athletes focus on substances other than alcohol.

NCAA regulations require, as a bare minimum, that member institutions provide student athletes with alcohol and drug prevention programming on a semester-by-semester basis. However, this requirement does very little to specify the nature or extent of this programming. Furthermore, the regulations have little or nothing to say about the availability of treatment services. Therefore, athletic departments could conceivably provide minimal educational information about the dangers of drug and alcohol abuse (which research has consistently shown is an ineffective intervention strategy in affecting behavior when used as the exclusive strategy; Larimer & Cronce, 2002) and be in compliance with NCAA standards. Further, there appears to be enormous variability with regard to the extent to which athletic departments have relationships with mental health professionals, as well as the nature of these relationships. For instance, a handful of NCAA member institutions have mental health professionals who are direct hires and thus are an integral part of athletic department operations (Hosick, 2005). Most programs, however, have a series of rather loosely defined relationships with service providers, including those who work at college counseling centers, psychology clinics, student health centers, and psychiatry departments. It would likely be very challenging for a provider who does not have a formal, integral relationship within the athletic department to develop or implement a comprehensive AOD prevention program.

In addition to NCAA regulations regarding AOD prevention/education programming, the NCAA also operates a drug-testing program (NCAA, 2007a). Extensive policies and procedures exist regarding banned substances lists, testing procedures, and consequences of positive test findings. Many member institutions have followed suit and now have drug-testing policies and procedures of their own. Although some research seems to indicate that formal drug testing may serve as a deterrent for those substances included in the testing (Coombs & Ryan, 1990; Goldberg et al., 2003), it is possible that many athletic department staff members believe that the deterrent effect of testing is itself enough to combat AOD problems among college athletes. This could temper any interest associated with implementing AOD prevention programs.

Strategies for Implementing AOD Prevention Programs

Despite these challenges associated with implementing AOD prevention programs in collegiate athletic departments, we believe that it is possible to persuade athletic departments that such efforts are useful. Achieving "buy in" on the part of athletic department leaders can be accomplished in a variety of ways. Certainly, pointing out the organizational linkages in terms of NCAA requirements regarding prevention/education, as well as the issue of dealing with athletes who test positive on drug screens, can be effective. However, although mental health issues in general may be receiving greater emphasis from the NCAA (e.g., NCAA, 2007b), efforts to convince the leadership of the value of substance abuse programming must take into account various unique aspects of the athletic department atmosphere previously referred to. These include such issues as the high profile of student athletes throughout the university community, as well as a generalized pressure throughout the department to win and perform. As one might expect, given the environment in which they work, athletic department leaders (including coaches) tend to be highly performance-oriented.

Thus, a rationale for the adoption of substance abuse programming should include an argument that is based on the empirically validated literature, but couched in terms that athletic directors and coaching staffs who may not be well-attuned to or very interested in these health-related issues can appreciate and understand. For example, if athletic department staff members can be convinced that implementing AOD prevention programs might positively affect the actual performance of the athletic teams on the field and in the classroom, they may be more likely to support such efforts. Further, given other time demands placed on athletes, programming needs to be implemented in a manner that is brief and cost-effective.

In this regard, many of the intervention and prevention programs discussed earlier in this chapter possess these characteristics. For instance, the BASICS program (Dimeff et al., 1999) is by nature a brief, targeted intervention, with a substantive literature demonstrating therapeutic effectiveness. The possibility that effective web-based interventions developed on the BASICS model could be implemented might represent an even more desirable alternative from a cost-effectiveness standpoint (see Walters & Neighbors, 2005). Further, environmentally based social norms interventions are generally inexpensive and presumably reach the entire targeted population (Perkins, 2002). It is important, though, that logistical considerations not dominate decision making in this area. For example, it is possible that many athletic departments rely on brief, information-only AOD prevention efforts primarily because of time-related concerns. Yet, as mentioned previously, there are data to suggest that programs that simply present information are generally ineffective.

A final consideration for effectively implementing AOD prevention programs in athletic departments involves obtaining the support of health care providers who have a more established role in these settings. Athletic trainers, for example, have a considerable amount of daily contact with athletes (especially when athletes are in-season), and college athletes often receive their medical services from a physician employed by the athletic department. We believe that it would be imperative for those attempting to develop or implement an AOD prevention program to obtain the support of these professionals. Besides providing political support within the culture of an athletic department, trainers and physicians could serve multiple roles in such programs. They could serve as excellent sources for identifying and referring athletes who could benefit from targeted prevention or treatment programs, or, if willing, be trained to deliver brief, motivational enhancing interventions that have been shown to be effective in other medical settings (e.g., Bertholet, Daeppen, Wietlisbach, Fleming, & Burnand, 2005; Fleming, Brown, & Brown, 2004; Monti et al., 1999). For example, in one author's experience (NCB) over an extended period of consultation with a Division I Athletic program, training staff was responsible for over half of the referrals received by the consulting psychologist. In some cases, training staff serve as intermediaries between the coaching staff and the psychologist, but in other cases they were instrumental in directly identifying student-athletes with substance abuse issues. We believe that it would be very difficult, if not impossible, to implement an AOD prevention program without the explicit support of other athletic department medical staff.

Summary

Research has established that AOD use, particularly with respect to alcohol, is a significant health problem among collegiate athletes. Although research in the area is relatively sparse, some studies do suggest that there are several sport-related social and environmental factors that could be associated with this pattern of substance use. Unfortunately, and despite a growing body of literature among college students in general supporting the effectiveness of certain types of prevention programs, few empirically supported programs have been implemented and/or tested among college athletes. We encourage clinicians working with college athletes to consider strategies for implementing a comprehensive, empirically supported AOD prevention in the settings in which they work, keeping in mind some of the considerations we noted regarding working with athletic departments. We also encourage researchers to engage in efforts that test the effectiveness of already established prevention programs with the unique population of college athletes, as well as designing and testing interventions that attempt to address some of the unique issues associated with college athlete alcohol and drug use.

References

American College of Sports Medicine. (1982). Position stand: The use of alcohol in sports. *Medical Science of Sports and Exercise, 14*, ix–xi.

Andersen, M. B., & Brewer, B. W. (1996). Organizational and psychological consultation in collegiate sports medicine groups. *Journal of American College Health, 44*, 63–69.

Baer, J. S., Marlatt, G .A., Kivlahan, D. R., Fromme, K., Larimer, M., & Williams, E. (1992). An experimental test of three methods of alcohol risk reduction with young adults. *Journal of Consulting and Clinical Psychology, 60*, 974–979.

Baum, A. (1998). Sports psychiatry: An outpatient consultation-liaison model. *Psychosomatics, 39*, 395–396.

Bertholet, N., Daeppen, J., Wietlisbach, V., Fleming, M., & Burnand, B. (2005). Reduction of alcohol consumption by brief alcohol intervention in primary care: Systematic review and meta-analysis. *Archives of Internal Medicine, 165*, 986–995.

Borsari, B., & Carey, K. B. (2000). Effects of a brief motivational intervention with college student drinkers. *Journal of Consulting and Clinical Psychology, 68*, 728–733.

Borsari, B., & Carey, K. B. (2003). Descriptive and injunctive norms in college drinking: A meta-analytic integration. *Journal of Studies on Alcohol, 64*, 331–341.

Bower, B. L., & Martin, M. (1999). African American female basketball players: An examination of alcohol and drug behaviors. *Journal of American College Health, 48*, 129–133.

Burke, B. L., Arkowitz, H., & Menchola, M. (2003). The efficacy of motivational interviewing: A meta analysis of controlled clinical trials. *Journal of Consulting and Clinical Psychology, 71*, 843–861.

Butler, G. K. L., & Montgomery, A. M. J. (2004). Impulsivity, risk taking and recreational "ecstasy" (MDMA) use. *Drug and Alcohol Dependence, 76*, 55–62.

Casillas, A., & Clark, L. A. (2002). Dependency, impulsivity, and self-harm: Traits hypothesized to underlie the association between cluster B personality and substance use disorders. *Journal of Personality Disorders, 16*, 424–436.

Chambless, D. L., Baker, M. J., Baucom, D. H., Beutler, L. E., Calhoun, K. S., Crits-Christoph, P., et al. (1998). Update on empirically validated therapies, II. *The Clinical Psychologist, 51*, 3–16.

Coombs, R. H., & Ryan, F. J. (1990). Drug testing effectiveness in identifying and preventing drug use. *American Journal of Drug and Alcohol Abuse, 16*, 173–184.

Curry, L. A., & Maniar, S. D. (2004). Academic course for enhancing student-athlete performance in sport. *The Sport Psychologist, 18*, 297–316.

Damm, J., & Murray, P. (1996). Alcohol and other drug use among college student-athletes. In E. F. Etzel, A. P. Ferrante, & J. W. Pinkney (Eds.), *Counseling college student-athletes: Issues and interventions* (2nd ed., pp. 185–220). Morgantown, WV: Fitness Information Technology.

Dansky, B. S., Brewerton, T. D., & Kilpatrick, D. G. (2000). Comorbidity of bulimia nervosa and alcohol use disorders: Results from the national women's study. *International Journal of Eating Disorders, 27*, 180–190.

Darkes, J., & Goldman, M. S. (1993). Expectancy challenge and drinking reduction: Experimental evidence for a mediational process. *Journal of Consulting and Clinical Psychology, 61*, 344–353.

Darkes, J., & Goldman, M. S. (1998). Expectancy challenge and drinking reduction: Process and structure in the alcohol expectancy network. *Experimental and Clinical Psychopharmacology, 6*, 64–76.

DeJong, W., Schneider, S. K., Towvim, L. G., Murphy, M. J., Doerr, E. E., Simonsen, N. R., et al. (2006). A multisite, randomized trial of social norms marketing campaigns to reduce college student drinking, *Journal of Studies on Alcohol, 67*, 868–879.

Diacin, M. J., Parks, J. B., & Allison, P. C. (2003). Voices of male athletes on drug use, drug testing, and the existing order in intercollegiate athletics. *Journal of Sport Behavior, 26*, 1–16.

Dimeff, L. A., Baer, J. S., Kivlahan, D. R., & Marlatt, G. A. (1999). *Brief alcohol screening and intervention for college students.* New York: Guilford Press.

Evans, M., Weinberg, R., & Jackson, A. (1992). Psychological factors related to drug use in college athletes. *The Sport Psychologist, 6*, 24–41.

Fischer S., Anderson K. G., & Smith G. T. (2004). Coping with distress by eating or drinking: Role of trait urgency and expectancies. *Psychology of Addictive Behaviors, 18*, 269–274.

Fleming, M., Brown, R., & Brown, D. (2004). The efficacy of a brief alcohol intervention combined with %CDT feedback in patients being treated for type 2 diabetes and/or hypertension. *Journal of Studies on Alcohol, 65*, 631–637.

Goldberg, L., Elliot, D. L., MacKinnon, D. P., Moe, E., Kuel, K. S., Nohre, L., et al. (2003). Drug testing athletes to prevent substance abuse: Background and pilot study results of the SATURN (Student Athlete Testing Using Random Notification) study. *Journal of Adolescent Health, 32*, 16–25.

Grant, B. F., Dawson, D. A., Stinson, F. S., Chou, S. P., Dufour, M. C., & Pickering, R. P. (2004a). The 12-month prevalence and trends in DSM-IV alcohol abuse and dependence: United States, 1991–1992 and 2001–2002. *Drug and Alcohol Dependence, 74*, 223–234.

Grant, B. F., Stinson, F. S., Dawson, D. A., Chou, S. P., Dufour, M. C., Compton, W., et al. (2004b). Prevalence and co-occurrence of substance use disorders and independent mood and anxiety disorders. *Archives of General Psychiatry, 61*, 807–816.

Grant, B. F., Stinson, F. S., Dawson, D. A., Chou, S. P., Ruan, W. J., & Pickering, R. P. (2004c). Co-occurrence of 12-month alcohol and drug disorders and personality disorders in the United States. *Archives of General Psychiatry, 61*, 361–368.

Green, G. A., Uryasz, F. D., Petr, T. A., & Bray, C. D. (2001). NCAA Study of Substance Use and Abuse Habits of College Student-Athletes. *Clinical Journal of Sport Medicine, 11*, 51–56.

Grossbard, J., Geisner, I. M., Neighbors, C., Kilmer, J. R., & Larimer, M. E. (2007). Are drinking games sports? College athlete participation in drinking games and alcohol related problems. *Journal of Studies on Alcohol and Drugs, 68*, 97–105.

Gundersheim, J. (1987). Sensation seeking in male and female athletes and nonathletes. *International Journal of Sport Psychology, 18*, 87–99.

Gutgesell, M., & Canterbury, R. (1999). Alcohol usage in sport and exercise. *Addiction Biology, 4*, 373–383.

Harvey, S. J. (1999). Hegemonic masculinity, friendship, and group formation in an athletic subculture. *Journal of Men's Studies, 8*, 91–125.

Hausenblas, H. A., & Carron, A. V. (1999). Eating disorder indices and athletes: An integration. *Journal of Sport and Exercise Psychology, 21*, 230–258.

Hosick, M. B. (2005, February 28). Forum places psychological focus on mental health issues. *The NCAA News*. Retrieved August 3, 2007, from http://www1.ncaa.org/membership/ed_outreach/health-safety/forummentalhealthpdf.pdf

Johnston, L. D., O'Malley, P. M., Bachman, J. G., & Schulenberg, J. E. (2006). *Monitoring the Future national survey results on drug use, 1975–2005. Volume II: College students and adults ages 19–45* (NIH Publication No. 06-5884). Bethesda, MD: National Institute on Drug Abuse.

Khantzian, E. J. (1985). The self-medication hypothesis of addictive disorders: Focus on heroin and cocaine dependence. *American Journal of Psychiatry, 142*, 1259–1264.

Kivlahan, D. R., Marlatt, G. A., Fromme, K., Coppel, D. B., & Williams, E. (1990). Secondary prevention with college drinkers: Evaluation of an alcohol skills training program. *Journal of Consulting and Clinical Psychology, 58*, 805–810.

Larimer, M. E., & Cronce, J. M. (2002). Identification, prevention, and treatment: A review of individual-focused strategies to reduce problematic alcohol consumption by college students. *Journal of Studies on Alcohol, S14*, 148–163.

Larimer, M. E., Kilmer, J. R., & Lee, C. M. (2005). College student drug prevention: A review of individually oriented prevention strategies. *Journal of Drug Issues, 35*, 431–456.

Larimer, M. E., Turner, A. P., Anderson, B. K., Fader, J. S., Kilmer, J. R., Palmer, R. S., et al. (2001). Evaluating a brief alcohol intervention with fraternities. *Journal of Studies on Alcohol, 62*, 370–380.

Leichliter, J. S., Meilman, P. W., Presley, C. A., & Cashin, J. R. (1998). Alcohol use and related consequences among students with varying levels of involvement with college athletics. *Journal of American College Health, 46*, 257–262.

Marcello, R. J., Danish, S. J., & Stolberg, A. (1989). An evaluation of strategies developed to prevent substance abuse among student-athletes. *The Sport Psychologist, 3*, 196–211.

Marijuana Treatment Project Research Group. (2004). Brief treatments for cannabis dependence: Findings from a randomized multisite trial. *Journal of Consulting and Clinical Psychology, 72*, 455–466.

Marlatt, G. A., Baer, J. S., Kivlahan, D. R., Dimeff, L. A., Larimer, M. E., Quigley, L. A., et al. (1998). Screening and brief intervention for high-risk college student drinkers: Results from a two-year follow-up assessment. *Journal of Consulting and Clinical Psychology, 66*, 604–615.

Martens, M. P., Dams-O'Connor, K., & Duffy-Paiement, C. (2006). Comparing off-season versus in-season alcohol consumption among intercollegiate athletes. *Journal of Sport and Exercise Psychology, 28*, 502–510.

Martens, M. P., Dams-O'Connor, K., Duffy-Paiement, C., & Gibson, J. T. (2006). Perceived alcohol use among friends and alcohol consumption among intercollegiate athletes. *Psychology of Addictive Behaviors, 20*, 178–184.

Martens, M. P., Dams-O'Connor, K., & Kilmer, J. (2007). Alcohol and drug abuse among athletes: Prevalence, etiology, and interventions. In G. Tenenbaum & R. C. Ecklund (Eds.), *Handbook of sport and exercise psychology* (3rd ed., pp. 859–878). New York: John Wiley & Sons, Inc.

Martens, M. P., Watson, J. C., Royland, E. M., & Beck, N. C. (2005). Development of the Athlete Drinking Scale. *Psychology of Addictive Behaviors, 19*, 158–164.

Martin, M. (1998). The use of alcohol among NCAA Division I female college basketball, softball, and volleyball athletes. *Journal of Athletic Training, 33*, 163–167.

Meilman, P. W. & Fleming, R. L. (1990). A substance abuse prevention program for student-athletes. *Journal of College Student Development, 31*, 477–479.

Miller, W. R., Andrews, N. R., Wilbourne, P., & Bennett, M. E. (1998). A wealth of alternatives: Effective treatments for alcohol problems. In W. R. Miller & N. Heather (Eds.), *Treating addictive behaviors* (2nd ed., pp. 203–216). New York: Plenum Press.

Miller, W. R., & Rollnick, S. (2002). *Motivational interviewing: Preparing people to change addictive behavior* (2nd ed.). New York: The Guilford Press.

Monti, P. M., Colby, S. M., Barnett, N. P., Spirito, A., Rohsenow, D. J., Myers, M. et al. (1999). Brief intervention for harm reduction with alcohol-positive older adolescents in a hospital emergency department. *Journal of Consulting and Clinical Psychology, 67*, 989–994.

National Collegiate Athletic Association. (2006). *NCAA Study of Substance Use of College Student-Athletes.* Indianapolis, IN: Author.

National Collegiate Athletic Association. (2007a). *Drug Testing Program 2007–2008.* Retrieved August 3, 2007, from http://www.ncaa.org/library/sports_sciences/drug_testing_program/2007-08/2007-08_drug_testing_program.pdf/

National Collegiate Athletic Association. (2007b). *Managing Student Athletes' Mental Health Issues.* Retrieved August 3, 2007, from http://www.ncaa.org/library/sports_sciences/mental_health/2007_managing_mental_health.pdf

National Institute of Alcohol Abuse and Alcoholism. (2002). *A call to action: Changing the culture of drinking at U.S. Colleges.* NIH Pub. No. 02-5010. Bethesda, MD: Author.

Nattiv, A., & Puffer, J. C. (1991). Lifestyles and health risks of collegiate athletes. *Journal of Family Practice, 33*, 585–590.

Nattiv, A., Puffer, J. C., & Green, G. A. (1997). Lifestyles and health risks of collegiate athletes: A multi-center study. *Clinical Journal of Sport Medicine, 7*, 262–272.

Neighbors, C., Larimer, M. E., & Lewis, M. A. (2004). Targeting misperceptions of descriptive drinking norms: Efficacy of a computer-delivered personalized normative feedback intervention. *Journal of Consulting and Clinical Psychology, 72*, 434–447.

Nelson, T. F., & Wechsler, H. (2001). Alcohol and college athletes. *Medicine and Science in Sports and Exercise, 33*, 43–47.

O'Brien, C. P., & Lyons, F. (2000). Alcohol and the athlete. *Sports Medicine, 29*, 295–300.

Perkins, H. W. (2002). Social norms and the prevention of alcohol misuse in collegiate contexts. *Journal of Studies on Alcohol, S14,* 164–172.

Perkins, H. W., & Craig, D. W. (2006). A successful social norms campaign to reduce alcohol misuse among college student-athletes. *Journal of Studies on Alcohol, 67,* 880–889.

Perna, F. M., Antoni, M. H., Baum, A., Gordon, P., & Schneiderman, N. (2003). Cognitive behavioral stress management effects on injury and illness among competitive athletes: A randomized clinical trial. *Annals of Behavioral Medicine, 25,* 66–73.

Ross, H. E., & Ivis, F. (1999). Binge eating and substance use among male and female adolescents. *International Journal of Eating Disorders, 26,* 245–260.

Schroth, M. L. (1995). A comparison of sensation seeking among different groups of athletes and nonathletes. *Personality and Individual Differences, 18,* 219–222.

Selby, R., Weinstein, H. M., & Bird, T. S. (1990). The health of university athletes: Attitudes, behaviors, and stressors. *Journal of American College Health, 39,* 11–18.

Sher, K. J., Walitzer, K .S., Wood, P. K., & Brent, E. E. (1991). Characteristics of children of alcoholics: Putative risk factors, substance use and abuse, and psychopathology. *Journal of Abnormal Psychology, 100,* 427–448.

Smolak, L., Murnen, S. K., & Ruble, A. E. (2000). Female athletes and eating problems: A meta-analysis. *International Journal of Eating Disorders, 27,* 371–380.

Sperber, M. A. (1990). *College sports inc.: The athletic department vs the university.* New York: Holt.

Stephens, R. S., Roffman, R. A., & Curtin, L. (2000). Comparison of extended versus brief treatments for marijuana use. *Journal of Consulting and Clinical Psychology, 68,* 898–908.

Thombs, D. L. (2000). A test of the perceived norms model to explain drinking patterns among university student athletes. *Journal of American College Health, 49,* 75–83.

Thombs, D. L., & Hamilton, M. J. (2002). Effects of a social norm feedback campaign on the drinking norms and behavior of Division I student-athletes. *Journal of Drug Education, 32,* 227–244.

Trenhaile, J., Choi, H. S., Proctor, T. B., & Work, P. (1998). The effect of anabolic steroid education on knowledge and attitudes of at-risk preadolescents. *Journal of Alcohol and Drug Education, 43*(2), 20–35.

Tricker, R. (2000). Painkilling drugs in collegiate athletics: Knowledge, attitudes, and use of student athletes. *Journal of Drug Education, 30,* 313–324.

Tricker, R., & Connolly, D. (1997). Drugs and the college athlete: An analysis of the attitudes of student athletes at risk. *Journal of Drug Education, 27,* 105–119.

Tricker, R., Cook, D. L., & McGuire, R. (1989). Issues related to drug abuse in college athletes: Athletes at risk. *The Sport Psychologist, 3,* 155–165.

Walters, S. T., & Neighbors, C. (2005). Feedback interventions for college alcohol misuse: What, why, and for whom? *Addictive Behaviors, 30,* 1168–1182.

Wechsler, H., Davenport, A. E., Dowdall, G. W., Grossman, S. J., & Zanakos, S. I. (1997). Binge drinking, tobacco, and illicit drug use and involvement in college athletics. *Journal of American College Health, 45,* 195–200.

Whiteside, S. P., & Lynam, D. R. (2001). The Five Factor Model and impulsivity: Using a structural model of personality to understand impulsivity. *Personality and Individual Differences, 30,* 669–689.

Wilson, G. S., Pritchard, M. E., & Schaffer, J. (2004). Athletic status and drinking behavior in college students: The influence of gender and coping styles. *Journal of American College Health, 52,* 269–273.

Zimbalist, A. (1999). *Unpaid professionals: Commercialism and conflict in big-time college sports.* Princeton, NJ: Princeton University Press.

ABOUT THE EDITOR

Edward F. Etzel is a licensed psychologist in the state of West Virginia, currently serving as the psychologist for the WVU Department of Intercollegiate Athletics. His duties include being a staff member of the WVU Carruth Center for Counseling and Psychological Services, and he is the liaison between the center and the Department of Intercollegiate Athletics. He is involved in the provision of individual and group counseling services for personal, career, and sport performance enhancement concerns and is the NCAA CHAMPS/Life Skills program coordinator at WVU.

Dr. Etzel also serves as an associate professor in the Department of Sport Sciences, teaching a variety of sport psychology courses at both the graduate and undergraduate level. He is a member of the WVU Faculty Senate and Faculty Senate Executive Committee, Council for Women's Concerns, and Alcohol and Other Drug Advisory Committee. He is listed as a consultant on the U.S. Olympic Committee's Sport Psychology Registry, serves as Chair of the American Psychological Association's Division 47 Education Committee, served as Chair of the Association of Applied Sport Psychology's Ethics Committee from 1998 to 2007, and is a Fellow in the Association of Applied Sport Psychology.

Dr. Etzel served as the coach of the WVU Rifle team from 1976-89, turning in a 101-3 career coaching record. He coached over 30 WVU All-Americans and guided his teams to five NCAA National Championships during the 1980s. He was the Gold Medalist at the 1984 Olympics in Los Angeles in the Men's English Match Rifle event and was a Gold Medalist in the 1978 World Championships and 1979 Pan American Games. He was 11-time National Champion and set numerous national rifle records as a member of the U.S. Shooting Team.

ABOUT THE AUTHORS

Rebecca Ahlgren-Bedics is the Associate Director of Education Services for the National Collegiate Athletic Association (NCAA). She earned her doctorate in sport and exercise psychology at West Virginia University, her masters in social psychology of sport at Southern Illinois University at Carbondale, and her undergraduate degree at the University of Dayton, where she competed as a softball student-athlete. Ahlgren-Bedics resides in Indianapolis with her husband, Mark, and sons, Kevin and Riley.

Niels C. Beck received his Ph.D. in clinical psychology from St. Louis University in 1977. He is a professor of psychiatry at the University of Missouri-Columbia Medical School and chief psychologist at the University of Missouri Health Sciences Center.

Britton W. Brewer is professor of psychology at Springfield College. He is a Certified Consultant, Association for the Advancement of Applied Sport Psychology, and is listed in the United States Olympic Committee Sport Psychology Registry, 2004–2008. He has received a series of grants from the National Institute of Arthritis and Musculoskeletal and Skin Diseases in support of his research on psychological aspects of sport injury.

Jennifer E. Carter is a psychologist at the Center for Balanced Living in Columbus, Ohio. She earned a Ph.D. in counseling psychology from the University of Notre Dame and completed a postdoctoral fellowship in sport psychology at The Ohio State University prior to serving as the Director of Sport Psychology at OSU from 2000–2008. Her main clinical and research interest is disordered eating in the athlete population, and she continues to stoke her competitive fires by participating in masters swimming.

Damien Clement, an assistant professor at West Virginia University's School of Physical Activity and Sport Sciences, teaches undergraduate sport and exercise psychology courses and graduate athletic training courses. He is a Certified Athletic Trainer and a National

Certified Counselor, as well as an Association for Applied Sport Psychology Certified Consultant. His research interests span both sport and exercise psychology and athletic training. More specifically, he is interested in attitudes toward sport psychology, professional issues in sport psychology, and psychology of injury.

Karen D. Cogan is a licensed psychologist at the University of North Texas Counseling Center and in private practice. She earned her Ph.D. in counseling psychology from The Ohio State University (1991) and an M.S. in kinesiology (1987) from UCLA. Her B.A. is in psychology, also from UCLA, where she competed for the nationally ranked gymnastics team. Currently she consults with Olympic athletes and teams in addition to university athletes. She is a member of APA and AASP and is currently the Council Representative for APA Division 47.

A. P. Ferrante has been an innovator in the conceptualization, development, and implementation of psychological support service programming and the provision of direct services for collegiate student-athletes since 1982. "Dr. Budd" was Psychologist for Athletics for the Ohio State Buckeyes beginning in 1991 and served on the sport psychology staff with the 1988 United States Olympic Team in Seoul, South Korea. A Diplomate of the American Board of Professional Psychology, he maintains a private practice in Columbus, Ohio, and consults with business, sport, and educational institutions.

Laura M. Finch is a professor in the Department of Kinesiology at Western Illinois University. Her areas of expertise include sport psychology, applied sport psychology, sport sociology, and gender and sport.

Lisa C. Hamilton is a staff psychologist and assessment coordinator at the Carruth Center for Counseling and Psychological Services at West Virginia University.

Douglas M. Hankes, Director of Student Counseling Services at Auburn University, completed his Ph.D. in counseling psychology from the University of North Texas and is a licensed psychologist in Alabama and Tennessee. He has been actively involved at the national level in sport and exercise psychology and has served on the Executive Boards of APA Division 47 (Exercise and Sport Psychology) and the Association for Applied Sport Psychology. He is currently listed on the 2008–2012 United States Olympic Committee Sport Psychology Registry.

Jason R. Kilmer is an acting assistant professor in psychiatry and behavioral sciences at the University of Washington, involved in research evaluating prevention and intervention efforts for substance use by college students. He is also actively involved in the coordination and delivery of prevention programs and brief interventions targeting alcohol and other drug use. He received his B. S. in psychology and his M.S. and Ph.D. in clinical psychology from the University of Washington.

Mary Jo Loughran is an assistant professor in the Counseling Psychology Department at Chatham University in Pittsburgh, Pennsylvania. She is a licensed psychologist and a certified consultant, AASP. In addition to her faculty responsibilities, she maintains a private practice in Pittsburgh, Pennsylvania, where she specializes in work with collegiate athletes.

Sam Maniar holds a doctorate in counseling psychology, with a specialization in sport psychology, and is a licensed psychologist in the state of Ohio. He gained diversified experience as a sport psychology consultant while at the University of Montana, West Virginia University, Washington State University, and The Ohio State University and offers a variety of services to individuals, teams, and corporations through his company, Optimal Performance Consulting. He has published in numerous scholarly journals, such as *The Sport Psychologist, Journal of Applied Sport Psychology, Personality and Social Psychology Bulletin, Journal of School Health,* and *Journal of School Nursing.*

Matthew P. Martens is an assistant professor in the Department of Educational and Counseling Psychology at the University at Albany–State University of New York. He is a licensed psychologist in the state of New York. He received his doctoral degree in counseling psychology from the University of Missouri-Columbia and his master's degree in sport psychology from the University of North Carolina at Chapel Hill. His research interests include student-athlete substance use (including steroids), college student drinking, and sports psychology.

Samantha Monda is a doctoral candidate in the Sport and Exercise Psychology Program and the CHAMPS/Lifeskills instructor at West Virginia University. She received a B.S. in Psychology from Carnegie Mellon University, where she competed in collegiate swimming for four years. Her research interests include leadership, athlete stress and coping, and professional issues in sport psychology.

William D. Parham serves currently in the role of Dean of the Graduate School of Professional Psychology at John F. Kennedy University in the San Francisco Bay Area. He is a licensed psychologist, board certified in counseling psychology, and is the immediate Past-President of the Society of Counseling Psychology, Division 17, of the American Psychological Association, wherein he also is a Fellow of Divisions 17, 45, and 47. Multiculturalism/diversity and sport and health psychology represent the foci of his scholarship, consultations, direct service, and social advocacy.

Albert J. Petitpas is a professor of psychology at Springfield College, where he directs the Center for Youth Development and Research. He is a licensed psychologist in Massachusetts and a Certified Consultant, Association for the Advancement of Applied Sport Psychology. He has provided consulting services to a wide range of sport organizations including The First Tee, the NCAA, the NBA, the NFL, and the United States Olympic Committee.

James W. Pinkney is a professor in the Counselor and Adult Education department at East Carolina University. He has published and presented at the state, regional, and national levels in the areas of academic performance, career development, and student-athlete for over thirty years. He is a distinguished reviewer for the *Buros' Mental Measurements Yearbook* series.

Deborah N. Roche is a licensed psychologist. She started working in collegiate athletics in 1999. Currently she is the Director for Counseling and Sport Psychology Services in New York City, where she provides clinical services to the general population as well as performance enhancement and consultation to athletes and teams. She continues her work in higher education as an adjunct professor at a local college teaching sport psychology.

Robin Scholefield is a senior staff psychologist at the University of Southern California (USC). She has provided psychological counseling services exclusively to student athletes at USC for ten years. In addition, she consults with and provides on-call services to athletic department coaches, staff/administration, trainers, and SAAS counselors about mental health issues related to student athletes. She was an Olympic medalist in swimming in the 1976 Olympic Games.

Jamie Shapiro is a doctoral candidate in the Sport and Exercise Psychology Program at West Virginia University. She received a B.S. in psychology from Brown University and she obtained her M.S. in athletic counseling from Springfield College. She is a graduate teaching assistant at WVU, which enables her to teach sport and exercise psychology classes. Her interests include psychology of sport injury, counseling student-athletes, performance enhancement, education and prevention of the female athlete triad, and learning life-skills through sport.

Ariane Smith Machín is a post-doctoral fellow at the University of Wisconsin-Madison Counseling and Consultation Services. She earned her doctoral degree in counseling psychology from the University of North Texas and her master's degree in kinesiology with a specialization in sport psychology from the University of Minnesota. Her clinical interests and expertise include providing performance enhancement and counseling services within the college student-athlete population, and in developing and implementing groups and intervention programs aimed toward college students experiencing difficulties associated with body image and disordered eating.

John Sommers-Flanagan is a faculty member in the School of Education, University of Montana–Missoula. He earned a bachelor's degree in psychology from Oregon State University, a master's degree in psychology from the University of Montana, and a Ph.D in psychology from the University of Montana. His research interest areas include anti-depressant medications, parent education, and adolescence.

Mark A. Stevens is the Director of the University Counseling Services at California State University Northridge (CSUN). His latest edited book with Matt Englar-Carlson is titled *In the Room with Men: A Casebook of Therapeutic Change* (2006) and is published by the

American Psychological Association. Dr. Stevens is also the featured therapist in an APA-produced video on counseling and psychotherapy with men.

Carmen Tebbe is in the Ph.D. Counseling Psychology Program at the University of North Texas. She is an intern with the PROS staff, assisting in provision of counseling and sport psychology services. She received her undergraduate degree from the University of South Carolina, Spartanburg, where she played four years of volleyball. She received her master's degree from Wake Forest University.

Roy Tunick is a professor in the Department of Counseling, Rehabilitation Counseling, and Counseling Psychology in the College of Human Resources and Education at West Virginia University. He earned his B.S.E. and M.S. from Emporia State University, and his Ed.D. from the University of Northern Colorado. He is a licensed psychologist, school psychologist, and professional counselor in the state of West Virginia. He is also a nationally certified counselor, certified rehabilitation counselor, and certified vocational evaluator.

Judy L. Van Raalte is a professor of psychology and co-director of the Athletic Counseling master's program at Springfield College in Springfield, Massachusetts. She is listed in the United States Olympic Committee Sport Psychology Registry and is a Certified Consultant, Association Applied Sport Psychology.

Jack Watson is an associate professor and department chair in the Department of Sport Studies at West Virginia University. He is a licensed psychologist in the state of West Virginia and teaches in the area of sport and exercise psychology. His primary research interests are in the areas of ethics, supervision, and mentoring within the field of sport and exercise psychology.

INDEX